CONTEMPORARY BUSINESS ISSUES
with *Readings*

Based on selected materials from the Ninth Edition of
Business and Society: Corporate Strategy, Public Policy, Ethics

James E. Post
Boston University

Anne T. Lawrence
San Jose State University

James Weber
Duquesne University

UNIVERSITY
OF PHOENIX

 McGraw-Hill Primis
Custom Publishing

New York St. Louis San Francisco Auckland Bogotá
Caracas Lisbon London Madrid Mexico Milan Montreal
New Delhi Paris San Juan Singapore Sydney Tokyo Toronto

CONTENTS

Post–Lawrence–Weber:
Business and Society,
Ninth Edition

Preface

© The McGraw–Hill
Companies, 1999

Preface

The relationship between business and society is changing in new and profound ways. At the beginning of the twenty-first century, the global economy is an intricate landscape of social, political and economic entities: highly advanced industrial nations such as the United States, Japan, and Germany; emerging economies in Asia and Latin America; Eastern European economies that are free after decades of political repression; and countries that are still struggling to devise economic strategies that will help produce prosperity and an improved quality of life for their citizens.

The prosperity that accompanies such growth is not shared equally among the countries in each group. Income and quality of life are unevenly distributed. People with education tend to gain a larger share of a nation's wealth than those who lack schooling. Knowledge commands a premium in a world of new and powerful technologies, and education is a powerful source of economic well-being. People who understand the complex interplay of economic, political, and social forces are better able to appreciate the impact of globalization of markets, advances in science, and the changing relationships between humans and nature. As we enter a new century, we are called to understand a very complicated and rapidly changing world. In the midst of this social change, the realities of managing a business are also changing.

Businesses have new roles and new responsibilities in the modern economy. Decisions are not made in the same ways as they were 10 or 20 years ago. The impact of business decisions is felt by more people, in more ways than in an earlier time. And because so many other things have changed in the new global economy, business leaders are required to think more carefully than ever about the effects of their actions on their company's employees, customers, suppliers, and investors. The actions of business are watched carefully by the media, government officials, and the communities in which business is conducted. In a very real sense, the world is watching as business executives chart their companies' future direction.

Business and Society is about how we as stakeholders—managers, consumers, employees, and community members—try to understand, influence, and shape business behavior and social change. Consider these factors:

- Businesses in the United States and other nations are once again transforming the employment relationship, abandoning practices that once provided job security to employees, in favor of highly flexible but less secure forms of employment. This historic shift in the social contract is driven by complex economic, technological, and social factors.

- The restructuring and redesign of businesses has been driven by vigorous competition in global markets, pressure to improve the quality of products and services, and the creation of information networks that facilitate rapid transfer of economic, social, and political information. Geography, technology, and time once provided buffers that protected companies and people from change. Today, those buffers are disappearing.

Post–Lawrence–Weber:
Business and Society,
Ninth Edition

Preface

© The McGraw–Hill
Companies, 1999

- Government policies toward individual industries and sectors of the economy have shaped and reshaped markets for goods and services. International trade policies are now critical to the competitive future of businesses everywhere and to the well-being of more than 5 billion people that now inhabit the earth.

- Ecological and environmental problems have forced businesses and governments to take action. Crises, accidents, and better understanding of how human activities affect natural resources is producing a consensus that environmental protection must be achieved *with* economic growth if development is to be sustainable.

- Public concern is growing about the ethical and moral behavior of business executives and government officials. As standards change, businesses are challenged to understand new public standards and norms, adjust business practices, and reconcile sometimes conflicting ethical messages. Social values differ from country to country, which challenges accepted notions of the moral order. Business executives must operate in many nations whose people hold very different values about the workplace and the marketplace.

- The challenge of corporate responsibility and ethical behavior is made more complex when companies conduct business in countries with very different social and political cultures. Companies are challenged to function in a world community where great differences still exist. For example, China's role as a powerful economic and political actor has produced conflict in light of the country's unwillingness to conform to Western views of human rights. Human rights advocates pressure governments to link trade policies to human rights, while others argue that unfettered trade with China will eventually produce a freer, more democratic Chinese society.

- A host of new technologies have become part of the everyday lives of billions of the world's population. Advances in basic sciences—physics, biology, and chemistry—are stimulating extraordinary changes in agriculture, telecommunications, and pharmaceuticals. The media uses superlatives such as *biotechnology revolution* and the *information age* to convey some of the exciting possibilities that these scientific and technological developments promise. New industries emerge, and new approaches to living and working follow from these advances. But serious public issues also arise, as with genetically cloned animals or use of the Internet for pornographic and exploitative purposes.

This Material *Business and Society* addresses this complex agenda of issues and their impact and influence on business and its stakeholders. The authors bring a broad background of business and society teaching, research, and case development to this endeavor. The development of this edition began by asking current users of the book to share their suggestions and insights with the author team. Many recommended changes are integrated into this new edition.

Since the 1960s, when Professors Keith Davis and Robert Blomstrom wrote the first edition of this book, *Business and Society* has maintained a position of leadership by discussing central issues of business performance in a form that students and faculty have found engaging and stimulating. The leadership of Professor Davis and Professor William C. Frederick helped *Business and Society* to consistently achieve a high standard

Post–Lawrence–Weber:
Business and Society,
Ninth Edition

Preface

© The McGraw–Hill
Companies, 1999

of quality and market acceptance in the field. Thanks to the authors' remarkable eye for the emerging issues that shape the organizational, social, and public policy environments in which students will soon live and work, the material has added value to the business education of many thousands of students.

Business and Society builds on this legacy of market leadership by reexamining such central issues as the role of business in society, the nature of corporate responsibility, business ethics practices, and the complex roles of government and business in the global economic community. Examples of individuals and companies of all sizes illustrate the concepts, theories, and ideas for action in each topical area.

New Themes

This material also addresses important new themes in modern business and management education.

- The rise of *cross-disciplinary* teaching has created a need for books that span the breadth of business activity, including strategic and operational management. *Business and Society,* ninth edition, helps meet this need by illustrating how all types of business decisions impact stakeholders within and outside the firm.

- Business schools often teach today's students how to *manage across business functions*. This edition presents examples of companies that have managed social issues across the business functions in a strategic, stakeholder-oriented manner.

- The growth of the *Internet* and the proliferation of *World Wide Web sites* creates new opportunities for students and faculty to enrich courses with information drawn from a nearly infinite universe of sources. A list of useful Web sites is included at the end of each chapter, and many text references include Web site references.

This is a book with a vision. It is not simply a compendium of information and ideas. *Business and Society* articulates the view that in a global community, where traditional buffers against change no longer protect business from external change, managers *can* create strategies that integrate stakeholder interests, respect personal values, support community development, and are implemented fairly. Most important, these goals can be achieved while also being economically sound and successful.

Acknowledgments

We are grateful for the assistance of many colleagues at universities in the United States and abroad who have made suggestions and shared ideas for this edition. We also note the feedback from students in our classes and from other colleges and universities that have helped make this book as user-friendly as possible. Among the special contributors to this project are Carla Galisin, Boston University; Stephanie Glyptis, Duquesne University; and Carol Anderson and Lisa Iha, San Jose State University, who helped with numerous research and developmental tasks. Sandra Waddock and Michael Ames of Boston College contributed the Unum case study. We also appreciate the efforts of the following reviewers: Leslie Conley, University of Central Florida; Susan Esiner, Ramapo College of New Jersey; Katharine Harrington, University of Southern California; Norma J. Carr-Rufino, San Francisco State University; Joseph Ford, Iona College; David Jacobs, American University; Harvey Nussman, Wayne State University; William Soderman, Southern Indiana University; Kurt Parkum, Pennsylvania State Uni-

Post–Lawrence–Weber:
Business and Society,
Ninth Edition

Preface

© The McGraw–Hill
Companies, 1999

versity, Harrisburg; Robert Boewaldt, Georgia College; and Marsha Silverman, University of Miami.

We are grateful to the excellent editorial and production team at Irwin/McGraw-Hill. Special thanks to Karen Mellon, sponsoring editor, for her leadership in this project. Kimberly Hooker, project manager; Linda Huenecke, supplement coordinator; and Steven Gomes, copyeditor have made contributions that we very much appreciate. You have given much meaning to the term *team*.

Finally, we wish to acknowledge the support and inspiration of Keith Davis and Bill Frederick, two pioneers in the business and society field, whose legacy of intellectual and editorial leadership we proudly continue in this edition.

James E. Post
Anne T. Lawrence
James Weber

Introduction and Overview

The material is divided into parts that are organized around major themes. In this introduction, we explain the overall design. Each topic contains a number of common features designed to enhance student learning.

The Corporation in Society

Readers are introduced to the basic conceptual themes and ideas of the interaction of business and society. "The Corporation and Its Stakeholders" introduces the corporation and its stakeholders and provides a focused way of mapping the relationships between an organization and its stakeholders. The chapter also discusses the central forces that are shaping business and society relations as we move into the new century. The role of the firm in its social, economic, and political setting is discussed.

"Business and Public Issues" introduces a strategic management approach that executives use in dealing with public issues. By understanding the relationship between stakeholder expectations and corporate performance, it is possible to follow the evolution of public issues through a normal life cycle. Business responses to public issues are discussed, with a close look at the corporate public affairs function and the development of issues management systems. The topic concludes with a discussion of crisis management and ways to strategically manage an organization's stakeholder relations.

Business and the Social Environment

"Corporate Social Issues" discusses public expectation that business will act in a socially responsible manner. This chapter looks at how corporate social responsibility is practiced around the world and the various limits to a firm's social obligations. Balancing its economic, legal, and social responsibilities is a major challenge for modern businesses.

"Socially Responsive Management" describes how a socially responsive firm manages its relations with stakeholders. Firms must address environmental forces before shaping a successful social strategy. This chapter provides a model for determining if a firm is acting in a socially responsive manner.

Business and the Ethical Environment

"Ethical Dilemmas in Business" and "Ethical Reasoning and Corporate Programs" introduce the concept of business ethics. Learning how to recognize ethical issues and understanding their importance to business are emphasized in "Ethical Dilemmas in Business." International efforts to curtail unethical practices are described. "Ethical Reasoning and Corporate Programs" focuses on business efforts to promote an ethical environment in the workplace. An ethical decision-making framework and ethical safeguards are discussed.

Post–Lawrence–Weber:
Business and Society,
Ninth Edition

Introduction and Overview

© The McGraw–Hill
Companies, 1999

"Global Challenges to Corporate Responsibility" focuses on the powerful global changes that are reshaping the business world. The influence of the multinational corporation, demise of communism, emergence of market economies, and the rise of ethnic, religious, and radical forces in the geopolitical world are all shaping the global processes of commerce. The business challenge of acting responsibly, managing issues well, and living by ethical norms is clearly developed for students.

Business and Government in a Global Society

"The Corporation and Public Policy" and "Managing Business-Government Relations" discuss the changing role of government in the global economy, especially its role as a strategist for national economic growth and social welfare. The many roles and responsibilities of government in advanced industrial nations are explored in comparative form, and the essential roles of governments in developing and newly industrialized countries is also discussed.

"Antitrust, Mergers, and Global Competition" revisits the century-old issue of antitrust in the context of today's rapid technological change and the globalization of markets. As the world economy has changed, policymakers have confronted new challenges in promoting free competition and curbing monopoly power.

The Corporation and the Natural Environment

"Ecology, Sustainable Development, and Global Business" and "Managing Environmental Issues" address the ecological and natural resource issues that will reshape entire industries as the next century unfolds. Rapid population growth and the explosive development of many of the world's economies have placed new pressures on scarce resources. Water, air, and land pollution have created new constraints for business around the globe. These chapters explore both the challenges and the opportunities presented by the need to move to a more sustainable business model.

Responding to Stakeholders

The central concepts and themes discussed in earlier chapters are applied to managing relations with the corporation's primary stakeholders and to a number of emerging social issue areas. "Stockholders and Corporate Governance" explores the changing roles and responsibilities of stockholders, managers, boards of directors, and other stakeholders in contemporary corporate governance. It also takes up the controversial debate over executive compensation.

"Consumer Protection" focuses on consumer protection, including such current topics as the social dimensions of advertising, product liability reform, and recent business efforts to use new technologies to communicate more effectively with their customers. It also explores issues of consumer privacy in the new information age.

The role of the corporation in the community is examined in "The Community and the Corporation," which looks at business's role in the community, addressing such issues as education reform. The importance of corporate giving, charitable contributions, and employee volunteerism to community life are also discussed.

"The Employee-Employer Relationship" focuses on the evolving employee-employer relationship. Governmental influences on this relationship from countries around the world are described in this chapter. Ethical challenges concerning employees' and employers' rights in the workplace are discussed.

Post–Lawrence–Weber:
Business and Society,
Ninth Edition

Introduction and Overview

© The McGraw–Hill
Companies, 1999

Social Issues

"Women, Work, and the Family" addresses the special issue of women at work. Where do women work? To what extent have women moved into the ranks of top management, and do women as a group manage differently than men? This chapter also explores programs companies have developed to support working parents and eliminate sex discrimination.

The complex relationships between science, technology, and society are creating numerous ethical and political issues for business. This topic is examined in "Technology as a Social Force." If the information superhighway emerges as experts believe it will, the careers of future managers will be inextricably tied to its features. Technological advances in many other fields promise equally complicated decisions for managers and companies. Business and society will be profoundly affected by this new age of science and technological change.

Case Studies in Corporate Social Policy

The material features nine full-length case studies, including a number of new cases prepared especially for this edition. The cases are written to provide rich discussion material and present a variety of opportunities for instructors to connect topics raised across individual chapters.

The Corporation and Its Stakeholders

Business has complex relationships with many segments of society. The existence and power of these stakeholders require careful management attention and action. A company's success can be affected — negatively or positively — by its stakeholders. In an era when business strategies are changing because of such forces as global competition, new political arrangements, shifting public values, and ecological concerns, managers are challenged to achieve good economic results while also considering the needs and requirements of their business's stakeholders.

This topic focuses on these key questions and objectives:

- Why are business, government, and society an interactive system?

- What kind of involvement does business have with other segments of society?

- Who are a corporation's primary and secondary stakeholders?

- Why are stakeholders important to a corporation, and how can they affect its success?

- What major forces of change are reshaping the business environment for companies?

- How do globalization, ecological concerns, and ethical norms affect corporate stakeholders?

Post–Lawrence–Weber:
Business and Society,
Ninth Edition

The Corporation and Its
Stakeholders

© The McGraw–Hill
Companies, 1999

E ach day, hundreds of newsworthy stories are made by businesses and managers making decisions on new products, employment policies, advertising campaigns, locations for production and manufacturing, and directions for future research and development. The face of business in today's society is ever-changing, highly dynamic, and extraordinarily diverse. Some events are exciting, others depressing. But many reflect the basic trends and underlying forces that are shaping business and society, as illustrated by the following examples.[1]

- In what was described as the largest merger and acquisition in U.S. business history, MCI, a global communications company, was acquired by WorldCom, a smaller but more prosperous global communications firm. The merger was valued at more than $34 billion, well beyond the previous high (the $22 billion merger of R.J. Reynolds and Nabisco). Other bidders for MCI included the British Telephone (BT), a European telecommunications giant, and GTE, a U.S. company with a vast domestic telephone market. The completed merger will affect hundreds of thousands of employees, thousands of suppliers of equipment, and millions of customers.

- Unionized workers at United Parcel Service (UPS), the world's largest package delivery company, went on strike for several weeks to protest the company's contract offer. A major issue in the dispute, which disrupted package delivery in the United States and abroad, involved the company's two-tier wage structure in which part-time employees received lower hourly wages than full-time employees and no benefits while doing the same work. The union argued that this system was fundamentally unfair since both types of workers were performing comparable tasks. The company claimed that the two-tier system was essential if it was to have needed flexibility in a very competitive marketplace. Direct mail and catalog retailers such as Lands' End and L.L. Bean desperately sought to meet delivery schedules. The U.S. Postal Service was a big winner: Its business grew substantially, and many new customers said they would stay with the Post Office rather than return to UPS. Throughout the strike, public sentiment and opinion polls firmly supported the strikers. Pollsters speculated that the strike was a way for the public to lash out at the uncertainty caused by a decade of downsizing and restructuring. News commentators and labor relations experts called the strike a watershed event in modern employer–union relations.

- Warner-Lambert, a global pharmaceutical company with headquarters in Morris Plains, New Jersey, was fined $3 million after pleading guilty to falsifying reports on the levels of pollutants released from a wastewater treatment plant in Puerto Rico, according to the U.S. Justice Department. The company will also pay a $670,000 civil penalty for releasing excessive levels of pollutants from 1992 to 1995, violating its wastewater discharge permit 347 times. The plant's supervisor, Juan Ruiz Orengo, pleaded guilty to similar charges and could be sentenced to up to 27 months in jail. He was responsible for collecting and

[1] Based on published material in *The Wall Street Journal,* the *New York Times,* and other business journals. See, for example, "Warner-Lambert Is Fined $3 Million," *New York Times,* October 24, 1997, p. D2; and "Deferring to Company's Will: Kodak Workers Say Layoffs May Be Needed Tonic," *New York Times,* November 16, 1997, pp. 41, 46.

analyzing wastewater samples for 34 pollutants, including fecal coliform, metals, oil, and grease.

- In Rochester, New York, officials at Eastman Kodak Company announced a reorganization and downsizing. The global photography company is Rochester's largest employer, taxpayer, and purchaser of goods and services. Its photographic film and imaging equipment is sold throughout the world, and the Kodak label is one of the world's best-known logos. For decades, Kodak "owned" the photographic film business and exercised its market power by charging relatively high prices for its products. Although profitable, the pricing strategy exposed the company to potential competition. In the 1990s, Fuji, a Japanese film manufacturer, introduced high-quality films that compared favorably with Kodak's and sold for much less. Big Father Yellow, as Kodak is called in Rochester, began to suffer sharply declining sales and plummeting profits. The problem worsened until late 1997, when CEO George Fisher, announced a major restructuring that included the elimination of 10,000 jobs. The company promised job placement assistance and generous benefits for displaced workers. Although shaken by the bad news, Rochester's mayor expressed both admiration for Kodak's commitment to the community and confidence that unemployed workers would find jobs in the local economy.

These examples highlight some of the powerful and central forces in the modern economy. The changing shape of competition is reflected in the MCI/WorldCom merger and in Kodak's failing film business. Technological change is evident in the merger case and the global package delivery business. The complex relationship between labor, capital, and competition in the modern global economy is illustrated by the changing employer–employee relations at UPS and Kodak. The importance of the natural environment and the need for government regulation to protect the public against unethical actions by companies and managers is clearly illustrated in the Justice Department's actions against Warner-Lambert. All of these issues, and many others as well, underline the complicated and challenging relationships that exist between modern businesses, the people they affect, and the society in which they operate.

Every business has complex involvements with other people, groups, and organizations in society. Some are intended and desired; others are unintentional and not desired. The people and organizations with which a business is involved have an interest in the decisions, actions, and practices of the firm. Customers, suppliers, employees, owners, creditors, and local communities are among those affected by the profitability and economic success of the business. Their support can be critical to a company's success or failure.

The modern business, whether small or large, *is* part of the global business environment. It will be affected by social issues, events, and pressures from around the world. Whether the company has 50 employees or 50,000, its links to customers, suppliers, employees, and communities are likely to be numerous, diverse, and vital to its success. This is why the relationship between business, government, and society is so important to understand as both a citizen and a manager. Whether looked at from outside business—as a member of the community—or from within business—as a manager, employee, or entrepreneur—it is important to see how businesses can blend economic and social purposes together, with minimum conflict and maximum benefits for all.

Post–Lawrence–Weber:
Business and Society,
Ninth Edition

The Corporation and Its
Stakeholders

© The McGraw–Hill
Companies, 1999

Business-Government-Society: An Interdependent System

As the introductory examples illustrate, business, government, and other elements of society are highly interdependent. Few business actions are without an impact on others in society, just as few actions by government are without direct or indirect impact on business. And, of course, business and government decisions continuously affect all segments of the general public. To manage these interdependencies, corporate managers need a conceptual understanding of the relationships and ideas for responding to issues.

A Systems Perspective

Management thinking has been greatly influenced by general systems theory. According to this theory, all living organisms (systems) interact with, and are affected by, other forces in their host environments. The key to survival is the ability to adapt—to be responsive to the changing conditions in the environment. For an organism such as the modern business corporation, systems thinking provides a powerful tool to help managers appreciate the relationships between their companies and the rest of the world.

Figure 1 illustrates the "systems" connections between broad, abstract ways of thinking about business-government-society relationships and specific, practical ways of doing so. The broadest view of that relationship is a societal perspective that emphasizes the systems connections between a nation's economic activity, its political life, and its culture. Every society is a mixture of economic, political, and cultural influences, each generated by its own system of people, institutions, and ideas.[2] In other words, reality for all of us is a mixture of economic, political, and cultural influences.

A somewhat narrower perspective is illustrated in the middle panel of Figure 1–1. *Business* is composed of many segments, industries, and sectors; *government* involves political life at the national, state, local, and, increasingly, international levels; and *society* is composed of many segments, ethnic and other groups, and stakeholders. Once, it was widely believed that business interacted with others in society only through the marketplace. But that view has long since been replaced by an understanding that business and society have many nonmarket interactions as well. Many social influences on business come from cultural and political forces in society; business also has an influence on the political life and culture of any society.

> About a decade ago, Bell Atlantic, a U.S. telecommunications company, formed a joint venture with the national telecommunications company of New Zealand. The joint venture made possible an expanded array of telecommunications services for citizens and businesses in New Zealand. Faxes between New Zealanders and others throughout the Pacific grew exponentially; the number of international telephone calls exploded. New Zealanders quickly became more connected to the rest of the world. Despite large geographic distances, New Zealand businesses were linked to important markets in the global economy in ways that had never before occurred.

Computer technology has also had pervasive effects on cultures and societies everywhere. These cultural effects are largely due to the success of computer pioneers such as IBM, Apple Computer, Microsoft, and others in developing technology (hardware and

---

[2] See, for example, Amitai Etzioni, *The New Golden Rule* (New York: Basic Books, 1996); and Amitai Etzioni, *The Spirit of Community* (New York: Crown Publishers, 1993).

Post–Lawrence–Weber:
Business and Society,
Ninth Edition

The Corporation and Its
Stakeholders

© The McGraw–Hill
Companies, 1999

Figure 1

A range of levels for
understanding
business–
government–society
relationships.

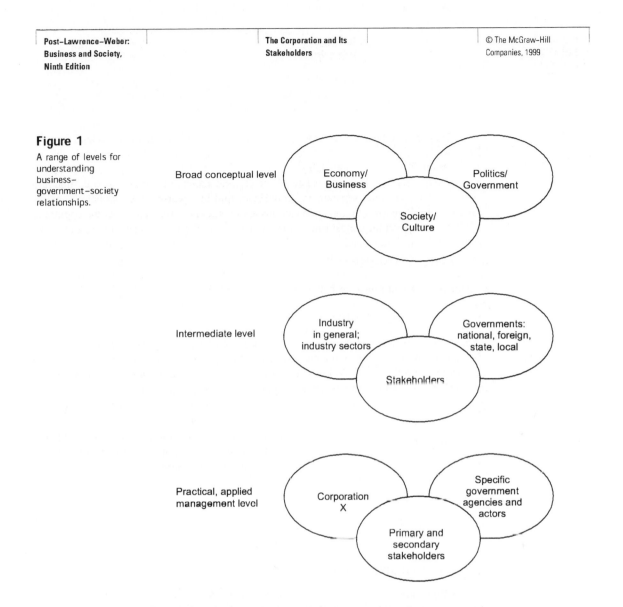

software), marketing it to many types of customers, and encouraging the public to use it for work and entertainment.

One result of this close, inseparable relationship between business and society is that all business decisions have a social impact, much as a pebble thrown into a pond creates ever-widening ripples. Another result is that the vitality and survival of business depend on society's actions and attitudes. Business can be smothered under a heavy blanket of social demands. Taxes can be set at levels that limit available funds for capital investment or encourage relocation to communities in countries with lower tax burdens. Environmental regulations may prove technically impossible or too costly to allow certain industries to continue operating, leading to plant closures and job losses. Labor unions can demand wages or working conditions that exceed a company's ability to pay or its ability to compete in the marketplace. So, while business decisions can have both positive and negative impacts on society, the actions of a society can also influence and affect whether a business firm will prosper or fail.[3]

[3] William C. Frederick, *Values, Nature, and Culture in the American Corporation* (New York: Oxford University Press, 1995).

Post–Lawrence–Weber:
Business and Society,
Ninth Edition

The Corporation and Its
Stakeholders

© The McGraw–Hill
Companies, 1999

That is why business and society, taken together, are an interactive social system. Each needs the other; each influences the other. They are entwined so completely that an action taken by one will inevitably affect the other. The boundary between the two is blurred and indistinct. Business is part of society, and society penetrates far and often into business. They are both separate and connected. And in a world where global communication is rapidly expanding, the connections are closer than ever before. At the beginning of the twentieth century, most travel was done by horse-drawn vehicles, trains, and ships. Fifty years later, autos and airplanes were transforming society. Today, as we enter the twenty-first century, equally momentous transformations are occurring in business and politics. Throughout this book are examples of organizations and people who are shaping the business-society relationships of the twenty-first century.

The Stakeholder Concept

When business interacts so often and so closely with society, a shared interest and interdependence develops between a company and other groups—the organization is interacting with its stakeholders.[4] **Stakeholders** are all the people and groups affected by, or that can affect, an organization's decisions, policies, and operations. The number of stakeholders and the variety of their interests can be quite large; thus, a company's decisions can become very complex.

Government, a stakeholder, creates conditions that can influence a company to stay in or withdraw from a particular market; still, the decision is ultimately the company's to make. However, a business cannot act without regard to its stakeholders' interests. In addition to profit and economic considerations, for example, the company must consider its customers, suppliers, employees, owners, and creditors. Simply stated, good managerial decisions are made by paying attention to the effects of those decisions—pro and con—on the people and interests that are affected. Weighing conflicting considerations such as these is a part of any manager's job.

The Three-Legged Stool

The relationships between companies and their stakeholders have changed over the years. Previously, managers had only to focus their attention on the product-market framework; they could concentrate on bringing products and services to market as efficiently and effectively as possible. The number of stakeholders was limited. Thomas J. Watson, Sr., chairman of IBM in the 1950s, described management's role as one of balancing a three-legged stool consisting of employees, customers, and shareholders. To emphasize their equality, he routinely changed the order in which he mentioned the three groups in his talks and speeches. In those days, it could be assumed that these were the important stakeholders. In contrast, the 1990 book about IBM by Thomas J. Watson, Jr., son of the senior Watson, emphasized the large number and variety of other stakeholders—communities, arts organizations, colleges and universities, foreign governments, and many more—with which the company interacted during the era of the younger Watson's leadership. Ironically, John Akers, one of the Watsons' successors as IBM chairman, was deposed as

[4]R. Edward Freeman, *Strategic Management: A Stakeholder Approach* (Marshfield, MA: Pitman, 1984); and Thomas Donaldson and Lee E. Preston, "The Stakeholder Theory of the Corporation: Concepts, Evidence, Implications," *Academy of Management Review*, January 1995, pp. 71–83.

Post-Lawrence-Weber:
Business and Society,
Ninth Edition

The Corporation and Its
Stakeholders

© The McGraw-Hill
Companies, 1999

the company's chief executive in 1993 because he was unable to meet expectations of critical stakeholders such as shareholders and creditors. The multilegged stool had become unbalanced and cost Akers his job as the economic stakeholders (i.e., investors) reasserted their importance and power. His successor, Lewis V. Gerstner, Jr., emphasized the importance of *all* the company's stakeholders and orchestrated a massive turnaround in IBM's fortunes by the end of the 1990s. The results benefited all of IBM's stakeholders, including investors, employees, customers, communities, and the many educational institutions the company supports through its philanthropic giving.

Managers have the challenge of weighing and balancing the interests of the corporate stakeholders. If their concerns are disregarded, the stakeholders may damage or halt the company's operations. The key point about corporate stakeholders is that they may, and sometimes do, share decision-making power with a company's managers. Their justification for seeking a voice is that they are affected by the company's operations. The interest created between a company and its stakeholders can be a powerful aid to business, or it can be turned against a company. When stakeholders demand a voice in decision making and policy making, the company's managers need to respond with great skill if their primary business mission—producing goods and services—is to be achieved.

On the positive side, a corporation's stakeholders can also be enlisted to aid and support a company that is in trouble.

For example, when Malden Mills, a textile manufacturer located in Methuen, Massachusetts, suffered a devastating fire that destroyed its mill, employees, community officials, the governor, state legislative leaders, and prominent business leaders were ready to help. The family-owned company and its chief executive, Aaron Feuerstein, had defied the odds for years by producing special textiles for the furniture and clothing industries. Malden Mills was New England's last textile producer, in large measure because of Feuerstein's refusal to walk away from the company's 1,400 employees. When the fire damage was surveyed, it appeared that the company could not continue. Feuerstein refused advice to close. He insisted that production continue in the buildings that were not damaged. Immediate repairs were made to equipment and additional space was rented. Injured workers were promised top medical care, and Feuerstein's daughter personally oversaw arrangements for families whose members had been transferred to Boston burn-treatment centers. Most important, Feuerstein promised all workers that he would continue their pay and medical benefits for one month despite the lack of actual work. He later extended these benefits for additional months, enabling many of the families to meet critical emergency expenses.

Feuerstein prepared an ambitious schedule to get the mill rebuilt. But he couldn't do it alone. Industrial facilities take many months, even years, to complete. Regulations are complex and extensive. At Malden Mills, the reconstruction occurred in record time. The state legislature quickly passed needed legislation, and local banks extended credit to the company, despite its immediate inability to pay. Customers, including clothing and furniture manufacturers with unforgiving seasonal demands, tried to reserve their business for Malden Mills. The Malden Mills stakeholder network was concerned and eager to help the company. The state's congressional representatives and senators urged the

Post–Lawrence–Weber:
Business and Society,
Ninth Edition

The Corporation and Its
Stakeholders

© The McGraw–Hill
Companies, 1999

secretary of labor and president of the United States to invoke federal law to help the company. In the end, the company did reopen and virtually all employees were offered jobs at the new facility. Aaron Feuerstein was hailed as a business hero and received many prizes, honorary degrees, and commendations. He insisted the credit belonged to others and always thanked the company's many friends and supporters.

There are many examples of companies disregarding their stakeholders' wishes, either out of the belief that the stakeholder is wrong or out of arrogance reflected in the attitude that one unhappy customer, employee, or regulator doesn't matter. Such attitudes are foolish and often prove costly to the company involved. Today, for example, builders know that they cannot locate a plant in a community that strongly objects. The only way to build a power plant or incinerator, for example, is to work with the community, to respond to concerns, and to invest in creating and maintaining a relationship of trust. John deButts, who once served as chairman of AT&T, commented about the three-legged stool in this way: "The only image which recurs with uncomfortable persistence is not a piece of furniture at all. It is a porcupine, with quills reversed!"[5]

Today, many stakeholders have the ability to stick quills into business. But, as the Malden Mills example suggests, stakeholder relationships are also a vital part of the company's assets. Companies need comprehensive approaches that take into account the needs of a larger and more diverse group of stakeholders. Business cannot be done in a social and political vacuum, and good management planning must take into account this web of stakeholder considerations.

Primary and Secondary Stakeholders

Business interacts with society in a variety of different ways, and a company's relations differ with different stakeholders. Figure 2 shows business interacting with groups that affect its ability to carry out its primary purpose of providing society with goods and services. Investors (stockholders) and creditors provide financial capital to the company; employees contribute their work skills and knowledge; suppliers provide raw materials, energy, and other supplies; and wholesalers, distributors, and retailers help move the product from plant to sales offices to customers. All businesses need customers who are willing to pay for the products or services being produced, and most companies compete against others offering similar products and services in the marketplace. These are the fundamental interactions every business has with society, and they help us define the primary economic mission of the company.

A business's primary involvements with society include all the direct relationships necessary for it to perform its major mission of producing goods and services for customers. These interactions normally occur in the marketplace and involve processes of buying and selling. The primary involvements shape a company's strategy and the policy decisions of its managers and reveal the importance of its **primary stakeholders.** These stakeholders, who are critical to the company's existence and activities, include customers, suppliers, employees, and investors.

However, as Figure 3 reveals, a business's relationships go beyond those primary involvements to others in society. Secondary interactions and involvements occur when

---

[5] John deButts, "A Strategy of Accountability," in William Dill, ed., *Running the American Corporation* (Englewood Cliffs, NJ: Prentice Hall, 1978), p. 141.

Figure 2

Relations between a business firm and its primary stakeholders.

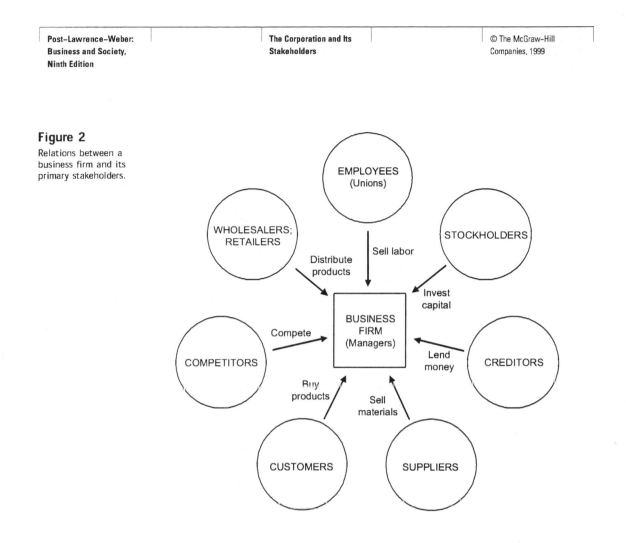

other groups express interest in or concern about the organization's activities. **Secondary stakeholders** are those people and groups in society who are affected, directly or indirectly, by the company's primary activities and decisions. They include the general public, various levels of government, social activist groups, and others.

Calling these involvements and stakeholders *secondary* does not mean that they are less important than business's primary relationships with society. It means that they occur *as a consequence* of the normal activities of conducting business. Moreover, primary and secondary areas of involvement are not always sharply distinguished; often, one area shades into the other. For example, while the safety or environmental effect of a product (e.g., an automobile) is a primary concern to a customer, the cumulative effect of the use of the product may represent a secondary safety or environmental concern for the entire community (e.g., smog from automobile emissions).

Combining a business's primary and secondary interactions gives an **interactive model of business and society.** The interactive model of business and society recognizes the fundamental role of business as an economic contributor to society. But it also suggests that managers must make decisions and take actions that benefit the society as a whole as well as the company's economic interests. The net effect is to enhance the quality of life in the broadest possible way, as that quality of life is defined by society. Business acts to produce the goods and services that society wants, recognizes the social effects of its activities, and is concerned with the social and economic effects on society.

13

Figure 3

Relations between a
business firm and
some of its other
(secondary)
stakeholders.

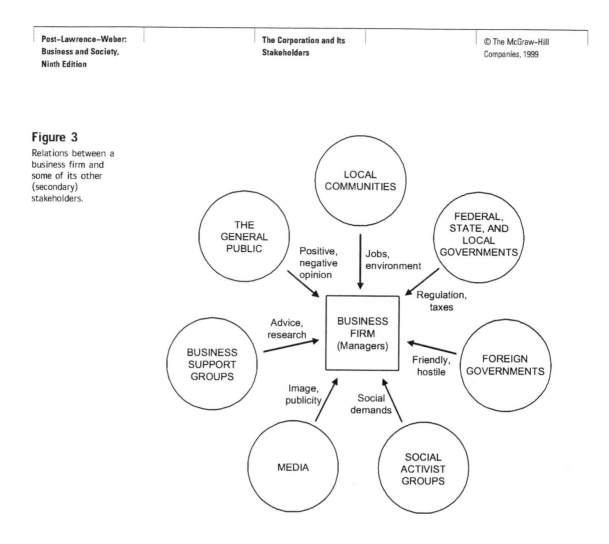

Stakeholder Interests and Power

Stakeholder groups exist in many forms, some well organized, others much less so. This variety makes it more difficult for a company's managers to understand and respond to stakeholder concerns. Each stakeholder has a unique connection with the organization, and managers must understand these involvements and respond accordingly. For example, stockholders have an ownership interest in the organization. The economic health and success of the corporation affect these people financially; their personal wealth is at stake. Customers, suppliers, and retailers have different interests. Owners are most interested in realizing a return on their investment, whereas customers and suppliers are most interested in gaining fair value in the exchange of goods and money. Neither has a great interest in the other's stake. And when we recognize that there are different kinds of owners, ranging from pension funds with large holdings to individual owners with small holdings, the picture grows more complicated.

Governments, public interest groups, and local communities have another sort of relationship with the company. In general, their stake is broader than the financial stake of owners or persons who buy products and sell services to the company. They may wish to protect the environment, assure human rights, or advance other broad social interests. Managers need to track these stakeholder interests with great care.

Different stakeholders also have different types and degrees of power. Stakeholder power, in this instance, means the ability to use resources to make an event happen or to

Post–Lawrence–Weber:
Business and Society,
Ninth Edition

The Corporation and Its
Stakeholders

© The McGraw–Hill
Companies, 1999

secure a desired outcome. Most experts recognize three types of stakeholder power: voting power, economic power, and political power.

Voting power (not referring to political, electoral voting) means that the stakeholder has the legitimate right to cast a vote. For example, each stockholder has a voting power proportionate to the percentage of the company's stock he or she owns. Stockholders typically have an opportunity to vote on such major decisions as mergers, acquisitions, and other extraordinary issues. Through the exercise of informed, intelligent voting, they may influence company policy so that their investment is protected and produces a healthy return.

Customers, suppliers, and retailers have *economic power* with the company. Suppliers can withhold supplies or refuse to fill orders if a company fails to meet its contractual responsibilities. Customers may refuse to buy a company's products if the company enacts an improper policy. Customers can boycott products if they believe the goods are too expensive, poorly made, unsafe, or inappropriate for consumption.

Government exercises *political power* through legislation, regulations, or lawsuits. Other stakeholders also exercise political power, using their resources to pressure government to adopt new laws or regulations or to take legal action against a company.

In a landmark case, a group of citizens in Woburn, Massachusetts, sued W.R. Grace and Company and Beatrice Foods for allegedly dumping toxic chemicals that leaked into underground wells used for drinking water. The deaths and illnesses of family members led the survivors to mobilize political power against the two companies. Investigations were conducted by private groups and public agencies. The lawsuits and political pressure helped make toxic dumping and the protection of water supplies very important political issues. (This case is the basis of Jonathan Haar's book A Civil Action *and the 1998 John Travolta movie of the same name.)*

Of course, a single stakeholder is capable of exercising more than one type of power. The Woburn families sued the two companies (political power), but they had other powers too. They could have led a boycott of the companies' products (economic power) or purchased shares of stock in the companies and attempted to oust the directors and management through a proxy fight (voting power).

Stakeholder Coalitions

Stakeholder coalitions are not static. Stakeholders that are highly involved with a company today may be less involved tomorrow. Issues that are most salient at one point in time may be replaced by other issues at another time; stakeholders who are most dependent on an organization at one time may be less so at another. To make matters even more complex, the process of shifting coalitions may not occur uniformly in all parts of a large corporation. Stakeholders involved with one part of a large company often have little or no involvement with other parts of the organization.

Groups are always changing their relationships to one another in society. Stakeholder coalitions are the temporary unions of stakeholder groups that come together and share a common point of view on a particular issue or problem. There are very broad coalitions whose member organizations span the nation and the world. Movements such as the environmental movement or the human rights movement involve hundreds of state, national, and international organizations and may operate with little or no coordination and policy making. Other movements may be very diverse but operate in a coordinated manner through a central policy-making board or group.

15

Post–Lawrence–Weber:
Business and Society,
Ninth Edition

The Corporation and Its
Stakeholders

© The McGraw–Hill
Companies, 1999

Coalitions of stakeholders have become increasingly internationalized as well. Sophisticated communications technology has enabled like-minded people to communicate quickly, irrespective of political boundaries. Telephones, fax machines, computers, and the Internet have become powerful tools in the hands of activist groups trying to monitor how multinational businesses are operating in different locations around the world.

For example, the Scott Paper Company, a U.S. multinational corporation head-quartered in Philadelphia, negotiated an agreement with the government of Indonesia to build a new paper mill and pulp-processing plant on Sumatra, one of Indonesia's principal islands. Indonesian environmental activists were outraged at the proposal, however, and fought to prevent it. They feared that the paper mill would inevitably lead to destruction of Sumatra's rain forest. Since pulp and paper mills are also notorious for their air and water pollution, the Indonesian environmentalists contacted friends in the United States, including the Natural Resources Defense Council (NRDC). NRDC staff focused on what kind of pressure they could apply against Scott. They concluded that a national boycott of Scott paper products, including such highly visible consumer products as Scotties tissues, was possible. Once this was communicated to Scott Paper's executives, they recognized the company's vulnerability to a consumer boycott and decided to withdraw from the Indonesia project. The Indonesian government was disappointed, having anticipated tax revenues and the creation of jobs. The government eventually turned to a Japanese company to build and operate the pulp and paper mill.[6]

This example illustrates how national and international networks of experienced activists, and the media's interest in a wide range of local, national, and international issues, make coalition development and issue activism an increasingly powerful factor in business.

Forces Shaping Business-Society Relations

Today's business firms do not operate in a social or political vacuum; rather, they find themselves in a virtual whirlwind of social and political problems and controversies. Business managers are buffeted by complicated and threatening forces, many of them global in scope. These trends now intrude into the very core of business operations, thus requiring careful attention and planning. Even small business firms that serve local markets are affected by disruptions in supply, price fluctuations, regional warfare, and uncertainty stemming from international political and economic events. Figure 4 illustrates six critical forces that are shaping business-society relations in the 1990s. Each of these forces is introduced below.

Force 1: Strategic and Social Challenges

Throughout the world, companies of all sizes and in all industries are rethinking critical business assumptions about where to compete and how. **Strategic rethinking** has produced major changes in virtually every company in every industry. Many companies have

---

[6] Based on an interview conducted by one of the authors with the head of the Indonesian Environmental Federation.

Post–Lawrence–Weber:
Business and Society,
Ninth Edition

The Corporation and Its
Stakeholders

© The McGraw–Hill
Companies, 1999

Figure 4

Six forces shaping
business-society
relations.

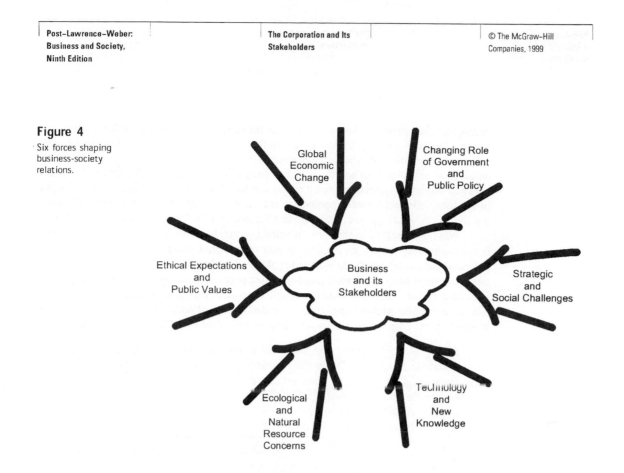

restructured their business operations, often eliminating those activities that seem too distant from the company's strengths or too vulnerable to competitors. Reorganization of business operations occurs frequently as companies have tried to improve the quality of their products and services, reduce costs, and improve the speed with which they respond to customers. This redesign of business operations is also known as **reengineering.**[7]

This broad process of reinventing the corporation has many social consequences. Employees are dismissed from jobs that no longer exist in a redesigned manufacturing or service-delivery system. People who have made long-term career commitments to one firm are asked to take an early retirement or face dismissal. The impact can be tempered by financial arrangements and efforts to train and relocate former employees in new jobs. But the overwhelming sense of loss that people feel in such circumstances is reflected in social indicators such as increased suicide, alcoholism, mental illness, and child and spouse abuse.

Strategic changes in a company's business also affect its relationships with other segments of society. External stakeholders are hurt when a business closes: suppliers, competitors, and other businesses (restaurants, retailers, banks, movie theaters) suffer. A multiplier effect leaves the community short on jobs, tax revenues, and morale.

Traditional concepts of the corporation's responsibility to its stakeholders may be challenged when a company begins to rethink its strategy. Many experts describe the

[7]Michael Hammer and James Champy, *Reengineering the Corporation* (New York: Harper Business, 1993). The popularity of the concept led to many abuses by companies and, in time, a reconsideration of the concept by the authors. See Michael Hammer, *Beyond Reengineering: How the Process-Centered Organization Is Changing Our Work and Our Lives* (New York: Harper Business, 1996).

Post–Lawrence–Weber:
Business and Society,
Ninth Edition

The Corporation and Its
Stakeholders

© The McGraw–Hill
Companies, 1999

corporation-stakeholder relationship as a **social contract,** an implied understanding between a business and stakeholders as to how they will act toward one another. Social contracts are often affected when a company's business strategy changes. Commitments to employees may change in bad times. A company's community involvements and charitable contributions may decline when it encounters severe economic problems. Such changes in the social contract between companies and their stakeholders occurred frequently during the 1990s, leading some observers to conclude that the "good corporation" is dead.[8]

What is emerging in the view of some experts, however, is a **new social contract** between the corporation, its employees, and other stakeholders.[9] As the dynamics of a business change, relationships with stakeholders also change. The roles and responsibilities a company acknowledges and accepts must necessarily change. The new social contract implies that stakeholders can reasonably expect that managers will acknowledge those relationships, deal with the impacts of their decisions, and respond to the people who are touched by the corporation's activities. That is the essence of "doing the right thing."

During the 1990s, more than four million job losses were announced by large American companies. Downsizing occurred in virtually every sector of the economy. Manufacturing, financial services, retailing, and transportation were among the industries greatly affected. A package of benefits was typically offered to departing employees, including compensation based on years of service, continuation of health care benefits for a period of time (ranging from 30 days to one or more years), and support for retraining or education. Research showed that surviving employees also felt the psychological impact of staff reductions, including fears of how management would act in the future. Companies such as Levi Strauss recognized the need to do the right thing for employees and responded to these concerns by stating in writing the commitments on which continuing employees could count. In some companies, these statements of commitment are called compacts, covenants, *or* social contracts, *symbolizing the special nature of the employee-employer relationship.*

Reinventing corporate strategy along these lines is often more a matter of mind and managerial attitude than anything else. It takes a business executive who is willing to look at more than the bottom line. Social sensitivity is possessed by a manager who realizes that employees are people first and producers second. Employees may take pride in their work, but at the same time they are family members, citizens of communities, members of churches, political adherents, and people with aspirations, problems, hopes, and desires who are often emotional, sometimes rational, and frequently confused.

Research has shown that companies with the best social reputations and the best social performance records have top managers who take a broad view of their company's place in society.[10] In fact, these managers often believe that their companies should take

---

[8] Robert J. Samuelson, "R.I.P.: The Good Corporation," *Newsweek,* July 5, 1993, p. 41; and John W. Houck and Oliver Williams, eds., *Is the Good Corporation Dead?* (South Bend, IN: University of Notre Dame Press, 1996).

[9] James E. Post, "The New Social Contract," in Oliver Williams and John Houck, eds., *The Global Challenge to Corporate Social Responsibility* (New York: Oxford University Press, 1995); and Severyn T. Bruyn, *A Future for the American Economy: The Social Market* (Stanford, CA: Stanford University Press, 1991).

[10] Charles J. Fombrun, *Reputation: Realizing Value from the Corporate Image* (Boston, MA: Harvard Business School Press, 1996). See also *Corporate Reputation Review* 1, nos. 1 and 2 (1997), which focus on reputation as one of an organization's strategic assets.

Post–Lawrence–Weber:
Business and Society,
Ninth Edition

The Corporation and Its
Stakeholders

© The McGraw–Hill
Companies, 1999

the lead in helping society solve its problems. Corporations with this attitude generally take a long-run view of the company rather than focusing exclusively on short-run gains. Social goals, as well as economic goals, are given a high priority in planning the company's future. Such an attitude will not prevent the company from facing the stern pressures of marketplace competition or enable them to avoid difficult issues of restructuring, reorganizing, and refocusing, but it will help ensure that the interests of the company and all of its stakeholders are integrated into the corporate strategy.

There are many companies, large and small, that are committed to finding ways to operationalize this new social contract. Anita Roddick, founder and managing director (CEO) of the Body Shop International, a company that manufactures and markets natural cosmetics, soaps, and toiletries through franchise stores, expressed a sentiment shared by members of such businesses:

> [O]ver the past decade, while many businesses have pursued what I call "business as usual," I have been part of a different, smaller business movement—one that has tried to put idealism back on the agenda. We want a new paradigm, a whole new framework, for seeing and understanding [that] business can and must be a force for positive social change. It must not only avoid hideous evil—it must actively do good.[11]

Whether or not this attitude will yield consistent, high levels of economic performance is not yet clear. What is clear is that the business-society relationship is always dynamic; it has been changing very rapidly in recent years and is likely to continue doing so in the next decade. Creating a successful business strategy will require managers who are concerned that business continue to perform a positive role in society.

Force 2: Ethical Expectations and Public Values

Ethical expectations are a vital part of the business environment. The public expects business to be ethical and wants corporate managers to apply **ethical principles**—in other words, guidelines about what is right and wrong, fair and unfair, and morally correct—when they make business decisions.

In the global arena, ethical standards—and even what is meant by *ethics*—can vary from one society to another. In spite of differences in ethical meanings, cultural variation does not automatically rule out common ethical agreement being reached among people of different societies. For example, the European Union's Social Charter promotes common job rights and humane workplace treatment among its member-nations. The International Chamber of Commerce has promoted a common code of environmental practices and principles to protect natural resources around the world. And the 29 member-nations of the Organization for Economic Cooperation and Development (OECD), the world's leading industrial economies, adopted a treaty banning bribery of foreign officials in international commerce.[12]

[11] Anita Roddick, "Corporate Responsibility: Good Works Not Good Words," Speech to the International Chamber of Commerce, October 21, 1993; reprinted in *Vital Speeches of the Day* 60, no. 7, (January 15, 1994), pp. 196–99.
[12] Edmund Andrews, "29 Nations Agree to Outlaw Bribing Foreign Officials," *New York Times*, November 21, 1997, pp. A1, C2.

Post–Lawrence–Weber:
Business and Society,
Ninth Edition

The Corporation and Its
Stakeholders

© The McGraw–Hill
Companies, 1999

Human rights issues have become more prominent and important for business. For many years, great pressure was exerted on South Africa's political leaders to halt racially discriminatory practices of apartheid and its business leaders to challenge the South African government's enforcement of the policy. More recently, pressures from many sources have focused on alleged abuses of human rights in countries such as China, Burma (Mynamar), and Nigeria. And religious organizations in the United States, Canada, and Britain have proposed Principles for Global Corporate Responsibility.

The question is not, Should business be ethical? Nor is it, Should business be economically efficient? Society wants business to be both at the same time. Ethical behavior is a key aspect of corporate social performance. To maintain public support and credibility—that is, **business legitimacy**—businesses must find ways to balance and integrate these two social demands: high economic performance and high ethical standards. When a company and its employees act ethically in dealings with other stakeholders, they are improving the organization's contribution as a social actor. When they fail to act ethically, there is the risk of losing the public support an organization needs to be credible and successful.

For example, in the early 1990s it was disclosed that William Aramony, chief executive officer of United Way of America, a nonprofit organization, was being paid a salary in excess of $400,000 per year, plus other expensive benefits. Moreover, there was alleged evidence that directors and others were misled by Aramony as to the extent of his compensation and spending habits. This was viewed as unethical and scandalous for a nonprofit organization that pays no taxes because it is a charitable institution. The negative publicity resulted in Aramony's dismissal, a shake-up of officers at United Way, and the naming of a new CEO at a significantly lower salary. Public financial support for United Way fell dramatically. It took more than five years for the organization—which supports a wide range of community groups—to restore its reputation and rebuild its donor support.

Business leaders are faced with the continuing challenge of meeting public expectations that are, themselves, always changing. Yesterday's acceptable behavior may not be tolerated today. Many forms of harassment and discrimination were once common. Today, however, social standards make such actions unacceptable. Public expectations of service and ethical behavior are as relevant to a business as customer expectations regarding products such as automobiles and computers.

Force 3: Global Economic Change

Foremost among the factors affecting business is **global economic change.** Dramatic changes have transformed the world's economic scene in recent times. Consider the following events: Asian economic growth, third-world economic development, Western European economic integration, the experiments of Eastern European economies with free markets and competition, and the North American Free Trade Agreement (NAFTA). Global changes of this magnitude create more than just new economic competition. As economies have changed, so have governments, politics, and social systems. Achieving business goals in the midst of such global change requires a keen understanding of interrelated social, economic, political, and cultural trends (see Exhibit A).

Post–Lawrence–Weber:
Business and Society,
Ninth Edition

The Corporation and Its
Stakeholders

© The McGraw–Hill
Companies, 1999

EXHIBIT A   General Motors Catches the Asian Flu

The General Motors Corporation is the world's largest automobile company. It operates around the world and has vast experience in dealing with the economic and political ups and downs of countries. As 1998 began, however, General Motors executives were stunned to see what happened to their business in many Asian countries. In what business observers were calling the Asian flu and Asian contagion, the economies of Thailand, South Korea, and Indonesia suffered huge economic losses.

For Ronald Frizzell, president of GM's Thailand subsidiary, the story began in July 1997, while he was on vacation in Scotland. One day, he received a fax requiring his immediate return to Thailand.

Thailand had been forced to devalue its currency, the baht, plunging the nation into financial turmoil. And as the crisis spread to other Asian countries, Frizzell and his GM colleagues faced a crisis of their own: They were in the midst of building a $500 million factory in Rayong, Thailand, on a former pineapple plantation to supply what they thought would be an endlessly booming Asian market.

"In the annals of poorly timed corporate investments, GM's history in Thailand looks at the moment like a doozy," opined *The Washington Post.* Along with other U.S. automakers, GM withdrew from Thailand and other Southeast Asian markets in the late 1970s, leaving Japanese competitors who quickly gained 90 percent of the market and reaped handsome profits as the Asian economic "miracle" generated the world's fastest growth in auto sales. A long decision process finally produced GM's decision to reenter the Asian car market in a big way.

GM's rush back into the market came just as auto sales slumped and an economic crunch gripped the region. At the the Tokyo Auto Show in October 1997, GM chairman Jack Smith said that the company was looking to the long term, not short-term gain. The plant's construction will continue although the product portfolio might change. The original plan called for production of 100,000 low- to-medium-end passenger cars annually. GM executives now believe production will be lower, and the models may be changed in light of new market conditions.

Across Asia, economic experts are changing their growth forecasts for what were called the tiger economies because of their high economic growth rates throughout the 1990s. Thailand seems to be slipping into an outright recession because of the flight of investment funds by investors who are concerned that the nation is laden with unproductive real estate, wasteful pork-barrel projects, and overly ambitious industrial investments. Car sales in July and August 1997 dropped 75 percent below year-earlier levels. Wealthy Thais were selling off their luxury vehicles at auction just to raise cash.

When Frizzell flew back to Detroit for meetings with GM's top brass to discuss options. Nobody in a position of authority wanted to pull the plug on the factory. "Detroit was concerned, as we are, but they realize this is a strategic decision, and if we're going to participate in Asian markets, we've got to build in Asia."

The timing could work in Frizzell's favor. The plant was not scheduled to be fully operational until 1999. As Frizzell said, "I anticipate that by the time we come to market, the economy might then be starting to recover. And what better time to come to market with a new product than when a recovery is taking place?"

Source: Paul Blustein, "GM's New Factory in Thailand Rises as Car Sales Fall," *Washington Post,* November 10, 1997, pp. A1, A33.

Post–Lawrence–Weber:
Business and Society,
Ninth Edition

The Corporation and Its
Stakeholders

© The McGraw–Hill
Companies, 1999

The emergence of Japan as a global economic power dramatically illustrates the nature of global economic change as a force in business-society relations. Japan was known for its success in steel, electronics, and automobile production in the 1970s and 1980s; so by the 1990s, no business leader anywhere in the world could ignore Japan's emergence as a leading competitor in major sectors of the global economy. Japan also became a large investor in the economies of other nations. For example, Japanese interests doubled their investment in Europe during the late 1980s and grew from 10 percent of foreign-owned business in the United States to more than 20 percent in less than a decade. Japan also became the dominant lender to other Asian economies and invested in industrial projects in the developing nations of Latin America and Africa. In the 1990s, Japan became a primary actor in the world's financial markets.

While Japan continued to grow, some of the world's less developed nations also began to make their economic influence felt. Nations that earlier had occupied only the outer margins of the world economy emerged as strong competitors in the 1990s. South Korea, Taiwan, Singapore, Brazil, Spain, and Mexico became world-class competitors in clothing, footwear, toy, and electronic assembly industries. As they shifted production into basic industries such as steel and other capital-intensive manufacturing industries, even poorer countries with lower wage rates began to produce consumer items such as clothing and footwear.

The new players in the world economy have greatly intensified competition. Their competitive success has disrupted social and economic relations in other countries. The jobs that have gone to people willing to work for low wages in poor nations have sometimes taken away jobs from workers in the wealthier, developed countries. By opening plants in the third world, companies have closed older operations in Europe and North America, creating economic and social distress there. The effects have been dramatic, signaling economic hope for poorer nations but sending a competitive chill through the highly industrialized nations. This new and intense competition from developing countries has helped reshape the economic and social strategies of the advanced industrial nations, as discussed above.

One exceptionally important development has been the opening of societies previously closed to trade and international competition. The opening of the People's Republic of China (PRC) to foreign investment and economic development, for example, stimulated an impressive boom of commercial activity. Billions of dollars of foreign investment have flooded into China to support infrastructure projects such as new roads, power plants, water systems, and investment in industries such as steel, electronics, textiles, and consumer products. With a population of 1.4 billion people, the PRC represents one of the world's largest potential markets for goods and services and an economic colossus as a producer.

During the 1990s, for example, China's gross domestic product grew by nearly 10 percent per year, the highest rate of any nation in the world. Its industrial production soared as well. Such success led many nations that once disdained economic trade with the capitalist world to rethink their policies. China's growth has led businesses everywhere to investigate how they too can do business with Chinese entrepreneurs, traders, and businesses.

Political reorganization and changes have also stimulated major economic changes during the past decade. Western European nations pursued the opening and integration of their economies as a way to establish a vibrant economic base that would create jobs and well-being for more than 300 million people, a population larger than the combined total of the United States, Canada, and Mexico. The member-nations of the European Economic Community (EEC) agreed to create a common market by the end of 1992. Since then, these nations have taken other steps—including creation of a common currency—to expand trade. As the 1990s end, such steps have produced a larger European market and encouraged additional countries to join the renamed European Union (EU).

The remarkable economic, political, and ideological upheavals that occurred in Eastern Europe, beginning with the fall of the Berlin Wall and including the breakup of the former Soviet Union, have also created a mixture of opportunities and threats to business. The opening of Eastern European nations to democracy and trade with the rest of the world provides economic opportunities, but it is also producing social strains as old ways crumble.

The basic lesson to be drawn from these examples is clear: Fundamental social and political change pressures businesses to adjust the way they conduct operations. A firm's economic and financial strategy is vitally affected by political events and changing public attitudes. In these rapidly changing political and social settings, a company's short-term and long-term success may depend greatly on how well its social and economic strategy work together.

Since the end of World War II in 1945, numerous international agreements have been crafted to encourage trade among nations. Much of this effort was coordinated through the General Agreement on Tariffs and Trade (GATT). Many nations have also established trade agreements with other nations with which they are economically interdependent. This drive to open markets and integrate economic activity across national borders in North America started in the late 1980s when the leaders of Canada, Mexico, and the United States began shaping a North American Free Trade Agreement to remove trade and investment restrictions. The agreement, which went into effect on January 1, 1994, will lower trade barriers among the three nations for the next decade.

The reorganization of global markets has not occurred without difficulties. People who think of themselves as citizens of France, Germany, the Netherlands, or any other nation will not quickly give up that sense of cultural identity simply because the European Union exists. Former Communists will not embrace capitalism just because the new political leadership thinks it is a good idea. American workers will remain concerned that high-paying jobs might be exported to Mexico by firms seeking to reduce labor costs. And the businesspeople of South Korea, Indonesia, and Thailand will not quickly forget the pain that they and their fellow citizens endured in 1998 as their economies collapsed under the weight of too much debt and heavy international financial burdens. The world economy may improve by establishing free trade and uniform economic standards and regulations, but the social and political environment will remain quite complex. Firms planning to do business in this challenging environment will need a sophisticated understanding of local customs, social institutions, and political systems. That is another way of saying they will need a sound social strategy at home and abroad.

Force 4: The Changing Role of Government and Public Policy

Beginning in the 1970s, new winds of reform began to blow through many of the world's economic, political, and social institutions. No one knew exactly what had set these new

Post–Lawrence–Weber:
Business and Society,
Ninth Edition

The Corporation and Its
Stakeholders

© The McGraw–Hill
Companies, 1999

currents in motion. They were not felt with the same strength in all nations, nor in all kinds of institutions in any one nation. But wherever these currents blew, the focal points seemed to be centralized power and authority. Governmental power and, especially, the role of government in society were challenged.

Demands were made to disperse power more widely within many societies and nations. "Power to the people" became a popular rallying cry that captured the essence of this new social force. Leaders discovered that their grip on institutional power was not as secure as it had been in earlier times. The public, less trusting of its leaders, wanted a piece of the action. Believing that too much power had been concentrated at the top of society's major institutions, the public demanded democratic reforms.

The best known of these political changes were deregulation and privatization in the Western world; **glasnost** (openness) and **perestroika** (reform, reconstruction, renewal) in the former Soviet Union; freer markets and a more decentralized economic system in China; and sweeping political upheavals in Eastern Europe. In each of these cases, centralized governmental power was being dispersed and moved out from the center toward the periphery. In many countries, this has been called the *devolution* of governmental power.

What does this global reform movement mean for business? First, and foremost, it creates new business opportunities. But it also poses new business risks. When free markets open up where none existed before, corporations can take advantage of profit opportunities. European, Japanese, and American business firms flocked to China in the early days of its reform movement. But just as quickly, they became more cautious when government authorities showed signs of reinstalling centralized power over all business decisions. When the nations of the former Soviet Union and Eastern European nations relaxed government controls and welcomed economic ties with Western nations, many corporations crossed over into that formerly forbidden territory, seeking profitable opportunities. The business risks were considerable, because these former socialist nations lacked free and open market systems, stable currencies, and competitive traditions.

As Eastern Europe struggled to transform its economic and political institutions, its governments faced formidable problems such as inflation, unemployment, and declining national income. Speaking of this difficult period, a Hungarian political scientist said, "The cold war is over, but this will be a very dangerous peace. . . . Conflicts are growing between nationalities, between rich people and poor, between the government and street protesters, between industrialists and laborers."[13] The view was prophetic: Ethnic, ideological, and economic conflicts have raged in Eastern Europe (e.g., Bosnia, Serbia) since the early 1990s, and the political winds have blown in different, often contradictory directions.

The global movement from centralized governmental authority toward freedom and democracy carries both pluses and minuses for business. Once again, corporations have found themselves facing large measures of uncertainty and risk.

Russia is one of the world's largest and most resource-abundant countries in the world. Since the fall of communism, Russia has suffered political convulsions as Mikhail Gorbachev, Boris Yeltsin, and Vladimir Zhiranovsky have contested for power. This political uncertainty has influenced the way Central

---

[13]"East Europe Offers Investors Big Profits and Big Perils," *The Wall Street Journal*, January 11, 1991, p. A6.

Post–Lawrence–Weber:
Business and Society,
Ninth Edition

The Corporation and Its
Stakeholders

© The McGraw–Hill
Companies, 1999

> *Asia's oil industry has been developing. Chevron Corporation, a U.S. multina-*
> *tional oil company, has invested heavily in Kazhakistan, a former Soviet repub-*
> *lic. As the political fortunes of the republics have ebbed and flowed, Chevron's*
> *political risk has also grown. Its traditional multinational oil competitors such*
> *as Royal Dutch Shell (Netherlands) and Total (France) are trying to acquire*
> *drilling rights in the area where Chevron has conducted explorations. Each*
> *company has its political friends. New state oil companies from Russia*
> *(Gazprom) and Malaysia (Petronas) are working to foreclose U.S. companies.*
> *Chevron executives know how bad it can get: In the 1980s, Chevron invested*
> *$1 billion in Sudan. But as that nation slid into anarchy, Chevron was forced*
> *to abandon its wells, refineries, and pipelines. Although Chevron sees business*
> *potential in Kazhakistan and Central Asia, its executives also recognize that*
> *political risk may overwhelm the business opportunity.*[14]

Such volatile political and ideological forces have become a central part of the world business climate. Corporations and their managers cannot ignore them; to do so could be fatal. Learning how to integrate changing political realities into a corporate business strategy has become a basic requirement for companies and managers. Looking ahead, it seems to loom even more important in the future.

The role of government has also changed in the United States. Deregulation of segments of the economy created change for the airlines, trucking, and communications industries in the 1970s. In the 1980s, presidents Ronald Reagan (1981–89) and George Bush (1989–93) pressed for an approach that would limit the role of the federal government and leave more responsibility with state and local governments to meet public needs. During the 1992 presidential campaign, candidates George Bush, Bill Clinton, and Ross Perot argued sharply different positions on the role government should play in education, environmental protection, and most important, creating a healthy economy. The election of President Clinton did not settle the debate. In 1994, Republicans swept into Congress on a campaign platform that called for downsizing the role of the federal government. Subsequent national elections have not clarified the picture, insofar as Clinton and many of his congressional opponents won reelection. As political pundit Chris Matthews suggested, "perhaps Americans *like* political gridlock."

The role of government and public policy, including regulation and antitrust, and the role of business in politics are discussed elsewhere. However, the importance of these issues in the modern world was succinctly expressed by Milton Friedman, a Nobel Prize–winning economist who has long urged that government not interfere with free markets:

> *It is today possible, to a greater extent than at any time in the world's history,*
> *for a company to locate anywhere, to use resources from anywhere to produce*
> *a product that can be sold anywhere. . . . [The challenge] is to use our influ-*
> *ence to make sure governments are not short-sighted and do not short-circuit*
> *the process.*[15]

---

[14]Sheila N. Heslin, "The New Pipeline Politics," *New York Times*, November 10, 1997, p. A37.
[15]Milton Friedman, quoted in Lindley H. Clark, Jr., "The New Industrial Revolution," *The Wall Street Journal*, November 23, 1993, p. A16.

Post–Lawrence–Weber:
Business and Society,
Ninth Edition

The Corporation and Its
Stakeholders

© The McGraw–Hill
Companies, 1999

Force 5: Ecological and Natural Resource Concerns

One of the most important social challenges to business is to strike a balance between industrial production and nature's limits. Industrial production, mining, and farming are bound to produce waste and pollution, along with needed goods and services. Waste and pollution are a price society pays for rising populations, urbanization, and more goods and services. All industrial societies—whether the United States, Japan, Germany, Russia, or South Korea—create a disproportionate (relative to population) share of the world's pollution and waste because these are the unavoidable by-products of a high level of economic activity. The emerging nations of the third world, with their rapid growth rates and limited pollution controls, also contribute to global ecological problems as their economies become more industrialized.

Consumers too are responsible for much solid waste and pollution because they demand, buy, and use pollution-generating products such as automobiles, refrigerators, air conditioners, and computers. The widespread use of product packaging and the proliferation of toxic products such as cleaners, lawn chemicals, batteries, and antifreeze all contribute to global pollution issues.

Ecological impacts extend far beyond national boundaries. Stratospheric ozone depletion potentially threatens health and agriculture on a worldwide basis. The industrial accident at the Chernobyl nuclear power station spread dangerous radiation across several European nations and sent a radiation cloud around the globe. Oil spills have fouled the oceans and beaches of many nations. The cutting and burning of tropical rain forests has the potential to affect weather climates throughout the world.

Environmental protection, involving pollution control, waste minimization, and natural resource conservation, has become a high priority for developing nations as well as the advanced industrialized nations. International agreements have been created to address the most pressing issues, such as ozone depletion, biodiversity, and global warming. But government and industry leaders recognize that this is just the beginning of what must be done to achieve a sustainable balance between economic activity, which requires the use of resources, and global environmental protection, which requires the preservation of resources. Business leaders and managers at every level of business activity from corporate headquarters to the local retail outlet are being challenged by the need to integrate ecological thinking into their decision making.

Today, companies are learning how to adjust their products, manufacturing processes, purchasing activities, and business strategies to the need for sustainable economic and ecological practices. Although much has already been improved, there is no doubt that reducing harmful ecological effects will continue to be a major social challenge for corporate managers. Pollution and waste cannot be stopped entirely, but their volume can be reduced through improved product designs, better controls, and the recycling of reusable materials. Environmental accidents such as oil spills can be prevented by careful planning, and cleanup efforts can be pursued vigorously with new techniques and technologies. The basic goal is to achieve a livable balance between human needs and nature's limits.[16]

[16]Andrew J. Hoffman, *From Heresy to Dogma* (San Francisco: New Lexington Press, 1997); and A. J. Hoffman, ed., *Global Climate Change* (San Francisco: New Lexington Press, 1997).

Post–Lawrence–Weber:
Business and Society,
Ninth Edition

The Corporation and Its
Stakeholders

© The McGraw-Hill
Companies, 1999

Force 6: Technology and New Knowledge

Technology is one of the most powerful forces affecting business and society. Improved technology includes machines of all sizes, shapes, and functions; processes that enable business to produce goods at faster speeds, with lower costs, and with less waste; and software that incorporates new forms of learning into formats that direct machines (hardware) to perform functions that would have taken much longer, and been less reliable, if done by other means. Technology involves harnessing human imagination to create new devices and new approaches to the needs, problems, and concerns of a modern society. Indeed, a government study showed that sales by the computing and telecommunications industries grew by 57 percent during the 1990s to more than $866 billion, making those businesses the nation's largest industry, ahead of construction, food products, and automotive manufacturing.[17]

Technology also involves drawing together fields of knowledge that converge, enabling new ways to solve problems or perform tasks. An example of such a convergence technology is biometrics.

Biometrics is a field that integrates biological science and computer science. One application of this new field of knowledge involves identification procedures. Scientists know that no two persons have the same fingerprint. This makes fingerprints a nearly foolproof method of identification. In the past, an individual's fingers were coated with ink, and impressions were made on paper, then compared with impressions made by others. Laboratories such as the Federal Bureau of Investigation (FBI) kept files containing thousands of fingerprints. In time, computers enabled researchers to digitalize fingerprints and reproduce them on computer screens. This enabled searches to occur much faster once fingerprints were on file. Biometrics has now made possible the next step in this evolution of identification science. New scanners enable a person to place his or her finger on an imaging surface and instantaneously receive confirmation that the fingerprint matched that of the owner of an identification card. This technology of identification has been used to speed health-care identification, eligibility for welfare benefits, and credit-card approvals.

Although new technologies have the potential to benefit large portions of the population, they may also negatively affect some people. If biometric scanners are generally adopted, for example, ink-based print systems will be rendered obsolete, costing manufacturers of inkpads and employees of inkpad companies their livelihood. Still, for society as a whole, biometric identification may prove to be a highly efficient and productive use of resources. It is in this way that new technologies put pressure on today's companies to understand and respond to new knowledge and its applications.

Many technologies have broader social impacts as well as competitive effects. New technologies force managers and organizations to examine all of the ethical implications of their use.

---

[17]Steve Lohr, "Information Technology Field Is Rated Largest U.S. Industry," *New York Times*, November 18, 1997, p. D12.

Post–Lawrence–Weber:
Business and Society,
Ninth Edition

The Corporation and Its
Stakeholders

© The McGraw–Hill
Companies, 1999

For example, as medical experts learned how to transplant living organs such as kidneys and hearts from one person to another, ethical concerns emerged about the criteria that hospitals would follow in deciding when, and under what conditions, transplants would occur. These decisions affect both the donors and the recipients. When is a person really dead? Should some organs be removed before the donor is dead but after a medical team is certain that death will soon occur? Is it safe for a living donor to give up a kidney, eye, lung, or other organ?

As new technologies become available, the challenges to sound decision making become even more ethically complicated. As experiments with fetal tissues show that it is possible to regenerate cells that once were thought to be dead, hospitals and medical staffs struggle to decide whether the tissue of aborted fetuses can be used to treat strokes, spinal cord injuries, and other health problems once thought to be beyond hope.

Technology is creating what experts call the *knowledge economy*. This is an economy in which new knowledge, in all of its many forms, is reshaping and transforming old industries and businesses, creating new industries and businesses, and ultimately affecting individuals, families, communities, and institutions throughout the world. For these reasons, technology must be understood as one of the major drivers of change in both business and society.

Corporate Strategy for the Twenty-First Century

Business, government, and society are interdependent and their relationship is complex in every nation. General systems theory tells us that all organisms or systems are affected by their host environments; thus, an organization must be appropriately responsive to changes and conditions in its environment to survive and succeed.

This web of interactions between business, government, and society creates a system of stakeholders—groups affected by and influential in corporate decisions and actions. The analysis of these stakeholders—who they are, what power they hold, and the ways in which they interact with one another—helps managers understand the nature of their concerns and needs and how these relationships are changing. If the creation of stakeholder networks is a natural process for organizations, managers must learn how to understand and utilize these relationships. The business of the twenty-first century must have managers who understand the importance of creating business strategies that include these considerations.

The relationship between business and society is also continuously changing. People, organizations, and social issues change; inevitably, new issues will arise and challenge managers to develop new solutions. To be effective, corporate strategy must respond to the biggest and most central questions in the public's mind. People expect businesses to be competitive, to be profitable, and to act responsibly by meeting the reasonable expectations of stakeholders. The corporation of the twenty-first century is certain to be affected by global economic and political trends, powerful new technologies, and a global population of stakeholders who will expect their interests to be integrated into the thinking of the companies from which they buy goods and services, to which they contribute labor and ideas, and to which they extend the hospitality and support of their communities.

Post–Lawrence–Weber:
Business and Society,
Ninth Edition

The Corporation and Its
Stakeholders

© The McGraw–Hill
Companies, 1999

Summary Points

- Business, government, and society form an interactive system because each affects and influences the other and because neither can exist without the others. Economic, political, and cultural life are thoroughly entwined with one another in every nation. Together, they define the uniqueness of a society.

- Every business firm has economic and social involvements and relationships with others in society. Some are intended, some unintended; some are positive, others negative. Those related to the basic mission of the company are its primary involvements; those that flow from those activities but are more indirect are secondary involvements.

- The people, groups, and organizations that interact with the corporation and have an interest in its performance are its stakeholders. Those most closely and directly in volved with a business are its *primary* stakeholders; those who are indirectly connected are its *secondary* stakeholders.

- Stakeholders can exercise their economic, political, and other powers in ways that benefit or challenge the organization. Stakeholders may also act independently or create coalitions to influence the company.

- Six key forces are affecting the business-society relationship as companies move into the late 1990s: strategic refocusing and restructuring of businesses; changing ethical expectations and public values; global economic change; a global trend toward rethinking the role of government; ecological and natural resource concerns; and the transformational role of technology.

- To deal effectively with globalization, ecological concerns, and ethical issues, a corporate strategy must take into account the interests, needs, and expectations of all of the company's stakeholders. Companies should have a strategy that combines business goals and broad social interests.

Key Terms and Concepts

- Stakeholders
- Primary stakeholders
- Secondary stakeholders
- Interactive model of business and society
- Strategic rethinking
- Reengineering
- Social contract

- New social contract
- Ethical principles
- Business legitimacy
- Global economic change
- Glasnost
- Perestroika
- Environmental protection

Internet Resources

- http://www.businessweek.com — *Business Week*—broad range of business topics
- http://www.economist.com — *The Economist*—strong international coverage
- http://www.fortune.com — *Fortune*—useful profiles of large corporations
- http://www.ethics.org — Ethics Resource Center
- http://www.whitehouse.gov/fsbr/ssbr.html — Executive Office of the President of the United States

Discussion Case Inland National Bank

Amy Miller, manager of community affairs at Inland National Bank (INB), was facing a problem. Inland had recently acquired another local bank, Home Savings Bank. INB's senior management was in the process of reorganizing the company's retail banking operations, and some branches were sure to be consolidated. Located in a medium-sized city in the midwestern United States, Inland National Bank had a good reputation for community involvement and solid financial performance. The decision to reorganize the bank's branches made economic sense, but Amy was troubled by how it would affect a number of local neighborhoods. She was especially concerned about two branches in her district.

Rockdale Branch

This was a small Home Savings branch. The problem here was obvious: The neighborhood was old and on the decline. Home Savings had not modernized the facility for many years, and a major upgrade was essential to improve the rundown facility. Miller thought the cost could be as much as $500,000. It was unclear whether the financial potential of the neighborhood warranted such an investment. Home Savings was the last bank to have a Rockdale branch; all of the other banks had closed their branch offices at least five years ago. If the local office was closed, Rockdale customers could use INB's branch in Culver Heights, about a 10-minute auto or bus ride from Rockdale. The Culver Heights branch was conveniently located on a local bus route.

North Madison Branch

Miller was also concerned about a branch office located in North Madison, a neighborhood adjacent to Rockdale. This was a poor neighborhood, with an average income about $2,000 per household below that of any other neighborhood in the city. Many of North Madison's residents were on welfare and public assistance. Home Savings Bank also had a branch office in North Madison's main commercial main district. INB had not offered local branch banking here in more than a decade. One of INB's senior executives had talked about closing the branch, replacing it with four automatic teller machines conveniently located in the North Madison shopping district. The move would

Post–Lawrence–Weber:
Business and Society,
Ninth Edition

The Corporation and Its
Stakeholders

© The McGraw–Hill
Companies, 1999

eliminate a total of 20 jobs at the branch. Only a few of these employees were likely to find other jobs within the bank. Miller understood that about half of the employees in the two branches lived in or near North Madison.

Other Factors

Rockdale residents had organized a group of picketers in front of the Home Savings branch a few days after the merger announcement was made. A local television station sent a crew to cover the story. One local resident who was interviewed said, "INB just hates old people, and old people is all that lives in Rockdale! They care more about money than people."

INB had also received angry telephone calls from several city officials. Sheila Thomas, an elected member of the city council whose district included both the Rockdale and North Madison neighborhoods, was especially vocal about the bank's plan. She questioned whether the bank was acting in good faith toward all of the city's residents. During a television interview she said, "It's wrong for this bank to cut the heart out of neighborhoods by replacing people with ATMs." Amy Miller knew and respected Sheila Thomas, but also recognized the political visibility this issue was providing an ambitious elected official.

Inland National Bank operated under the regulatory supervision of several federal and state banking agencies. The bank had a good record with these authorities, but the branch reorganization plan clouded the picture. Under the federal Community Reinvestment Act, INB had to disclose where its deposits came from and where they were being invested. This was to help ensure that money was being fairly reinvested in communities where depositors lived and worked. The law gave banking officials some leverage to force banks to pay attention to local community needs.

The Rockdale protest and phone calls from North Madison residents and merchants had gotten the attention of state banking officials who needed to approve INB's branch closings. The state's banking commissioner had given a number of speeches urging banks to invest "at home," and "in people, as well as technology." The traditional test for banking officials was whether the financial solvency of the bank would be improved or harmed by the proposed action. These communities were raising different issues.

The Decision

At a recent meeting with INB's president and senior management committee, Miller learned that the state banking officials had told INB to submit a plan that responded to the issues raised by the residents of Rockdale and North Madison. She was named to a team that had to recommend a course of action to INB's president by the end of the week.

The team's leader had called a meeting for this afternoon. He had suggested that one way for INB to get out of this problem was to close just one of the branches. Miller had been asked to bring her analysis of Rockdale and North Madison to the meeting.

Post-Lawrence-Weber:
Business and Society,
Ninth Edition

The Corporation and Its
Stakeholders

© The McGraw-Hill
Companies, 1999

Discussion Questions

1. Who are the stakeholders in this case? Which are primary, and which are secondary? What influence do they have? How are they related to each other? Draw a diagram of the stakeholder relationships to INB.

2. If INB decides to close the Rockdale and North Madison branches, how will the business-government-society relationship come into play? How might the issue develop? What considerations must be weighed by INB's management?

3. What should Amy Miller recommend to her team? Are there steps that can be taken to soften the impact of the closings? Should she recommend against closing the branches?

4. Compare the business and social considerations in the Rockdale and North Madison communities. Which branch seems to be more important to the community? Are there any meaningful differences between the two situations?

5. Identify the key terms and concepts in this chapter that apply to this discussion case.

Bibliography

Academy of Management Review. Special Topic Forum on Shifting Paradigms: Societal Expectations and Corporate Performance, vol. 20, no. 1, January 1995.

Dennis, Lloyd B., ed. *Practical Public Affairs in an Era of Change.* Lanham, MD: Public Relations Society of America and University Press of America, 1996.

Dertouzas, Michael L.; Richard K. Lester; and Robert M. Solow. *Made in America: Regaining the Productivity Edge.* Cambridge, MA: MIT Press, 1989.

Dickie, Robert B., and Leroy S. Rouner, eds. *Corporations and the Common Good.* South Bend, IN: University of Notre Dame Press, 1986.

Drucker, Peter. *The New Realities.* New York: Harper and Row, 1989.

Etzioni, Amitai. *The New Golden Rule.* New York: Basic Books, 1996.

_____. *The Spirit of Community.* New York: Crown Publishers. 1993.

Frederick, William C. *Values, Nature, and Culture in the American Corporation.* New York: Oxford University Press, 1995.

Freeman, R. Edward. *Strategic Management: A Stakeholder Approach.* Marshfield, MA: Pitman, 1984.

Heath, Robert L., ed. *Strategic Issues Management,* 2d ed. San Francisco, CA: Jossey-Bass, 1996.

Kennedy, Paul. *Preparing for the Twenty-First Century.* New York: Vintage/Random House, 1994.

Krugman, Paul. *The Age of Diminished Expectations.* Cambridge, MA: MIT Press, 1994.

Post, James E., ed. *Research in Corporate Social Performance and Policy.* "The Corporation and Public Affairs," Vol. 14. Greenwich, CT: JAI Press, 1994.

Werhane, Patricia H. *Adam Smith & His Legacy for Modern Capitalism.* New York: Oxford University Press, 1990.

Wolfe, Alan. *One Nation, After All.* New York: Viking, 1998.

Post–Lawrence–Weber:
Business and Society,
Ninth Edition

Business and Public Issues

© The McGraw–Hill
Companies, 1999

Business and Public Issues

Businesses face a large number of public and social issues. Each business must deal with a unique set of relationships and issues that are tied to its activities. Senior executives often spend large amounts of time managing relationships with their organization's stakeholders. Many companies also designate specific managers to the job of public affairs management; others believe that managing public and social issues effectively is a job that all managers must perform.

This topic focuses on these key questions and objectives:

- Why do the expectations of stakeholders matter to organizations and managers?
- What is the life cycle through which public issues evolve?
- What is the mission and purpose of a company's public affairs function?
- What strategies can an organization use to cope with specific public issues?
- What activities make up an issues management system?
- What are the elements of effective crisis management?
- What must a company do to strategically manage its stakeholder relations?

The Ford Motor Company is one of the world's largest and most successful automobile manufacturers. Building and selling cars, trucks, and other motorized vehicles of all sizes throughout the world, the company has earned a reputation as a high-quality manufacturer. Still, there are times when Ford vehicles fail to meet customer expectations. Such is the case in what some disgruntled Ford customers call the case of the Flaming Fords.[1]

Ford Motor Company has long manufactured a range of automobiles and light trucks. The popularity of these vehicles has led to many millions being sold in the North American market. Between 1988 and 1993, for example, Ford sold more than 26 million vehicles in North America. That five-year period is important for other reasons as well.

The problem that angered Ford customers involved an ignition system that appears to have experienced an internal short circuit, thereby overheating and creating smoke and fire in the steering column of the vehicle. By 1993, Ford received reports of at least 300 such fires among Canadian owners and more than 800 from owners in the United States. In many of these cases, the entire vehicle had been engulfed and the driver injured.

Lawyers representing victims of these fires sued Ford and charged that the company knew, or should have known, about risks involved with the ignition system. Ford denied that the ignition system was defective and defended its overall safety. To advance their case, lawyers for some of the victims tried to locate other Ford owners who have experienced such problems in the hope of joining forces in a class action lawsuit against Ford. To identify and inform prospective members of the class (Ford owners), the lawyers created a Web site entitled "Association of Flaming Ford Owners." One page on the site showed a burnt out truck and asked, "Are you one of the 26 million owners of a Ford manufactured vehicle that contains an ignition switch that starts fires?" The reader was prompted to click onto the model and year of Ford vehicle owned for information in the database.

The Web site was a boon to Ford owners. They have been able to access current information about the ignition system, pending lawsuits, and new plaintiffs. According to one attorney involved in the litigation, the Web site made it possible for customers to proceed much faster and with more complete information than in the past. In this respect, Flaming Fords story shows how a conflict between a manufacturer and some of its customers can be transformed into a larger, faster-developing, and more potent public issue.

Each year, hundreds of millions of dollars of new products and services are sold through the Internet. Digital commerce is a powerful commercial force. Indeed, in the late 1990s, Ford Motor Company is promoting and selling vehicles through Web-based marketing strategies. Technology such as the World Wide Web is changing the way both commerce and social issues must be managed. But customers and citizens are also using the Internet to learn about public issues and, as in the case of the Flaming Fords, to organize large numbers of other people into a powerful force for action. The Internet, then, is a tool for promoting commerce and for expanding public awareness of problems and issues involving products, business practices, and social impacts. In terms of the forces discussed in "The Corporation and Its Stakeholders," the case of the Flaming Fords underscores how technology is forcing ethics and business strategy closer together. For business today, there is no hiding from a world of stakeholders who are capable of closely observing every decision and every mistake a company makes.

[1] See http://www.flamingfords.com/flaming1.cgi.

Post–Lawrence–Weber:
Business and Society,
Ninth Edition

Business and Public Issues

© The McGraw–Hill
Companies, 1999

Why Public Issues Matter

As the case of the Flaming Fords illustrates, companies cannot afford to ignore their stakeholders. Customers, suppliers, and competitors are capable of quickly organizing forces to pressure a company's managers. Of course, not every claim is legitimate, and not every stakeholder has a request that is reasonable. But managers who ignore the concerns of their company's stakeholders do so at their peril and may place the company at risk.

In the modern business environment, no organization can long ignore legitimate stakeholders whose lives are entwined with the activities of the business. First, many stakeholders (e.g., owners, employees, suppliers) have a legitimate connection to the business, often sacrificing something of value for the success of the enterprise. Second, to ignore stakeholders is to risk the kind of campaign that Ford faced with the Flaming Fords. For this reason, many organizations have created systematic ways of responding to stakeholder issues as they arise and have developed more strategic, longer-term business approaches to their key stakeholder relationships.

Emergence of Public Issues

One reason companies are exploring new ways to build positive relationships with stakeholders is that other, more adversarial approaches have often failed. The first sign of a problem is often a complaint, objection, or protest from a stakeholder or stakeholder group whose expectations are not being met.

For example, a group of residents may object to the odor or smoke from a local plant. Citizens may protest the use of monkeys or mice for scientific research at a local university. Employees may claim that they became ill after eating food prepared in a company's cafeteria or breathing fumes from chemicals used in a manufacturing process. In each case, the complaint serves as an early warning of a problem that the company's management should examine more closely.

The Performance-Expectations Gap

In each of the instances described above, a gap has developed between the expectations of the stakeholder (person or group) and the actual performance of the corporation (see Figure 1). Stakeholder expectations are a mixture of the opinions, attitudes, and beliefs

Figure 1

The performance-expectations gap: A measure of stakeholder wants versus company actions and results.

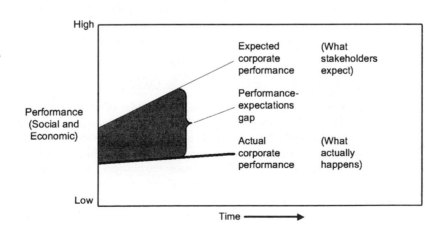

35

Post–Lawrence–Weber:
Business and Society,
Ninth Edition

Business and Public Issues

© The McGraw–Hill
Companies, 1999

of people about what constitutes reasonable business behavior. The residents do not believe that air emissions constitute reasonable behavior; some people who care about animals do not believe it is morally responsible to inflict pain on animals in the name of scientific research; employees who get sick from food or choke on fumes do not believe it is ethically responsible for a company to endanger their health in this way. The following example illustrates how one company has read the signs of stakeholder sentiment and decided to act before the **performance-expectations gap** grew any wider.[2]

> *A few days before Thanksgiving in 1997, the Mattel Toy Co. joined a number of other retailers in adopting a labor code of conduct. The company, which does a huge portion of its annual sales during the Christmas season, had been under pressure from consumers and activist organizations to ensure that the workers who manufacture these toys in countries such as India, Malaysia, and China were not being exploited by suppliers who have been shown to pay slave wages and operate in dangerous conditions. In announcing a code of conduct for its suppliers, Mattel pledged to monitor the conditions in its supplier's plants and halt contracts if they violated the company's wage and safety standards.*

Managers and organizations have a responsibility to identify the beliefs and expectations of their stakeholders as early as possible. Failure to understand their concerns, and to respond appropriately, will permit the performance-expectations gap to grow larger. This gap shows the magnitude of the difference between what the stakeholder expects and the firm's actual performance. The larger the gap, the greater the risk of stakeholder backlash.

The Public Issue Life Cycle

Effective management of stakeholder concerns begins with the understanding that public issues often develop in predictable ways. In other words, it is possible for managers to anticipate how pressures will build around an issue and possibly turn it into a high profile problem that attracts the attention of media and political figures.

A **public issue** exists when there is a gap between the *stakeholder expectations* of what an institution should do and the *actual performance* of those businesses, government agencies, or nonprofit organizations. Ford executives could have anticipated how the Flaming Ford members would act and responded to problems with the defective ignition issue when they were first recognized. One way companies can do so is to study the **public issue life cycle,** shown in Figure 2. This model illustrates the basic phases through which a public issue passes as it matures.

Phases of the Public Issue Life Cycle

Social concerns generally evolve through a series of phases that, because of their natural evolution, can be thought of as a life cycle. By recognizing the pattern through which issues evolve and spotting the early warning signs, managers can anticipate problems and work to resolve them before they reach crisis proportions. As shown in Figure 2, the public issue life cycle contains four phases: the changing of stakeholder expectations; polit-

---

[2] "Mattel Adopts Standards," *New York Times*, November 20, 1997, p. D5; and CNBC, "Nightly Business Report," November 20, 1997, interview with Prakash Sethi, chairman of Mattel's commission.

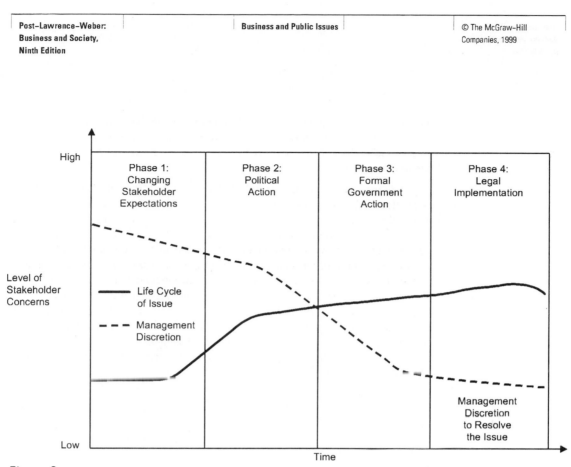

Figure 2

The Public issue life cycle.

ical action; formal government action; and legal implementation. Each phase is discussed below.

Phase 1: Changing stakeholder expectations

Public issues develop as stakeholder expectations of how business or government should behave are not met. This failure can take many forms, ranging from small groups of residents objecting to a local manufacturer's fouling of the air, to the concern of animal lovers for the welfare of monkeys being used in scientific research in a laboratory, to the anger of voters at officials who raise taxes. As discussed above, once a gap develops, the seeds of a public issue have been sown.

> *Few industries have faced as large a legitimacy gap in the 1990s as the American tobacco industry. The industry has battled an increasingly pervasive antismoking climate. For decades, smoking was considered to be glamorous and sophisticated. Advertisements during the 1940s featured movie stars dressed in military uniforms, which gave the impression that smoking was not only glamorous but patriotic. The perception of smokers and smoking is very different today. Smoking has become an unacceptable social behavior. Although the industry has argued that smokers are being unfairly turned into social pariahs, health experts argue that the public has a right to live free from smoke and its negative health effects. Cities, states, and even the federal government have taken steps to ensure that nonsmokers were free of unwanted smoke. In 1993, for example, antismoking advocates proposed legislation (the Smoke-Free*

Post–Lawrence–Weber:
Business and Society,
Ninth Edition

Business and Public Issues

© The McGraw–Hill
Companies, 1999

*Environment Act) in both houses of Congress to prohibit smoking in any build-
ing (other than private homes) that is regularly used by 10 or more workers a
week.[3] And in 1998, California started implementing a law that banned smoking in bars and nightclubs.*

Cigarette manufacturers, such as Philip Morris and R. J. Reynolds, have lived with
the health effects issue for many years. As criticism mounted, the companies identified
segments of the population that oppose and those that support smoking restrictions. Although nonsmokers want restrictions, the companies have effectively argued that smokers have rights too. By campaigning heavily on this theme, the companies have tried to
frame the debate in terms of nonsmokers' reasonable expectations, balancing the rights of
smokers and nonsmokers and finding ways to create accommodation.

What does it take to put a problem on the agenda for action by government? The
agenda of public issues on which officials are asked to act is enormous, and not all public issues warrant action by government. Of the thousands of issues to which government
is asked to respond each year, most fail to get needed support.

Strong and effective leadership is always needed to capture enough public attention
to lead a reform movement. The American civil rights movement, for example, had charismatic leadership in Dr. Martin Luther King, Jr., during the 1960s. Dr. King, a brilliant
public speaker whose speeches attracted large audiences and media coverage, helped to
build powerful support for the expansion of equal opportunity to citizens of all races. Other
movements have had leaders with very different personalities. Ralph Nader's fight for automobile safety won public support with detailed technical analyses of dangerous products, including his famous book, *Unsafe at Any Speed*,[4] Gloria Steinem and Betty Friedan
were effective advocates for women's rights. Cesar Chavez, a quiet and determined leader,
drew public attention to the plight of farm workers through hunger strikes and product
boycotts. Each of these leaders used his or her personality and knowledge to keep issues
in front of the public and its political leaders. There are times when a reform movement's
leadership comes from within the political system itself. In the mid-1990s, Congressman
Newt Gingrich led a political crusade to reduce the power of the federal government, and
more recently, U.S. Senator John McCain led a campaign to change the rules surrounding political campaign financing.

Dramatic events can also prompt government to act. Environmental crises such as
the nuclear power plant accident at Three Mile Island, the tragedy at Union Carbide's
chemical plant in Bhopal, India, or the discovery of chemical dangers in places such as
Love Canal (Niagara Falls, New York) or Times Beach, Missouri, all served to generate
public pressure on government to strengthen environmental protection laws.

Interest groups may signal the emergence of an issue by advocating government action to protect members. Managers must understand what others are asking government
to do and be prepared to ask government to act on behalf of their business. International

---

[3] Philip Morris and R. J. Reynolds developed advertising campaigns using the accommodation
theme. In one RJR-sponsored advertisement, three picture captions read, respectively, "The Berlin
Wall Crumbles," "Russia Approves New Constitution," and "Democracy's Victory in South
Africa." The fourth caption provided a contrast: "Nationwide, Reins on U.S. Smokers' Freedom
Tightens." The title to the ad read: "Where Exactly Is the Land of the Free?" See *New York
Times*, October 25, 1994, p. A17. For a discussion of cigarette companies' business strategies see,
Richard McGowan, *Business, Politics, and Cigarettes* (Westport, CT: Praeger/Quorum Books,
1995).

[4] Ralph Nader, *Unsafe at Any Speed* (New York: Grossman, 1965).

Post–Lawrence–Weber:
Business and Society,
Ninth Edition

Business and Public Issues

© The McGraw–Hill
Companies, 1999

trade conflicts, for example, prompted American companies to ask the federal government to challenge the unfair trade practices of foreign competitors.

U.S. auto manufacturers sought the assistance of the federal government in getting Japan to allow more U.S. vehicles to be sold in that country. The unwillingness of Japan to open its domestic market to the sale of more General Motors, Ford, and Chrysler automobiles contrasted sharply with the U.S. market, where Japanese auto companies have established major market positions with their Toyota, Nissan, and Honda vehicles. U.S. firms claimed Japanese governmental policy was behind the closed market. Hence, only the U.S. government could move Japan to change.

Phase 2: Political action

It may take months or even years for a concerned group of stakeholders to build a base of support sufficient to challenge a corporation. If an issue persists, however, the group may organize formally and campaign for its point of view through pamphlets, newsletters, Web pages, and other forms of print and electronic communication. They may attract the attention of the media, which will result in newspaper, television, or radio coverage. This moves the issue from one of citizen concern to one of political importance.

The political drive against passive smoking took off when the Civil Aeronautics Board ruled that smokers had to be separated from nonsmokers on airline flights. Political developments included the formation of various antismoking groups, including Group Against Smoking Pollution (GASP). GASP received calls from people complaining of illness caused by passive smoke—smoke from other people's cigarettes. They assisted companies that wished to establish smoking restrictions. Antismoking activists attribute corporate willingness to set up such policies to dozens of legal cases in which nonsmokers have sued companies for failing to protect them from passive smoke. The Environmental Protection Agency issued statistics that showed passive smoke kills thousands of people each year, and courts increasingly sided with nonsmokers in passive smoking lawsuits. In 1997, for example, 60,000 airline attendants sued tobacco companies to recover damages for injuries from passive smoke. Trial of the case began, but it ended when the companies negotiated a settlement with the airline attendants. The attendants claimed victory. Governments have also sued tobacco companies for the costs of smoking-related disease. Florida, for example, was the first state to sue tobacco product manufacturers to recover the costs of treating the tobacco-related illnesses of Florida Medicaid patients. Other states followed and the financial risk of such lawsuits led the industry to negotiate with states' attorneys general. (See "The Tobacco Deal" case study.)

Politicians are interested in citizens' concerns and often are anxious to advocate action on their behalf. The government officials become new stakeholders with different types of power to use in closing the gap between public expectations and business performance. The tobacco lobby once had the support of a powerful coalition of elected representatives and senators in Washington. But as antismoking pressures have grown, more elected officials and political candidates have spoken in favor of antismoking laws. Some have also become outspoken critics of the tobacco lobby. The involvement of political actors creates more stakeholders and, hence, makes the issue more complex for the company and its managers.

Post–Lawrence–Weber:
Business and Society,
Ninth Edition

Business and Public Issues

© The McGraw–Hill
Companies, 1999

Phase 3: Formal government action

As more people are drawn into a political conflict, ideas may emerge about how to use laws or regulations to solve the problem. When legislative proposals or draft regulations emerge, the public issue moves to a new level of action.

> *Much legislative action has been taken in favor of antismoking activists during the past decade. Antismoking legislation has been enacted nationally and in many states and cities. The federal government has required that health warnings on cigarette labels be in larger print and that messages be rotated quarterly to provide more effective warnings. Many communities set limits on the areas in restaurants that can be used by smokers, and nonsmokers in the workplace can legally declare their immediate work area a no-smoking zone. Some cities have even outlawed smoking entirely in office buildings, restaurants, and public buildings.*

Companies involved in legislative actions are usually represented by lawyers, lobbyists, and professional political consultants. Top management may be called to testify before government committees or regulatory agencies; corporate lawyers and lobbyists decide what proposals are best and worst for the company, and they make efforts to slow or alter legislative proposals that work against the company's interests.

> *Tobacco companies have hired dozens of lobbyists, lawyers, and political advisers to fight antismoking efforts. In 1997, it was estimated that the tobacco industry was spending $650 million dollars per year in legal and lobbying fees. Individually, and through the Tobacco Institute, an industry association, they have challenged scientific findings and worked to defeat antismoking proposals. Two powerful counterarguments have been used: first, that 50 million U.S. smokers are citizens who also have rights, including the personal freedom to smoke; and second, that taxes on tobacco products are an important source of revenue for cities and states, accounting for many millions of dollars. Legislators who might vote for an antismoking law are sometimes stopped by fears of what it will mean for government to lose tobacco tax revenue or to have angry smokers campaigning against them in the next election.*

Phase 4: Legal implementation

Making a public policy decision does not mean that the policy will be carried out automatically. The validity of new laws and regulations is often challenged through law suits. Once the legal issues are settled, however, the company must comply with the law.

Stakeholder interest in an issue tends to plateau or even decline as a new law or regulation is implemented. New laws often spark lawsuits to test the interpretation and limits of the statute. Once the test cases are over, affected parties will normally abide by the law and compliance will reduce public interest in the issue. If the law is violated or ignored, however, the issue may reemerge, as a new gap develops between stakeholder expectations and the corporation's actual performance.

Business still has a chance to influence how government policy is implemented at this stage of the process. A company may negotiate with a regulatory agency for extending

Post–Lawrence–Weber:
Business and Society,
Ninth Edition

Business and Public Issues

© The McGraw–Hill
Companies, 1999

compliance deadlines, as steel companies have done regarding pollution controls and auto manufacturers have done in introducing air bags and other safety devices. Legal steps can also be taken by appealing to a court to review the law or regulation's constitutionality. Or an industry may play off one branch of government against another. For example, presidential decisions can sometimes be overridden by congressional votes.[5]

Continuing Issues

Debates about some public issues may continue long after the implementation of policy. Advocacy groups may keep the issue alive, knowing that new government officials may be receptive to changing the law or interpreting it differently. Groups opposed to a policy may work to document its negative effects, whereas supporters work to document the positive effects. Government officials may try to find out whether the benefits have been worth more than the costs and whether the policy goals could have been achieved in other, more efficient or less expensive ways.

Public issues often overlap and interweave with one another, creating a complex web of advocacy groups, coalitions, government policies, programs, laws, regulations, court orders, and political maneuvers. Something is always happening in each stage, often involving issues of concern to the company and its management. Thus, the business, or any other interest group, must anticipate and respond to issues in a timely way. That is the essence of good management.

The Public Affairs Function

The pressures on business firms that arise from public issues, plus the increasingly complex relationships organizations have with stakeholders, have led many companies to create specialized staff departments to manage external affairs. The emergence of the corporate public affairs function has been a major innovation in U.S. management in the past two decades, especially as the number of stakeholder issues has grown and issues have become more complex and important to business.[6]

Public affairs management refers to the active management of a company's external relations, especially its relations with external stakeholders such as government, regulatory agencies, and communities. Other names that are sometimes used to describe the function are *external affairs* or *corporate relations*. Some companies have also created separate departments for *community relations, government relations,* and *media relations*. The creation of public affairs units appears to be a global trend as well, with many companies in Canada, Australia, and Europe developing sophisticated public affairs operations.[7]

[5] Hedrick Smith, *The Power Game: How It Works* (New York: Random House, 1988); and Haynes Johnson and David S. Broder, *The System: The American Ways of Politics at the Breaking Point* (Boston, MA: Little, Brown, 1996).
[6] The data for this discussion are reported in James E. Post and Jennifer J. Griffin, *The State of Corporate Public Affairs* (Washington, D.C.: Foundation for Public Affairs, 1997). These data are also discussed in James E. Post and Jennifer J. Griffin, "Corporate Reputation and External Affairs Management," *Corporate Reputation Review* 1 (1997), pp. 165–71.
[7] The survey of Australian companies can be found in James E. Post and Australian Centre for Corporate Public Affairs, "Australian Public Affairs Practice: Results of the 1992 National Public Affairs Survey," in J.E. Post, ed., *Research in Corporate Social Performance and Policy*, vol. 14 (Greenwich, CT: JAI Press, 1993), pp. 93–103.

Post–Lawrence–Weber:
Business and Society,
Ninth Edition

Business and Public Issues

© The McGraw–Hill
Companies, 1999

Although many names are used to describe the function, there is broad agreement among companies as to what activities have to be managed if an organization is to effectively address its external stakeholders. Figure 3 shows the profile of activities performed by public affairs units in more than 250 large and medium-sized companies in the United States.

These activities may seem quite diverse, but they are linked by a company's need to relate to its many stakeholders. Notice how many of the activities refer to a named stakeholder group (e.g., federal, state, and local government relations; community relations; media relations; employee communications; and investor relations). Others refer to activities that are clearly connected to one stakeholder or more (e.g., political action committees, grassroots programs, environmental affairs).

Organizations typically seek three distinct types of contribution from their public affairs operations. As one group of scholars has written,

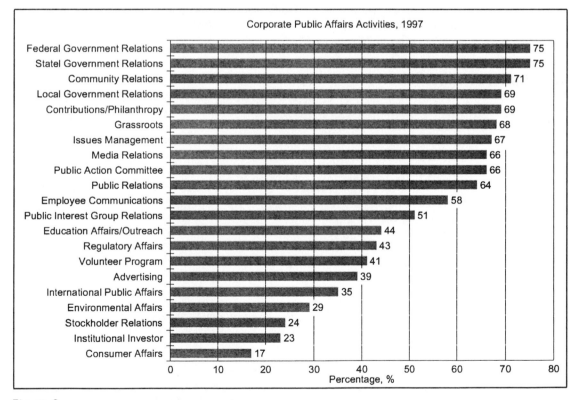

Figure 3

Public affairs activities in a sample of U.S. corporations, 1997.

Source: James E. Post and Jennifer J. Griffin, *The State of Corporate Public Affairs: Final Report* (Washington, DC: Foundation for Public Affairs, 1997). Used with permission.

Post–Lawrence–Weber:
Business and Society,
Ninth Edition

Business and Public Issues

© The McGraw–Hill
Companies, 1999

[T]he essential role of public affairs units appears to be that of a window out of the corporation through which management can perceive, monitor, and understand external change, and simultaneously, a window in through which society can influence corporate policy and practice. This boundary spanning role primarily involves the flow of information to and from the organization. In many firms it also involves the flow of financial resources in the form of political contributions to various stakeholder groups in society.[8]

As shown in Figure 4, three critical elements help define the responsibility of public affairs in relating to stakeholder issues and concerns. These include social and political intelligence, internal communication, and external action programs. Each is discussed below.

- *Social and political intelligence.* Public affairs is responsible for collecting, analyzing, and preparing social and political intelligence for other managers. Issues are identified, trends forecasted, and activists in the external environment are studied. If there is no public affairs unit or staff, the organization must develop alternative ways to gather such information.

- *Internal communication.* Public affairs must communicate what it learns to other managers throughout the company. Public affairs units typically produce daily

Figure 4

Three functions of public affairs management.

The "value added" that public affairs delivers to an organization consists of three parts:

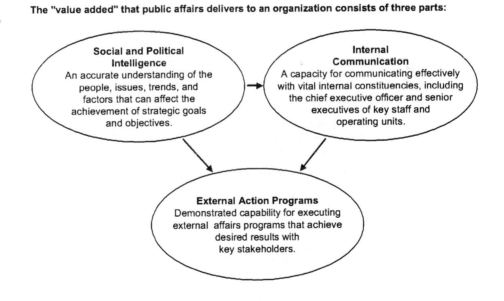

Social and Political Intelligence
An accurate understanding of the people, issues, trends, and factors that can affect the achievement of strategic goals and objectives.

Internal Communication
A capacity for communicating effectively with vital internal constituencies, including the chief executive officer and senior executives of key staff and operating units.

External Action Programs
Demonstrated capability for executing external affairs programs that achieve desired results with key stakeholders.

[8] Boston University Public Affairs Research Group, *Public Affairs Offices and Their Functions: A Summary of Survey Results* (Boston, MA: Boston University School of Management, 1981), p. 1.

reports for the CEO and regular reports for the board of directors and senior executives. Special reports are frequently prepared for strategic planners, heads of business units, and operating managers. Many public issues require that the interests and ideas of managers in many different parts of the organization be coordinated. This coordination is vital to the development of sound positions on complex issues.

- *External action programs.* Public affairs is responsible for developing and executing action programs that target key external stakeholders. Thus, a public affairs department will often have a media contacts program for building regular interaction with the press; a local community affairs program for strengthening contacts with the local community; and state and federal government lobbying operations that ensure the company's voice will be heard by legislators or other government officials.

Many companies have drafted a public affairs mission statement to define that function's purpose and focus. Most companies have appointed a senior manager or executive to lead the public affairs department, providing a direct voice and perspective on the company's major strategy and policy decisions. The size of the department and the support staff vary widely across companies. Many companies assign employees from other parts of the business to work on public affairs issues and to help plan, coordinate, and execute public affairs activities. In this way, the formulation and implementation of the policies and programs developed by a company's public affairs unit are closely linked to the primary business activities of the firm. The organization chart for the public affairs organization of a modern global corporation is illustrated in Figure 5.

Figure 5

Public affairs
organization for a
global corporation.

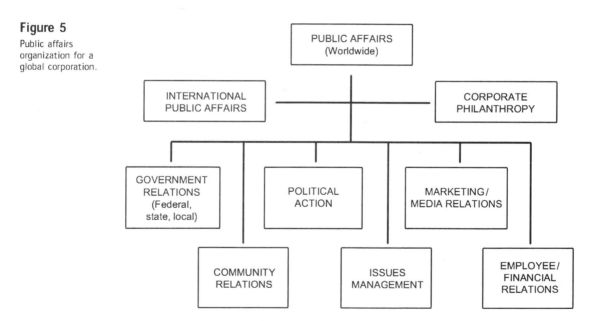

Post–Lawrence–Weber:
Business and Society,
Ninth Edition

Business and Public Issues

© The McGraw–Hill
Companies, 1999

Managing Issues

The Process

Issues management is a structured and systematic method through which companies respond to those public issues that are of greatest importance to the business. Companies rarely have full control of a public issue because of the many factors involved. But it is possible for an organization to create a management system that monitors issues as they emerge and involves managers in action to minimize the negative effects of a public issue or to maximize the positive effects to the organization's advantage. One of the foremost practitioners of systematic issues management is the Dow Chemical Company.

> *According to its executives, Dow Chemical created an issues management system to provide an early warning/early response capability so that a public issue's positive potential can be encouraged and enhanced and its negative potential can be discouraged or inhibited. "The objective is to identify issues in the early stages of development before options are narrowed and liabilities expanded. The difference between issues management and crisis management is timing."*[9]

Managers have less influence on a public issue as it evolves. That is another way of saying that the sooner a company can become involved in managing an issue, the more likely it can shape an outcome that is acceptable to the organization and others. The issues management process is a basic tool used to achieve this objective. Figure 6 illustrates the components of a typical issues management system.

Figure 6

The issues
management process.

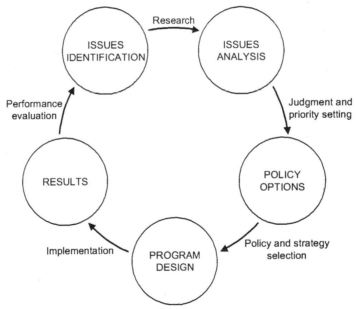
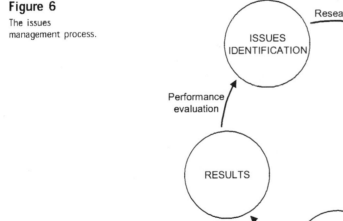

[9] Tony Jacques, Public Affairs Manager, Dow Chemical (Australia) Limited. Presentation at Public Affairs Institute, Melbourne, Australia, July 1994.

Post–Lawrence–Weber:
Business and Society,
Ninth Edition

Business and Public Issues

© The McGraw–Hill
Companies, 1999

Issues identification

This involves the active scanning of newspapers, other media, experts' views, and community concerns to identify issues of concern to the public. Because there are many ways to spot emerging issues, managers must decide how best to focus their efforts. Companies often use electronic databases, including the Internet, to track ideas, themes, and issues that may be relevant to their public policy interests.

Issues analysis

Once identified, the facts and implications of the issue must be analyzed. For example, an analysis of the dioxin issue would show that there is much discussion among scientists as to the chemical process of dioxin exposure and much debate as to whether, or how, dioxin contamination can be cleaned up. Similarly, tobacco companies have invested in having researchers examine every study that claims a link between passive smoking and health effects. Issue analysis is guided by management's need to answer two basic questions: (1) What impact can this issue have on our business? and (2) What is the probability that this issue will evolve into later stages of the public issue life cycle?

Policy options

An issue's impact and probability of occurrence tell managers how significant the issue is for the company; but they do not tell management what to do. Developing policy options involves creating choices. It requires complex judgments that incorporate ethical considerations, the company's reputation and good name, and other nonquantifiable factors. Management may decide to change internal practices, operating procedures, or even the product itself. Companies in the pulp and paper industry, for example, have invested in developing new bleaching technologies to eliminate chlorine from their manufacturing processes.[10] Management may also focus on changing the views of officials, the public, or the media. Doing nothing may also be an option if an issue is not ripe for immediate action. Research organizations, such as think tanks, can be useful sources of ideas about alternative policy options. These groups issue papers on many public policy topics, including environmental practices, taxation, minimum wages, and regulation.[11]

Program design

Once the policy option has been chosen, the company must design and implement an appropriate program. For example, tobacco companies made a policy choice to fight antismoking proposals in every city, state, and political district in which such proposals are made. Their program was designed to ensure that no antismoking law is created without efforts by the industry to shape, influence, or kill the proposal. This "fight on every front" policy requires a very expensive program, but it has been an integral part of the tobacco companies' strategy for years.

Early issues identification enables a company to build political capital before it is needed. Often, a company creates goodwill by helping other organizations, which, in time, can lead those organizations into becoming the company's allies.

---

[10]See "Ecology, Sustainable Development, and Global Business" and "Managing Environmental Issues" for additional examples.
[11]David Ricci, *The Transformation of American Politics: The New Washington and the Rise of Think Tanks* (New Haven, CT: Yale University Press, 1993).

Post–Lawrence–Weber:
Business and Society,
Ninth Edition

Business and Public Issues

© The McGraw–Hill
Companies, 1999

For many years, Philip Morris has been a patron of the arts. Millions of its dollars have supported museums, art galleries, and performing arts organizations across the nation. Philip Morris, which has its corporate headquarters in New York, faced the prospect of a complete ban on cigarettes in restaurants and other public places under an ordinance proposed by the New York City Council. Philip Morris executives telephoned arts institutions that had benefited from the company grants and asked them to put in a good word with the city council. The company said it would have to move away from New York if such a ban were passed, with inevitable loss of support for the arts organizations. The arts groups were asked to tell the city council how much that would mean to their organizations.[12]

Results

Once a company has tried an issues management program, it must study the results and make adjustments if necessary. Because political issues may take considerable time to evolve, it is important that the manager entrusted with a particular issue regularly update senior managers as to the actions and effectiveness of other stakeholders. The company may reposition or even rethink its approach to the issue.

Managing a Single Issue

Traditionally, public issues are managed by the company's public affairs or government relations staff. A new trend is for responsibility of managing an issue to be placed in the hands of managers from the area of the business most affected by the problem. For example, an issue involving tax rates or depreciation schedules would be assigned to an issues manager from the company's tax department; an issue involving local protests of truck traffic at a plant in Tulsa, Oklahoma, would properly be assigned to the plant manager of the Tulsa facility. TRW, a global manufacturer of defense and industrial products, pioneered the management of issues by operating managers when it created its "quarterback system," in which one manager coordinates the efforts of a team of people from across the company.

When an issue involves several areas of a company's business, an *issues management team* may be created to deal with the issue. Building on the quarterback concept, these teams are led by a manager from the area most directly affected by the problem. She or he will "own" the issue and be responsible for ensuring that the company is acting appropriately to manage the problem. Experts from other areas within the company will be included in the team as needed. Through the use of electronic mail and other technologies, teams can be organized from personnel at different locations.

For example, Dow Chemical created a global issues management team in the 1990s to deal with public issues surrounding chlorine. As one of the world's largest producers of chlorine, Dow had a very large stake in proposals to ban or regulate the use of chlorine, a widely used chemical in modern manufacturing. Members of the global issues management team were drawn from the United States, Europe, and Asia-Pacific and included scientists, plant man-

---

[12]"Hooked on Tobacco Sponsorships," *New York Times*, January 13, 1998, p. A22; for more background, see Maureen Dowd, "Philip Morris Calls in I.O.U.'s in the Arts," *New York Times*, October 5, 1994, pp. A1, C4.

Post–Lawrence–Weber:
Business and Society,
Ninth Edition

Business and Public Issues

© The McGraw–Hill
Companies, 1999

*agers, and managers from Dow's manufacturing businesses that would be af-
fected by any changes in the availability of chlorine. The global issues management team analyzed scientific studies of chlorine, followed government actions across the world, coordinated research into various aspects of the
problem, and worked with the company's lobbyists and government relations
staff to ensure Dow spoke with one voice when talking about chlorine.*

Issues management teams usually exist only as long as the issue is a high priority
for the company. This mirrors the modern management trend toward using task forces and
other temporary team assignments to manage issues in companies. Rather than create large
staffs and costly bureaucracies, companies have learned that flexibility is the key to managing public issues as well as other aspects of the business.

Managing Multiple Issues

Companies facing many public issues need to set priorities about which ones will receive
the most attention. Many companies use an *issues priority matrix* such as that shown in
Figure 7. The number of issues that a company can actively work on is limited by resources. If resources are limited, only high-priority issues (those with the greatest impact
on the firm and highest chance of occurring) will be assigned for managers to work on;
the company may use trade associations or consultants to follow less important issues.

Crisis Management

Crisis management is the process companies use to respond to short-term
and immediate shocks, such as accidents, disasters, catastrophes, and injuries.
It is not easy to generalize about how to manage in a crisis. As one crisis management

Figure 7

The issues priority matrix.

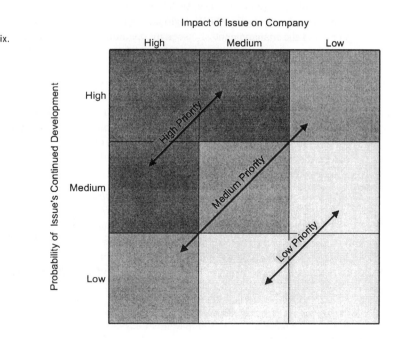

Post–Lawrence–Weber:
Business and Society,
Ninth Edition

Business and Public Issues

© The McGraw–Hill
Companies, 1999

adviser has written, "It is true that every corporate crisis is unique; that is to say, the underlying circumstances are unique, the individuals who are involved are unique to that company or to that organization, the facts, the timing and anything else going on in the marketplace is unique. Therefore, every situation has to be managed on its own terms."[13] There are, however, certain characteristics that emerge time and again. (See Exhibit A)

What Is a Crisis?

According to the consultant quoted above, four characteristics define a crisis.

1. *Surprise.* Surprise is the single-most defining characteristic of a crisis. The organization is not ready for the event, it happens without warning, and managers are left trying to react to events beyond their control. "Expect the unexpected," said one experienced observer of organizational crises.

2. *Lack of information.* Crises often put managers in the position of needing to act, but having to do so without reliable information. Today, most managers operate in an information-rich environment. But when a crisis strikes, managers may be forced to act quickly without full and complete information. When TWA Flight 800 crashed on takeoff over the Long Island Sound, for example, TWA executives and employees were caught without vital information about the aircraft and its passengers. Without an accurate passenger list, TWA could not confirm the number of people on board and presumed dead. Sixteen hours passed before the company's CEO arrived in New York and was able to speak to the media. Lack of information slowed communications between the airline, government officials, rescue workers, and the families of passengers on board.

3. *Escalating pace of events.* A crisis does not wait until a company is ready for it. Once a crisis begins, it often sets in motion a chain of events that increases in number and complexity for the company. For example, when the *Exxon Valdez* oil spill occurred in Alaska, government agencies and environmental groups were on the scene at Prince William Sound well before Exxon was able to establish its communications command center. Government officials and environmental spokespersons were able to hold press conferences and define the crisis their way. This enabled them to create expectations and set the agenda for what would be an adequate response by Exxon. All of this occurred before any Exxon officials were on site to make their own determination of the oil spill.

4. *Intense scrutiny.* During a crisis, the world is watching every move executives make. In the normal course of business, managers make decisions on the basis of research and analysis, extensive consultation within experts within the company, and careful deliberation, and they do so *in private*. During a crisis, every single decision is closely scrutinized and subject to immediate assessment by the media, government officials, and many other external stakeholders. Crisis management is management in a fishbowl. Feedback comes quickly, whether as praise, criticism, or condemnation. This makes it very hard for managers to internalize the feedback they are receiving and evaluate what others are saying.

---

[13] Ray O'Rourke, "Managing in Times of Crisis," *Corporate Reputation Review* 1 (1997), pp. 120–25.

Post–Lawrence–Weber:
Business and Society,
Ninth Edition

Business and Public Issues

© The McGraw–Hill
Companies, 1999

EXHIBIT A   Key Principles of Crisis Management

What does one do when a crisis occurs? According to experts, there are some principles, not *rules*, that can be useful to managers facing a crisis.

Define the Real Problem

Crises tend to force managers to think short term and focus on the narrow problem at hand. Experience suggests that the crisis management team should ask several reflective questions: What would constitute a good job in managing this crisis? What can we accomplish? What is impossible?

Set Goals and Define the Crisis Strategy in Light of Those Goals

The urge to act first, think later is hard to resist when facing a crisis. Experts suggest that the better course is to have some managers actively thinking about the goals—What do we want to accomplish? How do we want to be perceived by the media? By our shareholders? By our employees and customers?

Manage the Flow of Information

Experts advise managers to tell the story their way, consistently, and frequently. Because electronic media repeat crisis stories quite frequently in a typical news day, managers have an opportunity to correct errors and should not permit an erroneous statement to stand unchallenged.

Adopt a Team Approach

It is important to have one spokesperson designated at the outset and available to act on the company's behalf immediately. Successful companies have thought in advance about the skills each crisis team should possess. Legal, media, and government relations skills are essential in many crisis situations.

Plan for the Worst Case

A crisis always has the potential to worsen, and managers need to anticipate the worst-case possibility. It is tempting to assume a crisis will pass and the world will return to normal. Experience suggests it is wise to prepare for the worst.

Plan on the Situation Getting Worse

By doing so, an organization can begin to see ahead and create contingency plans for communicating with key stakeholders, deploying resources, and organizing other companies and people for action.

Follow Up after the Crisis is Over

Many contacts with stakeholders occur during a crisis. Experience suggests that a company can restore its image and reputation by dedicated follow-up to stakeholders.

Use Technology

Information technology can be a powerful aid to a company facing a crisis and needing to communicate with stakeholders. Experts also advise that a company should measure the effectiveness of communication messages through polling, surveys, and focus-group interviews.

Don't Give Up

As bad as it can be for an organization, a crisis rarely destroys a well-managed business. Leadership is vital if an organization's internal and external stakeholders are to believe that there is a bright future beyond the crisis.

Source: Adapted from Ray O'Rourke, "Managing in Times of Crisis," *Corporate Reputation Review* 1 (1997), pp. 120–25.

Post–Lawrence–Weber:
Business and Society,
Ninth Edition

Business and Public Issues

© The McGraw–Hill
Companies, 1999

Is it possible to really manage a crisis? Although managers are at a disadvantage, there are a number of principles that experts believe help minimize the impact of a crisis on the organization. And since no two crises are ever alike, managers can only try to learn the lessons from past crises to be more prepared for the future. As shown in Exhibit A, advisers to companies that have been caught in crises have learned some lessons that enable us to define some guidelines and suggestions. Still, a company's executives often have to rely on their own good sense and instincts for dealing with stakeholders when facing a crisis.

Strategic Management of Stakeholder Relations

Companies are learning that it is important to take a strategic approach to stakeholder relations. That requires thinking ahead, understanding what is important to each stakeholder, and determining when it is possible to cooperate and when it is necessary to disagree. Strategic thinking recognizes that while some disagreement may be inevitable, a company's long-term well-being is dependent on the continued support and cooperation of its many stakeholders.

To manage stakeholder relations in a strategic way, three types of actions must be undertaken. As illustrated in Figure 8, management must first be aware of the company's stakeholders and demonstrate an acceptance of their legitimate right to participate in decisions affecting them. Second, the company must think proactively about how its plans

Figure 8

Strategic management approach to managing external relations.

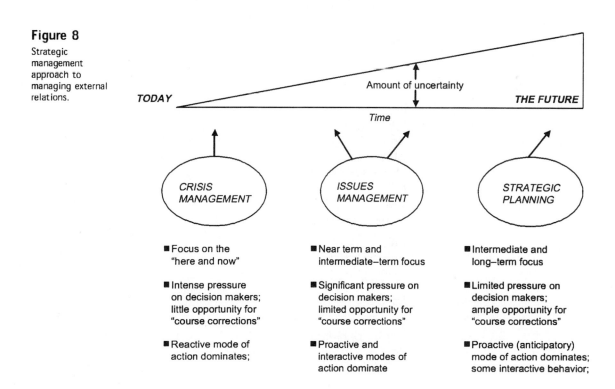

Post–Lawrence–Weber:
Business and Society,
Ninth Edition

Business and Public Issues

© The McGraw–Hill
Companies, 1999

will affect, positively and negatively, its many stakeholders. Plans should be developed to build support whenever possible and creatively address negative impacts when they occur. Third, the firm should manage issues carefully and consistently, recognizing the possibility that issues may explode if mishandled, possibly creating other unanticipated and unforeseen problems.

For example, Ford Motor Company has developed important relationships with suppliers, dealers, and customers. The company regularly surveys purchasers of its products, for example, to determine customer satisfaction with the automobiles and trucks, service problems, and other concerns. This approach helps the company meet the second principle of anticipating the impact of decisions on stakeholders and the reaction of those stakeholders. Ford knows its customers, many of whom are repeat purchasers of Ford products. Still, unexpected surprises can and do occur. Ford claims it was greatly surprised by the reactions of its customers when it refused to settle the ignition fire cases.

Strategies of Response

Businesses respond to stakeholder pressures in various ways. Some firms steadfastly adhere to their plans, no matter how strong the opposition or pressure from others. Some firms change only when forced to do so by strong outside pressures. Others actively attempt to move stakeholders in directions that will be to the company's advantage. And some try to find ways to harmonize the company's goals and objectives with the changing needs, goals, and expectations of the public. These approaches are respectively referred to as **inactive, reactive, proactive,** and **interactive strategies of response,** as illustrated in Figure 9.

Figure 9

Four basic strategies of response to stakeholder issues.

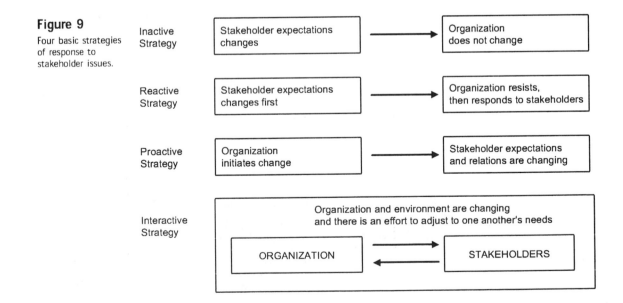

Post–Lawrence–Weber:
Business and Society,
Ninth Edition

Business and Public Issues

© The McGraw–Hill
Companies, 1999

Companies may use any of these strategies in responding to a particular issue or problem. Sometimes a company will quite deliberately be slow to respond (reactive) to an issue. At other times, the same company may be deliberately proactive in trying to head off an issue before it develops into a major problem. Some companies display a general preference for one or another of these strategies in dealing with many types of issues, although it is unclear whether this is just a style of management or a conscious strategy for use in responding to a particular issue. As the following example suggests, today's strategy may have to change—perhaps dramatically—if the business environment changes.

Petroleum companies have long explored for oil in remote and difficult-to-reach places. Offshore exploration has been one great challenge, as companies have sought to build and operate drilling rigs in deep ocean waters amidst hurricane winds, blizzard storms, and waves the size of high-rise buildings. And in the remote jungles of African, Asian, and Latin American nations another kind of problem has arisen. Having long been accused of operating with disregard for the enormous environmental impact of drilling and production activities and running roughshod over the rights of native peoples, companies such as Royal Dutch/Shell and Mobil have been the target of boycotts and other protests by global activist organizations. Stymied by such protests, Shell and Mobil are pursuing a different approach in developing the rich gas resources of Camisea, a remote area in Peru with enormous potential. Working with government officials, local environmental groups, and international advisers, the companies are making a major effort to work with local Indian tribes and critics. Plans have been adapted to local conditions, and the companies are earning respect for listening and changing their traditional practices.[14]

Summary Points

- Stakeholder expectations can, if unmet, trigger action to transform social concern into pressure on business and government. The existence of a gap between what is expected and actual performance stimulates the formation of a public issue.

- The public issue life cycle describes the evolution of a social concern through stages of politicalization, formal government action, and implementation of legally mandated change. Every public issue passes through these stages, and managers can predict what will happen if the performance-expectations gap is not closed.

- An organization's public affairs function is charged with collecting and analyzing information about the social and political environment, communicating with internal audiences, and interacting with stakeholders to achieve the organization's objectives.

- Companies can develop reactive, proactive, or interactive strategies to respond to public issues. Some steadfastly adhere to inactive strategies. Most organizations will develop separate strategies for each issue they are trying to manage.

[14]Jonathan Friedland, "Green Acres: Oil Companies Strive to Turn a New Leaf to Save Rain Forest," *The Wall Street Journal*, July 17, 1997, pp. A1, A8.

Post–Lawrence–Weber:
Business and Society,
Ninth Edition

Business and Public Issues

© The McGraw–Hill
Companies, 1999

- Issues management includes identification and analysis of issues; development of policy options; program design; implementation; and evaluation of the results of such activities.
- Crisis management is the process organizations use to respond to short-term and immediate shocks, such as accidents, distress, and catastrophes. A number of practical guidelines have emerged through experience. Effective crisis management always begins with the proactive step of being prepared.
- Strategic management of stakeholder relations involves awareness of stakeholders and their interests, proactive planning of relationship development with them, and readiness to respond quickly and effectively to issues and crises.

Key Terms and Concepts

- Performance-expectations gap
- Public issue
- Public issue life cycle
- Public affairs management

- Issues management
- Crisis management
- Inactive, reactive, proactive, interactive strategies of response

Internet Resources

- http://allpolitics.com
- http://nationaljournal.com

CNN/*Time* review of emerging social-
  political issues
National Journal index of current events

Discussion Case McDonald's Plays Tough in UK

Dave Morris and Helen Steel didn't look like they were capable of challenging a multi-billion (U.S.) corporation in the court of world opinion. But that's just what they did, and in doing so, they held their own against one of the world's best marketing organizations.

The Problem

Morris (age 43) and Steel (age 31) were accused of libeling McDonald's by passing out leaflets on London streets that charged the company with exploiting underpaid workers, despoiling the environment, and endangering human health. Entitled "What's Wrong with McDonald's?" the leaflet claimed that McDonald's sells products that are high in fat, sugar, and salt, and low in fiber, vitamins, and minerals, all factors associated with breast cancer and bowel and heart disease. It also charged that the company exploits children by using gimmicks to get them to eat junk food, underpays its staff, creates mountains of waste through discarded packaging, is cruel to animals, and helps destroy South American rain forests to make way for cattle ranches.

Following its worldwide strategy of defending its brand name and reputation, McDonald's decided to go to court to secure an injunction. To do so, it was necessary

Post–Lawrence–Weber:
Business and Society,
Ninth Edition

Business and Public Issues

© The McGraw–Hill
Companies, 1999

to sue Morris and Steel for damages to get a court hearing. The London media publicized the controversy and quickly christened the case, "McLibel." The David-and-Goliath imagery was enhanced when it was disclosed that the leafleteers were a $105-a-week welfare recipient and a part-time bartender.

Strategy and Counterstrategy

British libel law is relatively restrictive unlike U.S. law where free speech protections have created a broad immunity to libel suits. McDonald's decided to press its case in the British courts and hired Richard Rampton, a libel specialist, to head its legal team. Rampton, it was later disclosed, charges more than $3,285 (U.S.) per day. The proceedings involved 313 days of hearings and the testimony of more than 130 witnesses (some testified for as long as two weeks). The trial produced 40,000 documents and more than 20,000 pages of transcripts.

If McDonald's thought the lawsuit would discourage criticism of its business activities, it was badly mistaken. The McLibel Support Campaign raised donations for the defense and conducted a public campaign against the company by handing out two million leaflets in Britain since the controversy began in 1990. The group also used the World Wide Web (http://www.mcspotlight.org) to post such documents as the transcript of the trial, McDonald's 500-page summing-up document, film clips, and other documentation in 15 different languages.

Morris and Steel were unable to afford lawyers and chose to fight their own case. They flew in witnesses from around the world with donations from supporters. They cross-examined McDonald's executives and filed a countersuit for libel against McDonald's after the company issued leaflets that accused them of spreading lies.

Negotiations

McDonald's tried to reach a negotiated settlement with Morris and Steel. A McDonald's spokesman said there were two separate attempts to reach a mutually acceptable resolution. Morris and Steel said that McDonald's asked them for between $130,000 and $190,000 damages; but McDonald's stated it only wanted to ensure that the pair does not continue to libel the company, calling the claim for damages a legal formality. Morris and Steel claimed that McDonald's executives from corporate headquarters (Oak Brook, Illinois) tried on three occasions to persuade them to agree to an out-of-court settlement. They said they refused to do so unless McDonald's guaranteed to refrain from suing other people who make similar allegations, a condition the company rejected.

The Verdict

Morris and Steel said that if they lost the court proceeding to McDonald's, they would exercise their right to appeal the case. In addition, they threatened to bring the case before the European Court of Human Rights. A McDonald's spokesperson said that if the company lost the first round to Morris and Steel, it would appeal the decision to a higher court.

On June 19, 1997, Judge Rodger Bell handed down his verdict. The judge found that Morris and Steel had libeled McDonald's by making certain untrue statements regarding environmental damage in third-world countries and claiming that the company's food was unhealthy and dangerous for public consumption.

Post–Lawrence–Weber:
Business and Society,
Ninth Edition

Business and Public Issues

© The McGraw–Hill
Companies, 1999

The judge also found that Morris and Steel had *not* libeled McDonald's on such issues as child labor, wages rates, and some food-related claims. Finally, the judge ordered that Morris and Steel pay McDonald's the sum of $100,000 in damages.

The trial itself took over three years, making it the longest-running case in British history. Morris and Steel immediately declared victory.

Sources: Ray Moseley, "Three-year Trial Pits Burger Giant against a Pair of Leafleteers," *Boston Globe,* June 15, 1997, p. A23. Also, John Vidal, *Burger Culture on Trial* (New York: New Press,

Discussion Questions

1. Whose expectations are at stake in this case? What performance changes could McDonald's conceivably make to close the gap?
2. How did this issue evolve through the public issues life cycle? What were the drivers?
3. What kind of an issues management team would you want to assemble if you were an executive at McDonald's? What skills would you want represented on the team?
4. Using the suggested guidelines in Exhibit A, describe what steps McDonald's might have taken to deal with Morris and Steel.

Bibliography

Academy of Management Review. Special Topic Forum on Shifting Paradigms: Societal Expectations and Corporate Performance, vol. 20, no. 1, January 1995.

Dennis, Lloyd B., ed. *Practical Public Affairs in an Era of Change.* Lanham, MD: Public Relations Society of America and University Press of America, 1996.

Dertouzas, Michael L.; Richard K. Lester; and Robert M. Solow. *Made in America: Regaining the Productivity Edge.* Cambridge, MA: MIT Press, 1989.

Dickie, Robert B., and Leroy S. Rouner, eds. *Corporations and the Common Good.* South Bend, IN: University of Notre Dame Press, 1986.

Drucker, Peter. *The New Realities.* New York: Harper and Row, 1989.

Etzioni, Amitai. *The New Golden Rule.* New York: Basic Books, 1996.

——————. *The Spirit of Community.* New York: Crown Publishers. 1993.

Frederick, William C. *Values, Nature, and Culture in the American Corporation.* New York: Oxford University Press, 1995.

Freeman, R. Edward. *Strategic Management: A Stakeholder Approach.* Marshfield, MA: Pitman, 1984.

Heath, Robert L., ed. *Strategic Issues Management,* 2d ed. San Francisco, CA: Jossey-Bass, 1996.

Kennedy, Paul. *Preparing for the Twenty-First Century.* New York: Vintage/Random House, 1994.

Krugman, Paul. *The Age of Diminished Expectations.* Cambridge, MA: MIT Press, 1994.

Post, James E., ed. *Research in Corporate Social Performance and Policy.* "The Corporation and Public Affairs," Vol. 14. Greenwich, CT: JAI Press, 1994.

Werhane, Patricia H. *Adam Smith & His Legacy for Modern Capitalism.* New York: Oxford University Press, 1990.

Wolfe, Alan. *One Nation, After All.* New York: Viking, 1998.

Post–Lawrence–Weber:
Business and Society,
Ninth Edition

Corporate Social
Responsibility

© The McGraw–Hill
Companies, 1999

Corporate Social Responsibility

Corporate social responsibility challenges businesses to be accountable for the consequences of their actions affecting the firm's stakeholders while they pursue traditional economic goals. The general public expects businesses to be socially responsible, and many companies have responded by making social goals a part of their overall business operations. Guidelines for acting in socially responsible ways are not always clear, thus producing controversy about what constitutes such behavior, how extensive it should be, and what it costs to be socially responsible.

This topic focuses on these key questions and objectives:

- What is the basic meaning of corporate social responsibility?
- Where and when did the idea of social responsibility originate?
- What must a company do to be considered socially responsible?
- Is corporate social responsibility practiced by businesses around the world?
- What are the limits of corporate social responsibility?
- How does business meet its economic and legal obligations while being socially responsible?

Post–Lawrence–Weber:
Business and Society,
Ninth Edition

Corporate Social
Responsibility

© The McGraw–Hill
Companies, 1999

Do managers have a responsibility to their stockholders? Certainly, for the owners of the business have invested their capital in the firm. Do managers also have a responsibility, a social responsibility, to their employees? Since worker satisfaction appears closely related to productivity, being socially supportive of employees seems to make good economic sense; thus, social responsibility to employees may also benefit the firm's stockholders. What happens when these, and other, responsibilities seem to clash? The following two stories reflect different views of managerial responsibility, particularly to the firm's employees. The approaches are at different ends of the spectrum in the debate over corporate social responsibility.

At Caterpillar Inc., the chief executive officer, Donald V. Fites, was accused by many of his own employees of various antiworker practices. The workers claimed that Fites eliminated unions by beating back a strike attempt, closed plants, and provided management with huge paychecks while holding down wage increases for blue-collar employees. Yet, many of his colleagues cited his company's behavior as being a model of social responsibility. Fites was credited with turning around Caterpillar. His strategy may have saved tens of thousands of jobs for Americans when many of his competitors were shifting employment to low-wage sites abroad. "The first and most important responsibility of any corporation is to be economically viable," said Peter Feuille, the director of the Institute for Labor and Industrial Relations at the University of Illinois. Caterpillar's Fites seemed to embody that form of social responsibility.

Employees experienced a different version of corporate social responsibility at Harman International, a speaker manufacturing company. Recently President Clinton held up Sidney Harman, chief executive of Harman International, as a model of how treating workers well is not only the right thing to do but also good for business. Harman offered extensive training programs for his employees and experimented with allowing workers to share in the proceeds of cost savings they proposed to management. Despite a downturn in the industry in 1996, when layoffs at the company were inevitable, Harman sought to keep his workers employed by putting them on the payroll of a firm he called Off Line Enterprises. This firm made wiring for Harman International that would otherwise be purchased from suppliers. Laid-off employees also worked as security officers and gardeners at Harman International plants, jobs that would normally have gone to outside contractors. Keeping these 250 workers on the payroll cost the company $130,000 a week. Yet, Harman noted that most of the cost was made up in savings on what the company would otherwise have paid outside suppliers for parts and service. Harman planned to have these workers go back to their regular jobs as soon as industry demand picked up.[1]

Which firm, Caterpillar or Harman International, is practicing corporate social responsibility? Which firm will survive in the long run and why? Which firm would you want to work for?

We discuss the advantages and drawbacks of being socially responsible. Most of all, though, we argue that social responsibility is an inescapable demand made by society. Whether businesses are large or small, make goods or provide services, operate at home or abroad, willingly try to be socially responsible or fight against it all the way—there is no doubt about what the public expects. Many business leaders also subscribe to the idea

[1] Richard W. Stevenson, "Do People and Profits Go Hand in Hand? Different Views of Corporate Responsibility, but Companies Share Goals," *New York Times,* May 9, 1996, pp. C1, C2.

Post–Lawrence–Weber:
Business and Society,
Ninth Edition

Corporate Social
Responsibility

© The McGraw–Hill
Companies, 1999

of social responsibility. A *Business Week*/Harris poll revealed that U.S. top-level corporate executives (69 percent of those polled) and MBA students (89 percent) believe that corporations should become more involved in solving social problems. Similar beliefs were recorded in a study of 107 European corporations, in which a majority of CEOs surveyed agreed that addressing social issues, such as substance abuse, health care, and education, was needed.[2]

The Meaning of Corporate Social Responsibility

Corporate social responsibility means that a corporation should be held accountable for any of its actions that affect people, their communities, and their environment. It implies that negative business impacts on people and society should be acknowledged and corrected if at all possible. It may require a company to forgo some profits if its social impacts are seriously harmful to some of its stakeholders or if its funds can be used to promote a positive social good.

The Many Responsibilities of Business

However, being socially responsible does not mean that a company must abandon its other primary missions. As discussed later, a business has many responsibilities: economic, legal, and social. The challenge for management is the blending of these responsibilities into a comprehensive corporate strategy while not losing sight of any of its obligations. At times these responsibilities will clash; at other times they will work together to better the firm. Thus, having multiple and sometimes competing responsibilities does not mean that socially responsible firms cannot be as profitable as others less responsible; some are and some are not.

Social responsibility requires companies to balance the benefits to be gained against the costs of achieving those benefits. Many people believe that both business and society gain when firms actively strive to be socially responsible. Others are doubtful, saying that business's competitive strength is weakened by taking on social tasks. The arguments on both sides of this debate are presented later.

Social Responsibility and Corporate Power

The social responsibilities of business grow directly out of two features of the modern corporation: (1) the essential functions it performs for a variety of stakeholders and (2) the immense influence it has on the lives of the stakeholders. We count on corporations for job creation, much of our community well-being, the standard of living we enjoy, the tax base for essential municipal, state, and national services, and our needs for banking and financial services, insurance, transportation, communication, utilities, entertainment, and a growing proportion of health care. These positive achievements suggest that the corporate form of business is capable of performing a great amount of good for society, such as encouraging economic growth, expanding international trade, and creating new technology.

[2]David L. Mathison, "European and American Executive Values," *Business Ethics: A European Review*, April 1993, pp. 97–100.

The following well-known quotation, frequently appearing in journals for business executives, challenges the readers to assume a responsible role for business in society:

Business has become, in the last half century, the most powerful institution on the planet. The dominant institution in any society needs to take responsibility for the whole. . . . Every decision that is made, every action that is taken, must be viewed in light of that kind of responsibility.[3]

Consider the following statistics: the world's largest industrial corporations employ only .05 of 1 percent of the world's population, yet they control 25 percent of the world's economic output. The top 300 transnationals own nearly 25 percent of the world's productive assets. Of the world's 100 largest economies, 50 are corporations. In the world's international currency markets, more than $1 trillion changes hands each day; the traders are seeking instant profits unrelated to the production or trade of real goods and services.[4]

Many people are concerned about potential corporate influence. The focused power found in the modern business corporation means that every action it takes can affect the quality of human life—for individuals, for communities, and for the entire globe. This obligation is often referred to as the **iron law of responsibility.** The iron law of responsibility says that in the long run, those who do not use power in ways that society considers responsible will tend to lose it.[5] With such technology as computers, communications satellites, and television networks drawing the world into a tighter and tighter global village, the entire Planet Earth has become a stakeholder in all corporations. All societies are now affected by corporate operations. As a result, social responsibility has become a worldwide expectation.

How Corporate Social Responsibility Began

In the United States, the idea of corporate social responsibility appeared around the turn of the twentieth century. Corporations at that time came under attack for being too big, too powerful, and guilty of antisocial and anticompetitive practices. Critics tried to curb corporate power through antitrust laws, banking regulations, and consumer-protection laws.

Faced with this kind of social protest, a few farsighted business executives advised corporations to use their power and influence voluntarily for broad social purposes rather than for profits alone. Some of the wealthier business leaders—steelmaker Andrew Carnegie is a good example—became great philanthropists who gave much of their wealth to educational and charitable institutions. Others, like automaker Henry Ford, developed paternalistic programs to support the recreational and health needs of their employees. The point to emphasize is that these business leaders believed that business had a responsibility to society that went beyond or worked in parallel with their efforts to make profits.[6]

---

[3] David C. Korten, "Limits to the Social Responsibility of Business," The People-Centered Development Forum, no. 19, June 1, 1996.

[4] David C. Korten, *When Corporations Rule the World* (San Francisco: Kumarian Press, 1995).

[5] This concept first appeared in Keith Davis and Robert Blomstrom, *Business and Its Environment* (New York: McGraw-Hill, 1966).

[6] Harold R. Bowen, *Social Responsibilities of the Businessman* (New York: Harper, 1953); and Morrell Heald, *The Social Responsibility of Business: Company and Community, 1900–1960* (Cleveland: Case-Western Reserve Press, 1970). For a history of how some of these business philanthropists acquired their wealth, see Matthew Josephson, *The Robber Barons: The Great American Capitalists* (New York: Harcourt Brace, 1934).

Post–Lawrence–Weber:
Business and Society,
Ninth Edition

Corporate Social
Responsibility

© The McGraw–Hill
Companies, 1999

As a result of these early ideas about business's expanded role in society, two broad principles emerged. These principles have shaped business thinking about social responsibility during the twentieth century and are the foundation stones for the modern idea of corporate social responsibility.

The Charity Principle

The **charity principle,** the idea that the wealthier members of society should be charitable toward those less fortunate, is a very ancient notion. Royalty through the ages has been expected to provide for the poor. The same is true of those with vast holdings of property, from feudal times to the present. Biblical passages invoke this most ancient principle, as do the sacred writings of other world religions. When Andrew Carnegie and other wealthy business leaders endowed public libraries, supported settlement houses for the poor, gave money to educational institutions, and contributed funds to many other community organizations, they were continuing this long tradition of being "my brother's keeper."

> *Andrew Carnegie and John D. Rockefeller are usually credited with pioneering the path of the giant givers of modern philanthropy. For some years, the world's newspapers kept score on the giving. The* London Times *reported that in 1903 Carnegie had given away $21 million, Rockefeller $10 million. By 1913, the* New York Herald *ran a final box score: Carnegie, $332 million; Rockefeller, $175 million. All this was before the income tax and other tax provisions had generated external incentives to giving. The feeling of duty to the public good arose from inner sources.*[7]

This kind of private aid to the needy members of society was especially important in the early decades of this century. At that time, there was no Social Security system, no Medicare for the elderly, no unemployment pay for the jobless, and no United Way to support a broad range of community needs. There were few organizations capable of counseling troubled families, sheltering women and children who were victims of physical abuse, aiding alcoholics, treating the mentally ill or the physically handicapped, or taking care of the destitute. When wealthy industrialists reached out to help others in these ways, they were accepting some measure of responsibility for improving the conditions of life in their communities. In doing so, their actions helped counteract the critics who claimed that business leaders were uncaring and interested only in profits.

Before long, these community needs outpaced the riches of even the wealthiest persons and families. When that happened, beginning in the 1920s, much of the charitable load was taken on by business firms themselves rather than by the owners alone. The symbol of this shift from individual philanthropy to corporate philanthropy was the Community Chest movement in the 1920s, the forerunner of today's United Way drives that are widespread throughout the United States. Business leaders gave vigorous support to this form of corporate charity, urging all firms and their employees to unite their efforts to extend aid to the poor and the needy. Business leaders established pension plans, employee stock ownership and life insurance programs, unemployment funds, limitations on working hours, and higher wages. They built houses, churches, schools, and libraries, provided medical and legal services, and gave to charity.

[7]Michael Novak, *Business as a Calling: Work and the Examined Life* (New York: Free Press, 1996), p. 197.

Post-Lawrence-Weber:
Business and Society,
Ninth Edition

Corporate Social
Responsibility

© The McGraw-Hill
Companies, 1999

For some of today's business firms, corporate social responsibility means participating in community affairs by making paternalistic, charitable contributions. Ted Turner's sensational pledge of $1 billion ($100 million a year for 10 years) to the United Nations in October 1997 served as a gauntlet for other millionaire business leaders, challenging them to contribute in a similar fashion.[8] However, charitable giving is not the only form that corporate social responsibility takes.

The Stewardship Principle

Many of today's corporate executives see themselves as stewards, or trustees, who act in the general public's interest. Although their companies are privately owned and they try to make profits for the stockholders, business leaders who follow the **stewardship principle** believe they have an obligation to see that everyone—particularly those in need—benefits from the company's actions. According to this view, corporate managers have been placed in a position of public trust. They control vast resources whose use can affect people in fundamental ways. Because they exercise this kind of crucial influence, they incur a responsibility to use those resources in ways that are good not just for the stockholders alone but for society generally. In this way, they have become stewards, or trustees, for society. As such, they are expected to act with a special degree of social responsibility in making business decisions.[9]

This kind of thinking eventually produced the modern theory of stakeholder management, which was described in the opening chapter of this book. According to this theory, corporate managers need to interact skillfully with all groups that have a stake in what the corporation does. If they do not do so, their firms will not be fully effective economically or fully accepted by the public as a socially responsible corporation. As one former business executive declared, "Every citizen is a stakeholder in business whether he or she holds a share of stock or not, is employed in business or not, or buys the products and services of business or not. Just to live in American society today makes everyone a stakeholder in business."[10]

Modern Forms of Corporate Social Responsibility

These two principles—the charity principle and the stewardship principle—established the original meaning of corporate social responsibility. Figure 1 shows how these two principles have evolved to form the modern idea of corporate social responsibility.

[8] For a comprehensive discussion of millionaire business leaders turning philanthropists, see "A New Breed of Philanthropist," *Business Week*, October 6, 1997, pp. 40–44. Two sizable donations are discussed in Monica Langley, "How Turner Decided to Give Away $1 Billion," *The Wall Street Journal*, September 22, 1997, pp. B1, B18; and Karen Kaplan, "Microsoft's Gates to Donate $200 Million to Libraries," *Los Angeles Times*, June 24, 1997, p. A1.

[9] Two early statements of this stewardship-trustee view are Frank W. Abrams, "Management's Responsibilities in a Complex World," *Harvard Business Review*, May 1951, pp. 29–34; and Richard Eells, *The Meaning of Modern Business* (New York: Columbia University Press, 1960).

[10] James E. Liebig, *Business Ethics: Profiles in Civic Virtue* (Golden, CO: Fulcrum, 1990), p. 217. For stakeholder theory, see R. Edward Freeman, *Strategic Management: A Stakeholder Approach* (Boston: Pitman, 1984).

Figure 1

Foundation principles of corporate social responsibility and their modern expression.

	Charity Principle	Stewardship Principle
Definition	Business should give voluntary aid to society's needy persons and groups.	Business, acting as a public trustee, should consider the interests of all who are affected by business decisions and policies.
Modern Expression	■ Corporate philanthropy ■ Voluntary actions to promote the social good	■ Acknowledging business and society interdependence ■ Balancing the interests and needs of many diverse groups in society
Examples	■ Corporate philan-thropic foundations ■ Private initiatives to solve social problems ■ Employee volunteerism ■ Social partnerships with needy groups	■ Enlightened self-interest ■ Meeting legal requirements ■ Stakeholder approach to corporate strategic planning

Corporate Philanthropy

Corporate philanthropy is the modern expression of the charity principle. The stewardship principle is given meaning today when corporate managers recognize that business and society are intertwined and interdependent. This mutuality of interests places a responsibility on business to exercise care and social concern in formulating policies and conducting business operations. Exhibit A shows a few of the many organizations that foster modern day corporate philanthropy. Figure 2 shows a list of social priorities from the early 1970s developed by the Committee for Economic Development (CED), a group of about 200 top-level business executives. These recommendations were some of the first industrywide suggestions for social responsibility programs.

Most recent surveys identifying areas of corporate social involvement generally reflect the CED's 1971 list. Employment and training has expanded to include various health and wellness issues, such as employee fitness, AIDS education and treatment, and dependence on cigarettes, alcohol, and drugs.

Corporate Employee Volunteerism

Corporate employee volunteerism is a relatively new phenomenon. Many large corporations developed charitable contribution programs but left employee involvement in community service up to the individual. In the early 1970s, companies began to see

Post–Lawrence–Weber:
Business and Society,
Ninth Edition

Corporate Social
Responsibility

© The McGraw–Hill
Companies, 1999

EXHIBIT A Helping Business with Philanthropic Activities

Numerous organizations exist that seek to help business in their expressions of modern-day corporate philanthropy.

- **Business for Social Responsibility** Was formed in 1992 to work with its members to integrate a full range of socially responsible practices into the strategic, long-term vision of the firm. It recognizes the best practices of its members in the areas of the workplace, the community, and the environment.

- **The Cygnus Group** Helps businesses integrate environmental concepts into their strategic planning, marketing, and communications activities. The Cygnus Group is a pioneer in the use of the Internet for business information retrieval, analysis, and dissemination.

- **Business Council for Sustainable Development in the Gulf of Mexico** Was established by a group of Mexican and American corporate leaders to promote new partnerships, develop policy initiatives, and undertake regional sustainable development endeavors to support sound and sustained economic growth.

- **Prince of Wales Business Leaders Forum** Was established in 1990 to provide a focus for international business leaders who recognize that good corporate citizenship is important to global business success. It includes an international charity supported by business from North America, Europe, and the Far East.

Source: Key Organizations Focused on Business and Industry, compiled by IISD, © 1996, http://iisdl.iisd.ca/ic/sb/direct/SDBUSIN.HTM (June 27, 1997).

community service as a way to improve their images—internally and externally—as well as to serve the communities in which the business operates. According to The National Volunteer Center, more than 1,100 major U.S. corporations had established structured activities to involve their workers in community volunteerism by 1990. A 1996 survey of 180 leading U.S. companies found that 79 percent had volunteer programs.[11]

Today, workplace employee volunteer programs generally take two forms:

- The team model, in which a team of employees plan and implement group volunteer activities.

- The volunteer clearinghouse model, in which a full-time coordinator or a part-time employee provides volunteer opportunities to employees.[12]

Employee volunteer programs help companies attract and retain good employees, according to a study conducted by the Conference Board. Volunteerism helps develop characteristics such as creativity, trust, teamwork, and persistence. It builds skills and attitudes that foster commitment, company loyalty, and job satisfaction. Morale is as much as three

[11] Steve Levin, "Volunteer Spirit Lifts Morale, Bottom Line for Corporations," *Pittsburgh Post-Gazette,* May 25, 1997, pp. A1, A12–13.

[12] Loyce Haran, Siobhan Kenney, and Mark Vermilion, "Contract Volunteer Services: A Model for Successful Partnerships, Sun Microsystems, Jobs and Corporate Information," http://www.sun.com (June 27, 1997).

Post–Lawrence–Weber:
Business and Society,
Ninth Edition

Corporate Social
Responsibility

© The McGraw–Hill
Companies, 1999

Figure 2

Recommended social
responsibility
actions—Committee
for Economic
Development.

*Source: Social
Responsibilities of
Business
Corporations* (New
York: Committee for
Economic
Development,
1971).

- **Economic growth and efficiency**
  Improving productivity
  Cooperating with government

- **Education**
  Giving aid to schools and colleges
  Assisting in managing schools and colleges

- **Employment and training**
  Training disadvantaged workers
  Retraining displaced workers

- **Civil rights and equal opportunity**
  Ensuring equal job opportunities
  Building inner-city plants

- **Urban renewal and development**
  Building low-income housing
  Improving transportation systems

- **Pollution abatement**
  Installing pollution controls
  Developing recycling programs

- **Conservation and recreation**
  Protecting plant and animal ecology
  Restoring depleted lands to use

- **Culture and the arts**
  Giving aid to art institutions

- **Medical care**
  Helping community health planning
  Designing low-cost medical care programs

- **Government**
  Improving management in government
  Modernizing and reorganizing government

times higher in companies with volunteer programs.[13] Research has found a positive association between employees involved in corporate volunteer programs and better physical health, mental health, and social interaction. An example of an employee volunteer program is described in Exhibit B. A study conducted by IBM and the Graduate School of Business at Columbia University showed a clear link between volunteerism and return on assets, return on investment, and employee productivity. A company with a strong community involvement program is likely to score high in profitability and employee morale.

[13] Shari Caudron, "Volunteer Efforts Offer Low-Cost Training Options," *Personnel Journal,* June 1994, pp. 38, 40, 42, 44.

Post–Lawrence–Weber:
Business and Society,
Ninth Edition

Corporate Social
Responsibility

© The McGraw–Hill
Companies, 1999

EXHIBIT B   Community Service Improves Employee Job Skills

Helene Curtis, a Chicago-based personal care company, integrated community volunteerism into its management development program. The results benefited both the employees and the business. "The program gives employees the chance to learn and apply experiences gained through community service to their personal and professional growth," explained Ann Schwartz, manager of community relations at Helene Curtis. "Our goal is to help employees identify the skills they want to develop and then work with them to identify ways and venues in which to practice those skills."

The goals of the program are to formally recognize the value of business skills gained through community service, transfer practical skills from community work to business application, provide managers and employees with alternative ways to develop business skills, provide a low-risk learning experience for both the employees and the corporation, and contribute to the betterment of the organization and community. Managers at Helene Curtis see employee volunteerism as reinforcing the values at the firm. As one employee pointed out, "This program is such a natural fit with the Helene Curtis culture and reflects the values of our CEO."

Source: "Using Community Service Projects to Improve Employee Job Skills," *Issues in Corporate Social Responsibility,* Barnes and Associates publication, Spring 1996, p. 9.

Corporate Awards for Social Responsibility

Recognition of socially responsible behavior by business has increased dramatically. One of the first award programs was sponsored by the Council on Economic Priorities (CEP). The CEP is a corporate watchdog organization that reports periodically on the social behavior of large corporations. In 1987 the council began to accentuate the positive by citing companies that had demonstrated an outstanding record of socially responsible behavior. A selective list of the CEP award recipients is provided in Figure 3–3. In addition, companies have been given dishonorable mentions for a variety of socially irresponsible actions.

> *The Business Enterprise Trust, founded in 1989 by prominent leaders in business, academia, labor, and the media, recognizes business leaders and other individuals who have significantly advanced the cause of social responsibility through "acts of courage, integrity, and social vision." The Trust's annual awards have been presented to Merck & Company for developing a drug to combat river blindness, McKay Nursery Company for their employee stock ownership plan that included 60 migrant workers hired for eight months a year, DAKA International—a restaurant and food service business—for pioneering an aggressive AIDS education program, and Julia Stasch for developing the Female Employment Initiative to assist women in the pursuit of careers in the construction industry.[14]*

[14] A thorough analysis of the Business Enterprise Trust program can be found in James O'Toole, "Do Good, Do Well: The Business Enterprise Trust Awards," *California Management Review,* Spring 1991, pp. 9–24.

Post-Lawrence-Weber:
Business and Society,
Ninth Edition

Corporate Social
Responsibility

© The McGraw-Hill
Companies, 1999

Figure 3

Social responsibility honored by the Council on Economic Priorities.

Source: America's Corporate Conscience Awards, Council on Economic Priorities, http://www.accesspt.com/cep/research/cca/pastawards.html.

America's Corporate Conscience Awards, 1993–1997

Community Involvement

Brooklyn Union Gas	Kellogg
Clorox	Pfizer
Colgate-Palmolive	Timberland
Community Pride Food Stores	Working Assets

Employee Issues

Coca-Cola	Pitney Bowes
Cooperative Home Care	Polaroid
Federal National Mortgage	Quad Graphics
Hewlett-Packard	SAS Institute
Merck & Co.	

Environmental Stewardship

Aveda Corp.	New England Electric System
Digital Equipment	Novo Nordisk
Enron	S.C. Johnson
J. Sainsbury	Stoneyfield
Natural Cotton Colours	Wilkhahn Wilkening

Global Ethics

Cooperative Bank	Starbucks Coffee
Levi Strauss & Co.	Toys 'R' Us
Merck & Co.	

President Clinton announced in 1996 the establishment of the Ron Brown Award for Corporate Leadership, which is to be given each year by the president of the United States to corporations that demonstrate good corporate citizenship. The key criteria for receiving the award include: be at the "best practice" level—distinctive, innovative, and effective; have a significant, measurable impact on the people served; offer broad potential for social and economic benefits; be sustainable and feasible within a business environment and mission; and be adaptable to other businesses and communities.

Corporate Social Responsibility Around the World

Social responsibility, however, reflects cultural values and traditions and takes different forms in different societies. What may be the accepted custom in the United States, Japan, or South Korea may not be in Germany, Brazil, Indonesia, or the Ukraine. Determining what is socially acceptable around the world often is a difficult process.

Japanese firms have proven themselves to be model citizens on many dimensions of corporate social responsibility. Their support of local community activities and other philanthropic endeavors has led to increased goodwill in the communities where they operate. The firms help society in areas directly related to the operations of the business. Thus, Japanese firms clearly help themselves while helping others, showing a strong commitment to the harmonious relations between the corporation and society.

Post–Lawrence–Weber:
Business and Society,
Ninth Edition

Corporate Social
Responsibility

© The McGraw–Hill
Companies, 1999

From a U.S. perspective, however, this may seem to be a narrow understanding of corporate social responsibility. Victims of environmental disasters have been treated as outcasts when seeking compensation for harm caused by Japanese business. Employment practices that may favor certain groups have been generally accepted as a social practice in Japan.[15] However, as Japanese firms have become more integrated with the international community, a broader view of corporate social responsibility has begun to emerge.

The Japan External Trade Organization (JETRO) conducted a survey of Japanese philanthropy in the United States. They reported that approximately 80 percent of Japanese-affiliated operations in the United States responding to their survey engaged in corporate philanthropy. Making cash contributions was the most common form of philanthropy (91 percent), followed by participation in community organizations (57 percent). Community development and education were the primary beneficiaries of cash donations, and encouragement of employee volunteerism was up 36 percent from 1992. Over 95 percent of responding organizations maintained or increased both cash donations, and other philanthropic activities since the last survey in 1992.[16]

Dong Ah Company, a South Korean construction firm, demonstrated its belief in corporate social responsibility in October 1994. One week after a 17-year-old bridge in Seoul, South Korea, collapsed killing 32 people, Dong Ah pledged to build a new bridge even though the company was not blamed for the accident. (Several Seoul officials were arrested on charges of neglecting to maintain the bridge.) The cost of replacing the structure was 150 billion won, or $188.1 million. In addition, the company donated 10 billion won, about $12.5 million, to a program designed to improve South Korean commuters' safety.

Corporate social responsibility has assumed a different form in European countries. Governments have provided many social services often received as benefits from private employers in the United States. For example, debate by government representatives over social responsibility issues resulted in the adoption of a social policy for the European Union countries, called the Social Charter. Rather than relying on private corporate initiatives, governments represented in the EU drafted a public policy that provided incentives and rewards for corporate social actions within the EU.

Embodied within the Social Charter is the Social Action Programme (SAP). The SAP established health and safety guidelines, regulations on working hours, Europe-wide rules for worker consultation, and rules for gender equality at work. Thus, European businesses' response toward social responsibility is actually often a matter of compliance with various governmental policy guidelines and program initiatives.

Other acts of corporate social responsibility are performed by McCarthy Retail, a South African firm. The company has an active Corporate Social Involvement program aimed at supporting and facilitating community

[15] For a thorough discussion of corporate social responsibility Japanese style, see Richard E. Wokutch and Jon M. Shepard, "Corporate Social Responsibility, Moral Unity, and the Maturing of the Japanese Economy," http://www.nd.edu/~isbee/p_wokut.htm (June 27, 1997); and "Kyosei: Japanese Firms Must Pick Up the Social Tab as Well," *Tokyo Business Today*, January–February 1993, pp. 33–34.
[16] Japanese External Trade Organization, "Executive Summary," http://www.jetro.go.jp/ JETROINFO/SURVEY/PHILAN/lexe.html (June 27, 1997).

Post–Lawrence–Weber:
Business and Society,
Ninth Edition

Corporate Social
Responsibility

© The McGraw–Hill
Companies, 1999

development. According to the firm, the programs exist because the company sees pressing needs at the community level and is in a position to contribute to the long-term development of communities; the company realizes that its future business success depends on stable and thriving communities. Education has become the main focus of the company's efforts, particularly by establishing networking computer centers in schools in disadvantaged communities and actively supporting classroom-building projects in rural communities.[17]

In many of the world's developing nations where poverty is widespread or civil strife is frequent, economic goals and military activities tend to be given a higher priority than the pursuit of social goals. Environmental protection, for example, may be considered less critical than having a polluting steel plant that creates jobs. In these cases, social responsibility initiatives by business may be slow in coming.

The Limits of Corporate Social Responsibility

Social responsibility is widely expected of business. It can benefit both the business and the stakeholders of the firm. There are strong arguments in favor of corporate social responsibility; however, corporate social responsibility has its critics. The key arguments for and against social responsibility are noted in Figure 4.

Even if corporate social responsibility is a welcomed business strategy, it has limits. The main limits are legitimacy, cost, efficiency, and scope and complexity. As a result of these constraints, the amounts and kinds of social actions pursued by businesses are sometimes less than the public wants to see.

Figure 4

The pros and cons of corporate social responsibility.

Arguments for corporate social responsibility	Arguments against corporate social responsibility
■ Balances corporate power with responsibility.	■ Lowers economic efficiency and profit.
■ Discourages government regulation.	■ Imposes unequal costs among competitors.
■ Promotes long-term profits for business.	■ Imposes hidden costs passed on to stakeholders.
■ Responds to changing stakeholders' demands.	■ Requires social skills business may lack.
■ Corrects social problems caused by business.	■ Places responsibility on business rather than individuals.

[17]The McCarthy Retail social programs are described in the company's Web site, http://www.mccarthy.co.za/corporate/community.html (July 9, 1997).

Post–Lawrence–Weber:
Business and Society,
Ninth Edition

Corporate Social
Responsibility

© The McGraw–Hill
Companies, 1999

Legitimacy

Is this social problem any of our affair? Is it seriously affecting our business? Do we have the needed in-house talent? Can solving it help us, as well as others? These are questions corporate officials would be wise to ask. A yes answer to these questions might lead a company to an understanding that it has a legitimate obligation to take socially responsible action. If, for example, drug use is causing serious safety problems in a plant, a company might be justified in spending money on a drug education and treatment center that can help its employees and others in the community.

However, a no or a not sure answer to the questions should cause company executives to think twice. Social expenditures by corporations can be justified, and are considered to be a lawful use of stockholders' funds, if they promote the interests of the company while simultaneously helping society. This legal principle was established in a famous 1951 lawsuit when a judge ruled that corporations were justified in contributing company funds to a university because these corporate gifts benefited the company in the long run. Judgments about the legitimacy of any social activity are usually made by a firm's top-level executives who, in the words of the court, must take "a long-range view of the matter" and exercise "enlightened leadership and direction."[18]

Costs

Every social action is accompanied by costs of one kind or another. Consider, for instance, a company's contributions to a worthy charity or its establishing a child-care center for its employees. A United Way contribution could have been paid instead to company stockholders as a dividend. Money spent on a child-care center could have been used instead to boost employees' wages. As worthy as some social actions may be, they do impose costs either on the business firm or on some groups in society, or both.

Efficiency

The costs of social responsibility, like all business expenses, can potentially reduce a company's efficiency and affect its ability to compete in the marketplace. For example, if a company is pressured by a local community to keep an outmoded, inefficient plant in operation because closing it would mean a big job loss for local people, while its competitors close their old plants and move operations to foreign nations where wage rates are lower, which company is more likely to survive in the long run? The managers who make what seems to be a socially responsible decision by putting the interests of their local employees first may not be able to compete with their lower-cost, more efficient competitors.

Scope and Complexity

Some of society's problems are simply too massive, too complex, and too deep-seated to be solved by even the most socially conscientious company or by all companies acting together.

---

[18] *Barlow et al.* v. *A.P. Smith Manufacturing Company* (1951, New Jersey Supreme Court), discussed in Clarence C. Walton, *Corporate Social Responsibility* (Belmont, CA: Wadsworth, 1967), pp. 48–52.

Examples are environmental problems such as acid rain, ozone depletion in the upper atmosphere, and destruction of rain forests. What is required is joint action by corporations and governments in several nations, as happened when companies producing the chemicals that destroy the planet's ozone layer agreed to phase out production gradually.[19]

Some of today's health problems—AIDS, on-the-job drug abuse, and tobacco use—frequently reflect complex social conditions. Although socially responsive businesses can adopt workplace policies and programs regarding these and other health problems, solutions are most likely to be found through joint actions of government, business, community groups, and the individuals involved.

Other social problems are even more persistent. These may include the deep-seated issues of race relations, sex discrimination, and ethnic and religious animosities. No single business firm can be expected to root out these long-standing features of society. The most it can do is to adopt socially responsible attitudes and policies about these issues, being certain that company practices do not make things worse.

These four limits often produce disagreements among those who want corporations to be socially responsible and those who think business is doing enough. The latter group usually declares, Business cannot do more because of these limits. Their opponents in the debate usually respond by saying, Business should be socially active in spite of these constraints, because it is obligated to help society solve its problems.

Balancing Economic, Legal, and Social Responsibilities

Any organization and manager must seek to juggle multiple responsibilities. The popular belief that the business of business is solely profit making was dispelled by a 1997 *Business Week*/Harris poll in which 95 percent of the American adults surveyed rejected that corporations' only role was to make money. As shown in Figure 5, business is challenged by managing its economic responsibilities to its stockholders, its legal requirements to societal laws and regulations, and its social responsibilities to various stakeholders. Although these obligations may conflict at times, a successful firm is one for which management finds ways to meet each of its critical responsibilities and develops strategies to enable these obligations to help each other.

Figure 5

The multiple responsibilities of business.

[19]The Montreal Protocol, the multinational government-business agreement that banned or phased out the use of various materials harmful to the earth's ozone layer, is discussed in "Ecology, Sustainable Development, and Global Business."

Post–Lawrence–Weber:
Business and Society,
Ninth Edition

Corporate Social
Responsibility

© The McGraw–Hill
Companies, 1999

Enlightened Self-Interest

Being socially responsible by meeting the public's continually changing expectations requires wise leadership at the top of the corporation. Companies with an ability to recognize profound social changes and anticipate how they will affect operations have proven to be survivors. They get along better with government regulators, are more open to the needs of the company's stakeholders, and often cooperate with legislators as new laws are developed to cope with social problems. Corporate leaders who possess this kind of social vision believe that business should help create social change rather than block it. With such an attitude, they know that their own companies will have a better chance of surviving in the turbulent social currents of today's world.[20]

Companies with this outlook are guided by **enlightened self-interest,** which means that they are socially aware without giving up their own economic self-interest. According to this view, profits are the reward for the firm as it continues to provide true value to its customers, to help its employees to grow, and to behave responsibly as a corporate citizen.[21] These goals are reflective of the fastest-growing, most-profitable firms in the United States.

> *An emphasis on social responsibility can attract customers. A poll conducted by Opinion Research Corporation shows that 89 percent of purchases by adults are influenced by a company's reputation. Social responsibility also benefits companies by enabling them to recruit a high-quality labor force. The reputation of the firm and the goodwill associated with socially responsible actions attract talented prospective employees, people seeking an employer for which they would be proud to work.*

Economic Obligations and Social Responsibility

Do socially responsible companies sacrifice profits by working conscientiously to promote the social good? Do they make higher profits, better-than-average profits, or lower profits than corporations that ignore or flout the public's desires for a high and responsible standard of social performance? Efforts to discover an observed relationship between a company's financial performance and its social performance have produced mixed results.

Some studies seem to demonstrate that good social performers also tend to have good records of profit making, which could be an example of enlightened self-interest. For example, scholars found no support for the belief that social responsibility and profitability were trade-offs for businesses. In fact, they discovered "a positive association between social and financial performance in large U.S. corporations." However, other research reported that the relationship between profits and social responsibility is sequential. In this view, once the company is profitable, it can "afford" to be socially responsible in its actions. Others have argued that being socially responsible attracts investors to the firm.

---

[20]Robert H. Miles, *Managing the Corporate Social Environment: A Grounded Theory* (Englewood Cliffs, NJ: Prentice Hall, 1987).

[21]Jeff Frooman, "Socially Irresponsible and Illegal Behavior and Shareholder Wealth," *Business and Society,* September 1997, pp. 221–49, he argues that negative effects on shareholder wealth when a firm acts irresponsibly support the enlightened self-interest view: Act responsibly to promote shareholders' interests.

Post–Lawrence–Weber:
Business and Society,
Ninth Edition

Corporate Social
Responsibility

© The McGraw–Hill
Companies, 1999

The relationship between social responsibility and profitability is extremely complex and difficult to prove.[22]

Any social program—for example, an in-company child-care center, a drug education program for employees, or the lending of company executives as advisers to community agencies—will usually impose immediate monetary costs on the participating company. These short-run costs certainly have a potential for reducing the company's profits unless the social activity is designed to make money, which is not usually the purpose of these programs. Therefore, a company may sacrifice short-run profits by undertaking social initiatives. But what is lost in the short run may be gained back over a longer period. For example, if a drug education program prevents and reduces on-the-job drug abuse, the firm's productivity may be increased by lower employee turnover, fewer absences from work, a healthier workforce, fewer accidents and injuries, and lower health insurance costs. In that case, the company may actually experience an increase in its long-run profits, although it had to make an expensive outlay to get the program started.

Legal Requirements versus Corporate Social Responsibility

Accompanying a firm's economic responsibility to its stockholders are its **legal obligations.** As a member of society, a firm must abide by the laws and regulations governing the society. How are a firm's legal obligations related to its social responsibilities? Laws and regulations are enacted to ensure socially responsible conduct by businesses. The high standard of social behavior expected by society are embodied in the society's laws. Can't businesses voluntarily decide to be socially responsible? Of course, but legal rules set standards for businesses to follow. Some firms go beyond the law; others seek to change the law to require its competitors to be more socially responsible.

Laws and regulations help create a level playing field for businesses that compete against one another. By requiring all firms to meet the same social standards—for example, the safe disposal of hazardous wastes—one firm cannot gain a competitive advantage over its rivals by dumping its wastes carelessly without the risk of lawsuits, fines, possible jail terms for some of its managers and employees, and unfavorable publicity for its actions.

Businesses that comply with laws and public policies are meeting a minimum level of social responsibility expected by the public. According to one leading scholar of corporate social performance, even legal compliance is barely enough to satisfy the public:

> *The traditional economic and legal criteria are necessary but not sufficient*
> *conditions of corporate legitimacy. The corporation that flouts them will not*

---

[22]The positive relationship between social and financial performance is reported in Lee E. Preston and Douglas P. O'Bannon, "The Corporate Social–Financial Performance Relationship," *Business and Society,* December 1997, pp. 419–29. The "profits first, then social action" argument is discussed by Jean B. McGuide, Alison Sundgeon, and Thomas Schneeweis, "Corporate Social Responsibility and Firm Financial Performance," *Academy of Management Journal* 31 (1988), pp. 854–72. The "social responsibility attracts investors" argument is supported by research reported in Samuel B. Graves and Sandra A. Waddock, "Institutional Owners and Corporate Social Performance," *Academy of Management Journal* 37 (1994), pp. 1034–46. Prior studies investigating this relationship are summarized in Jennifer J. Griffin and John F. Mahon, "The Corporate Social Performance and Corporate Financial Performance Debate," *Business and Society,* March 1997, pp. 5–31.

Post–Lawrence–Weber:
Business and Society,
Ninth Edition

Corporate Social
Responsibility

© The McGraw–Hill
Companies, 1999

survive; even the mere satisfaction of these criteria does not ensure the corporation's continued existence. . . .

Thus, social responsibility implies bringing corporate behavior up to a level where it is in congruence with currently prevailing social norms, values, and performance expectations. . . . [Social responsibility] is simply a step ahead—before the new societal expectations are codified into legal requirements.[23]

Stockholder Interests versus Other Stakeholder Interests

Top-level managers, along with a corporation's board of directors, are generally expected to produce as much value as possible for the company's owners and investors. This can be done by paying high dividends regularly and by running the company in ways that cause the stock's value to rise. Not only are high profits a positive signal to Wall Street investors that the company is being well run—thereby increasing the stock's value—but those profits make possible the payment of high dividends to stockholders. Low profits have the opposite effects and put great pressure on managers to improve the company's financial performance.

However, stockholders are not the only stakeholder group that management must keep in mind. The leaders of the world's largest organizations from Europe, Asia, and North America have formed the Caux Roundtable. In its publications, these corporate leaders have recognized that all the stakeholders must be considered; none can be ignored. A top manager's job is to interact with the totality of the company's stakeholders, including those groups that advocate high levels of social responsibility by business. Management's central goal is to promote the interests of the entire company, not just any single stakeholder group, and to pursue multiple company goals, not just profit goals. These two contrasting views of corporate social responsibility are shown in Exhibit C.

This broader and far more complex task tends to put more emphasis on the long-run profit picture rather than an exclusive focus on immediate returns. When this happens, dividends paid to stockholders may be less than they desire, and the value of their shares may not rise as rapidly as they would like. These are the kinds of risks faced by corporate managers who have a legal responsibility to produce high value for the company's stockholder-owners but who also must try to promote the overall interests of the entire company. Putting all of the emphasis on short-run maximum profits for stockholders can lead to policies that overlook the interests and needs of other stakeholders. Managers may also downgrade social responsibility programs that increase short-run costs, although it is well-known that the general public strongly approves socially responsible companies.

As a response to the conflict between long- and short-term profit making, an enlightened self-interest point of view may be the most useful and practical approach. That means incurring reasonable short-run costs to undertake socially responsible activities that benefit both the company and the general public in the long run.

[23] S. Prakash Sethi, "A Conceptual Framework for Environmental Analysis of Social Issues and Evaluation of Business Response Patterns," in S. Prakash Sethi and Cecilia M. Falbe, eds., *Business and Society: Dimensions of Conflict and Cooperation* (Lexington, MA: Lexington Books, 1987), pp. 42, 43.

EXHIBIT C   Two Views of Corporate Social Responsibility

Shareholder Wealth

In a market-based economy that recognizes the rights of private property, the only social responsibility of business is to create shareholder value and to do so legally and with integrity. Yet we do have important unresolved social challenges—from drug abuse to education and the environment—that require collective action. Corporate management however has neither the political legitimacy nor the expertise to decide what is in the social interest. It is our form of government that provides the vehicle for collective choice via elected legislators and the judicial system.

Whether corporate social responsibility is advocated by political activists or the chief executive officer, the costs of these expenditures, which don't increase the value of the company or its stock, will be passed on to consumers by way of higher prices, or to employees as lower wages, or to shareholders as lower returns.

Source: Copyright © 1990 by The New York Times Company. Reprinted by Permission.

Multiple Stakeholders

We believe in treating all customers with dignity irrespective of whether they purchase our products and services directly from us or otherwise acquire them in the market. . . .

We believe in the dignity of every employee and in taking employee interests seriously. . . .

We believe in honoring the trust our investors place in us. . . .

Our relationship with suppliers and subcontractors must be based on mutual respect. . . .

We believe that fair economic competition is one of the basic requirements for increasing the wealth of nations and, ultimately for making possible the just distribution of goods and services. . . .

We believe that as global corporate citizens, we can contribute to such forces of reform and human rights . . . at work in the communities [where we operate]. . . .

Source: "The Caux Principles," Section 3, *The Caux Roundtable,* http://www.arq.co.uk/ethicalbusiness/archive/caux/caux3.htm (July 9, 1997).

Summary Points

- Corporate social responsibility means that a corporation should be held accountable for any of its actions that affect people, their communities, and their environment. Businesses must recognize their vast power and wield it to better society.

- The idea of corporate social responsibility in the United States was adopted by business leaders in the early twentieth century. The central themes of social responsibility have been charity—which means giving aid to the needy—and stewardship—acting

Post–Lawrence–Weber:
Business and Society,
Ninth Edition

Corporate Social
Responsibility

© The McGraw–Hill
Companies, 1999

as a public trustee and considering all corporate stakeholders when making business decisions.

- Social responsibility most often is demonstrated through philanthropic contributions and employee volunteerism.
- Examples of corporate social responsibility are increasing around the world. However, some cultures, such as Japan, take a more limited view of social responsibility.
- Business firms are limited in their efforts to be socially responsible. Usually excluded are actions that are unrelated to company goals and abilities, are too costly, impair business efficiency, and are highly complex.
- Socially responsible businesses should attempt to balance economic, legal, and social obligations. Following an enlightened self-interest approach, a firm may be economically rewarded while society benefits from the firm's actions. Abiding by legal requirements can also guide businesses in serving various groups in society. Managers should consider all of the company's stakeholders and their interests.

Key Terms and Concepts

- Corporate social responsibility
- Iron Law of Responsibility
- Charity principle
- Stewardship principle
- Corporate philanthropy
- Corporate employee volunteerism
- Enlightened self-interest
- Legal obligations

Internet Resources

- http://www.capitalresearch.org/crc/patterns   Patterns in Corporate Philanthropy
- http://www.rpbooks.com/visitors/newsroom   Corporate Philanthropy News
- http://www.iquest.com/~hats/promos.html   Corporate Aspects of Volunteerism
- http://www.bsr.org   Business for Social Responsibility

Discussion Case   Cummins Engine Company

One admirer called it "capitalism at its best." Another said its chief executive officer "believed in superb products, concern for employees, involvement in the community—all those qualities that made American corporations the envy of the world."

The subject of this commentary was Cummins Engine Company, a leading maker of heavy-duty diesel engines for trucks. From its founding in 1919, Cummins was known for a benevolent attitude, mainly a result of the religious convictions and social philosophy of Clessie Cummins, the founder. It also was famous for high-quality, reliable, and efficient engines.

Cummins's long record of social responsibility is well-known. Its headquarters town of Columbus, Indiana, is sprinkled with public buildings designed by some of the world's leading architects whose fees were paid by Cummins. The management staff was racially integrated as early as the 1960s, and Cummins became an early leader in reducing pollution caused by its engines. Employees are protected against unwarranted use of personal data in company files, and Cummins's chairman helped develop privacy

Post–Lawrence–Weber:
Business and Society,
Ninth Edition

Corporate Social
Responsibility

© The McGraw–Hill
Companies, 1999

guidelines for other employers. Many local causes draw upon the company's charitable funds, along with the voluntary help of company executives and employees. Townspeople remained fiercely loyal to the company, even after over 4,000 were laid off during the 1980s. Cummins employees receive good wages and benefits and take much pride in producing high-quality engines.

But as the 1990s began, this paragon of social responsibility appeared to be in trouble. It had lost over $100 million in 1986, almost as much in 1988, and had only a tiny net profit in 1987. It had fended off one British corporate raider at a cost of $72 million but faced another potential hostile takeover by a Hong Kong investor who held around 15 percent of the company's stock. In spite of shaky profits, the company refused to cut long-term research spending to improve its products or to reduce charitable contributions which were among the highest in industrial America. Neither would company officials listen to those who urged a move from its midwestern home to nonunion lower-cost areas in the South. When Hurricane Hugo devastated large sections of South Carolina in 1989, the company sent free engines and generators to some of the victims. Near its new factory in Brazil, it helped build a school, a clinic, and a gymnasium in a poor neighborhood. Viewing this situation, one financial analyst declared, "Cummins is one big social slush fund. An incredibly naive attitude exists at the company."

Henry B. Schacht, Cummins's chairman, disagreed. He commented: "Some say the company's main goal should be to maximize shareholder value . . . I say no. [The company's goal is] being fair and honest and doing what is right even when it is not to our immediate benefit." Hearing this, a Wall Street skeptic declared that Cummins has been "in a long-term mode for 10 years. . . . Schacht sounds great, but at some point there's got to be a payout for all this spending."

An outside observer responded by saying, "Wall Street stubbornly ignores the success of Japanese industrial enterprises—success achieved in long-term planning for market penetration, in lieu of a consuming emphasis on short-term results. If the financial community would lay off the hounding of public-company managements [like Cummins], allowing them to run their businesses instead of wasting valuable time reacting to the ill-conceived criticisms of these Wall Street gurus, domestic enterprises would be all the better for it." A former chairman of the company summed up his own view: "Cummins has a fantastic future because it isn't just factories, machines and cash. It's outstanding people who take intense pride in their work and their community."

Demonstrating that his social skills were matched by an equal financial ability, Cummins's CEO in mid-1990 sold a 27 percent stake of the company to Ford Motor, Tenneco, and Kubota, a Japanese firm. The deal gave Cummins needed new business for its diesel engines and $250 million to reduce debt and invest in modernization. Cummins's continued international expansion and diversification from the mid-1980s into the 1990s proved its worth in 1996. While the heavy-duty truck market in North America had a cyclical downturn, Cummins's annual sales increased by $12 million to $5.257 billion. This marked the second year in a row that Cummins had exceeded the $5 billion mark in total revenue. Cummins Engine Company appears to provide an example that profits and social responsibility can coexist.

Sources: All quotations are from Robert Johnson, "Survivor's Story: With Its Spirit Shaken but Unbeaten, Cummins Shows Decade's Scars," *The Wall Street Journal,* December 13, 1989, pp. A1, A6; and "Letters to the Editor," *The Wall Street Journal,* January 15, 1990, p. A11. Current financial data are from the 1996 Cummins Engine Company annual report.

Post–Lawrence–Weber:
Business and Society,
Ninth Edition

Corporate Social
Responsibility

© The McGraw–Hill
Companies, 1999

Discussion Questions

1. Is Cummins's commitment to social responsibility fair to the company's stockholders? If you were Cummins's CEO, would you cut back on social expenditures so you could pay higher dividends to the company's owners?

2. Which principle of social responsibility—the charity principle or the stewardship principle—is the basis of Cummins's approach to social responsibility? Give some examples from the case.

3. Of the four major limits to social responsibility discussed in this chapter, which ones seem to apply to Cummins?

4. Is Cummins an example of what this chapter calls "enlightened self-interest?" Explain your answer.

Bibliography

Ackerman, Robert. *The Social Challenge to Business.* Cambridge, MA: Harvard University Press, 1975.

Block, Peter. *Stewardship: Choosing Service over Self Interest.* San Francisco, CA: Berrett-Koehler, 1996.

Bollier, David. *Aiming Higher.* New York: American Management Association, 1996.

Bowen, Howard R. *Responsibilities of the Businessman,* New York: Harper, 1953.

Bradshaw, Thornton, and David Vogel, eds. *Corporations and Their Critics.* New York: McGraw-Hill, 1981.

Chamberlain, Neil W., *The Limits of Corporate Social Responsibility.* New York: Basic Books, 1973.

Himmelstein, Jerome. *Looking Good and Doing Good.* Bloomington, IN: Indiana University Press, 1997.

Houck, John, and Oliver F. Williams, eds. *Is the Good Corporation Dead? Social Responsibility in a Global Economy.* Lanham, MD: Rowman and Littlefield Publishers, 1996.

Kuhn, James W., and Donald W. Shriver, Jr. *Beyond Success: Corporations and Their Critics in the 1990s.* New York: Oxford University Press, 1991.

Miles, Robert. *Managing the Corporate Social Environment: A Grounded Theory.* Englewood Cliffs, NJ: Prentice-Hall, 1987.

Scott, Mary, and Howard Rothman. *Companies with a Conscience: Intimate Portraits of Twelve Firms That Make a Difference.* New York: Citadel Press Book/ Carroll Publishing Group, 1994.

Socially Responsive Management

Socially responsive corporations consider and carefully seek to foster mutually beneficial relationships with their stakeholders. This topic discusses how businesses must assess environmental forces before attempting to implement a successful social strategy. Once implemented, the social strategy must be evaluated to determine if the firm is acting in a socially responsive manner.

This topic focuses on these key questions and objectives:

- What groups and social forces changed the way management responds to the social environment?
- What influences and forces should be monitored by managers when developing a socially responsive program?
- What are the stages in the model of social responsiveness?
- What elements are critical for a business to effectively manage the corporate social environment?
- Can a firm's management of the social environment be assessed?

S trategic alliances became common in the 1990s as leading corporations faced an increasing number of social issues. To respond to the complex social problems affecting business, companies joined together and with their key stakeholders (government agencies, community or special interest groups, schools, etc.) to form **collaborative partnerships** (see Exhibit A). By pooling their financial and human resources, a network of organizations could better address the challenges presented by the various social concerns and more effectively achieve their mutual goals.

A collaborative partnership was formed when businesses in Milwaukee, Wisconsin, realized that dramatic changes required dramatic responses. Gangs, drug dealers, and prostitutes became familiar residents of the Avenues West area, a 100-square-block section of the city on the fringe of the downtown business district. Crime in the Milwaukee area was up 22 percent; residential housing was decaying. By 1990, 60 percent of the buildings in the Avenues West area contained 20 or more rental units. Only a small percentage of the housing units were owner-occupied. Absentee landlords frequently let dwellings fall into disrepair or be taken over by drug dealers to become crack houses where drugs are easily purchased. These and other factors led to a collaborative partnership involving business and its stakeholders to seriously address these social challenges. The plan was called the Campus Circle Project.[1]

Announced in November 1991, the project created a partnership with numerous organizations and community groups to redevelop the Avenues West neighborhood. Four local corporations—Wisconsin Energy Corporation, Wisconsin Bell, Catholic Knights Insurance Company, and Aurora Health Care—pledged nearly $15 million. Marquette University, a Jesuit Catholic college located in the Avenues West area, joined the partnership and committed cash, land, and in-kind contributions worth $9 million. The City of Milwaukee created a special tax structure to help pay for public improvements. Finally, a $20 million, five-year federal grant was received to provide further support for the project.

The multiphase project of crime prevention, community planning, housing rehabilitation and construction, and economic development for the Avenues West neighborhood continued throughout the 1990s. Minority- and women-owned businesses and laborers completed more than 30 percent of the work. Green spaces were created in neighborhoods in response to the children, who make up one-third of the community's population. Initial assessments indicate that this type of cooperative partnership between corporate, academic, and governmental institutions may be one way to combat high crime and declining housing in neighborhoods.

But what gave rise to the change in corporate social responsiveness of the 1980s and 1990s? What events or social movements triggered these changes in stakeholder management analysis and the programs developed from the analysis?

The Corporate Social Climate

Decades of challenges by corporate stakeholders seeking social control of business, most evident during the 1960s and 1970s in the United States, created a corporate social environment filled with opportunities for socially responsive strategies. Challenges by corporate stakeholders came from many diverse groups.

[1]"Marquette University Leads Urban Revival of Blighted Environs," *The Wall Street Journal,* February 1, 1994, pp. A1, A6.

Post–Lawrence–Weber:
Business and Society,
Ninth Edition

Socially Responsive
Management

© The McGraw–Hill
Companies, 1999

EXHIBIT A   Business and Government Partnering to Create Jobs

A partnership among businesses and government to address various social issues was reflected in the actions taken by a group of companies in support of a national service program, AmeriCorps. AmeriCorps was run by the Corporation for National Services, a nonprofit organization that selected proposals submitted by thousands of communities seeking to employ local youths or the unemployed. At a time when conservative business interests often attack government-sponsored social programs, the AmeriCorps partnership between business and government has been overwhelmingly supported.

For example, U.S. Health pledged over $150,000 over three years to City Year, a nonprofit organization that sent AmeriCorps members to work with community projects. An executive at the firm pointed out that AmeriCorps recouped more than $376 million of its costs in one year by giving youths skills to become productive adults in the economy. Other corporate support included the following: General Electric contributed $250,000 to 11 United Way chapters for literacy training and food pantries; Tenneco Gas gave $35,000 and provided printing and accounting services to Serve Houston Youth Corps, an AmeriCorps affiliate; Nike promised $150,000 for programs designed to set up fitness-oriented sports leagues and for the renovation of playgrounds; and Fanny May contributed $100,000 to three housing groups to train AmeriCorps members to counsel low-income renters on home-ownership.

Since the creation of AmeriCorps in 1993, businesses contributed cash, equipment, and employee volunteers to help 20,000 youths to perform services that range from rehabilitating low-income housing to cleaning up rivers.

Source: "A Social Program CEOs Want to Save," *Business Week,* June 19, 1995, pp. 120–21.

- Consumer advocates, spearheaded by Ralph Nader's fight against the U.S. automobile industry for safer vehicles, demanded safe products, accurate information, and competitive pricing of products.

- Environmentalists held the first Earth Days in the 1970s, calling for businesses to be accountable for air and water quality.

- Anti–Vietnam War activists demanded that businesses participating in what they termed the military industrial complex abandon conventional and chemical weapons production and convert to the manufacture of peacetime goods.

- African-American groups, organized under the civil rights movement, pressed for an end to discriminatory practices in the hiring, promotion, and training of employees.

- Women's groups accused businesses of gender bias and discrimination.

- Workers, of all races and both genders, pushed for safer working conditions.

- Communities protested both the use and transportation of toxic materials by businesses and the construction and operation of nuclear energy plants.

Post-Lawrence-Weber:
Business and Society,
Ninth Edition

Socially Responsive
Management

© The McGraw-Hill
Companies, 1999

These and other corporate stakeholders dramatically altered the business environment within which managers attempted to perform their tasks. Most of the groups mentioned are discussed in greater detail in other material. The overall contribution of these groups to the collective social movements demanded a different response from businesses in addition to those embodied in the notions of *corporate social responsibility*. Firms are now required to develop a sense of *corporate social responsiveness.*

Corporate social responsibility is based on the principles of charity and stewardship. Expressions of these concepts are seen in corporate philanthropy and the care of the public's resources. However, the basis for **corporate social responsiveness** does not rely on the generosity of a firm's senior management or their awareness of their role as trustees of the public's interests. Corporate social responsiveness is seen in the *processes* a firm establishes to address social demands initiated by corporate stakeholders or in the *social actions* taken by the firm that affect its stakeholders. The contrast between corporate social responsibility and what has been labeled corporate social responsiveness is highlighted in Figure 1.

Formulating Socially Responsive Strategies

Before it can form a social strategy, a corporation must skillfully analyze various influences and forces and then weigh the information collected. This section discusses the multiple environments that affect business and the techniques available to analyze them.

The Macroenvironment of Business

To begin formulating a socially responsive strategy, a firm needs a framework of environmental information. Managers must understand what is occurring in many sectors of the external world. According to two authorities, the environment that is relevant for businesses and their managers consists of four distinct segments: social, economic, political, and tech-

Figure 1

Contrast between corporate social responsibility and corporate social responsiveness.

	Corporate Social Responsibility	Corporate Social Responsiveness
Origin	1920s	1960s
Basis	Principles of charity and stewardship	Demands made by numerous social stakeholder groups
Focus	Moral obligations to society at large	Practical reponses by businesses to corporate stakeholders
Action	Philanthropy, trustee of the public's interests	Social programs

Post–Lawrence–Weber:
Business and Society,
Ninth Edition

Socially Responsive
Management

© The McGraw–Hill
Companies, 1999

nological.[2] This **macroenvironment of business** consists of an almost unlimited amount of information, including facts, trends, issues, and ideas; and each of these segments represents a focused area of information, some of it important and relevant to the business. Figure 2 illustrates each of the four segments of the macroenvironment of business.

As shown in the figure, the *social segment* focuses on information about (1) demographics, (2) lifestyles, and (3) social values of a society. Managers have a need to understand changes in population patterns, characteristics of the population, emergence of new lifestyles, and social values that seem to be in or out of favor with the majority of the population.

The information from the social segment in the case of the Campus Circle Project, described earlier, was a critical motivation in the formulation of a socially responsive strategy. The Avenues West neighborhood was quickly deteriorating. Housing decay and increases in drug traffic, prostitution, and violent crimes began to challenge the business community's lack of social involvement in the neighborhood. These social conditions had a direct impact on the viability of business and its stakeholders (local community, customers, employees).

The *economic segment* focuses on the general set of economic factors and conditions confronting industries in a society. For example, information about interest rates, unemployment, foreign imports, and many other such factors is relevant to virtually all businesses. The economic segment obviously has a large impact on all business organizations.

Figure 2

The macroenvironments of business.

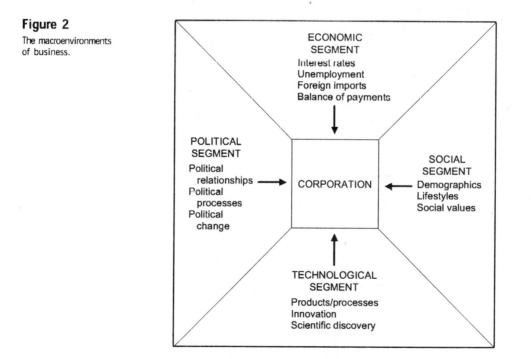

[2]Liam Fahey and V.K. Narayanan, *Macroenvironmental Analysis for Strategic Management* (St. Paul, MN: West, 1986), pp. 28–29.

Post–Lawrence–Weber:
Business and Society,
Ninth Edition

Socially Responsive
Management

© The McGraw–Hill
Companies, 1999

This impact was also central to the Campus Circle Project. The conditions in the neighborhood contributed to the overall economic decline in the area. Businesses were considering relocating to a safer, more prosperous suburban Milwaukee industrial park. The costs of doing business near the Avenues West area increased as safety programs were created to protect employees as they walked from the parking lot to work. The economic segment of the macroenvironment of business was central to the project's strategic focus. The socially responsive strategy had to deal with the economic objectives and needs of those involved in the partnership, as well as the social ones.

The *political segment* deals with specific political relationships in society, changes in them, and the processes by which society makes political decisions. Changes in the tax code, for example, redistribute income and tax burdens. This involves political relationships between various segments of society. The creation and dissolution of regulatory institutions that set standards for business behavior are examples of changes in the political process.

A critical participant in the Campus Circle Project was the City of Milwaukee. The partnership relied on a special tax structure to help pay for numerous public improvements to the Avenues West area. Another political relationship was evident on the federal level, as the Campus Circle Project secured a $20 million, five-year grant to supplement the private funding for the project.

The *technological segment* is concerned with the technological progress and potential hazards that are taking place in society. New products, processes, or materials, including any negative social impacts; the general level of scientific activity; and advances in fundamental science (e.g., biology) are the key concerns in this area.

Although the technological segment is often understood in terms of manufacturing development or processes, the Campus Circle Project utilized a somewhat unique technology: urban planning. Extensive drafting and revisions were made to plans calling for housing demolition, construction, or rehabilitation. The relocation of numerous businesses into a centrally located mall was carefully planned and coordinated with the business owners. The city was petitioned to close a stretch of a major avenue that cut through the Avenues West area to ensure greater safety for the residents and to create a buffer between the residential neighborhood and the downtown business district.

The macroenvironment, as presented in Figure 2, is a system of interrelated segments, each one connected to and influencing the others. In the Campus Circle Project, social decay had economic consequences for businesses and other organizations in the neighborhood. To turn around the Avenues West area, a collaborative partnership of business, government, and educational organizations was formed. This group had to integrate the social, economic, political, and technological segments of their macroenvironment to formulate a socially responsive strategy to address the challenge facing them.

A manager must understand each of these segments, their interrelationships, and those facts that are of direct importance to the corporation. This knowledge will improve his or her understanding of the relevant environment in which strategies must be formulated.

Scanning and Environmental Analysis

To effectively formulate socially responsive strategies, managers must learn about the company's external environment. **Environmental scanning** is a managerial process of analyzing the external social, economic, political, and technological environments. Scanning can be done informally or formally by individual managers or teams. It is largely an in-

Post–Lawrence–Weber:
Business and Society,
Ninth Edition

Socially Responsive
Management

© The McGraw–Hill
Companies, 1999

formation collection, analysis, and processing activity, and it is a valuable first step in building a socially responsive strategy for an organization.

Generally, scanning can be done by focusing on one or more of the following: trends that are occurring in government, society, or segments of each; issues that are emerging in the company's industry or sector of the economy or in nations where it conducts business; and stakeholders that are currently important to the organization or appear to be potentially important in the future.

Trend analysis attempts to understand and project the implications and consequences of current trends into the future. Companies whose products or services have particularly long life spans have a special need for understanding long-term trends. The life insurance industry, for example, regularly enters into individual contracts that have a life span of 20, 30, or even 50 years. A policyholder may pay premiums on life insurance for decades before the insurer is required to pay a benefit. Trends such as increasing life spans and more active lifestyles also can alter the calculation of how many years an insurer may have to pay out on a pension plan or annuity. The failure to understand such trends and their implications can result in poor financial planning that injures the company and the insurance beneficiary or pension recipient.

Issues analysis involves a careful assessment of specific concerns that are having, or may have, an impact on the company. In many companies, public affairs managers do detailed tracking and monitoring of numerous social issues, seeking opportunities for economic and social benefit. Warner-Lambert, for example, believes that responding to critical social issues enhances the company's image, builds company pride among its employees, and helps those in need. The firm addresses various social issues such as hospice care for the terminally ill and the problem of domestic violence. The company has created educational and community outreach programs in response to these emerging social issues.[3]

Stakeholder analysis places the scanner's focus on the people, groups, and organizations that populate the external environment. By trying to understand the issues that are of concern to the company's primary and secondary stakeholders, managers are better able to predict what types of demands are going to be made in the months ahead. There are many ways to collect such information, ranging from professional reporting services that track leaders of activist groups to direct contacts and discussions with stakeholder representatives. Informal discussions with union leaders or local environmentalists can go a long way toward providing managers with an understanding of what is critical to these groups and why.

Implementing Social Responsiveness

Companies do not become socially responsive overnight. The process takes time. New attitudes have to be developed, new routines learned, and new policies and action programs designed. Once a company is prepared to implement a social strategy, it must follow specific guidelines to achieve its social objectives. Many obstacles must be overcome in implementing socially responsive strategies. Some are structural, such as the reporting relationships between groups of managers; others are cultural, such as a historical pattern of only men or women in a particular job category.

[3]"Warner-Lambert's World, Social Responsibility," http://www.warner-lambert.com/info/social.html (July 9, 1997).

Post–Lawrence–Weber:
Business and Society,
Ninth Edition

Socially Responsive
Management

© The McGraw–Hill
Companies, 1999

A Model of Corporate Social Responsiveness

An early model of how large corporations effectively implement socially responsive policies is illustrated in Figure 3. There are three stages to the responsiveness process depicted in this model. Each is discussed below.

The Policy Stage

In the first stage of social responsiveness, the company becomes aware of those parts of the surrounding environment to which it needs to respond and act on. Awareness may occur after stakeholder expectations change, or it may result from a systematic environmental analysis. Whether or not stakeholder pressure exists, a company's management may think, based on environmental analysis, that it should respond to emerging issues, concerns, or social trends.

> *For example, a group of Boston businesses announced a $6 million program designed to guarantee financial aid to all graduates of the city's public high schools who get into college and to provide jobs for those who complete their education. This effort was taken in reaction to a dramatic increase in the dropout rate among Boston-area high school students. In addition to the funds provided, 350 Boston-area companies pledged to help provide jobs to high school graduates, and many offered to help pay for guidance counselors in the schools. This commitment served two purposes: The students and schools were helped, and the companies ensured themselves a future pool of applicants for entry-level jobs. By 1997, businesses managed about 10 percent of the 750 charter schools in the United States, educational institutions owned and operated by for-profit companies.*[4]

A company's social responses need to be guided by policies that are carefully and deliberately developed by its top management and board of directors. Those policies provide a framework for shaping other aspects of the organization's response. New production policies, for example, may result in better quality control for consumer products, may remove job hazards, and may reduce water pollution all at the same time.

The Learning Stage

Once it has identified a social problem—for example, excessive numbers of high school dropouts—and adopted a general policy—an educational opportunity policy—the company must learn how to tackle the problem and make the new policy work. Two kinds of learning are needed: specialized learning and administrative learning.

Specialized learning occurs when a sociotechnical expert—for example, an inner-city educator who is thoroughly familiar with the culture, lifestyles, motivations, and special problems of high school youth—is employed to advise company officers and managers. The kind of specialized knowledge that the sociotechnical expert can provide is particularly helpful in the early stages of social responsiveness when the company is deal-

---

[4]Fox Butterfield, "Funds and Jobs Pledged to Boston Graduates," *New York Times,* September 10, 1986, p. D25; and Steve Stecklow, "Businesses Scramble to Run Charter Schools," *Wall Street Journal,* August 21, 1997, p. B1. Business involvement in public school education is discussed in detail in "Breaking the Mold: The Private Sector's Accelerating Role in Public Education," *Business Week,* October 17, 1994, pp. 122–53.

Post–Lawrence–Weber:
Business and Society,
Ninth Edition

Socially Responsive
Management

© The McGraw–Hill
Companies, 1999

Figure 3

A three-stage model
of corporate social
responsiveness.

Source: Adapted from
Robert W. Ackerman
and Raymond A.
Bauer, Corporate
Social Responsiveness:
The Modern Dilemma.
(Reston, VA: Reston,
1976).

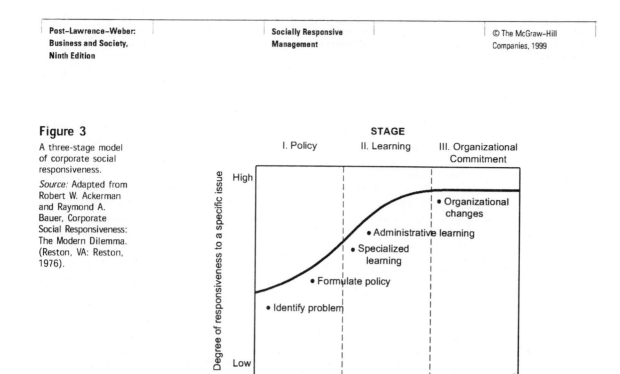

ing with an unfamiliar social problem, whether it is high school dropouts, prejudice against minorities in hiring practices, excessive pollution, or toxic chemical hazards.

Administrative learning occurs when a company's supervisors and managers—those who administer the organization's daily affairs—become familiar with new routines that are necessary to cope with a social problem. A technical expert can assist the company in taking its first steps to solve a problem but cannot do the whole job alone. Social responsiveness requires the full cooperation and knowledge of line managers and staff experts. Personal involvement is essential.

> *The AT&T Learning Network is a $150 million, five-year program designed to assist America's youth in electronic communication. AT&T provides three months of free voice-messaging service and free voice mailboxes to thousands of students, who the company sees as potential customers. To fully implement this program, on-line mentoring is essential. The mentoring aspect of the program involves AT&T managers, technical experts, and other employees across the corporate organization.[5]*

The Organizational Commitment Stage

A final step is needed to achieve full social responsiveness: An organization must *institutionalize* its new social policy.[6] The new policies and routines learned in the first two stages should become so well accepted throughout the entire company that they are considered to be a normal part of doing business. In other words, they should be a part of the

[5]Gautan Naik, "AT&T to Give 110,000 Schools Free Services," *The Wall Street Journal,* November 1, 1995, pp. A3, A12.
[6]Robert Ackerman, "How Companies Respond to Social Demands," *Harvard Business Review,* July–August 1973, pp. 88–98.

Post–Lawrence–Weber:
Business and Society,
Ninth Edition

Socially Responsive
Management

© The McGraw–Hill
Companies, 1999

company and its standard operating procedures. For example, when managers respond to the needs of the local education system or to the students without having to rely on special directives from top management, the socially responsive policy can be considered to be institutionalized.

The normal organizational pressures to resist change mean that both effort and time are needed to improve a corporation's responsiveness. In the past, it took large corporations an average of six to eight years to progress from the first stage to the third stage on any given social issue or problem such as equal employment opportunity or pollution control. Yet some firms are more flexible than others, and some social problems are easier to handle than others, so the time involved may vary considerably. It is clear, however, that a combination of internal factors, especially management willpower, and external factors, especially continued stakeholder action on the problem, is necessary for effective change to occur.

Framework for Social Policy

After reaching the organizational commitment stage, the company must develop specific guidelines to direct the strategic social policy. Two scholars in the strategic management field have created a set of guidelines to enhance the success of a business's social policy.[7] They believe that social policies should:

- *Concentrate action programs on limited objectives.* No company can take significant action in every area of social responsibility. It can achieve more if it selects areas in which to concentrate its efforts. Vermont National Bank targets socially responsible investing that has community impact. The Socially Responsible Banking Fund has attracted more than $85 million in investments. As a result, thousands of loans are made to affordable housing projects, organic farms, small businesses, environmental and conservation projects, and education.

- *Concentrate action programs related to the firm's products or services.* The program should focus on areas strategically related to the present and prospective economic functions of the business. Mario J. Antoci, chairman and CEO of American Savings Bank, initiated a community outreach and urban lending program for California's low-income and minority populations. This initiative gives thousands of Californians the opportunity to purchase homes and has helped American Savings become one of the most stable and profitable thrifts in the country.

- *Begin action programs close to home.* The program should address local issues or social needs before spreading out or acting in far-distant regions. Rachel's Bus Company, a Chicago-based school transportation company, targets inner-city Chicago and its economic devastation when developing its social program guidelines. Rachel Hubka, the company's president, located the company headquarters in the inner-city and hires qualified applicants from the local community. These guidelines foster a stronger pride in the inner-city area that the company serves.

---

[7]Archie B. Carroll and Frank Hoy, "Integrating Corporate Social Policy into Strategic Management," *Journal of Business Strategy,* Winter 1984, pp. 48–57; also see Craig Smith, "The New Corporate Philanthropy," *Harvard Business Review,* May–June 1994, pp. 105–16.

Post–Lawrence–Weber:
Business and Society,
Ninth Edition

Socially Responsive
Management

© The McGraw–Hill
Companies, 1999

- *Facilitate employee action.* Programs in which employees can become involved as individuals rather than as representatives of the company encourage future participation and commitment. As part of its ongoing commitment to Habitat for Humanity, Coldwell Banker selects sales employees to travel to various sites to help build homes for deserving families. In 1997, four Coldwell Banker employees were flown to Godollo, Hungary, for the project. In past years, employees assisted Habitat for Humanity in various cites located in the United States.

Becoming a Socially Responsive Firm

How does a firm become more socially responsive? Robert Miles, American scholar and consultant, observed that:

Executive leaders of America's largest corporations have been confronted . . . during the last two decades with an unprecedented increase in the social issues impinging upon their business policies and practices. Not only have a variety of social regulations been developed that apply universally to all industries, but each industry has also experienced to varying degrees a proliferation of industry-specific challenges for the corporate social environment.[8]

In response to these pressures, businesses have increased their efforts to manage the corporate social environment. The social environment encompasses business activities influenced by various community and government groups. Many chief executives spend more time on the external affairs of the business than any other activity. Most executives allocate significant personnel, time, and budget to the creation of elaborate staff groups to help them understand and manage this environment and its challenges.

Some firms may be more vulnerable to social group pressure and social regulation than others. A number of factors have been identified as contributing to this vulnerability. A firm may be more vulnerable to social forces if the firm is:

- A large-sized or well-known company thus presenting a big target.
- Located in an urban area and under increased scrutiny by the media and social groups.
- Producing a consumer-oriented product viewed as a necessity by the public.
- Providing a product or service that may cause harm or injury to the user.
- Part of a heavily regulated industry that is expected to meet high public expectations.

Top Management Philosophy

How a firm addresses its exposure to the corporate social environment heavily depends on the values and beliefs of the company managers—the philosophy they hold about the role of the corporation in society. This is called the **top management philosophy.**

Managers sensitive to the impact of social forces and seeking to strategically manage their stakeholders will adopt the view that the firm is a social as well as an economic institution. They embrace the view that the firm has a duty to adapt to a changing social

[8]Robert H. Miles, *Managing the Corporate Social Environment* (Englewood Cliffs, NJ: Prentice Hall, 1987). Miles develops a corporate social strategy similar to the one presented here.

Post-Lawrence-Weber:
Business and Society,
Ninth Edition

Socially Responsive
Management

© The McGraw-Hill
Companies, 1999

environment. In response to emerging social issues, these managers are more likely to modify their business policies and practices than managers who understand their responsibilities to the firm only in an economic context. Managers in socially responsive firms recognize and consider not only the interests of their immediate, core stakeholders but the interests of all of the firm's stakeholders. They see corporate social performance in broad terms extending over the long term and having an impact on their industry. Most important, these managers merge the economic and social goals of their company into the firm's planning, measurement, and reward systems developed to guide and monitor business operations and managers' performance.

Socially Responsive Strategy

Using a socially responsive top management philosophy as a foundation, a firm must develop a **socially responsive strategy.** This strategic orientation tends to emphasize a collaborative and problem-solving approach, as opposed to one that emphasizes only the firm's interests and is adversarial in nature.

Collaborative, problem-solving strategies are distinguished by their emphasis on maintaining long-term relationships based on trust and open communication with all of the company's stakeholders. Managers demonstrate this collaborative characteristic by participating in regulatory advisory committees and trade associations that seek mutually beneficial compromises. However, these managers are quick to explain that their strategy is not purely altruistic. They acknowledge that maintaining ongoing relationships with their stakeholders and seeking mutually beneficial problem-solving strategies will ensure the company's long-term survival. This is an expression of enlightened self-interest.

> *An example of a collaborative strategy is IBM Corporation's "Reinventing Education" grants program. With education as the primary focus of IBM's social strategy, the firm has created partnerships with other businesses, foundations, and educational groups. IBM's involvement includes financial pledges, donations of technology, and expert assistance to participating schools. In cooperation with other institutions, IBM seeks economic profit as well as attempting to manage various forces in the corporate social environment.*[9]

Socially Responsive Structure

The next step in becoming a socially responsive organization is to change the organizational structure to be more responsive to external social challenges and better able to implement socially responsive strategies. This structure evolves from the values and beliefs held by the company's top managers and is expressed through socially responsive business strategies. There are four basic design dimensions that help to distinguish a **socially responsive structure** in an organization. They are breadth, depth, influence, and integration.[10]

Breadth is the number of different staff units that specialize in the socially responsive strategies undertaken by the company. The breadth of the design must be sufficient to enable the firm to adequately monitor and respond to the demands made by social forces.

[9]"IBM Corporate Contributions Program," http://www.technogrants.com/4.html (June 27, 1997).
[10]See Miles, *Managing the Corporate Social Environment,* for his observations of these characteristics in his study of the insurance industry.

Post–Lawrence–Weber:
Business and Society,
Ninth Edition

Socially Responsive
Management

© The McGraw–Hill
Companies, 1999

Depth is the intensity of the organizational learning process in response to the potential for social challenges and is addressed by the socially responsive strategy process. Companies more vulnerable to social challenges require more developed social response functions, which provide a wide range of perspectives and responses.

Influence and *integration* are the final two dimensions of the socially responsive organizational structure. They refer to the quality of relationships that exist among the company's staff units. The absence of this influence and integration could undermine or bias the corporation's socially responsive strategy process since it could lead to one staff unit, or a few, dominating the process at the sake of other units. The ultimate effectiveness often is due to the degree of integration achieved among the staff units.

Line Manager Involvement

The final element in becoming a socially responsive firm is the extent to which line managers are involved in the strategic process. The degree of **line manager involvement** depends on the sophistication of the company's socially responsive strategy process. The more elaborate the process, the more essential is involvement by line managers.

A high degree of line manager involvement often is difficult to achieve. Initially the strategic process is developed by staff units, but line managers must quickly become involved and assume responsibility for the implementation of the company's socially responsive strategies. For example, if a firm develops a strategy that includes a highly integrated philanthropic contribution and employee volunteerism program with local charities, line managers often are in the best position to screen worthy recipients, determine appropriate levels of contributions, and assign employee volunteers.

In contrast, corporations that rely on staff personnel and do not foster line manager involvement will tend to exhibit a narrow, defensive, and protective socially responsive posture. This approach will buffer the company's line managers and line operations from corporate social environment influences. The degree of line manager involvement is heavily influenced by top management philosophy and generally is consistent with the socially responsive strategy and structure adopted by the company.

Corporate Social Audits

In 1953, Howard Bowen introduced the idea of bringing social impacts to the attention of managers. He proposed a specialized group of social auditors to work within the organization and present their audit findings to managers. A recent definition of **social auditing** challenges businesses to be socially responsive:

> *Today, a social audit examines the social and ethical impact of the business from two perspectives: from the inside, assessing performance against the company's mission statement of objectives; and from the outside, using comparisons with other organizations' behavior and social norms.*[11]

Since the 1960s, the demand for social auditing has gained momentum in Europe, as well as in the United States. A British scholar, George Goyder, made the following passionate plea:

[11] Howard R. Bowen, *Social Responsibilities of the Businessman* (New York: Harper, 1953).

Post–Lawrence–Weber:
Business and Society,
Ninth Edition

Socially Responsive
Management

© The McGraw–Hill
Companies, 1999

> *Has the time come for the country which led the first industrial revolution to
> lead the industrialized nations a second time, by returning to those mutual aid
> principles which are also the principles of the natural law? For Britain, time is
> running out. We need the responsible company now.*[12]

Modern Day Social Assessment

Throughout the 1970s, managers remained unconvinced that financial measures involved
in social auditing could be used in business decision making. They believed that social
costs and benefits were too removed from the firm's mainstream functions, especially from
its profits. As a result, they argued that financial accounting for social impacts was not
helpful in the quest for developing socially responsible strategies or in the assessment of
such strategies.[13]

In response to this skepticism, researchers have tried to develop a **social performance audit** or corporate ratings approach. This type of audit involves measuring a firm's
corporate activities on an ideal socially responsible scale or comparing the resulting rating of a firm's actions against those of other, similar organizations.[14] For example, if a
company supports a tutorial program at a local school, the performance audit might look
at not only the number of hours of employee volunteerism but also assess the change in
student test scores as an indicator of the program's social impact.

> *Organizations concerned about stakeholder issues use performance audits to
> evaluate the impact of corporate social efforts. Examples include universities,
> churches, charitable groups, and socially responsible mutual funds who invest
> their money in companies that behave like good neighbors.*[15]

As businesses approach the twenty-first century, interest in social auditing is once
again rising. Many corporate stakeholders—community groups, employee unions and consumer activists—expect businesses to act responsibly and be contributing members to the
society to which the firms and the stakeholder groups belong. One such example of a social audit involves the Body Shop. A social audit was commissioned by Body Shop executives to provide an independent assessment of the company's social and ethical achievements. In the report, high marks were given to the Body Shop in areas such as the quality
of its mission statement, corporate philanthropy, and environmental and animal welfare.
But, according to Stanford professor Kirk Hanson, who conducted the audit, the company
was weak in accepting outside criticism and had a poor relationship with the public and
the media.[16] Another example of a corporate social audit is shown in Exhibit B.

---

[12] George Goyder, *The Just Enterprise—A Blueprint for the Responsible Company* (London:
Adamantine Press, 1993).

[13] William C. Frederick, "Auditing Corporate Social Performance: The Anatomy of a Social Research Project," in Lee E. Preston, ed., *Research in Corporate Social Performance and Policy*
(Greenwich, CT: JAI Press), vol. 1 (1978), pp. 123–37.

[14] See Carolyn Kay Brancato, "New Corporate Performance Measures," Report No. 1118-95-RR,
The Conference Board, New York, 1995, for examples of corporate performance measure models
from many countries.

[15] Kim Davenport, "Social Auditing: The Quest for Corporate Social Responsibility," in Jim Weber and Kathleen Rehbein, eds., *IABS 1997 Proceedings 8th Annual Conference* (1997), pp. 196–
201. Davenport's paper also provides a very complete historical review of corporate social auditing.

[16] Matthew Rose, "Body Shop Gets Taken to Task in 'Social Audit,'" *The Wall Street Journal*,
April 19, 1996, p. B9B.

Post–Lawrence–Weber:
Business and Society,
Ninth Edition

Socially Responsive
Management

© The McGraw–Hill
Companies, 1999

EXHIBIT B   The Citizen's Bank Social Audit

The social audit developed at Citizens Bank, a Canadian financial institution, reported the firm's corporate social performance score. This score measured a number of key issues such as employee relations, the environment, the community, and ethical business practices.

For example, employee relations emphasized workplace safety, occupational stress, employment equity, and other variables that contributed to the firm's overall performance. The audit was performed on a regular basis—every 12 to 18 months. Like a financial audit, the social audit intended to allow the bank's customers and local communities to assess the social performance over time, to see whether or not the firm was living up to its commitment to being a team leader in corporate social responsibility in Canada.

Source: http://www.citizensbank.ca/difference/reportcard.html (August 6, 1997).

Summary Points

- In response to the numerous social challenges facing businesses, managers have recognized the need to develop formal social response strategies and programs.

- Business should monitor the multiple segments within the macroenvironment of business and conduct rigorous environmental scanning before developing a socially responsive program.

- The model of social responsiveness includes the policy stage, the learning stage, and the organizational commitment stage.

- A framework for managing the corporate social environment includes four critical elements: top management philosophy, socially responsive strategy, socially responsive structure, and line manager involvement.

- Corporate social auditing and performance audits are used to assess a firm's management of the corporate social environment.

Key Terms and Concepts

- Collaborative partnerships
- Corporate social responsiveness
- Macroenvironment of business
- Environmental scanning
- Top management philosophy
- Socially responsive strategy
- Socially responsive structure
- Line manager involvement
- Social auditing
- Social performance audit

Post–Lawrence–Weber:
Business and Society,
Ninth Edition

Socially Responsive
Management

© The McGraw–Hill
Companies, 1999

Internet Resources

- http://www.charitynet.org/caf/cafcompanies   Corporate Community Involvement Resource Center
- http://www.hbsp.harvard.edu   Business Enterprise Trust teaching material
- http://www.mcs.net/~commnews   Community News Project

Discussion Case   Aaron Feuerstein—A Socially Responsive Owner

The evening of December 11, 1995, was a special time for Aaron Feuerstein, CEO of Malden Mills. A small surprise 70th birthday party quietly was held in his honor at a local Boston restaurant. But Feuerstein's life took a dramatic turn that evening for a different reason: A boiler at his company's plant exploded, setting off a fire that injured 33 employees and destroyed three of the factory's century-old buildings. Malden Mills was a privately owned firm, with Feuerstein owning a majority share. The firm was located in a small Massachusetts town, Methuen, and employed nearly 3,000 people in the economically depressed area. The fire was a devastating blow for the community. According to Paul Coorey, local union president, "I was standing there seeing the mill burn with my son, who also works there, and he looked at me and said, 'Dad, we just lost our jobs.' Years of our lives seemed gone."

Unexpected tragedies happen all too often, and the aftermath is frequently devastating to the owners, employees, suppliers, local community, and customers of the firm. But the December 1995 tragedy at Malden Mills had a different outcome than most, primarily due to the owner of the factory—Aaron Feuerstein—and the deep sense of corporate social responsiveness he showed through his actions following the tragedy at Malden Mills.

Aaron Feuerstein typically awoke at 5:30 A.M. and began each day by memorizing passages from the scriptures and Shakespeare. He firmly believed in loyalty and fairness to his workers. He often said that the average American wanted businesses and their owners to treat workers as human beings, with consideration and thoughtfulness. Feuerstein tried to meet these expectations. "I have to be worthy," he told his wife over and over again. "Too many people depend on me." He simply could not let anyone down—even after the unexpected and devastating tragedy of the December 1995 fire at his plant.

Aaron Feuerstein knew he had many options after the fire. He could close the factory and walk away with tens of millions of dollars in fire insurance. He could turn over to his industry rivals his profitable, flagship product, Polartec. This synthetic fiber was in great demand by the sport outerwear industry. Its production required a highly skilled, experienced workforce, and Malden Mills basically held a market monopoly. Many of the company's competitors would have paid a high price for the rights to produce Polartec.

Yet, Feuerstein's commitment to his employees led him to a different strategy. "I was telling myself I have to be creative. Maybe there's some way out of this." In an announcement to his employees at a local high school gymnasium four days after the tragic fire, Feuerstein explained that he would keep all the nearly 3,000 employees on the payroll for a month while he started to rebuild the family business. One month later,

Post–Lawrence–Weber:
Business and Society,
Ninth Edition

Socially Responsive
Management

© The McGraw–Hill
Companies, 1999

as the rebuilding process continued at a slow pace, Feuerstein extended the salary offer to his employees for another month; a month later, he extended it for yet a third month. "What I did was merely the decent thing to do," he insisted. "The worker is not just a cuttable expense, a pair of hands. I consider the employees the most valuable asset Malden Mills has."

With the first announcement of guaranteed salaries just days before Christmas, the reactions from employees were understandably positive. "When he did it the first time, I was surprised," said Bill Cotter, a 49-year-old Malden Mills employee. "The second time was a shock. The third . . . well, it was unrealistic to think he would do it again." Nancy Cotter finished her husband's thought: "It was the third time that brought tears to everyone's eyes." By March 1996, most of the company's employees were back to work. Those who were not were offered assistance in making other arrangements or finding other employment in the area.

Another surprising twist to this story of social responsiveness was shown by the outpouring of support by Malden Mills' customers and other local organizations. An apparel company, Dakotah, sent Feuerstein a $30,000 check after the fire. The Bank of Boston donated $50,000, the company's union sent $100,000, and the Chamber of Commerce in nearby Lawrence, Massachusetts, contributed $150,000. Many of Malden Mills' customers promised to stick with the company and wait for them to rebuild and regain their production capacity rather than switch to a competitor.

Just eight months after the fire, three of the four production lines at Malden Mills were fully operational and all but 500 of the nearly 3,000 employees were back to work in the factory. In December 1996, a year after the tragic fire, the company projected sales revenue of $358 million, compared to $400 million in 1995. Malden Mills apparently had weathered the storm following the destructive fire. One of the strongest factors contributing to the firm's reemergence was Aaron Feuerstein's commitment to *both the company's economic and social mission and goals.*

Sources: Tom Mitkowski, "A Glow from a Fire," *Time,* January 8, 1996; Mitchell Owens, "A Mill Community Comes Back to Life," *New York Times,* December 26, 1996, p. B12; Louis Uchitelle, "The Risks of Keeping a Promise," *New York Times,* July 4, 1996, p. C1, C3; Bruce D. Butterfield, "What Flames Could Not Destroy," *Boston Globe,* September 8, 1996, p. A28; Michael Ryan, "They Call Their Boss a Hero," *Parade Magazine,* September 8, 1996, pp. 4–5; Alison S. Lebwohl, "Rising from the Ashes," http://www.afscme.org/afscme/press/peso9614.htm (July 11, 1997); and Bruce D. Butterfield, "More Than a Factory," *Boston Globe,* December 8, 1996, p. E1.

Discussion Questions

1. Conduct a corporate social audit of Malden Mills. What social factors appear to economically benefit the company? What score or grade would you give Malden Mills for its social performance after the December 1995 fire?
2. What factors do you believe influenced Aaron Feuerstein's choice of a socially responsive strategy in reaction to the tragic fire at his factory?
3. Could Feuerstein's actions be a model of corporate social responsiveness for other corporate managers?

Post–Lawrence–Weber:
Business and Society,
Ninth Edition

Socially Responsive
Management

© The McGraw–Hill
Companies, 1999

Bibliography

Ackerman, Robert. *The Social Challenge to Business.* Cambridge, MA: Harvard University Press, 1975.

Block, Peter. *Stewardship: Choosing Service over Self Interest.* San Francisco, CA: Berrett-Koehler, 1996.

Bollier, David. *Aiming Higher.* New York: American Management Association, 1996.

Bowen, Howard R. *Responsibilities of the Businessman,* New York: Harper, 1953.

Bradshaw, Thornton, and David Vogel, eds. *Corporations and Their Critics.* New York: McGraw-Hill, 1981.

Chamberlain, Neil W., *The Limits of Corporate Social Responsibility.* New York: Basic Books, 1973.

Himmelstein, Jerome. *Looking Good and Doing Good.* Bloomington, IN: Indiana University Press, 1997.

Houck, John, and Oliver F. Williams, eds. *Is the Good Corporation Dead? Social Responsibility in a Global Economy.* Lanham, MD: Rowman and Littlefield Publishers, 1996.

Kuhn, James W., and Donald W. Shriver, Jr. *Beyond Success: Corporations and Their Critics in the 1990s.* New York: Oxford University Press, 1991.

Miles, Robert. *Managing the Corporate Social Environment: A Grounded Theory.* Englewood Cliffs, NJ: Prentice-Hall, 1987.

Scott, Mary, and Howard Rothman. *Companies with a Conscience: Intimate Portraits of Twelve Firms That Make a Difference.* New York: Citadel Press Book/ Carroll Publishing Group, 1994.

Post–Lawrence–Weber:
Business and Society,
Ninth Edition

Ethical Dilemmas in
Business

© The McGraw–Hill
Companies, 1999

Ethical Dilemmas in Business

People who work in business—managers and employees alike—frequently encounter and must deal with on-the-job ethical issues. Learning how to recognize the different kinds of ethical dilemmas and knowing why they occur is an important business skill. The costs to business and to society of unethical and illegal behavior are very large. A business firm is more likely to gain public approval and social legitimacy if it adheres to basic ethical principles and society's laws.

This topic focuses on these key questions and objectives:

- What is ethics? What is business ethics?
- Why should business be ethical?
- Why do ethics problems occur in business?
- What efforts are being made to curtail unethical practices around the world?
- Are ethical behavior and legal behavior the same?

Roger Worsham had just graduated as an accounting major with a business degree and had landed a job with a small regional accounting firm in northern Michigan. Working there would give him the experience he needed to qualify as a certified public accountant (CPA). He, his wife, and their two small children settled in to enjoy small-town life. Roger's employer was experiencing tough competition from large accounting firms that were able to offer more varied services, including management consulting, computerized data processing services, and financial advice. Losing a big client could mean the difference between staying open or closing down one of the local offices.[1]

During one of his first audit assignments of a local savings and loan (S&L) company, Roger uncovered evidence of fraud. Law restricted the S&L at that time to mortgages based on residential property, but it had loaned money to a manufacturing company. To conceal this illegal loan from Roger, someone had removed the file before he began the audit. Roger suspected that the guilty party might have been the S&L president, who, in addition to being the largest owner of the manufacturing firm, was also a very influential lawyer in town.

Roger took the evidence of wrongdoing to his boss, expecting to hear that the accounting firm would include it in the audit report, as required by standard accounting practices. Instead, he was told to put the evidence and all of his notes through a shredder. His boss said, "I will take care of this privately. We simply cannot afford to lose this client." When Roger hesitated, he was told, "You put those papers through the shredder or I'll guarantee that you'll never get a CPA in Michigan, or work in an accounting office in this state for the rest of your life."

Question: If you were Roger, what would you do? If you were Roger's boss, would you have acted differently? What is the ethical thing to do?

Ethical puzzles like this occur frequently in business. They are troubling to the people involved. Sometimes, a person's most basic ideas of fairness, honesty, and integrity are at stake. This material explores the meaning of ethics, identifies the different types of ethical problems that occur in business, and tells why these dilemmas arise. A discussion of corporate crime illustrates the relationship of law and ethics. "Ethical Reasoning and Corporate Programs" tells how ethical performance in business can be improved by providing some tools for grappling with on-the-job ethical dilemmas.

The Meaning of Ethics

Ethics is a conception of right and wrong conduct. It tells us whether our behavior is moral or immoral and deals with fundamental human relationships—how we think and behave toward others and how we want them to think and behave toward us. **Ethical principles** are guides to moral behavior. For example, in most societies lying, stealing, deceiving, and harming others are considered to be unethical and immoral. Honesty, keeping promises, helping others, and respecting the rights of others are considered to be ethically and morally desirable behavior. Such basic rules of behavior are essential for the preservation and continuation of organized life everywhere.

These notions of right and wrong come from many sources. Religious beliefs are a major source of ethical guidance for many. The family institution—whether two parents, a single parent, or a large family with brothers and sisters, grandparents, aunts, cousins,

---

[1] More details about this episode are in LaRue Tone Hosmer, *The Ethics of Management*, 3d. ed. (Homewood, IL: Irwin, 1991), pp. 164–68.

Post–Lawrence–Weber:
Business and Society,
Ninth Edition

Ethical Dilemmas in
Business

© The McGraw–Hill
Companies, 1999

and other kin—imparts a sense of right and wrong to children as they grow up. Schools and schoolteachers, neighbors and neighborhoods, friends, admired role models, ethnic groups—and of course, the ever-present electronic media —influence what we believe to be right and wrong in life. The totality of these learning experiences creates in each person a concept of ethics, morality, and socially acceptable behavior. This core of ethical beliefs then acts as a moral compass that helps to guide a person when ethical puzzles arise.

Ethical ideas are present in all societies, organizations, and individual persons, although they may vary greatly from one to another. Your ethics may not be the same as your neighbor's; one particular religion's notion of morality may not be identical to another's; or what is considered ethical in one society may be forbidden in another society. These differences raise the important and controversial issue of **ethical relativism,** which holds that ethical principles should be defined by various periods of time in history, a society's traditions, the special circumstances of the moment, or personal opinion. In this view, the meaning given to ethics would be relative to time, place, circumstance, and the person involved. In that case, there would be no universal ethical standards on which people around the globe could agree. For companies conducting business in several societies at one time, whether or not ethics is relevant can be vitally important, and we discuss those issues in more detail later.

For the moment, however, we can say that in spite of the diverse systems of ethics that exist within our own society and throughout the world, all people everywhere do depend on ethical systems to tell them whether their actions are right or wrong, moral or immoral, approved or disapproved. Ethics, in this sense, is a universal human trait, found everywhere.

What Is Business Ethics?

Business ethics is the application of general ethical ideas to business behavior. Business ethics is not a special set of ethical ideas different from ethics in general and applicable only to business. If dishonesty is considered to be unethical and immoral, then anyone in business who is dishonest with its stakeholders—employees, customers, stockholders, or competitors—is acting unethically and immorally. If protecting others from harm is considered to be ethical, then a company that recalls a dangerously defective product is acting in an ethical way. To be considered ethical, business must draw its ideas about what is proper behavior from the same sources as everyone else. Business should not try to make up its own definitions of what is right and wrong. Employees and managers may believe at times that they are permitted or even encouraged to apply special or weaker ethical rules to business situations, but society does not condone or permit such an exception. People who work in business are bound by the same ethical principles that apply to others.

Employees often admit that they feel pressure at work, which may lead to unethical behavior. A national study released by the Ethics Officers Association and two professional groups claimed that over half of the workers felt some pressure to act unethically on the job. Nearly half of the workers, 48 percent, reported that they had engaged in unethical or illegal actions during the past year and attributed their actions to workplace pressure. Figure 1 shows the breakdown of factors that contributed to pressure to act unethically, as reported by the employees in the study.

Post–Lawrence–Weber:
Business and Society,
Ninth Edition

Ethical Dilemmas in
Business

© The McGraw–Hill
Companies, 1999

Figure 1

Factors contributing
to pressure in the
workplace.

Source: Ethics
Officer Association
and American
Society of Chartered
Life Underwriters
and Chartered
Financial
Consultants, April
1997.

Responses by employees to a national study showed the following factors contributed to pressure to act unethically on the job:			
Balancing work and family	52%	Need to meet goals (e.g., sales)	46%
Poor leadership	51%	Company politics	44%
Poor internal communications	51%	Insufficient resources	40%
Work hours/workload	51%	Incompetent subordinates	39%
Lack of management support	48%	Downsizing effects	33%
Little or no recognition of achievements	46%		

Figure 2

Why should business
be ethical?

- Fulfill public expectation for business.
- Prevent harming others.
- Improve business relations and employee productivity.
- Reduce penalties under the U.S. Corporate Sentencing Guidelines.
- Protect business from others.
- Protect employees from their employers.
- Promote personal morality.

Why Should Business Be Ethical?

Why should business be ethical? What prevents a business firm from piling up as many profits as it can, in any way it can, regardless of ethical considerations? For example, what is wrong with Roger Worsham's boss telling him to destroy evidence of a client's fraudulent conduct? Why not just shred the papers, thereby keeping a good customer happy (and saving Roger's job, too)? Figure 2 lists the major reasons business firms should promote a high level of ethical behavior.

We mentioned one reason when discussing social responsibility in "Business and the Social Environment." Corporate stakeholders expect business to exhibit high levels of ethical performance and social responsibility. Companies that fail to fulfill this public demand can expect to be spotlighted, criticized, curbed, and punished.

> *For example, Gtech Holding Corporation was one of the largest on-line betting companies in the United States. But during the past year, Gtech's management and security analysts pointed to the firm's recent ethical investigations and allegations of bribery as an explanation for the firm's marginal revenue decrease. Consistently Gtech's clients switched to competitor firms when contracts with Gtech expired. Allegations of shady business dealings prompted numerous federal grand jury investigations and may have contributed to Gtech's former clients' wariness of doing business with the firm. Although*

Post-Lawrence-Weber:
Business and Society,
Ninth Edition

Ethical Dilemmas in
Business

© The McGraw-Hill
Companies, 1999

Gtech stressed it had never been found guilty of corporate wrongdoing, the impression of ethical impropriety seemed to affect the firm's business relations and its profitability.[2]

A second reason businesses and their employees should act ethically is to prevent harm to the general public and the corporation's many stakeholders. One of the strongest ethical principles is stated very simply: Do no harm. A company that is careless in disposing of toxic chemical wastes that cause disease and death is breaking this ethical injunction. Many ethical rules operate to protect society against various types of harm, and businesses are expected to observe these commonsensical ethical principles.

Some people argue that another reason for businesses to be ethical is that it pays. In a recent study, scholars concluded that organizations that promote ethics by adopting a code of conduct to guide their operations were "more effective in managing their ethical activities and were more successful and profitable—both in the short term and the long term."[3] Further support for the relationship between being ethical and being profitable was found in a study conducted by Rutgers University. Researchers found that investors in firms that fostered an ethical work environment realized an annual shareholder rate of return that was about 45 percent higher than firms that ignored ethics.[4]

Being ethical imparts a sense of trust, which promotes positive alliances among business partners. If this trust is broken, the unethical party may be shunned and ignored. This situation occurred when Malaysian government officials gave the cold shoulder to executives of a French company. When asked why they were being unfriendly, a Malaysian dignitary replied: "Your chairman is in jail!"[5] The nurturing of an ethical environment and the development of ethical safeguards can be critical incentives for improving business relations and employee and organizational productivity.

The **U.S. Corporate Sentencing Guidelines** provide a strong incentive for businesses to promote ethics at work.[6] The sentencing guidelines come into play when an employee of a firm has been found guilty of a criminal wrongdoing. To determine sentencing, a federal judge computes a culpability (degree of blame) score using the equations contained in the guidelines. The score is significantly affected if a firm's ethics program monitors and aggressively responds to reported criminal violations at work. Under the sentencing guidelines, corporate executives found guilty of criminal activity could receive lighter penalties if their firm has developed a strong ethics program. According to a U.S. Sentencing Commission report, the most frequent target of the sentencing guidelines have been firms that are relatively young (less than 10 years old) and small (fewer than 50 em-

---

[2] William M. Bulkeley and Steve Stecklow, "Long a Winner, Gtech Faces Resistance Based on Ethical Concerns," *The Wall Street Journal,* January 16, 1996, pp. A1, A6.

[3] Michael K. McCuddy, Karl E. Reichardt, and David L. Schoeder, "Exploring the Relationships between Ethical Business Practices and Organizational Success and Profitability," paper presented at the 1996 national annual Academy of Management meeting, Cincinnati, OH.

[4] Dale Kurschner, "5 Ways Ethical Busine$$ Creates Fatter Profit$," *Business Ethics,* March–April 1996, pp. 20–23.

[5] "Scandals Crimp Business for French Firms," *The Wall Street Journal,* October 20, 1994, p. A20.

[6] For a thorough discussion of the U.S. Corporate Sentencing Guidelines, see Jeffrey M. Kaplan and William K. Perry, "The High Cost of Corporate Crime," *Management Accounting,* December 1991, pp. 43–46; and Dan R. Dalton, Michael B. Metzger, and John W. Hill, "The 'New' U.S. Sentencing Commission Guidelines: A Wake-Up Call for Corporate America," *Academy of Management Executive* 8 (1994), pp. 7–13.

Post–Lawrence–Weber:
Business and Society,
Ninth Edition

Ethical Dilemmas in
Business

© The McGraw–Hill
Companies, 1999

ployees). The commission report said that "97 percent of the 280 firms sentenced under the guidelines since they took effect have been privately held or controlled by only a small group of shareholders."[7] However, it is believed that within the next decade older and larger firms will feel the effect of the U.S. Sentencing Commission guidelines.

A fifth reason for promoting ethical behavior is to protect business firms from abuse by unethical employees and unethical competitors. Security experts estimate that employee pilferage (stealing) has caused more businesses to go into bankruptcy than any other crime. Stealing by employees accounts for 60 to 75 percent of all business losses, according to a U.S. government survey. A study by the U.S. Department of Commerce showed that employee theft in manufacturing plants alone amounted to $8 million a day nationwide.[8] For the retail industry, it is a larger cost to store owners than customer shoplifting. One of the reasons for the magnitude of the problem is the difficulty of detecting the crime. Store owners admit that they are often at the mercy of the employees to act honestly.

> *A startling example of employee theft was discovered in 1994 involving an MCI Communications employee. U.S. Secret Service agents arrested the employee after it was alleged that he stole more than 60,000 telephone-card numbers, which were sold on the international black market. The four major telephone carriers lost more than $50 million in revenues.*[9]

High ethical performance also protects people who work in business. Employees resent invasions of privacy (such as obtrusive video surveillance in workplace restrooms) or being ordered to do something against their personal convictions (such as falsifying an accounting report) or being forced to work in hazardous conditions (such as entering unventilated coal mines or being exposed to dangerous agricultural pesticides in the fields). Businesses that treat their employees with dignity and integrity reap many rewards in the form of high morale and improved productivity. It is a win-win-win situation for the firm, its employees, and society.

A final reason for promoting ethics in business is a personal one. Most people want to act in ways that are consistent with their own sense of right and wrong. Being pressured to contradict their personal values creates much emotional stress. Knowing that one works in a supportive ethical climate contributes to one's sense of psychological security. People feel good about working for an ethical company because they know they are protected along with the general public.

Business Ethics across Organizational Functions

Not all ethics issues in business are the same. Because business operations are highly specialized, ethics issues can appear in any of the major functional areas of a business firm. **Functional-area ethics** tends to have its own particular brand of ethical dilemmas, as discussed next.

---

[7] Joe Davidson, "Corporate Sentencing Guidelines Have Snagged Mostly Small Firms," *The Wall Street Journal*, August 28, 1995, p. B5.

[8] Landmark Investigators, http://www2.thecia.net/users/landmark/employee.html (October 30, 1997).

[9] "MCI Worker Charged in U.S. Investigation of Phone-Card Fraud," *The Wall Street Journal*, October 4, 1994, p. B7.

Post–Lawrence–Weber:
Business and Society,
Ninth Edition

Ethical Dilemmas in
Business

© The McGraw–Hill
Companies, 1999

Accounting Ethics

The accounting function is a critically important component of every business firm. Accounting reports tell owners and managers whether the firm is doing well or poorly. Company managers, external investors, government regulators, tax collectors, and labor unions rely on accounting data to make key decisions. Honesty, integrity, and accuracy are absolute requirements of the accounting function. No other single issue is of greater concern to accountants in industry and public accountancy than ethics. Roger Worsham's dilemma, discussed at the beginning of this material, highlights the importance of honest accounting.

Professional accounting organizations—such as the American Institute of Certified Public Accountants and the Financial Accounting Standards Board—have developed generally accepted accounting principles whose purpose is to establish uniform standards for reporting accounting and auditing data. In 1993, the American Institute for Certified Public Accountants dramatically changed its professional code by requiring CPAs to act as whistle-blowers when detecting "materially misstated" financial statements or face losing their license to practice accounting. Examples of this profession's efforts toward promoting ethics are shown in Exhibit A. Spurred by the increasing threat of liability suits filed against accounting firms and the desire to reaffirm professional integrity, these standards go far toward ensuring a high level of honest and ethical accounting behavior.

EXHIBIT A
Professional Codes of Conduct in Accounting and Finance
American Institute of Certified Public Accountants (AICPA)
Code of Professional Conduct

Membership in the American Institute of Certified Public Accountants is voluntary. By accepting membership, a certified public accountant assumes an obligation of self-discipline above and beyond the requirements of laws and regulations.

These Principles of the Code of Professional Conduct of the American Institute of Certified Public Accountants express the profession's recognition of its responsibilities to the public, to clients, and to colleagues. They guide members in the performance of their professional responsibilities and express the basic tenets of ethical and professional conduct. The Principles call for an unswerving commitment to honorable behavior, even at the sacrifice of personal advantage. . . .

- Responsibilities—In carrying out their responsibilities as professionals, members should exercise sensitive professional and moral judgments in all their activities. . . .

- The Public Interest—Members should accept the obligation to act in a way that will serve the public interest, honor the public interest, and demonstrate commitment to professionalism. . . .

- Integrity—To maintain and broaden public confidence, members should perform all professional responsibilities with the highest sense of integrity. . . .

- Objectivity and Independence—A member should maintain objectivity and be free of conflicts of interest in discharging professional responsibilities. A member

Post–Lawrence–Weber:
Business and Society,
Ninth Edition

Ethical Dilemmas in
Business

© The McGraw–Hill
Companies, 1999

in public practice should be independent in fact and appearance when providing auditing and other attestation services. . . .

- Due Care—A member should observe the profession's technical and ethical standards, strive continually to improve competence and the quality of services, and discharge professional responsibility to the best of the member's ability. . . .

- Scope and Nature of Services—A member in public practice should observe the Principles of the Code of Professional Conduct in determining the scope and nature of services to be provided.

"Reprinted with permission from the AICPA Code of Professional Conduct, copyright © 1997 by the American Institute of Certified Public Accountants, Inc."

Chartered Financial Analyst (CFA)

Code of Ethics and Standards of Professional Conduct

The financial analyst shall inform his* employer, through his direct supervisor, that the analyst is obligated to comply with the Code of Ethics and Standards of Professional Conduct, and is subject to disciplinary sanctions for violations thereof. He shall deliver a copy of the Code and Standards to his employer if the employer does not have a copy.

The financial analyst shall maintain knowledge of and shall comply with all applicable laws, rules and regulations . . . shall not knowingly participate in, or assist, any acts in violation of any applicable law, rule or regulation . . . [and] shall exercise reasonable supervision over subordinate employees . . . to prevent violations.

Areas of ethical concern for the financial analyst include reasonable basis for investment recommendations and representations, accuracy of research reports, suitability of portfolio recommendations for the client, avoidance of plagiarism, avoidance of misrepresentation of services, fair dealing with customers and clients, disclosure of conflicts of interest, reporting of compensation, preservation of confidentiality, objectivity, and fiduciary duties.

---

*Masculine personal pronouns, used throughout the Code and Standards to simplify sentence structure, shall apply to all persons, regardless of sex.
Source: Excerpted with permission from *Standards of Practice Handbook, Seventh Edition*, Copyright 1996, Association for Investment Management and Research, Charlottesville, VA. All rights reserved.

Failure to observe these professional ethical standards can produce ethics problems that also occur in other nations; and member-nations of the European Union have discussed the desirability of adopting uniform accounting rules that would apply to all members.[10] The **U.S. Foreign Corrupt Practices Act** requires U.S. companies with foreign operations to adopt accounting procedures that ensure a full disclosure of the company's relations with sales agents and government officials; the purpose is to prevent bribery and other legally questionable payments.

[10]Andrew Likierman, "Ethical Dilemmas for Accountants: A United Kingdom Perspective," *Journal of Business Ethics* 8 (1989), pp. 617–29. For several excellent examples of ethical dilemmas in accounting, see Leonard J. Brooks, *Professional Ethics for Accountants: Text, Readings and Cases* (St. Paul, MN: West Publishing, 1995).

Post–Lawrence–Weber:
Business and Society,
Ninth Edition

Ethical Dilemmas in
Business

© The McGraw-Hill
Companies, 1999

Financial Ethics

Finance produced some of the most spectacular ethics scandals of recent times. Wall Street financiers were found guilty of insider trading, illegal stock transactions, and various other financial abuses. Three examples of ethical abuses within the financial community follow.

> *Officers at the Bank of Credit and Commerce International fraudulently spent over $20 billion of its investors' deposits to support the financing of illegal arms sales, nuclear weapon production, and laundering of drug-trade profits. Executives involved in the fraud were sentenced to as many as 14 years in prison and fined $9.13 billion.*
>
> *Prudential Insurance improperly sold partnerships without appropriate licenses through a commission-sharing scheme with its subsidiary, Prudential-Bache Securities. From 1983 to 1990, Prudential received $777 million in partnership fees while ignoring warning signs that partnerships may be a highly risky venture.*
>
> *Hundreds of savings and loan associations failed after their managers misused their depositors' funds, rewarded themselves and family members with lavish salaries and perks, misled bank examiners, published false accounting reports, and left U.S. taxpayers to pay the cost of the largest corporate bailout in the nation's history. These lapses in ethical conduct were evident despite efforts by the finance professions to foster an ethical environment, as shown in Exhibit A.*

Several other kinds of financial transactions are potential ethical minefields: investment banks that finance hostile corporate takeovers that threaten employees' jobs and local communities; trust departments that are charged with safely investing funds entrusted to them; money market managers who must vote on shareholder resolutions dealing with controversial ethical issues; banks that must decide whether to side with a corporation's management team that has been a good customer even though management's policies cause damage to the company's stockholders; and stockbrokers' relationships with clients who seek sound investment advice.[11]

Marketing Ethics

Relations with customers tend to generate many ethical problems. Pricing, promotions, advertising, product information, relations between advertising agencies and their clients, marketing research—all of these are potential problem areas. To improve the marketing profession, the American Marketing Association (AMA) adopted a code of ethics for its members (see Exhibit B). The AMA code advocates professional conduct guided by ethics, adherence to applicable laws, and honesty and fairness in all marketing activities. The code also recognizes the ethical responsibility of marketing professionals to the consuming public and specifically opposes such unethical practices as misleading product information, false and misleading advertising claims, high-pressure sales tactics, bribery and

---

[11] For several good examples of these and other areas, see John L. Casey, *Ethics in the Financial Marketplace* (New York: Scudder, Stevens & Clark, 1988); James B. Stewart, *Den of Thieves* (New York: Simon and Schuster, 1991); and Larry Alan Bear and Rita Maldonado-Bear, *Free Markets, Finance, Ethics, and Law* (Englewood Cliffs, NJ: Prentice Hall, 1994).

Post–Lawrence–Weber:
Business and Society,
Ninth Edition

Ethical Dilemmas in
Business

© The McGraw–Hill
Companies, 1999

EXHIBIT B   Professional Codes of Conduct in Marketing and Information Systems

American Marketing Association (AMA)

Code of Ethics

Members of the American Marketing Association (AMA) are committed to ethical professional conduct. They have joined together in subscribing to this Code of Ethics embracing the following topics: . . .

- Responsibilities . . . —Marketers must accept responsibility for the consequences of their activities and make every effort to ensure that their decisions, recommendations, and actions function to identify, serve, and satisfy all relevant publics: customers, organizations, and society. . . .

- "Honesty and Fairness—Marketers shall uphold and advance the integrity, honor, and dignity of the marketing profession . . .

- "Rights and Duties of Parties . . . —Participants in the marketing exchange process should be able to expect that: (1) products and services offered are safe and fit for their intended uses; (2) communications about offered products and services are not deceptive; (3) all parties intend to discharge their obligations, financial and otherwise, in good faith; and, (4) appropriate internal methods exist for equitable adjustment and/or redress of grievances concerning purchases. . . .

- Organizational Relationships—Marketers should be aware of how their behavior may influence or impact on the behavior of others in organizational relationships. They should not demand, encourage or apply coercion to obtain unethical behavior in their relationships with others. . . .

Any AMA members found to be in violation of any provision of this Code of Ethics may have his or her Association membership suspended or revoked.

"Reprinted with permission from the American Marketing Association's Code of Ethics, published by the American Marketing Association.

Association for Computing Machinery (ACM)

Code of Ethics and Professional Conduct

Preamble. Commitment to ethical professional conduct is expected of every member (voting members, associate members, and student members) of the Association for Computing Machinery (ACM).

This Code, consisting of 24 imperatives formulated as statements of personal responsibility, identifies the elements of such a commitment. It contains many, but not all, issues professionals are likely to face. . . . The code and its supplemented Guidelines are intended to serve as a basis for ethical decision making in the conduct of professional work. Secondarily, they may serve as a basis for judging the merit of a formal complaint pertaining to violation of professional ethical standards.

The general imperatives for ACM members include contribute to society and human well-being, avoid harm to others, be honest and trustworthy, be fair and take

Continued

Post–Lawrence–Weber:
Business and Society,
Ninth Edition

Ethical Dilemmas in
Business

© The McGraw–Hill
Companies, 1999

action not to discriminate, honor property rights, including copyrights and patents, give proper credit for intellectual property, respect the privacy of others, and honor confidentiality.

Adherence of professionals to a code of ethics is largely a voluntary matter. However, if a member does not follow this code by engaging in gross misconduct, membership in ACM may be terminated.

Courtesy of the Association for Computing Machinery, Inc.

kickbacks, and unfair and predatory pricing. These code provisions have the potential for helping marketing professionals translate general ethical principles into specific working rules.[12]

Information Systems Ethics

One of the fastest-growing areas of business ethics is in the field of information systems. Exploding in the 1990s were ethical challenges involving invasions of privacy; the collection, storage, and access of personal and business information; confidentiality of communications over the telephone, electronic mail, and facsimile machine; copyright protection regarding software copying; and numerous other related issues. The explosion of information technology raised serious questions of trust between individuals and businesses. Questions centering on who should monitor and possibly control access to information were also raised as important ethical concerns in the field of information systems. In response to calls by businesspeople and academics for an increase in ethical responsibility in the information system field, professional organizations have developed or revised professional codes of ethics, as shown in Exhibit B.[13]

Other Functional Areas

Production and maintenance functions, which may seem to be remote from ethics considerations, can be at the center of some ethics storms. Dangerously defective products can injure or kill innocent persons, and toxic production processes may threaten the health of workers and the general public. Flawed manufacturing and lack of inspection of aircraft fuse pins, which hold the engines to the wing on Boeing 747 jet airplanes, were suspected in some accidents, endangering the lives of passengers as well as innocent bystanders. Union Carbide's pesticide plant in Bhopal, India, was allegedly not properly

[12]The AMA Code for Market Researchers and a discussion of numerous marketing ethics issues can be found in Gene R. Laczniak and Patrick E. Murphy, *Ethical Marketing Decisions* (Boston: Allyn and Bacon, 1993); and Lawrence B. Chonko, *Ethical Decision Making in Marketing* (Thousand Oaks, CA: SAGE Publications, 1995).
[13]For further discussion of ethics in information systems see Richard O. Mason, Florence M. Mason, and Mary J. Culnan, *Ethics of Information Management* (Thousand Oaks, CA: SAGE Publications, 1995); M. David Ermann, Mary B. Williams, and Michele S. Shauf, *Computers, Ethics, and Society*, 2d ed. (New York: Oxford University Press, 1997); and Effy Oz, "Ethical Standards for Computer Professionals: A Comparative Analysis of Four Major Codes," *Journal of Business Ethics* 12 (1993), pp. 709–26.

Post–Lawrence–Weber:
Business and Society,
Ninth Edition

Ethical Dilemmas in
Business

© The McGraw–Hill
Companies, 1999

maintained, and this failure was believed to be a contributing cause of the tragic leak that killed over 2,000 people.

Ethics issues also arise in purchasing departments. Kmart Corporation launched a formal investigation involving many of its real estate purchasing officials after allegations of corruption and bribery. This investigation followed a federal grand jury indictment of a former Kmart real estate executive on taking more than $750,000 in bribes.[14]

A survey by the National Association of Purchasing Management reported common ethics problems: exaggerating a problem to receive a better price from a supplier; providing preferential treatment to a supplier who is also a good customer; allowing personal friendships to enter into selection decisions; providing information to a competing supplier; accepting promotional prizes or purchase volume incentives; accepting trips, meals, or entertainment; and giving special treatment to vendors preferred by higher management.[15]

These examples make one point crystal clear: All areas of business, all people in business, and all levels of authority in business encounter ethics dilemmas from time to time. Ethics issues are a common thread running through the business world.

Why Ethical Problems Occur in Business

Obviously, ethics problems in business appear in many different forms. Although not common or universal, they occur frequently. Finding out just what is responsible for causing them is one step that can be taken toward minimizing their impact on business operations and on the people affected. Some of the main reasons are summarized in Figure 3 and are discussed next.

Figure 3

Why ethical problems occur in business.

Reason	Nature of Ethical Problem	Typical Approach	Attitude
Personal gain and selfish interest	Selfish interest vs. others' interests	Egoistical mentality	"I want it!"
Competitive Pressures on Profits	Firm's interest vs. others' interests	Bottom–line mentality	"We have to beat the others at all costs!"
Business Goals vs. Personal Values	Boss's interests vs. subordinates' values	Authoritarian mentality	"Do as I say, or else!"
Cross-Cultural Contradictions	Company's interests vs. diverse cultural traditions and values	Ethnocentric mentality	"Foreigners have a funny notion of what's right and wrong"

[14]"Kmart Is Dismissing 12 Managers from Its Purchasing Department," *The Wall Street Journal*, July 30, 1996, p. B4.
[15]Renee Florsheim and Eduardo S. Paderon, "Purchasing Practices in a Hospital Environment: An Ethical Analysis," *Hospital Material Management Quarterly* 13, no. 4 (1992), pp. 1–10.

Post–Lawrence–Weber:
Business and Society,
Ninth Edition

Ethical Dilemmas in
Business

© The McGraw-Hill
Companies, 1999

Personal Gain and Selfish Interest

Personal gain, or even greed, causes some ethics problems. Businesses sometimes employ people whose personal values are less than desirable. They will put their own welfare ahead of all others, regardless of the harm done to other employees, the company, or society. In the process of hiring employees, managers make efforts to weed out ethically undesirable applicants, but ethical qualities are difficult to anticipate and measure. The embezzler, the expense-account padder, the bribe taker, and other unethical persons can slip through. Lacking a perfect screening system, businesses are not likely to eliminate this kind of unethical behavior entirely. Moreover, firms have to proceed carefully when screening applicants, taking care not to trample on individuals' rights in the search for potentially unethical employees.

A manager or an employee who puts his or her own self-interest above all other considerations is called an **ethical egoist**. Self-promotion, a focus on self-interest to the point of selfishness, and greed are traits commonly observed in an ethical egoist. The ethical egoist tends to ignore ethical principles accepted by others, believing that ethical rules are made for others. **Altruism**—acting for the benefit of others when self-interest is sacrificed—is seen to be sentimental or even irrational. "Looking Out for Number One" is the ethical egoist's motto.[16]

Competitive Pressures on Profits

When companies are squeezed by tough competition, they sometimes engage in unethical activities to protect their profits. This may be especially true in companies whose financial performance is already substandard. Research has shown that poor financial performers and companies with lower profits are more prone to commit illegal acts.[17] However, a precarious financial position is only one reason for illegal and unethical business behavior, because profitable companies also can act contrary to ethical principles. In fact, it may be simply a single-minded drive for profits, regardless of the company's financial condition, that creates a climate for unethical activity.

Price-fixing is a practice that often occurs when companies vigorously engage in a market with limited growth potential. Besides being illegal, price-fixing is unethical behavior toward customers, who pay higher prices than they would if free competition set the prices. Companies fix prices to avoid fair competition and to protect their profits, as happened in the following cases.

> One of the most sensational and costly incidences of price-fixing involved companies in the citric acid and lysine industries. Archer-Daniels Midland Company, whose role in this ethics scandal is presented in the discussion case at the end of Chapter 13, was at the forefront. But other firms have been indicted or pleaded guilty, leading to the realization of a global price-fixing conspiracy

---

[16] For a compact discussion of ethical egoism, see Tom L. Beauchamp and Norman E. Bowie, *Ethical Theory and Business,* 5th ed. (Englewood Cliffs, NJ: Prentice Hall, 1997), pp. 14–19.

[17] For a discussion, see Peter C. Yeager, "Analyzing Corporate Offenses: Progress and Prospects," in William C. Frederick, ed., *Business Ethics: Research Issues and Empirical Studies* (Greenwich, CT: JAI Press, 1990), pp. 168–71; and Michael K. McCuddy, Karl E. Reichardt, and David L. Schroeder, "Ethical Pressures: Fact or Fiction?" *Management Accounting* 74, no. 10 (1993), pp. 57–61.

Post–Lawrence–Weber:
Business and Society,
Ninth Edition

Ethical Dilemmas in
Business

© The McGraw–Hill
Companies, 1999

*occurred involving Switzerland's F. Hoffmann–La Roche and Jungbunzlauer
International and German-based Bayer Corporation.*[18]

In another case, Japan's Fair Trade Commission demonstrated its aggressiveness toward uncovering unfair trade practices in two separate incidents. In May 1993, eight Japanese plastic food-wrapping companies were fined between $54,225 and $72,300, and several executives were suspended for conducting an elaborate price-fixing cartel. Later that year, the commission raided the nation's largest electronic companies to uncover evidence of bid-rigging. Close ties between Japanese businesses and government officials had effectively shut out foreign competition in bidding for public works projects.[19]

Price-fixing among competing companies is not the only kind of unethical behavior that can occur.

Senior Honda executives pleaded guilty in 1995 to accepting bribes and expensive gifts from U.S. dealers as a condition of providing them with an adequate supply of the most popular cars. The former Honda executives could face up to 35 years in prison and fines up to $5 million. Dozens of dealers contend that the corruption began in the 1970s and dramatically escalated later when Honda automobiles were in great demand but import quotas limited supply.[20]

Other kinds of unethical behavior also occur under competitive pressures. Companies can coerce suppliers into lowering their prices through nonmarket pressures, thereby receiving less than a fair price. When company officials have a strict bottom-line mentality shaped almost exclusively by market competition, they may overlook the ethical claims of their stakeholders. Doing so has the unfortunate and needless effect of pitting business against society.

Business Goals versus Personal Values

Ethical conflicts in business sometimes occur when a company pursues goals or uses methods that are unacceptable to some of its employees. *Whistle-blowing* may be one outcome, if an employee goes public with a complaint after failing to convince the company to correct an alleged abuse. Another recourse for employees caught in these situations is a lawsuit. This option has become less of a financial and professional risk for employees in recent years as a result of various governmental protection acts.

Paul Blanch blew the whistle on his employer, Connecticut's Northeast Utilities. Blanch identified safety lapses in plant operations. Shortly after his complaints, Blanch was subjected to negative job evaluations and harassing inter-

---

[18]"Investigators Suspect a Global Conspiracy in Archer-Daniels Case," *The Wall Street Journal,* July 28, 1995, pp. A1, A5; and Scott Kilman, "Two Swiss Chemical Firms Will Plead Guilty, Pay Fines in Price-Fixing Case," *The Wall Street Journal,* March 27, 1997, p. B5.

[19]"Japan's Court Fines Eight Firms," *The Wall Street Journal,* May 24, 1993, p. A6; and Jathon Sapsford, "Japanese Electronics Firms Are Raided by Agency on Suspicion of Bid-Rigging," *The Wall Street Journal,* November 16, 1993, p. A15.

[20]Angelo B. Henderson, "Two Former Honda Officials Convicted of Accepting Bribes From Auto Dealers," *The Wall Street Journal,* June 2, 1995, p. B2; and "Former Honda Officials Sentenced for Kickbacks," *The Wall Street Journal,* August 22, 1995, p. B16.

Post–Lawrence–Weber:
Business and Society,
Ninth Edition

Ethical Dilemmas in
Business

© The McGraw–Hill
Companies, 1999

nal audits. After Blanch sought government protection, the Nuclear Regulatory Commission imposed a $100,000 fine on Northeast Utilities for its actions against him.

Former GE employee Chester Walsh sued General Electric for overcharging the government on aircraft parts destined for Israel. After GE agreed to settle the suit for $39.5 million, a federal judge ordered the firm to pay $11.5 million to Walsh.[21]

The protesting employees in these companies were not troublemakers. They tried to work through internal company procedures to get the problems corrected. The ethical dilemmas arose because the companys' goals and methods required the employees to follow orders that they believed would harm themselves, other employees, customers, the company, and the general public. As far as they were concerned, they were being asked or ordered to do something unethical. Their own internal ethical compass was at odds with the goals and methods of their company.

Cross-Cultural Contradictions

Some of the knottiest ethical problems occur as corporations do business in other societies where ethical standards differ from those at home. Today, the policymakers and strategic planners in all multinational corporations, regardless of the nation where they are headquartered, face this kind of ethical dilemma. Consider the following situations:

U.S. sleepwear manufacturers discovered that the chemicals used to flameproof children's pajamas might cause cancer if absorbed through the child's skin. When these pajamas were banned from sale in the United States, some manufacturers sold the pajama material to distributors in other nations where there were no legal restrictions against its use.

Question: Although the foreign sales were legal, were they ethical? Is dumping unsafe products ethical if it is not forbidden by the receiving nation?

When Honda began building automobile plants in Ohio, it located them in two mostly white rural areas and then favored job applicants who lived within a 30-mile radius of the plant. This policy excluded African-Americans who lived in Columbus, the nearest big city. Earlier, Honda also had agreed to pay nearly half a million dollars to settle an age-discrimination suit brought by older job applicants who had been refused work there.

Question: Were Honda's job-hiring policies, which would have caused few problems in Japan, unethical in Ohio?

These episodes raise the issue of ethical relativism, which was defined earlier in this chapter. Should ethical principles—the ones that help chart right and wrong conduct—take their meaning strictly from the way each society defines ethics? Are Japanese attitudes toward job opportunities for minorities, older workers, and women as ethically valid as U.S. attitudes? Were the children's pajama makers on solid or shaky ethical ground

---

[21]Matthew L. Ward, "Regulator Says Connecticut's Largest Power Company Harassed Worker," *The New York Times*, May 5, 1993, p. B6; and Amal Kumar Naj, "Whistle-Blower at GE to Get $11.5 Million," *The Wall Street Journal*, April 26, 1993, p. A3, A4.

Post–Lawrence–Weber:
Business and Society,
Ninth Edition

Ethical Dilemmas in
Business

© The McGraw–Hill
Companies, 1999

when they sold the cancer-risky pajama cloth in countries where government officials did not warn parents about this possible health risk? Who should assume the ethical responsibility? What or whose ethical standards should be the guide?

As business becomes increasingly global, with more and more corporations penetrating overseas markets where cultures and ethical traditions vary, these questions will occur more frequently. Employees and managers need ethical guidance from clearly stated company policy if they are to avoid the psychological stresses mentioned earlier. One U.S. corporate executive emphasized this point by saying that he and his company recognize that the world consists of a wide array of races, religions, languages, cultures, political systems, and economic resources: "We accept these differences as legitimate and desirable; we recognize that each country must determine its own way. . . . However, we must not use local custom as an excuse for violating applicable laws or corporate policies. We regard observing local law to be the minimum acceptable level of conduct; PPG's own standards frequently oblige us to go beyond that legal minimum and to conduct our affairs according to a higher standard."[22]

Ethics in a Global Economy

Examples of unethical conduct by business employees are reported from nearly every country. One example of unethical activity is **bribery,** a questionable or unjust payment to ensure or facilitate a business transaction. It is found in nearly every sector of the global marketplace.

A Berlin-based watchdog agency, Transparency International, published a survey that ranked corruption by country according to perceptions of executives and the public. Countries where having to pay a bribe is least likely included New Zealand, Denmark, Sweden, Finland, and Canada. At the other end of the index—countries most likely to demand or accept bribes—were Nigeria, Pakistan, Kenya, Bangladesh, and China. The United States ranked as the 15th least corrupt nation out of 54 countries. Other rankings included: Germany, 13; Japan, 17; and Russia, 47.

Examples of bribery and corruption in business have been frequently reported. Payoff scandals plagued Japan throughout the 1990s, involving some of the nation's largest firms: Ito-Yokado, Kirin Brewery, Fuji Photo Film, Takashimaya, Nomura Securities, Ajinomoto, and Dai-Ichi Kangyo Bank. Companies operating in South Korea considered bribery to be a part of business. Executives seeking to conduct business in South Korea believed they were obligated to pay each cabinet minister *ttuk kab,* or "rice-cake expenses," ranging from $6,500 to $19,500 to honor the major holidays of the year. Two IBM executives were indicted in 1997 on bribery charges in connection with a $249 million contract to modernize an information technology system at a state-owned Argentine bank.[23]

Executives representing U.S.-based companies are prohibited by the U.S. Foreign Corrupt Practices Act from paying bribes. According to a U.S. Department of Commerce study, United States competitors lose out on $36 billion of international business deals since they are banned from paying bribes. Some American firms try unusual approaches to comply with the law while conducting business in countries that expect special payments.

[22] Vincent A. Sarni, chairman, PPG Industries, Inc., Worldwide Code of Ethics, Pittsburgh, PA, n.d.
[23] For a comprehensive look at the state of ethics around the globe, see "Special Issue: Region- and Country-Related Reports on Business Ethics," *Journal of Business Ethics,* October 1997.

Post–Lawrence–Weber:
Business and Society,
Ninth Edition

Ethical Dilemmas in
Business

© The McGraw–Hill
Companies, 1999

Chubb Corporation, a New Jersey–based insurance company, wanted to tap the vast Chinese insurance market. Rather than illegally paying a bribe to Chinese officials, the company set up a $1 million program to teach insurance at a Shanghai university. Through this philanthropic gift, the Chubb Company attempted to circumvent the typical approach of bribing officials to gain entrance into a new market in this country. According to a Chubb spokesperson, the company spent millions of dollars on similar projects to improve its prospects overseas.[24]

Efforts to Curtail Unethical Practices

Numerous efforts are underway to curb unethical business practices throughout the world. The most common control is through government intervention and regulation. Efforts to address unethical business behavior often begin with national governments, which can enact stiff legislative controls or empower government agencies with more authority. Many governments are attempting to establish a moral minimum as a guide for proper behavior or to draw the line to control unethical action.

Various international organizations, such as the International Labor Organization or the United Nations, have attempted to develop an international code of conduct for multinational corporations. These efforts have emphasized the need for companies to adhere to universal ethical guidelines when conducting business throughout the world. These codes and the ethical issues they address are shown in Figure 4.

In addition, a transnational effort toward minimizing corruption in the global marketplace was launched in 1996. This anticorruption campaign was evident

Figure 4

International ethics codes and ethics issues addressed in these codes.

Source: This chart is adapted from William C. Frederick, "The Moral Authority of Transnational Corporate Codes," *Journal of Business Ethics* 10 (1991), pp. 165–77, particularly table 1, p. 168; and Kathleen A. Getz, "International Codes of Conduct: An Analysis of Ethical Reasoning," *Journal of Business Ethics* 9 (1990), pp. 567–77.

Ethics Issues Addressed	International Ethics Codes*			
	ICC	OECD	ILO	UN/CTC
Economic Development	X	X	X	X
Technology Transfer	X	X	X	X
Regulatory Action	X	X		X
Employment	X	X	X	
Human Rights			X	X
Environmental Protection	X	X		X
Consumer Protection		X		X
Political Action		X		X

*Key for the international codes of conduct:

ICC = International Chamber of Commerce code (1972)
OECD = Organization for Economic Cooperation and Development code (1976)
ILO = International Labor Organization code (1977)
UN/CTC = United Nations Commision on Transnational Corporations code (1984)

[24]"How U.S. Concerns Compete in Countries Where Bribes Flourish," *The Wall Street Journal,* September 29, 1995, pp. A1, A14.

Post–Lawrence–Weber:
Business and Society,
Ninth Edition

Ethical Dilemmas in
Business

© The McGraw–Hill
Companies, 1999

*from many fronts, and organizations appeared to draw energy from each other.
In November 1997, members of the Organization for Economic Cooperation
and Development agreed to an accord that banned international bribery by
criminalizing overseas bribes and eliminating the tax deductibility of these
payoffs. The Organization of American States approached its members to approve similar rules. For the first time in its history, the World Bank vowed to
revoke loans to governments that let bribes influence business transactions.
"The trend line is very positive," said Tony Imler, policy director at Merck &
Company, a multinational pharmaceutical company. "This is the issue for the
next 10 years [in world trade]."*[25]

Some businesses have joined their governments in efforts to control unethical employee behavior. As discussed in the next chapter, corporate codes of ethics have been
drafted or recently revised to cover instances of undesired practices in the global marketplace. An example of corporate policy addressing global ethical challenges is shown in
Exhibit C. In addition, a consortium of European, Asian, and North American business
leaders formed the Caux Roundtable. This group drafted the Caux Principles, an international standard for ethical conduct emphasizing *kyosei* (that is, working for the common
good) and a respect for human rights.

Some people question the effectiveness of governmental legislation or corporate
policies. Rather than establishing rules, some businesses are trying to educate and motivate their employees worldwide to both respect the customs of other nations and adhere
to basic ethical principles of fairness, honesty, and respect for human rights. Some who
study international business ethics say that such higher standards of ethics already exist.
Thomas Donaldson, a leading ethics scholar, has outlined a set of fundamental human
rights—including the right to security, to freedom of movement, to subsistence income,
and other rights—that should be respected by all multinational corporations. These standards and other ethical values are at the core of the development of transnational codes
of conduct promoted by the United Nations and other international organizations.[26]

Ethics, Law, and Illegal Corporate Behavior

Before discussing specific ways to improve business's ethical performance
(in the next chapter), we want to consider the relationship of law and ethics. Some people have argued that the best way to assure ethical business conduct is to insist that business firms obey society's laws. However, this approach is not as simple as it seems.

Law and ethics are not quite the same. Laws are similar to ethics because both define proper and improper behavior. In general, laws are a society's attempt to formalize—
that is, to reduce to written rules—the general public's ideas about what constitutes right
and wrong conduct in various spheres of life. However, it is rarely possible for written
laws to capture all of the subtle shadings that people give to ethics. Ethical concepts—
like the people who believe in them—are more complex than written rules of law. Ethics

---

[25] "Anticorruption Drive Starts to Show Results," *The Wall Street Journal,* January 27, 1997, p.
A1; and "Bribery Ban Is Approved by OECD," *The Wall Street Journal,* November 24, 1997,
p. A14.
[26] For a complete list of fundamental human rights, see Thomas Donaldson, *The Ethics of International Business* (New York: Oxford University Press, 1989).

EXHIBIT C   Levi Strauss & Co. Global Sourcing & Operating Guidelines

Introduction
Levi Strauss & Company developed the following policy to guide the firm through the maze of international business and maintain its high standard of ethical integrity. Levi Strauss & Co. has a heritage of conducting business in a manner that reflects its values. Because we source in many countries with diverse cultures, we must take special care in selecting business partners and countries whose practices are not incompatible with our values. Otherwise, our sourcing decisions have the potential of undermining this heritage, damaging the image of our brands and threatening our commercial success.

Business Partner Terms of Engagement
Terms of Engagement address issues that are substantially controllable by our individual business partners.

We have defined business partners as contractors and subcontractors who manufacture or finish our products and suppliers who provide material (including fabric, sundries, chemicals and/or stones) utilized in the manufacturing and finishing of our products.

1. **Environmental Requirements** We will only do business with partners who share our commitment to the environment and who conduct their business in a way that is consistent with Levi Strauss & Co.'s Environmental Philosophy and Guiding Principles.

2. **Ethical Standards** We will seek to identify and utilize business partners who aspire as individuals and in the conduct of all their businesses to a set of ethical standards not incompatible with our own.

3. **Legal Requirements** We expect our business partners to be law abiding as individuals and to comply with legal requirements relevant to the conduct of all their businesses.

4. **Employment Practices** We will only do business with partners whose workers are in all cases present voluntarily, not put at risk of physical harm, fairly compensated, allowed the right of free association and not exploited in any way. In addition, . . . specific guidelines [are provided in the areas of]: wages and benefits, . . . working hours, . . . child labor, . . . prison labor/forced labor, . . . health and safety, . . . discrimination, [and] . . . disciplinary practices.

5. **Community Involvement** We will favor business partners who share our commitment to contribute to the betterment of community conditions.

Source: Levi Strauss & Co.

Post–Lawrence–Weber:
Business and Society,
Ninth Edition

Ethical Dilemmas in
Business

© The McGraw–Hill
Companies, 1999

deals with human dilemmas that frequently go beyond the formal language of law and the meanings given to legal rules. The following situation demonstrates that there is not always a perfect match between the law and important ethical principles.

> *In 1994, educators and parents voiced their concern over the significant increase in sexually explicit language and violence depicted in video games and computer software. Congress joined in the criticism and called for a system of warnings for consumers. The Interactive Digital Software Association, which represents video game makers, established a five-category system that was voluntarily adopted by the industry. The labeling system informed consumers of the intended target audience: early childhood (3 years old and up), children to adults (ages 6 and up), teenagers (13 and over), mature audience (17 and up), and adults only. The video game industry also agreed to provide content warnings, such as "mild profanity," and to use warning symbols: a hand grenade means violence, a hand partly covering an eye indicates sexual scenes, and an exclamation point warns of foul language.*[27]

This example suggests that legality cannot always define when something is believed to be ethical or unethical. Although laws attempt to codify a society's notions of right and wrong, they are not always able to do so completely. Obeying the law is usually one way of acting ethically, and the public generally expects business to be law-abiding. But at times, the public expects business to recognize that ethical principles are broader than the law. Because of the imperfect match between law and ethics, business managers who try to improve their company's ethical performance need to do more than comply with the law. Society will generally insist that they heed ethical principles and the law.

Corporate Lawbreaking and Its Costs

Although estimates vary, lawbreaking in business may cause serious financial losses. A Department of Justice estimate puts the total annual loss from reported and unreported violations of federal regulations by corporations at $10 to $20 billion. The Chamber of Commerce of the United States, a conservative probusiness organization, has estimated that various white-collar crimes cost the public some $41 billion a year. Ten percent of the $1 trillion spent on U.S. health care is believed lost due to fraud every year. One of the most thorough attempts to calculate the financial loss to the country from corporate crimes was that of a U.S. Senate subcommittee, which put the cost of corporate crime at between $174 and $231 billion a year. Compared with even the lesser of these estimates, the $3 to $4 billion annual loss to street crime—robbery, burglary, assault, and so forth—represents only a small proportion of the economic cost of crime. The United States is not the only nation suffering losses from illegal acts. German officials believed that over 50 billion marks ($29.07 billion) a year was lost from the German economy as a result of inflated accounting, tax evasion, and illegal kickbacks.[28]

[27]"Games Industries Introduce Voluntary Ratings System," *The Wall Street Journal*, July, 29, 1994, p. B3.

[28]See Jeffrey S. Hornsby, Donald F. Kuratko, and William Honey, "Emerging Growth Companies and the At-Risk Employee: The Viability of Pre-Employment Honesty Testing," *SAM Advanced Management Journal* 54, no. 4 (1992), pp. 24–29; and Brandon Mitchener, "Germany Says Business Bribes on the Rise," *The Wall Street Journal*, April 14, 1997, p. A12.

Post–Lawrence–Weber:
Business and Society,
Ninth Edition

Ethical Dilemmas in
Business

© The McGraw–Hill
Companies, 1999

Beyond these dollar costs of illegal behavior are the physical and social costs. Over 100,000 deaths each year are attributed to occupational diseases, and many of these result from violations of health and safety laws. Annually over 6,000 workers die from on-the-job injuries. This amounts to an average of nearly 17 workplace deaths each day. Tragically, many of these deaths might have been avoided if employers and workers were informed about the risks and complied with established safety and health regulations.[29]

Summary Points

- Ethics is a conception of right and wrong behavior, defining for us when our actions are moral and when they are immoral. Business ethics is the application of general ethical ideas to business behavior.

- Ethical business behavior is expected by the public, prevents harm to society, fosters business relations and employee productivity, reduces criminal penalties, protects business against unscrupulous employees and competitors, protects business employees from harmful actions by their employer, and allows people in business to act consistently with their personal ethical beliefs.

- Ethics problems occur in business for many reasons, including the selfishness of a few, competitive pressures on profits, the clash of personal values and business goals, and cross-cultural contradictions in global business operations.

- Similar ethical issues, such as bribery, are evident throughout the world, and many international agencies and national governments are actively attempting to minimize such actions through economic sanctions and international codes.

- Although law and ethics are closely related, they are not the same; ethical principles tend to be broader than legal principles. Illegal behavior by business and its employees imposes great costs on business and the general public.

Key Terms and Concepts

- Ethics
- Ethical principles
- Ethical relativism
- Business ethics
- U.S. Corporate Sentencing Guidelines
- Functional-area ethics

- U.S./Foreign Corrupt Practices Act
- Ethical egoist
- Altruism
- Bribery
- Law

Internet Resources

- http://www.dii.org   Defense Industry Initiative on Business
                         Ethics and Conduct

[29] An extensive analysis of the U.S. census data on workplace fatalities is in Guy Toscano and Janice Windau, "Fatal Work Injuries: Results from the 1992 National Census," *Monthly Labor Review*, October 1993, pp. 39–48.

Post–Lawrence–Weber:
Business and Society,
Ninth Edition

Ethical Dilemmas in
Business

© The McGraw–Hill
Companies, 1999

- http://www.per2per.com   Gaia Friends: Ethics Information Center
- http://www.depaul.edu/ethics/ethg1.html   The On-Line Journal of Ethics
- http://www.us.kpmg.com/ethics   KPMG Business Ethics Practice

Discussion Case   **Unethical Practices at Daiwa Bank**

In November 1995, Daiwa Bank, Japan's 10th-largest financial institution, was rocked
by allegations of questionable bank practices and criminal actions by bank employees at
their New York–based U.S. operations. As the situation unfolded in the international
press, the bank was accused by U.S. banking regulators of

- Not recording more than $1 billion of trading loss between 1983 and 1995 and falsi-
  fying records to conceal these losses.

- Concealing this information from U.S. regulators for almost two months under direct
  orders by Daiwa's senior management.

- Deceiving U.S. federal bank regulators in 1992 and 1993 when Daiwa told the government in writing that custody and trading operations were separated when they had
  not been.

- Knowingly concealing another $97 million in losses between 1984 and 1987.

In addition, Toshihide Iguchi, a New York–based bond trader for Daiwa Bank,
pleaded guilty in a U.S. federal court to six counts of fraud, including money laundering, falsifying bank documents, embezzling $500,000 for personal use, and misappro-
priating $1.1 billion in Daiwa funds. In defense of his actions, Iguchi filed a letter with
the U.S. court claiming that "he suffered years of anguish as he wrestled with whether
to confess about the losses." He claimed that "he would have divulged the losses seven
years earlier, when they were only $200 million, but the Daiwa executive he intended to
tell died unexpectedly." A federal judge sentenced Iguchi to four years in prison and ordered him to pay nearly $2.6 million in fines and restitution for concealing trading
losses at Daiwa Bank.

Daiwa Bank was one of Japan's most profitable and fastest-growing financial institutions at the time of the incident. The bank employed over 9,000 people, with 200
Japanese branches and an expanding international network overseas. As of September
1996, Daiwa's assets were more than 18 trillion yen ($162 billion in U.S. currency).
The bank reported a quarterly income in September 1996 of nearly 12 billion yen ($108
million).

The U.S. position was one of outrage. On November 3, 1995, the Federal Reserve
gave Daiwa Bank 90 days to get out of the country. "It's unprecedented," said Peter
Wallison, an international banking expert and former Treasury general counsel. U.S.
Senator Alfonse D'Amato, head of the Senate Banking Committee, said that this action
sent an important message to the Japanese government that the United States would not
tolerate this type of action, since it was evident that the Japanese government knew of
the illegality but kept it quiet.

The severity of the punishment to this financial institution that had previously
held the respect of the international banking community sent shock waves around the
world. Since Daiwa's U.S. operations accounted for 15 percent of its global profits, it

Post–Lawrence–Weber:
Business and Society,
Ninth Edition

Ethical Dilemmas in
Business

© The McGraw-Hill
Companies, 1999

was predicted that the impact of the U.S. directive would be a takeover of Daiwa's U.S. operations by another Japanese bank. Threats of a merger circulated for months after the incident, but a year later, Daiwa appeared to have avoided this outcome. Other experts predicted that the bank's unethical behavior might have a profound impact on U.S.–Japan trade relations. Representative Jim Leach, head of the House Banking Committee, felt that the Daiwa incident highlighted the growing lack of international cooperation on bank regulation and the increasing risk of inadequate oversight of financial institutions.

In the aftermath of this ethics scandal, Daiwa attempted to right itself. Takashi Kaiho, the new president of Daiwa, announced a new medium-term management plan aimed at renewing growth in the bank's operations and restoring confidence in the bank's practices. Kaiho stated, "We apologize sincerely for any inconvenience that might have arisen in the wake of this [the November 1995] incident and express our warmest gratitude to a number of people who stood by and supported us during [this] trying period." He continued to say that the bank would treat the incident as a learning experience and outlined a three-step program that emphasized increasing bank controls of overseas management, inspection of overseas offices, and a reorganization of oversight duties to strengthen overseas compliance with regulations. He concluded by saying, "we aim to build a solid internal control system so that customers can deal with the Bank in full confidence."

Yet, some pointed to other actions taken by Daiwa Bank after the guilty plea as less than adequate. For example, former Daiwa president Tetsuya Horie resigned on October 9, 1995, in the midst of the scandal. Yet a month later, Horie was given the title of bank adviser at Daiwa Bank and received a salary, office, and chauffeured limousine. The bank defended these actions by saying that Horie's resignation was intended to defend the honor of the bank and that no one ever suggested that he had any culpability in the incident.

Sources: Information and quotations for this discussion case were taken from Norihiko Shirouzu, "Daiwa Confirms It Told Trader to Hide Losses," *The Wall Street Journal,* October 23, 1995, p. A16; "In a Signal to Japan, U.S. Bars Daiwa Bank and Indicts Institution," *The Wall Street Journal,* November 3, 1995, pp. A1, A5; Frances A. McMorris and Michael Rapoport, "Former Daiwa Bank Trader Gets Four Years in Jail, Fines for Losses," *The Wall Street Journal,* December 17, 1995, p. B10; and Daiwa Bank, http://www.infoweb.or.jp/daiwabank (November 6, 1997).

Discussion Questions

1. Why did these ethical problems occur at Daiwa Bank? Use Figure 3 to help you in your analysis.
2. Assess the position and actions taken by Daiwa Bank and the U.S. Federal Reserve. Were these positions and actions unethical or ethically necessary given the competitive world of international finance?
3. Was the punishment by the U.S. federal court just?
4. Was Daiwa Bank's new medium-term management plan a sufficient response to the firm's unethical practices?

Post–Lawrence–Weber:
Business and Society,
Ninth Edition

Ethical Dilemmas in
Business

© The McGraw–Hill
Companies, 1999

Bibliography

Cavanaugh, Gerald F. *American Business Values: With International Perspective,* 4th ed. Englewood Cliffs, NJ: Prentice-Hall, 1998.

Colby, Anne, and William Damon. *Some Do Care: Contemporary Lives of Moral Commitment.* New York: The Free Press, 1992.

Colby, Anne, and Lawrence Kohlberg. *The Measurement of Moral Judgment: Volume 1, Theoretical Foundations and Research Validation.* Cambridge, MA: Harvard University Press, 1987.

Dobson, John. *Finance Ethics: The Rationality of Virtue.* Lanham, MD: Rowman and Littlefield, 1997.

Dunfee, Thomas W., and Yukimasa Nagayasu. *Business Ethics: Japan and the Global Economy.* Dordrecht, Netherlands: Kluwer Academic, 1993.

Estes, Ralph. *Tyranny of the Bottom Line: Why Corporations Make Good People Do Bad Things.* San Francisco, CA: Berrett Kochler, 1996.

Etzioni, Amitai. *The Moral Dimension: Toward a New Economics.* New York: Free Press, 1988.

Freeman, R. Edward, and Daniel R. Gilbert, Jr. *Corporate Strategy and the Search for Ethics.* Englewood Cliffs, NJ: Prentice-Hall, 1988.

Fukuyama, Francis. *Trust: The Social Virtues and the Creation of Prosperity.* New York: The Free Press, 1995.

Harding, Harry. *China's Second Revolution: Reform after Mao.* Washington: Brookings, 1987.

Jackall, Robert. *Moral Mazes: The World of Corporate Managers.* New York: Oxford University Press, 1988.

Kennedy, Paul. *The Rise and Fall of the Great Powers.* New York: Random House, 1987.

Kidder, Rushworth M. *How Good People Make Tough Choices.* New York: William Morrow & Co., 1995.

Korten, David. *When Corporations Ruled the World.* San Francisco, CA: Berrett-Kochler, 1996.

Levine, Marvin J. *Worker Rights and Labor Standards in Asia's Four New Tigers: A Comparative Perspective.* New York: Plenum Press, 1997.

Messick, David M., and Ann E. Tenbrunsel, eds. *Codes of Conduct: Behavioral Research into Business Ethics.* New York: Russell Sage Foundation, 1996.

Nash, Laura L. *Good Intentions Aside: A Manager's Guide to Resolving Ethical Problems.* Boston: Harvard Business School Press, 1990.

_____. *Believers in Business,* Nashville, TN: Thomas Nelson Publishers, 1994.

Neilsen, Richard P. *The Politics of Ethics.* New York: Oxford University Press, 1996.

Rawls, John. *A Theory of Justice.* Cambridge, MA: Harvard University Press, 1971.

Rest, James L., and Darcia Navarez, eds. *Moral Development in the Professions.* Hillsdale, NJ: Lawrence Erlbaum Associates, 1994.

Stone, Christopher D. *Where the Law Ends: The Social Control of Corporate Behavior.* Prospect Heights, IL: Waveland Press, 1975.

Tavis, Lee A. *Power and Responsibility: Multinational Managers and Developing Country Concerns.* South Bend, IN: University of Notre Dame Press, 1997.

Velasquez, Manuel G. *Business Ethics: Concepts and Cases,* 4th ed. Upper Saddle River, NJ: Prentice Hall, 1998.

Post–Lawrence–Weber:
Business and Society,
Ninth Edition

Global Challenges to
Corporate Responsibility

© The McGraw–Hill
Companies, 1999

Global Challenges to Corporate Responsibility

The globalization of business poses new social, ethical, and political challenges for managers and corporations. Diverse cultural values and the differing ways in which political systems treat economic activity challenge managers to develop a sophisticated and global concept of corporate responsibility. Today's managers regularly interact with people from other cultures and socioeconomic systems. The global business environment of the twenty-first century will reflect more change and present more complex problems for corporations and their managers.

This topic focuses on these key questions and objectives:

- What are the leading factors encouraging the globalization of business?

- What are the critical differences among systems of free enterprise, central state control, and mixed state and private enterprise?

- Why does global economic activity conflict with national sovereignty?

- What do host countries do to encourage or discourage multinational companies from doing business?

- What political and social pressures do companies and their managers face as they engage in international business transactions?

Post–Lawrence–Weber:
Business and Society,
Ninth Edition

Global Challenges to
Corporate Responsibility

© The McGraw–Hill
Companies, 1999

The twenty-first century, according to some experts, is likely to be China's century.[1] For much of the twentieth century, China has been a nation facing war, internal strife, political revolution, and an ancient system of social and economic relationships that reminded many of feudalism. But in the 1990s, China's fortune improved as powerful economic and political changes occurred. The country's size and promise have led some to believe that the twenty-first century will be a time for China to become a dominant power.

The drive to improve life for China's two billion people has produced many political conflicts. Chinese leaders have sometimes desired that the country remain closed to foreign influence and foreign trade. More recently, they have sought foreign trade to help unlock China's vast economic potential. China's role in the global economy is clearly linked to trade and to its political relations with the rest of the world. Normal political relations rest, in turn, on the belief that China's political repression has ended. To many who remember events of a decade ago, that will take some further convincing.

In June 1989, tens of thousands of students demonstrated in Beijing's Tiananmen Square and generated worldwide media coverage of China's democracy movement. When the Chinese military intervened after weeks of protests, television showed the world the raw power of soldiers, tanks, and armored personnel vehicles killing and arresting hundreds of student protesters. People in democratic nations were outraged at the brutality of the Chinese government's response and pressured their governments to condemn China's actions and force release of protestors. Chinese leaders refused to buckle to the pressure and a war of political wills began. A number of countries retaliated by imposing trade sanctions that banned companies from doing business with China. The U.S. government condemned the massacre but refused to impose trade sanctions.

When Bill Clinton won the 1992 presidential election, he promised that human rights would guide U.S. policy toward China and that trade restrictions would follow unless China improved its human rights record. The point of leverage would be the renewal of China's most favored nation (MFN) trading status in 1994. The congressional debate would coincide with the fifth anniversary of events in Tiananmen Square.

Under international law, designation as a most favored nation, would give China special rights to import technology from and export finished products to the United States without any tariffs, duties, and other trade restrictions. President Clinton's willingness to consider China's human rights record during the MFN debate was applauded by human rights groups but criticized by business groups that believed it was a diplomatic mistake to connect commerce and human rights.

Direct and indirect pressures grew as the decision neared. China refused to make concessions; human rights groups lobbied Congress, the White House, and businesses with commercial investments in China. One full-page advertisement in national newspapers named individual business leaders and called on them to ask the president to support human rights in China. Pressures mounted on all sides until Clinton finally announced that MFN status would be renewed despite China's disappointing record on human rights. The president said:

> *Our relationship with China is important to all Americans. We have significant interests in what happens there and what happens between us. China has an*

---

[1] "Can China Reform Its Economy?" *Business Week,* September 29, 1997, pp. 116–24.

Post–Lawrence–Weber:
Business and Society,
Ninth Edition

Global Challenges to
Corporate Responsibility

© The McGraw–Hill
Companies, 1999

atomic arsenal and a vote and veto in the U.N. Security Council. . . . We share important interests, such as in a nuclear-free Korean peninsula and in sustaining the global environment. China is also the world's fastest growing economy. Over $8 billion of United States exports to China last year supported over 150,000 American jobs. . . . Extending M.F.N. will avoid isolating China and instead will permit us to engage the Chinese with not only economic contacts but with cultural, educational and other contacts, and, with a continuing aggressive effort in human rights—an approach that I believe will make it more likely that China will play a responsible role, both at home and abroad.[2]

Many political and business leaders praised the decision as the best possible under difficult circumstances. But some newspapers ran headlines that implied the United States was backing away from democratic principles (e.g., "Profit Motive Gets the Nod," "Back to Business on China Trade," and "Clinton Eats Some Crow over China"). Foreign policy experts pointed to the U.S. need for China's assistance in dealing with the threat of North Korea's nuclear arms as a factor that ultimately influenced the decision. Others argued the view that trade with China is a form of constructive engagement that supports and encourages political and economic freedom.

The decision regarding China's MFN status demonstrates how entwined economic, political, and social interests are in the modern global economy. Commercial and political interdependencies are intricate, and governments and businesses both need to manage this complicated web of relations with great skill. This can only be done when the people involved understand the workings of different socioeconomic systems. As the twenty-first century unfolds, we are certain to encounter difficult situations involving human rights, turbulence in national economies, and social policy problems. Sound business and governmental decisions will depend on managers who understand the dynamics of a global economy and the ethical challenges inherent in such a business environment.

Globalization of Business

Nearly all businesses, large and small, are drawn to doing business across national borders today. This may involve purchasing raw materials from foreign suppliers, assembling products from components made in several nations, or selling finished goods or services to customers in other countries. One of most important trends in the late twentieth century has been the lowering of barriers to such international trade. The list of firms affected by international competitive forces grows longer each day, and even small retailers—such as those that surround college campuses—are affected by the global production and the sales practices of companies that manufacture, import, and sell clothing, CDs, snack foods, books, and computers. Many U.S. companies have subsidiaries, affiliates, and joint venture partners in other countries. In some instances, the number of foreign employees exceeds those from the company's home nation.

Drivers of Globalization

Only a few decades ago, the opportunities for global business were limited. Communication was much slower, travel and shipping took longer, and international commerce was

---

[2] The decision was announced on May 26, 1994, at a White House press conference. This excerpt is from President Clinton's statement. See "Clinton's Call: Avoid Isolating China," *New York Times*, May 27, 1994, pp. A1, A8.

Post–Lawrence–Weber:
Business and Society,
Ninth Edition

Global Challenges to
Corporate Responsibility

© The McGraw–Hill
Companies, 1999

expensive. Today, people can get to virtually any place on the globe in one day and international communication is instantaneous.[3] Federal Express, the international package-shipping company, claims to provide one-day delivery service to destinations representing 96 percent of the world's gross domestic product. Business operations can be managed effectively and profitably in many countries simultaneously. Resources are sometimes more plentiful and less costly in other countries; labor may be cheaper; taxes may be lower. In some cases, it may even be beneficial if the weather is better. Leading factors encouraging the globalization of business include the following:

- *Trade barriers are falling.* Western Europe's democratic nations have agreed to move toward integration of their economies. Liberalization of trade through the North American Free Trade Agreement and expansion of the General Agreement on Tariffs and Trade are also producing new opportunities for doing business with more of the world's populations.

- *Social and political reforms have opened nations once closed to international business.* The former Communist nations of Eastern Europe are now open to doing business around the world. Millions of people in these countries are now able to take advantage of goods and services that global commerce provides in an open and free marketplace. The reunification of East and West Germany and integration of their economies is also creating a powerful global competitor.

- *New regions of the world are becoming dynamic competitors in global markets.* A great wave of change has occurred in the Pacific region. Japan became a leading global economic power in the 1970s and 1980s, producing competitive, high-quality products. During the 1990s, Asian nations such as Taiwan, South Korea, Malaysia, Thailand, and Indonesia grew rapidly and China blossomed as the world's fastest-growing economy. China, India, and Brazil are among the emerging nations that are likely to contribute new markets, new products, and new technologies to the global economy of the twenty-first century. These are among the "must" locations for companies seeking to be where the economic action is in the years ahead.

Doing Business in a Diverse World

Doing business in other nations is much more than a step across a geographical boundary; it is a step into different social, political, cultural, and economic realities. Even businesses operating in one community or one nation cannot function successfully without taking into account a wide variety of stakeholder needs and interests. When companies do business in several countries, the number of stakeholders to be considered in decision making increases dramatically. And companies such as Coca Cola, McDonald's, and Microsoft, which operate in most of the 200 sovereign nations that exist today, have had no choice but to address this great diversity in building their organizations.

Historically, companies that operated internationally often had an **ethnocentric perspective**. This perspective views the home nation as the major source of the company's capital, revenues, and human resource talent. The home country's laws are viewed as dominant, and the company flies the flag of its home nation. Today's businesses have discov-

---

[3] Comments of Allen Grau, chief financial officer of Federal Express, in an interview on CNBC, September 16, 1997.

Post–Lawrence–Weber:
Business and Society,
Ninth Edition

Global Challenges to
Corporate Responsibility

© The McGraw–Hill
Companies, 1999

ered that they must consider the world, not just one nation, as their home. Companies that have such a **geocentric perspective** adapt their practices to different cultures and environments while maintaining their worldwide identity and policies. They develop managers at all levels from a worldwide pool of talent and seek to use the best people for all jobs regardless of their country of origin.

> *Companies such as IBM, General Electric, and Exxon have long histories of bringing their managers from around the world to meetings and workshops for the purpose of broadening everyone's understanding of the world in which their company operates. At Dow Chemical, technical specialists from plants around the world are connected by information technology and physically meet several times each year to discuss advances in science and technology. European firms, such as Nestlé (Switzerland), ABB (Asea, Brown, Boveri, a Swedish-Swiss company), and Unilever (Great Britain–Netherlands) have led the way toward internationally diverse corporate board membership.*

Small companies also develop a geocentric perspective when they do business across borders and among different cultures. Managers throughout the southwestern United States, for example, speak Spanish, understand Mexican culture, and engage in cross-border commerce. Citizens of Maine, New York, Michigan, and Washington State know the importance of business with Canadians and are likely to understand such issues as Quebec's movement for independence from Canada. It is not the size of the business that accounts for a geocentric outlook. Geographic location and awareness of the social and cultural features of the firm's stakeholders reinforce the importance of an open approach to cultural differences. To be a global company in the modern economy is to build a geocentric perspective into the very fiber of the business organization.

A World of Diversity

Business opportunities depend greatly on the size and wealth of a population. The population is growing around the world but at quite different rates. Birthrates in Africa, Latin America, and South Asia, for example, are two or three times greater than those in Europe and North America. Companies that sell consumer products such as packaged food, clothing, and even automobiles need to go where the people are. Eventually, fast-food restaurants, entertainment, telecommunications, and other consumer products will find their way to all of the world. To do business in world markets, a company must design a business plan that fits with the cultural, competitive, and political realities of diverse societies defined by features such as language, customs, religion, and traditions.[4]

Basic Types of Socioeconomic Systems

Ideas about the way political power should be held and exercised in society ultimately affect the way economic activity is conducted. Societies differ greatly in their preferences for cooperation versus competition. They also differ in their views about who owns property,

[4]Lee A. Tavis, *Power and Responsibility: Multinational Managers and Developing Country Concerns* (South Bend, IN: University of Notre Dame Press, 1997).

Post–Lawrence–Weber:
Business and Society,
Ninth Edition

Global Challenges to
Corporate Responsibility

© The McGraw–Hill
Companies, 1999

who sets the rules for using common resources (e.g., water), and who must approve social investments in technology, public works projects, and care for people. Because these societal arrangements involve decisions about social, political, and economic matters, they are called **socioeconomic systems.**

Four types of socioeconomic systems dominate the modern world. Each system entails some combination of private efforts and government controls, although the balance differs quite greatly. As shown in Figure 1, varying amounts of freedom and coercion are present in each system. Some systems are democratic and open; others are dominated by one political party that controls the government and centralizes economic and social decisions.

The socioeconomic system of any nation depends on that nation's history and culture. But history and culture are not the whole story. Socioeconomic systems can and do change. This may occur with dramatic speed, as in the collapse of the Soviet Union and demise of Communist regimes in Eastern Europe in the late 1980s or the rapid change in South Africa, where, following decades of conflict, the system of racial separatism called *apartheid* gave way in the 1990s to a more integrated and democratic way of life.

Business leaders know that the grounds on which they do business are constantly shifting. As commerce becomes more global, with customers, suppliers, and competitors from other nations and cultures, it is important that managers understand how diverse socioeconomic systems affect the markets and the social-political environment for business. Businesses of all sizes have a stake in understanding these issues.

Figure 1

Basic types of socioeconomic systems.

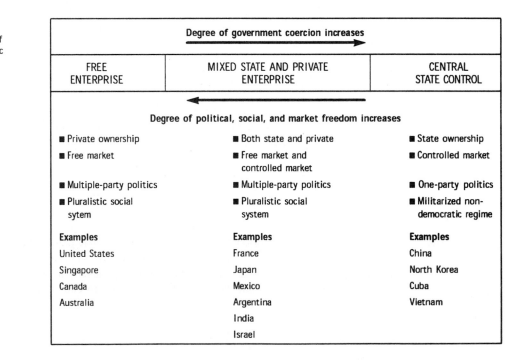

Degree of government coercion increases →		
FREE ENTERPRISE	MIXED STATE AND PRIVATE ENTERPRISE	CENTRAL STATE CONTROL

← Degree of political, social, and market freedom increases

■ Private ownership	■ Both state and private	■ State ownership
■ Free market	■ Free market and controlled market	■ Controlled market
■ Multiple-party politics	■ Multiple-party politics	■ One-party politics
■ Pluralistic social sytem	■ Pluralistic social system	■ Militarized non-democratic regime
Examples	**Examples**	**Examples**
United States	France	China
Singapore	Japan	North Korea
Canada	Mexico	Cuba
Australia	Argentina	Vietnam
	India	
	Israel	

Post–Lawrence–Weber:
Business and Society,
Ninth Edition

Global Challenges to
Corporate Responsibility

© The McGraw–Hill
Companies, 1999

*The small business in Michigan that sells machine parts to customers in
Canada, or the insurance agency in San Antonio, whose customers speak
Spanish and have relatives and relationships in Mexico, are also part of the international business community. Under current trade laws, small businesses
are expected to greatly expand the number and value of international transactions.*

Free Enterprise

A **free enterprise economy** is based on the principle of voluntary association and exchange. People with goods and services to sell take them voluntarily to the marketplace,
seeking to exchange them for money or other goods or services. Other people with wants
to satisfy go to the marketplace voluntarily hoping to find the things they want to buy. No
one forces anybody to buy or to sell. Producers are drawn voluntarily to the market by
their desire to make a profit. Consumers likewise go willingly to the marketplace in order to satisfy their many wants. The producer and the consumer then make an economic
exchange in which normally both of them receive an economic benefit. The producer earns
a profit, and the consumer has a new good or service that satisfies some want or desire.

In this system, members of society satisfy most of their economic wants through
voluntary market transactions. Business firms (like supermarkets) that sell goods and services to consumers for a profit are also fulfilling a social or public need. Usually there is
a very large overlap between society's needs and business's efforts to meet those needs
through profit-making activities.

Very few economic systems conform strictly to the ideal conception of a free enterprise system. The United States comes the closest of any of the major industrial powers, partly because its historical traditions have favored free markets and partly because
the American public has urged leaders to favor less centralized government. All socioeconomic systems have an *ideology*—a guiding philosophy—that explains and justifies
the way economic activities are organized. This philosophy shapes the attitudes of people and influences their thinking about how economic problems should be addressed.

Free enterprise ideology originated over 200 years ago in Great Britain. Adam Smith,
the Scottish philosopher, first outlined the main components of this capitalist philosophy
in 1776 when he wrote *An Inquiry into the Nature and Causes of the Wealth of Nations*.
This book has guided business thinking in free market nations ever since. A resurgence
of interest in Smith's ideas was sparked when Eastern European nations broke away from
the domination of the Soviet Union and struggled to build democratic societies characterized by the core elements of free enterprise ideology (see Exhibit A).

The attraction of a system built on principles of individualism, freedom, private
property, competition, and profit remains very powerful. Free enterprise systems have incorporated other principles into their ideology. Foremost among these is the belief in limited government. Beyond protecting private property, enforcing contracts, and providing
for public security, the government is expected to do little. A hands-off policy toward business, often called *laissez faire*, is a preferred ideal of free enterprise theory, although many
things have changed since that theory was first advanced.

Central State Control

Corporations doing business under a system of **central state control** encounter entirely
different rules. In such a system, economic and political power is concentrated in the hands

---

EXHIBIT A   Free Enterprise Philosophy/Ideology

Advocates of the free enterprise system build their case on several basic ideas. The following ideas are the core of this free enterprise ideology.

- *Individualism.* The individual person is considered to be more important than society or its institutions. Social institutions exist to protect and promote the interests of individuals. The opposite is true in a collectivist state, where individuals are subordinate to the powers of government, the military, or organized religion.

- *Freedom.* All individuals must be free to promote and protect their own personal interests. This means that they must have freedom to own property, to choose a job and career, to move freely within a society and to other societies, and to make all of life's basic decisions — where to live, whom to marry, personal life-style — without being coerced by others. In business affairs, it means that companies should be free to pursue profits, and markets should be free of government intervention.

- *Private property.* The bedrock institution on which free enterprise is founded is private property. Unlike socialist states, where government owns the productive system, private property is held by individuals or companies in a free enterprise system. The ownership and use of property allows one to control one's own destiny, rather than to have important decisions made by others.

- *Competition.* Competition is an indispensable part of free enterprise thinking. It encourages the most skilled, the most ambitious, and the most efficient to succeed. Competition is society's way of encouraging high levels of economic performance from all of its citizens. The behavior of firms and individuals is regulated in a system of competition by what Adam Smith called an "invisible hand," rather than the "visible hand" of government regulation. In this way, competition signals business to do its best, or else a competitor will win customers away with a better product or service.

- *Profit.* Profit is a gain made by owners who use their property for productive purposes. Although profits are sometimes made by using property inappropriately (e.g., illegal drug sales), or by not using property at all (e.g., subsidies for not using farmland), a free enterprise economy tends to draw all property into productive uses because that is the way to make profits. Profits are a reward for making a productive contribution to society. They act as a powerful incentive to produce goods and services that are of value to a society.

---

of government officials and political authorities. The central government owns property used to produce goods and services. Private ownership may be forbidden or greatly restricted, and most private markets are illegal. People need government permission to move from one job to another. Wages and prices are strictly controlled by government planners and bureaucrats. Foreign corporations, if permitted to operate at all, may find it difficult or impossible to take their profits out of the country.

The political system is usually organized around one political party. Not all citizens are permitted to join this one party, so the party's members may form a privileged elite

Post–Lawrence–Weber:
Business and Society,
Ninth Edition

Global Challenges to
Corporate Responsibility

© The McGraw–Hill
Companies, 1999

of powerful people. With no political opposition, elections are a formality used by the nation's leaders to reinforce their control over politics, government, and other spheres of society. These leaders also set the terms and conditions under which any businesses, including foreign corporations, are permitted to operate. This means that the business owners, or the corporation's managers, must be skilled in political negotiations with government officials. Moreover, since the decision-making process in government bureaucracies is often slow, business owners or managers must exercise patience.

In this type of socioeconomic system, government is the central actor, making decisions about meeting social and economic needs. Governments in state-controlled systems typically resort to elaborate five-year plans that spell out what goods are to be produced by state-managed factories, in what volume, and what services (e.g., health care) will be available through what institutions (e.g., hospitals, clinics). Government bureaucrats then allocate budget resources to those factories, hospitals, and other organizations and oversee the way in which they meet their goals. All of the key functions performed by individual companies and managers in a free enterprise system—determining what to produce, allocating resources, setting wages and prices—are performed by government officials in a centrally controlled state system.

Under such circumstances, government planners and party leaders may decide economic production is more important than safe factories, clean air and water, and healthy workers. Central state control, exercised through the party or other means, gives them the power to make such decisions. Coercion is the dominant feature of this type of system. There are fewer such regimes in the late 1990s than in earlier times, but Cuba, North Korea, and Nigeria are among nations that still reflect key features of central state control.

Mixed State and Private Enterprise

Standing between the extremes of free enterprise and central state control is another type of socioeconomic system that combines some elements of both of those systems. In a **mixed state and private enterprise** system, a portion (but not all) of a nation's industrial and financial sectors is owned and operated by the government. This may include the central bank through which the country's overall monetary policies are determined; the railroads, bus lines, and airline companies; public utilities such as telephone, water, electric, and gas companies; and basic industries such as steel, auto manufacturing, coal mining, nuclear power, and health care.

Mixed systems provide opportunities for private sector business activity. Private businesses may compete alongside the state enterprises and transact business according to free market principles; they make profits for owners or stockholders, serve consumers, and face the risk of business failure if the market does not value their products and services. This type of socioeconomic system is popular, and many countries have built economies with a mixture of private and state-owned businesses. These countries often provide more economic and political freedom than the central state control systems but with a significant role for the public sector. Political elections are open and free, and the social system tends to be pluralistic and diverse. The amount of market freedom is considerably less than in purely free enterprise economies.

> *Mexico's government has committed itself to a program of change that will expand private sector activities in an increasingly free enterprise environment. But the government has refused to allow competition to challenge its state-*

Post–Lawrence–Weber:
Business and Society,
Ninth Edition

Global Challenges to
Corporate Responsibility

© The McGraw–Hill
Companies, 1999

owned petroleum industry. The state-owned oil industry is a traditional source of Mexico's wealth and a matter of national pride. Fears that competition would damage this national treasure have led political leaders to insist on maintaining the state enterprise. It is noteworthy that this industry is among Mexico's worst environmental offenders.

Eastern European economies evolved from communism toward a form of mixed state and private enterprise in the 1990s. Poland, Hungary, Czechoslovakia (which became two nations, the Czech Republic and Slovakia), and East Germany (which joined with West Germany to form a single German nation) opened their economies to market competition while trying to protect government-run health plans, retirements, housing, and other social services. Some resisted abandoning price controls and state assistance in the form of subsidies to farmers and other groups. Railroads, airlines, and public utilities continued under state-enterprise management for a time, although many are now privatized.

Militarized Nondemocratic Systems

Militarized nondemocratic systems operate in many countries of the world. Central America, for example, has been the scene of powerful military rulers and attempted takeovers in nations such as Panama, Nicaragua, Guatemala, and El Salvador. A small, wealthy class is sometimes allied with the military government, with its members serving in high-level government posts. Human rights and democratic freedoms may be severely curtailed by the government. The press and media are normally government controlled and used for propaganda purposes. Labor unions, religious organizations, and some professional groups (e.g., artists, teachers, writers) are watched carefully by government authorities to keep them from becoming vocal political opponents.

Outwardly, the socioeconomic system may appear to be a mixed system of private and state enterprise. Private markets may be tolerated and many privately owned businesses may exist. The government may welcome foreign investment and foreign corporations. There may be opposition political parties, although the opposition is unlikely to win in elections, which are usually controlled by the government and military. These regimes have sometimes been pawns of the superpowers as they engaged in skirmishes in different parts of the world. (Iran's military rulers were long supported by the United States and its allies as a way of keeping Iran's oil resources away from the Soviet Union.) Sometimes they have been the result of the ambition of local military officers, impatient with other forms of democratic self-government (e.g., Nigeria, North Korea, and Myanmar—formerly Burma—are among the current restrictive military regimes).

Military-political regimes present serious ethical and strategic problems for business leaders. In an effort to generate economic activity, such regimes may make attractive deals with foreign companies. Low taxes, low wages, freedom from criticism in the press, and weak environmental rules and regulations are among the attractions that a military regime can create through its power. Still, if a company knows that human rights are suppressed, that military leaders are lining their own pockets with money that should go to the country, and that corruption and abuse of power are part of the standard operating procedure, business leaders must pause and think about long-term consequences. The strategic business question *is* an ethical question: Do the benefits of doing business in such a system outweigh the economic, human, and social costs?

Post–Lawrence–Weber:
Business and Society,
Ninth Edition

Global Challenges to
Corporate Responsibility

© The McGraw–Hill
Companies, 1999

The New World Economic Order

Political leaders refer to the *new world order* to describe relations among countries no longer facing threats of the cold war. From the 1940s to the 1990s, the world's nations organized into Communist and non-Communist political blocs. The Warsaw Pact and the North Atlantic Treaty Organization (NATO) were alliances created to deter nations from military actions and geopolitical threats. Today, we are witnessing a world order organized around economic interests more than ideology or politics.

Economic relationships are redrawing world maps. As illustrated in Figure 2, the European Union provides a framework for trade and commerce on the European continent. In North America, the North American Free Trade Agreement is encouraging integration of the economies of Canada, the United States, and Mexico. Steps are underway to link NAFTA with other Latin American countries, including members of Mercosur, the Latin American trade group that includes Argentina, Brazil, and Chile. In the Asia-Pacific region, trade arrangements are creating links between Australia, China, Indonesia, Taiwan, Thailand, Singapore, Malaysia, and South Korea. Figure 3 shows the nations of Southeast Asia that are creating a powerful regional economy. Southeast Asia, in the view of many experts, will remain one of the world's most-promising economic regions despite the serious financial problems facing the region in the late 1990s. The members of the Association of Southeast Asia Nations (ASEAN)—Brunei, Indonesia, Malaysia, Philippines, Singapore, and Thailand—have lowered trade barriers and are creating an integrated market of 330 million people.

The socioeconomic systems of nations in the EU, NAFTA, and ASEAN are quite diverse. These nations do not see the world the same way, and each nation's policies and political systems reflect its unique culture and history. In the end, these features will affect the willingness of people to do business with a foreign company and will shape the way in which that business is done.

The Global Business Enterprise

Much of the world's commerce is done through corporations that operate beyond the borders of any single country. It is estimated that 37,000 multinational corporations do business around the world. United Nations agencies refer to *transnational corporations* (TNCs); other experts prefer the terms *multinational corporation* (MNC), *multinational enterprise* (MNE), or *global corporation* (see Exhibit B). There is no common agreement as to which of these terms is best.

Corporations that do business across national borders are sometimes so large that their annual revenues from worldwide operations exceed the value of goods and services (gross domestic product) of entire nations. For example, General Motors had revenues of $164 billion in 1996, more than the entire GDP of Norway ($114 billion) or Thailand ($130 billion) and nearly equal to the GDP of Indonesia ($167 billion). Other companies of comparable size in 1996 included Toyota, with worldwide revenues of $108 billion, General Electric ($79 billion), IBM ($75 billion), and Exxon ($116 billion).[5]

In this context, the chief executives of General Motors, Toyota, IBM, and Exxon are responsible for economic activities equal to or greater than those managed by the political leaders of some of the world's most significant economies.

---

[5]"The International 500" and "The World Super Fifty," *Forbes,* July 28, 1997, pp. 178–80.

131

Post–Lawrence–Weber:
Business and Society,
Ninth Edition

Global Challenges to
Corporate Responsibility

© The McGraw–Hill
Companies, 1999

Figure 2

European Union and
NAFTA and Mercosur
countries.

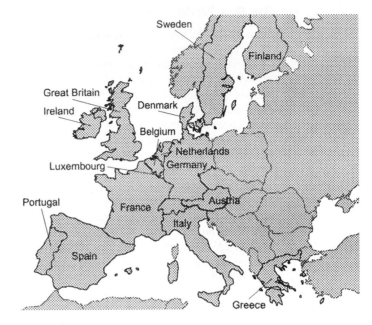

(a) Countries of the European Union (EU).

(b) Countries of the North American Free Trade
Agreement (NAFTA) shown in gray and
Mercosur in dark gray.

Post–Lawrence–Weber:
Business and Society,
Ninth Edition

Global Challenges to
Corporate Responsibility

© The McGraw–Hill
Companies, 1999

Figure 3
Southeast Asian
countries.

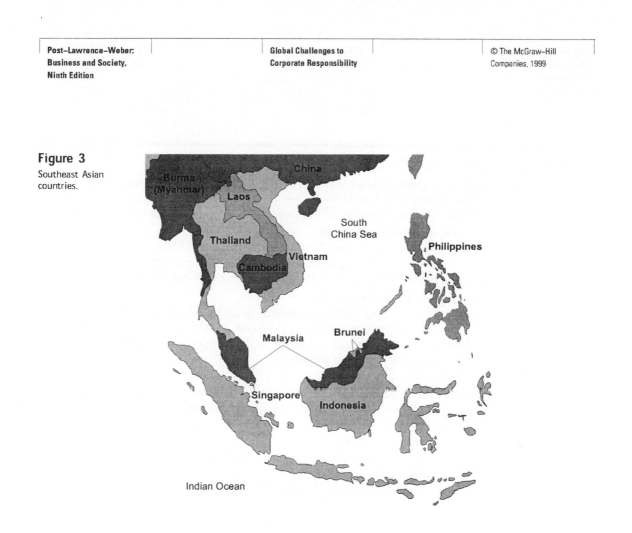

Size, Power, and Accountability

Years ago, Keith Davis defined the iron law of responsibility as a way of pointing out the
relationship between corporate size, power, and responsibility. As he stated, "In the long
run, those who do not use power in a way that society considers responsible will tend to
lose it."[6] As modern corporations become larger and more global, they affect more people in more nations. Responsibility grows with size. Business is the powerful engine that
drives economic growth; it is an incomparable creator of wealth. The creation of wealth
is only part of the story; the impact and effect of wealth-creating activities on employees,
communities, and nations must also be considered. Business leaders must recognize their
accountability to society and the importance of harmonizing business goals with other responsibilities everywhere they operate.

Three ideas guide much of modern understanding about a corporation's private and
public roles and responsibilities, whether it is operating at home or in foreign countries.
First, it is generally accepted that a company is responsible for the direct consequences
that flow from its business activities. Thus, a chemical firm is accountable for its discharges into local rivers, for the quality of products it sells, and for the safety of its op-

[6]The iron law of responsibility was first presented in Keith Davis and Robert L. Blomstrom,
Business and Its Environment (New York: McGraw-Hill, 1966), pp. 174–75.

Post–Lawrence–Weber:
Business and Society,
Ninth Edition

Global Challenges to
Corporate Responsibility

© The McGraw–Hill
Companies, 1999

EXHIBIT B   What's in a Name?

There is a debate about what to call a company whose business ranges across national borders, tying together home and host countries through corporate policies and practices. Here are some of the terms used to describe these companies:

Transnational Corporation (TNC)

Because companies "transcend" or operate across national borders, some experts prefer the term *transnational corporation,* or TNC. The United Nations favors this term and has created a Research Center for the Study of Transnational Corporations.

Multinational Corporation (MNC)

The fact that companies operate in multiple countries has led some experts to adopt the term *multinational corporation,* or MNC. This term is very popular in the business press and in textbooks. It seems to be the most generic name to describe corporations operating around the world.

Multinational Enterprise (MNE)

Because some of the international giants are state-owned enterprises, rather than corporations, the term *multinational enterprise,* or MNE, has entered the vocabulary of international trade.

Global Corporation

This term became very popular in the 1990s. The term seems to have first been used to describe a small number of companies whose business was conducted in dozens of—perhaps more than 100—nations. Hence, Nestlé has long been described as truly global because the scope of its operations extends to more than 150 nations around the globe. The term is often applied to companies doing business in several areas of the world (e.g., Europe, Latin America, Asia-Pacific, and North America).

---

erations. When a company fails to meet these expectations—as Union Carbide did at its Bhopal, India, plant, where leaking chemical vapors killed more than 2,000 residents in 1984—government is entitled to take action to hold the corporation accountable for the consequences.

Second, a company's responsibilities are not unlimited. The chemicals discharged by a local plant, for example, cannot be distinguished from those discharged by dozens of other facilities. At that point, government is required to correct the collective problem and allocate the costs among all businesses. In Bhopal, Union Carbide was the only company involved. When dealing with air pollution in Mexico City, for example, there are so many contributors to the pollution that government must find a fair way to set standards and allocate pollution costs.

Third, businesses should reconcile and integrate their private, profit-seeking activities with their public responsibilities. No society holds the view that human beings are accountable only for themselves. Societies cannot function when such ideas prevail. Thus, when a corporation or a business enterprise is part of a community, the leaders of that business are expected to assume responsibility for the community's well-being. Managers must find ways to harmonize the drive for profits with its public responsibilities.

Post–Lawrence–Weber:
Business and Society,
Ninth Edition

Global Challenges to
Corporate Responsibility

© The McGraw–Hill
Companies, 1999

National Sovereignty and Corporate Power

Multinational corporations present real challenges to a nation's sovereignty and independence. The **national sovereignty principle** holds that a nation is a sovereign state whose laws, customs, and regulations must be respected. It means that a national government has the right, power, and authority to create laws, rules, and regulations regarding business conducted within its borders.

The second principle that shapes business-government relations in most countries is the **business legitimacy principle.** This principle holds that a company's behavior is legitimate if it complies with the laws of the nation and responds to the expectations of its stakeholders. In theory, the principles of national sovereignty and business legitimacy are not in conflict. There may be times, however, when conflicts arise.

India has had a long and difficult struggle with foreign corporations. In 1977, Coca Cola was forced to leave India for refusing to disclose its secret product formula. Coca Cola was finally able to renegotiate entry into India in 1989 by setting up a bottling plant in one of the country's export processing zones (free trade zone). The plant was to ship 75 percent of its production to markets outside India, thereby helping India's foreign trade balance.

As multinational corporations reach across national borders, their global operations may exceed the regulatory influence of national governments. This has raised concerns about the emergence of a **stateless corporation.** These corporations have facilities, shareholders, and customers everywhere. Therefore, they seem to owe loyalty to no single nation and are able to organize and reorganize around the globe. There are economic and political advantages to being, or appearing to be, stateless.

For example, when countries impose trade bans on products from another nation, a company may be able to continue its business if it operates through a subsidiary that is incorporated in a nation that is not the target of a ban. Taiwan and South Korea have banned Japanese automobiles as part of their national trade policy. But because Honda Motor Co., another Japanese automaker, had U.S. operations in Marysville, Ohio, it was able to circumvent the restrictions by shipping Honda automobiles from the United States to Taiwan and South Korea. For the purpose of such trade, Honda was considered a U.S. corporation.

Political and Social Challenges of Doing Business Abroad

The multinational firm, the host nation, and the company's home country have important stakes in harmonizing one another's goals and objectives. Conflicts do occur, however, especially when other stakeholders become involved.[7] This forces managers to adjust business activity in light of challenges to economic and ethical decision making.

Political Challenges

International business is affected by political and governmental factors on two levels. First, business operates in an environment shaped by the relationships between governments

[7]See, for example, "The Explosive Trade Deal You've Never Heard Of," *Business Week,* February 9, 1998, p. 51, on the Clinton administration's negotiations of the Multilateral Agreement on Investment (MAI), which has been called "NAFTA on steroids" because of its limitations on labor and environmental rules.

135

Post–Lawrence–Weber:
Business and Society,
Ninth Edition

Global Challenges to
Corporate Responsibility

© The McGraw–Hill
Companies, 1999

(home country and host country), which may range from friendly to hostile. Second, even in an atmosphere of normal relations between governments, companies must recognize that the host government is a powerful political actor that sets the rules of the game by which businesses will operate in the foreign country.

Intergovernmental Relations

Relations between national governments have influence on international business. If two countries are at war, for example, there will be no trade between them.

When Great Britain and Argentina went to war over ownership of the Falkland Islands, for example, British companies, such as Unilever, a large consumer products company, found themselves in a serious dilemma. Unilever subsidiaries conducted business in Argentina but were barred by the government from doing business with the "enemy" (i.e., Great Britain). Similarly, Great Britain ordered all British companies to cease commercial transactions with the "enemy" (i.e., Argentina). Unilever was therefore under orders from the warring governments not to send or receive messages between its headquarters and its Argentinean businesses. The dilemma facing Unilever's managers was resolved when it was determined that the headquarters and business units could both report to Unilever's office in a neutral country (e.g., Brazil) without violating the dealing-with-the-enemy rules of the two warring nations.

Business transactions may be influenced by the political relations of home and host country governments even when there is no war. Japan and the United States have had an important, but difficult, relationship since the end of World War II. The United States helped rebuild Japan's steel, shipbuilding, and auto industries, and by the 1970s Japan had become an industrial giant. It used its efficiencies to export steel, automobiles, and semiconductors to the huge U.S. market. At first, the United States did not object, but as the market share of U.S. firms in these industries declined, business leaders urged Washington to act. Charges of Japanese dumping—selling below real costs—became familiar. Congress threatened to retaliate if Japan did not stop anticompetitive dumping; companies filed lawsuits; government agencies flexed their muscles. The result was a war of words as the U.S. and Japanese governments engaged in trade negotiations while maintaining an uneasy peace. Progress has been uneven: In 1998, for example, Japan agreed to allow U.S. airlines more access to Japanese airports. Only a few months earlier, the United States refused to allow Japanese ships to enter U.S. ports because of a dispute surrounding Japan's refusal to pay unpaid import taxes.[8]

The United States has shifting political relations with Russia, China, Brazil, Great Britain, and many other nations. Economic relations are affected, for better or worse, by political change, and national political priorities shape commercial relations. The United States, for example, banned U.S. companies from selling military products to countries that government agencies believe may threaten U.S. security; it restricts high-technology exports; and it has banned U.S. companies from doing business in Cuba.

Export-oriented industries, like agriculture and high-technology equipment, are especially vulnerable to such policy changes. Sometimes the changes can be positive for businesses, and business and government have often become partners in achieving

---

[8]"Tax Dispute Threatens US–Japan Trade," *New York Times*, October 17, 1997, p. A14.

economic and political goals. When the United States reestablished economic relations with Nicaragua, for example, it removed sanctions and pledged $500 million to help rebuild that country's stagnant economy. Much of the aid was in the form of credits to buy products and services from U.S. companies.

Host Government Influence

Multinational firms are subject to the regulations, controls, licenses, and rules imposed by the host government. Host countries use a variety of sanctions and incentives ("sticks and carrots") to shape and regulate foreign investment, attempting to lure investors but also trying to prevent excessive manipulation by them. The host government must weigh the benefits of technology, jobs, and tax revenues that foreign investment can bring versus the costs of power that the foreign investor will acquire.

National governments use laws, rules, and regulations to ensure that companies do not engage in certain types of conduct. These standards usually apply to all companies in a nation or in a specific industry. In some countries, however, national governments may wish to single out multinational businesses for special treatment. To prevent such discrimination, a *principle of national treatment* has been adopted that guarantees that all companies operating in a country are treated the same as home companies.

Interference becomes extreme when the host government insists on becoming a partial owner of the foreign business. This has happened in basic or natural resources industries such as petroleum and mining. Resource-rich countries such as Brazil, Chile, Papua New Guinea, Saudi Arabia, and Indonesia have often insisted that foreign mining and oil exploration firms share ownership with the government. (See the case study of Shell in Nigeria at the end of the book.) For many years, state-owned enterprises—such as Mexico's national petroleum company—were the rule; then, shared ownership followed. In recent times, some of these countries have allowed foreign ownership of resources that are deemed national assets.

Changes in government control can lead a country to *expropriate,* or seize, a foreign company's assets. The government takes ownership of the property, and it may or may not pay for what it takes. In 1960, Fidel Castro nationalized billions of dollars of assets from U.S. firms in Cuba; in 1990, Iraq seized all of Kuwait's assets, including its oil fields. Such expropriations are relatively rare and are estimated at no more than 5 percent of all foreign-owned assets. More common, by far, is the taking of assets from local owners—especially the political opposition—when a government changes hands or an ethnic war or a revolution occurs.

Social Challenges

The social and cultural differences among nations present challenges for managers, businesses, and families. Language, physical surroundings, and values of the population can create important business and human conflicts. Concepts of human rights, equality among sexes, races, and ethnic groups, and business responsibilities differ around the world. The amount of difference between two social systems, or *cultural distance,* can be very significant.

> *Southern China is industrializing and developing at an explosive rate. In Guangzhu province, change is staggering: Construction sites are everywhere, with companies racing to get their businesses under way. There are many*

Post–Lawrence–Weber:
Business and Society,
Ninth Edition

Global Challenges to
Corporate Responsibility

© The McGraw-Hill
Companies, 1999

problems, but the one most often identified by managers was "people." Procter & Gamble, Motorola, and Johnson & Johnson are companies whose human resources practices are admired. But they cannot get enough people to staff their Chinese operations. U.S. managers face family pressures since housing, schools, and amenities seem very limited. Chinese managers with the proper skills are so scarce that they are regularly recruited away from one employer to another for much more money and responsibility. What is the answer? Managers who were interviewed from many different firms agreed: There are no easy answers.[9]

Inadequate facilities may require a company to build housing, establish schools, and create transportation systems to ease the difficulties for employees. International business needs not only a proper physical infrastructure of airports, telephones, and fax machines but a social infrastructure as well. Whether the project is in the remote highlands of Papua New Guinea, the deep jungle of the Republic of Congo, or the desert city of Amman, Jordan, there are certain requirements that the host country must provide for the business to be successful. There must be a system of law that ensures that contracts will be honored; essential civil services, such as fire and police protection; and a social tolerance for people from different nations and cultures. If the government is unable to provide these, the company may have to do so or conclude that it cannot do business in the host country.

Adherence to a host country's cultural norms may be complicated by a company's home country values. Cultural conflicts can pose serious issues. Stakeholders in the home nation will be watching the company's conduct abroad; if they discover policy violations or unacceptable behavior, there will be pressure on management to change.

When U.S. companies conducted business in South Africa during the 1970s and 1980s, the nation's apartheid system of racial separation offended many U.S. citizens. A campaign was organized to force individual companies to practice racial integration in South Africa, despite the country's public policy, or to withdraw and stop doing business in that setting. Pressures grew, and Congress passed a law imposing economic sanctions on South Africa in 1986 that pressured some U.S. companies to close their South African operations.[10]

Conflicts between the home country and the host country arise for many different reasons. Often, the cultural and political practices of the home country simply are not applied in the host nation. Two examples are familiar to virtually any company doing business around the world: questionable payments and labor standards.

Questionable Payments

Questionable payments are those that raise significant questions of ethical right or wrong in the host or home nation. Some people condemn all questionable payments as bribes, but real situations are not that simple. Managers of a foreign subsidiary may find themselves forced to choose between the host country's laws or customs and the policies of corporate headquarters.

[9]Interviews conducted by researchers at the Human Resources Policy Institute at Boston University.
[10]Robert Kinloch Massie, *Loosing the Bonds* (New York: Doubleday, 1998).

Post–Lawrence–Weber:
Business and Society,
Ninth Edition

Global Challenges to
Corporate Responsibility

© The McGraw–Hill
Companies, 1999

The Foreign Corrupt Practices Act regulates questionable payments of all U.S. firms operating in other nations. Passed in 1977 in response to disclosure of questionable foreign payments by U.S. corporations, the law has two purposes: (1) to establish a worldwide code of conduct for any kind of payment by U.S. businesses to foreign government officials, political parties, and political candidates, and (2) to require proper accounting controls for full disclosure of the firm's transactions. The law applies even if a payment is legal in the nation where it is made. The intention is to assure that U.S. firms meet U.S. standards wherever they operate. The law has the following major provisions:

- It is a criminal offense for a firm to make payments to a foreign government official, political party, or candidate for political office to secure or retain business in another nation.

- Sales commissions to independent agents are illegal if the business has knowledge that any part of the commission is being passed to foreign officials.

- Government employees "whose duties are essentially ministerial or clerical" are excluded; expediting payments to customs agents and bureaucrats are permitted.

- Payments made in genuine situations of extortion are permitted.

- Companies whose securities are regulated by the Securities Exchange Act must establish internal accounting controls to assure that all payments abroad are authorized and properly recorded.

Many business leaders criticized the U.S. Congress for imposing such regulations. They complained that companies from other nations did not have to operate in similar ways and were permitted to make payments that ultimately tipped the competitive scales against U.S. firms. Proponents of the standards argued that the United States should not slip to the lowest competitive level and should prove its superiority in product quality, service, and other factors, not questionable payments. The latter position seems to have prevailed. In 1997, the 29 leading industrial countries that make up the Organization for Economic Cooperation and Development adopted a code of conduct that bars companies from engaging in corruption and bribery. Twenty years after the U.S. law was written, the concept of business without bribery is becoming a world standard.[11]

Labor Standards

Labor standards refer to those conditions that affect a company's employees or the employees of its suppliers, subcontractors, or others in the commercial chain. For example, in some countries, sweatshop conditions exist in which women and children labor long hours in extreme heat for very little money and with virtually no safety protection.

Levi Strauss, a U.S. company with a reputation for progressive social programs, was accused of using an unethical contractor in Saipan. The contractor was accused of keeping some workers as virtual slaves. Wages were below the legal minimum, and conditions were wretched and unsafe. Levi fired the con-

---

[11] Kathleen A. Getz, "International Instruments on Bribery and Corruption," paper presented at the Conference on Global Codes of Conduct: An Idea Whose Time Has Come? University of Notre Dame, October 6–8, 1997. Also, see Transparency International, "Global Corruption Index," http://www. transparency.de.

Post–Lawrence–Weber:
Business and Society,
Ninth Edition

Global Challenges to
Corporate Responsibility

© The McGraw–Hill
Companies, 1999

tractor and formed a committee of managers to review procedures for hiring contractors. The company became the first multinational to adopt a wide-ranging set of guidelines for its hired factories. The guidelines cover treatment of workers and environmental impacts of production. Levi Strauss now sends inspectors to conduct audits of work and safety conditions at all of its contractors. Deficiencies must be corrected or the company will cancel the contract. The company also led the effort to create industrywide standards.[12]

There is growing pressure to ensure that workers who are willing to work for low wages in developing countries are not exploited by unscrupulous businesses.[13] When the North American Free Trade Agreement was being debated in the United States, labor unions focused on the abuses that could occur as high-paying jobs in the United States became low-paying jobs in Mexico. The creation of labor standards and business commitments to honor them could ease some of this concern. But as the following example suggests, implementation of such commitments has been uneven in recent years.

Sony Corporation, Honeywell, and General Electric were among the first companies alleged to have broken U.S. labor laws under NAFTA. In 1994, Sony (Japanese) and the two U.S. companies were accused of actions to stifle union organizing campaigns at plants in Mexico. Activist organizations filed a complaint with the National Administrative Office, a U.S. agency established to enforce the terms of the agreement. The group claimed that Sony and Mexican authorities failed to enforce laws that give workers in Sony's plant in Nuevo Laredo, along the U.S. border, rights to hold union elections. The company was charged with forcing workers to work beyond the 48-hour maximum under Mexican law, harassing employees who favored unions, and creating dangerous working conditions. Although Sony denied the charges, the complaints foretell a continuing battle to create standards that all stakeholders will support.[14]

Human Rights

Human rights codes of conduct are the newest development in this area of concern. Companies such as Reebok International have created codes of conduct that will be applied to all of its suppliers (see Exhibit C). Some business leaders doubt that company codes can stop labor abuses in other nations, in part because foreign competitors may not abide by similar standards. This has led to calls on the U.S. Congress to create a labor standards law similar to the Foreign Corrupt Practices Act that would set the global labor standards for all U.S. companies wherever they operate. Despite some interest in such action, the Congress has so far failed to develop such legislation.

[12] G. Pascal Zachary, "Exporting Rights: Levi Tries to Make Sure Contract Plants in Asia Treat Workers Well," *The Wall Street Journal,* July 28, 1994, pp. A1, A9.
[13] Martin J. Levine, *Worker Rights and Labor Standards in Asia's Four New Tigers: A Comparative Perspective* (New York: Plenum Press, 1997). The author compares the state of worker rights in China, Indonesia, Thailand, and Malaysia.
[14] Asra Q. Nomani, "Sony Is Targeted in Rights Action Based on NAFTA," *The Wall Street Journal,* August 18, 1994, p. A2.

Post–Lawrence–Weber:
Business and Society,
Ninth Edition

Global Challenges to
Corporate Responsibility

© The McGraw–Hill
Companies, 1999

EXHIBIT C   Reebok's Human Rights Code (circa 1998)

Reebok has adopted the following human rights production standards in seven specific areas:

Non-discrimination—Reebok will seek business partners that do not discriminate in hiring and employment practices on grounds of race, color, national origin, gender, religion, or political or other opinion.

Working hours/overtime—Reebok will seek business partners who do not require more than 60 hour work weeks on a regularly scheduled basis, except for appropriately compensated overtime in compliance with local laws, and we will favor business partners who use 48 hour work weeks as their maximum normal requirement.

Forced or compulsory labor—Reebok will not work with business partners that use forced or other compulsory labor, including labor that is required as a means of political coercion or as punishment for holding or for peacefully expressing political views, in the manufacture of its products. Reebok will not purchase materials that were produced by forced prison or other compulsory labor and will terminate business relationships with any sources found to utilize such labor.

Fair wages—Reebok will seek business partners who share our commitment to the betterment of wage and benefit levels that address the basic needs of workers and their families so far as possible and appropriate in light of national practices and conditions. Reebok will not select business partners that pay less than the minimum wage required by local law or that pay less than prevailing local industry practices (whichever is higher).

Child Labor—Reebok will not work with business partners that use child labor. The term "child" generally refers to a person who is less than 14 years of age, or younger than the age for completing compulsory education if that age is higher than 14. In countries where the law defines "child" to include individuals who are older than 14, Reebok will apply that definition.

Freedom of association—Reebok will seek business partners that share its commitment to the right of employees to establish and join organizations of their own choosing. Reebok will seek to assure that no employee is penalized because of his or her non-violent exercise of this right. Reebok recognizes and respects the right of all employees to organize and bargain collectively.

Safe and healthy work environment—Reebok will seek business partners that strive to assure employees a safe and healthy workplace and that do not expose workers to hazardous conditions.

Source: Reebok International, Ltd., *Human Rights Productions Standards*, (Stoughton, MA: Reebok International. Ltd., 1998). Also available at http://www.reebok.com/humanrights

Human rights codes have an impact when individual companies take actions based on their codes. For example, Reebok acted on the code principles in Exhibit C when it threatened one of its Chinese contractors, Yue Yuen International (Holdings), Ltd., with cancellation of orders if workers were not moved out of unsafe dormitories and into safer housing. A story in the *Asian Wall Street Journal* described hundreds of women working

Post–Lawrence–Weber:
Business and Society,
Ninth Edition

Global Challenges to
Corporate Responsibility

© The McGraw–Hill
Companies, 1999

in conditions that were unsafe and violated labor regulations in Guangdong province. After Reebok's protests, Yue Yuen relocated 800 workers from the unsafe dormitories to newer, safer facilities.[15]

Corporate Social Strategy

Doing business in international settings presents many challenges to managers. There is no magic solution to meeting these issues as they arise. Companies can prepare for the types of challenges discussed in this chapter, however, by designing a **corporate social strategy** that matches and balances the company's economic strategy.[16] These questions are a good place to start the process:

- Are we being socially responsible in what we do? Do we meet the expectations of our host country as well as our home country? Would stakeholders in either country question our behavior?

- Are we responsive to the stakeholders in each country where we do business? Do we treat employees, customers, suppliers, local communities, and others in a fair and just way?

- Do we recognize emerging issues, as well as immediate social issues, in the countries and communities where we operate? Are we anticipating change rather than just reacting to it?

- Do we abide by the host government's regulations and policies? Do we have good systems for ensuring that our employees and the agents who represent us follow our corporate policies?

- Do we conduct business in ways that respect the values, customs, and moral principles of each society? Do we recognize that there may be times when they conflict with principles of other societies? Are we ready to address these conflicts in thoughtful, positive ways?

Companies that address these questions before trouble strikes are better prepared to meet global challenges to corporate responsibility. They are better prepared to prevent crises, anticipate change, and avoid situations that compromise the values and principles for which the company stands. A corporate social strategy helps managers achieve both the economic and the social goals of the company.

Summary Points

- The globalization of business is driven by many factors. The demand for many goods and services is global, and modern transportation and communication systems enable companies to meet consumer demand around the world. The decline of trade barriers,

[15]"Reebok Compels Chinese Contractors to Improve Conditions for Workers," *The Wall Street Journal*, August 16, 1994, p. A9; also, Pamela Varley, ed., *The Sweatshop Quandry: Corporate Responsibility on the Global Frontier* (Washington, D.C.: Investor Responsibility Research Center, 1998).

[16]Lee A. Tavis, *Power and Responsibility: Multinational Managers and Developing Country Concerns* (South Bend, IN: University of Notre Dame Press, 1997).

Post–Lawrence–Weber:
Business and Society,
Ninth Edition

Global Challenges to
Corporate Responsibility

© The McGraw–Hill
Companies, 1999

opening of markets in economies that were once closed to trade, and dynamic growth in developing nations all contribute to worldwide economic activity.

- Free enterprise, central state control, and mixed state and private enterprise differ from one another in the amount of freedom permitted for making economic choices, including how much government coercion and regulation is present. Militarized non-democratic regimes present special ethical challenges for global businesses.

- Global business enterprises, or multinational corporations, are powerful actors in the world economy. The size and wealth of the largest of these companies rivals those of nations. National sovereignty is thereby challenged in a world where economic power, global communications, and human mobility are increasing while political barriers are more difficult for nations to enforce. Because they are able to span national boundaries, MNCs are sometimes referred to as stateless corporations.

- Home countries and host countries encourage international business but try to structure the rules of the game in ways that benefit their citizens. Laws and regulations are created to protect national interests as global business expands.

- Businesses face the challenge of maintaining ethical norms and standards when operating in other nations. Host country customs, traditions, and business norms may conflict with home country standards in the workplace and in dealing with government officials.

Key Terms and Concepts

- Ethnocentric perspective
- Geocentric perspective
- Socioeconomic systems
- Free enterprise economy
- Central state control
- Mixed state and private enterprise
- Militarized nondemocratic regime

- National sovereignty principle
- Business legitimacy principle
- Stateless corporation
- Questionable payments
- Human rights codes
- Corporate social strategy

Internet Resources

- http://www.census.gov
- http://www.esd.worldbank.org
- http://www.citizen.org/pctrade/
  tradehome.html

Census data on global population
World Bank
Public Citizen Global Trade Watch

Discussion Case   General Electric in Hungary

The iron curtain came down in Europe a decade ago. Countries living under Soviet Union domination since World War II celebrated freedom and began to chart a new economic direction. The collapse of communism and its central state control created new opportunities but many uncertainties as well. How would businesses that had lived under central planning do when exposed to the forces of the marketplace? One answer

Post–Lawrence–Weber:
Business and Society,
Ninth Edition

Global Challenges to
Corporate Responsibility

© The McGraw–Hill
Companies, 1999

came from Hungary, where Tungsram, an old and well-known lighting company, joined the General Electric Company. This is Tungsram's report card.

In 1989, after the iron curtain fell, the General Electric Company, a U.S.-based multinational company with operations around the world, made a major investment in Hungary when it purchased Tungsram, a maker of lighting products. Tungsram was one of Hungary's leading state-owned companies under Communist rule. Under Hungary's new democratic government, however, state-owned companies were to be privatized. Foreign investment and management experience were sought for companies that would have to operate in competitive market environments. The Hungarians wanted to learn how to compete, and General Electric was eager to have Tungsram as a part of its global business.

Things quickly turned unpleasant. Tungsram was losing large amounts of money on its operations. The equipment was old, work practices were inefficient, communication was poor, and the workforce had a lackadaisical attitude. GE's business strategy was to use Tungsram as an entry point into the Eastern European markets that had been closed to its products. It intended to bring product quality, customer service, and aggressive pricing to the marketplace. By using GE management principles, manufacturing quality could be improved; by using the company's marketing experience, customers could be satisfied and profits could be made. However, nearly every aspect of the strategy ran into problems.

GE managers saw that costs had to be reduced and quality improved if Tungsram's products were to be competitive. When markets were controlled under Communist regimes, neither cost nor quality seemed very important. If plants ran at an operating deficit, the government subsidized the operation. With GE, that was to change. GE's analysis showed that Tungsram had far too many workers for the volume of production. The workforce would have to be cut. GE designed a plan to lay off those who were nearest retirement. Employees received nine months of wages, considerably more than Hungarian law required. But many women who were on leave under Hungary's generous three-year maternity leave were not rehired. In 1992 and 1993, GE's productivity goals became more ambitious and more employees were dismissed. Between 1989 and 1996, Tungsram's employee headcount went from 17,640 to 10,500.

Workers who remained had to undergo a changed mind-set about their work. GE used its American system of *action workouts* at Tungsram to improve productivity. Teams of workers are formed to tackle specific problems. Problems are solved by changing work routines, altering the mix of people and machines, and finding better ways to achieve goals. Communication requires a common language and employee commitment to the company's goals. At Tungsram, workers had to attend English classes and read a book containing many of GE chairman Jack Welch's favorite sayings, including "If we're not No. 1 or No. 2 in a business, improve it, close it or sell it!" A culture change was underway, but progress was slow and difficult to achieve.

In 1993, GE announced that it lost all of the $150 million it had invested when it bought 50.1 percent of Tungsram in 1989. Much more money was required to achieve results. GE would invest more than $550 million in Tungsram by 1995. The strategy that had looked so appealing in 1989 looked very costly after five years.

By 1994, however, progress began to show. Tungsram was successfully competing in the European lighting business. Costs were brought in line with the best lighting manufacturers in the world, and Hungarian scientific expertise helped produce innova-

Post–Lawrence–Weber:
Business and Society,
Ninth Edition

Global Challenges to
Corporate Responsibility

© The McGraw–Hill
Companies, 1999

tive new products. Innovative new processes were making Tungsram's plants more efficient. Sales were approximately $288 million in 1989; they dipped sharply in 1992 and 1993, then began to rise slowly. By 1994 the trajectory was up; and in 1996, Tungsram's total sales exceeded $376 million. GE had invested $700 million, according to observers.

Some problems remain. Workers' pay has not kept pace with Hungary's inflation rate and about one-third of Tungsram's workers live close to the poverty line. Still, GE claims that Tungsram's wages average more than $300 per month, an amount that is in the top 25 percent in each of the eight towns where the company has plants. Peter Wohl, Tungsram's vice president and managing director, says that Tungsram has helped make GE's lighting division run neck and neck with leading competitors Philips and Osram Sylvania. GE, he said, has made a profit on the deal. "Sure they have made [a profit]," he said, "but the problem for the foreign investors looking at the Tungsram acquisition is that they cannot compare it. An almost-100-year-old, relatively good working company like Tungsram, having a good reputation, high technological standards and a huge product range and export markets and a good brand name, that's something [special, compared] . . . to what other Hungarian companies can offer for investors."

Source: "GEL Tungsram—Hungary: Interview—GE Hungary Light Unit Turns Corner," October 26, 1997, Reuters Limited, 1997, DIALOG(R) File, 799, Reuters Info, Services.

Discussion Questions

1. What business objectives led General Electric to invest in Hungary in 1989? What challenges confronted General Electric when it started the process of changing Tungsram into a competitive enterprise?
2. Assess General Electric's decision to lay off workers. Why would they pay more than Hungarian law required to departing employees?
3. In the United States, its home country, GE would be required to rehire women on maternity leave. In Hungary, however, it has not done so. Is it proper for GE to operate with different standards in different countries?
4. Did GE have a corporate social strategy for its business in Hungary? Using the questions on page 165, explain what GE could have done to anticipate the problems it encountered.

Bibliography

Cavanaugh, Gerald F. *American Business Values: With International Perspective,* 4th ed. Englewood Cliffs, NJ: Prentice-Hall, 1998.

Colby, Anne, and William Damon. *Some Do Care: Contemporary Lives of Moral Commitment.* New York: The Free Press, 1992.

Colby, Anne, and Lawrence Kohlberg. *The Measurement of Moral Judgment: Volume 1, Theoretical Foundations and Research Validation.* Cambridge, MA: Harvard University Press, 1987.

Dobson, John. *Finance Ethics: The Rationality of Virtue.* Lanham, MD: Rowman and Littlefield, 1997.

Dunfee, Thomas W., and Yukimasa Nagayasu. *Business Ethics: Japan and the Global Economy.* Dordrecht, Netherlands: Kluwer Academic, 1993.

Estes, Ralph. *Tyranny of the Bottom Line: Why Corporations Make Good People Do Bad Things.* San Francisco, CA: Berrett Kochler, 1996.

Etzioni, Amitai. *The Moral Dimension: Toward a New Economics.* New York: Free Press, 1988.

Post-Lawrence-Weber:
Business and Society,
Ninth Edition

Global Challenges to
Corporate Responsibility

© The McGraw-Hill
Companies, 1999

Freeman, R. Edward, and Daniel R. Gilbert, Jr. *Corporate Strategy and the Search for Ethics.* Englewood Cliffs, NJ: Prentice-Hall, 1988.

Fukuyama, Francis. *Trust: The Social Virtues and the Creation of Prosperity.* New York: The Free Press, 1995.

Harding, Harry. *China's Second Revolution: Reform after Mao.* Washington: Brookings, 1987.

Jackall, Robert. *Moral Mazes: The World of Corporate Managers.* New York: Oxford University Press, 1988.

Kennedy, Paul. *The Rise and Fall of the Great Powers.* New York: Random House, 1987.

Kidder, Rushworth M. *How Good People Make Tough Choices.* New York: William Morrow & Co., 1995.

Korten, David. *When Corporations Ruled the World.* San Francisco, CA: Berrett-Kochler, 1996.

Levine, Marvin J. *Worker Rights and Labor Standards in Asia's Four New Tigers: A Comparative Perspective.* New York: Plenum Press, 1997.

Messick, David M., and Ann E. Tenbrunsel, eds. *Codes of Conduct: Behavioral Research into Business Ethics.* New York: Russell Sage Foundation, 1996.

Nash, Laura L. *Good Intentions Aside: A Manager's Guide to Resolving Ethical Problems.* Boston: Harvard Business School Press, 1990.

_____. *Believers in Business,* Nashville, TN: Thomas Nelson Publishers, 1994.

Neilsen, Richard P. *The Politics of Ethics.* New York: Oxford University Press, 1996.

Rawls, John. *A Theory of Justice.* Cambridge, MA: Harvard University Press, 1971.

Rest, James L., and Darcia Navarez, eds. *Moral Development in the Professions.* Hillsdale, NJ: Lawrence Erlbaum Associates, 1994.

Stone, Christopher D. *Where the Law Ends: The Social Control of Corporate Behavior.* Prospect Heights, IL: Waveland Press, 1975.

Tavis, Lee A. *Power and Responsibility: Multinational Managers and Developing Country Concerns.* South Bend, IN: University of Notre Dame Press, 1997.

Velasquez, Manuel G. *Business Ethics: Concepts and Cases,* 4th ed. Upper Saddle River, NJ: Prentice Hall, 1998.

Post−Lawrence−Weber:
Business and Society,
Ninth Edition

Consumer Protection

© The McGraw−Hill
Companies, 1999

Consumer Protection

Safeguarding consumers while continuing to supply them with the goods and services they want is a prime social responsibility of business. Many companies recognize that providing customers with excellent service and product quality is an effective, as well as ethical, business strategy. Consumers, for their part, have become increasingly aware of their rights to safety, to be informed, to choose, and to be heard— and, increasingly, of their right to privacy. Government agencies serve as watchdogs for consumers, supplementing the actions taken by consumers to protect themselves and the actions of socially responsible corporations.

This topic focuses on these key questions and objectives:

- Why did a consumer movement develop in the United States?
- What are the major rights of consumers?
- In what ways do government regulatory agencies protect consumers? To what extent *should* government protect consumers?
- Why has advertising become a target of consumer activists and government regulators?
- Is there a product liability crisis, and what reforms, if any, should be made?
- How have socially responsible corporations responded to consumer needs?

I n 1997, the Food and Drug Administration (FDA) ordered two of the nation's most popular diet drugs off the market after they were linked to serious heart problems in some users. The drugs, *dexfenfluramine* and *fenfluramine,* had been used with another medicine called *phentermine* in a combination popularly known as fen-phen. Fen-phen had enabled many obese people to lose weight, and many patients and doctors were enthusiastic. The two diet drugs had been big moneymakers for their manufacturer, Wyeth-Ayerst Laboratories, producing over $300 million in sales in 1996. But doctors found that some patients developed potentially fatal heart-valve problems while taking the medication, and several previously healthy dieters died. When the government showed Wyeth-Ayerst officials the clinical data, the company readily agreed to withdraw the drugs. "Our first commitment is to our patients and their doctors," said a representative of Wyeth-Ayerst. "Even though this new information . . . is difficult to evaluate, the company is taking the most prudent course of action." Wyeth-Ayerst placed full-page advertisements in newspapers announcing the drugs' withdrawal and established a toll-free number for patients.[1]

A Texas man had to have his foot amputated after a hunting rifle he was unloading, the Remington Model 700, accidentally discharged, seriously wounding him. Five years later, in 1994, a jury returned a verdict of $17 million against Remington, including $15 million in punitive damages. The company called the rifle "a safe and reliable sporting firearm" and disputed that it was in any way defective. But the Texan's attorney introduced internal documents showing that Remington had received complaints about the rifle dating back to 1982 and that the company had designed a safer firing mechanism but had decided not to use it. Guns are among the few consumer products for which the government has no authority to regulate safety. Although firearm accidents cause as many as 1,400 deaths a year, the National Rifle Association and gun manufacturers have vigorously opposed federal oversight.[2]

In 1993, after nearly a decade of controversy, the U.S. government approved bovine somatropin (BST), a genetically engineered hormone to boost milk production in cows. Years of testing by the FDA and health organizations showed that milk produced with BST was indistinguishable from milk that was not. But the day before the hormone was released for use, several of the country's largest food companies—including Kroger, Pathmark, and Southland, operator of 7-Eleven convenience stores—announced that they would not buy milk produced by cows given the drug. "Food is an emotional issue," a spokesperson for Southland said. "We felt a responsibility to take this action because of concern expressed by our customers."[3]

These three episodes demonstrate some of the complexities of serving consumers today. New standards of business performance are being demanded. Today's consumers are increasingly aware of the broad impact that consumption can have not only on themselves but on society generally. This material examines these issues and the various ways that consumers, government regulators, and business firms have dealt with them.

[1]"How Fen-Phen, a Diet 'Miracle,' Rose and Fell," *New York Times,* September 23, 1997, p. F1; and "Two Top Diet Drugs Are Recalled Amid Reports of Heart Defects," *New York Times,* September 16, 1997, p. A1.
[2]"Remington Faces a Misfiring Squad," *Business Week,* May 23, 1994, pp. 90–91.
[3]"Crying over Unnatural Milk," *Business Week,* November 22, 1993, p. 48; and "Grocers Challenge Use of New Drug for Milk Output," *New York Times,* February 4, 1994, pp. A1, A8.

Post–Lawrence–Weber:
Business and Society,
Ninth Edition

Consumer Protection

© The McGraw–Hill
Companies, 1999

Pressures to Promote Consumer Interests

As long as business has existed—since the ancient beginnings of commerce and trade—consumers have tried to protect their interests when they go to the marketplace to buy goods and services. They have haggled over prices, taken a careful look at the goods they are buying, compared the quality and prices of products offered by other sellers, and complained loudly when they felt cheated by shoddy products. So, consumer self-reliance has always been one form of consumer protection. The Latin phrase, *caveat emptor*—meaning "let the buyer beware"—has put consumers on the alert to look after their own interests. This form of individual self-reliance is still very much in existence today.

However, the increasing complexity of economic life in the twentieth century, especially in the more advanced industrial nations, has led to organized, collective efforts to safeguard consumers. These organized activities are usually called consumerism or the **consumer movement.**

The Anatomy of Consumerism

At the heart of consumerism in the United States is an attempt to expand the rights and powers of consumers. The goal of the consumer movement, which began in the 1960s as part of a broader movement for social change, is to make consumer power an effective counterbalance to the rights and powers of business firms that sell goods and services.

Within an advanced, industrialized, private-enterprise nation, business firms tend to grow to a very large size. They acquire much power and influence. Frequently, they can dictate prices. Typically, their advertisements sway consumers to buy one product or service rather than another. If large enough, they may share the market with only a few equally large competitors, thereby weakening some of the competitive protections enjoyed by consumers where business firms are smaller and more numerous. The economic influence and power of business firms may therefore become a problem for consumers unless ways can be found to promote an equal amount of consumer power.

Most consumers would feel well protected if their fundamental rights to fair play in the marketplace could be guaranteed. In the early 1960s, when the consumer movement in the United States was in its early stages, President John F. Kennedy told Congress that consumers were entitled to four different kinds of protection:

1. *The right to safety*—to be protected against the marketing of goods that are hazardous to health or life.
2. *The right to be informed*—to be protected against fraudulent, deceitful, or grossly misleading information, advertising, labeling, or other practices, and to be given the facts to make an informed choice.
3. *The right to choose*—to be assured, wherever possible, access to a variety of products and services at competitive prices, and in those industries in which competition is not workable and government regulation is substituted, to be assured satisfactory quality and service at fair prices.
4. *The right to be heard*—to be assured that consumer interests will receive full and sympathetic consideration in the formulation of government policy and fair and expeditious treatment in its administrative tribunals.

The **consumer bill of rights,** as it was called, became the guiding philosophy of the consumer movement. If those rights could be guaranteed, consumers would feel more

Post–Lawrence–Weber:
Business and Society,
Ninth Edition

Consumer Protection

© The McGraw–Hill
Companies, 1999

confident in dealing with well-organized and influential corporations in the marketplace. In the mid-1990s, some activists and government regulators began to call for laws protecting a fifth consumer right, the *right to privacy*. This issue is discussed in the case at the end of this chapter.

Reasons for the Consumer Movement

This consumer movement exists because consumers want to be treated fairly and honestly in the marketplace. Some business practices do not meet this standard. Consumers may be harmed by abuses such as unfairly high prices, unreliable and unsafe products, excessive or deceptive advertising claims, and the promotion of some products known to be harmful to human health, such as cigarettes or farm products contaminated with pesticides.

Additional reasons for the existence of the consumer movement are the following:

- *Complex products have enormously complicated the choices consumers need to make when they go shopping.* For this reason, consumers today are more dependent on business for product quality than ever before. Because many products are so complex—a personal computer or an automobile, for example—most consumers have no way to judge at the time of purchase whether their quality is satisfactory. Many of the component parts of such products are not visible to consumers, who, therefore, cannot inspect them even if they have the technical competence to do so. Consumers find that they are almost entirely dependent on business to deliver the quality promised. In these circumstances, unscrupulous business firms can take advantage of uninformed consumers.

- *Services, as well as products, have become more specialized and difficult to judge.* When choosing lawyers, dentists, colleges, or hospitals, most consumers do not have adequate guides for evaluating whether they are good or bad. They can rely on word-of-mouth experiences of others, but this information may not be entirely reliable. Or, when purchasing expensive items such as refrigerators, consumers have to judge how well the items will perform and know what to do when they break down. The consumer faces a two-tier judgment problem in making purchases: First, is the product a good one? Then, what will good service cost? The uninformed or badly informed consumer is frequently no match for the seller who is in the superior position.

- *When business tries to sell both products and services through advertising, claims may be inflated or they may appeal to emotions having little to do with how the product is expected to perform.* An example was an ad for a stereo that declared, "She's terrific in bed, she's witty and intelligent and makes her own pasta." But, the ad continued, "she didn't own [the advertised sound system], so he married a woman who did." The ad was withdrawn after numerous complaints poured in to the manufacturer.[4] A survey by *American Demographics* magazine found that nearly a third of adults found sexual references or images in advertising offensive.[5] Ad-industry critics have also frequently found fault with advertise-

---

[4]"Does Sex Sell? Yes, But . . . ," *The Detroit News*, June 12, 1994.
[5]Doris Walsh, "Safe Sex in Advertising," *American Demographics*, April 1994, pp. 24–30.

Post–Lawrence–Weber:
Business and Society,
Ninth Edition

Consumer Protection

© The McGraw-Hill
Companies, 1999

ments that air during children's television programs and feature violence, sell sweetened cereals, or promote toys—for example, the Ninja Turtle or G.I. Joe characters—by building program plots around these products, thus taking advantage of young children unable to differentiate between a fictional program and a commercial advertisement.[6] Beer commercials that feature "good old boys" relaxing after work and auto advertisements that link male virility with horsepower and speed have come under attack for ignoring the negative impacts of alcohol abuse and high-speed automobile deaths and injuries.

- *Product safety has often been ignored.* The symbolic beginning of consumerism in the United States was Ralph Nader's well-publicized charges in the early 1970s about the hazards of driving the Corvair.[7] As public interest in health and nutrition grew, many consumers worried about food additives, preservatives, pesticide residues left on fruits and vegetables, diet patterns that contributed to obesity, and the devastating health effects of long-term tobacco use. If the public could not count on business to screen out these possible dangers to consumers, to whom could they turn for help? This question was raised more and more often, which led eventually to corrective actions by business, government, and consumer advocacy groups.

Consumer Advocacy Groups

One of the impressive features of the consumer movement in the United States is the many organized groups that actively promote and speak for the interests of millions of consumers. One organization alone, the Consumer Federation of America, brings together over 240 nonprofit groups to espouse the consumer viewpoint; they represent some 50 million Americans. A nonprofit organization, Consumers Union, conducts extensive tests on selected consumer products and services and publishes the results, with ratings on a brand-name basis, in *Consumer Reports* magazine. Consumer cooperatives, credit unions, Web sites catering to consumers, and consumer education programs in schools and universities and on television and radio round out a very extensive network of activities aimed at promoting consumer interests.

The most-publicized consumer advocate is Ralph Nader, who with his associates formed a network of affiliated organizations. Public Citizen, founded in 1971, became the umbrella organization for specialized units, the main fund-raising organization, and a publishing arm for consumer publications. The Health Research Group has taken the lead in urging a ban on harmful color dyes used in various foods, putting warning labels on dangerous products, setting exposure limits on hazardous substances, and alerting the public to possibly dangerous medical products on the market, such as silicone breast implants. Other organizations under the Public Citizen umbrella include the Litigation Group, which gives legal assistance to people who have difficulty in gaining adequate access to the court system; Congress Watch, which monitors Congress; and Global Trade Watch, which ed-

[6]"Watch What Your Kids Watch," *Business Week,* January 8, 1990, pp. 50–52.
[7]Ralph Nader, *Unsafe at Any Speed: The Designed-In Dangers of the American Automobile* (New York: Grossman, 1972).

Post–Lawrence–Weber:
Business and Society,
Ninth Edition

Consumer Protection

© The McGraw–Hill
Companies, 1999

ucates consumers about the impact of economic globalization. Nader's organization is also allied with a network of state and local activist groups.[8]

How Government Protects Consumers

The federal government's involvement in protecting consumers' interests is extensive. During the 1960s and 1970s, Congress passed important laws to protect consumers, created new regulatory agencies, and strengthened older consumer protection agencies. These developments meant that consumers, rather than relying solely on free market competition to safeguard their interests, could also turn to government for protection. During most of the 1980s, a deregulatory attitude by the federal government tended to blunt federal initiatives on behalf of consumers. However, state governments became more active, particularly regarding price-fixing, car insurance rates, and corporate takeovers that threatened jobs and consumer incomes. The mid- and late-1990s have witnessed a revival of government regulatory activism in many areas of consumer protection.

Goals of Consumer Laws

Figure 1 lists some of the safeguards provided by **consumer protection laws.** Taken together, these safeguards reflect three goals of government policymakers and regulators.

First, some laws are intended to provide consumers with better information when making purchases. Consumers can make more rational choices when they have accurate information about the product, thereby making comparison with competing products easier. For example, the Truth in Lending Act requires lenders to inform borrowers of the annual rate of interest to be charged, plus related fees and service charges. The laws requiring health warnings on cigarettes and alcoholic beverages broaden the information consumers have about these items. Knowing the relative energy efficiency of household appliances, which must be posted by retailers, permits improved choices. Manufacturers, retailers, and importers must specify whether warranties (guarantees or assurances by the seller) are full or limited, must spell them out in clear language, and must give consumers the right to sue if warranties are not honored.

Deceptive advertising is illegal. Manufacturers may not make false or misleading claims about their own product or a competitor's product.

A 1993 law requires food manufacturers to adopt a uniform nutrition label, specifying the amount of calories, fat, salt, and other nutrients contained in packaged, canned, and bottled foods. The same kind of information about fresh fruits and vegetables, as well as fish, must be posted in supermarkets.

A second aim of consumer legislation is to protect consumers against possible hazards from products they may purchase. Required warnings about possible side effects of pharmaceutical drugs, limits placed on flammable fabrics, the banning of lead-based paints, and inspections to eliminate contaminated or spoiled meats are examples of these safeguards. In 1997, following several outbreaks of bacterial poisoning, President Clinton proposed new rules designed to reduce the risk of food-borne illness. One incident of bacterial contamination in food, involving fresh fruit juice made by Odwalla, Inc., is described in a case study entitled "Odwalla, Inc., and the E. Coli Outbreak."

---

[8]Further information about Public Citizen is available at http://www.citizen.org.

Post–Lawrence–Weber:
Business and Society,
Ninth Edition

Consumer Protection

© The McGraw–Hill
Companies, 1999

Figure 1

Major consumer
protections specified
by consumer laws.

Information protections

Hazardous home appliances must carry a warning label.

Home products must carry a label detailing contents.

Automobiles must carry a label showing detailed breakdown of price and all related costs.

Credit loans require lender to disclose all relevant credit information about rate of interest, penalties, and so forth.

Tobacco advertisements and products must carry a health warning label.

Alcoholic beverages must carry a health warning label.

All costs related to real estate transactions must be disclosed.

Warranties must specify the terms of the guarantee and the buyer's rights.

False and deceptive advertising can be prohibited.

Food and beverage labels must show complete information.

Food advertising must not make false claims about nutrition.

Direct hazard protections

Hazardous toys and games for children are banned from sale.

Safety standards for motor vehicles are required.

National and state speed limits are specified.

Hazardous, defective, and ineffective products can be recalled under pressure from FPA, CPSC, NHTSA, and FDA.

Pesticide residue in food is allowed only if it poses a negligible risk.

Pricing protections

Unfair pricing, monopolistic practices, and noncompetitive acts are regulated by FTC and Justice Department and by states.

Liability protections

When injured by a product, consumers can seek legal redress.

Other protections

No discrimination in the extension of credit.

Congress has also recently addressed the problem of pesticide and herbicide residues left on farm products. Some of these chemicals cause nerve damage if consumed in large quantities; others have produced cancers in test animals. Children are thought to be especially at risk. In 1996, Congress repealed the 1958 Delaney Clause, which had banned all food additives known to cause cancer, and replaced it with a single standard for fresh and processed food. The new standard allowed pesticide residue in food only if it posed a negligible risk, except for some stronger provisions designed to protect children. The goal of the new law was to protect the public's health without causing unnecessary harm to agricultural producers.

A third goal of consumer laws is to encourage competitive pricing. When competitors secretly agree to divide markets among themselves, to rig bidding so that it appears to be competitive, or to fix prices of goods and services at a noncompetitive, artificially high level, they are taking unfair advantage of consumers. Both federal and state laws forbid these practices. Competitive pricing also was promoted by the deregulation of rail-

Post–Lawrence–Weber:
Business and Society,
Ninth Edition

Consumer Protection

© The McGraw–Hill
Companies, 1999

roads, airlines, intercity bus lines, trucking, telephones, and various financial institutions in the 1970s and 1980s. Prior to deregulation, government agencies frequently held prices artificially high and, by limiting the number of new competitors, shielded existing businesses from competition.

Major Consumer Protection Agencies

Figure 2 depicts the principal consumer protection agencies that operate at the federal level, along with their major areas of responsibility. The oldest of the six is the Food and Drug Administration, which, along with the Department of Agriculture's meat and poultry inspection programs, dates back to the first decade of the twentieth century. The Federal Trade Commission was established in 1914 and has been given additional powers to protect consumers over the years. Three of the agencies—the Consumer Product Safety Commission, the National Highway Traffic Safety Administration, and the National Transportation Safety Board—were created during the great wave of consumer regulations in the 1960s and early 1970s. Not listed in Figure 2 is the Antitrust Division of the Department of Justice, which indirectly protects consumers by policing monopolistic and anticompetitive practices of business firms.

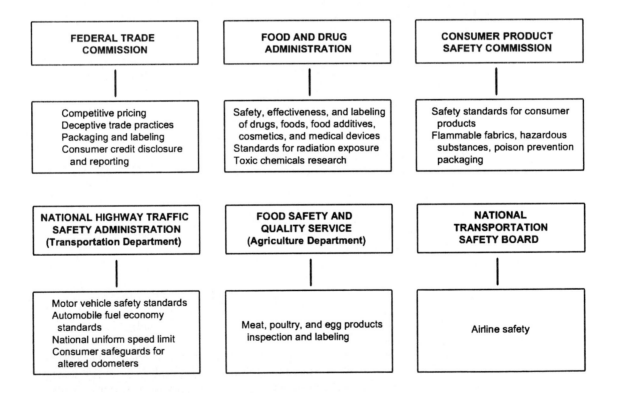

Figure 2

Major federal consumer protection agencies and their main responsibilities.

Post–Lawrence–Weber:
Business and Society,
Ninth Edition

Consumer Protection

© The McGraw–Hill
Companies, 1999

A recent controversy surrounding rule-making by the National Highway Traffic Safety Administration, concerning air bags, is profiled in Exhibit A.

Of these agencies, the one with perhaps the greatest impact on the business community is the Food and Drug Administration. The FDA's mission is to assure the safety and effectiveness of a wide range of consumer products, including pharmaceutical drugs, medical devices, foods, and cosmetics. The agency has authority over $960 billion worth of products, about a quarter of all consumer dollars spent each year.

EXHIBIT A   Air Bags: Do They Help or Hurt Safety?

Should consumers have the right to refuse to use safety equipment mandated by the government? Should the government mandate equipment that, while helping many, might hurt a few? Should manufacturers and dealers be held responsible if a consumer did not use safety equipment provided? These questions were raised in connection with automobile air bags.

An air bag is a safety device that works by inflating rapidly during a collision, preventing the occupant from moving forward and striking the steering wheel, dashboard, or other hard object. In 1995, the National Highway Traffic Safety Administration (NHTSA) required automatic seat belts or driver-side air bags in most cars sold in the United States and driver *and* passenger-side air bags were required as standard equipment on most cars by 1998.

But in 1996, concern emerged about possible hazards of the air bags themselves to children and small adults. Although air bags were believed to have saved more than 1,750 lives since their introduction in 1986, they had also apparently killed 52 people, over half of them children, when they deployed forcefully and struck passengers. Many of those killed or injured had not been wearing seat belts, or had not been properly belted, and had been thrown toward the dashboard in emergency braking. As news of these deaths spread, some consumers complained to the safety agency, and some even tried to disable their own air bags.

In 1997, the NHTSA announced new rules. Beginning with the following model year, automakers could offer less powerful bags as an option. Eventually, the government said it would require so-called smart air bags that would adjust the force of deployment according to the weight of the occupant. The government also proposed that consumers be allowed to request that their dealer or mechanic disconnect their vehicle's air bags.

The response of auto dealers and manufacturers was mixed. Some dealers were worried about shutting off air bags at the customer's request. "What if a dealer disables an air bag [and] the owner drives out of the lot and gets into an accident?" asked a representative of the National Automobile Dealers Association. Manufacturers were also worried about liability, but they also saw the new rules as a way to alleviate customers' concerns about possible air bag hazards.

Sources: "New Government Rule Seeks to Stem Danger from Air Bags," *New York Times,* March 15, 1997, p. A11; "U.S. to Propose Air Bag Rule Changes Today to Protect Children, Small Adults," *The Wall Street Journal,* December 30, 1996, p. A14; and the National Highway Traffic Safety Administration, http://www.nhtsa.dot.gov/cars/rules/rulings. In November 1997, the government announced that, effective immediately, consumers would be allowed to install switches to disable passenger-side air bags, if they could demonstrate a good reason, such as the need to place a small child in the front seat.

Post–Lawrence–Weber:
Business and Society,
Ninth Edition

Consumer Protection

© The McGraw–Hill
Companies, 1999

One of the FDA's jobs is to review many new products prior to their introduction. This job requires regulators to walk a thin line as they attempt to protect consumers. Two types of regulatory errors may occur. On one hand, the agency must not approve products that do not work or are harmful, as illustrated by the example of fen-phen at the beginning of this chapter. On the other hand, the agency must also not delay beneficial new products unnecessarily, as shown by the following example.

> *The Sensor Pad is a simple $7 medical device, consisting of two sealed plastic sheets separated by a layer of lubricant, designed to help women conduct monthly breast self-exams. Many doctors praised the product, and its developer was honored as a finalist in an inventor-of-the-year contest. The Sensor Pad product was readily approved in Canada and many European and Asian countries. But its manufacturer in Decatur, Illinois, Inventive Products, Inc., fought unsuccessfully for almost a decade to win FDA approval. Regulators expressed concern that the device would give women a false sense of security, and they demanded that the company conduct exhaustive clinical trials comparing the number of cancers detected with and without use of the Sensor Pad. In 1994, Inventive Products' president laid off all the company's workers except two and stated, "We're at the point of surrender."[9]*

The FDA has been criticized both for overly zealous regulation and for lax oversight of consumer safety. In the early 1990s, the agency undertook a major internal reorganization aimed at better serving the public and easing the regulatory burden on business.[10]

All six government regulatory agencies shown in Figure 2 are authorized by law to intervene directly into the very center of free market activities if that is considered necessary to protect consumers. In other words, consumer protection laws and agencies substitute government-mandated standards and the decisions of government officials for decision making by private buyers and sellers.

The Social Dimension of Advertising

One issue long of concern to both consumer activists and government regulators is the social dimension of advertising. Commercial advertisements, whether on billboards or television, in magazines or newspapers, or in newer media such as on-line services, do more than simply attempt to sell products. Many advertisements carry strong, sometimes controversial social messages as well. Advertising's social influence is seen in the pictures and images of people depicted in ads, in the health claims made for some products, and in the promotion of alcohol and tobacco products—particularly to young people.

Advertising Images

It is natural for all groups in society to want to be fairly and accurately represented in advertisements. Advertising images, because they are sent out to so many viewers, have the

[9]"How a Device to Aid in Breast Self-Exams Is Kept off the Market," *The Wall Street Journal,* April 12, 1994, pp. A1, A5.
[10]"Getting the Lead out at the FDA," *Business Week,* October 25, 1993, pp. 96–98; and "Inside FDA: Building New Consensus to Improve Public Safety," *Washington Post,* July 15, 1993, p. A25.

Post–Lawrence–Weber:
Business and Society,
Ninth Edition

Consumer Protection

© The McGraw–Hill
Companies, 1999

potential to influence the way people think about other people, as well as about the product or service being advertised. Some advertisers have learned this lesson the hard way, as shown in the following illustration.

> *Many people were offended when a county police officers' association in Virginia ran an advertisement promoting its annual dinner-dance in a local newspaper. The drawing used in the ad appeared to portray a white couple dancing, a black bellhop, and a dark-skinned waiter. An organization of black police officers demanded an apology, saying that the ads depicted African-Americans in stereotyped, demeaning roles. "It was really offensive as soon as I saw the faces," commented one African-American captain in the department. The police chief apologized, and said that "In today's society, we need to be more aware of issues like this that can be perceived as insensitive."[11]*

Another controversy over the depiction of groups in the media, concerning the use of sexual images of young people in advertising by the designer Calvin Klein, is profiled in Exhibit B.

Health-Related Claims

Even more serious impacts can occur when companies make excessive health claims for their products.

The Food and Drug Administration pressured U.S. drug firms to stop promoting aspirin as an aid in reducing the risk of a first heart attack. The companies' claims were based on a scientific study that said taking an aspirin every other day had lowered the risk of heart attacks in middle-aged men. The FDA said that the study's findings were preliminary, were restricted to the test group, and could not be recommended for the general population. After meeting with FDA officials, the companies voluntarily stopped their advertising claims.

Five of the country's largest commercial diet programs, including Weight Watchers International, Nutri/System, and Jenny Craig, were sued by the Federal Trade Commission for making unsubstantiated promises of weight loss. The agency wanted the diet programs to back up their advertising claims and to warn consumers that weight loss was often temporary. A FTC representative stated, "The bottom line is that losing weight is hard work—and keeping it off is harder still. . . . Consumers who buy into these programs need to understand that all too often, promises of long-term weight loss raise false hopes of an easy fix for a difficult problem."[12]

Food manufacturers must also be careful not to make exaggerated claims for their products. Under new food-labeling rules, companies must follow strict guidelines when using words such as *healthy, light,* or *low-fat* to describe their products. For example, the FDA ruled that Tang, an orange-flavored drink, could not be called healthy because it did not restore nutrients that were originally in fresh oranges. Since 1994, food advertisers have been required to follow these guidelines.[13]

[11]"Blacks' Portrayal in Police Union Ad Draws Complaints," *Washington Post,* February 27, 1996, p. B1.
[12]"Five Diet Firms Charged with Deceptive Ads," *Los Angeles Times,* October 1, 1993, pp. A1, A15.
[13]"U.S. Issues Rules for Labeling Food 'Healthy,'" *New York Times,* May 5, 1994, p. B8; and "FTC to Require Food Ads to Follow FDA Label Guides," *The Wall Street Journal,* May 16, 1994, p. A6.

Post–Lawrence–Weber:
Business and Society,
Ninth Edition

Consumer Protection

© The McGraw–Hill
Companies, 1999

EXHIBIT B   Calvin Klein's "Pornographic" Ads

During the summer of 1995, Calvin Klein, the clothing designer, unveiled a new advertising campaign for CK jeans. A series of print advertisements, bus posters, billboards, and TV spots featured adolescent-looking models in a variety of provocative poses, many with their underwear casually exposed.

In one of the most notorious television spots, a young man was shown leaning against a dingy paneled wall as an off-camera male voice talked to him. "You got a real nice look," the gravelly voice said. "How old are you? Are you strong? You think you could rip that shirt off you? That's a real nice body. You work out? I can tell."

The ad campaign, which was produced by the company's in-house CRK Advertising, generated a storm of protest. Commentators denounced the ads as just a step short of child pornography. The conservative American Family Association threatened a boycott of stores selling the jeans and called for a government investigation. Some magazines, including *Seventeen,* refused to carry the ads. Even President Clinton weighed in with critical remarks.

At the end of August, after the campaign had run for only a few weeks, Klein withdrew the ads voluntarily. He refused to apologize, however, defending the ads as a tribute to the "spirit, independence, and inner worth of today's young people."

The brief ad campaign and flurry of negative publicity that followed had the combined effect of powerfully boosting sales of CK jeans to young people. In September, the editor of *Fashion Network Report* noted that the jeans were "flying out of the stores" and called Klein a "marketing genius" who had cleverly timed the controversy to coincide with the back-to-school buying period.

In response to public protest, the Justice Department launched an investigation. Two months later, however, government regulators backed off after determining that the company had not used underage models or in any other way violated child pornography laws.

In 1997, Calvin Klein changed course, introducing a new ad campaign for perfume showing a wholesome family relaxing at the beach. The company's ad agency described the spots as showing "the eternal love between parents and child." The very conservatism of the new campaign, ironically, prompted some to attack the company for hypocrisy. Once again, Calvin Klein's ads had generated their own publicity.

Source: "Calvin Klein Finds Family Values," *Boston Globe,* February 28, 1997, p. C2; "Calvin Klein Ads Cleared," *Washington Post,* November 16, 1995, p. D7; and "Where Calvin Crossed the Line," *Time,* September 1, 1995, p. 64.

Curbing Alcohol and Tobacco Promotions

Alcoholic beverages and tobacco carry health risks, not just for users but for others as well. For that reason, when liquor and tobacco companies advertise their products, they are having an impact on public health that goes beyond a company's goal of persuading smokers and drinkers to use a particular brand.

Awareness of this public health problem is widespread. Some activists have been particularly concerned with beer ads that are apparently designed to attract young drinkers

Post–Lawrence–Weber:
Business and Society,
Ninth Edition

Consumer Protection

© The McGraw-Hill
Companies, 1999

by featuring popular rock stars or clever cartoon frogs and lizards. A group called Center for Media Education attacked liquor companies for developing slick Web sites to "find and woo the younger generations . . . in the open fields of cyberspace." A survey commissioned by *The Wall Street Journal* found that almost half of U.S. consumers favor banning all television ads for beer and wine.[14]

Cigarette advertising is increasingly restricted, in the United States and other nations. In 1997, cigarette manufacturers negotiated an agreement with a group of state attorneys general and public health officials that would, among other things, ban most cigarette advertising in the United States, including the use of cartoon characters such as Joe Camel to promote tobacco products. (This historic agreement is discussed in more detail in a case study at the end of the textbook.) Several other nations, including Italy, Portugal, Norway, Sweden, Canada, Singapore, China, and Thailand, have already banished tobacco ads from television and the print media. Even the Moscow city council passed a resolution barring most cigarette promotions.[15]

In all of these ways, consumers and their government representatives were sending strong signals to the manufacturers and their advertising agencies that alcohol and tobacco promotions should be strictly curbed. It is another example, among many mentioned in this book, that firms operate within a web of social values and social attitudes that can have a vital impact on how they should conduct business.

Product Liability: A Special Problem

In today's economy, consumers' relationships with products they use and their relationships with producers of those products are complicated and abstract. The burden of responsibility for product performance has been shifted to the producer, under the legal doctrine of **product liability**. Although many businesses have attempted to assume much of the responsibility through money-back guarantees and other similar policies, consumers have thought that this is not enough and have demanded that business assume a larger burden of responsibility. The result has been a strengthening of product liability laws and more favorable court attitudes toward consumer claims. Walls protecting producers from consumer lawsuits have crumbled, and there has been a dramatic increase in product liability suits. These trends have led many business groups to call for reforms of the nation's product liability laws.

Strict Liability

Within the last few years courts have increasingly taken the position that manufacturers are responsible for injuries resulting from use of their products. One result has been a rapid rise in the number of product liability lawsuits—from about 12,437 in 1992 to 27,584 in 1996 in the federal courts.[16] Eighty-three percent of executives in a recent poll felt that their decisions were increasingly affected by the fear of lawsuits, and 62 percent said the

[14]"Besieged on Most Fronts, Tobacco Companies and Booze Makers Are Setting Their Sites on the Web, Where They're Running up against–What Else? More Opposition," *Entertainment Weekly,* April 25, 1997, p. 75. For the survey data, see "Rebelling against Alcohol, Tobacco Ads," *The Wall Street Journal,* January 14, 1989, pp. B1, B11.

[15]For regulations in other countries, see "A Red Flag in Moscow on Tobacco and Liquor Ads," *New York Times,* July 20, 1993, p. C1.

[16]John Gibeaut, "At the Crossroads," *American Bar Association Journal,* March, 1998.

Post–Lawrence–Weber:
Business and Society,
Ninth Edition

Consumer Protection

© The McGraw–Hill
Companies, 1999

civil justice system significantly hampered the ability of U.S. firms to compete with Japanese and European companies.[17] Small companies are especially vulnerable to lawsuits and may be driven out of business by sky-high liability insurance rates.

Under existing court interpretations, it is not necessary for consumers to prove either negligence or breach of warranty by the producer. Nor is the consumer's own negligence an acceptable defense by the manufacturer. If a product is judged to be inherently dangerous, manufacturers can be held liable for injuries caused by use of the product. This doctrine, known as **strict liability,** extends to all who were involved in the final product—suppliers, sellers, contractors, assemblers, and manufacturers of component parts. The following case illustrates the extent to which businesses can be held liable.

> *In 1994, an 81-year-old woman was awarded $2.9 million by a jury in Albuquerque, New Mexico, for burns suffered when she spilled a cup of hot coffee in her lap. The woman, who had purchased the coffee at a McDonald's drive-through window, was burned when she tried to open the lid as she sat in her car. In court, McDonald's argued that customers like their coffee steaming, that their cups warned drinkers that the contents are hot, and that the woman was to blame for spilling the coffee herself. But jurors disagreed, apparently swayed by arguments that the woman's burns were severe—requiring skin grafts and a seven-day hospital stay—and by evidence that McDonald's had not cooled down its coffee even after receiving many earlier complaints. McDonald's appealed the jury's verdict and later settled the case with the elderly woman for an undisclosed amount.[18]*

In this case, McDonald's was held liable for damages even though it provided a warning and the customer's actions contributed to her burns.

Business Efforts to Reform Product Liability Laws

Many businesses have argued that the evolution of strict liability has unfairly burdened them with excess costs. Liability insurance rates have gone up significantly, as have the costs of defending against liability lawsuits and paying large settlements to injured parties.

Businesses have also argued that concerns about liability exposure sometimes slow research and innovation. For example, many pharmaceutical companies halted work on new contraceptive methods because of the risk of being sued. Despite the need for new contraceptives that would be more effective and also provide protection against viral diseases, such as herpes and AIDS, research had virtually come to a halt by the late 1990s, according to some public health groups.[19]

Faced with increasing liability suits and the costs of insuring against them, business has lobbied for changes in laws and court proceedings. In the 1980s and 1990s, bills were

---

[17]"Guilty! Too Many Lawyers and Too Much Litigation: Here's a Better Way," *Business Week,* April 13, 1992, p. 66.

[18]"How a Jury Decided that a Coffee Spill Is Worth $2.9 Million," *The Wall Street Journal,* September 1, 1994, pp. A1, A5; and "McDonald's Settles Lawsuit over Burn from Coffee," *The Wall Street Journal,* December 2, 1994, p. A14.

[19]"Birth Control: Scared to a Standstill," *Business Week,* June 16, 1997, pp. 142–44; and "Fears, Suits, and Regulations Stall Contraceptive Advances," *New York Times,* December 27, 1995, pp. A1, A9.

Post–Lawrence–Weber:
Business and Society,
Ninth Edition

Consumer Protection

© The McGraw–Hill
Companies, 1999

introduced in Congress that would establish the following principles in product liability suits:

- *Set up uniform federal standards for determining liability.* Companies would not have to go through repeated trials on the same charges in many different states, which would lower legal costs for companies and help them develop a uniform legal strategy for confronting liability charges in court.

- *Shift the burden of proving liability to consumers.* Consumers would have to prove that a manufacturer knew or should have known that a product design was defective before it began producing the item. Under present law and judicial interpretations, a company is considered to be at fault if a product injures the user, whether or not the company was negligent.

- *Eliminate some bases for liability claims.* Products not measuring up to a manufacturer's own specifications—for example, poorly made tires that blow out at normal speeds—could be the basis for a liability claim, but the vast majority of liability cases go further and blame poorly designed products or a failure of the manufacturer to warn of dangers.

- *Require the loser to pay the legal costs of the winner.* If a plaintiff (consumer) refused an out-of-court settlement offer from the company and then received less in trial, he or she would have to pay the company's legal fees, up to the amount of his or her own fees. This would discourage many plaintiffs from proceeding to trial.

- *Limit punitive damages.* Punitive damages punish the manufacturer for wrongdoing rather than compensate the victim for actual losses. Punitive damage awards over the past 25 years have averaged $625,000, and some awards in recent years—like the one in the Remington case, mentioned at the beginning of this chapter—have been for multimillions of dollars.[20] One proposal would limit punitive damages to $250,000 or three times compensatory damages, whichever was greater.

In 1997, Congress once again took up the issue of product liability law reform. Although supported by many business groups, including the Business Roundtable and the National Association of Manufacturers, these reform proposals faced vigorous opposition from consumers' organizations and from the American Trial Lawyers Association, representing plaintiffs' attorneys. These groups defended the existing product liability system, saying that it put needed pressure on companies to make and keep products safe.[21]

One alternative to product liability lawsuits is described in Exhibit C.

Positive Business Responses to Consumerism

The consumer movement has demonstrated to businesses that they must perform at high levels of efficiency, reliability, and fairness to satisfy the consuming public. Because firms have not always responded quickly or fully enough, consumer advo-

---

[20] "Product Suits Yield Few Punitive Awards," *The Wall Street Journal,* January 6, 1992, p. B1.
[21] For a discussion of the consumer viewpoint on product liability reform, see Peter Nye, "The Faces of Product Liability: Keeping the Courthouse Door Open," *Public Citizen,* November–December 1992, pp. 16–21.

Post–Lawrence–Weber:
Business and Society,
Ninth Edition

Consumer Protection

© The McGraw–Hill
Companies, 1999

EXHIBIT C An Alternative to Product Liability Lawsuits

Product liability lawsuits cost businesses and consumers a lot of money, and many cases are held up for years in backlogged courts. Often, large proportions of any settlement go to attorneys rather than to the people who were injured by defective products. Businesses are unable to predict the extent of their liability exposure. Is there a better way to resolve disputes between businesses and consumers?

Some people think that alternative dispute resolution (ADR) may be an answer. In ADR, a professional mediator works with both sides to negotiate a settlement outside the traditional court system. Generally, if the negotiation fails, the parties can still proceed to trial. The nonprofit American Arbitration Association has developed a panel of experts skilled in resolving liability claims. Several for-profit organizations, such as JAMS/Endispute of Irvine, California, also provide ADR services.

Supporters of ADR say it saves money that would be spent on lawyers' fees, so more can go to plaintiffs in a settlement. Cases can be resolved quickly, rather than waiting for an opening on a busy judge's calendar. Critics, however, worry that ADR deprives plaintiffs of their day in court, and injured consumers may get less than if their cases were heard before a jury.

Eventually, ADR may be widely used to settle individual complaints brought under mass torts, such as those involving injuries from asbestos, tobacco, or defective medical devices. In this situation, a court would set up a procedure and a set of rules by which individuals could negotiate a settlement tailored to the facts of their own case. Some businesses feel that such a process would enable them to better predict, and budget for, future liabilities.

Source: John Gibeaut, "At the Crossroads," *American Bar Association Journal*, March 1998.

---

cates and their organizations have turned to government for protection. On the other hand, much effort has been devoted by individual business firms and by entire industries to encourage voluntary responses to consumer demands. Some of the more prominent positive responses are discussed next.

Total Quality Management

In the 1980s and 1990s, many businesses adopted a philosophy of management known as **total quality management (TQM).** This approach, which borrows from Japanese management techniques, emphasizes achieving high quality and customer satisfaction through teamwork and continuous improvement of a company's product or service. TQM businesses seek to "delight the customer," as shown in the following example.

> *At the Saturn plant in Spring Hill, Tennessee, TQM methods have been used to produce a car of superior quality. Joint labor–management teams designed the car from the start to compete head-on with popular Japanese imports. Workers can stop the assembly line if they see a defect. Saturn keeps in close contact with car buyers, so it can correct any problems that crop up. The result has*

Post–Lawrence–Weber:
Business and Society,
Ninth Edition

Consumer Protection

© The McGraw–Hill
Companies, 1999

been a vehicle that has been extremely popular with customers. In 1997, Saturn topped all other cars, foreign and domestic, in the J. D. Power survey of customer satisfaction.[22]

Total quality management is a response to pressure from consumer activists and an attempt by business to address its customers' needs. It is an example of interactive strategy, where by companies try to anticipate and respond to emerging stakeholder expectations. One of the primary changes created by the TQM movement has been for companies to focus on the customer. This occurs in many different ways.

Consumer Affairs Departments

Many large corporations operate consumer affairs departments, often placing a vice president in charge. These centralized departments normally handle consumer inquiries and complaints about a company's products and services, particularly in cases where a customer has not been able to resolve differences with local retailers. Some companies have installed **consumer hot lines** for dissatisfied customers to place telephone calls directly to the manufacturer.

One of the largest hot lines, General Electric's Answer Center, fields three and a half million questions a year on thousands of products. One technician diagnosed a mysterious refrigerator noise by asking the customer to hold the phone to up to the appliance. Another advised a frantic caller on how to extract a pet iguana from the dishwasher. "This isn't a job for the faint of heart," said one consultant who works with company consumer hot lines.[23]

Many companies now communicate with their customers and other interested persons through Web sites on the Internet. Eighty percent of the 500 biggest companies had Web sites by 1997, according to one survey. Some sites are interactive, allowing customers to post comments or questions that are answered via e-mail by customer relations staff.[24]

Experienced companies are aware that consumer complaints and concerns can be handled more quickly, at lower cost, and with less risk of losing goodwill by a consumer affairs department than if customers take a legal route or if their complaints receive widespread media publicity.

Arbitration

In the 1990s, the use of **arbitration** to handle consumer complaints became much more common. Many companies, especially in the health care and financial services industries, required customers to bring disputes before a private arbitrator rather than sue the company. An arbitrator, a neutral person not related to either party, would make a final decision resolving the dispute.

---

[22] Barry Bluestone and Irving Bluestone, "Reviving American Industry: A Labor–Management Partnership," *Current*, May 1993, pp. 10–16; and "German Cars Follow Saturn in Buyer Satisfaction Ratings," *Seattle Times*, June 7, 1997, p. D1.

[23] "What's This? Confused or Curious, Consumers Know Where to Call," *Newsday*, October 18, 1995, p. B37.

[24] "Simplest E-Mail Queries Confound Companies," *The Wall Street Journal*, October 21, 1996, pp. B1, B9.

Post–Lawrence–Weber:
Business and Society,
Ninth Edition

Consumer Protection

© The McGraw–Hill
Companies, 1999

Many businesses favored arbitration because it tended to reduce their legal costs and the risk of big jury awards. Some consumers favored the process as well, because their complaints could often be resolved more quickly and cheaply. But some advocates were wary of any action by firms that unilaterally took away customers' rights to sue if they were injured or mistreated.[25]

Product Recalls

Companies also deal with consumer dissatisfaction by recalling faulty products. A **product recall** occurs when a company, either voluntarily or under an agreement with a government agency, takes back all items found to be dangerously defective. Sometimes these products are in the hands of consumers; at other times they may be in the factory, in wholesale warehouses, or on the shelves of retail stores. Wherever they are in the chain of distribution or use, the manufacturer tries to notify consumers or potential users about the defect so that they will return the items. A recalled product may be repaired, replaced, or destroyed, depending on the problem.

> In 1997, Shimano American Corp., in cooperation with the Consumer Product Safety Commission, announced it would voluntarily recall more than one million cranks installed on bicycles, after it had received numerous complaints that the cranks had broken, injuring riders. (The crank connects the pedal to the front gear.) Shimano offered to have all defective cranks replaced, for free, at authorized repair shops.[26]

The four major government agencies responsible for most mandatory recalls are the Food and Drug Administration, the National Highway Traffic Safety Administration, the Environmental Protection Agency (which can recall polluting motor vehicles), and the Consumer Product Safety Commission.

Consumerism's Achievements

After 35 years of the consumer movement, its leaders could point to some important gains for U.S. consumers. Consumers today are better informed about the goods and services they purchase, more aware of their rights when something goes wrong, and better protected against inflated advertising claims, hazardous or ineffective products, and unfair pricing. Several consumer organizations serve as watchdogs of buyers' interests, and a network of federal and state regulatory agencies acts for the consuming public.

Some businesses, too, have heard the consumer message and reacted positively. They have learned to assign high priority to the things consumers expect: high-quality goods and services, reliable and effective products, safety in the items they buy, fair prices, and marketing practices, such as advertising, that do not threaten important human and social values.

All of these achievements, in spite of negative episodes that occasionally occur, have brought the U.S. consuming public closer to realizing John F. Kennedy's four consumer rights: to be safe, to be informed, to have choices, and to be heard.

[25]"In Fine Print, Customers Lose Ability to Sue; Arbitrators, Not Courts, Rule on Complaints," *New York Times,* March 10, 1997, pp. A1, C7.
[26]"Product Recalls: Kid's Clothing, Bike Parts, and Fans Pulling a Fast One," *Newsday,* July 16, 1997, p. A47.

Post-Lawrence-Weber:
Business and Society,
Ninth Edition

Consumer Protection

© The McGraw-Hill
Companies, 1999

Summary Points

- The U.S. consumer movement that began in the 1960s represents an attempt to promote the interests of consumers by balancing the amount of market power held by sellers and buyers.

- The four key consumer rights are the rights to safety, to be informed, to choose, and to be heard. Recent discussion has focused on consumers' right to privacy.

- Consumer protection laws and regulatory agencies attempt to assure that consumers are treated fairly, receive adequate information, are protected against potential hazards, have free choices in the market, and have legal recourse when problems develop.

- The general public's growing awareness of the ability of advertising to exert widespread social influence brought new demands for business to be socially responsible in serving consumers.

- Business has complained about the rising number of product liability lawsuits and the high cost of insuring against them. But efforts to reform product liability laws have been opposed by consumer groups and lawyers representing people injured by dangerous or defective products.

- Socially responsible companies have responded to the consumer movement by giving serious consideration to consumer problems, increasing channels of communication with customers, instituting arbitration procedures to resolve complaints, and recalling defective products. They have also pursued total quality management in an effort to meet, and even anticipate, consumers' needs.

Key Terms and Concepts

- Consumer movement
- Consumer bill of rights
- Consumer protection laws
- Deceptive advertising
- Product liability

- Strict liability
- Total quality management (TQM)
- Consumer hot lines
- Arbitration
- Product recalls

Internet Resources

- http://www.cpsc.gov   U.S. Consumer Product Safety Commission
- http://www.ftc.gov   U.S. Federal Trade Commission
- http://www.igc.apc.org:80/cbbb   Better Business Bureau

Post–Lawrence–Weber:
Business and Society,
Ninth Edition

Consumer Protection

© The McGraw–Hill
Companies, 1999

Discussion Case ## Consumer Privacy in the Information Age

In 1996, Netscape, maker of the widely used Navigator Web browser, generated a storm of controversy over a new technology somewhat whimsically called a *cookie*.

The new release of Netscape's browser was designed so that the software would automatically record which Web sites the user visited and which Web pages had been accessed at each site. This information would then be stored on the user's own computer in a site called a cookie. The user, in many cases, would not even be aware that the cookie had been created.

The problem, from the standpoint of privacy, was that the cookie could be accessed and read by each subsequent Web site visited by the user, without the user's consent. Netscape's software was designed to permit the Web site to learn only about previous visits to that specific site, not other sites the user might have visited. However, the technology could potentially be modified to permit the Web site to read the entire cookie.

Many commercial Web sites welcomed the cookie technology as a valuable way to learn more about the characteristics and preferences of their customers. For example, an operator of cruise lines would be able to learn that most visitors to its site were interested in Caribbean vacations, prompting it to develop more detailed coverage of this subject.

Users were concerned, however, that access to their cookies represented an unauthorized use of personal information and a violation of their privacy. Businesses in turn worried that concerned customers were less likely to use the Internet and to shop there. In response to numerous complaints, Netscape announced that subsequent versions of the software would give users the option of enabling or disabling cookies.

The controversy over Netscape's cookie software highlighted the broader issue of consumer privacy in the information age. New technologies made collection of data about consumer behavior, often without the consumer's knowledge or consent, increasingly possible. Not only could data be collected from a Web user's cookie, but stores, banks, pharmacies, airlines and other businesses often had access to considerable information about consumers that could be collected, used, sold, or even stolen.

Research showed that consumers were increasingly concerned about the potential threat to their privacy in the information age. A 1995 Louis Harris poll, for example, reported that 82 percent of respondents were very concerned about their personal privacy, up from 64 percent in 1978. The dilemma over how best to protect consumer privacy while fostering legitimate Internet commerce generated a wide-ranging debate. Some consumer advocacy organizations and privacy activists favored new government regulations requiring that consumers be notified when information was collected, be allowed to opt out, and have access to their files and a means of correcting errors. Some even called for a new regulatory agency charged with protecting privacy.

Many Internet-related businesses, on the other hand, argued that they should be allowed to regulate themselves. In May 1997, a group of about 60 companies, including Netscape, proposed a new voluntary privacy scheme called an Open Profiling Standard (OPS). Under this system, users would store facts about themselves on a protected file on their own hard drive. When users visited a participating Web site, they would be able to determine what information, if any, the site could access.

Post-Lawrence-Weber:
Business and Society,
Ninth Edition

Consumer Protection

© The McGraw-Hill
Companies, 1999

Evolving technologies also gave Web surfers new ways to protect themselves. Software like the Cookie Crusher helped manage cookies, and surfing through special intermediary sites provided user anonymity. "We have to develop mechanisms that allow consumers to control information about themselves," commented a representative of the Center for Democracy and Technology, a civil liberties group.

In June 1997, the Federal Trade Commission convened public hearings on Internet privacy issues. "Three things must exist for electronic commerce to prosper," commented the FTC commissioner. "Ease, ubiquity, and trust. Technology can take care of the first two. But how can consumers be sure that their transactions are secure and private? . . . The question we're grappling with is whether government has a role in creating that trust."

Sources: "Exposed Online," *U.S. News & World Report,* June 23, 1997, pp. 59 ff.; Andrew L. Shapiro, "Privacy for Sale: Peddling Data on the Internet," *The Nation,* June 23, 1997, pp. 11–16; "Making America Safe for Electronic Commerce," *New York Times Week in Review,* June 22, 1997, p. 4; "Fear of Prying," *Marketing Tools,* June, 1997, pp. 46 ff.; "Privacy Watch: Is Your Computer Spying on You?" *Consumer Reports,* May, 1997, p. 6; John Hagel III and Jeffrey F. Rayport, "The Coming Battle for Consumer Information," *Harvard Business Review,* January–February 1997, pp. 53 ff.; "They're Watching You Online," *Business Week,* November 11, 1996, p. 19; "How to Practice Safe Surfing," *Business Week,* September 9, 1996, p. 120.

Discussion Questions

1. In his consumer bill of rights, President Kennedy outlined four basic consumer rights. Do you believe consumers have an additional right to privacy? Why or why not?

2. In the case Netscape's cookie technology, do you believe Netscape acted in a socially responsible way? Identify all the stakeholders in this situation, and tell how each would answer this question.

3. Who do you believe should be mainly responsible for protecting consumer privacy on the Internet? Should it be the individual consumer, the companies that make Internet-related technology, the companies that gather or use information, or the consumer-protection agencies of government? Why do you think so?

Bibliography

Adler, Nancy, and Dafna N. Israeli, eds. *Competitive Frontiers: Women Managers in the Global Economy.* Cambridge, MA: Basil Blackwell, 1995.

Bloom, Paul, and Ruth Belk Smith, eds. *The Future of Consumerism.* Lexington, MA: Lexington Books, 1986.

Caplan, Lincoln. *Up Against the Law: Affirmative Action and the Supreme Court.* New York: Twentieth Century Fund Press, 1997.

Edley, Christopher F. *Not All Black and White: Affirmative Action, Race and American Values.* New York: Hill and Wang, 1996.

Fagenson, Ellen A., ed. *Women in Management: Trends, Issues, and Challenges in Management Diversity.* Newbury Park, CA: Sage, 1993.

Faludi, Susan. *Backlash: The Undeclared War against American Women.* New York: Doubleday, 1991.

Goldin, Claudia. *Understanding the Gender Gap: An Economic History of American Women.* New York: Oxford University Press, 1990.

Gray, Barbara. *Collaborating: Finding Common Ground for Multiparty Problems.* San Francisco: Jossey-Bass, 1989.

Post–Lawrence–Weber:
Business and Society,
Ninth Edition

Consumer Protection

© The McGraw–Hill
Companies, 1999

Gunderson, Martin; David J. Mayo; and Frank S. Rhame. *AIDS: Testing and Privacy.* Salt Lake City: University of Utah Press, 1989.

Gutek, Barbara A. *Sex and the Workplace: The Impact of Sexual Behavior and Harassment on Women, Men, and Organizations.* San Francisco: Jossey-Bass, 1985.

Herman, Edward S. *Corporate Control, Corporate Power.* Cambridge, England: Cambridge University Press, 1981.

Hochschild, Arlie. *The Second Shift: Working Parents and the Revolution at Home.* New York: Viking, 1989.

Kester, Carl W. *Japanese Takeovers: The Global Contest for Corporate Control.* Boston: Harvard Business School Press, 1991.

Kittrie, Nicholas N., *The War against Authority: From the Crisis of Legitimacy to a New Social Contract.* Baltimore, MD: Johns Hopkins University Press, 1995.

Kuenne, Robert E. *Economic Justice in American Society.* Princeton, NJ: Princeton University Press, 1993.

Linowes, David F. *Privacy in America: Is Your Private Life in the Public Eye?* Urbana, IL: University of Illinois Press, 1989.

Lorsch, Jay William. *Pawns or Potentates: The Reality of America's Corporate Boards.* Boston: Harvard Business School Press, 1989.

Mann, Jonathan M., and Daniel J. M. Tarantola, eds. *AIDS in World War II: Global Dimensions, Social Roots and Responses.* New York: Oxford University Press, 1996.

Matteo, Sherri, ed. *American Women in the Nineties.* Boston: Northeastern University Press, 1993.

Morrison, Ann M.; Randall P. White; and Ellen Van Velsor. *Breaking the Glass Ceiling: Can Women Reach the Top of America's Largest Corporations?* updated ed. Reading, MA: Addison-Wesley, 1992.

Powell, Gary N. *Women and Men in Management,* 2d ed. Newbury Park, CA: Sage Publications, 1993.

Puckett, Same B., and Alan R. Emery. *Managing AIDS in the Workplace.* Reading, MA: Addison-Wesley, 1988.

Rix, Sara E. *The American Woman 1990–91: A Status Report.* New York: Norton, 1990.

Singer, Merrill, ed. *The Political Economy of AIDS.* Amityville, NY: Baywood Publishers, 1998.

United Nations. *The World's Women, 1970–1990: Trends and Statistics.* New York: United Nations Publications, June 1991.

Post–Lawrence–Weber:
Business and Society,
Ninth Edition

The Community and the
Corporation

© The McGraw–Hill
Companies, 1999

The Community and the Corporation

When a business has a good relationship with its community, it can make an important difference in the quality of that community's life and in the successful operation of the company. Communities look to businesses for civic leadership and for help in coping with local problems, while firms expect to be treated in fair and supportive ways by the local community. Corporate restructuring can create special problems that require cooperation between business and community groups.

This topic focuses on these key questions and objectives:

- What critical links exist between the community and business?

- How do businesses respond to community problems and needs?

- What goals and objectives are achieved when businesses contribute to the community?

- How does volunteerism contribute to building strong relationships between businesses and communities?

- What are the community impacts of corporate restructuring, and what strategies do companies and communities use in responding?

- How are social partnerships between businesses and the communities used to address today's pressing social problems?

Post–Lawrence–Weber:
Business and Society,
Ninth Edition

The Community and the
Corporation

© The McGraw–Hill
Companies, 1999

The Walt Disney Company is one of America's leading entertainment corporations. Founded by Walt Disney, and best known for animated movies such as *Fantasia, The Little Mermaid,* and *The Lion King,* and characters such as Mickey Mouse and Donald Duck, Disney has also created the famous theme parks Disneyland and Disney World in the United States and international theme parks in France and Japan. The company has had unparalleled success integrating its movies, theme parks, and related products into a commercial colossus. Imagination, creativity, and dedicated people have enabled Disney to become a leader in the multibillion dollar entertainment industry.

Disney began planning a new generation of theme parks in the early 1990s. In November 1993, the company announced that it had purchased an option on a 3,000-acre tract of land in Haymarket, Virginia, on which it intended to build an American history theme park called Disney's America. The land, located in Prince William County about 35 miles southwest of Washington, DC, is near the Manassas National Battlefield Park, site of the battles of Bull Run, two of the Civil War's bloodiest battles. Plans called for building a theme park, as many as 2,281 homes, 1,340 hotel rooms, and about 1.96 million square feet of retail and commercial space.

Critics immediately argued that the thousands of visitors expected at such a theme park would overwhelm the ability of local communities to absorb and manage side effects. A group calling itself Protecting Prince William County was quickly formed to provide organized opposition to the Disney plan. But local and county officials, working with Disney staff, concluded that the negative effects were being exaggerated and would, in any event, be outweighed by benefits the region would reap, including 19,000 jobs and nearly $50 million in new tax revenues. Both the jobs and the tax revenues were seen as vital to the long-term well-being of the county's communities and residents.

For nearly a year, hearings were held by local, state, and federal government legislatures and agencies. Repeatedly, local opponents presented arguments against the project while Disney executives and local government officials tried to argue the benefits of the project. According to participants, Disney representatives were always cordial, evidenced a willingness to compromise, and sought to find win-win solutions to the concerns being raised. But opponents had no interest in compromise. A group of historians, including several famous Civil War experts, campaigned against the Disney project through an organization called Project Historic America. They argued that Disney's proposed virtual reality battles would trivialize and sanitize the true battles that had occurred at the site. The Piedmont Environmental Council, a coalition of 70 organizations and more than 5,000 families from northern Virginia, took a different approach: they sued Disney, alleging violations of state and federal environmental laws. Lobbying occurred at all levels of government, and it was estimated that hundreds of lawyers, lobbyists, and political advisers were employed on behalf of Disney, its opponents, and interested parties.

By 1995, Disney was forced to announce plans to drop the project. Its option on the land was about to expire, forcing it to either renew the option or buy the land outright. Either would be costly, and in the face of opposition generated since the announcement, it was unlikely that the company could complete the project by its intended completion date in 1998. In announcing the decision, John Cooke, chairman of Disney's America, said, "We are starting afresh and are reaching out to historians who have opposed us to make sure our portrayal of the American experience is responsible." Recognizing that his community would get neither jobs nor new tax revenues, Mayor Jack Kapp

Post-Lawrence-Weber:
Business and Society,
Ninth Edition

The Community and the
Corporation

© The McGraw-Hill
Companies, 1999

of Haymarket, Virginia, spoke more directly: "People around here are devastated. It's an economic blow to Prince William County. I feel like I've been to a funeral today."[1]

Disney's America illustrates some of the complex issues that can arise between a company and the community in which it operates. What did the company do wrong? Why didn't others see the benefits of the proposal as Mayor Kapp did? What could Disney have done differently? This material examines how companies try to integrate community and citizenship concerns with their financial goals and objectives. Although it is not always possible to do so, as Disney's America shows, businesses and communities can often do much together to create win-win solutions to common problems.

Community Relations

The **community** discussed here involves a company's area of local business influence. It includes many individual stakeholders, and may include more than one geographic or political community, for such boundaries do not necessarily follow economic and social impacts. A bank in a large metropolitan area, for example, has numerous stakeholders and may define its community as the central city and the towns and cities in which it does business. A local merchant's community may comprise several surrounding cities or towns. A multinational firm may have a separate community for each of the local areas it serves around the world. In all cases, both company and community have a mutual dependence that is significant in economic and social terms.

The involvement of business with the community is called **community relations.** Community relations today are quite different from those of 50 or 100 years ago. Advances in technology, especially information technology, population shifts in the United States and much of the industrialized world, and the globalization of business operations are putting great pressures on the business-community relationship. Community relationships in the United States and other countries are also entwined with cultural norms. Business decisions have become more complex, and the impact of those decisions has loomed larger in the life of communities. Keeping community ties alive, well, and relevant is a major task for today's businesses.

Many corporations have established community relations offices to coordinate community programs, manage donations of goods and services, work with local governments, and encourage employee volunteerism in nonprofit and civic groups.[2] Companies have increasingly become involved with local communities on diverse issues, including education reform, environmental risk management, local taxes, and improving the lives of the homeless. Their aims are to improve local conditions that produce or attract a workforce qualified to meet the company's needs and to build a positive relationship between the firm and important local groups. Community relations officers work closely with other corporate offices that link the corporation to the external world, such as the employee re-

[1] Based on articles in the *New York Times* and *The Wall Street Journal* appearing in 1993–1998. See especially Sallie Hofmeister, "Disney Vows to Seek Another Park Site," *New York Times,* September 30, 1994, p. A12; and Michael Janofsky, "Town 'Devastated' by Loss of Project," *New York Times,* September 30, 1994, p. A12.

[2] James E. Post and Jennifer J. Griffin, *The State of Corporate Public Affairs* (Washington, D.C.: The Foundation for Public Affairs, 1997). Trends in this area are discussed in James E. Post and the Foundation for Public Affairs, "The State of Corporate Public Affairs in the United States: Results of a National Survey," in J. Post, ed., *Research in Corporate Social Performance and Policy,* vol. 14 (Greenwich, CT: JAI Press, 1993), pp. 79–89; and Lee Burke, Jeanne Logsden, and David Vogel "Corporate Community Involvement in the San Francisco Bay Area," *California Management Review,* Spring 1986, pp. 121–41.

Post–Lawrence–Weber:
Business and Society,
Ninth Edition

The Community and the
Corporation

© The McGraw–Hill
Companies, 1999

lations, public relations, or public affairs offices. These links form important bridges between the corporation and community groups.[3]

Limited Resources Face Unlimited Community Needs

Every community has many social needs requiring far more resources than are available. Choices must be made and priorities established. In some instances, the community decides the priorities, but in other instances, business influences community priorities very directly. Further, in all cases, once management has decided to help serve a need, it still must decide how its resources can best be applied to that need. This means that any action management takes will result in some dissatisfaction from those who get no help and from those who do not get as much help as they want.

Figure 1 illustrates the variety of expectations that communities have of business. Each year, companies receive requests for artistic, educational, and charitable assistance serving both special groups and the community as a whole. A company may agree to sup-

Figure 1

What the community and business want from each other.

Requests Made by the Community to Business
- Assistance for less-advantaged people
- Support for air and water pollution control
- Support for artistic and cultural activities
- Employment and advancement of minorities and women
- Assistance in urban planning and development
- Support of local health-care programs
- Donation of equipment to local school system
- Support of local bond issues for public improvements
- Aid to community hospital drive
- Support of local program for recycling
- Executive leadership for United Way fund-raising campaign

Community Services Desired by Business
- A cultural and educational environment that supports a balanced quality of life for employees
- Adequate family recreational activities
- Public services, such as police and fire protection, and sewage, water, and electric services
- Taxes that are equitable and do not discriminate for or against business
- Acceptance of business participation in community affairs
- A fair and open public press
- An adequate transportation system to business and residential areas (e.g., suitable public transportation and well-maintained streets)
- Public officials, customers, and citizens who are fair and honest in their involvement with business
- Cooperative problem-solving approach to addressing community problems

---

[3] Boston College Center for Corporate Community Relations, "Profile of the Community Relations Profession," *Community Relations Letter,* (Chestnut Hill, MA: Boston College Center for Corporate Community Relations, March 1993).

Post–Lawrence–Weber:
Business and Society,
Ninth Edition

The Community and the
Corporation

© The McGraw–Hill
Companies, 1999

port some, but not all, of these requests, and its work with these groups will consume hundreds of days of employee time and thousands of dollars of company resources. Meanwhile, the company must still meet its business objective of serving customers competitively throughout the nation.

Community Involvement and Firm Size

Community involvement has become a part of most business lifestyles. Studies show that both large and small businesses, whether they are local firms or branches of national firms, tend to be active in community affairs.[4] Business leaders bring knowledge and ability to civic and community matters. Much of this activity involves participation in local and regional groups (e.g., business councils, associations, and roundtables); leadership on civic task forces; and personal involvement of executives as directors, trustees, or advisers to schools, community groups, and collaboratives. Through such activities executives become familiar with local needs and issues and involved in finding ways for businesses and communities to cooperate.

Large companies usually have more public visibility in community affairs. These well-known firms are more established and help to characterize their surrounding towns.[5] Executives, often acting as board members and consultants, tend to participate more actively in philanthropy, volunteerism, and community issues when the headquarters is located in the community.[6]

When a company has numerous *branches,* its community involvements extend into those cities and towns, and corporate policy has to be implemented in different local situations. An effective policy has to recognize the unique needs of each community in which the firm is involved. This makes it desirable for corporate headquarters to give local managers broad leeway to make community-related decisions.

> *Target Stores is a retailer with more than 600 stores throughout the United States. Community involvement—which Target calls its Good Neighbor program—is a basic part of every store's business strategy. Local store managers are expected to develop innovative community outreach programs to reinforce the message that Target is a good neighbor whose deeds make the community a better place for all to live. Target Stores are not alone in assigning community relations responsibility to local managers. Research studies have found that nearly 60 percent of firms have delegated local community relations responsibilities, including corporate contributions, to managers in local plants, branch offices, and service branches.[7]*

Foreign-owned companies also participate in community affairs. As shown in Figure 2, their profile of activities is quite similar to that of domestic companies. This pattern seems to operate in many countries and suggests that communities in many countries

---

[4] Center for Corporate Public Involvement, *Helping Families, Strengthening Communities: The Life and Health Insurance Industry Annual Report on Community Involvement* (Washington, DC: American Council of Life Insurance and Health Insurance Association of America, 1995).
[5] Ibid.
[6] See Burke et al., "Corporate Community Involvement," for a discussion of these involvements.
[7] Target Stores data provided by company. The program is dicussed in Molly McKaughan, *Corporate Volunteerism: How Families Make a Difference,* (New York: The Conference Board, 1997). See also, Audris Tillman, *Corporate Contributions in 1995* (New York: The Conference Board, 1996).

Post–Lawrence–Weber:
Business and Society,
Ninth Edition

The Community and the
Corporation

© The McGraw–Hill
Companies, 1999

Figure 2

Community
involvement of
foreign-owned
corporations in the
United States.

Source: David
Logan, *Community
Involvement of
Foreign-Owned
Companies in the
United States,*
Research Report
1089–94 (New York:
The Conference
Board, 1994).

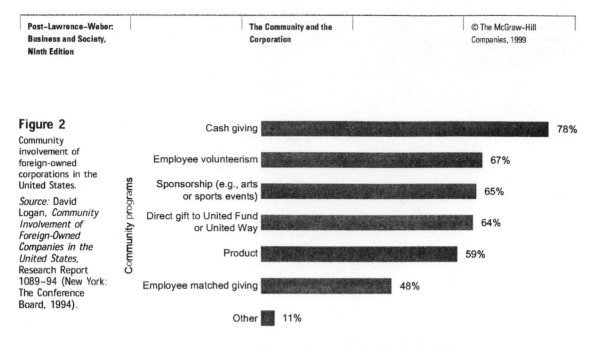

Cash giving — 78%
Employee volunteerism — 67%
Sponsorship (e.g., arts or sports events) — 65%
Direct gift to United Fund or United Way — 64%
Product — 59%
Employee matched giving — 48%
Other — 11%

Community programs

Percent of companies participating (*n* = 108)

tend to develop local norms of business-community relations. When a new company enters a community and begins to do business with local stakeholders, expectations develop as to the proper role and responsibilities of that firm to the new community.

Small business participation in community activities is just as important as large business involvement. Small business representatives, such as automobile dealers, restaurants, real estate brokers, supermarkets, and other retail merchants, significantly influence the quality of community life. They tend to be personally and professionally involved in community affairs, often expressing a deep commitment to the community based on many years of residence. In large urban areas, different ethnic neighborhoods may exist, often with family-operated stores, restaurants, and services. Cultural norms may affect the willingness of such business owners to participate in community development activities. In many cities, Community Development Corporations (CDCs) have been formed to help bring together and focus the energy of local residents and businesses to improve neighborhood life for all.

Local businesses are often part of a community's Chamber of Commerce, Kiwanis, and Rotary clubs. These organizations work on community issues such as parking and traffic, business development, and cooperation with local schools. In one community, for example, a real estate brokerage donated the time of its employees to several local middle schools that needed adult assistance to run a weekly bottle and can recycling collection. Every Friday morning, teams of real estate brokers worked with students at each middle school to receive the bottles and cans dropped off by residents during the morning commuting hours.

Community Support of Business

The relationship of business and community is one of mutual interdependence. Each has responsibilities to the other because each has social power to affect the other. This power-responsibility equation applies to both parties and reminds that success is a matter of mutual support, rather than opposition. The concept of a *social contract* is fundamental to the relationship between business and the community.

Post–Lawrence–Weber:
Business and Society,
Ninth Edition

The Community and the
Corporation

© The McGraw–Hill
Companies, 1999

Businesses normally expect various types of support from the local communities in which they operate. As previously shown in Figure 1, businesses expect fair treatment, and they expect to be accepted as a participant in community affairs because they are an important part of the community. They also expect community services such as a dependable water supply and police protection. Companies are encouraged to remain in the community and grow if there are appropriate cultural, educational, and recreational facilities for their employees and, of course, if taxes remain reasonable. Businesses also have come to recognize that they rely heavily on the public school system and other local services to run their businesses efficiently.

This combination of business-community mutual support is illustrated in Figure 3. The diagonal line in the diagram illustrates the situation when a business receives support from the community that is equal to that which it provides to the community. Sometimes, a business will invest more in the community than the community seems to provide to it in return. This is illustrated by the area above the diagonal line. Conversely, a community sometimes provides much more support to a business than the business seems to contribute to the community. This is shown by the area below the diagonal line. Ideally, the business and community provide relatively equal amounts of support to each other and, more important, their interaction moves from the lower left end of the box to the upper right. This signifies a high degree of interaction and relatively equal amounts of support for one another. As a company grows, for example, it provides more jobs, tax revenues, volunteers for community projects, support to local charities, and so forth. But positive relationships between a company and a community are sometimes difficult to develop.

Wal-Mart has encountered serious local objection to its plans to build superstores and distribution centers in a number of local communities. Wal-Mart's founder, Sam Walton, now deceased, was fond of saying that he would never try to force a community to accept a Wal-Mart store. "Better to go where we are wanted," he is reported to have said. In recent years, however, that view is less often endorsed by Wal-Mart management. In a series of high-profile local conflicts, Wal-Mart sparked intense local opposition from several communities

Figure 3

Business and the community need support from each other.

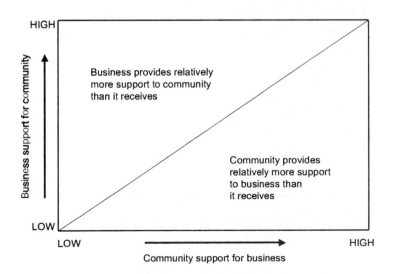

175

Post–Lawrence–Weber:
Business and Society,
Ninth Edition

The Community and the
Corporation

© The McGraw–Hill
Companies, 1999

that were worried about traffic patterns, safety, and negative effects on local small businesses from the opening of giant Wal-Mart facilities. The problem seems likely to grow more complex for Wal-Mart as it continues its expansion into international markets.[8]

Strengthening the Community

Business initiatives have helped improve the quality of life in communities in many ways, some of which are listed in Figure 4. Although not exhaustive, the list suggests the range of community needs that a corporation's executives are asked to address. These community concerns challenge managers to apply talent, imagination, and resources to develop creative ways to strengthen the community while still managing their businesses as profitable enterprises.

Improving Economic Development

Business leaders and their companies are frequently involved in local or regional economic development, which is intended to bring new businesses into an area or to otherwise improve local conditions.[9] Central business districts, unlike older and often neglected

Figure 4

Community projects of 320 insurance companies.

Source: Center for Corporate Public Involvement, *Helping Families, Strengthening Communities: The Life and Health Insurance Industry Annual Report on Community Involvement* (Washington, DC: Center for Corporate Public Involvement and American Council of Life Insurance and Health Insurance Association of America, 1995).

Types of Projects	Percentage of Reporting Companies Involved
Education	87%
Arts and culture	77
Youth activities	76
Local health programs	72
Neighborhood improvement programs	68
Programs for hunger/homeless	61
Minority affairs	47
Programs for the handicapped	45
Drug or alcohol abuse programs	45
AIDS education and treatment	44
Housing programs	42
Activities for senior citizens and retired persons	41
Safety programs	38
Environmental programs	36
Hard-to-employ programs	31
Crime prevention	29
Prenatal and well-baby care	27
Day-care programs	26
Health promotion/low-income and minority	26
Other	32

[8] In a short period of time, Wal-Mart encountered opposition in several Massachusetts and Vermont communities. See "Town Residents Oppose Proposed Wal-Mart Center," *The Wall Street Journal,* August 22, 1994, p. B5.

[9] George Peterson and Dana Sundblad, *Corporations as Partners in Strengthening Urban Communities,* Research Report 1079–94 (New York: The Conference Board, 1994).

Post–Lawrence–Weber:
Business and Society,
Ninth Edition

The Community and the
Corporation

© The McGraw–Hill
Companies, 1999

poorer residential areas, have benefited from businesses during recent decades. Business has helped transform these business areas in major U.S. cities into a collection of shining office buildings, entertainment facilities, fashionable shopping malls, conference centers, and similar urban amenities. In spite of these developments, many urban areas have become forbidding and inhospitable places, fraught with drugs, violence, and frighteningly high crime rates.[10]

Through extensive cooperative efforts, planners are trying to control development so that the central business districts will again become attractive to all citizens. Some of the ingredients needed are police protection that ensures safety, open spaces devoted to fountains, green grass, and trees, outdoor sitting areas, arcades, a variety of attractive stores, outdoor cafes, theaters, and interesting people.

The rush of business development can present problems, as well as opportunities, for a community.

> *When Toyota announced that it would build an automobile plant in Georgetown, Kentucky, residents were both pleased and anxious. The plant was expected to add as many as 3,500 jobs, but local people worried about how the community would be able to absorb the influx of outsiders and how their tightly knit community would be affected. Acknowledging its responsibility for the expected changes, Toyota gave Georgetown $1 million to build a community center. By working closely with local government officials, acknowledging their responsibility, and communicating openly about expected problems, Toyota helped the community become a more dynamic place to live while expanding its business presence. In 1998, the company announced another expansion of its facility, adding more than 1,000 jobs to the payroll. Toyota executives cited the positive relationship with the community as a contributing factor in the expansion decision.[11]*

The congestion and other problems that accompany metropolitan growth are not limited to large cities. Office building has mushroomed in many suburban areas; almost two-thirds of new office space built in the late 1980s was in the suburbs, creating in many metropolitan areas what is called **urban sprawl.** Technological changes permit many business operations to be located away from central headquarters, and suburban building and rental costs are usually much less than those of center-city locations. In the San Francisco suburb of Walnut Creek, for example, local citizens voted to bar large-scale office buildings and retail projects until traffic congestion was relieved. The most celebrated case in recent years, however, may have been the failed efforts of the Disney Company to build a history theme park in Virginia near Civil War battle sites (see the opening example in this chapter). Residents were concerned about traffic from the park, but they were also worried about the long-term impact of office and residential construction on their communities.

---

[10]Dennis R. Judd and Todd Swanstrom, *City Politics: Private Power and Public Policy* (New York: HarperCollins College Publishers, 1994).

[11]The community involvements of foreign-owned companies are discussed in David Logan, *Community Involvement of Foreign-Owned Companies in the United States,* Research Report 1089–94 (New York: The Conference Board, 1994). See also, "Toyota in Bluegrass Country," *Industry Week,* June 5, 1989, pp. 30–33; and "As U.S. Car Makers Cut Back, Toyota Is Expanding Briskly," *New York Times,* January 1, 1991, p. A1.

Post–Lawrence–Weber:
Business and Society,
Ninth Edition

The Community and the
Corporation

© The McGraw–Hill
Companies, 1999

Housing

Suburban areas appeal to businesses because of generally less crowded conditions. Many people choose to live in suburban communities, which usually feature space and some sense of the small-town atmosphere that is rooted in American culture. Many suburban communities have grown during periods of prosperity, as families sought to move from apartments to houses or from smaller homes to more spacious dwellings. When communities have been battered by layoffs and plant closings, they are often pleased to have any new businesses open. But rarely will communities ignore public concerns about the types of growth and businesses that locate in a town. To avoid community backlash and an anti-growth attitude, business leaders need to work with community groups in balancing business growth with respect for community values. Community planning efforts by municipal governments, done in cooperation with private industry, represent one of the steps that businesses can take to achieve this balance.

Life and health insurance companies have taken the lead in programs to revitalize neighborhood housing through organizations such as Neighborhood Housing Services (NHS) of America. NHS, which is locally controlled, locally funded, nonprofit, and tax-exempt, offers housing rehabilitation and financial services to neighborhood residents. Similar efforts are being made to house the homeless. The New York City Coalition for the Homeless includes corporate, nonprofit, and community members. In Los Angeles, Transamerica Life Companies, a founding partner of the Greater Los Angeles Partnership for the Homeless, has provided money and sent trained people to assist the partnership's efforts. Banks are also involved in meeting the housing needs of low-income residents.

Under the federal Community Reinvestment Act, banks are required to demonstrate their commitment to local communities through low-income lending programs and to provide annual reports to the public. This has led many banks to begin viewing the inner city as a new opportunity for business development. In the late 1990s, leading banks have even created special subsidiaries that have as their mission the development of new lending and development in needy urban neighborhoods.

Education Reform

The aging of the post–World War II baby boom generation and the subsequent decline in the number of entry-level workers have forced businesses to pay attention to the quality of the workforce. In assessing how the available workforce can be improved, many businesses have recognized that local public schools are a critical resource. Amidst the severe criticism of America's public schools, which began with the publication, *A Nation at Risk*,[12] businesses have become significantly involved in education reform.

Thousands of local school-business partnerships were formed during the 1980s and 1990s. Many of these collaborations, or adopt-a-school partnerships, engaged businesses in working with school teachers for the first time. Business leaders began participating on school boards and as advisers to schools and government officials who needed business-specific training. The National Alliance of Business (NAB), for example, developed a social compact project in which local businesses pledged their assistance and support to lo-

---

[12]National Commission on Excellence in Education, *A Nation at Risk: The Imperative for Educational Reform* (Washington, DC: U.S. Government Printing Office, 1983).

Post–Lawrence–Weber:
Business and Society,
Ninth Edition

The Community and the
Corporation

© The McGraw–Hill
Companies, 1999

cal schools. Demonstration projects in 12 cities led to an improved understanding of the factors required for successful business-education collaboration.[13]

According to one leading research organization, business involvement in education has passed through four stages, or waves.[14] Beyond business support for programs (first wave) and the application of management principles to school administration (second wave), business has become increasingly committed to public policy initiatives (third wave) and collaboration with all of education's stakeholders to reform of the entire system (fourth wave). An example of systemic reform in Kentucky is described in Exhibit A; also see the case about the efforts of Unum Corporation and the State of Maine Education Excellence initiative entitled "Unum Corporation and the Maine Coalition for Excellence in Education."

EXHIBIT A   Kentucky's Educational Reform Partnership

Kentucky, one of America's five commonwealth states,* has become a leader in the nation's efforts to reform public education. The active involvement of the state's largest business corporations and the personal involvement of chief executives and managers from companies of all sizes have been key factors in Kentucky's commitment to reforming the entire educational system.

Public education faced a crisis in Kentucky when a court decision declared the system unconstitutional because of discrimination among racially divided schools. The decision was a wake-up call for political leaders, many of whom had not been previously involved in education reform. Business leaders recognized that without a functioning school system, Kentucky businesses would not be able to hire new employees with the fundamental skills needed for productive activity in the workplace.

Kentucky has become home to a wide range of manufacturing and service industries. Among the largest and best-known companies headquartered in Kentucky are Ashland Oil, Humana, and United Parcel Service. Financial services have also grown rapidly, including General Electric's credit operations, which are located in Louisville. These each employ many thousands of people whose skills are vital to the productivity and success of the companies. With such a large stake in an educated workforce, Kentucky's business leaders stepped forward and announced the Partnership for Kentucky School Reform in 1990. At an inaugural meeting in 1991, 50 business leaders formally committed their efforts to the passage of the Kentucky Education Reform Act (KERA)—a state law that would radically restructure the schools—thereby joining dozens of other political and education leaders to form a powerful coalition for educational improvement.

(continued next page)

[13] Sandra A. Waddock, *Not by Schools Alone: Sharing Responsibility for America's School Reform* (New York: Praeger, 1995); and Sandra Waddock, "Understanding Social Partnership: An Evolutionary Model of Partnership Organizations," *Administration and Society* 21 (May 1989), pp. 78–100. The NAB project is described in National Alliance of Business, *The Compact Project: School-Business Partnerships for Improving Education* (Washington, DC: National Alliance of Business, 1989).

[14] Sandra A. Waddock, *Business and Education Reform: The Fourth Wave,* Research Report 1091–94 (New York: The Conference Board, 1994), p. 13.

Post–Lawrence–Weber:
Business and Society,
Ninth Edition

The Community and the
Corporation

© The McGraw–Hill
Companies, 1999

The Partnership for Kentucky School Reform set forth three goals: (1) to promote support for the implementation of KERA's provisions and goals; (2) to provide an ongoing forum for discussion of problems and concerns; and (3) to serve as a vehicle for securing the technical assistance and expertise needed to facilitate implementation of school reform. Most important, the companies that agreed to become Partnership members have made a 10-year commitment. As Kent "Oz" Nelson, chairman and chief executive officer of United Parcel Service, said, "KERA has been recognized by many as the most comprehensive education reform legislation in the nation. . . . It is also a vast undertaking, which requires a serious and deep commitment if it is to be implemented successfully." Kentucky businesses have made that commitment and will be engaged in the cause of improving public education well into the twenty-first century.

---

*The other commonwealth states are Maryland, Massachusetts, Pennsylvania, and Virginia.
Source: Sandra A. Waddock, *Business and Education Reform: The Fourth Wave,* Research Report 1091–94 (New York: The Conference Board, 1994) pp. 26–27.

Efforts at workforce improvement involve direct business participation in worker training and retraining, especially efforts to train the disadvantaged. Much of this participation has come about as a result of federal job legislation, which requires that public sector job-training programs be supervised by private sector managers through private initiative councils (PICs) in every community where federal funds are used. Businesses have generally welcomed this chance to participate as a way to better match school and community efforts with business workforce opportunities and needs.

Jobs, Training, and Welfare Reform

In the late 1990s, government leaders have called on American businesses to help address one of the most vexing and costly social problems—welfare reform. Welfare is a form of public assistance to those who are unable to work and live an independent and self-sufficient life. Most societies have some basic form of public assistance to the needy, and some countries (Germany, France, and the United States) are known for their relatively generous assistance programs. As the costs of such programs have risen, however, many citizens have pressured their governments to curb the cost of welfare-assistance programs.

In the United States, a movement to reform welfare programs included tightened eligibility for assistance, limits on the length of time one can claim welfare benefits, and most important in the views of many, requirement that welfare recipients earn their eligibility by working in an approved public job. These programs—known as *workfare* in many states—depend heavily on businesses to provide job opportunities. President Clinton called on American businesses to come forward with innovative job-training opportunities to help move people from welfare to workfare, and a number of companies, such as Marriott and Pennsylvania Blue Shield, created new job and training programs. George Grode, senior vice president of Pennsylvania Blue Shield, noted:

> *Training, realistic goal-setting, and steady, constructive feedback are three key
> elements of any successful program intended to promote movement from the*

Post–Lawrence–Weber:
Business and Society,
Ninth Edition

The Community and the
Corporation

© The McGraw–Hill
Companies, 1999

*world of welfare to the world of work. Collaboration between the private sec-
tor employers and public sector support agencies is also essential. The rewards can be high for the employer, the employee, and all taxpayers, as is
shown by our experience. Over a three-year period, 208 former welfare workers were trained, hired, and retained as productive members of our workforce.
The government saved 2.4 million (dollars) in welfare benefits, and collected
1.3 million (dollars) in payroll taxes.*[15]

Technical Assistance to Government

In a number of cities, businesses have spearheaded programs to upgrade the quality of local government. They provide special advice and technical expertise on budgeting, financial controls, and other management techniques. Many of the techniques of total quality
management pioneered in the private sector are now being adapted to the analysis and improvement of government programs. Business know-how in these matters can inject vitality and efficiency into government systems that are often overburdened, obsolete, and
underfinanced.[16]

Aid to Minority Enterprise

In addition to programs to hire and train urban minorities for jobs in industry, private enterprise has extended assistance to minority-owned small businesses that must struggle for
existence in the inner cities. These businesses are often at a great economic disadvantage:
they do business in economic locations where high crime rates, congestion, poor transportation, low-quality public services, and a low-income clientele combine to produce a
high rate of business failure. Large corporations, sometimes in cooperation with universities, have provided financial and technical advice to minority entrepreneurs and have
helped launch programs to teach managerial, marketing, and financial skills. They also
have financed the building of minority-managed inner-city plants and sponsored special
programs to purchase services and supplies from minority firms. Still, in the view of many,
there is the need, and opportunity, for businesses to do much more.

*In January 1998, Reverend Jesse Jackson announced a new campaign by his
Rainbow/PUSH coalition to get Wall Street firms and the nation's largest companies to expand diversity programs and extend more economic opportunity to
people of color. Reverend Jackson put the issue in these terms: "We'll pay for
not investing; we're in one big tent." The view was endorsed by U.S. Treasury
Secretary Robert Rubin, a former Wall Street banker himself, who said: "Our
economy is going to fall short of its potential unless it is for all of us. . . . Inclusion is critical to the bottom line."*

*Jackson continued, "Riker's Island [a New York prison] is a more expen-
sive university than NYU [New York University]," referring to the high cost per
year of caring for prisoners who do not contribute to the nation's well-being.
"What's missing in this dialogue has been corporate America. They must lead*

---

[15] Felice Davidson Perlmutter, *From Welfare to Work* (New York: Oxford University Press, 1997).
See C-SPAN, November 26, 1997, comments of Eli Segal, "The Welfare to Work Partnership,"
speech to the U.S. Chamber of Commerce. Also, John C. Winfrey, *Social Issues: The Ethics and
Economics of Taxes and Public Programs* (New York: Oxford University Press, 1998).
[16] Peterson and Sundblad, *Corporations as Partners.*

Post–Lawrence–Weber:
Business and Society,
Ninth Edition

The Community and the
Corporation

© The McGraw–Hill
Companies, 1999

the way on making the case, as educators and in skills and training. There is this wealth gap here. The biggest since 1929."[17]

Environmental Programs

The positive impacts of business on the community are balanced by a number of negative effects, including environmental problems. As local landfills near capacity, for example, communities have become concerned about the disposal of solid wastes. Citizen groups using slogans like NIMBY ("not in my back yard") or GOOMBY ("get out of my back yard") have resisted development of additional landfills to handle solid-waste disposal, to which businesses contribute in great quantities. So high was public concern about solid-waste disposal in Seattle, for example, that Procter & Gamble began a pilot project there to collect and recycle disposable diapers. Seattle's families provided an enthusiastic test case for Procter & Gamble's experiment in recycling, and P&G learned important lessons about public perceptions of the environmental impact of its products.

Community perceptions of environmental risk can have a powerful effect on the ability of companies to operate existing facilities and to expand their businesses. Chemical companies are among the industrial manufacturers facing such problems. They have created **community advisory panels (CAPs)** to bridge communications between managers of their facilities and residents of local communities. These advisory panels have a continuing dialogue with plant managers and bring issues of public concern to the meetings. The chemical industry formally adopted this approach as part of the Responsible Care Program commitments all its members make to the communities in which they operate.

Disaster Relief

One common form of corporate involvement in the community is disaster relief. Throughout the world, companies, like individuals, tend to provide assistance to local citizens and communities when disaster strikes. When major floods occurred in the midwestern United States in 1994, for example, assistance worth millions of dollars poured into affected communities from companies across the country and overseas. And when eastern Canada, including Montreal and much of the province of Quebec was devastated by ice storms in the winter of 1998, assistance poured in from Canadian and U.S. companies. Hundreds of volunteers from electric companies in the United States rushed to help restore electric power to more than 3 million Canadian residents.[18]

The willingness of companies to provide emergency assistance is an international phenomenon. When an earthquake seriously damaged the Japanese port city of Kobe in 1995, individuals and businesses from all over the world sought to provide assistance.

Abbott Laboratories, a health-care products company headquartered near Chicago, Illinois, joined dozens of other companies to provide needed medical products for Kobe's survivors. Abbott contributed 1,600 cases of sterile water, intravenous solutions, antibiotics, and pharmaceuticals to a coordinated relief effort organized by AmeriCares, a private international relief organization based in New Canaan, Connecticut. A shipment of more than 200,000 pounds

[17] Peter Truell, "On Wall St., Fervent Pleas for Minorities," *New York Times*, January 16, 1998, p. C4.

[18] News reports published in *New York Times* and *Boston Globe*, January 11–16, 1998. Also, network news television reports January 11–16, 1998, and http://www.cnn.org.com.

Post-Lawrence-Weber:
Business and Society,
Ninth Edition

The Community and the
Corporation

© The McGraw-Hill
Companies, 1999

of materials was airlifted to Japan where another organization, the Japan International Rescue Action Committee, distributed the products to earthquake victims in Kobe.

Networks of volunteer agencies, such as the American Red Cross and AmeriCares, are instrumental in aligning resources with needs in such instances. International relief efforts are becoming more important, as communications improve and people around the world are able to witness the horror of disasters. Corporate involvement in such efforts, then, is an extension of the natural tendency of people to help one another when tragedy strikes.

Corporate Giving

America is a generous society. According to information collected by the Internal Revenue Service, individuals and organizations give more than $150 billion each year to churches, charities, and other nonprofit organizations. American businesses are a small, but important, part of this broad cultural tradition of giving. One of the most visible ways in which businesses help communities is through gifts of money, property, and employee service. This **corporate philanthropy,** or **corporate giving,** demonstrates the commitment of businesses to assist the communities by supporting such nonprofit organizations as United Way, Community Chest, and individual hospitals, schools, homeless shelters, and other providers of important community services.

The federal government has encouraged corporate giving for educational, charitable, scientific, and religious purposes since 1936.[19] The current IRS rule permits corporations to deduct from their taxable income all such gifts that do not exceed 10 percent of the company's before-tax income. In other words, a company with a before-tax income of $1 million might contribute up to $100,000 to nonprofit community organizations devoted to education, charity, science, or religion. The $100,000 in contributions would then reduce the income to be taxed from $1 million to $900,000, thus saving the company money on its tax bill while providing a source of income to community agencies. Of course, there is nothing to prevent a corporation from giving more than 10 percent of its income for philanthropic purposes, but it would not be given a tax break above the 10 percent level.

As shown in Figure 5, average corporate giving in the United States is far below the 10 percent deduction now permitted. Though it varies from year to year, corporate giving has been closer to 1 percent of pretax income since the early 1960s, with a rise that reached a peak in 1986. Although a few corporations, including a cluster headquartered in the Minneapolis–St. Paul metropolitan area, have pledged 5 percent of their pretax income, most companies average between 1 and 2 percent of pretax income.[20] Even at the national average of 1 percent giving, substantial amounts of money are channeled to education, the arts, and other community organizations. Corporate giving totaled more than $8 billion in 1997, including more than $2.5 billion for education.[21]

[19]The evolution of corporate philanthropy is summarized in Mark Sharfman, "Changing Institutional Rules: The Evolution of Corporate Philanthropy, 1883–1953," *Business and Society,* 33, no. 3 December 1994), pp. 236–69; and "Charities Tap Generous Spirit of Hong Kong," *The Wall Street Journal,* November 3, 1994, pp. B1, B8.

[20]Audris Tillman, *Corporate Contributions in 1995* (New York: The Conference Board, 1996).

[21]Useful references include The Conference Board, *Corporate Contributions, annual 1964–1998*; and Ann Kaplan, ed., *Giving USA, 1998* (New York: AAFRC Trust for Philanthropy, 1998).

Post–Lawrence–Weber:
Business and Society,
Ninth Edition

The Community and the
Corporation

© The McGraw–Hill
Companies, 1999

Figure 5

Corporate contributions as a percentage of pretax net income.

Source: Audris Tillman, *Corporate Contributions in 1995* (New York: The Conference Board, 1996). This chart is derived from Internal Revenue Service data presented in an appendix to Tillman's book.

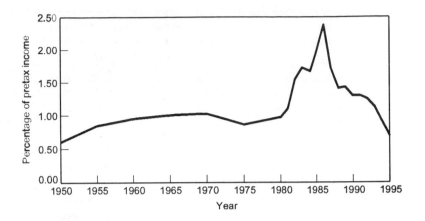

Some critics have argued that corporate managers have no right to give away company money that does not belong to them. According to this line of reasoning, any income earned by the company should be either reinvested in the firm or distributed to the stockholders who are the legal owners. The courts have ruled, however, that charitable contributions fall within the legal and fiduciary powers of the corporation's policymakers. Corporate contributions are one additional way in which companies link themselves to the broader interests of the community, thereby advancing and strengthening the company rather than weakening it.

Companies also help local communities through the substantial number of business donations that are not recorded as philanthropy because they are not pure giving. Routine gifts of products and services for local use often are recorded as advertising expenses; gifts of employee time for charity drives and similar purposes usually are not recorded; and the costs of soliciting and processing employee gifts, such as payroll deductions for the United Way, usually are not recorded as corporate giving. Still, they add value to the local community of which the company is a part.

Many large U.S. corporations have established nonprofit **corporate foundations** to handle their charitable programs. This permits them to administer contributions programs more uniformly and provides a central group of professionals that handles all grant requests. Foreign-owned corporations use foundations less frequently, although firms such as Matsushita (Panasonic) and Hitachi use highly sophisticated corporate foundations to conduct their charitable activities in the United States. As corporations expand to more foreign locations, pressures will grow to expand international corporate giving. Foundations, with their defined mission to benefit the community, can be a useful mechanism to help companies implement philanthropic programs that meet this corporate social responsibility.

Corporate Giving in a Strategic Context

One way to stretch the corporate contributions dollar is to make sure that it is being used strategically to meet the needs of both the recipient and the donor. Creating a strategy of mutual benefits for business and society is one of the major themes of this material, and this type of **strategic philanthropy** is a means of achieving such win-win outcomes. As

Post–Lawrence–Weber:
Business and Society,
Ninth Edition

The Community and the
Corporation

© The McGraw-Hill
Companies, 1999

shown in Figure 6, strategic philanthropy blends traditional corporate philanthropy with giving programs that are directly or indirectly linked to business goals and objectives. In the 1990s, more companies have transformed their corporate philanthropic giving to this strategic focus.[22]

One example of linking business goals to charitable giving is **cause marketing,** pioneered by American Express as a way to promote wider use of its credit cards. Today, following the lead of American Express, many companies have created formulas for making contributions to nonprofit organizations based on how many of the particular nonprofit organization's members use the company's credit card or purchase its products. In 1994, Johnson & Johnson broke new ground when it introduced Arthritis Foundation pain-relief medicine. It agreed to make a contribution to the Arthritis Foundation for each package of pain reliever sold under the AF name. Such activities increase corporate giving while enhancing the revenues of the donors.

One group of scholars pointed out that strategic philanthropy occurs in two forms. One, called *strategic process giving,* applies a professional business approach to determine the goals, budgets, and criteria for specific grants. The second approach, called *strategic outcome giving,* emphasizes the links between corporate contributions and business-oriented goals such as introducing a new product, providing needed services to employees (e.g., child-care centers), or maintaining positive contacts with external stakeholder groups

Figure 6

Corporate giving and community relations.

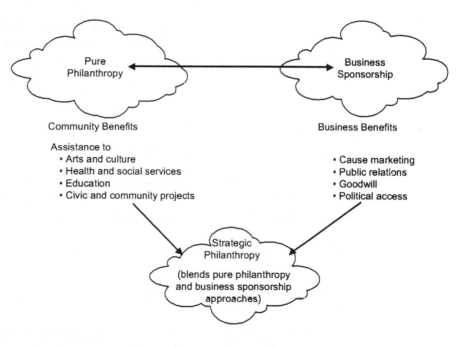

[22] Barbara W. Altman, *"Corporate Community Relations in the 1990s: A Study in Transformation,"* unpublished doctoral dissertation, Boston University, 1997. Abstract published in *Business and Society,* forthcoming, 1998. See also Craig Smith, "The New Corporate Philanthropy," *Harvard Business Review* 72, no. 3 (May–June 1994), pp. 105–112, and Myra Alperson, *New Strategies for Corporate Giving* (New York: The Conference Board, 1995).

Post–Lawrence–Weber:
Business and Society,
Ninth Edition

The Community and the
Corporation

© The McGraw–Hill
Companies, 1999

(e.g., Asian-Americans).[23] Pressures to justify the use of every corporate dollar are leading managers to think about new ways to tie charitable contributions to business goals.

Priorities in Corporate Giving

The distribution of corporate contributions reflects how the businesses view overall community needs. As shown in Figure 7, corporate giving from 1982 to 1995 varied somewhat among categories, but the pie was divided in approximately the same way. These percentages are not identical among different companies and industries, however; some companies tend to favor support for education, whereas others give relatively greater amounts to cultural organizations or community groups.

The actual contributions of an individual company will depend on company goals and priorities. Corporate giving is often justified as a *social investment* that benefits business in the long run by improving the community, its labor force, the climate for business, or other conditions affecting business. An alternative view is that routine local gifts are a *normal expense* of operating a business in the community and should be treated like other public relations expenses. Another view holds that the corporation is a citizen and, as such, has a *citizenship responsibility* to give without regard to self-interest. Some believe that giving should be *linked to business purposes* as exemplified in the cause-related marketing pioneered by American Express. The customer gets the product or service, the charity receives a contribution, and company sales grow.

Another point of view is that some corporate gifts take on the characteristics of taxes. Since it is widely believed that corporations should be good citizens, helpful neighbors, and human institutions, the community's expectations come close to imposing some

Figure 7

Distribution of corporate contributions, 1982–1996.

Source: Audris Tillman, *Corporate Contributions in 1995* (New York: The Conference Board, 1996).

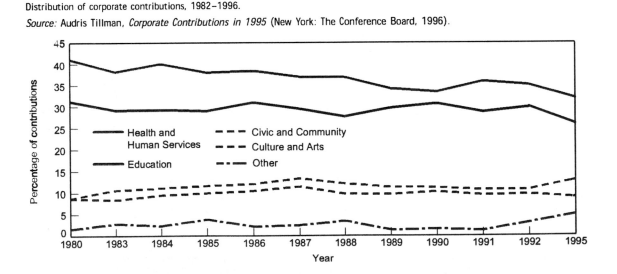

[23] Jeanne M. Logsdon, Martha Reiner, and Lee Burke, "Corporate Philanthropy: Strategic Responses to the Firm's Stakeholders," *Nonprofit and Voluntary Sector Quarterly* 19, no. 2 (Summer 1990), pp. 93–109.

Post–Lawrence–Weber:
Business and Society,
Ninth Edition

The Community and the
Corporation

© The McGraw–Hill
Companies, 1999

types of gift giving on the corporation as a form of *unofficial tax*. The gifts are given to retain public approval.

Regardless of whether gifts are considered to be an investment, an expense, philanthropy, or a tax, most of their costs are ultimately passed on to consumers, making corporate giving in the long run a cost of doing business. Businesses are then acting partly as agents and trustees for the community, receiving funds and distributing them according to perceived and expressed community needs. In the trusteeship role, businesses respond to various stakeholder claims in the community, and one of these responses is gifts to those whose claims are perceived as being either legitimate or so powerful that they threaten the business if not satisfied. Thus, both the legitimacy of claim and the power of claimants are considered when making a decision concerning corporate giving.

The Role of Volunteerism

Volunteerism involves the efforts of people to assist others in the community through unpaid work. The United States has a long and distinguished tradition of volunteerism, with many examples dating back to the founding of communities as the population moved west across the continent. In the 1980s, the spirit of volunteerism was invoked by presidents Ronald Reagan and George Bush as an alternative to government programs to solve community problems. The business community formed the Council on Private Sector Initiatives as a mechanism to encourage voluntary business-community activities.

Volunteerism received a highly publicized boost in the 1980s when Bush launched his 1,000 Points of Light campaign to celebrate 1,000 voluntary efforts by individuals and organizations to solve problems in American communities. In the 1990s, volunteerism was spurred by the work of the Points of Light Foundation, a catalyst for stimulating voluntary action programs in local communities.[24] Volunteerism received another push in 1997 when former presidents Jimmy Carter, Gerald Ford, and George Bush and President Bill Clinton supported an initiative led by General Colin Powell to tackle the problems of youth, education, and community in a bipartisan call for broad voluntary action. The campaign was high profile, with extensive media coverage of events and General Powell's personal involvement.[25]

Businesses, large and small, are often enlisted as allies in such efforts to improve communities. Managers are asked to announce, publicize, and promote such efforts among staff members, employees, and associates. Some companies may also provide money, supplies, T-shirts, transportation, or other resources to these community efforts. Corporate community relations managers are frequently the executives who are asked to coordinate these efforts.

For example, Coca Cola, Bell South, and other leading companies operating in Atlanta became leaders of that city's campaign to host the 1996 Summer Olympic Games. Corporate volunteer commitments were an important element of the city's bid. By the time the Olympic Games were actually held, the com-

---

[24] Points of Light Foundation, "Special Report: The 1994 National Community Service Conference," *News-letter* 2, no. 7 (Washington, DC: Points of Light Foundation, July–Aug. 1994).
[25] Jonathan Alter, "Powell's New War," *Newsweek,* April 28, 1997, pp. 28–32. The cover of *Newsweek* showed General Powell pointing toward the reader and saying "I Want You." The tag line read, "Why Colin Powell Is Asking America to Volunteer."

Post–Lawrence–Weber:
Business and Society,
Ninth Edition

The Community and the
Corporation

© The McGraw–Hill
Companies, 1999

munity relations staffs at Coca Cola, Bell South, and dozens of other Atlanta-based companies had coordinated tens of thousands of employee days of volunteer work in support of the Olympics.

Although most companies and communities are involved in activities that are less visible than the Olympic Games, nearly every city and local community has community needs that require the helping hands of volunteers. This means that in addition to providing jobs, paying taxes, and directing charitable contributions dollars to worthy causes, there is a role for companies as catalysts in encouraging volunteerism that helps build local communities.

Corporate Restructuring and Community Relations

Since the 1980s, and continuing on through the 1990s, American businesses have gone through massive corporate restructuring, reorganization, and reengineering. This change process, which many believe is vital if American firms are to be successful in global competition, has also become a serious and disruptive fact of life for communities.

Corporate restructuring means that companies are reshaping their business activities in some fundamental way so as to become more competitive. Restructured companies often close down older, less productive facilities, improving the firm's ability to produce goods more efficiently. Sometimes they sell off assets to other corporations that may not have the same relationship to the local community as the previous owner. Management may voluntarily restructure the company to avoid being taken over by hostile corporate raiders or simply to meet the forces of global competition by introducing labor-saving technology, moving production facilities to low-wage regions of the world, or using new, substitute materials such as plastic and ceramic auto parts.

Social Costs of Restructuring

Whatever the reasons for the restructuring, the effects on the community are similar: local plants close, workers are laid off, jobs are lost, and individuals are relocated. Studies show that displaced workers seldom have managed to find new jobs as good or as well paying as the ones they lost when a plant closed. Single-income families may be so hard hit that they cannot make home mortgage payments, and some may sell homes to meet back taxes. Sometimes pension benefits and health-care insurance are lost. Older workers, minorities, and women suffer more than other groups of displaced workers, taking longer to find new jobs and receiving lower pay when they do. Family tensions build up; divorce rates increase; depression and mental illness increase; suicides become more frequent; alcoholism and drug abuse grow; child abuse and spouse abuse occur more often. The impact was summed up in a *Time* cover story: "We're #1 and It Hurts."[26]

---

[26]George J. Church, "We're #1 and It Hurts," *Time,* October 24, 1994, pp. 50–56. Job cuts in large companies have become a way of life in American business. In 1997, 434,350 jobs were eliminated; this was the lowest annual total since 1991. The largest 1997 layoffs occurred at Eastman Kodak (19,900) and Boeing (12,000), well below the 40,000 job cuts announced at AT&T in January 1996. Companies may go through several rounds of cuts. In early 1998, for example, AT&T announced a further job cut (15,000). See "The Falling Ax," *Fortune,* March 2, 1998, p. 224, based on data provided by the job outplacement firm, Challenger Gray & Christmas.

Post–Lawrence–Weber:
Business and Society,
Ninth Edition

The Community and the
Corporation

© The McGraw–Hill
Companies, 1999

Community Responses

Communities may be unable to adjust as corporate restructuring reshapes the local business community. Many cities are dependent on one or a few large employers to anchor the economic base of the community. Rochester, New York, for example, suffered severe effects when Eastman Kodak—known as "Father Yellow" for its high level of community involvement in its headquarters city—announced major job reductions in 1997. The following example illustrates how difficult in can be for communities to deal with such losses.

> *Akron, Ohio, was for many years known as the Rubber Capital. Millions of tires and inner tubes were produced in Akron's massive tire factories until more than 10,000 jobs were lost in the tire industry's intense global competition during the 1980s. Struggling to recover from these devastating losses, Akron's city government worked hard to attract and develop smaller and mid-sized businesses in the city to replace some of the jobs that were lost. Although local supporters boast of the New Akron, economic recovery is slow, requiring many more smaller businesses to provide an equivalent number of jobs to offset those that were lost. The new industries also require more cooperation between public and private sector officials to create the conditions for business success.*

The human and community problems created by restructuring are not confined to the industrial Rust Belt of the midwestern United States. California's Silicon Valley and Massachusetts's high-technology belt also have been squeezed by foreign competition in the 1990s. Texas, Louisiana, and other oil-producing states have faced falling oil prices since the 1980s, resulting in dramatic and well-publicized failures of savings and loan institutions, a decline in the local housing markets, and in the mid-1990s, a wave of job reductions and downsizings by major oil companies. These job losses have resulted in the same negative impacts on people and communities that have occurred elsewhere.

The end of the cold war also meant the reduced need for large military forces and a defense industry that employed millions of workers. California alone suffered the loss of hundreds of thousands of jobs in the early 1990s because of what were called **defense industry conversion** pressures.

> *Lockheed was one of Southern California's largest employers for more than 30 years from the 1960s to the early 1990s. The company manufactured airplanes and other aerospace equipment, developing a reputation as one of the American defense industry's most reliable contractors. As defense budgets began to shrink in the post–cold war era, Lockheed began to trim its business operations. From a high of more than 100,000 employees, the company reduced its workforce to less than 30,000 by early 1994. Then, in an announcement that shocked many, Lockheed management announced that the company would be merged into Martin Marietta, another defense contractor.[27]*

In the United States, each year during the 1980s plant closings displaced about 500,000 workers who had more than three years on the job; in the 1990s, corporate re-

---

[27]"Aerospace: Swords into Satellites," *The Economist,* September 3, 1994, pp. 60–61.

Post–Lawrence–Weber:
Business and Society,
Ninth Edition

The Community and the
Corporation

© The McGraw–Hill
Companies, 1999

structurings continued to eliminate jobs at the rate of more than 400,000 jobs per year, including a high of more than 600,000 jobs in 1993. As shown in Figure 8, job losses have a cascading effect in the community. Job losses were once primarily felt by lower-wage, hourly workers, including members of minority groups. But in the 1990s, the impact has affected workers at all income levels, including professional staffs and managers.

Many stakeholder groups are affected by these restructuring activities. Local, state, and federal governments, company management, employees, labor unions, local businesses, and community organizations all suffer the impact of restructuring-induced job losses. There is no official estimate of the social costs that have resulted from restructuring during the 1990s, but the cumulative costs of unemployment taxes, social assistance to unemployed workers and their families, and economic-adjustment assistance to affected businesses attributable to corporate restructuring is thought to have surpassed $100 billion from 1990 to 1994. In 1994 alone, corporate America spent more than $10 billion on restructuring while communities spent much more.[28]

As the number of plant closings grew, and their impact became better understood, state and federal governments stepped up their efforts to protect workers and communi-

Figure 8

The cascading effects of job losses on a community.

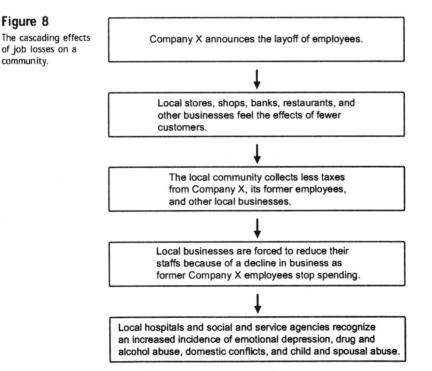

[28]"When Slimming Down Is Not Enough," *The Economist,* September 3, 1994, pp. 59–60; "Downsizing Government," *Business Week,* January 25, 1995, pp. 34–41; and "Defense Improvement," *Business Week,* February 6, 1995, pp. 144–45. See Sylvia Nasar, "Layoff Law Is Having Slim Effect," *New York Times,* August 3, 1993, pp. C1, C2; and Ronald G. Ehrenberg and George H. Jakubson, "Advance Notification of Plant Closing: Does It Matter?" *Industrial Relations,* Winter 1989, pp. 60–71.

Post–Lawrence–Weber:
Business and Society,
Ninth Edition

The Community and the
Corporation

© The McGraw–Hill
Companies, 1999

ties. State legislatures created **plant closing laws** that required a company to give advance warning before closing a plant. In 1988, the U.S. Congress enacted the Worker Adjustment and Retraining Notification Act (WARN). WARN required employers to give 60 days' advance notice of plant closings and major layoffs that result in permanent job losses. Many state legislatures have also created plant closing laws that require a company to give advance warning before closing a plant. The business community has generally opposed such laws.

Business argued that the need for companies to become more efficient in the face of competition required faster action than these laws would permit. Some research suggests, however, that most of the negative impacts on business were temporary, and there is little evidence that such laws have deterred corporate restructuring in the 1990s. Much of the current U.S. worker legislation is modeled on Western European government requirements that employers provide notice to employees, job training, and job search assistance when layoffs are necessary. European laws often require compensation payments to the community as well. The European Union, for example, tried to create common standards of compensation and provided funds to communities and regions that lost jobs to the new competition of the international marketplace.[29]

Company Responses

Management practices vary from company to company when corporate restructuring occurs. In some cases, management gives advance notice, makes an effort to find new jobs for displaced workers, and works with local citizens' groups and municipal officials to ease the impact of a closing. At other times, only the minimum legal requirements are met by a company that does not want to be pressured to reverse its decision. It may offer little aid to employees, local government, or the community.

Restructuring does not always work as planned; some companies have discovered that employees they wished to retain have taken advantage of early retirement or other voluntary programs. Others have learned that employees who remain with the company are disillusioned, unhappy, and fearful of the next round of layoffs. This can result in lack of loyalty and low morale among remaining employees, making it more difficult for the company to respond effectively to the competitive pressures that forced the restructuring in the first place.[30]

The Age of Anxiety

Employees faced with job loss suffer a variety of fates. Some may move to another job with the same company but in a different location. Some are retrained and enter a new skill or craft. Others hang on to false hopes: one steel mill worker with 20 years of experience with a company simply refused to accept reality, saying, "I think the mill is going to open again." Those who find new jobs often end up with lower pay, have less desirable jobs, and lose their seniority. Former U.S. secretary of labor Robert Reich led a highly visible campaign to convince employees and employers that lifelong learning and continued development of job skills are the only real security that people can have in a

[29]See, for example, "Steel Region Wins £36 Million EU Funds," *Financial Times,* October 14, 1994, p. 9. The EU's rules on plant closing are updated in *European Labor Law,* Washington, D.C., BNA Research, 1994–98.
[30]William Bridges, "The End of the Job," *Fortune,* September 19, 1994, pp. 62–74.

Post–Lawrence–Weber:
Business and Society,
Ninth Edition

The Community and the
Corporation

© The McGraw–Hill
Companies, 1999

world of rapid competitive change. As Secretary Reich delivered his message around the nation, he began referring to the 1990s as "The Age of Anxiety."[31]

The era of corporate restructuring has led some corporations to downsize and reevaluate activities, including corporate giving. As the following example shows, even charitable contributions are no longer a sacred cow in the highly competitive, global business environment.

> *In 1994, the senior management of ARCO, one of the world's largest petroleum companies, informed the senior executive of the ARCO Foundation that a decision had been made to reduce its funding and eventually eliminate the foundation. ARCO had been a highly visible and much-admired corporate citizen in its headquarters community of Los Angeles. The company provided important leadership in Los Angeles in such efforts as education reform, community development, and Rebuild LA, a major attempt to address the city's complex social and racial issues after the 1992 riots. Through the ARCO Foundation, millions of dollars had been focused on meeting community needs. Still, persistently low prices for oil forced petroleum companies to reduce staffs, trim expenses, and reengineer operations. A consulting firm was called in by ARCO's top management and concluded that no lasting damage would be done to ARCO's image or profits by cutting out its contributions program. Despite its record of good works, the cost-cutting ax fell on the ARCO Foundation.*

The Need for Partnership

The need for **public–private partnerships** between business and government are very apparent when dealing with community problems. The idea of such partnering is not new. As one group of business executives said in 1982:

> *Whether growing or contracting, young or old, large or small, in the Frost Belt or Sun Belt, America's urban communities possess the resources of an advanced and affluent society: highly educated and skilled individuals, productive social and economic institutions, sophisticated technology, physical infrastructure, transportation and communications networks, and access to capital. Developing this potential will require cooperation. . . . Public–private partnerships are a source of energy and vitality for America's urban communities.*[32]

Corporate restructuring and refocusing has underscored the importance of this point nearly 15 years later. Many community problems are people problems involving hopes, attitudes, sentiments, and expectations for better human conditions. Neither government nor business can simply impose solutions or be expected to find quick and easy answers to problems so long in the making and so vast in their complications. Moreover, neither government nor business has the financial resources to solve these issues. Grassroots involvement is needed, where people are willing and able to confront their own needs, imagine solutions, and work to fulfill them through cooperative efforts and intelligent planning. In that community-oriented effort, government and business can be partners,

[31] Robert Reich, Address to the National Alliance of Business, September 25, 1994, Washington, D.C. See Catherine S. Manegold, "Reich Urges Executives to Aid Labor," *New York Times*, September 25, 1994, p. 25.

[32] Committee for Economic Development, *Public-Private Partnership: An Opportunity for Urban Communities* (New York: Committee for Economic Development, 1982), p. 1.

Post–Lawrence–Weber:
Business and Society,
Ninth Edition

The Community and the
Corporation

© The McGraw–Hill
Companies, 1999

contributing aid and assistance where feasible and being socially responsive to legitimately expressed human needs. Exhibit B describes such an effort in communities along the U.S.-Mexico border.

A study by the Conference Board and the Urban Institute identified three distinct strategies that corporations can use to become effective partners with urban communities.[33] One is to become *directly involved* in addressing specific problems in specific neighborhoods or communities. A second approach is to develop *partnerships* with the community wherein the community's needs and priorities guide the form and type of corporate activity. The third strategy is for the corporation to be involved in the community through an *intermediary organization,* such as a citywide umbrella organization that helps to coordinate the efforts of many local businesses and nonprofits.

Communities need jobs, specialized skills, executive talents, and other resources that business can provide. Business needs cooperative attitudes in local government, basic

---

EXHIBIT B   Business Meets the Maquiladoras*

The South Texas border with Mexico is not the usual hotbed of corporate community affairs. It is, however, a hotbed of commercial expansion as companies from around the world establish manufacturing and assembly operations called *maquiladoras.* Inexpensive Mexican labor and easy access to American markets make the maquiladoras the vehicle for boomtown development.

The boomtowns are growing in areas where social problems—including no schools, no housing, and no social infrastructure to hold together the community—abound. In El Paso, for example, low wages and the prestige of a Made in the USA label have helped keep employment high, with more than 20,000 jobs in the apparel industry in 1994. More than 100 million pairs of jeans are made in El Paso each year. But the stiff competition also helps keep El Paso as the poorest metropolitan region in the United States, with personal incomes only 59 percent of the national average. Patricia Fogerty, a former NYNEX community affairs officer who lives in McAllen, Texas, says, "Some [companies] are finding they have to develop the entire social infrastructure in the towns."

A model for doing so is being developed by the El Paso Community Foundation. It organizes Hispanic wives of workers to do community work and serves as a bridge between employers and social problems in the border communities. Among the leadership companies that have partnered with community groups are Levi Strauss, General Electric, Sierra West, and Alcoa. Yet the maquiladora conditions are so bad that many church groups in the United States are campaigning to press companies to do much more in dealing with these poor and needy communities on both sides of the border.

---

*There are two accepted spellings for this word. We have chosen to use "maquiladora" rather than "machiladora," which also appears in published materials.
Source: Allen R. Myerson, "Jeans Makers Flourish on Border," *New York Times,* September 29, 1994, pp. D1, D9; and "Machiladora Blues," in Craig Smith, ed., *Corporate Philanthropy Report,* vol. 5, no. 1 (August–September 1989), p. 12. See also, "Doing Business in the Maquiladoras."

---

[33] Peterson and Sundblad, *Corporations as Partners.*

Post–Lawrence–Weber:
Business and Society,
Ninth Edition

The Community and the
Corporation

© The McGraw–Hill
Companies, 1999

public services, and a feeling that it is a welcome member of the community. Under these circumstances much can be accomplished to upgrade the quality of community life. The range of specific business-community involvements is extensive, giving business many opportunities to be socially responsible. Corporate restructurings, erratic growth patterns, and an explosion of community needs challenge business involvement with the community. Still, by using management skills, corporate philanthropy, employee volunteerism, and other creative means, companies can have a positive impact on the quality of community life.

Summary Points

- Businesses and the communities have a mutual dependence that is both economically and socially significant. Thus, businesses work to be accepted as participants in community affairs by supporting community interests as well as their own.

- Many corporations have established a community relations office that links their activities to local needs and community groups and develops strategies for creating win-win approaches to solving community problems.

- Corporate contributions to educational, charitable, scientific, and community programs help sustain vital community institutions while benefiting business in a variety of ways. Strategic philanthropy represents a way of linking corporate giving and business goals.

- Corporate volunteerism involves encouraging employees to participate in projects that address a wide range of community needs. Some companies have made volunteerism an explicit part of their strategy.

- Corporate restructuring and layoffs can affect many community groups, including merchants, employees, school systems, local government, and charitable organizations. Successful strategies for coping with the social consequences and pressures that restructuring can place on community life involve cooperation among business, government, employees, labor unions, and community organizations.

- The development of public-private partnerships has proven to be effective in tackling some problems in education, economic development, and social service needs. Partnerships and volunteerism provide models of a shared responsibility in which business and communities address social problems. Many businesses and communities are creating new strategies based on these models.

Key Terms and Concepts

- Community
- Community relations
- Urban sprawl
- Community advisory panels (CAPs)
- Corporate philanthropy, corporate giving
- Corporate foundations
- Strategic philanthropy
- Cause marketing
- Volunteerism
- Corporate restructuring
- Defense industry conversion
- Plant closing laws
- Public-private partnerships

Post–Lawrence–Weber:
Business and Society,
Ninth Edition

The Community and the
Corporation

© The McGraw–Hill
Companies, 1999

Internet Resources

- http:// www.disney.com   Walt Disney Company
- http://www.fdncenter.org   The Foundation Center
- http://www.cof.org   Council on Foundations
- http://www.bs.edu/bc_org/avp/csom/cccr   Boston College Center for Corporate Community Relations
- http:// www.impactonline.org/points   Points of Light Foundation

Discussion Case   Abbott Laboratories Helps Habitat for Humanity

Habitat for Humanity is a worldwide organization that builds homes and sells them to low-income families on a no-profit, no-interest basis. Habitat was founded in 1976 and has built more than 30,000 homes throughout the world. It has more than 1,000 affiliates in its worldwide network.

Among Habitat's many affiliates are groups of people who are employed by companies such as Abbott Laboratories, a pharmaceutical and health-care products manufacturer that employs more than 50,000 people. About 15,000 Abbott employees and retirees live in Lake County, Illinois, where Abbott's world headquarters is located. Employees of Abbott Laboratories are involved in many types of volunteer activity in their local communities, so it was no surprise when a group decided to form the Abbott Chapter of Habitat for Humanity. The Abbott Chapter has worked closely with Lake County's Habitat organization to identify needs and plan a construction project. Local government officials have also been instrumental in identifying sites for Habitat projects and for obtaining needed permits. Since its formation, the Abbott Chapter has helped renovate several buildings in North Chicago and Waukegan, Illinois.

Robin Coleman and her four children learned that they had been selected as the family to work with the Abbott Chapter in building a new house in North Chicago. Habitat families are selected on the basis of need, ability to make a low mortgage payment, and a willingness to help construct the homes of others as well as their own. With the help of more than 200 Abbott employee volunteers, a $38,000 grant for materials from the Abbott Laboratories Fund, and more than 500 hours of sweat equity by the Coleman family, Habitat volunteers built the house in less than one year. Cheers and tears of joy were abundant when Coleman and her family received the keys to their new home.

A dedication ceremony was held at the new Coleman family home. Abbott officials, the mayor of North Chicago, Habitat for Humanity officials, and many of the volunteers attended. Jim Donovan, an R&D quality manager in Abbott's diagnostic division and president of the Abbott chapter of Habitat, said, "All the people involved in this project have felt a great sense of pride in contributing to the future of the Coleman family as well as to the community."

Source: Information provided by the corporate communications department, Abbott Laboratories, Abbott Park, Illinois.

Post–Lawrence–Weber:
Business and Society,
Ninth Edition

The Community and the
Corporation

© The McGraw–Hill
Companies, 1999

Discussion Questions

1. What is the motivation for Abbott employees to participate in the Habitat project? What is the motivation for Abbott to provide charitable contributions to the project?
2. What do you believe the Abbott/Habitat project means to the long-term relationship between the company and the North Chicago community? Use Figure 3.
3. What are the elements of community partnership that are essential to the success of this effort?
4. If you were an employee of Abbott Laboratories, what would attract you to participate in such a project?

Bibliography

Adler, Nancy, and Dafna N. Israeli, eds. *Competitive Frontiers: Women Managers in the Global Economy.* Cambridge, MA: Basil Blackwell, 1995.

Bloom, Paul, and Ruth Belk Smith, eds. *The Future of Consumerism.* Lexington, MA: Lexington Books, 1986.

Caplan, Lincoln. *Up Against the Law: Affirmative Action and the Supreme Court.* New York: Twentieth Century Fund Press, 1997.

Edley, Christopher F. *Not All Black and White: Affirmative Action, Race and American Values.* New York: Hill and Wang, 1996.

Fagenson, Ellen A., ed. *Women in Management: Trends, Issues, and Challenges in Management Diversity.* Newbury Park, CA: Sage, 1993.

Faludi, Susan. *Backlash: The Undeclared War against American Women.* New York: Doubleday, 1991.

Goldin, Claudia. *Understanding the Gender Gap: An Economic History of American Women.* New York: Oxford University Press, 1990.

Gray, Barbara. *Collaborating: Finding Common Ground for Multiparty Problems.* San Francisco: Jossey-Bass, 1989.

Gunderson, Martin; David J. Mayo; and Frank S. Rhame. *AIDS: Testing and Privacy.* Salt Lake City: University of Utah Press, 1989.

Gutek, Barbara A. *Sex and the Workplace: The Impact of Sexual Behavior and Harassment on Women, Men, and Organizations.* San Francisco: Jossey-Bass, 1985.

Herman, Edward S. *Corporate Control, Corporate Power.* Cambridge, England: Cambridge University Press, 1981.

Hochschild, Arlie. *The Second Shift: Working Parents and the Revolution at Home.* New York: Viking, 1989.

Kester, Carl W. *Japanese Takeovers: The Global Contest for Corporate Control.* Boston: Harvard Business School Press, 1991.

Kittrie, Nicholas N., *The War against Authority: From the Crisis of Legitimacy to a New Social Contract.* Baltimore, MD: Johns Hopkins University Press, 1995.

Kuenne, Robert E. *Economic Justice in American Society.* Princeton, NJ: Princeton University Press, 1993.

Linowes, David F. *Privacy in America: Is Your Private Life in the Public Eye?* Urbana, IL: University of Illinois Press, 1989.

Lorsch, Jay William. *Pawns or Potentates: The Reality of America's Corporate Boards.* Boston: Harvard Business School Press, 1989.

Mann, Jonathan M., and Daniel J. M. Tarantola, eds. *AIDS in World War II: Global Dimensions, Social Roots and Responses.* New York: Oxford University Press, 1996.

Matteo, Sherri, ed. *American Women in the Nineties.* Boston: Northeastern University Press, 1993.

Morrison, Ann M.; Randall P. White; and Ellen Van Velsor. *Breaking the Glass Ceiling: Can Women Reach the Top of America's Largest Corporations?* updated ed. Reading, MA: Addison-Wesley, 1992.

Powell, Gary N. *Women and Men in Management,* 2d ed. Newbury Park, CA: Sage Publications, 1993.

Puckett, Same B., and Alan R. Emery. *Managing AIDS in the Workplace.* Reading, MA: Addison-Wesley, 1988.

Rix, Sara E. *The American Woman 1990–91: A Status Report.* New York: Norton, 1990.

Singer, Merrill, ed. *The Political Economy of AIDS.* Amityville, NY: Baywood Publishers, 1998.

United Nations. *The World's Women, 1970–1990: Trends and Statistics.* New York: United Nations Publications, June 1991.

The Employee-Employer Relationship

Employees and employers are engaged in a critical relationship affecting the corporation's performance. There is a basic economic aspect to this relationship. Employees provide labor for the firm; employers compensate workers for their contribution of skill or productivity. Yet, also present in the employee-employer exchange are numerous social, ethical, legal, and public policy issues. Attention to the multiple aspects of this association can benefit the firm, its workers, and society.

This topic focuses on these key questions and objectives:

- Do employers have a duty or obligation within the employer-employee contract to provide job security and equal opportunities for employment to their workers?

- What rights do workers have to organize and bargain collectively?

- As governmental intervention into employee safety and health issues increases, what are a business's duties in protecting its workers?

- How does greater diversity in the workforce affect a business's obligations to its employees?

- Does a business's acquiring information about its workers violate an employee's right to privacy? For example, do monitoring employee communication, AIDS testing, and honesty tests violate an employee's privacy?

- Do employees have a duty to blow the whistle on corporate misconduct, or should employees always be loyal to their employer?

Post–Lawrence–Weber:
Business and Society,
Ninth Edition

The Employee–Employer
Relationship

© The McGraw–Hill
Companies, 1999

Santo Alba began working for Raytheon Company in February 1988. Nine years later, on May 15, 1997, he died, decapitated by a circular saw used for cutting sheet metal in one of the shops he supervised. The coroner ruled the death a suicide. Yet the Alba family had a different version of the circumstances that led to Santo's grisly death.

The Alba family alleged that Santo sent several memos to his manager in 1996 that said he felt overwhelmed by increased responsibilities at work. Restructuring had slashed over half the people in his department. According to the Alba family, because of Raytheon's workforce reductions, Santo Alba had been required to work 70 to 80 hour weeks, including weekends.

In March 1994, Alba had sought counseling and was hospitalized for several days. According to his medical records, he was admitted for "severe anxiety/depression related to fear of job loss, stress, [and] working very long hours in highly driven work atmosphere." His family said he told doctors that he had considered suicide because he was so anxiety-ridden. The Albas filed charges, claiming that Raytheon drove Santo to his death by overloading him with work and failing to make accommodations for his depression.[1]

Is Raytheon responsible for Santo Alba's suicide? Legally? Ethically? What obligation does a firm have to attend to the needs of the workers still employed after corporate downsizing? What obligations does a firm have to a worker with a documented mental illness?

The Employee–Employer Contract

Employees and employers are engaged in a stakeholder relationship that includes numerous expectations by both parties. The employer, for example, has assumed various duties and obligations. Some of these responsibilities are economic or legal; others are social or ethical in nature.

The relationship is clearly more than simply paying a worker for the labor provided. Cultural values and traditions also play a role. In Europe, employers feel they have a duty to include workers on the board of directors to assist in forming company policy. For many years, Japanese employers have offered their workers lifelong employment, although this practice has become less widespread in recent years. In the United States, since the late 1800s, the contractual basis for employee labor has been employment-at-will. **Employment-at-will** means that employees are hired and retain their jobs "at the will of," or as decided by, the employer. However, over time, an increase in wrongful discharge claims by employees has dramatically curtailed American employers' freedom to terminate workers.

The New Social Contract

In recent years, basic expectations underlying the employee-employer relationship have changed, both in the United States and in other countries around the globe. Beginning in the late 1980s and continuing through the 1990s, fierce global competition and greater attention to improving the bottom line resulted in significant corporate restructuring and downsizing (termination) of employees. Along with corporate restructuring came a new way of thinking about the employee-employer relationship. As described in Figure 1, the new **employer-employee social contract** shifted the focus of employers' obligations away

[1] Audrey Choi, "Family Claims Raytheon Caused Suicide," *Wall Street Journal*, November 3, 1995, p. B5.

Post–Lawrence–Weber:
Business and Society,
Ninth Edition

The Employee–Employer
Relationship

© The McGraw-Hill
Companies, 1999

Figure 1

The new employer-
employee social
contract.

Sources: James E.
Post, "The New
Social Contract," in
Oliver Williams and
John Houck, eds.,
*The Global Challenge
to Corporate Social
Responsibility* (New
York: Oxford
University Press,
1995); and Barbara
W. Altman and
James E. Post,
"Challenges in
Balancing Corporate
Economic and Social
Responsibilities,"
Boston University
Working Paper,
Boston, MA, 1994.

Emphasizes

- The burden of maintaining employment shifts from the employer to the employee.
- Job security is no longer based on seniority but on job performances.
- Worker employability is enhanced by training and development programs.

Positive Results for Employers	Negative Results for Employers
• Greater ability to move employees job to job	• Lower employee morale
• Greater ease in removing marginal performers	• Reduced productivity
• Greater ability to recruit and retain high performers	• Employee mistrust of the firm
• More flexibility due to temporary workforce	• Temporary workforce more difficult to manage
• More self-directed, independent employees	• Increase in unplanned turnover
• Development of diversity and work/family programs	• Uncertainty of job skills possessed by future workforce
	• Pressure to develop social programs to replace job security

from long-term job security. The new relationship was aimed at satisfying employees at work by emphasizing interesting and challenging work, performance-based compensation, and training to help workers become more employable within and outside the company. In return, employees were expected to contribute to the employer-employee social contract by providing a strong commitment to the job task and work team. Employees were expected to share in the responsibility of achieving company success. The new message for employees was: *you* are responsible for your lifetime employment. It is not the responsibility of the employer.[2]

Although initially seen in the United States, evidence of this change of contractual employment is appearing in many countries. The International Labor Organization reported that in 1995, 30 percent of the world's labor force, or 750 million people, were either unemployed or underemployed. Throughout the 1990s, U.S. firms continued to restructure their organizations, often leading to a dramatic reduction of the number of employees. In 1994, employers announced more than 3,100 job terminations *per day.* Three years later, 10 of the nation's largest employers—including Eastman Kodak, Woolworth, Citicorp and International Paper—announced layoffs exceeding 4,000 employees per firm, averaging more than 16 percent of the firms' workforces. The dramatic financial tumble of the Asian economies impacted workers there. Experts estimated that layoffs could reach two million employees in Indonesia, Thailand, South Korea, Japan, and Hong Kong alone.[3]

[2]See a collection of papers in *Human Resources Briefing: The New Employer-Employee Contract* (New York: The Conference Board, 1994); "Writing a New Social Contract," *Business Week,* March 11, 1996, pp. 60–61; and "Rewriting the Social Contract," *Business Week,* November 20, 1995, pp. 120–ff., 120–123, 126, 130, 134.
[3]"Jobs Shock," *Business Week,* December 22, 1997, pp. 48–49; and G. Pascal Zachary, "Study Predicts Rising Global Joblessness," *The Wall Street Journal,* February 22, 1995, pp. A2, A5; Eric Rolfe Greenberg, "Downsizing AMA Survey Results," *Compensation and Benefits Review,* July–August 1991, pp. 33–38; and "Big Knives of 1997," *Business Week,* December 15, 1997, p. 6.

Post–Lawrence–Weber:
Business and Society,
Ninth Edition

The Employee–Employer
Relationship

© The McGraw–Hill
Companies, 1999

The Government Role in the Employment Relationship

The relationship between employers and employees in the United States is influenced in important ways by laws and regulations that shape worker rights to organize and bargain collectively and that prescribe standards of equal opportunity and occupational safety and health. Some of the roles that government plays are described in this section.

The Role of Labor Unions

An important voice for employees on the job is a labor union. The influence of labor unions in the United States has waxed and waned over the years. During the New Deal, federal laws were passed that gave many employees the right to organize unions and to bargain collectively with their employers. Many workers, particularly in manufacturing industries such as automobiles and steel, joined unions, and the ranks of organized labor grew rapidly during the 1930s and 1940s. Unions negotiated with employers for better wages, benefits such as pensions and health insurance, and improved working conditions. Since the mid-1950s, however, the proportion of American workers represented by unions has declined. In 1997, only about 14 percent of all employees were union members. (The percentage was somewhat higher in government employment.)

Some observers believe, however, that unions in the United States may be poised for recovery. The AFL-CIO, the major federation of labor unions, elected new leaders in 1995 who vowed to devote more resources to organizing new members. A possible indicator of labor's resurgence was the 1997 Teamsters' strike against the United Parcel Service (UPS). After a several day strike that crippled the ability of many businesses to transport important documents and packages, management agreed to a new contract that included higher wages and more full-time job opportunities for part-time workers. The Teamsters believed that strong support from the public for the rights of part-time workers was an important factor in their victory. Polls showed a 2-to-1 margin of support for striking workers over management. Experts believed that public confidence might encourage other unions to take a harder line against management in future negotiations.

Labor union power was evident in other ways in the late 1990s. Time Warner faced an unexpected foe at the company's 1996 annual stockholder meeting: its labor union. A total of 12 labor unions used shareholder activism to score a number of victories regarding union representation in corporate governance. New alliances were formed between labor unions and diverse activist organizations such as the Sierra Club and the National Association for the Advancement of Colored People.[4]

Some labor unions also sought to work cooperatively with employers for their mutual benefit. At Saturn, AT&T, and Kaiser Permanente (a large health maintenance organization), management and unions forged new partnerships aimed both at giving workers a greater say in the business and improving quality and productivity. However, the adversarial tone that had so often characterized management-union relations could also be found. At Caterpillar, management took a tough stance when the machinists union called a strike. The firm hired replacement workers, used retirees, salaried employees, and clerical staff in plant operation positions, and shifted work to outside contractors. When the United Auto Workers went on strike months later at a McDonnell Douglas plant, the firm followed Caterpillar's strategy.

[4]Joann S. Lublin, "Unions Brandish Stock to Force Change," *Wall Street Journal,* May 17, 1996, pp. B1, B2; and Aaron Bernstein, "Big Labor Invites a Few Friends Over," *Business Week,* April 21, 1997, p. 44.

Post-Lawrence-Weber:
Business and Society,
Ninth Edition

The Employee-Employer
Relationship

© The McGraw-Hill
Companies, 1999

Equal Job Opportunity

Working to ensure **equal job opportunity** continues to be a socially desirable goal for U.S. businesses. This area of employee relations calls for positive responses and initiatives if businesses are to continue evolving toward social responsiveness and public approval.

Government Policies and Regulations

Government efforts against workplace discrimination began in the United States on a major scale in the 1960s. U.S. presidents issued directives, and Congress enacted laws intended to improve equal treatment of employees. These government rules apply to most businesses in the following ways:

- Discrimination based on race, color, religion, sex, national origin, physical or mental disability, or age is prohibited in all employment practices. This includes hiring, promotion, job classification, and assignment, compensation, and other conditions of work.

- Government contractors must have written affirmative action plans detailing how they are working positively to overcome past and present effects of discrimination in their workforce. However, affirmative action plans must be temporary and flexible, designed to current past discrimination, and cannot result in reverse discrimination against whites or men.

- Women and men must receive equal pay for performing equal work, and employers may not discriminate on the basis of pregnancy.

Governmental efforts to eliminate discrimination in the workplace vary from country to country. As shown in Figure 2, more regulatory control exists in the United States, Canada, and France than in Venezuela and Hong Kong.

The major agency charged with enforcing federal equal employment opportunity laws and executive orders in the United States is the **Equal Employment Opportunity**

Figure 2

Prohibition of workplace discrimination around the world.

Country	Age	Sex	National Origin	Race	Religion	Marital Status
United States	yes	yes	yes	yes	yes	no
France	some	yes	yes	yes	yes	yes
Greece	no	yes	no	yes	yes	yes
Great Britain	no	yes	yes	yes	no	no
Venezuela	no	no	no	no	no	no
Canada	yes	yes	yes	yes	yes	yes
Hong Kong	no	no	no	no	no	no
Japan	no	yes	yes	yes	yes	no
Italy	yes	yes	some	yes	yes	no
Spain	no	yes	yes	yes	yes	yes
Belgium	some	yes	yes	yes	yes	yes
Netherlands	no	yes	yes	yes	yes	yes

Post–Lawrence–Weber:
Business and Society,
Ninth Edition

The Employee–Employer
Relationship

© The McGraw–Hill
Companies, 1999

Commission (EEOC). The EEOC was created in 1964 and given added enforcement powers in 1972 and 1990. This agency is primarily responsible for enforcing provisions of the Civil Rights Acts of 1964 and 1991, the Equal Opportunity Act, the Equal Pay Act, the Age Discrimination in Employment Act, and the Americans with Disabilities Act.

Regulators and courts first used a results-oriented approach to these laws. In other words, a company would be considered in violation of the law if statistical analysis revealed that its jobs were out of line with the proportions of whites and nonwhites or men and women potentially available for such work. Later, other judicial interpretations were handed down. In the early 1980s, these decisions were seen as gains for business because companies were less vulnerable to discrimination lawsuits and freer to make personnel decisions on their own. In the 1990s, however, government efforts placed additional responsibilities on businesses and overturned the effects of the U.S. Supreme Court decisions from the early 1980s. For example, under the 1990 EEOC guidelines, employers faced greater liability for employee conduct involving sexual harassment. In addition, employers were obligated to demonstrate that alleged discriminatory practices were job related and consistent with practices necessary to operate a business, according to the 1991 Civil Rights Act.

Corporate Responses

Generally, businesses have developed a number of approaches to curb discrimination and equalize employment opportunities. An example of one company that has done a particularly good job at this is the Inland Steel Company, shown in Exhibit A. Companies that

---

EXHIBIT A   Addressing Discrimination at Inland Steel

In the mid-1980s, four African-American managers at Inland Steel, two men and two women, came forward with a complaint. Although they had been with the company for many years and had excellent performance evaluations, they had not advanced in their careers as far as they felt they should have. They perceived that their way up the corporate ladder was blocked because of race and gender discrimination.

Inland responded proactively. White, male managers were encouraged to attend workshops sponsored by the Urban Crisis Center in Atlanta and directed by the charismatic civil rights activist, Reverend Charles King, Jr. At these workshops, participants were helped to understand what it really felt like to be a minority and to be excluded from contributing to the decision process.

The company increased its number of affirmative action focus groups. Their goal was to ensure that all people at Inland were treated equally and fairly and had the opportunity to achieve their potential. The groups also tried to draw attention to subtle forms of discrimination and to give minorities and women a greater voice in the company.

These efforts paid off. Hiring of minorities and women increased. Many employees who had been passed over for years were promoted to positions commensurate with their years of experience and performance evaluations. Inland Steel had made real progress in incorporating affirmative action practices into its everyday culture.

In 1992, the company won an award from the Business Enterprise Trust for its efforts to reduce discrimination.

Post–Lawrence–Weber:
Business and Society,
Ninth Edition

The Employee–Employer
Relationship

© The McGraw–Hill
Companies, 1999

have failed to promote equal opportunity in employment often find themselves facing expensive lawsuits based on charges of employee discrimination.

> *One of the more sensational examples of racial discrimination in the workplace involved Texaco. A number of African-American employees sued the big oil company, charging discrimination. In the course of investigating the case, these employees' attorneys obtained a copy of a tape recording, apparently of top Texaco executives at a meeting to discuss how to respond to the lawsuit. The tape seemed to contain offensive racial epithets as well as some discussion of destroying evidence that would be harmful to Texaco's position. When a transcript of the tape was published, it was very embarrassing for the company.*
>
> *Texaco settled the lawsuit out of court. The firm agreed to pay $176.1 million over five years, the largest settlement in the history of racial discrimination suits in the United States. The company also created organizational programs promoting racial sensitivity at work. An Equality and Tolerance Task Force was created with committee members appointed by the firm and the plaintiff's lawyers. Willie Stamfield, an African-American Texaco executive, was appointed as an assistant to the task force chairperson to oversee diversity issues at the firm.[5]*

Potentially costly lawsuits can involve other forms of discrimination as well. Age discrimination was the charge made by 239 former First Union Corporation employees. The nation's sixth-largest bank agreed to pay $58.5 million to settle the class-action suits. Charges of age discrimination were also filed against the Adolph Coors brewing company, Schering-Plough pharmaceutical firm, and investment bankers and traders at Kidder, Peabody & Company. Although the cases against the last three firms have not been proven in court, it does illustrate the widespread potential for costly discrimination lawsuits in business.

> *In a survey of 515 trial verdicts involving wrongful termination lawsuits from 1988 to 1992, successful age-bias claims resulted in an average award of more than $300,000, compared with approximately $250,000 awarded for sex discrimination actions. Race bias and disability discrimination claims, on average, received approximately $200,000 per claim.[6]*

Promoting equal opportunity in hiring, promotion, and job assignment is good business, both because it allows firms to use the widest possible range of talent and it avoids expensive lawsuits.

Affirmative Action

One way to promote equal opportunity and remedy past discrimination is through **affirmative action.** Since the mid-1960s, major government contractors have been required by presidential executive order to adopt written affirmative action plans specifying goals, actions, and timetables for promoting greater on-the-job equality. Their purpose is to

---

[5]"Texaco to Pay $176.1 Million in Bias Suit," *Wall Street Journal,* November 187, 1996, pp. A3, A6.
[6]"Age-Bias Cases Found to Bring Big Jury Awards," *Wall Street Journal,* December 17, 1993, pp. B1, B8.

Post–Lawrence–Weber:
Business and Society,
Ninth Edition

The Employee–Employer
Relationship

© The McGraw–Hill
Companies, 1999

reduce job discrimination by encouraging companies to take positive (that is, affirmative) steps to overcome past employment practices and traditions that may have been discriminatory.

Affirmative action became increasingly controversial in the late 1990s. In some states, new laws (such as Proposition 209 in California) were passed banning or limiting affirmative action programs in public hiring and university admissions, and the issue was debated in Congress and in the courts. Backers of these programs argued that affirmative action was an important tool for achieving equal opportunity. Roger Wilkins, a well-known African-American historian, supported this view: "We believe that minorities and women are still disadvantaged in our highly competitive society and that affirmative action is absolutely necessary to level the playing field." Some large corporations have found that legally required affirmative action programs are helpful in monitoring the company's progress in providing equal job opportunity. General Electric, AT&T, and IBM have said that they would continue to use affirmative action goals and timetables even if they were not required by law.

Critics of affirmative action, however, argued that affirmative action was inconsistent with the principles of fairness and equality. Some pointed to instances of so-called **reverse discrimination,** which occurs when one group is unintentionally discriminated against in an effort to help another group. For example, if a more qualified white man were passed over for a job as a firefighter in favor of a less qualified Hispanic man to remedy past discrimination in the fire department, this might seem unfair to the white candidate. Critics of affirmative action also argued that these programs could actually stigmatize or demoralize the very groups they were designed to help. For example, if a woman were hired for a top management post, other people might *think* she got the job just because of affirmative action preferences, even if she was truly the best qualified. This might undermine her effectiveness on the job or even cause her to question her own abilities. Some women and members of minority groups actually wanted *less* emphasis on affirmative action, preferring to achieve personal success without preferential treatment.[7]

In 1995, the Supreme Court ruled in an important decision that affirmative action plans were legal but only if they were temporary and flexible, designed to correct past discrimination, and did not result in reverse discrimination against men or whites. Under this ruling, *quotas* (e.g., a hard-and-fast rule that 50 percent of all new positions will go to women, say, or African-Americans) would no longer be permitted in most cases. Clearly, affirmative action is an issue that will continue to be debated, not just in the courts but in business, society, and government generally.

Americans with Disabilities Act

The Americans with Disabilities Act (ADA) of 1990 requires employers to make accommodations for disabled workers and job applicants and prohibits employers from discriminating on the basis of a person's disability. A more elaborate description of the provisions in the ADA is shown in Figure 3.

---

[7] Peter Coy, "The Best Kind of Affirmative Action," *Business Week,* May 19, 1997, p. 35; and "A 'Race-Neutral' Helping Hand?" *Business Week,* February 27, 1995, pp. 120–121.

Post–Lawrence–Weber:
Business and Society,
Ninth Edition

The Employee–Employer
Relationship

© The McGraw–Hill
Companies, 1999

Figure 3

Provisions of the Americans with Disabilities Act of 1990.

Source: Adapted from The Equal Employment Opportunity Commission, *The Americans with Disabilities Act of 1990* (Washington, DC: 1991. U.S. Government Printing Office, (Washington D.C.: U.S. Government Printing Office, 1991).

Prohibits employers when hiring from inquiring about

- Medical history
- Prior insurance claims
- Work absenteeism due to illness
- Past treatment for alcoholism
- Mental illness

Defines a qualified disabled worker as

- One who can perform the "essential functions" of a job, with or without reasonable accommodations

Requires employers to make reasonable accommodations to disabled workers by

- Modifying work equipment
- Providing readers or interpreters
- Adjusting work schedules
- Making existing facilities accessible

Even before the law was signed, employers complained that the definition of disability was unclear. Nonetheless, the act was passed, and those with disabilities began to exercise their new rights. The EEOC reported it had received over 16,000 ADA-related complaints by the end of 1993. Nearly half of the charges involved the discharge of a disabled employee. Other complaints accused employers of failing to provide reasonable accommodations for the disabled at work, discriminatory hiring practices, or the harassment of disabled workers. By 1995, the EEOC relaxed restrictions on what questions employers could ask job applicants with disabilities.

Corporate responses were generally slow. However, leaders of the country's largest firms and labor unions joined forces to form the National Organization on Disability and the Industry-Labor Council of the National Center for Disability Services. These organizations seek to promote the hiring and advancement of people with disabilities. Many employers have been encouraged to hire people with disabilities, based on the good results others have achieved through this practice.

Courts have interpreted the ADA to cover persons with acquired immunodeficiency syndrome (AIDS). Discrimination against persons with AIDS or infected with the virus that causes AIDS is prohibited under the ADA, so long as the person can perform essential elements of the job. The employment rights of workers with AIDS are discussed later.

Job Safety and Health

Much industrial work is inherently hazardous because of the extensive use of high-speed and noisy machinery, production processes requiring high temperatures, an increasing reliance on sophisticated chemical compounds, and the nature of such work as construction, underground, and undersea tunneling, drilling, and mining. Accidents, injuries, and illnesses are likely to occur under these circumstances.

Over the past decade, new categories of accidents or illnesses have emerged, including the fast-growing job safety problem of office injuries. Stress from rising produc-

Post–Lawrence–Weber:
Business and Society,
Ninth Edition

The Employee–Employer
Relationship

© The McGraw–Hill
Companies, 1999

tivity pressure and escalating job demands can cause cumulative trauma disorders, such as the wrist pain sometimes experienced by supermarket checkers, meatcutters, or keyboard operators. The number of health problems attributed to the use of video display terminals and computer keyboards and to tasks requiring repetitive motion have increased tenfold in the past decade. *Ergonomics* quickly became an office buzzword in the 1990s. **Ergonomics** means adapting work and work conditions and equipment to suit the worker rather than forcing the worker to adapt to the design of the machine, for example. Office furniture that lacks ergonomic features may be partly responsible for poor productivity and lost time due to illness and injury.

Annually, nearly 10,000 workers are killed, 6 million are injured, and 300,000 become ill while on the job, according to union reports. As the workforce continues to get older, workplace injuries are of greater concern. According to the Bureau of Labor Statistics, older workers are nearly four times as likely as younger ones to die from job-related injuries. Despite some decreases in worker fatalities and injuries, "the annual death rate is still radically higher than other industrialized nations," stated Donald Millar, director of the National Institute for Occupational Safety and Health. Corporate liability for on-the-job injuries also is escalating. Employers in 14 states have been sentenced to prison for ignoring warnings to improve safety at work. One plant owner was sentenced to serve 20 years in jail for a workplace fatality.[8]

Occupational Safety and Health Administration

The **Occupational Safety and Health Administration (OSHA),** created by Congress in 1970, has been one of the most controversial of the government agencies established in the great wave of social legislation during the 1970s. Congress gave OSHA important powers over employers, requiring them to provide for each employee a job "free from recognized hazards that are causing or likely to cause death or serious physical harm." Employers found in violation of OSHA safety and health standards can be fined and, in the case of willful violation causing the death of an employee, jailed as well.

Over the years, OSHA has sometimes been more aggressive, sometimes less aggressive, in policing the health and safety of American workplaces. In the late 1980s and early 1990s, the agency vigorously pursued significant safety violations and imposed large fines on violators.

> *In 1988, Chrysler agreed to pay $1.6 million to settle OSHA charges of worker overexposure to lead and arsenic and other alleged health and safety violations. In 1993, OSHA charged the Wyman-Gordon Company with 149 safety violations at its Massachusetts metal forging plant. Over $1 million in penalties was proposed.[9]*

By the mid-1990s, however, OSHA appeared to be more cooperative. From 1995 to 1997, OSHA inspections declined 43 percent, citations for serious safety violations dropped 64 percent, and the agency appeared more open to business concerns in seeking collaborative solutions to workplace hazards.

---

[8]Helen L. Richardson, "Accept Responsibility for Safety," *Transportation and Distribution,* August 1992, pp. 29–32; and Michael Moss, "For Older Employees, On-the-Job Injuries Are More Often Deadly," *The Wall Street Journal,* June 17, 1997, pp. A1, A10.

[9]"Chrysler to Pay Record Penalty in OSHA Case," *The Wall Street Journal,* February 2, 1987, p. 20; and "OSHA Asks Safety Penalties of More than $1 Million," *The Wall Street Journal,* August 13, 1993, p. B2.

Post-Lawrence-Weber:
Business and Society,
Ninth Edition

The Employee–Employer
Relationship

© The McGraw–Hill
Companies, 1999

Management's Responses

Although some have praised OSHA as an aggressive government watchdog, businesses have generally criticized it as being too costly. Small businesses in particular had a difficult time carrying the paperwork required by OSHA's rules. Other companies objected to the high cost of redesigning machinery and production processes, saying that these expenses far outweighed any tangible or marginal benefit in increased safety and health for workers. Some employees themselves refused to wear required safety goggles, earplugs, respirators, and other special equipment to protect them from harm, but if they were to be injured while not wearing such items, the employer, not the employee, would be subject to penalty.

Some businesses have developed their own systems to reduce the threats of workplace injuries. One of the more popular and widespread methods is **workplace safety teams.** Safety teams are generally made up of equal numbers of workers and managers. In operation, these teams not only reduce employee accidents, they also lower workers' compensation costs. The effect is particularly dramatic at small companies that typically do not have the financial or human resources to develop the more elaborate and costly safety programs and committees found in large corporations.

The experience with employee safety teams has been encouraging. Norfolk Southern reduced its number of injuries by two-thirds while reducing the size of its safety staff by 84 percent. The rise in worker compensation costs at State Fair Foods was reversed after the firm initiated worker-safety teams and gave them the authority to correct problems immediately.[10]

Businesses seem to be responding with cautious cooperation to government regulations designed to protect employees. Some appear to be complying only with the letter of the law; others are exceeding government standards to avoid regulatory investigation. In spite of these mixed results, many firms accept their responsibility to protect their employees' health and safety.

Workplace Violence

Another social issue affecting their employees' safety is challenging employers: violence in the workplace. Stories of angry or distraught employees, ex-employees, or associates of employees attacking workers, coworkers, or superiors at work are becoming more frequent. For example, there is a growing trend for workers who have lost their jobs to seek vengeance against individuals who terminated them, often in calculated and cold-blooded fashion. In a three-year period there were six shootings at a Detroit-area auto plant. In another incident, an employee fired eight years earlier from James River Corporation, a Pennsylvania paper products manufacturer, faked a family emergency to gain access to the company's executive offices. The former employee shot Brenton F. Halsey, Jr., vice president and the son of the company's founder, eight times before turning the gun on himself.

Nearly one-fourth of the 311 companies surveyed reported that at least one of their employees had been attacked or killed on the job since 1990. Another 31 percent claim threats have been made against workers. The Justice Department reported that nearly

[10]Michael A. Verespej, "Better Safety through Empowerment," *Industry Week,* November 15, 1993, pp. 56–68.

Post–Lawrence–Weber:
Business and Society,
Ninth Edition

The Employee–Employer
Relationship

© The McGraw–Hill
Companies, 1999

one million people every year were victims of violent crimes while working, costing 1.75 million days of lost work and over $55 million in lost wages.[11]

Unfortunately, many companies are poorly prepared to deal with these situations. Only 24 percent of employers offer any type of formal training to their employees in coping with workplace violence, and just 10 percent offer this type of training to *all* employees. Government intervention in this area of employee safety is also lacking.

Working Conditions around the World

Recent headlines have turned the public's attention to the problem of sweatshops, factories where employees are forced to work long hours at low wages, under abhorrent working conditions. One of the most publicized scandals involved shoe manufacturer Nike. A study of the work conditions at Nike's factory in Vietnam reported that workers were paid below minimum wages, limited to one trip to the bathroom and two drinks of water per shift, verbally abused, sexually harassed, and commonly subjected to corporal punishment. Similar charges were made against four of the nation's largest retailers—Wal-Mart, Kmart, Nordstroms, and Limited—whose merchandise was made at New York City factories.[12]

In an effort to address the worldwide issue of work conditions, the Council on Economic Priorities introduced Social Accountability 8000, or SA 8000. Modeled after the quality initiative developed by the International Organization for Standardization, ISO 9000 (now used in 80 countries), SA 8000 established criteria for companies to meet in order to receive a "good working condition" certification. The criteria include:

- Do not use child or forced labor.
- Provide a safe working environment.
- Respect workers' rights to unionize.
- Do not regularly require more than 48-hour workweek.
- Pay wages sufficient to meet workers' basic needs.

Workplace Diversity

The sheer diversity of the U.S. workforce spawns many new employee issues and problems. Women, African-Americans, Hispanics, Asians, the physically or mentally challenged, and other entrants are changing the nation's labor pool in dramatic ways. According to the Hudson Institute, 85 percent of the growth expected in the U.S. workforce by the year 2000 will come from white and nonwhite women, nonwhite men, and immigrants of both sexes and various races. As the large group of white men now dominant in the labor force ages and retires, they will occupy a smaller share of the total labor pool, only about 39 percent by the year 2000, according to the U.S. Department of Labor.

Businesses adjusting to these changes in the workforce may be in a position to reap the benefits of a well-integrated yet culturally diverse work population. These advantages

---

[11]"Disgruntled Workers Intent on Revenge Increasingly Harm Colleagues and Bosses," *The Wall Street Journal,* September 15, 1992, pp. B1, B10; "Waging War in the Workplace," *Newsweek,* July 19, 1993, pp. 30–31, 34; "Companies See More Workplace Violence," *The Wall Street Journal,* April 12, 1994, pp. B1, B6; "Murder in Workplace Is a Major Part of the Latest Death-on-the-Job Statistics," *The Wall Street Journal,* August 11, 1994, p. A4; and Jim McKay, "Worked Over at Work," *Pittsburgh Post-Gazette,* May 28, 1995, p. C1.
[12]"Nike Workers in Vietnam Suffer Abuse, Group Says," *The Wall Street Journal,* March 28, 1997, p. B15.

Post–Lawrence–Weber:
Business and Society,
Ninth Edition

The Employee–Employer
Relationship

© The McGraw–Hill
Companies, 1999

include attracting applicants from a large potential labor pool, a work environment enriched by multiple cultures, and the ability to meet the needs of a culturally diverse customer base in the United States and abroad.

Voice Processing Corporation, which manufactures speech-recognition software, has 11 nationalities represented among its 40 corporate headquarters' staff members. Combined, these employees speak 30 languages, including Mandarin Chinese, Russian, Hindi, Turkish, Thai, and Serbo-Croatian. The multilingual workforce enabled Voice Processing to more easily introduce and market its products in countries all over the world.[13]

Language in the Workplace

About one of five workers seeking jobs in the 1990s was a recent immigrant. For employers, that often meant relying on employees whose limited knowledge of English could interfere with their work.

Motorola confronted the problem by offering to meet employees halfway. English communication classes were provided at the company's expense and, increasingly, on company time. The company spent over $30 million on the program, which included basic literacy for English speakers. Motorola says about 6,000 employees received language training.

The push for on-the-job language efficiency can lead to problems, however, if a company decides that all of its rules and regulations must be exclusively in English. The U.S. Supreme Court has upheld these English-only rules. In 1994, the Court refused to overturn a lower court ruling that permitted a California company to require its employees to speak English on the job. However, according to the U.S. Equal Employment Opportunity Commission, these practices can be used to discriminate against certain groups at work, thereby heightening ethnic tensions. Where non-English-speaking employees make up a large bulk of a company's workforce, employers need to demonstrate a commitment to fairness by adopting a flexible language policy.

Managing a Diverse Workforce

Managers have many new lessons to learn if they are to be effective in motivating and directing their multicultural employees. One lesson is to listen—to hear the distinct and often subtle ways of speaking and communicating that are routinely used by various ethnic groups, and to hear the often submerged voices of women employees, Hispanics, Native Americans, African-Americans, Asian-Americans, the physically or mentally challenged, and others. Yet, as shown in Exhibit B, it may require a costly lawsuit to become more attentive to workplace diversity issues.

A group of regional and national companies have formed the Diversity Council. The purpose of the organization is to help member firms manage diversity issues through cooperative efforts. Through the council, member firms are able to share ideas and participate in group problem solving for workforce diversity management and training. Managing the corporate culture regarding diversity

---

[13]"Small Company Goes Global with Diverse Work Force," *Wall Street Journal,* October 12, 1994, p. B2.

Post–Lawrence–Weber:
Business and Society,
Ninth Edition

The Employee–Employer
Relationship

© The McGraw–Hill
Companies, 1999

EXHIBIT B   Diversity at Shoney's

Raymond Danner, cofounder of Shoney's restaurants, liked to shake up the staffs at his restaurants because some of them "were too dark." Employees claimed that he ordered managers to fire black employees if they seemed too visible to white customers. He would often make racial slurs at work. Now retired, Danner gives heavily to black causes and believes that the restaurant staffs need to be more representative of minorities in America's ever-changing business environment. "We have a policy of zero tolerance [at Shoney's]," said Juanita Presley, a black lawyer and one of two employees investigating discrimination and harassment complaints at the company.

So what took Shoney's from racial insensitivity to a company aggressively pursuing workplace diversity? A costly, attention-grabbing lawsuit, changing times, and, some think, an actual change of heart by Shoney's leadership.

Since 1989, the family-style restaurant chain added 83 black dining-room supervisors. Two of its 24 vice presidents were black, and an African-American was on the company's nine-member board of directors. Black-owned franchises had increased from 2 in 1989 to 13 in 1996. The firm spent $17 million annually to buy goods and services from minority-owned companies in 1996, compared with $2 million in 1989.

The company operated an 800-number, posted in all corporate offices and its 700 restaurants, to field complaints about racial discrimination or harassment. In 1996, it fired an employee who left racial slurs on a tape recording, reinforcing its claim of having a zero tolerance policy on racism.

The firm came a long way since taking a $77.2 million charge to settle the class-action lawsuit, which claimed that Shoney's was a racist enterprise. In total, Shoney employees who filed the lawsuit received $105 million, with Raymond Danner paying over $50 million out of his own pocket.

Source: Dorothy J. Gaiter, "How Shoney's, Belted by a Lawsuit, Found the Path to Diversity," *The Wall Street Journal,* April 16, 1996, pp. A1, A6.

---

involves providing a work environment that encourages all employees to perform their best and to feel that they are part of the company. To be successful, firms must adopt cultural diversity as a corporate priority and recognize the different ways people think, see, and respond to the world around them.

When employees believe they are respected, rather than ridiculed, for the way they talk, for the way they approach business problems, or for their gender or ethnic background, their morale is higher and a company's productivity tends to be higher.

Corporations in the United States are slowly beginning to acknowledge differences in employee sexual orientation and lifestyles. Gay and lesbian employees are becoming a vocal minority, winning important victories in the courts. Spurred by this mounting pressure, firms are responding.

More than 350 U.S. and Canadian corporations offered domestic-partner benefits, including coverage for the partners of gay employees. Lotus Development

Post–Lawrence–Weber:
Business and Society,
Ninth Edition

The Employee–Employer
Relationship

© The McGraw–Hill
Companies, 1999

*was the first major employer to offer spousal benefits to same-sex partners.
AT&T, Chase Manhattan, General Motors Canada, and Microsoft are among
other firms responding to employee sexual orientation diversity. A few firms
also cover heterosexual unmarried couples, including Ben and Jerry's, Levi
Strauss, Federal National Mortgage Association, and Borland International.*[14]

Addressing issues of cultural or sexual diversity in the workplace is simply another
way of saying what other materials say: business operations always occur within a social
and cultural setting, and the best managers are those who make their decisions on that
basis.

Challenging Employees' Privacy

Privacy rights in the business context refer primarily to
protecting a person's private life from intrusive and un-
warranted business actions. The employees believe that their religious, political, and social beliefs, as well as personal lifestyles, are private matters and should be safeguarded
from snooping or analysis. Exceptions are permitted grudgingly only when job involvement is clearly proved. For example, it may be appropriate to know that an employee is
discussing with a competitor, through e-mail messages, the specifications of a newly developed product not yet on the market. Other behaviors are not so clear-cut. For example, should a job applicant who is experiencing severe financial problems be denied employment out of fear that he may be more inclined to steal from the company? Should an
employee be terminated after the firm discovers that she has a serious medical problem,
although it does not affect her job performance, since the company's health insurance premiums may dramatically increase? At what point do company interests weigh more heavily than an employee's right to freedom and privacy?

Information Technology

The technology age brought many ethical issues to the forefront. A company's need for
information, particularly about employees, to conduct business may be at odds with an
employee's privacy. Several federal laws govern the dissemination of information: the Fair
Credit Reporting Act (1970), Privacy Act (1974), Right to Financial Privacy Act (1978),
Video Privacy Protection Act (1988), and Computer Matching and Privacy Protection Act
(1988). Each of these laws has loopholes. For example, under the Fair Credit Reporting
Act, anyone with a "legitimate business need" can gain access to personal information in
credit files. The Right to Financial Privacy Act is intended to forbid access to individuals' bank accounts; however, the act makes exceptions for state agencies, law enforcement
officials, and private employers.

Besides the collection and storage of employee information, corporations are actively involved in observing workers' activities. Since employers are exempt from the Electronic Communications Privacy Act (1986), they are free at any time to view employees
on closed-circuit televisions, to tap their telephones, e-mail, and network communications,
and to rummage through their computer files with or without employee knowledge or
consent.

[14]"Gay Employees Win Benefits for Partners at More Corporations," *Wall Street Journal,* March
18, 1994, pp. A1, A2.

Post–Lawrence–Weber:
Business and Society,
Ninth Edition

The Employee–Employer
Relationship

© The McGraw–Hill
Companies, 1999

The ability of employers to monitor employee activities exploded in the 1990s with the greater availability of sophisticated surveillance equipment, the greater affordability of this equipment, and the ease of access to employee activity through technological advances in e-mail and facsimile machines (faxes), as the following example illustrates.

Procter & Gamble's (P&G) company practices were exposed in a book, Soap Opera: The Inside Story of Procter & Gamble, *by Alecia Swasy. In the book, the company's activities of routinely obtaining medical records of employees, watching them with video cameras, monitoring their telephone calls from P&G offices and their homes, and following them on business trips were described. For years, the firm employed former agents from the government's Central Intelligence Agency and Federal Bureau of Investigation, as well as former police officers, as part of a security department that conducted investigations that bordered on harassment and invasions of privacy, according to Swasy.*[15]

Management justifies the increase in employee monitoring for a number of reasons: to achieve greater efficiency at work, to maintain an honest workforce and protect the firm from employee theft, and to reduce health insurance premiums by reducing employee negligence or failure to comply with safety regulations. Yet employees are becoming more aware of corporate monitoring and are challenging it in court as an invasion of privacy. Judges have ruled that workers must prove that their reasonable expectations for privacy outweigh the company's reasons for secretive monitoring. Employers sometimes satisfy the court's demands by simply informing workers of the company's surveillance policies. Others require job applicants to sign a privacy waiver before being hired.

AIDS Testing

AIDS has become a major public health problem. Emerging first among homosexual males and drug users, the AIDS epidemic now affects all segments of the world's population. It was estimated that by the year 2005 approximately 1 in every 250 Americans would be infected with the human immunodeficiency virus (HIV) that causes AIDS. The problem of exposure is far greater in other countries, particularly in Africa and Asia. Education seems to be the key in controlling the spread of AIDS. New drug therapies have also allowed those infected with the disease to live longer. The Center for Disease Control reported in 1996 that for the first time fewer of those infected with AIDS were dying than in the previous year.[16]

In business, employees with AIDS are protected against discrimination. In 1990, the federal government passed the strongest anti-AIDS discrimination legislation embodied in the Americans with Disabilities Act, introduced earlier. More than 30 states have laws that bar job discrimination against people with AIDS. Yet the issue of AIDS testing is a highly volatile topic. Opponents of AIDS testing argue that employees should not be tested for the presence of HIV because it would be an invasion of privacy, the available tests are frequently inaccurate, and the tests do not reveal whether a person having AIDS antibodies

[15]"Is Your Boss Spying on You?" *Business Week,* January 15, 1990, pp. 74–75; "P&G Keeps Tabs on Workers, Others, New Book Asserts," *The Wall Street Journal,* September 7, 1993, pp. A3, A10; and Alecia Swasy, *Soap Opera: The Inside Story of Procter & Gamble* (New York: Times Books, 1993).
[16]"Insurance Industry and the AIDS Epidemic," the Insure Foundation, June 1995; and Oscar Suris, "AIDS Deaths Drop Significantly for First Time," *The Wall Street Journal,* February 28, 1997, pp. B1, B16.

Post–Lawrence–Weber:
Business and Society,
Ninth Edition

The Employee–Employer
Relationship

© The McGraw–Hill
Companies, 1999

will ever develop the disease. According to guidelines issued in 1985 by the U.S. Department of Health and Human Services, since AIDS cannot be contracted by casual and normal workplace contacts, employees with the illness should not be segregated from others nor should they be restricted in performing jobs for which they are qualified.

As noted earlier, many firms believe that information is the best defense against AIDS. The benefits of such an information program are listed in Figure 4. Even so, AIDS imposes costs on companies, especially through their health benefit programs. Insurance companies favor trying to isolate high-risk applicants by means of AIDS antibody tests, fighting off attempts by some states to ban such blood tests and using substitutes for tests where they are banned. Insurers also favor denying new policies on grounds of the enormous costs to society; they aggressively fight existing policyholders' claims in court. According to the National Commission on AIDS, if this nation is to conquer AIDS then "strong, positive leadership is needed to overcome ignorance and fear, as well as to rectify the serious flaws and deficits in care and prevention strategies."[17]

Smoking in the Workplace

The life-threatening health dangers of tobacco for smokers have been repeatedly proven in medical research studies, as reported in the case study "The Tobacco Deal" at the end of this textbook. In addition, health officials estimate that environmental tobacco smoke—smoke emitted from a lit cigarette, cigar, or pipe, or exhaled by a smoker—causes nearly 50,000 nonsmoker deaths in the United States each year. Concern about the effects of smoking on nonsmokers has led many companies to restrict smoking to designated areas and private offices. Other firms have completely banned smoking on company grounds. A more extreme corporate policy is described in the following example.

> *As you enter the lobby of Kimball Plastics, an electronic manufacturer, receptionist Jennifer Walsh administered the "sniff test." If a whiff of tobacco smoke was detected on your breath, hair or clothes, you were asked to step outside. According to the firm's antismoking policy, to protect its employees' health, no one who has smoked in the previous two hours or smells of smoke is admitted into the company's laboratories. Kimball Plastics' 50 employees were on the honor system, but if any employee complained of a tobacco smell, the offending coworker faced disciplinary charges.*

Figure 4

Advantages of an
AIDS information
program.

- Minimizes disruption in the workplace
- Decreases chances of costly litigation
- Establishes consistent company guidelines
- Reduces health-care costs
- Enhances employee-employer relations
- Provides up-to-date AIDS information to employees
- Promotes a responsible corporate public image

[17]"How Insurers Succeed in Limiting Their Losses Related to the Disease," *The Wall Street Journal,* May 18, 1987, p. 12; and "Who Will Pay the AIDS Bill?" *Business Week,* April 11, 1988, p. 71. Quotation by the National Commission on AIDS is from Romuald A. Stone, "AIDS in the Workplace: An Executive Update," *Academy of Management Executive* 8, no. 3 (1994), pp. 52–64.

Post–Lawrence–Weber:
Business and Society,
Ninth Edition

The Employee–Employer
Relationship

© The McGraw–Hill
Companies, 1999

Estimates of the cost of smoking in the workplace provide additional support for corporate smoking bans. Over $47 million is lost annually because of productivity loss and disability time related to smoking. A smoker, on average, costs his or her firm $753 annually in medical expenses and misses two more workdays per year than a nonsmoker. Many firms offer their employees smoking-cessation programs, which cost about $165 per person.

Employees who smoke were divided in their reaction to smoking restrictions or bans at work. Some smokers welcomed the opportunity to stop smoking, and many took advantage of company-paid smoking-cessation programs. Others, however, were incensed at what they perceived as a violation of personal rights and freedoms. Some employers have sought government protection from the growing intolerance of workplace smoking and have joined the tobacco industry in appealing to state legislatures. By the mid-1990s, 28 states and the District of Columbia had passed laws making job discrimination against smokers illegal. Although the laws do not affect office smoking bans or smoke-free areas in the workplace, they do prohibit companies from refusing to hire smokers and from firing employees who choose to continue to smoke.

Employees' Rights and Responsibilities

Just as an employer must assume certain duties and obligations in the employee-employer relationship, so must the employee as a corporate stakeholder assume certain responsibilities. Employees have rights that must be protected from violation by the employer, yet workers can lose their privileged rights through irresponsible or illegal activities. It is possible that employees' responsibilities to coworkers, an industry, or society can place the employee at odds with the employer.

Whistle-Blowing

Sometimes the loyal bonds between a company and an employee are strained to the breaking point, especially when a worker thinks the company is doing something wrong or harmful to the public. When an employee reports alleged organizational misconduct to the public or to high-level company officials, **whistle-blowing** has occurred. In the United States, employee whistle-blowers exposed fraud in the country's defense contracting system and in the health-care, municipal bond, and pharmaceutical industries. One of the most publicized whistle-blowers in the 1990s alleged fraud within the tobacco industry.[18]

Government protection for whistle-blowers has increased at federal and state levels. The federal False Claims Act permits employees to sue companies suspected of government fraud and then to share in any financial restitution. Another federal law protects federal employees from retaliation by their supervisors when they expose government waste or fraud. Under the growing possibility of similar legal assistance for employees of private companies, employees are more willing to challenge employers' actions in the courts.

Whistle-blowing has both defenders and detractors. Those defending whistle-blowing point to the millions of dollars of fraudulent activities detected in the defense and health-care industries. Under the False Claims Act, more than $1.2 billion was returned

[18]For a sample of articles on whistle-blowers, see Randall Smith, "Whistle-Blower Rattles the Muni Industry," *Wall Street Journal*, July 17, 1995, pp. C1, C14; and Suein L. Hwang, "The Executive Who Told Tobacco's Secrets," *Wall Street Journal*, November 28, 1995, pp. B1, B6.

to the federal government, otherwise lost to fraud. However, opponents of whistle-blowing cite the hundreds of unsubstantiated cases, often used by disgruntled workers seeking to blackmail their employers.[19]

Generally, employees are not free to speak out against their employers because there is a public interest in allowing companies to operate without harassment from insiders. Company information is generally considered to be proprietary and private. If employees, based on their personal points of view, are freely allowed to expose issues to the public and allege misconduct, the company may be thrown into turmoil and be unable to operate effectively. On the other hand, there may be situations in which society's interests override those of the company, so an employee may feel an obligation to blow the whistle. According to one expert, certain conditions must be satisfied to morally justify blowing the whistle to outsiders (e.g., informing the media or government officials):

- The unreported act would do serious and considerable harm to the public.
- Once such an act has been identified, the employee has reported the act to his or her immediate supervisor and has made the moral concern known.
- If the immediate supervisor does nothing, the employee tries other internal pathways for reporting the problem.[20]

Only after each of these conditions has been met should the whistle-blower go public.

Testing to Control Employees' Actions

The issues discussed in this section focus on actions taken by businesses to control particular employee behavior. For example, the rampant increase in employee drug and alcohol use on the job or its affect on job performance prompted companies to institute drug and alcohol testing. Employee theft gave impetus to employers conducting honesty tests of their employees and job applicants.

Employee Drug Use and Testing

Abuse of drugs, particularly hard drugs such as heroin and cocaine, has become an epidemic problem for employers. By the late 1980s, 75 percent of drug users reported that they had used drugs on the job, and 64 percent said that they had sold drugs on the job. Eighteen percent of drug users had drug-related job accidents, and 60 percent reported impaired job performance. Nearly one in five said they stole from their employer to pay for drugs. Drug abuse costs the U.S. industry and taxpayers an estimated $176 billion in health claims, compensation, and lost workdays, including $99 billion in lost productivity.

One way business has dealt with on-the-job drug abuse is through drug testing. Company drug testing increased from 5 percent in 1982 to almost 50 percent in 1988 to 84 percent in 1993. Some of this increase may be attributed to the Drug-Free Workplace Act of 1988, which requires federal contractors to establish and maintain a workplace free of drugs. Tests of job applicants in several different industries revealed that, in 1988, 12 percent of prospective employees tested positive. The SmithKlein Beecham Clinical Labo-

[19]Catherine Yang and Mike France, "Whistle-Blowers On Trial," *Business Week*, March 24, 1997, pp. 172–174, 178.
[20]Richard DeGeorge, *Business Ethics*, 4th ed. (Englewood Cliffs, NJ: Prentice Hall, 1995), pp. 231–38.

Post–Lawrence–Weber:
Business and Society,
Ninth Edition

The Employee–Employer
Relationship

© The McGraw–Hill
Companies, 1999

ratories, which performed more than 3.6 million workplace drug tests annually, reported a decline in positive tests over seven consecutive years.[21]

Typically, drug testing is used on three different occasions.

- *Preemployment screening.* Some companies test all job applicants or selected applicants before hiring, usually as part of a physical examination, often informing the applicant ahead of time that there will be a drug screening.

- *Random testing of employees.* This type of screening may occur at various times throughout the year. In many companies, a member of a particular job category (e.g., an operator of heavy machinery) or job level (e.g., a supervisor) is eligible for screening at any time.

- *Testing for cause.* This test occurs when an employee is believed to be impaired by drugs and unfit for work. It is commonly used after an accident or some observable change in behavior.

Small businesses are also becoming more involved in employee drug testing. "The word on the street is that people with drug problems are going to small companies because they know that the IBMs and the Xeroxes and the GTEs are drug screening and have been for years," said an operations vice president at Corporate Wellness, a drug consulting firm.[22] So, employers at small businesses see a growing need to protect themselves from drug abusers.

The debate over employee drug testing is summarized in Figure 5. In general, proponents of testing emphasize the need to control the potential harm to others and the cost

Figure 5

Pros and cons of employee drug testing.

Arguments favoring employee drug testing

- Business cooperation with U.S. "War on Drugs" campaign
- Improves employee productivity
- Promotes safety in the workplace
- Decreases employee theft and absenteeism
- Reduces health and insurance costs

Arguments opposing employee drug testing

- Invades an employee's privacy
- Violates an employee's right to due process
- May be unrelated to job performance
- May be used as a method of employee discrimination
- Lowers employee morale
- Conflicts with company values of honesty and trust
- May yield unreliable test results
- Ignores effects of prescription drugs, alcohol, and over-the-counter drugs
- Drug use an insignificant problem for some companies

[21] For a presentation of the 1993 American Management Association study of workplace drug testing, see "Fewer People Fail as Workplace Drug Testing Increases," *HR Focus,* June 1993, p. 24. Also see, "Workplace Drug Tests Show Fewer Positives," *The Wall Street Journal,* March 7, 1995, p. B6.
[22] "Small Companies Move to Increase Anti-Drug Programs," *The Wall Street Journal,* November 6, 1990, p. B2.

Post–Lawrence–Weber:
Business and Society,
Ninth Edition

The Employee–Employer
Relationship

© The McGraw–Hill
Companies, 1999

to business and society attributed to drug use on the job. Opponents challenge the benefits of drug testing and its intrusion on individual privacy.

Alcohol Abuse at Work

Another form of employee substance abuse, which causes twice the problems of all illegal drugs combined, also challenges employers: alcohol use and addiction. Studies show that up to 40 percent of all industrial fatalities and 47 percent of industrial injuries are due to alcohol abuse. U.S. businesses lose an estimated $102 billion per year in productivity directly related to alcohol abuse.[23]

Company programs for drug abusers and alcohol abusers are often combined. Since the 1980s, an increasing number of firms recognized that they had a role to play in helping alcoholics control or break their habit. As with drug rehabilitation programs, most alcoholism programs work through employee assistance programs (EAPs) that offer counseling and follow-up. In 1994, 84 percent of companies responding to a survey indicated that they provide EAPs for alcohol and drug abusers. United Airlines' EAP reported dramatic reductions of absenteeism plus excellent recovery rates during a 10-year period, and it is considered a model for other firms.

Employee Theft and Honesty Testing

Employees can irresponsibly damage themselves, their coworkers, and their employer by stealing from the company. Employee theft has emerged as a significant economic, social, and ethical problem in the workplace. It accounts for an estimated 60 percent of all retail losses, and employee-related thefts occur 15 times more often than shoplifting. The U.S. Department of Commerce estimates that employee theft of cash, merchandise, and property costs businesses $40 to $50 billion a year. Employee theft accounts for 20 percent of the nation's business failures. In Canada, employee theft costs firms $20 billion a year.[24]

Many companies in the past used polygraph testing as a preemployment screening procedure or on discovery of employee theft. In 1988, the Employee Polygraph Protection Act became law. This law severely limited polygraph testing by employers and prohibited approximately 85 percent of all such tests previously administered in the United States. In response to the federal ban on polygraphs, many corporations have switched to written psychological tests, or **honesty tests,** that seek to predict employee honesty on the job. These pen-and-paper tests rely on answers to a series of questions that are designed to identify undesirable qualities in the test taker. When a British chain of home improvement centers used such tests to screen more than 4,000 applicants, theft dropped from 4 percent to 2.5 percent, and actual losses from theft were reduced from 3.75 million pounds to 2.62 million pounds.

The use of honesty tests, like polygraphs, is controversial. The American Psychological Association noted that there is a significant potential for these tests to generate false positives, indicating that the employee probably would or did steal from the company even though this is not true. After extensively studying the validity of honesty tests

[23]"Alcohol and Other Drugs in the Workplace," National Council on Alcoholism and Drug Dependencies, http://www.ncadd.org/workplace.html (January 12, 1998).
[24]"A Critical Look at Loss Prevention and Employee Theft," *Vito's Private Investigation Newsletter,* http://www.americasbright.com/employer/vito/new961101.html (November 1–15, 1996).

Post–Lawrence–Weber:
Business and Society,
Ninth Edition

The Employee–Employer
Relationship

© The McGraw–Hill
Companies, 1999

and the behavior they try to predict, Dan Dalton and Michael Metzger, leading academic researchers in this field, concluded that the tests are only 13.6 percent accurate at best and only 1.7 percent accurate at their worst. Critics also argue that the tests intrude on a person's privacy and discriminate disproportionately against minorities.[25]

Employees as Corporate Stakeholders

The issues discussed here illustrate forcefully that today's business corporation is open to a wide range of social forces. Its borders are very porous, letting in a constant flow of external influences. Many of these social forces are brought inside by employees whose personal values, lifestyles, and social attitudes become a vital part of the workplace.

Managers and other business professionals need to be aware of these employee-imported features of today's workforce. The employee-employer relationship is central to getting a corporation's work done and to helping satisfy the wishes of those who contribute their skills and talents to the company. The task of a corporate manager is to reconcile potential clashes between employees' human needs and the requirements of corporate economic production. Acknowledging the important stake that employees have in the successful pursuit of a corporation's economic mission enables business leaders to cope more effectively with the many issues that concern employees.

Summary Points

- Fierce global competition and other economic factors led to dramatic employee downsizing worldwide. Employers no longer assumed the responsibility of maintaining long-term job security for their employees. Instead, employees were expected to contribute to the firm's success and thus increase their employability.

- U.S. labor laws give most workers the right to organize unions and to bargain collectively with their employers. Some believe that unions are poised for a resurgence after many years of decline.

- Job safety and health concerns have increased as a result of rapidly changing technology in the workplace. Employers must comply with expanding OSHA regulations and respond to the growing trend toward violence at work.

- An increasingly diverse workforce requires corporate managers to respect and be able to deal effectively with a wide range of cultures and social attitudes among today's employees.

- Employees' privacy rights are frequently challenged by employers' needs to have information about their health, their work activities, and even their off-the-job lifestyles.

[25] Support for the reliability of honesty tests can be found in Denis S. Ones, Cockalingam Viswesvaran, and Frank L. Schmidt, "Comprehensive Meta-Analysis of Integrity Test Validities: Findings and Implications for Personnel Selection and Theories of Job Performance," *Journal of Applied Psychology,* August 1993, pp. 679–703; and H. John Bernardin and Donna K. Cooke, "Validity of an Honesty Test in Predicting Theft among Convenience Store Employees," *Academy of Management Journal,* October 1993, pp. 1097–108. The American Psychological Association's challenge to these tests and the opinions noted in this paragraph can be found in Dan R. Dalton and Michael B. Metzger, "'Integrity Testing' for Personnel Selection: An Unsparing Perspective," *Journal of Business Ethics,* February 1993, pp. 147–56.

Post–Lawrence–Weber:
Business and Society,
Ninth Edition

The Employee–Employer
Relationship

© The McGraw–Hill
Companies, 1999

When these issues arise, management has a responsibility to act ethically toward employees while continuing to work for a high level of economic performance.

• Blowing the whistle on one's employer is often a last resort to protest company actions considered to be harmful to others. It can usually be avoided if corporate managers encourage open communication and show a willingness to listen to their employees.

Key Terms and Concepts

• Employment-at-will
• Employer-employee social contract
• Equal job opportunity
• Equal Employment Opportunity Commission (EEOC)
• Affirmative action
• Whistle-blowing
• Reverse discrimination

• Ergonomics
• Occupational Safety and Health Administration (OSHA)
• Workplace safety teams
• Privacy rights
• Honesty tests

Internet Resources

• http:// www.drugfreeworkplace.org
• http:// www.eeoc.gov

• http://www.osha.gov

• http://www.whistleblowers.org

Institute for a Drug-Free Workplace
United States Equal Employment Opportunity Commission
United States Department of Labor, Occupational Safety and Health Administration
National Whistleblowers Center

Discussion Case   Responding to AIDS in the Workplace

Tim, a service-support manager for San Francisco—based Wells Fargo Bank, had been an exemplary employee for several years. A strong leader who had a good reputation, 32-year-old Tim was well liked by upper management and the 15 employees he supervised.

This up-and-coming individual also had a medical condition that was beginning to wear down his body's immune system. Infected with the human immunodeficiency virus, Tim had developed a form of AIDS, which can result in such symptoms as shortness of breath, a lingering dry cough, skin rashes, extreme fatigue, and lightheadedness. Symptoms never surface in many people who are infected, and others develop conditions years after infection.

Extreme fatigue became part of Tim's daily life and was a detriment to his usual top-notch performance. As his health deteriorated, he began to realize his physical limitations. About 15 months earlier, Tim revealed the information about his health to his middle-management supervisor, Sandra. He asked her to keep the news confidential. Tim was aware of his condition several months before he informed his manager. Because HIV is not contagious through casual contact, this individual was not a health

219

Post–Lawrence–Weber:
Business and Society,
Ninth Edition

The Employee–Employer
Relationship

© The McGraw–Hill
Companies, 1999

risk to other bank employees and therefore was under no obligation to share such personal information with his employer. Because he could not keep up with his workload, however, Tim wanted to inform Sandra that the problem was medical. Knowing that Wells Fargo's policy on HIV ensured his confidentiality, Tim believed that the company would accommodate him by not disclosing his illness.

After her discussion with Tim, Sandra consulted Bryan Lawton, the bank's employee assistance director and a clinical psychologist. She asked how to respond to managers and employees who have questions about workers who have HIV. "Sandra was distressed because she was concerned about Tim's health," said Lawton. Tim was showing signs of fatigue and was missing work. His coworkers began to wonder if he was ill. "Sandra was afraid that Tim was wearing himself down," Lawton added. "She also was concerned about the impact the illness was having on the people he supervised—people who had suspicions about him being infected with the disease, but who didn't know what to say or do."

Sandra was aware of the company's four-point policy:

- Keep confidential all information about the medical condition and medical records of an employee who has AIDS.
- Consult Employee Assistance Services (EAS) immediately after learning that an employee has been diagnosed with AIDS.
- Work with EAS and your personnel officer to arrange job accommodations that are deemed medically necessary for the employee with this condition.
- Help employees learn about AIDS by asking EAS for the AIDS Education Program.

Yet, even though Sandra was aware of the policy, she had never had to implement it or manage its effects. She had several questions and needed assistance in how to implement company policy on Tim's behalf. She also wanted to demonstrate concern and compassion for her fellow employee while staying within the legal boundaries of confidentiality. One particular point of interest for Sandra was possible job-based adjustments that Tim might need in the months ahead. Because Tim was a valued employee, Sandra wanted to minimize his concerns while maximizing his tenure.

Source: Jennifer Laabs, copyright April 1990. Used with permission of ACC Communications Inc./*Personal Journal* (now known as *Workforce*), Costa Mesa, CA. All rights reserved.

Discussion Questions

1. Given the passage of the Americans with Disabilities Act, does the bank's AIDS policy adequately protect the rights of all Wells Fargo employees?
2. Is the protection of Tim's privacy rights more important than, less important than, or equally as important as the bank's need to be efficient in getting its day-to-day work done? Should Tim be removed from his job?
3. If Tim is given special job privileges because of his illness, would other bank employees have a right to complain about unequal and discriminatory treatment?

Post–Lawrence–Weber:
Business and Society,
Ninth Edition

The Employee–Employer
Relationship

© The McGraw–Hill
Companies, 1999

Bibliography

Adler, Nancy, and Dafna N. Israeli, eds. *Competitive Frontiers: Women Managers in the Global Economy.* Cambridge, MA: Basil Blackwell, 1995.

Bloom, Paul, and Ruth Belk Smith, eds. *The Future of Consumerism.* Lexington, MA: Lexington Books, 1986.

Caplan, Lincoln. *Up Against the Law: Affirmative Action and the Supreme Court.* New York: Twentieth Century Fund Press, 1997.

Edley, Christopher F. *Not All Black and White: Affirmative Action, Race and American Values.* New York: Hill and Wang, 1996.

Fagenson, Ellen A., ed. *Women in Management: Trends, Issues, and Challenges in Management Diversity.* Newbury Park, CA: Sage, 1993.

Faludi, Susan. *Backlash: The Undeclared War against American Women.* New York: Doubleday, 1991.

Goldin, Claudia. *Understanding the Gender Gap: An Economic History of American Women.* New York: Oxford University Press, 1990.

Gray, Barbara. *Collaborating: Finding Common Ground for Multiparty Problems.* San Francisco: Jossey-Bass, 1989.

Gunderson, Martin; David J. Mayo; and Frank S. Rhame. *AIDS: Testing and Privacy.* Salt Lake City: University of Utah Press, 1989.

Gutek, Barbara A. *Sex and the Workplace: The Impact of Sexual Behavior and Harassment on Women, Men, and Organizations.* San Francisco: Jossey-Bass, 1985.

Herman, Edward S. *Corporate Control, Corporate Power.* Cambridge, England: Cambridge University Press, 1981.

Hochschild, Arlie. *The Second Shift: Working Parents and the Revolution at Home.* New York: Viking, 1989.

Kester, Carl W. *Japanese Takeovers: The Global Contest for Corporate Control.* Boston: Harvard Business School Press, 1991.

Kittrie, Nicholas N., *The War against Authority: From the Crisis of Legitimacy to a New Social Contract.* Baltimore, MD: Johns Hopkins University Press, 1995.

Kuenne, Robert E. *Economic Justice in American Society.* Princeton, NJ: Princeton University Press, 1993.

Linowes, David F. *Privacy in America: Is Your Private Life in the Public Eye?* Urbana, IL: University of Illinois Press, 1989.

Lorsch, Jay William. *Pawns or Potentates: The Reality of America's Corporate Boards.* Boston: Harvard Business School Press, 1989.

Mann, Jonathan M., and Daniel J. M. Tarantola, eds. *AIDS in World War II: Global Dimensions, Social Roots and Responses.* New York: Oxford University Press, 1996.

Matteo, Sherri, ed. *American Women in the Nineties.* Boston: Northeastern University Press, 1993.

Morrison, Ann M.; Randall P. White; and Ellen Van Velsor. *Breaking the Glass Ceiling: Can Women Reach the Top of America's Largest Corporations?* updated ed. Reading, MA: Addison-Wesley, 1992.

Powell, Gary N. *Women and Men in Management,* 2d ed. Newbury Park, CA: Sage Publications, 1993.

Puckett, Same B., and Alan R. Emery. *Managing AIDS in the Workplace.* Reading, MA: Addison-Wesley, 1988.

Rix, Sara E. *The American Woman 1990–91: A Status Report.* New York: Norton, 1990.

Singer, Merrill, ed. *The Political Economy of AIDS.* Amityville, NY: Baywood Publishers, 1998.

United Nations. *The World's Women, 1970–1990: Trends and Statistics.* New York: United Nations Publications, June 1991.

Post–Lawrence–Weber:
Business and Society,
Ninth Edition

Women, Work, and the
Family

© The McGraw–Hill
Companies, 1999

Women, Work, and the Family

Developing opportunities for women who work in business has become a major social challenge for corporations. Barriers to women's equal participation in the workplace are yielding to the forces of economic change, greater need for skilled people in all categories, the demands of women to be treated equally, and equal opportunity laws. Achieving full workplace parity remains a goal to be reached. Women's greater participation in the nation's labor force has brought adjustments in family life and social values, requiring changes in corporate practices and policies.

This topic focuses on these key questions and objectives:

- Why have women entered the workforce in such large numbers, and what problems have women faced as workers?

- What roles do women play as managers and business owners, and do women manage differently from men?

- What role does the government play in securing women's workplace rights and opportunities?

- What can companies do to develop policies and practices that promote women's workplace opportunities and support both women and men in their efforts to balance work and family responsibilities?

223

Post–Lawrence–Weber:
Business and Society,
Ninth Edition

Women, Work, and the
Family

© The McGraw–Hill
Companies, 1999

I n 1997, Jill Barad was promoted to the position of chief executive officer of Mattel, Inc., the toy maker. Barad, then 45 years old, had earned her spurs at Mattel by giving the venerable Barbie doll a makeover, transforming her into a doctor, teacher, and businesswoman, quadrupling the doll's revenues in a decade. Barad was the first woman to take leadership of a major U.S. corporation.

The same year, the Equal Employment Opportunity Commission (EEOC) announced that it would join a private lawsuit against Home Depot, Inc. The suit alleged that Home Depot, a retailer of home improvement products, hired women into low-level jobs, such as cashier, with little chance for advancement into sales or management positions. "Home Depot traps its female employees into what amounts to a glass basement," said a lawyer for the EEOC.[1]

These two examples capture some of the contradictions that face women in the business world in the United States. Nearly half of all U.S. workers, and more than 4 of every 10 managers, are women. For a half century, women have been entering the workforce in increasingly larger numbers, finding jobs formerly denied to them. Women have made great strides in the professions, skilled trades, and middle ranks of management. A few, like Jill Barad, have reached the pinnacle of success in corporate America. Yet most women, like those who are alleged to have experienced discrimination at Home Depot, still work in relatively low-paying jobs with poor prospects for upward mobility in traditionally female-dominated occupations.

The enormous transition that has occurred as women have entered the workforce in greater numbers has produced new social challenges. In this chapter, we discuss these changes and their implications for business. Understanding the history of women in society is a key to seeing what business can do today to meet these challenges.

The Status of Women in Society: Historical Background

The status of both women and men in society is largely a product of social custom and tradition. Customs evolve over extremely long periods of time, and they resist change. In all societies it is customary for men to perform certain tasks and for women to perform others. Once established, these distinctions between women's tasks and men's tasks—the **sexual division of labor**—tend to be accepted as proper and are reinforced over time by habit and custom. The sexual division of labor exerts a strong influence on the relative amounts of power and influence possessed by men and women within the family, clan, tribe, and larger society. Societies around the world and throughout history have varied greatly in how they arrange this basic division of labor.

Most societies in human history have been both patriarchal—men serve as head of the family or clan—and patrilineal—family lineage is traced through the father's ancestors. Because these male-centered social customs allocate power and privileges mainly to men, women have generally found themselves with relatively less social standing. Matriarchal societies—where women are politically, economically, and socially dominant—have occasionally existed but not as frequently. Generally it has been men, rather than women, who become chiefs, clan heads, tribal elders, shamans and priests, monarchs, presidents, prime ministers, generals, and corporate executives. Women's social standing

[1] "She Reinvented Barbie; Now, Can Jill Barad Do the Same for Mattel?," *The Wall Street Journal*, March 5, 1997, pp. A1, A8; and "U.S. to Intervene in Suit against Home Depot," *Los Angeles Times*, March 25, 1997, p. D3.

Post–Lawrence–Weber:
Business and Society,
Ninth Edition

Women, Work, and the
Family

© The McGraw–Hill
Companies, 1999

in these patriarchal (male-dominated) societies has been tied closely to childbearing and family sustenance.[2]

This general pattern of male-female relations continues in modern societies. Sex segregation based on custom has meant that today's women in general possess less economic and political power than men. Until quite recently, leadership positions in politics, government, business, religion, trade unions, sports, engineering, university teaching, military service, space exploration, science, and other fields have been considered off-limits to women. Although today's research demonstrates that women are as well qualified and capable as men to hold these high-level positions, sex discrimination based on custom, social habit, and gender bias has limited their opportunities.

Exhibit A explains how these persistent, gender-based customs have affected the jobs women hold, even long after explicit sex discrimination was outlawed.

The Women's Movement

The women's movement that began in the 1960s and has continued to the present is the most recent phase of women's efforts to redress the unequal balance that cultural history has left on contemporary society's doorstep. The fight for equal rights for women in modern times began over a century earlier in England as women sought the right to vote. In the United States, women secured that same right in 1920 with the passage of the Nineteenth Amendment to the U.S. Constitution.

The women's movement that renewed itself among American women in the 1960s proved to be a watershed. On one side were customs that cast most women in their traditional roles of homemaker and helpmate to their male companions—loyal sister, dutiful

---

EXHIBIT A   The Long Shadow of Sex Segregation

"The explicit policies to segregate the workplace and to fire married women that I have uncovered in the historical records of hundreds of firms would be clearly illegal today. . . . Many of these discriminatory policies, at least as the written procedures of firms, were abandoned sometime after 1950. Some were changed in the 1950s as a response to tighter labor supply conditions, while others were altered only later when the policies became clearly illegal. *But their impact remained long after.* If few women worked for extensive periods of time, even fewer would remain when jobs were dead end and when women were barred from promotional ladders. When virtually no woman was an accountant, for example, few would train to be accountants. And if women's work was defined in one way and men's in another, few individuals would choose to be the deviant, for deviance might cost one dearly outside the workplace. Thus change in the economic sphere is slowed not only by the necessity for cohorts (age groups) to effect change, but also by the institutionalization of various barriers and by the existence of social norms maintained by strong sanctions."

Source: Claudia Goldin, *Understanding the Gender Gap: An Economic History of American Women.* Copyright © 1990 by Oxford University Press, Inc. Reprinted by permission. Emphasis added.

---

[2]For a discussion of the history of patriarchy, see Gerda Lerner, *The Creation of Patriarchy* (New York: Oxford University Press, 1986).

Post–Lawrence–Weber:
Business and Society,
Ninth Edition

Women, Work, and the
Family

© The McGraw-Hill
Companies, 1999

daughter, faithful wife, nurturing mother. On the other side, events produced a new attitude toward women's place in society. This attitude supported the liberation of women from customary restraints and emphasized the importance of equality, greater choice, and personal control. Without rejecting the vital social contributions women had long made, leaders of the movement nevertheless advocated greater independence for women and a reexamination of long-accepted social habits and attitudes. In this new climate, women began to question their roles, their lives, their relationships, and where it all was leading them.[3]

This questioning ran deeper than had the earlier struggles of women to gain the right to vote, to own and control property, and to regulate family size. None of those earlier campaigns, even when successful, had seriously challenged society's prevailing distribution of power, privileges, and jobs that favored men. Women now were seeking equal rights, equal privileges, and the kind of liberty that would permit them to pursue lives determined largely by options of their own choosing. Their aims were self-determination and social justice, which meant having an equal claim on human rights and an equal standing with others around them.

Some believe that the women's movement lost ground in meeting these goals during the 1980s, a decade characterized by author Susan Faludi as one of backlash against women. A 1995 survey found that 45 percent of women believed that women were still mostly given low- or mid-level jobs, while men held the real power.[4]

Why Women Have Entered the Workplace

Women have always worked, whether paid or not. In farming-based societies, including the United States through the mid-1800s, the family was the primary economic unit. Women's work was essential to the family economy and involved farming, food preparation, the manufacture of household items, and the care of children. In the slave-based system of the southern states prior to the Civil War, the labor of African-American women made essential contributions to the plantation economy. The advent of the industrial revolution in the early and mid-1800s profoundly altered the nature of women's work by bringing females into the wage labor force. During the late 1800s and the first half of the 1900s, with the exception of periods of wartime, women who worked outside the home were mostly young and single, widowed or divorced, or married to men unable for some reason to support their families.

During the post–World War II period, the proportion of women working outside the home rose dramatically, as shown in Figure 1. In 1950, about a third of adult women were employed. This proportion has risen almost steadily since, standing at 59 percent in 1996. Participation rates (the proportion of women in the workforce) have risen for all groups of women, but the most dramatic increases have been among married women, mothers of young children, and middle-class women, those who had earlier been most likely to stay at home. Men's participation rates declined somewhat during this period; by the year 2005, the proportions of adult women and men at work are projected to be within 7 percentage points of each other (66 percent and 73 percent, respectively). The expanding participation of women in the workforce has posed many challenges for business.

[3]The seminal work that energized the U.S. women's movement is Betty Friedan's *The Feminine Mystique,* first published in 1963. For her views of what the movement had accomplished after 20 years, see the foreword of *The Feminine Mystique,* 20th anniversary ed. (New York: Norton, 1983).
[4]Susan Faludi, *Backlash: The Undeclared War against American Women* (New York: Doubleday, 1991); and "Women More Pessimistic about Work," *New York Times,* September 12, 1995, p. D5.

Post–Lawrence–Weber:
Business and Society,
Ninth Edition

Women, Work, and the
Family

© The McGraw–Hill
Companies, 1999

Figure 1

Proportion of women
in the labor force,
1950–1996.

Source: U.S. Bureau
of Labor Statistics.

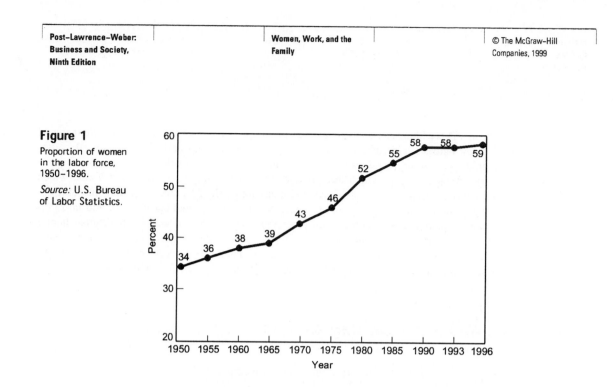

Women have entered the workforce for many of the same reasons men do. They need income to support themselves, their children, their aging, retired, or sick parents or other close relatives, and their marital partner, and to enjoy a satisfying lifestyle. A paycheck is a ticket to economic freedom, a symbol of freeing oneself from having to ask others for money to pursue one's own interests. Having a job with pay also gives a woman psychological independence and security. It can open up new vistas of opportunity, permitting and encouraging higher degrees of self-actualization. Being economically productive and contributing to society through paid work contributes as much to women's as to men's sense of self-esteem.

When marriages terminate, through either divorce or the death of one partner, the remaining person usually needs a paying job. Many women who choose not to work outside the home during their married life confront this necessity when joint savings or life insurance are inadequate for their post-marriage life. Research reveals that most women, even those with jobs, suffer a decline in their living standard following divorce. During the 1980s and 1990s, when many corporate takeovers and mergers, along with increased global competition, resulted in massive job layoffs, working women often found themselves the sole breadwinners in their families.

Inflation also puts financial pressure on families, frequently pushing women into the labor force just to sustain an accustomed standard of living or to put children through college or to care for aging parents. The inadequacies and uncertainties of retirement plans and health-care programs frequently mean that women, as well as men, need to save, invest, and plan for the future.

The rapid rise of female labor force participation also reflects the expansion of segments of the economy that were major employers of women. In 1940, about one-third of all U.S. jobs were white-collar (not requiring manual labor); by 1980, over half were white-collar. Professional, technical, and service jobs also grew relative to the economy. The creation of many new positions in fields traditionally staffed by women produced what economists call a *demand-side* pull of women into the labor force. More "women's jobs" meant more women working.

Post–Lawrence–Weber:
Business and Society,
Ninth Edition

Women, Work, and the
Family

© The McGraw–Hill
Companies, 1999

The widespread entry of women into the labor force has changed the character of many families and some kinds of family life. In 1996, in half of U.S. married households—29 million families in all—both husband and wife worked, far outnumbering the traditional family in which the husband works while the wife remains at home, which comprised only 13 percent of married households. (In 24 percent, neither husband nor wife worked; in 8 percent, only the wife or other family member worked; and in 5 percent, one spouse and another family member worked.) The decline of traditional family arrangements, as more and more women have entered the labor force, has been responsible for much of the criticism directed toward women who work outside the home. It also has focused attention on the numbers and types of jobs actually held by women, which we examine next.

Where Women Work and What They Are Paid

Highlights about working women in the United States include the following:[5]

- Over half (59 percent) of all women are employed.
- Women make up nearly half (46 percent) of the entire labor force.
- Three-quarters of all working women (74 percent) have full-time jobs.
- Women now own nearly 8 million businesses, an increase of 78 percent in the decade ending in 1996.
- Almost two-thirds (63 percent) of married women with children under the age of six hold jobs outside the home.
- The main jobs held by women are administrative support and clerical work (25 percent of all women's jobs), service work (18 percent), and sales (13 percent). About one of every eight working women (13 percent) is a manager.
- Women hold 44 percent of all executive, administrative, and managerial posts, but most of these are at low and middle levels of organizations.
- Women make up 10 percent of *all* corporate officers, but only 2.4 percent of *top* corporate officers (chairman, vice chairman, CEO, president, chief operating officer, or executive vice president) at Fortune 500 companies.

Although women have become major participants in doing the paid work of U.S. society, their distribution among jobs and industries remains lopsided. They have found more places in the service industries than in manufacturing, mining, or agriculture. They serve more as clerks and low-level administrative helpers than as high-level leaders in organizational life, and as staff workers more than as workers in line jobs with central authority over policies and practices.

One persistent feature of the working world is that women on average receive lower pay than men. This **gender pay gap** narrowed during the 1980s and the early 1990s, but as Figure 2 shows, it widened again more recently. Women as a group still earned only

[5]Bureau of Labor Statistics, Division of Labor Force Statistics, private communication; National Foundation for Women Business Owners, "Women-Owned Businesses in the United States 1996: A Fact Sheet," 1996; and Catalyst, "The 1996 Catalyst Census of Women Corporate Officers and Top Earners of the Fortune 500," New York, 1996. All data are for 1996.

Post–Lawrence–Weber:
Business and Society,
Ninth Edition

Women, Work, and the
Family

© The McGraw–Hill
Companies, 1999

Figure 2

The gender pay gap,
1980–1996.

Source: U.S. Bureau
of Labor Statistics.

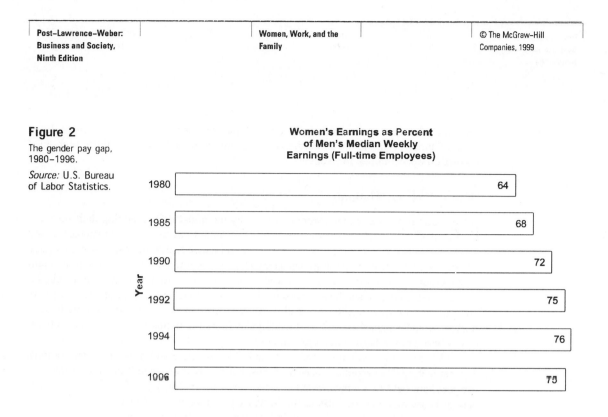

Women's Earnings as Percent
of Men's Median Weekly
Earnings (Full-time Employees)

Year	
1980	64
1985	68
1990	72
1992	75
1994	76
1996	75

three-quarters of men's pay in 1996. The gap is narrower in some jobs that call for more education, or among younger workers or where the experience of men and women is more balanced. The gender pay gap is smaller between African-American and Hispanic women and men than between white women and men, reflecting the lower wages of nonwhite men.

Most observers believe that the pay gap persists because of what is called **occupational segregation,** which concentrates women in traditionally female-dominated jobs. In 1996, over a quarter (29 percent) of all working women were employed in what has been called the *pink-collar ghetto* of jobs dominated by women—clerk, waitress, nurse, childcare worker, cashier, elementary school teacher, secretary, retail salesworker, and health technologist (e.g., dental hygienist). Because so many women hold these relatively low-paying jobs, women's average income is pulled down below the average wages of men. The labor market produces this kind of occupational segregation partly because women find better-paying jobs less accessible to them when they look for work. In some cases, an entire occupational category such as bank teller or clerical worker will shift from employing all men to hiring virtually all women, as men move on to more attractive and high-paying job opportunities. Occupational segregation frequently means that women cannot get the jobs that could break the cycle of relatively low pay.[6]

Women in Management

The most prestigious and highest-paying jobs in a corporation are in top management. Because corporations are organized hierarchically, top management jobs are few in number. For that reason, only a minority of either men

[6]Diana M. Pearce, "Something Old, Something New: Women's Poverty in the 1990s," in Sherri Matteo, ed., *American Women in the Nineties,* (Boston: Northeastern University Press, 1993), pp. 79–97; and U.S. Department of Labor, private communication.

or women can hope to reach the upper levels of management. Men have traditionally filled most of these desirable spots. Business's challenge now is to broaden these high-level leadership opportunities for women.[7]

Where Women Manage

Almost 8 million U.S. women were managers by the mid-1990s, doubling their numbers in one decade. In 1996, as Figure 3 reveals, more than 4 out of every 10 managers—and a majority of managers in some categories, such as finance and health care—were women. Clearly, women have broken into management ranks. Women are more likely to be managers, though, in occupational areas where women are more numerous at lower levels, including medicine and health care, personnel, labor relations, and education. They also are concentrated in service industries and in finance, insurance, real estate, and retail businesses. Women managers have also made gains in newer industries, such as biotechnology, where growth has created opportunity.[8]

Where women managers are scarce is in the executive suites of large corporations. Ten percent of all corporate officer positions, but barely more than 2 percent of the very top jobs, are held by women. Women are also scarce on corporate boards; only 10 percent of board members of Fortune 500 firms were women in 1996. Occasional exceptions do occur, as at Student Loan Marketing Association, where women held 57 percent of corporate officer positions in 1995.[9]

Access to management jobs is restricted in most areas of the world, according to a study of women managers in several nations.

> In country after country, the proportion of women holding managerial positions falls short of men's share. Corporations, it appears, have systematically ignored women as a potential resource. In all countries, the higher the rank within the organization, the fewer the women found there. In some countries, the percentages, though small, have increased over the last decade; but in none have they approached equality. This pattern prevails in oriental and occidental cultures, communist, socialist, and capitalist systems, and [in] both economically developed and developing countries.[10]

---

[7] For a variety of perspectives on women in corporate management, see the special edition of *Journal of Business Ethics*, vol. 16, no. 9 (June 1997).

[8] "Biotech Industry Is Bonanza for Women," *The Wall Street Journal*, June 6, 1994, pp. B1, B10.

[9] Catalyst, "1996 Catalyst Census of Women Board Members of the Fortune 500," New York, 1996; and Catalyst, "Fact Sheet: 1996 Census of Women Corporate Officers and Top Earners," New York, 1996.

[10] Nancy Adler and Dafna N. Izraeli, eds., *Women in Management Worldwide* (Armonk, NY: Sharpe, 1988), pp. 7–8. For a discussion of international aspects, see also Nancy Adler and Dafna N. Izraeli, eds., *Competitive Frontiers: Women Managers in the Global Economy* (Cambridge, MA: Basil Blackwell, 1994); and Ariane Berthoin Antal and Dafna N. Izraeli, "A Global Comparison of Women in Management: Women Managers in Their Homelands and as Expatriates," in Ellen A. Fagenson, ed., *Women in Management: Trends, Issues, and Challenges in Management Diversity* (Newbury Park, CA: Sage, 1993). A recent account of the status of women managers in Europe may be found in "Out of the Typing Pool, into Career Limbo," *Business Week*, April 15, 1996, pp. 92–94. Profiles of women managers in several countries appear in "Women in Business: A Global Report Card," *The Wall Street Journal*, July 26, 1995, pp. B1, B12.

Post–Lawrence–Weber:
Business and Society,
Ninth Edition

Women, Work, and the
Family

© The McGraw–Hill
Companies, 1999

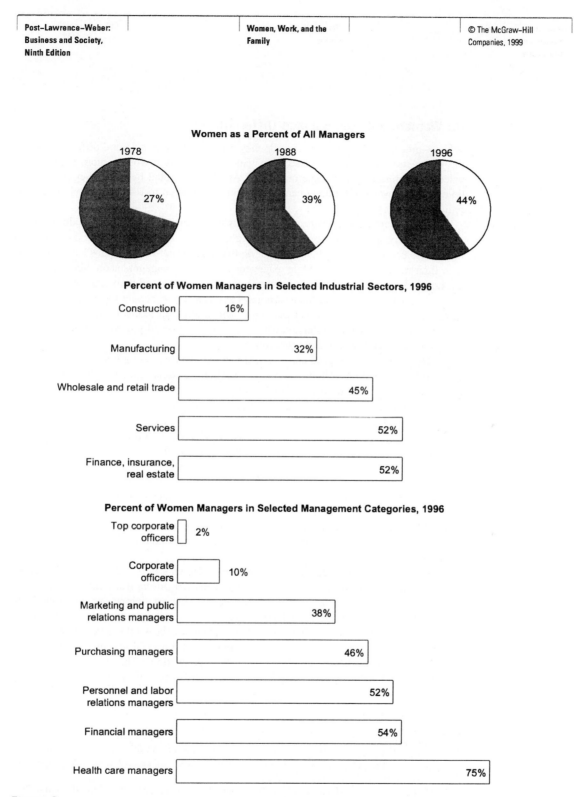

Figure 3

Where women manage.

Source: U.S. Bureau of Labor Statistics.

Post–Lawrence–Weber:
Business and Society,
Ninth Edition

Women, Work, and the
Family

© The McGraw–Hill
Companies, 1999

Do Women and Men Manage Differently?

When women do become managers, do they bring a different style and different skills to the job? Are they better, or worse, managers than men? Are women more highly motivated and committed than male managers? Are they accepted by those they manage, or do customary ways of thinking cause both men and women to react negatively to having female managers?

The research evidence strongly suggests that managers of both sexes do not seem to differ in any significant way in performing their tasks. Female managers do not appear to be more people-oriented than men, nor do they tackle task-oriented jobs less effectively than their male counterparts. Male managers and female managers score about the same on motivation tests. Women are sometimes more job-committed than men, at other times less. For both sexes, commitment is always stronger when people have satisfying jobs, when they believe their work is meaningful, and when their skills are used and appreciated. On-the-job sex discrimination can contribute to lowered job commitment by making the workplace less attractive for women.

The amount of time and commitment that anyone brings to a job and career is also affected by the amount of home-based support the individual receives. Women who bear a disproportionately large share of household tasks and family care may be unable to make as full a commitment to job and career as they would prefer.

Reactions of subordinates to female managers vary, but "once subordinates have worked for both female and male managers, the effects of [traditional sex-role] stereotypes disappear and managers are treated as individuals rather than representatives of their sex."[11]

Some research supports the idea that women bring different attitudes and skills to management jobs, such as greater cooperativeness, an emphasis on affiliation and attachment, nurturance, and a willingness to bring emotional factors to bear in making workplace decisions. These differences are seen to carry advantages for companies, because they expand the range of techniques that can be used to help the company manage its workforce effectively.[12]

A study commissioned by the International Women's Forum discovered a management style used by some women, and by some men, that differs from the command-and-control style traditionally used by male managers. Using an "interactive leadership" approach, "women encourage participation, share power and information, enhance other people's self-worth, and get others excited about their work. All these things reflect their belief that allowing employees to contribute and to feel powerful and important is a win-win situation—good for the employees and the organization." The study's director predicted that "interactive leadership may emerge as the management style of choice for many organizations."[13]

[11]Gary N. Powell, "One More Time: Do Female and Male Managers Differ?" *Academy of Management Executive,* August 1990, pp. 68–75. For a discussion of similarities and differences among male and female managers, see Powell's book *Women and Men in Management,* 2d ed. (Newbury Park, CA: Sage, 1993).

[12]Jan Grant, "Women as Managers: What They Can Offer to Organizations," *Organizational Dynamics,* Winter 1988, pp. 56–63.

[13]Judy B. Rosener, "Ways Women Lead," *Harvard Business Review,* November–December 1990, pp. 119–125.

Post–Lawrence–Weber:
Business and Society,
Ninth Edition

Women, Work, and the
Family

© The McGraw–Hill
Companies, 1999

The Glass Ceiling

Although women are as competent as men in managing people and organizations, they very rarely attain the highest positions in corporations. Their ascent seems to be blocked by an invisible barrier, or what is called a **glass ceiling**.

Failure to attain the topmost jobs in some cases is due to lack of experience or inadequate education. Because gender bias has kept women out of management until recent years, most women have not had time to acquire the years of experience that are typical of most high-ranking executives. Also in earlier years, women were discouraged from entering graduate schools of engineering, science, business, and law, which have been pathways to corporate management. Even as those barriers have been lowered, though, women remain underrepresented at executive levels. As a group, they have not yet broken through the glass ceiling to become chief executive officers, presidents, or board chairpersons.

What continues to hold women back? Recent studies by the U.S. Department of Labor and others have identified several reasons for the persistence of the glass ceiling. One barrier women face is **glass walls**: fewer opportunities to move sideways into jobs that lead to the top. Female managers are often found in staff positions, such as finance or public relations, rather than in line positions in such core areas as marketing, sales, or production where they can acquire the broad management skills necessary for promotion. Many women also experience what one sociologist called the "sticky floor." This means that sometimes women do not advance because they are concentrated in low-level jobs that do not lead to well-defined career paths. One study shows that the sticky floor was particularly evident for Hispanic, African-American, and Native-American women.[14]

Another problem women face is reliance on word-of-mouth by recruiters for top positions, the old boys' network from which women are often excluded. Other causes include a company's lack of commitment to diversity and too little accountability at the top management level for equal employment opportunity.[15]

The success of a few women, however, has demonstrated that the glass ceiling can be shattered. A 1994 study of a group of highly successful executive women found that most had been helped by top-level supporters and multiple chances to gain critical skills. Some companies have promoted women's mobility by assigning mentors—more-senior counselors—to promising female managers and by providing opportunities that include wide-ranging line management experience. In 1989, for example, Motorola revamped its career planning process to identify high-potential women and give them the opportunities they needed to merit promotion. By 1997, Motorola had 38 female vice presidents, up from just 2 when the program started.[16]

Women Business Owners

Some women have risen to the top by founding or taking over their own businesses. By 1996, nearly eight million businesses—over one-third of all those in the United States—

[14]"Study Says Women Face Glass Walls as Well as Ceilings," *The Wall Street Journal*, March 3, 1992, pp. B1, B2; and "At Work: And Now the 'Sticky Floor,'" *New York Times*, November 22, 1992, p. F23.

[15]Ann M. Morrison, Randall P. White, and Ellen Van Velsor, *Breaking the Glass Ceiling: Can Women Reach the Top of America's Largest Corporations?* 2nd ed. (Reading, MA: Addison-Wesley, 1992); and U.S. Department of Labor, "Good for Business: Making Full Use of the Nation's Human Capital: A Fact Finding Report of the Federal Glass Ceiling Commission," March 1995.

[16]Lisa A. Mainiero, "Getting Anointed for Advancement: The Case of Executive Women," *Academy of Management Executive*, May 1994, pp. 53–63; and "Breaking Through," *Business Week*, February 17, 1997, p. 64.

Post–Lawrence–Weber:
Business and Society,
Ninth Edition

Women, Work, and the
Family

© The McGraw–Hill
Companies, 1999

were owned or controlled by women, according to the National Foundation for Women Business Owners. Many of these businesses are in services, retail trade, finance, insurance, and real estate. Women are now forming new businesses at roughly twice the rate that men are. Although most female-headed firms are small, collectively they employ over 18 million people in the United States, more than the Fortune 500 firms do worldwide.[17]

> *An example of a successful female entrepreneur is Judy Figge, CEO of In Home Health, a company that provides nursing care to patients in their homes. A registered nurse, Figge bought the company in 1981, when revenues were $300,000 annually. 1993 sales were $104 million, with an annual growth rate of 76 percent over the past five years. "I always wanted to run my own business, and this [nursing] is what I knew," Figge said.*[18]

Contrary to popular belief, female entrepreneurs are just as successful as men, according to a mid-1980s study of over 400 midwestern small firms. The study's researchers reported that "the determinants of survival and success operated in much the same way for men and women. . . . Despite the widely shared assumption that women are less apt than men to innovate, for example, we found no evidence of women's being less likely to do this in their businesses. Moreover, we found no evidence that men were more confident of their business abilities."[19]

Government's Role in Securing Women's Workplace Rights

From early in the twentieth century, government laws and regulations—nearly all of them enacted at the state level—were used to protect women from some of the harsh and risky conditions found in factories, mines, construction sites, and other places of business. These protective laws were adopted on grounds that women were weaker physically than men, that their childbearing powers should be shielded from workplace harms, and that whatever work they performed was generally to supplement family income rather than to provide the main income. However, "protection" often meant being excluded from certain jobs and occupations, thus contributing to occupational segregation and unequal pay. Protective laws, however well intentioned, put women at a competitive disadvantage in the labor market.

Equal Pay and Equal Opportunity

The idea that women should be paid the same as men has been around for a long time. In the 1860s, for example, male printers demanded that female printers should receive equal pay for equal work, mainly so that their own wages would not be depressed by competition from lower-paid women. The same fear that female workers would lower all wage rates was observed during the First and Second World Wars, when women took over jobs formerly held by men who were in the armed forces. It was not until 1945 that an equal

---

[17]The National Foundation for Women Business Owners, "Women-Owned Businesses in the United States 1996: A Fact Sheet"; and "Women Entrepreneurs: They're Forming Small Businesses at Twice the Rate of Men," *Business Week,* April 18, 1994, pp. 104–10.

[18]"Lessons from America's Fastest Growing Companies," *Fortune,* August 8, 1994, p. 59.

[19]Arne L. Kalleberg and Kevin T. Leicht, "Gender and Organizational Performance: Determinants of Small Business Survival and Success," *Academy of Management Journal,* March 1991, pp. 157–58.

Post–Lawrence–Weber:
Business and Society,
Ninth Edition

Women, Work, and the
Family

© The McGraw–Hill
Companies, 1999

pay bill was introduced in Congress; even then, it was a tactic to defeat or forestall a more comprehensive equal rights amendment to the U.S. Constitution. The Equal Pay Act finally became law almost 20 years later in 1963.

One year after that, Congress adopted the Civil Rights Act, which prohibits employment discrimination on the basis of race, color, religion, sex, or national origin. When the Civil Rights Act was strengthened in 1972 and again in 1991, working women—along with minorities—had additional legal machinery to use in their quest for workplace equality.[20] For more than half a century, an equal rights amendment to the U.S. Constitution has been advocated but never ratified by the necessary number of states. The proposed amendment declares: "Equality of rights under the law shall not be denied or abridged by the United States or any state on account of sex."

Figure 4 outlines the major laws and one executive order that are intended to promote women's on-the-job opportunities.

Comparable Worth

Equal pay for equal work combats pay discrimination within the same job categories within the same firm—for example, providing equal pay rates for men and women carpenters and equal salaries for men and women managers performing identical work. However, it does little to reduce pay inequities when men and women hold different jobs that require approximately equal skills but are paid at unequal rates. Much of the gender pay gap discussed earlier occurs because many women are employed in jobs and occupational categories that are lower paying than those held predominantly by men. Equalizing pay levels in the same job category does nothing about the unequal rates paid to different jobs or occupations. The problem is especially unfair when these different jobs call for about the same degree of skill, effort, and responsibility. For example, the chief bookkeeper and payroll manager of the city of Princeton, Minnesota—a woman—earned $5,678 a year less than supervisors of road maintenance and sewer repair, typically men. When the state legislature required city governments to equalize the pay of women and

Figure 4

Major federal laws and an executive order to protect women's workplace rights.

> **Equal Pay Act (1963)**—Mandates equal pay for equal work.
> **Civil Rights Act (1964)** (amended 1972, 1991)—Forbids sex discrimination in employment.
> **Executive Order 11246 (1965)**—Mandates affirmative action for all federal contractors and subcontractors.
> **Equal Employment Opportunity Act (1972)**—Increased power and Equal Employment Opportunity Commission to combat sex and other types of discrimination.
> **Pregnancy Discrimination Act (1978)**—Forbids employers to discharge, fail to hire, or otherwise discriminate against pregnant women.
> **Family and Medical Leave Act (1993)**—Requires companies with 50 or more employees to provide up to 12 weeks unpaid leave for illness, care of a sick family member, or the birth or adoption of a child.

[20]Claudia Goldin, *Understanding the Gender Gap: An Economic History of American Women* (New York: Oxford University Press, 1990), pp. 201–2. The word *sex* was inserted in the 1964 civil rights bill, just one day before Congress voted on it, by a congressional opponent who was said to believe that its inclusion would help defeat the bill.

Post–Lawrence–Weber:
Business and Society,
Ninth Edition

Women, Work, and the
Family

© The McGraw–Hill
Companies, 1999

men in jobs requiring similar levels of education, skill, and responsibility, the bookkeeper got a raise.[21]

Comparable worth is an attempt to overcome this kind of pay inequity. Jobs are matched with each other in terms of skills, effort, responsibility, and working conditions, and pay is made equal when these factors for the two jobs are about equal or comparable with one another. As of the mid-1990s, pay equity based on comparable worth had been rejected by U.S. federal courts, but some states—like Minnesota, mentioned in the example above—have laws authorizing comparable worth plans for public employees. The European Union now requires that companies assess jobs and pay women and men the same for jobs of comparable value. Canada, Great Britain, and Australia have national comparable worth laws that appear to be effective in lessening pay discrimination.[22]

What Firms Can Do: Policies and Strategies

As women enter the labor force in large numbers, seeking permanent, well-paying, full-time jobs and aspiring to lifelong business careers, and as new laws pass protecting equal workplace rights for women, some changes are bound to take place in the way business firms organize and conduct their affairs. Three types of changes are needed. First, firms must reform their personnel policies to assure equal opportunities. Second, they must provide support programs to make a working life and a family life possible and rewarding for both men and women. Finally, businesses must remove sexist attitudes and behavior toward working women. Gender bias occurs throughout society, not just in the workplace, so these business reforms represent only those steps that firms themselves can take to provide equal workplace opportunities for women.

Reforming Personnel Policies

If women are to be treated equally in the workplace, all jobs and occupations must be open to them so that they may compete on the same terms as all others. A company's recruiters need to seek qualified workers and not assume that women are unqualified. Rates of pay and benefits need to be matched to the work to be done not to the gender of the jobholder. Pay raises for doing a current job well, along with promotions to more attractive jobs, also require equal treatment. Job assignments should be made on the basis of skills, experience, competence, capability, and reliability—in other words, proven ability to get the job done, not whether women have traditionally worked at one task rather than another.

Career ladders, whether short ones going only a few steps or longer ones leading into the higher reaches of corporate authority, should be placed so that both men and women can climb them as high as their abilities can carry them.

Providing Support Programs for Work and Family

No other area of business illustrates the basic theme of this book better than the close connection between work and family life. *Our basic theme is that business and society—in*

---

[21]Naomi Barko, "Equal Pay in Your Pocketbook," *Working Mother,* November 1993, p. 42.
[22]Laura B. Pincus and James A. Belohlav, "Legal Issues in Multinational Business Strategy," *Academy of Management Executive,* August 1996, pp. 52–61; and Kenneth A. Kovach and Peter E. Millspaugh, "Comparable Worth: Canada Legislates Pay Equity," *Academy of Management Executive,* May 1990, pp. 92–101.

Post–Lawrence–Weber:
Business and Society,
Ninth Edition

Women, Work, and the
Family

© The McGraw–Hill
Companies, 1999

this case, the family symbolizes society—are closely and unavoidably intertwined, so that what affects one also has an impact on the other. When large numbers of women began to enter the ranks of business in the 1940s, 1950s, and 1960s, they did not shed their usual roles in society. Women continued to marry and bear children. The customary roles of wife, homemaker, and child-caretaker did not disappear. Women were still expected to be "feminine" even as they filled what had formerly been "masculine" jobs. So when women came to work, they carried more than a lunch pail or a briefcase; they also bundled their customary family roles on their backs.

Study after study has demonstrated that women continue to do more housework than their male partners. Caring for children, preparing meals, cleaning house, shopping, and other household functions are still seen to be the responsibility of the mother more than the father, even when both parents work full-time. Many women thus work what has been called a "second shift" before and after their paying job.[23] In the 1960s and 1970s, women worked a month longer each year in combined job and housework than men did, and later studies show a continuation of the general pattern.

In other words, many women and men work within a surrounding network of social obligations imposed by tradition. For them and for their employers, business and the family are inseparably intertwined. This close relationship between family and work presents business with new kinds of challenges and requires changes in customary routines. Some of these are discussed next.

Child Care and Elder Care

The demand for **child care** is enormous and growing. Millions of children need daily care, especially the nearly 7 out of every 10 children whose mothers hold jobs. A major source of workplace stress for working parents is concern about their children; and problems with child care are a leading cause of absenteeism. Businesses lose an estimated $3 billion a year because of child-related absences.[24]

Business has found that child-care programs, in addition to reducing absenteeism and tardiness, also improve productivity and aid recruiting by improving the company's image and helping to retain talented employees. Eighty-six percent of large U.S. companies provide some type of child-care assistance, including referral services, parent education, dependent-care accounts, and vouchers. Slightly fewer than 1 in 10 large companies provides on-site child-care services. An example is Johnson Wax, a consumer products firm that cares for 400 children in a state-of-the-art center at its Racine, Wisconsin, headquarters. "This isn't a benefit," explained a company spokesperson. "It's a good business decision because we want to attract the best." Fel-Pro, an auto parts manufacturer in Skokie, Illinois, offers a summer day camp for employees' school-aged children.[25]

Other companies have combined child care with **elder care**, since many of today's families must find ways to care for aging parents and other older relatives. This issue will become increasingly important to businesses in the coming decade as baby boomers pass through their 40s and 50s, the prime years for caring for elderly parents. According to

[23] Arlie Hochschild, *The Second Shift: Working Parents and the Revolution at Home* (New York: Viking, 1989); see especially the appendix, "Research on Who Does the Housework and Child-care."

[24] Catalyst, "INFObrief: Childcare," New York, 1994.

[25] "Balancing Act Is Gaining Ground," *Seattle Times,* April 28, 1997, p. E1; and "What Price Child Care?" *Business Week,* February 8, 1993, pp. 104–5.

Post–Lawrence–Weber:
Business and Society,
Ninth Edition

Women, Work, and the
Family

© The McGraw–Hill
Companies, 1999

the consulting firm Work/Family Directions, the proportion of workers with elder-care responsibilities will rise from around 15 percent in 1994 to 37 percent by 2005.[26] Many businesses have found that job flexibility and referrals to services for the elderly can greatly help affected employees.

Parental Leaves

What was once called a maternity leave has become a **parental leave;** or when care of elderly parents is involved, it is called a **family leave.** Both parents may need time off from work when children are born and during the important early months of the child's physical and emotional development, and men and women may need time to care for elderly or ill parents or other family members. Under the Family and Medical Leave Act (FMLA), passed in 1993, companies that employ 50 or more people must grant unpaid, job-protected leaves of up to 12 weeks to employees faced with serious family needs, including the birth or adoption of a baby. Smaller companies, not covered by the FMLA, usually do less for expectant and new parents.

How many fathers actually take leave to care for children? Several studies have demonstrated that men are reluctant to take advantage of parental leave programs. Because a man typically makes more money than his spouse, taking a long unpaid job leave may impose greater financial hardships on the family. Men also fear, as do women, that being away from the job will interfere with their careers. However, there is some evidence that this pattern has begun to shift in the wake of the FMLA. In 1993, for example, 32 fathers at Du Pont Corporation took advantage of the company's parental leave policy, up from 18 the year before.[27]

Work Flexibility

Companies have also accommodated the changing roles of women and men by offering workers more flexibility through such options as flextime, part-time employment, job sharing, and working at home.

Aetna Life & Casualty, one of America's biggest insurance companies, demonstrates the benefits of the many kinds of work flexibility for both company and employees.[28]

> *In some departments at Aetna, as many as 40 percent of employees work flextime schedules, beginning and quitting at different times of the day. Others share jobs, with each working half a week. Many jobs are held on a part-time basis, leaving the worker time to be at home with children or elderly parents. Several hundred Aetna employees telecommute—work with computers—from their homes. The company has a Work/Life Strategies unit to assist employees in using these programs to meet family needs without seriously disrupting company routines. Aetna estimates it saves $1 million a year by not having to train new workers.*

Aetna is not the only corporation introducing these practices. A 1996 survey of large companies revealed that 72 percent had flexible schedules, 64 percent offered part-time work,

[26]"The Aging of America Is Making 'Elder Care' a Big Workplace Issue," *The Wall Street Journal,* February 16, 1994, p. A1, A8.
[27]"More Dads Take Off to Look After Baby," *The Wall Street Journal,* December 17, 1993, p. B1.
[28]"As Aetna Adds Flextime, Bosses Learn to Cope," *The Wall Street Journal,* June 18, 1990, pp. B1, B5; "Work and Family," *Business Week,* June 28, 1993, p. 83; and "The Childless Feel Left Out When Parents Get a Lift," *New York Times,* December 1, 1996, p. C12.

and 36 percent permitted job sharing. Twenty percent allowed employees to work from home.[29]

Reforming Attitudes in the Workplace

The largest obstacle to equity for working women is conventional attitudes about the place of women in society. Both men and women hold these attitudes. Such views contribute to continued occupational segregation, unequal pay and job opportunities, stymied career paths, and the failure of society to draw fully on all of its human resources for greater productivity and higher living standards. A key problem that symbolizes the need for changed workplace attitudes is sexual harassment.

Sexual Harassment

Sexual harassment at work occurs when any employee, woman or man, experiences repeated, unwanted sexual attention or when on-the-job conditions are hostile or threatening in a sexual way. It includes both physical conduct—for example, suggestive touching—as well as verbal harassment, such as sexual innuendoes, jokes, or propositions. Women are the target of most sexual harassment. Guidelines issued by the U.S. Equal Employment Opportunity Commission give limited legal protection to employees.

Harassment can occur whether or not the targeted employee cooperates. Jobs can be lost or gained by sexual conduct; if such behavior is treated as a requirement or strong expectation for holding a job or getting a promotion, it is clearly a case of unlawful sexual harassment. This kind of sex discrimination is not limited to overt acts of individual coworkers or supervisors. If a company's work climate is blatantly and offensively sexual or intimidating to employees—through prevailing attitudes, bantering, manner of addressing coworkers, lewd photographs, or suggestive behavior—then sexual harassment exists.[30]

> *An important legal case decided by the Supreme Court in 1993 made it easier for women to win sexual harassment lawsuits against their employers. In this case,* Harris v. Forklift Systems Inc., *a woman manager at a truck-leasing firm was subjected to repeated offensive comments by the company president. For example, he asked her in front of other employees if she used sex to get a particular account and suggested that the two of them "go to the Holiday Inn to negotiate [her] raise." The manager quit her job and sued.*
>
> *The Supreme Court upheld her charges, saying that the president's behavior would reasonably be perceived as hostile or abusive, even though it had not caused "severe psychological injury" or caused the woman to be unable to do her job. Some employers' attorneys expressed concern that this decision would open the door to frivolous claims of sexual harassment. Others welcomed the ruling and believed it would encourage many employers to develop policies and training to prevent such incidents.[31]*

[29] *Work and Family Benefits Provided by Major U.S. Employers in 1996* (Lincolnshire, IL: Hewitt Associates, 1996), cited in "Lies Parents Tell Themselves about Why They Work," *U.S. News and World Report,* May 12, 1997, p. 58.

[30] Catalyst, "INFObrief: Sexual Harassment," New York, 1993. For a discussion of legal issues, see Titus E. Aaron with Judith A. Isaksen, *Sexual Harassment in the Workplace* (Jefferson, NC: McFarland & Co., 1993); for a discussion of workplace strategies for women, see Ellen Bravo and Ellen Cassedy, *The 9 to 5 Guide to Combating Sexual Harassment* (New York: John Wiley, 1992).

[31] "Court, 9-0, Makes Sex Harassment Easier to Prove," *New York Times,* November 10, 1993, pp. A1, A15.

Post–Lawrence–Weber:
Business and Society,
Ninth Edition

Women, Work, and the
Family

© The McGraw–Hill
Companies, 1999

Women employees regularly report that sexual harassment is common. From 38 to 60 percent of working women have told researchers that they have been sexually harassed on the job. Managers and supervisors are the most frequent offenders, and female office workers and clerical workers are the main targets. As many as 90 percent of incidents of harassment are never reported.

Like most other problems that confront women in the workplace, sexual harassment stems from customary attitudes about women's functions in society. One expert explains these attitudes as **sex-role spillover,** meaning that many men continue to think of women mainly as performing their traditionally defined roles of sex partners, homemakers, and childbearers and only secondarily as coworkers and qualified professionals. These attitudes spill over into the workplace, leading to improper behavior that has no relation to the work to be done. This kind of conduct is most likely to occur where jobs and occupations are sex-segregated and where most supervisors and managers are men.[32]

What can companies do to combat sexual harassment? Exhibit B summarizes four major steps recommended by one authority. The twin keys to success are (1) a written

---

EXHIBIT B   Controlling Sexual Harassment

Barbara Gutek, an authority on sexual harassment in the workplace, advocates companies adopt a four-point action program to curb sexual harassment.

1. *Adopt a companywide policy forbidding sexual harassment, and communicate it to all employees and others who deal with the company.* Specific actions include orientation of new employees, training films and seminars, posters, a personal statement by top management, and designation of a neutral third party to hear complaints and field questions from employees.

2. *Vigorously investigate all complaints and act on the findings.* Specific actions include giving investigative responsibility to a qualified person who understands the psychological and organizational dimensions of sexual harassment. Follow-up based on the findings is required if the policy is to have meaning for everyone in the company.

3. *Include sexual harassment in performance appraisals of all employees, punishing those who violate company policy.* Treat sexual harassment as a form of unprofessional conduct that lowers the victim's job satisfaction, affects her or his progress and career in the company, and lowers overall company performance and productivity. Promoting or otherwise rewarding a harasser sends the wrong message about sexual harassment.

4. *Create and reinforce a climate of professional behavior that discourages sexual harassment.* Specific steps include frequent reminders of the importance of acting professionally, alerting employees to professional forms of addressing one another (avoiding *girlie, doll,* and *sweetie,* for example), and striving for sex-neutral interchanges when men and women work together.

Source: Adapted from Barbara A. Gutek, *Sex and the Workplace: The Impact of Sexual Behavior and Harassment on Women, Men, and Organizations* (San Francisco: Jossey-Bass, 1985), pp. 173–178.

---

[32]Barbara A. Gutek, *Sex and the Workplace* (San Francisco: Jossey-Bass, 1985), chap. 8.

policy, visibly supported by a company's top management, and (2) rewards for sex-neutral behavior and punishments for harassment. Only then is there a chance that the company's culture and work climate will begin to encourage attitudes that welcome women as full and equal workers and professionals.

A recent case involving sexual harassment at Mitsubishi Motors is profiled in the discussion case at the end of this chapter.

The Gender-Neutral, Family-Friendly Corporation

As a desirable goal for both business and society, a gender-neutral, **family-friendly corporation** would be one that has removed sex discrimination from all aspects of its operations and that has supported both men and women in their efforts to balance work and family responsibilities. Job advantages would not be granted or

---

EXHIBIT C A Family-Friendly Company

The most family-friendly company in the United States, according to a recent survey conducted for *Business Week* by the Center on Work and Family, is First Tennessee National Corp., a midsized regional bank based in Memphis, Tennessee. In 1993, First Tennessee initiated a Family Matters program that integrates family considerations into every aspect of the bank's operations. Some of the program's innovations include:

- On-site child care, or vouchers for employees who prefer to use other providers.
- Flexible scheduling, including condensed workweeks, job sharing, and telecommuting.
- Fitness centers.
- Jobs designed to accommodate family needs.
- A classroom visitation program that allows parents time off to participate in school activities.

The Family Matters program, managers believe, has had important bottom-line benefits. An internal study showed that employees were less likely to leave the bank, and so were customers. First Tennessee's customer retention rate was 95 percent, well above the industry average. Over a three-year period, profits at the bank were up 55 percent.

"We flip-flopped our entire corporate philosophy," said First Tennessee's CEO Ralph Horn. "Here it's employees first versus putting the shareholders first like at other financial institutions. The philosophy is that profit begins with satisfied employees."

Source: "Family Values: Corporations Find Family Programs Increase Employee Motivation as Well as the Bottom Line," *Incentive,* December 1996, pp. 23–27; and "Balancing Work and Family," *Business Week,* September 16, 1996, p. 74.

Post–Lawrence–Weber:
Business and Society,
Ninth Edition

Women, Work, and the
Family

© The McGraw–Hill
Companies, 1999

denied on the basis of gender. People would be hired, paid, evaluated, promoted, and extended benefits on the basis of their qualifications and ability to do the tasks assigned. The route to the top, or to satisfaction in any occupational category, would be open to anyone with the talent to take it. The company's stakeholders, regardless of their gender, would be treated in a bias-free manner. All laws forbidding sex discrimination would be fully obeyed. Programs to provide leaves or financial support for child care, elder care, and other family responsibilities would support both men and women employees and help promote an equitable division of domestic work.

Many companies believe that adopting gender-neutral, family-friendly policies improve business performance by reducing turnover and absenteeism and by increasing employee loyalty and commitment. An example of such a company is given in Exhibit C. Gender-neutral and family-friendly companies, such as First National Tennessee, embody the ethical principles of social justice and respect for human rights and demonstrate the kind of social responsiveness that serves the corporation's stakeholders.

Summary Points

- Women have entered the workforce in large numbers to gain economic security, find satisfying work, and achieve psychological independence. Working women continue to encounter job discrimination, including unequal pay and occupational segregation, but they have registered some gains in the last half of the twentieth century.

- The proportion of women in management has grown, although women continue to face a glass ceiling blocking their access to top executive ranks. The number of women-owned businesses has increased sharply, and women now form businesses at twice the rate men do. Research shows that men and women managers do not differ significantly in their leadership styles.

- Government laws and regulations prohibit employment discrimination on the basis of sex, mandate equal pay for equal work, and require unpaid family and medical leave under some circumstances.

- To provide equal opportunity, corporations need to support the career development of female employees, provide family-friendly programs, and help create positive workplace attitudes about working women. Corporations also need written policies prohibiting sexual harassment.

Key Terms and Concepts

- Sexual division of labor
- Gender pay gap
- Occupational segregation
- Glass ceiling
- Glass walls
- Comparable worth

- Child care
- Elder care
- Parental leave (family leave)
- Sexual harassment
- Sex-role spillover
- Family-friendly corporation

Post–Lawrence–Weber:
Business and Society,
Ninth Edition

Women, Work, and the
Family

© The McGraw–Hill
Companies, 1999

Internet Resources

- http://www.dol.gov/dol/wb — Women's Bureau of the U.S. Department of Labor

- http://www.workfamily.com — Work & Family Connection; information about work-life issues and practices

- http://www.hewittassoc.com — Hewitt Associates; information about family-friendly benefits at U.S. Corporations

- http://www.wfd.com — Work/Family Directions, Inc.; consulting firm specializing in workforce commitment

- http://www.now.org — National Organization for Women; advocacy organization

Discussion Case   Sexual Harassment at Mitsubishi

In April 1996, the Equal Employment Opportunity Commission sued Mitsubishi Motor Manufacturing of America, Inc. (MMMA) for sexual harassment. If the charges were upheld, total damages against the company could run as high as $150 million, potentially the biggest sexual harassment case in U.S. history.

The EEOC suit alleged that several hundred female employees at the company's assembly plant in Normal, Illinois, had been subject to "gross discrimination." The EEOC claimed that male workers and managers had propositioned women, grabbed their breasts and genitals, and called them *bitches* and *whores*. In one particularly shocking incident, a man was said to have shoved an air gun between a woman's legs and pulled the trigger. "It's very much a hostile environment," said one woman who had filed a complaint.

MMMA, a subsidiary of Mitsubishi Motors Corp. of Japan—itself part of a large group of affiliated companies all using the Mitsubishi name—operated the firm's only automobile assembly plant in the United States. The Illinois facility employed 4,233 people, about a fifth of them women, and was the second-largest employer in the region.

Mitsubishi's U.S. unit had a written policy forbidding sexual harassment, and 10 people had been fired for violating it since the plant opened in 1988. However, the company's contract with its union did not have specific procedures for dealing with sexual harassment, unlike contracts at the Big Three automakers. Prior to the EEOC suit, 29 women had filed private sexual harassment lawsuits against the company.

Mitsubishi's American subsidiary vigorously denied the EEOC's charges and immediately went on the offensive. The company offered to give its employees the day off and a free lunch to travel by bus to the EEOC's regional headquarters in Chicago to protest the lawsuit. Almost 3,000 workers participated. Management also installed phones in the plant and encouraged employees to call lawmakers, at company expense, to complain about the charges.

Many workers expressed concern that the suit might hurt sales, causing layoffs. "I have only a high school education," commented one welder. "Where else will I make $19 an hour with benefits?" Hundreds of women employees signed a petition supporting the company.

Post–Lawrence–Weber:
Business and Society,
Ninth Edition

Women, Work, and the
Family

© The McGraw–Hill
Companies, 1999

With the crisis on the front pages of U.S. newspapers, Mitsubishi Motors Corp. chairman Minoru Makihara intervened. On May 15, the Japanese company announced that it had hired former U.S. secretary of labor Lynn Martin to review its workplace policies and develop a new master plan to prevent sexual harassment.

As news of Mitsubishi's troubles reached Japan, many Japanese firms began sensitivity training sessions for their executives posted in the United States. Some practices alleged at Mitsubishi "would hardly raise an eyebrow in Japan," commented one reporter. "Businessmen openly thumb through porn at work, drink at hostess bars with clients, and typically know few professional women. Tradition dictates that women belong in the home."

In February 1997, Secretary Martin announced a comprehensive set of recommendations, including a policy of zero tolerance of harassment and a system to investigate and resolve complaints. The lawsuit, however, remained unresolved. Two months later, an exasperated EEOC official commented that Mitsubishi continued to be "extraordinarily aggressive in defending the . . . lawsuit. They have not indicated any interest in resolving it promptly."

Sources: "EEOC Sues Mitsubishi Unit for Harassment," *The Wall Street Journal,* April 10, 1996, pp. B1, B8; "Mitsubishi Plant Reeling over Harassment Lawsuit," *Boston Globe,* May 1, 1996, Metro Section, p. 1; "Fear and Loathing at Mitsubishi," *Business Week,* May 6, 1996, p. 35; "A Mitsubishi Unit Is Taking a Hard Line in Harassment Battle," *The Wall Street Journal,"* April 22, 1996, pp. A1, A12; "Japanese Firms Fight against Sexual Harassment," *Chicago Tribune,* April 27, 1997, Business Section, p. 8; and "Cramming for the Exotic U.S. Workplace," *The Wall Street Journal,* July 9, 1996, p. A14.

Discussion Questions

1. In your opinion, did sexual harassment occur at Mitsubishi? Please review the definition of sexual harassment. Did the alleged incidents meet all elements of the definition?

2. In your opinion, what factors, either internal or external, contributed to sexual harassment at Mitsubishi? What steps should management have taken, or should it take, to prevent sexual harassment from occurring?

3. How did Mitsubishi managers respond to EEOC charges of sexual harassment? Identify at least three actions taken by management. Do you believe these actions were ethical and socially responsible? Why do you think so?

Post–Lawrence–Weber:
Business and Society,
Ninth Edition

Women, Work, and the
Family

© The McGraw–Hill
Companies, 1999

Bibliography

Adler, Paul S., ed. *Technology and the Future of Work.*
New York: Oxford University Press, 1992.

Barbour, Ian G. *Ethics in an Age of Technology.* San Francisco: Harper, 1993.

Barcus, F. Earl. *Images of Life on Children's Television: Sex Roles, Minorities, and Families.* New York: Praeger, 1983.

Bradley, Stephen P.; Jerry A. Hausman; and Richard L. Nolan. *Globalization, Technology, and Competition: The Fusion of Computers and Telecommunications in the 1990s.* Boston, MA: Harvard Business School Press, 1993.

Corrado, Frank M. *Media for Managers: Communications Strategies for the Eighties.* Englewood Cliffs, NJ: Prentice-Hall, 1984.

Dates, Jannette L., and William Barlow, eds. *Split Image: African-Americans in the Mass Media.* Washington, D.C.: Howard University Press, 1990.

Dertouzas, Michael L.; Richard K. Lester; and Robert M. Solow. *Made in America: Regaining the Productivity Edge.* Cambridge, MA: MIT Press, 1989.

Drlica, Karl. *Double-edged Sword: The Promises and Risks of the Genetic Revolution.* Reading, MA: Addison-Wesley, 1994.

Etzioni, Amitai. *The Spirit of Community: Rights, Responsibilities, and the Communitarian Agenda.* New York: Crown Publishers, 1993.

Hernstein, Richard J., and Charles Murray, *The Bell Curve: Intelligence and Class Structure in American Life.* New York: Free Press, 1994.

Kolata, Gina. *Clone: The Road to Dolly and the Path Ahead.* New York: Morrow Publications, 1998.

Kuenne, Robert E. *Economic Justice in American Society.* Princeton, NJ: Princeton University Press, 1993.

Linowes, David F. *Privacy in America: Is Your Private Life in the Public Eye?* Urbana, IL: University of Illinois Press, 1989.

Oskamp, Stuart, ed. *Television as a Social Issue.* Newbury Park, CA: Sage Publications, 1988.

Reiss, Michael J. *Improving Nature? The Science and Ethics of Genetic Engineering.* New York: Cambridge University Press, 1996.

Schlesinger, Arthur M., Jr. *The Disuniting of America: Reflections on a Multicultural Society.* New York: Norton, 1993.

Steele, Shelby. *Content of Our Character: A New Vision of Race in America.* New York: St. Martin's Press, 1990.

Stoll, Clifford. *Silicon Snake Oil: Second Thoughts on the Information Highway.* New York: Doubleday, 1995.

Ten Berge, Dieudonne. *The First 24 Hours: A Comprehensive Guide to Successful Crisis Communications.* Cambridge, MA: Basil Blackwell, 1990.

Wilson, James Q., and Joan Petersilia, eds. *Crime.* Cambridge, MA: ICS Press, 1994.

Post–Lawrence–Weber:
Business and Society,
Ninth Edition

Technology as a Social
Force

© The McGraw-Hill
Companies, 1999

Technology as a Social Force

Technology is an unmistakable social force in our lives whether we are at home, in school, or in the workplace. The latest wave of technological innovations has dramatically changed how we live, play, learn, work, and interact with others. Accompanying these marvels of technology are equally powerful social and ethical challenges for business, government, and society. Can we use technology to enhance the quality of our lives and not be controlled by it?

This topic focuses on these key questions and objectives:

- What are the dominant features of technology?
- How has technology changed our lifestyle at home, our education at school, and our health?
- How has business utilized the advantages of technology in the workplace?
- What are some of the social and ethical threats emerging from rapid technological change?
- How have governments and businesses taken responsibility to monitor and control technological advancements?

Post–Lawrence–Weber:
Business and Society,
Ninth Edition

Technology as a Social
Force

© The McGraw–Hill
Companies, 1999

"Technology in the home is about to take off. Consumer demand for technology will be the fastest-growing area for technology providers in the next few years," predicted high-tech guru George Forrester Colony.[1] Colony envisioned homes transformed by multimedia personal computers and on-line services. Already "software helpers" have become available to home computer users. These helpers provide access to local weather forecasts, movie reviews, stock quotes, and business news. Others predicted that consumers would soon have access to affordable computers with speech recognition capabilities, 3-D graphic animation, and wearable computers. Another technological revolution is upon us and life looks very good—easier access to information, more information available at affordable prices, and greater opportunities to improve our lives through technological assistance.

But, not so fast, cried a group of technology critics concerned about the impact of technological advancement on the quality of our lives. They extolled traditional values and lifestyles, advocating families gathering together in their homes for singing or storytelling rather than relying on stereos, televisions, or computers for entertainment. Technology was seen as a source of ecological irresponsibility, an inappropriate substitute for family and social group interaction, and a catalyst for automation in the workplace that destroys job satisfaction, creativity, and jobs themselves.

Is technological change happening too fast? Is there too much technological development? Technology has improved the quality of our lives and our ability to communicate with others, yet has it also taken away something from our lives and the way we interact with others?

The Technology Invasion

Throughout history technology has had an enormous effect. It has pressed onward like a glacier, slowly and steadily exerting its influence. It appears virtually impossible to stem the advancement of technology. Though the Industrial Revolution created new and serious human problems for some people in society, it was a great advance in the history of civilization. New jobs and skills replaced older ones, living standards were raised, and economic abundance extended life expectancy for millions of people.

Technology continues to grow because of people themselves. Human beings have sampled and embraced the fruits of knowledge. It seems that people have acquired an insatiable desire for it. They forever seek to expand knowledge of their environment, probably because of the excitement of learning and their belief that more knowledge will help them adapt to their environment.

Features of Technology

The dominant feature of **technology** is *change* and then more change. Technology forces change on people whether they are prepared for it or not. In modern society it has brought so much change that it creates what is called *future shock,* which means that change comes so fast and furiously that it approaches the limits of human tolerance and people lose their ability to cope with it successfully. Although technology is not the only cause of change, it is the primary cause. It is either directly or indirectly involved in most changes that occur in society.

[1]G. Christian Hill, "Talking Technology," *The Wall Street Journal,* June 19, 1995, p. R33.

Post–Lawrence–Weber:
Business and Society,
Ninth Edition

Technology as a Social
Force

© The McGraw–Hill
Companies, 1999

Some years ago, right after the start of the personal computer revolution, industry experts observed that if automobiles had developed at the same rate as the computer business, a Rolls Royce would cost $2.75 and go 3 million miles on a gallon of gasoline. Today's microcomputers cost less than those of a decade or even a few years ago and offer many times the power and many more times the speed of their predecessors.

Another feature of technology is that its effects are *widespread,* reaching far beyond the immediate point of technological impact. Technology ripples through society until every community is affected by it. For example, **telecommunications,** the transmission of information over great distances via electromagnetic signals, has played a historically significant and positive role in our society's development. This innovation enhanced international commerce, linked relatives living great distances apart, and enabled us to discover many of the mysteries of outer space. Yet, along with these advances came the potential for a greater invasion of privacy through databases and telemarketing practices. The human touch in our communication with others has been diminished through the convenience of electronic voice mail.

The shock waves pushed their way into even the most isolated places. People could not escape it. Even if they traveled to remote places like the Grand Canyon, technology was still represented by vapor trails from airplanes flying overhead, microwave communication signals from satellites moving at the speed of light, and a haze from air pollution often preventing a view of the other side.

An additional feature of technology is that it is *self-reinforcing.* As stated by Alvin Toffler, "Technology feeds on itself. Technology makes more technology possible."[2] This self-reinforcing feature means that technology acts as a multiplier to encourage its own faster development. It acts with other parts of society so that an invention in one place leads to a sequence of inventions in other places. Thus, invention of the microprocessor led rather quickly to successful generations of the modern computer, which led to new banking methods, electronic mail, bar-code systems, and so on.

Phases of Technology in Society

Looking at technology in a very general way, we can see that five broad phases of technology have developed, as shown in Figure 1. In history, nations have tended to move sequentially through each phase, beginning with the lowest technology and moving higher with each step, so the five phases roughly represent the progress of civilization throughout history.

The current phase of technology is the **information society.** This phase emphasizes the use and transfer of knowledge and information rather than manual skill. It dominates work and employs the largest proportion of the labor force. Work becomes abstract, the electronic manipulation of symbols. Businesses of all sizes, including the smallest firms, are exploring the benefits of the information age.[3] Examples of people in information jobs are news editors, accountants, computer programmers, and teachers. Even a transplant surgeon, who must use a delicate manual skill, is primarily working from an information or intellectual base. Examples of information industries are newspaper publishing, television, education, book publishing, telecommunications, and consulting.

[2]Alvin Toffler, *Future Shock* (New York: Bantam, 1971), p. 26.
[3]Shoshanah Zuboff, *In the Age of the Smart Machine* (New York: Basic Books, 1988); and "Mom and Pop Go High Tech," *Business Week,* November 21, 1994, pp. 82–90.

Post–Lawrence–Weber:
Business and Society,
Ninth Edition

Technology as a Social
Force

© The McGraw–Hill
Companies, 1999

Figure 1

Phases in the
development of
technology in the
United States.

Technology Level	Phases in the Development of Technology	Approximate Period of Dominance in U.S.	Activity	Primary Skill Used
1	Nomadic-agrarian	Until 1650	Harvests	Manual
2	Agrarian	1650 – 1900	Plants and harvests	Manual
3	Industrial	1900 – 1960	Builds material goods	Manual and machine
4	Service	1960 – 1975	Focuses on providing services	Manual and intellectual
5	Information	1975 – 1990s and beyond	Abstract work	Intellectual and electronic

An information society's technology is primarily electronic in nature and is heavily dependent on the computer and the semiconductor silicon chip. The power of these devices rests on their ability to process, store, and retrieve large amounts of information with very great speed. With the arrival of the 1990s, the information age exploded into nearly every aspect of business and society. Civilization had never experienced that much change that fast. The information age radically transformed the way people learn, think, conduct business, and live their lives. These inventions have catapulted societies into **cyberspace,** where information is stored, ideas are described, and communication takes place in and through an electronic network of linked systems. The technology developed in this new age provided the mechanisms for more information to be produced in a decade than in the previous 1,000 years.

Technology in Our Daily Lives

People around the world are acquiring easier access to more technological innovations than ever before. Residents in economically developing countries enjoy energy-powered appliances, entertainment devices, and communication equipment at a rapidly increasing pace. Individuals and businesses in economically developed countries, like the United States and many European and Asian countries, are multiplying their dependence on electronic communication devices, thus increasing access to information needed for decision making and conducting business transactions.

> The United States, for example, is spawning a technological-gadget generation. By 1996, 90 percent of all U.S. households had a color television, radio, telephone, and videocassette recorder. Most homes in the United States had a cordless telephone, telephone answering machine, stereo system, and compact disc player. Other technological gadgets, such as personal computers, printers, cellular telephones, and pagers, electric car alarms, and camcorders, had also found their place in American homes.[4] Moreover, the speed in which technological change occurs is rapidly shortening, as shown in Figure 2.

The technological invasion also targeted schools. Spending on technology in American public schools, grades kindergarten through 12, doubled in six years in the 1990s.

[4]"The Technology Culture," *The Wall Street Journal,* June 16, 1996, p. R4.

Post–Lawrence–Weber:
Business and Society,
Ninth Edition

Technology as a Social
Force

© The McGraw–Hill
Companies, 1999

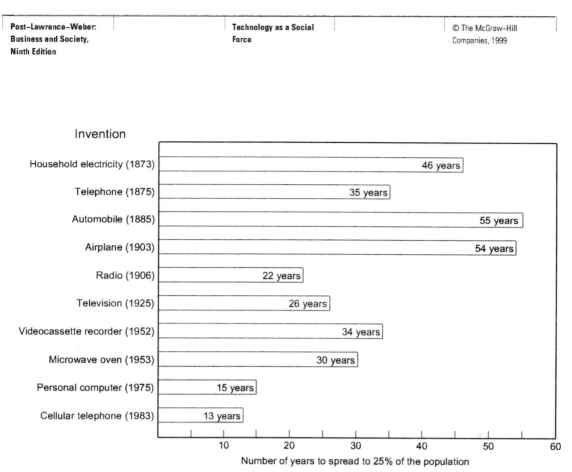

Figure 2

The speed of technological change.

Source: Republished by permission of Dow Jones, Inc. via Copyright Clearance Center, Inc © 1996 Dow Jones and Company, Inc. All Rights Reserved Worldwide.

Fees levied on business telephone service bills directed $2.25 billion over five years to subsidize access to the Internet for schools and libraries in the United States. In the United States, the ratio of computers to students plummeted from 125 to 1 in the mid-1980s to about 12 to 1 in the mid-1990s.[5]

> *In 1990, as part of a desegregation plan, Dillard High School in Fort Lauderdale, Florida, turned to financial aid from the school district, state and federal governments, and private donations to buy computer equipment. By 1996, it had acquired more than $1 million of computer hardware, software, and peripherals, enabling the establishment of a technology magnet school, a school within a school where students needed a C-grade average for admission.*
>
> *The results by any standard were impressive. Students in the technology program scored higher in test scores and grade-point average than students at Dillard High School not involved in the technology program. Only 3 of the program's 200 students failed Florida's mandatory high school competency test on the first try, compared with a 47 percent failure rate schoolwide. About 60 percent of the program's graduates entered college, nearly double the rate for the rest of Dillard's student body.[6]*

[5]William M. Bulkeley, "Back to School," *The Wall Street Journal*, November 13, 1995, p. R6.
[6]Steve Stecklow, "Magnet Miracle," *The Wall Street Journal*, November 13, 1995, p. R14.

Post–Lawrence–Weber:
Business and Society,
Ninth Edition

Technology as a Social
Force

© The McGraw–Hill
Companies, 1999

Seemingly, everywhere we turn—whether in our homes, in school, or at work—the technology invasion is all around us and its influence and opportunities seem inescapable.

The Internet

Certainly one of the most visible and widely used technological innovations in the 1990s was the **Internet** or **World Wide Web.** Springing to life in 1994, this conduit of information revolutionized how business was conducted, students learned, and households operated. The *Wall Street Journal* reported in 1996 that "the number of U.S. households with *Internet* access more than doubled to 14.7 million in the past year." Roughly nine million adult Americans log onto the Internet daily, and twice as many sign on weekly.[7] Increased Internet usage was predicted with continued innovations like WebTV networks, new devices that enable users Internet access via their television sets, and technology that allows people to make telephone calls and access the Internet via electric outlets in walls.

As depicted in Figure 3, most users of the Internet in 1997 were males between the ages of 30 and 49 with a college degree or some college education and an annual income over $25,000. Besides helping with work-related tasks, the Internet's influence expanded to help people plan their leisure time, as described in Exhibit A. Experts predicted that use of the Internet would continue to expand dramatically over the next few years, especially with the wiring of schools to the World Wide Web.

Technological Medical Breakthroughs

Technological breakthroughs in the medical and health-care fields have also dramatically affected people's lives. How people are examined, diagnosed, and treated, how health-related information is collected and stored, and the time and costs associated with health care have been changed by technological innovations within the past few years.

Figure 3

World Wide Web users.

Source: Amy Cortese, "A Census in Cyberspace," *Business Week,* May 5, 1997, p. 84.

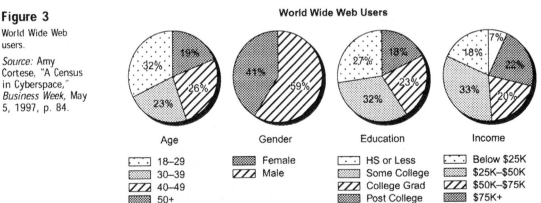

World Wide Web Users

[7]Jared Sandberg, "U.S. Households with Internet Access Doubled to 14.7 Million in Past Year," *The Wall Street Journal,* October 21, 1996, p. B9.

252

Post–Lawrence–Weber:
Business and Society,
Ninth Edition

Technology as a Social
Force

© The McGraw-Hill
Companies, 1999

EXHIBIT A Vacation Planning on the World Wide Web

Vacation planners discovered a new and exciting source for getaway ideas, exotic locations, and travel information—the World Wide Web. Thousands and thousands of travel-related Web sites cropped up on the Internet, blanketing nearly every corner of the globe and representing airlines, hotels, car-rental agencies, cruise companies, travel agencies, and tourist offices. The Web provides consumers an opportunity to make reservations, research fares, or converse with travelers who had already visited vacation paradises they were considering.

For example, the Subway Navigator site (http://metro.jussieu.fr: 10001/bin/cities/english) allows consumers to download maps and display routes for dozens of cities' public railway systems. Using the U.S. Department of Transportation's Bureau of Transportation Statistics (http://www.bts.gov), an individual can learn about on-time performance of airline carriers for flights between his or her home city and vacation destination. Commercial sites, such as Kroll Travel Watch Advisories (http://www.krollassociates.com/kts), offer safety and security tips, healthcare precautions, and much other traveler friendly advice for people venturing to cities around the world, although this site is only open to subscribing businesses. Individuals could receive this information by fax for a modest fee.

At the Association for Computing Machinery's 1997 conference, 100 people volunteered for a "telepresent" medical exam—their medical information was being diagnosed 3,000 miles away at a medical facility. Fifteen volunteers were found to have serious, previously undiagnosed medical problems.

Technology has revolutionized how people are treated. At Johns Hopkins University, a robotic arm was developed to deliver radioactive therapy to patients with liver cancer. The robotic technology can deliver the treatment faster than previous technology, which is critical since a patient's slightest movement through breathing can reduce the effectiveness of the treatment.[8]

The Integration of Technology into Business

The integration of technological innovation into routine business operations can be observed in nearly every workplace function. Communications and access to information are two of the more visible areas. Firms look to improve internal communication through electronic messages, or **e-mail.** Firms can keep better track of their inventory, orders, or project schedules through technologically enhanced information systems. The corporate Web site emerged as an effective marketing tool, and on-line merchandising helped firms shorten their purchase-to-delivery cycle time. "The integration of database, Internet, and CD-ROM is where the real breakthrough thinking is going on. The beautiful thing is it's equally available to small and large companies," explained marketing consultant Richard Cross.

[8]Bob Metcalfe, "We Do Not Need Science Fiction for Today's Telemedicine Wonders," *InfoWorld,* March 24, 1997, p. 50; and "Robots May Plant Seeds for Recovery," *R&D,* February 1997, pp. 33–34.

Post–Lawrence–Weber:
Business and Society,
Ninth Edition

Technology as a Social
Force

© The McGraw–Hill
Companies, 1999

Richard A. Penn, vice president of Puritan Clothing Company, a $20 million Massachusetts firm, created a database to track store sales and coordinate customer mailings. Bill Tuszynski, manager at Inolex Chemical, spent hours in front of his personal computer monitoring cybermarketing tactics of his competitors, scanning bulletin boards for product ideas, and checking out home pages of emerging businesses for materials or new technologies.[9]

Information as Corporate Power

The explosion of the general public's use of the Internet or World Wide Web was mirrored by business. In the 1990s, business connections to the Internet increased from 1,000 firms to an estimated 21,000 or more by 1996. Experts predict this growth to increase rapidly into the year 2000.

The Internet can provide firms with many advantages. For example, developing a marketing strategy that relies on the Internet can benefit firms by replacing electronic mail systems, providing a global reach to customers, selling products and services in cyberspace, and creating on-line databases, media lists, and other marketing tools. Firms discovered that customer service was enhanced with the Internet.

Federal Express Corporation emerged as a World Wide Web success story in the mid-1990s. The package-delivery company moved 2.4 million pieces every day in 1994, serving over 12,000 customers. In November 1994, the firm gave its customers a direct window into the FedEx package-tracking database. By enabling its customers to click their way through the FedEx Web pages to locate and determine the status of their parcels, rather than having a FedEx employee do it, the firm estimated that it saved up to $2 million a year.[10]

Use of the Internet became one of the hottest new strategies in the securities trading industry. Brokers had more information available to them to assist their clients since resources were available electronically. In addition, Internet-based brokers can be reached anytime from any computer with a secure Web browser, making them more accessible to their clients.

Paperless libraries dramatically changed the way information was stored and significantly reduced costs to businesses. Rather than printing information on paper, firms documented information on CD-ROMs, videodiscs, and the Internet, where it was stored and retrieved at less cost.

Supplementing the Internet as a communication tool are **intranets,** private or limited information network systems cordoned off from public access by software programs called *firewalls.* The corporate use of intranets exploded as companies found that these information communication systems were very inexpensive. A survey in 1997 found that the average time needed to train a typical intranet user was 2.4 hours, costing about $46. Comparable training for traditional software took 4.4 hours per user and cost $85.[11] Firms quickly discovered that intranet systems were an inexpensive yet powerful alternative to other forms of internal communication.

---

[9]Gary McWilliams, "Small Fry Go On-Line," *Business Week,* November 20, 1995, pp. 158–64.
[10]Amy Cortese, "Here Comes the Intranet," *Business Week,* February 26, 1996, pp. 76–84.
[11]"Corporate Use of Intranets Is Taking Off, Study Says," *The Wall Street Journal,* March 28, 1997, p. B3.

Post–Lawrence–Weber:
Business and Society,
Ninth Edition

Technology as a Social
Force

© The McGraw–Hill
Companies, 1999

From AT&T to Levi Strauss to 3M, hundreds of companies jumped into the intranet arena in the mid-1990s. Employees at Compaq Computer Corporation could reallocate investments in their 401(k) retirement funds. An intranet link at Ford Motor Company helped engineers in Asia, Europe, and the United States work together on projects for the 1996 Taurus. Other managers, engineers, and scientists found that intranet systems enabled them to exchange ideas and information quickly and inexpensively with colleagues around the world.[12]

Satellite imaging was another technological advancement that showed promise for integrating technology into business. For decades, governments used satellite imaging to spy on their enemies. In the 1990s, companies were finding other uses for this technology. Coldwell Banker Corporation offered real-estate shoppers pictures from space of homes, neighborhoods, and traffic patterns rather than maps and ground photographs. Pacific Bell, a telecommunications company, plotted the laying of telephone lines through satellite imaging, bypassing the costly practice of sending out crews to study and map the terrain.

Medical Research Breakthroughs

Experts believed that humankind was poised for a remarkable revolution in medical knowledge, based on advances in biological science. "This was the century of physics and chemistry," proclaimed 1996 Nobel prize–winning chemist Robert F. Curl. "But it is clear that the next century will be the century of biology."[13]

In February 1997, the century of biology predicted by Professor Curl appeared to arrive with the announcement of the first successful **cloning** of an animal. Scottish embryologist Ian Wilmut stunned the medical community and the world with Dolly, a cloned Dorset lamb. Dolly was created when researchers took cells from a sheep's mammary gland, put them into a test tube, and forced the cells into an inactive state by limiting their intake of nutrients. Next, medical researchers took unfertilized eggs from female sheep and mechanically removed the DNA nucleus from each egg. Finally, the DNA cells were inserted into the cells taken from the mammary glands. Of the 277 experiments, only 29 survived for a few days and were surgically implanted into the womb of 13 ewes. One of the 13 sheep became pregnant and gave birth to a lamb who was an exact genetic copy of the adult sheep whose mammary gland was tapped for DNA cells.

Recent advances in biological research may have potential business applications. Agricultural companies believe breaking down the genetic code will enable them to better combat bacteria and other crop-destroying elements. Genetic testing enabled a Canadian scientist to identify Alzheimer's disease patients who might benefit from the only approved drug in the United States. Continued advancements in genetic testing could help companies in the pharmaceutical industry as well as reduce medical costs for businesses in general.

Economic Effects of Technology

Perhaps the most fundamental effect of technology is *greater efficiency* in terms of quality and quantity. Seeking a more efficient method or means of production is the main rea-

[12]Cortese, "Here Comes the Intranet."
[13]John Carey, Naomi Freundlich, Julia Flynn, and Neil Gross, "The Biotech Century," March 10, 1997, pp. 78–90.

Post–Lawrence–Weber:
Business and Society,
Ninth Edition

Technology as a Social
Force

© The McGraw–Hill
Companies, 1999

son that most technology is adopted. Numerous scientific studies support the claim that using computers increases employee productivity.

> *For example, Famous Footware used technology to automate its human resource processes to reduce or eliminate paperwork tied to hiring, payroll changes, attendance reporting, personnel reviews, labor scheduling, and terminations. The company reported that the new-generation technologies integrated with human resource information systems resulted in markedly greater efficiency for its human resource personnel.*[14]

Technology places more emphasis on *research and development* (R&D). Research concerns the creation of new ideas, and development is their useful application. Growth in R&D expenditures for technological development is seen in both government and private business. The Japanese parliament passed a law in 1996 designed to produce a world-class research system for technological innovation. The law mandated a 12.5 percent annual rise in government R&D spending. When fully implemented, Japanese R&D spending on technology will exceed that of the United States by the year 2002.[15]

> *Thousands of R&D projects have been undertaken by private corporations. For example, IBM launched a $32 million project to develop holographic data storage technology. This new technology stores 12 times more data at the same cost as magnetic data storage. At Bell Laboratories a technique for transmitting data over fiber-optic lines at a rate of one terabit per second—400 times faster than current technology—was the result of a successful R&D strategy.*

The third economic effect of technology is that it creates an *insatiable demand for capital.* Large capital investments are required to build the enormous production systems that save labor time and provide other benefits of technology. At the turn of the century, an investment of $1,000 for each worker often was adequate in a factory, but modern investments in pipelines and petroleum refining exceed $200,000 for each worker.

Technology is costly but essential for business, thereby creating a problem for managers. The failure to maintain up-to-date technology can mean a loss of competitiveness, as occurred in the U.S. steel industry in the 1980s. Both productivity and product quality can suffer. However, such expenditures do not tell the entire story. New technology requires other expenditures to keep the labor force up to date with the machinery and technological changes. This in turn requires managers to select their technology carefully, train people properly, and encourage the continuous improvement of employees' understanding about the best ways to make use of technological capability. These demands also require businesses to generate large amounts of capital and engage in more long-range planning and budgeting for capital use. Global competitiveness requires each nation to invest heavily in its technological future.[16]

---

[14]Randall K. Fields, "Leveraging Information Technology Can Increase Professionalism," *Human Resources Professional,* January–February 1996, pp. 29–32.

[15]Wil Lepkowski and Richard Seltzer, "Japan Reinvents Its R&D Effort, Aims to Develop First-Class Universities," *Chemical and Engineering News,* September 9, 1996, pp. 27–28. For an analysis of the R&D policies for technological development created by the five major industrialized countries, see Rolf G. Sternberg, "Government R&D Expenditure and Space: Empirical Evidence form Five Industrialized Countries," *Research Policy,* August 1996, pp. 741–58.

[16]See, for example, Michael L. Dertouzos, Richard K. Lester, and Robert M. Solow, *Made in America* (Cambridge, MA: MIT Press, 1989), which was influential in public discussion of this issue in the early 1990s.

Post–Lawrence–Weber:
Business and Society,
Ninth Edition

Technology as a Social
Force

© The McGraw–Hill
Companies, 1999

Social and Ethical Concerns

Technological change has brought dramatic enhancements to our lives, work, and health. Few people would argue against the belief that technological advances have improved the quality of life. Yet there are signs that technological change may need to have limits or guidance to best serve business, government, and society.

Too Much, Too Fast?

Despite the explosion of Internet users, medical breakthroughs to enhance the quality of our lives, and numerous other technology advances, there remain people whom the technology invasion has left behind. A 1996 survey of business executives found that 20 percent of the 245 CEOs and senior executives did not have a personal computer on their desk and half of all CEOs surveyed did not use a computer at work.[17] This resistance to computers is often related to age, reflecting a generation gap between those proficient in information technology and those whose business training predates the availability of personal computers.

Technology was developing so fast that **information overload,** the availability of too much information to process or assist in decision making, occurred and more information became useless information.

> *The Direct Marketing Association estimated that a mailing to one million people would cost about $827,000 in 1996. Yet, Internet advertisers could reach the same number of people for the cost of local telephone calls and a few hundred dollars for on-line costs. Software was available that would allow businesses to send thousands of messages to prospective customers for only a few hundred dollars.*[18]

The emergence of junk e-mail and the saturation of the World Wide Web with advertisers quickly inundated businesses and customers with more information than they could handle.

The threat of technological inefficiency was attributed to not only those unskilled in using computers but those highly skilled: **computer hackers.** Computer hackers are individuals who break into company databases or other secure information banks to steal or delete information or cause confusion for those trying to use the information. It is difficult to estimate the cost hackers impose on businesses since most firms do not report hacker trespass, either out of embarrassment or because they do not realize the breach of security. According to a survey by a U.S. Senate subcommittee, major banks and other large corporations incurred an estimated $800 million in losses in 1995 because of hacker intrusions into their computer systems.[19]

Questions of Privacy

With the emergence of mass marketing, consumers gave away their **privacy** piece by piece. Long before the Internet, consumers provided data when applying for credit cards,

[17]Joann S. Lublin, "Computer Illiterates Still Roam Executive Suites," *The Wall Street Journal,* June 24, 1996, pp. B1, B8.
[18]Randi Feigenbaum, "Garbage In—And In and In," *Business Week,* September 9, 1996, p. 110.
[19]John J. Fialka, "Intrusions by Computer Hackers Cost Big Business $800 Million in 1995," *The Wall Street Journal,* June 6, 1996, p. B6.

Post–Lawrence–Weber:
Business and Society,
Ninth Edition

Technology as a Social
Force

© The McGraw–Hill
Companies, 1999

signing up for frequent flier programs, or receiving supermarket discount cards. But the information age dramatically changed the extent that personal information was stored and available to others.

Some Web sites, for example, will provide your name, address, telephone number, driving record, and even your Social Security number to any interested paying party. Embedded in Netscape software are what are called *cookies.* Cookies help merchants using the Internet to track what a particular customer purchases and how long he or she takes in making the selection. In response to consumer objections to cookies as invasions of privacy, Netscape Communications Company informed consumers that it was changing its Internet browser so customers could prevent on-line merchants from tracking their purchasing patterns on the Internet.

Invasions of privacy also occurred at work. An individual's electronic mail to a coworker could be read by his or her boss. An employee's squandering of company time by browsing the World Wide Web, visiting sex-related sites, or sending massive quantities of private e-mail could be detected by the company's monitoring of computer activity. E-mail, whether at work or in a university computer lab, is the property of the company or university, not the private property of the sender. Stored in the company or university databases, these messages are available to authorities at any time.

Monitoring of workplace communication over the Internet or e-mail is seen as warranted when employees use these forms of communication technology in ways viewed as socially unacceptable, for example, sending racist or sexist messages. Three examples of inappropriate e-mail disseminated at work are described in Exhibit B.

Intellectual Property

Ethical issues arise over obtaining copyrighted or patented material without acquiring permission or purchasing the rights. **Intellectual property** was a hotly contested issue in the 1990s. The copying of compact discs, or CD piracy, soared in 1997 as the availability of machines used to copy movies, music, and CD-ROMs flooded the marketplace from Europe, mostly into Asian countries. According to one estimate, nearly 200 million illegal CDs annually were stamped in the mid-1990s, almost 60 percent of them from China. The International Federation of the Phonographic Industry claimed annual losses of $2 billion to intellectual property pirates in 1996.[20]

The U.S. government responded to the intellectual piracy crisis by drafting a hit list of countries known to be the biggest violators. Those with inadequate protection against intellectual piracy included Argentina, Greece, Indonesia, India, Japan, and countries in the European Union.

China was singled out and threatened with economic sanctions because of the magnitude of its participation in illegal copyright violations. In June 1996, China agreed to close entirely or partly factories known to manufacture illegal CDs, shut down six major distribution markets of illegal CDs, and stop more than 5,000 minitheatres from showing pirated videos for a fee. The Chinese Ministry of Public Security added intellectual property violations to its Severe Campaign Against Crime. Chinese custom agents stepped up border surveillance, seizing 80,000 pirated discs in just a few months in 1996. China also

[20]Robert S. Greenberger and Craig S. Smith, "CD Piracy Flourishes in China, and West Supplies Equipment," *The Wall Street Journal,* April 24, 1997, pp. A1, A12.

Post–Lawrence–Weber:
Business and Society,
Ninth Edition

Technology as a Social
Force

© The McGraw–Hill
Companies, 1999

EXHIBIT B   Racist E-Mail at Work

In the space of six weeks, employees at three different companies claimed that racist e-mail messages were sent via their company's communications network. The first was at Morgan Stanley & Company. Two African-American employees charged that they should not have been subjected to racist jokes sent via electronic mail at the firm. After the two employees complained about the messages they allegedly were denied promotions. The firm denied discriminating against the two employees and stated that after the employees filed their internal complaints, three managers were found to have spread racist e-mail messages and were placed on probation.

Just four days later, a racial discrimination suit was filed against R.R. Donnelly & Sons Company, a Chicago-based commercial printing company. More than 500 African-American employees joined the racial discrimination charges against the firm and released documents that included a list of 165 racial, ethnic, and sexual jokes that allegedly were sent through the electronic mail system. Donnelly officials said that senior management had no knowledge of the documents, but if these messages did exist it would be a clear violation of company policy.

A month later, two African-American employees of Citibank, a unit of Citicorp, filed a racial discrimination lawsuit after racist jokes were allegedly sent via electronic mail by several bank supervisors. The employees claimed that supervisors, including company vice presidents, spread offensive e-mail to colleagues around the country. According to the employees, the e-mail created a "pervasively abusive, racially hostile work environment." When reported in the press, the company had no comment since officials had not yet had time to review the charges.

Sources: Frances A. McMorris, "Morgan Stanley Employees File Suit, Charging Race Bias over E-Mail Jokes," *The Wall Street Journal,* January 13, 1997, p. B2; Alex Markels, "Racist E-Mail Messages as Donnelly Show Pattern of Bias, Attorneys Claim," *The Wall Street Journal,* January 17, 1997, p. B2; and Frances A. McMorris, "Citibank Workers File Bias Lawsuit over Racist E-Mail," *The Wall Street Journal,* February 19, 1997, p. B5.

established an enforcement verification system to prevent piracy, including inspectors on the job 24 hours a day at every CD factory. Any CD found on the market without a registry number issued by the state was subject to immediate seizure.[21]

Fears of Cloning

The medical breakthrough of cloning an animal, described earlier, was received not only as a giant technological advancement but also as the terror of science fiction becoming reality. Whether it is visions of Jurassic Park dinosaurs running loose in a metropolitan downtown area or the eerie absurdity of cloning multiple Adolph Hitlers in the film *The Boys of Brazil,* fears of cloning living tissue have invaded our lives.[22] In February 1997, there were no laws on record that prevented scientists from attempting human cloning. Experts recognized that

[21]Kathy Chen and Helene Cooper, "U.S. and China Reach an Agreement, Averting Trade Sanctions by Both Sides," *The Wall Street Journal,* June 18, 1996, pp. A2, A6.
[22]Robert Langreth, "Cloning Has Fascinating, Disturbing Potential," *The Wall Street Journal,* February 24, 1997, pp. B1, B2; and George Johnson, "Ethical Fears Aside, Science Plunges On," *New York Times,* December 7, 1997, p. 6.

Post–Lawrence–Weber:
Business and Society,
Ninth Edition

Technology as a Social
Force

© The McGraw–Hill
Companies, 1999

the technique used in Scotland to clone a sheep was so simple, requiring little high-tech equipment, that it could be attempted by most biology laboratories with a budget of a few hundred thousand dollars. The ease with which this experiment could be attempted using human DNA cells and the lack of governmental control quickly brought the public and the scientific community's fears over cloning to an unprecedented level.

In June 1997, the U.S. National Bioethics Advisory Commission proposed that scientists be barred from implanting a cloned embryo into a woman's uterus. However, this proposal did not ban scientists from cloning embryos used for research but not implanted into a woman. The group of scientists, lawyers, and ethicists based much of their opposition on concerns for a fetus's safety and urged that the ban be respected for at least through the year 2002.[23] This debate will inevitably continue into the next century.

Responsibilities for Technological Advancements

Many technological advancements, including the unprecedented development of cloning living cells, outpaced government regulation, business oversight, and professional standards. As with most issues in society, the public looked to governmental regulation of business or voluntary self-regulation to ensure that societal interests were considered along with corporate economic interests. Businesses joined consumer advocates and employee watchdog groups to impose controls on the fast-growing technological frontier.

The Role of Government

Numerous efforts were taken as governments tried to bring control to cyberspace. Some countries attempted to censor subversive or socially unacceptable material on the Internet by banning access to it or criminalizing its distribution. Since the Internet is a global medium, however, national laws did little to stop the crossnational transmission of information or images. Internet users themselves or those with authority over the users, such as parents or companies, may need to provide the necessary controls to restrict access to some Internet sites.

> Five German police officers spent much of their time in 1997 surfing the Internet for pornographic material. They were attempting to build a case against CompuServe's German subsidiary based on allegations that the firm's general manager was an accessory to the dissemination of pornography.
>
> In Finland, the courts ordered Johan Helsingius to shut down what was reported to be the world's largest anonymous electronic-mail service after one of his service's users was linked to child pornography. The court made this ruling even though the Finnish police who were directly involved in the investigation reported that Helsingius's service the service was not designed to transmit photographs and there was no reason to believe that pornography was disseminated. Nonetheless, antipornography crusaders said that the service was used to help people find child prostitutes.[24]

---

[23]Laurie McGinley, "U.S. Bioethics Panel to Recommend Ban on Cloning to Produce a Human Being," *The Wall Street Journal,* June 9, 1997, p. B3.

[24]Silvia Ascarelli and Kimberley A. Strassel, "Two German Cases Show How Europe Still Is Struggling to Regulate Internet," *The Wall Street Journal,* April 21, 1997, p. B7B; and "Finnish E-Mail Service Closed after Charges of Child Pornography," *The Wall Street Journal,* September 4, 1996, p. B8.

Post–Lawrence–Weber:
Business and Society,
Ninth Edition

Technology as a Social
Force

© The McGraw–Hill
Companies, 1999

In 1996, the U.S. government launched an eight-month investigation aimed at uncovering software piracy in businesses and homes. Primary targets were computer bulletin boards used, according to the FBI, to distribute copyrighted software from some of the industry's most prominent suppliers. According to official reports, software piracy activities spilled over into the theft of telephone calling cards, the distribution of stolen credit cards, the spread of computer viruses, and the unauthorized access into corporate computer networks to steal proprietary information.

Other governments attacked information technology on the grounds of political subversion. Singapore officials blacklisted numerous Web sites, stating that they contained "content which may undermine public morals, political stability and religious harmony of Singapore."[25]

Similar bans of access to Internet information occurred in China. This country blocked over 100 sites on the World Wide Web, according to Chinese and Westerners who monitor the Internet. Chinese officials shut down access to some English-language sites sponsored by such U.S. news media giants as *The Wall Street Journal,* the *Washington Post,* and CNN because of what they perceived to be anti-Beijing messages. Chinese-language sites were not exempt; added to the list of Web sites found to be offensive to the Chinese government were those that presented news and commentaries from Taiwan, which government leaders in Beijing considered to be "a renegade province of China."

Business Responsibility for Technological Change

Although governmental control of technology increased in the 1990s, businesses also served as society's designated agents responsible for monitoring new technology. In light of the economic self-interest involved, corporate control of the use of technology emerged, and society's interests were protected as well.

Electronic games are often useful in education, but they tend to be a temptation for inappropriate behavior for employees in the workplace. In response, many corporations monitor employee use of computers at work and encourage the appropriate use of these productivity tools.

The 17,000 employees at Compaq Computer Corporation saw a warning flashing on their computer screen when they logged onto the company network. The warning read: improper and illegal duplication of corporate data will be punished. It also reminded employees that the firm reserved the right to read all e-mail messages sent over the network (see Exhibit B). Twelve workers at Compaq's Houston headquarters were fired when it was discovered that they had visited sexually explicit Web sites while at work.

SurfWatch developed a software that allowed companies to block employee access to any Internet site. Although it was originally developed for parents to block pornographic Web sites from their children's viewing, companies such as Lockheed Martin Corporation encouraged the software manufacture to develop a version for the corporate market. Other firms, such as IBM, Microsoft, AT&T, and America Online, joined the movement to develop ways that pornography and other offensive material could be blocked from

[25]Wayne Arnold, "Internet Censorship in China, Singapore May Affect Law-Abiding Citizens Most," *The Wall Street Journal,* September 13, 1996, p. B11B.

Post–Lawrence–Weber:
Business and Society,
Ninth Edition

Technology as a Social
Force

© The McGraw–Hill
Companies, 1999

company Internet networks. Business firms identified temptations for employees' abusive use of technology in the workplace and developed or acquired controls to minimize these opportunities.

Summary Points

- One of the dominant features of technology is change and more change. Technology also has widespread effects and tends to be self-reinforcing.

- The current phase of technology—the information society—has changed our lifestyle, our education, and the field of medical research by providing more information with easier access at a quicker pace. One of the most visible technological innovations in the 1990s was the creation of the Internet.

- Businesses seized many opportunities to enjoy the advantages of technology by understanding that information is power. This power can be seen in new corporate communication systems, such as e-mail, intranets, and satellite imaging.

- Technology brought social and ethical challenges along with the advantages of innovation. Information overload, invasions of privacy, violations of intellectual property, and fears of medical research going too far all caused people to question the benefits of technology.

- Governments have attempted to protect the public from technological infringements on social values, such as the dissemination of child pornography, software piracy, or political subversion. Likewise, businesses have tried to ensure the appropriate use of technology in the workplace and aggressively monitored employee use of e-mail and the Internet.

Key Terms and Concepts

- Technology
- Telecommunications
- Information society
- Cyberspace
- Internet, or World Wide Web
- E-mail

- Intranets
- Cloning
- Information overload
- Computer hackers
- Privacy
- Intellectual property

Internet Resources

- http://www.bnt.com — BizNet Technologies
- http://www.compinfo.co.uk/index.html — Computer Information Centre
- http://ciber.bus.msu.edu/busres.htm — International Business Resources on the WWW
- http://ds.internic.net/ds/dsdirofdirs.html — InterNIC Directory of Directories

Post–Lawrence–Weber:
Business and Society,
Ninth Edition

Technology as a Social
Force

© The McGraw–Hill
Companies, 1999

Discussion Case Pornography on the Internet

Doug Jackson logged onto the Internet nearly every day. It provided Doug with volumes and volumes of information that allowed him to complete educational assignments, explore new worlds, and communicate with people in many countries. One day Doug clicked on a search button and typed in *nude photos*. Within seconds thousands of Web sites were available to him. After randomly selecting one site, Doug was asked: "Are you 18 years of age? If no, click on the EXIT button and leave this adult site. If yes, click on the ENTER button." Doug did not hesitate to click on the ENTER button. There he found hundreds of explicit sexual photographs of women. Also listed on this Web site were directories of stories describing men and women having bizarre sexual encounters, contact information for women waiting to talk to Doug on the telephone for a fee, and telephone numbers for escort services in his hometown.

Social and religious values vary across cultures and countries, but in the United States in the 1990s, Doug—a 26-year-old man—was allowed to view these Web sites. But what if Doug were a 15-year-old high school student who was encouraged by his friends at school to browse these sites, or simply a curious adolescent?

Access to pornographic material or entertainment is controlled by law and enforced by those providing the material or entertainment. For example, a clerk at a convenience store that sells adult magazines is required to ask for identification to verify that buyers are of legal age. A manager of an adult bookstore or nightclub featuring nude or topless dancers is required to check identification of all patrons who enter the establishment. Yet who monitors access to adult Web sites on the Internet and validates that all browsers are of legal age to view the adult-oriented material?

The question of censorship or supervising the Internet was a growing problem in 1997. Who should control access to adult material on the Internet? Should it rest with the user, the provider, parents or other authorities, or the government?

Adult Web sites ask users if they are of legal age to access sexually oriented material. It seems unlikely that this type of regulation would be successful. Most of the larger commercial on-line and Web servers either say they examine advertisements individually or accept all ads but regulate their content or limit their display to specific search words. Only a few of the servers, including America Online and Starwave Corporation (producers of ESPNet Sportszone and other sites), ban adult material advertisers. Yet these companies also admit that they can not keep up with the massive flow of new advertisers on their services and that the cost of this control is enormous.

Parents, school officials, or company supervisors have another option. Numerous censors offer their services to parents or institutions to control what users can see on the Internet, such as WebTrack, SurfWatch, NetNanny, CyberPatrol, CYBERsitter, and SafeSurf. CYBERsitter is a content-intelligent system that identifies and blocks inappropriate Web sites for its subscribers. The firm also offers CYBERtimer, which defines allowable times during the day when on-line access is permitted.

SurfWatch is another popular Web screen. This firm offered software for parents and educators for $49.95 (in 1997) to deal with the flood of sexually explicit material on the Internet. As reported in one of the company's advertisements, "since creating the market for Internet filtering technology in May 1995, SurfWatch has shipped more than 7.2 million copies of the software and has become the industry-standard tool for blocking access to unwanted materials on the Internet."

Post–Lawrence–Weber:
Business and Society,
Ninth Edition

Technology as a Social
Force

© The McGraw–Hill
Companies, 1999

Traditionally the government has stepped in as the regulator of adult-oriented material or entertainment. This appeared to be the path the United States was taking to censor the Internet in 1996 when the Communications Decency Act was signed into law. The outcry from free-speech advocates and marketers using the Internet was deafening, and in June 1997, the U.S. Supreme Court declared the act unconstitutional. As Justice John Paul Stevens wrote, "We presume that governmental regulation of the content of speech is more likely to interfere with the free exchange of ideas than to encourage it." Thus, the question of who will control access to the Internet bounced back into the free market.

The presence of the Internet and its recent massive growth makes the question of monitoring access to pornography or adult-oriented Web sites critical. Should this material be controlled, and if so, who should say what is inappropriate material for minors and how would monitoring Web access be achieved?

Discussion Questions

1. Since the Internet is a widely used, free-access source of information, should pornographic material be banned from the World Wide Web?
2. Who do you believe should be responsible for monitoring access to adult material on the Internet: the user, the provider, parents, schools, or the government? Why do you think so?
3. Should Web screens, such as SurfWatch, be provided free to all parents, educators, or managers who want them? Should the government pay for this software technology?

Bibliography

Adler, Paul S., ed. *Technology and the Future of Work.* New York: Oxford University Press, 1992.

Barbour, Ian G. *Ethics in an Age of Technology.* San Francisco: Harper, 1993.

Barcus, F. Earl. *Images of Life on Children's Television: Sex Roles, Minorities, and Families.* New York: Praeger, 1983.

Bradley, Stephen P.; Jerry A. Hausman; and Richard L. Nolan. *Globalization, Technology, and Competition: The Fusion of Computers and Telecommunications in the 1990s.* Boston, MA: Harvard Business School Press, 1993.

Corrado, Frank M. *Media for Managers: Communications Strategies for the Eighties.* Englewood Cliffs, NJ: Prentice-Hall, 1984.

Dates, Jannette L., and William Barlow, eds. *Split Image: African-Americans in the Mass Media.* Washington, D.C.: Howard University Press, 1990.

Dertouzas, Michael L.; Richard K. Lester; and Robert M. Solow. *Made in America: Regaining the Productivity Edge.* Cambridge, MA: MIT Press, 1989.

Drlica, Karl. *Double-edged Sword: The Promises and Risks of the Genetic Revolution.* Reading, MA: Addison-Wesley, 1994.

Etzioni, Amitai. *The Spirit of Community: Rights, Responsibilities, and the Communitarian Agenda.* New York: Crown Publishers, 1993.

Hernstein, Richard J., and Charles Murray, *The Bell Curve: Intelligence and Class Structure in American Life.* New York: Free Press, 1994.

Kolata, Gina. *Clone: The Road to Dolly and the Path Ahead.* New York: Morrow Publications, 1998.

Kuenne, Robert E. *Economic Justice in American Society.* Princeton, NJ: Princeton University Press, 1993.

Linowes, David F. *Privacy in America: Is Your Private Life in the Public Eye?* Urbana, IL: University of Illinois Press, 1989.

Oskamp, Stuart, ed. *Television as a Social Issue.* Newbury Park, CA: Sage Publications, 1988.

Reiss, Michael J. *Improving Nature? The Science and Ethics of Genetic Engineering.* New York: Cambridge University Press, 1996.

Post–Lawrence–Weber:
Business and Society,
Ninth Edition

Technology as a Social
Force

© The McGraw–Hill
Companies, 1999

Schlesinger, Arthur M., Jr. *The Disuniting of America: Reflections on a Multicultural Society.* New York: Norton, 1993.

Steele, Shelby. *Content of Our Character: A New Vision of Race in America.* New York: St. Martin's Press, 1990.

Stoll, Clifford. *Silicon Snake Oil: Second Thoughts on the Information Highway.* New York: Doubleday, 1995.

Ten Berge, Dieudonne. *The First 24 Hours: A Comprehensive Guide to Successful Crisis Communications.* Cambridge, MA: Basil Blackwell, 1990.

Wilson, James Q., and Joan Petersilia, eds. *Crime.* Cambridge, MA: ICS Press, 1994.

Post–Lawrence–Weber:
Business and Society,
Ninth Edition

Case Studies: Odwalla,
Inc., and the E. Coli
Breakout

© The McGraw–Hill
Companies, 1999

Case Study:
Odwalla, Inc.,
and the E. Coli Outbreak

October 30, 1996, was a cool, fall day in Half Moon Bay, California, a coastal town an hour's drive south of San Francisco. At the headquarters of Odwalla, Inc., a modest, two-story wooden structure just blocks from the beach, company founder and chairman Greg Steltenpohl was attending a marketing meeting. Odwalla, the largest producer of fresh fruit and vegetable-based beverages in the western United States, had just completed its best-ever fiscal year, with sales of $59 million, up 40 percent over the past 12 months.

The company's CEO, Stephen Williamson, urgently knocked on the glass door and motioned Steltenpohl into the hall. Williamson, 38, a graduate of the University of California at Berkeley and a former investment banker, had served as president of Odwalla from 1992 and 1995, when he became CEO.

It was unlike him to interrupt a meeting, and he looked worried. "I just got a call from the King County Department of Health," Williamson reported. "They've got a dozen cases of E. coli poisoning up there in the Seattle area. A number of the families told health officials they had drunk Odwalla apple juice." E. coli O157:H7 was a virulent bacterium

Note: This is an abridged version of a longer case: Anne T. Lawrence, "Odwalla, Inc., and the E. Coli Outbreak (A), (B), and (C), presented at the annual meeting of the North American Case Research Association, October 24, 1997. This case was written with the cooperation of management, solely for the purpose of stimulating student discussion. Sources include articles appearing in the *Natural Foods Merchandiser, Nation's Business, San Jose Mercury News, Rocky Mountain News, San Francisco Chronicle, Seattle Times, Fresno Bee, New York Times, The Wall Street Journal,* and *Squeeze* (Odwalla's in-house newsletter); press releases issued by Odwalla and by the American Fresh Juice Council; and Odwalla's annual reports and prospectus. Odwalla's Web site may be found at http://www.odwallazone.com.

Post–Lawrence–Weber:
Business and Society,
Ninth Edition

Case Studies: Odwalla,
Inc., and the E. Coli
Breakout

© The McGraw–Hill
Companies, 1999

that had been responsible for several earlier outbreaks of food poisoning, including one traced to undercooked Jack-in-the-Box hamburgers in 1993.

Steltenpohl was puzzled. "What do they know for sure?"

"Right now, not a whole lot. It's just epidemiology," Williamson replied. "They don't have any bacteriological match-ups yet. They said it might be a while before they would know anything definitive."

"We'd better see what else we can find out."

Steltenpohl and Williamson returned to their offices, where they began placing calls to food safety experts, scientists at the Food and Drug Administration and the Centers for Disease Control, and the company's lawyers. A while later, Steltenpohl came out to speak to his next appointment, who had been waiting in the lobby for over an hour. "I'm awfully sorry," the chairman said apologetically. "I'm not going to be able to see you today. Something important's happening that I've got to deal with right away."

History of Odwalla, Inc.

Odwalla, Inc., was founded in 1980 by Steltenpohl, his wife Bonnie Bassett, and their friend Gerry Percy. Steltenpohl, then 25, was a jazz musician and Stanford graduate with a degree in environmental science. The group purchased a used hand juicer for $200 and began producing fresh-squeezed orange juice in a backyard shed in Santa Cruz, California. They delivered the juice to local restaurants in a Volkswagen van. Steltenpohl later said that he had gotten the idea from a book, *100 Businesses You Can Start for Under $100*. His motivation, he reported, was simply to make enough money to support his fledgling career as a musician and producer of educational media presentations. The company's name came from a jazz composition by the Art Ensemble of Chicago, in which Odwalla was a mythical figure who led the "people of the sun" out of the "gray haze," which the friends chose to interpret as a reference to overly processed food.

During the 1980s, Odwalla prospered, gradually extending its market reach by expanding its own distribution and production capabilities and by acquiring other juice companies. In 1983, the company moved into a larger production facility and added carrot juice to its product line. In 1985—the same year Odwalla incorporated—the company purchased a small local apple juice company, Live Juice. With apple added to the line, the company expanded its distribution efforts, moving into San Francisco and further north into Marin County. In 1986, Odwalla purchased Dancing Bear Juice Company in Sacramento and assimilated that company's juice products and distribution network in central California.

The company financed its rapid growth in its early years through bank loans and private stock offerings in 1991, 1992, and 1993. In December 1993, the company went public, offering for sale one million shares of common stock at an initial price of $6.375 a share. The proceeds of the initial public offering were used in part to construct a 65,000 square foot state-of-the-art production facility in Dinuba, in California's agricultural Central Valley.

The company also made additional acquisitions. In June 1994, the company acquired Dharma Juice Company of Bellingham, Washington, to distribute its products in the Pacific Northwest. In January, 1995, Odwalla purchased J.S. Grant's, Inc., the maker of Just Squeezed Juices, which became the distributor for Odwalla products in the Colorado market. The strategy appeared to be successful. By 1996, Odwalla, which already controlled more than half the market for fresh juice in northern California, had made significant inroads in the Pacific Northwest and Colorado and was poised to extend its market dominance into New Mexico, Texas, and southern California.

Post–Lawrence–Weber:
Business and Society,
Ninth Edition

Case Studies: Odwalla,
Inc., and the E. Coli
Breakout

© The McGraw–Hill
Companies, 1999

Product Line

The company considered its market niche to be "fresh, minimally processed juices and juice-based beverages."

The company produced a range of products from fresh juice, some single strength and some blended. Odwalla chose fun, clever names, such as Strawberry C-Monster (a vitamin C-fortified fruit smoothie), Femme Vitale (a product formulated to meet women's special nutritional needs), and Guava Have It (a tropical fruit blend). Packaging graphics were brightly colored and whimsical. Pricing was at the premium level; a half gallon of fresh-squeezed orange juice retailed for around $5.00; a 16-oz. blended smoothie for $2.00 or more.

Odwalla was committed to making a totally fresh product. In the company's 1995 annual report, for example, the letter to shareholders stated:

> Our juice is FRESH! We believe that fruits, vegetables and other botanical nutrients must be treated with respect. As a result, we do not heat-treat our juice, like the heavily processed products made by most other beverage companies.

The company's products were made without preservatives or any artificial ingredients, and the juice was not pasteurized (heat treated to kill microorganisms and to extend shelf life). Unpasteurized juice, the company believed, retained more vitamins, enzymes, and what Steltenpohl referred to as the "flavor notes" of fresh fruits and vegetables.

Although Odwalla did not pasteurize its juice, it took many steps in the manufacturing process to assure the quality and purity of its product. To avoid possible contamination, the company did not accept ground apples, only those picked from the tree. Inspectors checked field bins to see if there was any dirt, grass, or debris; and bins with evidence of ground contact were rejected. The company's manufacturing facility in Dinuba was considered the most advanced in the industry. The plant operated under a strict code of Good Manufacturing Practices. At Dinuba, apples were thoroughly washed with a sanitizing solution of phosphoric acid and scrubbed with whirling brushes. All juice was produced under extremely strict hygienic standards.

Marketing

Odwalla marketed its products through supermarkets, warehouse outlets, specialty stores, natural food stores, and institutions such as restaurants and colleges. Slightly over a quarter of all sales were with two accounts—Safeway, a major grocery chain, and Price/Costco, a discount warehouse.

A distinctive feature of Odwalla's strategy was the company's direct store distribution, or DSD, system. Most sites, from supermarkets to small retailers, were provided with their own stand-alone refrigerated cooler, brightly decorated with Odwalla graphics. Accounts were serviced by route sales people (RSPs), who were responsible for stocking the coolers and removing unsold juice that had passed its "enjoy by" date. RSPs kept careful records of what products were selling well, enabling them to adjust stock to meet local tastes. As an incentive, salespeople received bonuses based on their routes' sales, in addition to their salaries.

Although the DSD system was more expensive than using independent distributors, it allowed the company to maintain tight control over product mix and quality. Moreover, because the company assumed responsibility for ordering, stocking, and merchandising its own products within the store, Odwalla in most cases did not pay "slotting" and other handling fees to the retailer.

Post–Lawrence–Weber:
Business and Society,
Ninth Edition

Case Studies: Odwalla,
Inc., and the E. Coli
Breakout

© The McGraw–Hill
Companies, 1999

Corporate Culture

The fresh juice company was always, as Steltenpohl put it, "values driven." In 1992, around 80 Odwalla employees participated in a nine-month process that led to the creation of the company's vision, mission, and core values statements. These focused on nourishment, ecological sustainability, innovation, and continuous learning.

Concerned that rapid growth might erode common commitment to these values, in 1995 the company initiated annual three-day training sessions, held on site at multiple locations, known as Living Vision Conferences, for employees to talk about the application of the vision to everyday operating issues. An internal process the company called Vision Link sought to link each individual's job to the Odwalla vision. Managers were expected to model the company's values. The company called its values a "touchstone [for employees] in assessing their conduct and in making business decisions."

In addition, Odwalla instituted a "strategic dialogue" process. A group of 30 people, with some fixed seats for top executives and some rotating seats for a wide cross-section of other employees, met quarterly in San Francisco for broad discussions of the company's values and strategic direction.

Social responsibility and environmental awareness were critical to Odwalla's mission. Community service efforts included aid to farm families in the Central Valley, scholarships to study nutrition, and gifts of cash and juice to many local community organizations. The company instituted a recycling program for its plastic bottles. It attempted to divert all organic waste away from landfills—for example, by selling pulp for livestock feed and citrus peel for use in teas and condiments and past-code juice for biofuels. In the mid-1990s, the company began the process of converting its vehicle fleet to alternative fuels. Odwalla's corporate responsibility extended to its employees, who received innovative benefits that included stock options, extensive wellness programs, and an allowance for fresh juice. The company won numerous awards for its environmental practices, and in 1993, *Inc.* magazine honored Odwalla as Employer of the Year.

During these years, the Odwalla brand name became widely identified with a healthful lifestyle, as well as with California's entrepreneurial business climate. In an oft-repeated story, Steve Jobs, founder of Apple Computer, was said to have ordered unlimited quantities of Odwalla juice for all employees working on the original development of the Macintosh Computer.

The E. Coli Bacterium

The virulent strain of bacteria that threatened to bring down this fast-growing company was commonly known in scientific circles as Escherichia coli, or E. coli for short.

The broad class of E. coli bacteria, microscopic rod-shaped organisms, are common in the human intestinal tract, and few pose a danger to health. In fact, most E. coli play a beneficial role by suppressing harmful bacteria and synthesizing vitamins. A small minority of E. coli strains, however, cause illness. One of the most dangerous of these is E. coli O157:H7. In the intestine, this strain produces a potent toxin that attacks the lining of the gut. Symptoms of infection include abdominal pain and cramps, diarrhea, fever, and bloody stools. Most cases are self-limiting, but approximately 6 percent are complicated with hemolytic uremic syndrome, a dangerous condition that can lead to kidney and heart failure. Young children, the elderly, and those with weakened immune systems are most susceptible.

E. coli O157:H7 lives in the intestines of cows, sheep, deer, and other animals. The meat of infected animals may carry the infection. E. coli is also spread to humans through

270

Post–Lawrence–Weber:
Business and Society,
Ninth Edition

Case Studies: Odwalla,
Inc., and the E. Coli
Breakout

© The McGraw–Hill
Companies, 1999

fecal contamination of food. For example, apples may be contaminated when they fall to the ground and come in contact with cow or deer manure. Secondary infection may also occur, for example, when food is handled by infected persons who have failed to wash their hands after using the toilet. Unfortunately, only a small amount of 157—as few as 500 bacteria—is required to cause illness. As one epidemiologist noted, "It does not take a massive contamination or a major breakdown in the system to spread it."

E. coli O157:H7 is known as an emergent pathogen, meaning that its appearance in certain environments is viewed by researchers as a new phenomenon. The organism was first identified in 1982, when it was involved in a several outbreaks involving undercooked meat. Since then, poisoning incidents had increased dramatically. By the mid-1990s, about 20,000 cases of E. coli poisoning occurred every year in the United States; about 250 people died. Most cases were believed to be caused by undercooked meat. Although a serious threat, E. coli is not the most common food-borne illness. In the United States, five million cases of food poisoning are reported annually, with 4,000 of these resulting in death. Most cases are caused by mistakes in food preparation and handling, not by mistakes in food processing or packaging.

E. coli in Fresh Juice

It was widely believed in the juice industry that pathogens like E. coli could not survive in an acidic environment, such as citrus and apple juice. Odwalla apple juice had a pH (acidity) level of 4.3. (On the pH scale, 7 is neutral, and levels below 7 are increasingly acidic.) Odwalla did conduct spot testing of other, more pH-neutral products. The Food and Drug Administration, although it did not have specific guidelines for fresh juice production, indicated in its Retail Food Store Sanitation Code that foods with a pH lower than 4.6 were *not* potentially hazardous.

In the early 1990s, however, scattered scientific evidence emerged that E. coli O157:H7 might have undergone a critical mutation that rendered it more acid-tolerant. In 1991, an outbreak of E. coli poisoning sickened 23 people in Massachusetts who had consumed fresh, unpasteurized apple cider purchased at a roadside stand. A second, similar incident occurred in Connecticut around the same time. In a study of the Massachusetts outbreak published in 1993, the *Journal of the American Medical Association* reported that E. coli O157:H7, apparently introduced by fecal contamination of fresh apples, had unexpectedly survived in acidic cider. The journal concluded that E. coli O157:H7 could survive at a pH below 4.0 at the temperature of refrigerated juice. The journal recommended strict procedures for sanitizing apples used to make fresh juice, all of which Odwalla already followed.

Although the FDA investigated both instances in New England, it did not issue any new regulations requiring pasteurization of fresh juice, nor did it issue any advisories to industry. At the time of the Odwalla outbreak, neither the FDA nor state regulators in California had rules requiring pasteurization of fresh apple juice.

Considering the Options

In the company's second-floor conference room, later in the day of October 30, Steltenpohl and Williamson gathered the company's senior executives to review the situation.

King County officials had identified about a dozen cases of E. coli infection associated with Odwalla apple juice products. But, as Steltenpohl later described the situation, "It was all based on interviews. They didn't yet have bacteriological proof." Washington

271

Post–Lawrence–Weber:
Business and Society,
Ninth Edition

Case Studies: Odwalla,
Inc., and the E. Coli
Breakout

© The McGraw-Hill
Companies, 1999

health officials had not yet made a public announcement, nor had they ordered or even recommended a product recall.

Conversations with federal disease control and food safety specialists throughout the day had turned up troubling information. From them, Odwalla executives had learned of the two earlier outbreaks of E. coli illness associated with unpasteurized cider in New England. And they had been told that 157 could cause illness in very minute amounts, below levels that would reliably show up in tests. The FDA had indicated that it planned to launch an investigation of the incident but did not suggest that Odwalla had broken any rules.

Management understood that they had no *legal* obligation to order an immediate recall, although this was clearly an option. Another possibility was a nonpublic recall. In this approach, the company would quietly pull the suspect product off the shelves and conduct its own investigation. If a problem were found, the company could then choose to go public with the information.

The company carried general liability insurance totaling $27 million. It had little debt and about $12 million in cash on hand. The cost of various options, however, was hard to pin down. No one could be sure precisely how much a full or partial product recall would cost, if they chose that option, or the extent of the company's liability exposure.

Ordering a Recall

At 3 P.M., Steltenpohl and Williamson, about four hours after they had received the first phone call, issued a public statement.

Odwalla, Inc., the California-based fresh beverage company, issued today a national product recall of fresh apple juice and all products containing fresh apple juice as an ingredient. . . . Our first concern is for the health and safety of those affected. We are working in full cooperation with the FDA and the Seattle/King County Department of Public Health.

The recall involved 13 products, all containing unpasteurized apple juice. At the time, these 13 products accounted for about 70 percent of Odwalla's sales. The company did not recall its citrus juices or geothermal spring water products.

"Stephen and I never batted an eyelash," Steltenpohl later remembered. "We both have kids. What if it had turned out that something was in the juice, and we left it on the shelf an extra two weeks, or week, or even two days, and some little kid gets sick? What are we doing? Why are we in business? We have a corporate culture based on values. Our mission is nourishment. We really never considered *not* recalling the product. Looking back, I suppose the recall was the biggest decision we made. At the time, it seemed the only possible choice."

Once the decision to recall the product had been made, the company mobilized all its resources. On Thursday morning, October 31, 200 empty Odwalla delivery trucks rolled out from distribution centers in seven states and British Columbia with a single mission: to get the possibly tainted product off the shelves as quickly as possible. Organizing the recall was simplified by the facts that Odwalla operated its own fleet of delivery vehicles and that, in most cases, the product was displayed in the company's own coolers. The delivery drivers simply went directly to their own accounts, and removed the recalled juices. In cases where the product was shelved with other products, Odwalla worked with retailers to find and remove it.

Post–Lawrence–Weber:
Business and Society,
Ninth Edition

Case Studies: Odwalla,
Inc., and the E. Coli
Breakout

© The McGraw–Hill
Companies, 1999

A group of employees in San Francisco, one of the company's major distribution centers, later recounted the first day of the recall:

> Every single person who is or was an RSP (route salesperson), express driver, or merchandiser, worked that first full day and the next.
> What was amazing was there were a lot of people who we didn't even have to call to come in. It might have been their day off, but they'd call to ask, "What can I do?"
> Right. They'd ask, "When should I come in? Where do you need me to be?" . . . It was an amazing effort. . . . We were able to make it to every single account on that first Thursday. That's a thousand accounts.

Within 48 hours, the recall was complete. Odwalla had removed the product from 4,600 retail establishments in seven states and British Columbia. "This is probably as speedy as a product recall gets," a stock analyst commented. "They probably accomplished it in world-record time."

On October 31, as it was launching its recall, the company also took several additional steps.

- The company announced that it would pay all medical expenses for E. coli victims, if it could be demonstrated that Odwalla products had caused their illness.
- The company offered to refund the purchase price of any of the company's products, even those that had not been recalled.
- The company established a crisis communications center at its headquarters and hired a PR firm, Edelman Public Relations Worldwide, to help it handle the crush of media attention. It also set up a Web site and an 800 hot line to keep the public and the media apprised of the most recent developments in the case. Twice-daily media updates were scheduled.
- The company decided to extend the recall to include three products made with carrot juice. Although these products did not contain apple juice, carrot juice was produced on the same line. Until the company had determined the cause of the outbreak it felt it could not guarantee the safety of the carrot juice products.

On October 31, as the company's route sales people were fanning out to retrieve the juice, Odwalla's stock price was plummeting. The company's stock lost 34 percent of its value in one day, falling from $18\frac{3}{8}$ to $12\frac{1}{8}$ on the NASDAQ exchange. Trading volume was 20 times normal, as 1.36 million shares changed hands.

Tracking the Outbreak

Over the next few days, the full extent of the outbreak became clearer. In addition to the cases in Washington, new clusters of E. coli poisoning were reported by health authorities in California and Colorado. As the company received reports about individual cases, Steltenpohl and Williamson attempted to telephone families personally to express their concern. They were able to reach many of them.

On November 8, a 16-month-old toddler from a town near Denver, Colorado, who had developed hemolytic uremic syndrome, died following multiple organ failure. Tests later showed antibodies to O157:H7 in the girl's blood. It was the first, and only, death associated with the E. coli outbreak. Steltenpohl immediately issued a statement that read:

273

Post–Lawrence–Weber:
Business and Society,
Ninth Edition

Case Studies: Odwalla,
Inc., and the E. Coli
Breakout

© The McGraw–Hill
Companies, 1999

On behalf of myself and the people at Odwalla, I want to say how deeply saddened and sorry we are to learn of the loss of this child. Our hearts go out to the family, and our primary concern at this moment is to see that we are doing everything we can to help them.

Steltenpohl, who had spoken with the girl's parents several times during her hospitalization, flew to Denver, with the family's permission, to attend the child's funeral. The girl's father later told the press, "We don't blame the Odwalla company at all. They had no bad intentions throughout all this, and they even offered to pay all of [our child's] hospital bills. I told them yesterday that we don't blame them, and we're not going to sue."

By the time the outbreak had run its course, 61 people, most of them children, had become ill in Colorado, California, Washington, and British Columbia. Except for the Colorado youngster, all those who had become ill, including several children who had been hospitalized in critical condition, eventually recovered.

Investigation of the Outbreak

As the outbreak itself was running its course, the investigation by both the company and federal and state health authorities proceeded. On November 4, the FDA reported that it had found E. coli O157:H7 in a bottle of unopened Odwalla apple juice taken from a distribution center in Washington State. As it turned out, this was the only positive identification of the pathogen in any Odwalla product. Eventually, 15 of the 61 reported cases (5 in Colorado and 10 in Washington) were linked by molecular fingerprinting to E. coli found in the Odwalla juice sample. The origin of contamination in the other 46 cases remained unknown.

Meanwhile, federal and state investigators converged on Odwalla's Dinuba manufacturing plant, inspecting it from top to bottom, in an attempt to find the source of the pathogen. On November 18, the FDA announced that it had completed its review of the Dinuba facility and had found no evidence of E. coli O157:H7 anywhere in the plant. The investigators then turned their attention to the growers and packers who supplied apples to the Dinuba plant, on the theory that the company might have processed a batch of juice containing some ground apples contaminated by cow or deer feces. In their interim report, the FDA noted that although no E. coli was found at Dinuba, "microbial monitoring of finished product and raw materials used in processing [was] inadequate." Odwalla sharply challenged this conclusion, noting that the FDA did not have any requirements for microbiological testing.

Searching for a Solution

The recall placed enormous financial pressure on the company, and challenged its executives to decide how and when to reintroduce its products to the market.

As a short-term measure, Odwalla announced on November 7 that it would immediately reintroduce three of its recalled products, all juice blends, that had been reformulated without apple juice. These products would continue to be produced at Dinuba, but not on the apple processing line. In announcing the reformulation, Steltenpohl told the press, "Until we are assured of a completely safe and reliable method of producing apple juice, we will not include it in our juices."

But the reformulation of a few blended juice smoothies was hardly a long-term solution, since apple juice was a core ingredient in many of the company's top-selling products. Odwalla urgently needed to find a way to get apple juice safely back on the market. How to do so, however, was not obvious.

Post–Lawrence–Weber:
Business and Society,
Ninth Edition

Case Studies: Odwalla,
Inc., and the E. Coli
Breakout

© The McGraw–Hill
Companies, 1999

To assist it in finding a solution to the problem, Odwalla assembled a panel of experts, dubbed the Odwalla Nourishment and Food Safety Advisory Council, to recommend ways to improve product safety. In late November, with the help of these experts, Odwalla executives conducted detailed scenario planning, in which they reviewed a series of possible options. Among those they considered were the following:

- **Discontinue all apple juice products.** In this scenario, the company would eliminate all apple juice and blended juice products until it could be fully assured of their safety.

- **Improve manufacturing processes.** In this scenario, the company would take a number of steps to improve hazard control at various points in the production process, for example, through modified product handling procedures, multiple antiseptic washes, routine sample testing, and stricter controls on suppliers.

- **Modify labeling.** Another option was to disclose risk to the consumer through product labeling. For example, an unpasteurized product could be sold with a disclaimer that it was not suitable for consumption by infants, the elderly, or those with compromised immune systems, because of the very rare but still possible chance of bacterial contamination.

- **Use standard pasteurization.** Standard pasteurization involved slowly heating the juice to a point just below boiling and holding it at that temperature for several minutes. The heat killed dangerous microorganisms and also had a side benefit of extending the shelf life of the product. Standard pasteurization, however, also destroyed many of the nutritional benefits of raw juice.

- **Use modified pasteurization.** Modified pasteurization, also known as flash pasteurization, involved quickly heating the juice to a somewhat lower temperature, 160 degrees F., and holding it very briefly at that temperature to kill any harmful bacteria. In tests of this procedure, Odwalla technicians found that it yielded an apple juice that had a "lighter" taste than unpasteurized juice, but with a more "natural" taste than standard pasteurized apple juice. The process destroyed some nutrients, but fewer than standard pasteurization. Flash pasteurization did not, however, extend the shelf life of the product.

- **Use alternative (non–heat-based) technologies for removing pathogens.** The company also examined a number of alternative methods of killing pathogens. These included a high-pressure process in which pressure was used to explode the cell walls of bacteria; a process in which light waves were directed at the juice to destroy pathogens; the use of electricity to disrupt bacteria; and the use of herbal antiseptic products.

A key factor in the decision, of course, was what customers wanted. The company commissioned some market research to gauge consumer sentiment; it also carefully monitored public opinion as revealed in calls and letters to the company and discussions on public electronic bulletin boards, such as America Online.

The company also had to consider its financial situation. Remarkably, despite the recall, sales for the quarter ending November 30, 1996, were actually 14 percent ahead of the same period for 1995 because of excellent sales prior to the outbreak. The E. coli

Post–Lawrence–Weber:
Business and Society,
Ninth Edition

Case Studies: Odwalla,
Inc., and the E. Coli
Breakout

© The McGraw–Hill
Companies, 1999

incident, however, had caused significant operating losses. By the end of November, the recall had cost the company about $5 million. Expenses had included the cost of retrieving and destroying product, legal and professional fees, and increased marketing costs. At the end of the fiscal quarter, Odwalla had a cash position of about $9 million, down from $12 million at the time of the outbreak.

On December 5, Odwalla announced that it had decided to flash pasteurize its apple juice. In a statement to the press, Williamson stated:

> Odwalla's first priority is safety. After much consideration and research, we chose the flash pasteurization process as a method to produce apple juice. It is safe, yet largely preserves the great taste and nutritional value allowing Odwalla to remain true to its vision of optimal nourishment. Importantly, we will continue to aggressively pursue the research and development of alternative methods to bring our customers safe, unpasteurized apple juice.

The following day, all apple juice and blended juice products were reintroduced to the market with flash pasteurized juice. The label had been redesigned to indicate that the product had been flash pasteurized, and Odwalla coolers prominently displayed signs so advising customers.

At the same time, the company moved forward with its expert panel to develop a comprehensive Hazard Analysis Critical Control Points (HACCP) (pronounced hassip) plan for fresh juice production. HACCP was not a single step, but a comprehensive safety plan that involved pathogen control at multiple points in the juice production process, including sanitation of the fruit, testing for bacteria, and quality audits at several points in the process. The company also continued to monitor new, alternative technologies for controlling bacterial contamination.

Regulating the Fresh Fruit Juice Industry

In the wake of the E. coli outbreak, public concern about food safety mounted, and federal and state regulators began considering stricter regulation of the fresh fruit juice industry. On December 16, the FDA sponsored a public advisory hearing in Washington, D.C., to review current science and to consider strategies for improving the safety of fresh juice. Debate at the two-day hearings was wide-ranging.

Steltenpohl and Williamson represented Odwalla at the hearing. In their testimony, the Odwalla executives reported that they had decided to adopt flash pasteurization, but argued *against* government rules requiring all juice to be heat-treated. "Mandatory pasteurization would be a premature and unnecessary step in light of the vast new technologies emerging," Steltenpohl told the hearing. He warned the panel that mandates could "lead to widespread public fears about fresh food and beverages."

Steltenpohl and Williamson called on the FDA to continue to explore different methods for producing fresh juice safely. In addition, they called for industry self-regulation aimed at adoption of voluntary standards for safe manufacturing practices and hazard control programs. The Odwalla executives reported that they viewed flash pasteurization as the last line of defense in a comprehensive program to eliminate pathogens.

Some other juice makers and scientists supported Odwalla's position. Several small growers vigorously opposed mandatory pasteurization, saying they could not afford the expensive equipment required. A representative of Orchid Island Juice Company of Florida asked, "What level of safety are you trying to achieve? We don't ban raw oysters and steak tartar, although the risks are much higher. Nor do we mandate that they be cooked, because it changes the flavor." A number of food safety experts testified about emerging technologies able to kill pathogens without heat treatment.

Some scientists and industry representatives, however, were on the other side. Two major firms, Cargill and Nestlé, both major producers of heat-treated juice products, argued vigorously for a government mandate, saying that "other technologies just won't do the job." Dr. Patricia Griffin of the Centers for Disease Control and Prevention noted that "current production practices do not guarantee the safety of apple cider, apple juice, and orange juice." She called for pasteurization of apple juice and cider, as well as product labels warning customers of potential risk. A representative of the Center for Science in the Public Interest called for a label warning the elderly, infants, and persons with suppressed immune systems to avoid fresh, unpasteurized juice.

Several days after the hearing, the advisory panel recommended against mandatory pasteurization, for the moment at least, calling instead for "good hazard control" at juice manufacturing plants and in the orchards that supplied them. However, an FDA spokesman added, "we can never say that forced pasteurization is completely off the boards." The agency indicated that it would continue to study a number of alternative approaches to improving juice safety, including mandatory pasteurization.

Looking to the Future   In May, 1997, Steltenpohl reflected on the challenges facing Odwalla:

> Our task now is to rebuild a brand and a name. How you rebuild . . . these are important decisions. You can make what might be good short-term business decisions, but they wouldn't be the right thing. The decisions we make now become building blocks for the [company's] culture. We have to look at what's right and wrong. We need a clear moral direction.

Discussion Questions

1. What factors contributed to the outbreak of E. coli poisoning described in this case? Do you believe that Odwalla was responsible, wholly or in part, for the outbreak? Why or why not?
2. What do you believe Odwalla should have done as of October 30, 1996? As of November 11, 1996? In each instance, please list at least three options and state the arguments for and against each.
3. What steps, if any, should Odwalla take as of the point the case ends?
4. Do you consider Odwalla's voluntary recall decision to be an act of corporate social responsibility? Why or why not?
5. What is the appropriate role for public policy in the area of food safety? Assess the role of government authorities in this case. In your view, did they act properly?

Post–Lawrence–Weber:
Business and Society,
Ninth Edition

Case Studies: Unum Corp.
and the Maine Coalition for
Excellence in Education

© The McGraw–Hill
Companies, 1999

Case Study:
Unum Corporation and the Maine Coalition for Excellence in Education

> There are things you can do as a group, things that you can do as a collaborative entity, that you could never do as a single company, no matter how powerful you are, no matter how small your state is, no matter how much money you spend.
>
> —Kevin Healey

Kevin Healey, director of public involvement initiatives for Unum Corporation, considered what steps the company should take next in its role as a central player in the Maine Coalition for Education. A comprehensive coalition of primary stakeholders promoting systemic change throughout Maine's kindergarten through twelfth grade (K-12) education system, the Maine Coalition for Excellence in Education (MCEE) had played a critical role in the passage of statewide education reform legislation. Now, in 1997 and seven years into the process, Healey wondered what the future of the Coalition should be. More important, he wondered how Unum could continue to participate in the Coalition in a way that fostered the company's core philosophy of finding a better way in all it did.

Note: This case was written by Michael Ames, MBA/MSW, Boston College (May 1998) and Sandra Waddock, Carroll School of Management, Boston College. ©1998 by the authors. Used by permission. All rights reserved.

Post–Lawrence–Weber:
Business and Society,
Ninth Edition

Case Studies: Unum Corp.
and the Maine Coalition for
Excellence in Education

© The McGraw–Hill
Companies, 1999

Unum Corporation

Unum Corporation was chartered in 1848 as Union Mutual, a small life insurance company. Originally headquartered in Boston, Massachusetts, the company moved to Portland, Maine, in 1881. Founder Elisha B. Pratt had been committed to the notion of finding "the better way," a philosophy that became deeply ingrained in Unum's culture. Over the years, the company had grown into one of the leaders in the insurance industry by focusing on disability insurance and special risks. In the mid-1980s, in order to continue to succeed in the intensely competitive insurance industry, Union Mutual reorganized as a publicly held corporation and renamed itself Unum (meaning "one" in Latin). The company concentrated its efforts in three areas: streamlining operations, diversifying in domestic markets, and expanding overseas. The shift from a mutual company into one that was publicly held required Unum's managers to focus on building long-term value for shareholders while still retaining the company's historical values with respect to customers, employees, and the community.

At the time the company went public, Unum created new mission and vision statements, as shown in Exhibit A. These emphasized the company's intention to act with integrity and high ethical standards, to treat employees "as we would like to be treated," and to build long-term relationships with customers.

EXHIBIT A Unum Corporation: Mission and Vision Statement

Mission

To relieve clients of insurable financial risk. We protect clients from financial hardships that result from retirement, death, sickness and from disability or other casualty events.

Vision

We will achieve leadership in our businesses. Leadership does not necessarily mean a dominant market share. Rather, we will achieve leadership in areas which are meaningful and important to our business and the market, e.g., profitability, quality, reputation.

We will focus our business on specialty, risk-relieving products for which we can establish and sustain profitable positions. Development of these products will be driven by the needs of customers, in both domestic and international markets.

We will be a products-offered company: Developing products which meet customer needs and leveraging our expertise and strengths. Our product development efforts will focus on providing the right solution. Seeking market segments which are appropriate for our products. Delivering our products in a high-quality and efficient manner utilizing existing and new channels. Our products will be perceived by customers as representing superior value in quality and price, and will consist of a total offering including risk, service, delivery and reliability.

We will be known for: Superior knowledge, expertise and risk management, quality service, being responsive to the needs of customers and intermediaries, being reliable, dependable and trustworthy providing the right solutions to current and emerging needs, implementing good ideas well.

We will be a well-managed company: Consistently-growing profits, an efficient cost structure, leadership returns and financially sound, anticipating, shaping and effectively responding to relevant external forces and events, making decisions in the best long-term interests of our stakeholders, planning well; making clear and sound business decisions.

Post–Lawrence–Weber:
Business and Society,
Ninth Edition

Case Studies: Unum Corp.
and the Maine Coalition for
Excellence in Education

© The McGraw–Hill
Companies, 1999

Values

We take pride in ourselves and the organization's leadership position:

Acting with integrity and high ethical standards.

Achieving leadership in performance, the community and the industry.

Setting and meeting individual goals consistent with business goals, and owning our individual performance.

Being motivated and excited about the organization.

Believing in what we are doing.

Emphasizing the positives, celebrating our successes and strengths, and constantly striving to improve our performance.

Delivering results.

We value and respect people:

Dealing with each other as individuals, and treating each other as we would like to be treated.

Developing people to their fullest potential.

Working together in a common endeavor: recognizing each other as important elements to the success of the whole.

Having a common understanding of each other's role and how we fit with the corporate objectives.

Collaborating with each other and having a sense of team.

Recognizing and accepting differences among people, but sharing the same values.

We value customers:

Building long-term relationships with our customers and intermediaries.

Maintaining a strong orientation to service and the customer.

Delivering what we promise.

We value communications:

Communicating clearly, consistently and openly with everyone we deal with.

Building an environment which encourages open communication, participation, honesty and candor.

Listening.

A Strategic Focus on Education

In the late 1980s, executives recognized that the changing insurance market would increasingly demand greater name recognition for Unum. Although the company had been in existence for almost 150 years, Unum was hardly a household name. In the past, Union Mutual had sold its insurance products mainly through insurance brokers, who in turn sold to end-users. Now, however, this traditional model was rapidly changing, and Unum intended to sell policies directly to the public. Unum executives knew they needed to increase their profile among potential customers.

Management felt that by addressing a public policy issue Unum could both make a difference within the community and raise the profile of the company and its CEO, James F. Orr. In 1990 Janice Hird, director of the Unum Foundation, began thinking about enhancing Unum's public involvement. Numerous public policy issues were in the spotlight. Orr and Hird quickly focused on public education. According to John Carroll of the Unum Foundation:

Post–Lawrence–Weber:
Business and Society,
Ninth Edition

Case Studies: Unum Corp.
and the Maine Coalition for
Excellence in Education

© The McGraw–Hill
Companies, 1999

[Unum] picked education purposefully for two reasons. One, because education is obviously critical to the nature of the business. Education's success and workforce quality is critical. [And two,] . . . to help raise the visibility of the CEO. At the time, when you looked around at the issues you might get involved with, and how to do that, there were environmental issues, crime, the economy, a whole host of issues. . . . Education was . . . central to the company's success, it has a lot of public interest and visibility, but it really did provide a good opportunity to influence and raise the profile of the CEO. . . . Education was an issue waiting to be addressed. There wasn't any clear logical [business] leadership that was already in place [in Maine].

At the time that Unum was considering a possible role in education reform, fully one in five students in Maine did not graduate from high school with their class. Fewer than half who went onto college completed their studies. Additionally, a survey of public and private employers conducted in 1992 reported that over 70 percent said that their young employees did not have the skills they expected of an educated worker. These problems had persisted despite significant raises in average teacher salaries in Maine during the 1980s, as well as nearly 50 percent (inflation adjusted) increases in total spending on education. Since spending alone seemed to be ineffective in achieving significant improvements in educational achievement, it was rapidly becoming clear that Maine needed a major shift in educational policy. Unum's Orr decided to take the lead.

Changing the Company First

Orr wisely understood that before a company like Unum would have credibility to ask the schools, the legislature, parents, or anyone else to change, the company needed to start by reforming its own policies. Unum focused initially on parental leave for school-related matters. Healey noted:

Recently, I was asked to suggest some easy steps other businesses might take to become better partners for education. . . . I came up with a surprising answer, "Let them begin where we did—with their human resources policies."

When we took our first steps for education reform, our Human Resources Department responded by introducing the School Release policy. The policy allows parents to attend parent/teacher conferences, classroom presentations, field trips, or just to join their child in the classroom for a day. We offer this as a paid benefit specifically because we think they have a special obligation to their children's education, and school activities almost always conflict with the workday.

Later, Orr announced that the company would begin asking for "proof of performance in high school" in its hiring process to reinforce the message that all students, not just the college-bound, need to work hard and get good grades in school.

In addition to looking within, Unum undertook a careful strategic planning process for its education reform efforts. According to Healey:

Too many companies jump right in and they say, "Well, we're business. We know how to get things done, lets just jump right in and fix it." Big mistake! You wouldn't do that if they were launching a product, or if you were thinking about a major change in your organization. What you would do is get smart and ask yourselves a lot of questions around customers, "What the customers expect? What's the market? What's the focus?" The same approach is true for the education initiative. We took a

Post–Lawrence–Weber:
Business and Society,
Ninth Edition

Case Studies: Unum Corp.
and the Maine Coalition for
Excellence in Education

© The McGraw–Hill
Companies, 1999

look at learning everything we could about education, about what attempts had been made, who are our partners, what had happened nationally, what does the department of education do [before acting].

Unum's analysis led it to conclude that systemic change in education was needed. Since the mid-1980s, hundreds of school-business partnerships had been established throughout the United States. Most of them, Unum's analysis concluded, could be characterized as "feel good" partnerships. That is, the companies gave money to always-needy school systems, felt good about it, washed their hands of involvement, and went on to other more pressing business matters. And nothing much changed within the schools, because new band uniforms or more funds for trips had no impact on curriculum, structure, or standards. Despite spending considerable amounts of money on partnerships with schools and a variety of reform efforts, many business leaders nationally had expressed frustration at the slowness of change.

In contrast, Unum management understood that real involvement meant change, both internal and external, if the educational system itself were to change. Schools needed to change, but so did standards, structure, and curriculum. So did the relationships among all stakeholders interested in better educational achievement. And, as the parental leave policy suggested, businesses themselves needed to change. For such change to be successful, Unum CEO Orr figured, it needed to be supported and implemented at three different levels: at the grassroots, involving parents and the rest of the community; within the educational system, involving teachers, administrators, and teachers' unions; and in the public policy arena at the state level. Healey later described these levels as being interconnected, building on top of one another as in the levels in a pyramid.

The bottom level, the grassroots, he noted, is comprised of the education system stakeholders. Initiatives directed at the grassroots, alone, do nothing to change the system but can provide the foundation on which change at other levels can be built. Grassroots initiatives range from changing corporate culture to enable parents to attend to their children's educational needs, to providing assistance to schools by volunteering or providing financial and in-kind donations to schools and PTAs.

The second level, the educational system, includes all aspects of the system, from the teachers and the ways they are trained, to the curriculum they teach, how schools and school days are structured, and standards. Initiatives at this level include working with schools and school administrators through the provision of grants and training resources to change the way they teach.

The third level, the public policy arena, includes the laws and regulations that drive and provide mandates for the educational system. This level, Unum felt, provided the greatest opportunity to impact the educational system. Unum realized, however, that without support and ownership of policy change from the grassroots and educational system levels, such change would be doomed, much as similar initiatives had been elsewhere in the country. Thus, Orr concluded that the only way to effectively work toward systemic change was for Unum to work at each level and to integrate initiatives across all three, in order to maximize support for systemic change.

The Maine Coalition for Excellence in Education (MCEE)

Realizing that there was a need for legislative change involving all stakeholders, not simply business, Unum took the lead in forming a coalition aimed at educational reform. With financial support from Unum, the Maine

Post–Lawrence–Weber:
Business and Society,
Ninth Edition

Case Studies: Unum Corp.
and the Maine Coalition for
Excellence in Education

© The McGraw–Hill
Companies, 1999

Development Foundation, a Maine-based foundation whose charge is to promote development in Maine, brought together a group that included business leaders, students, parents, educators, and government officials in what became the Maine Coalition for Excellence in Education. One of the coalition's first actions was to hold a symposium in 1990 called "Rethinking Education: Maine's Future in the Balance." At that symposium, James Orr spelled out his vision, derived from the strategic planning effort on education.

In all our talks and studies with these and other experts, we learned . . .

- Measurable improvements . . . demand fundamental changes in the attitudes and practices of educators and in society's attitudes toward and responsibilities to education.
- There are no quick fixes. Real change will not happen quickly. It must happen, ultimately, if our economy and society are to prosper and grow. So we're prepared to make support of education improvements a fundamental component of our corporate public policy. Not just for today, or this year, but for a minimum of five years, with the intention it will carry on much longer.
- Substantive, long-term solutions are going to take not only financial commitment but human and technical resources as well. We will not sit in criticism of you; rather we will work beside you. We will not give only our money, but share with you our many resources. And we will not judge the system, but will, with you, evaluate its results regularly.

After this symposium, Orr convened a meeting of MCEE, with participation by leading educators, businesspeople, citizens, and government officials. MCEE identified three primary means through which it could help restructure the Maine public education system: by developing a comprehensive *vision* for better education along with a plan for achieving that vision; by creating an independent, consistent *voice* for education reform to sustain this effort and by fostering a collaborative spirit and *understanding among stakeholders.*

The first goal of the Coalition was to develop a plan for Maine's educational system that could be used to drive legislative change. All stakeholders were included in the process of formulating this plan. According to Healey:

[We] made a conscious choice that [the plan] shouldn't be top down. . . . [Rather,] it *should* be driven by the stakeholders. . . . The Maine Coalition for Excellence in Education . . . included people from the legislature—state senators—members from the Department of Education, the state superintendent. We had business leaders from the banks, to Unum, to [L.L.] Bean. We had the president of the teachers union. We had a couple of students. We tried to get everyone we thought had a stake in this on that coalition.

The involvement of multiple stakeholders was important in two critical ways. First, having representatives of all of education's stakeholders meant that the plan received inputs from a range of sources with different perspectives. The result was a plan that represented all viewpoints. Second, representatives from each sector were able to take ownership of the plan and subsequently present it to other members of their particular group, creating support throughout every sector.

Learning to Work Together

Having so many stakeholders work together, however, was not always easy. Stereotypes existed on both sides. Educators were used to asking for a check from business and doing what they wanted with the money. Unum, however, wanted to engage in a real hands-on partnership in which it would have significant involvement over a long period of time. It was difficult for both sides to give up their unique positions of strength to engage in a more equal collaborative partnership.

One issue the Coalition faced early on was that of school choice. Business leaders tended to take a pro-choice position, which would allow parents and students to choose their schools, presumably permitting market forces to operate in what is traditionally a monopoly situation. Educators, on the other hand, tended to say, "School isn't just like business. This is not a business; we are talking about what is best for kids." Educators tended to take the position that all children need to be educated to succeed in the modern world, that choice will "cream off" the best students for the best schools leaving poorer students in weaker schools that are underfunded. Further, educators tended to believe that education is a public good that not only prepares students for work but also enhances citizenship. These positions created tension between two well-meaning groups.

Rather than allow this potentially divisive issue to split the Coalition, members were able to engage in a productive dialogue because of a culture of openness and trust. According to many observers, Unum CEO James Orr played an important role in creating such a culture. Commented school superintendent Robert Kautz, "Orr as an individual created the climate of openness. He personally facilitated the steps as chairman that created an open climate and trusting culture necessary for the coalition to work. His example also set the stage for others in the coalition to take an approach that all voices must be heard." According to Kautz, Orr demonstrated that an ability to listen to all viewpoints, disagree without personalizing the disagreement, and work through difficult issues in an open and trusting fashion.

Legislative Action

After two years of hard work, MCEE finally issued its own vision and reform plan. The plan, called *Success Begins with Education,* outlined 15 goals. Goals focused on four levels. First was creating successful students by developing a common core of learning and a certificate of initial mastery to be earned by all students effective 1998. Next was successful schools through enhanced accountability measures and an integrated school-assessment process based on specified performance standards. In addition, the goals set forth the resources needed to prepare schools for success, including shared vision, collaboration, leadership, and an emphasis on meeting high expectations for student learning, as well as meeting the expectations of the business community for workforce preparedness. Finally, the goals outlined the steps necessary to prepare communities for success, including providing resources to parents, training for collaboration, and support for parents, children, and schools by employers.

The presence of legislators in MCEE proved vital to successful legislative action. Within nine months of the release of *Success Begins with Education*, the Maine Legislature had approved *An Act to Enhance the Role of the State Board of Education*. But this was only a first step. Continued legislative work, with significant political pressures from the Coalition, resulted in 1994 in the passage of a reform package that mirrored MCEE's plan. Throughout 1994, the Legislature's Task Force on Learning Results worked on state standards. By 1996, Coalition members were able successfully to petition the state to ap-

Post–Lawrence–Weber:
Business and Society,
Ninth Edition

Case Studies: Unum Corp.
and the Maine Coalition for
Excellence in Education

© The McGraw-Hill
Companies, 1999

propriate public money for its continued work. Finally, in 1996, the 117th Maine Legislature adopted six guiding principles proposed by the Task Force to define a successfully educated Maine student. It asked the Task Force to return in 1997 with specific learning standards and performance indicators in eight subjects: career preparation, English and language arts, foreign languages, health and physical education, mathematics, science and technology, social studies, and visual and performing arts. These standards were submitted in February 1997 and passed later in the legislative session.

Other Unum Initiatives

Outside of MCEE, Unum developed initiatives to support change at all three levels. At the grassroots, Unum addressed its company culture and the way this affects and is affected by the education system, as illustrated by its policy to encourage employees to go to their children's school meetings. Further, Unum brought in speakers and trainers to speak to employees and their children about educational issues. And the company assigned an employee to coordinate schools' volunteer needs with volunteers from the company. As a result, parents employed at Unum were able to become more involved in their children's schools, employees were encouraged to volunteer in the schools, and employees had more opportunities to learn more about the public school system. Healey commented:

> We have tried very hard . . . to get the mind-set of our employees moved to not only how important education is, but that the company values education and supports the employees as they try to make a difference in their kids education and in the local school systems. . . . A few years ago the Portland school district bought a new centralized computer system and they wanted to input all of the student records onto the system so they could start tracking student performance better. They didn't have the labor to do that. We were able to go to employees and say Portland needs help. . . . Hundreds of people responded. . . . It didn't cost the school system a dime in labor.

Working within the second level, the education system, Unum supported change through the provision of grants to schools. For example, the Unum Foundation funded a project called the Extended Teacher Education Program (ETEP). ETEP changed the way teachers were trained at the University of Southern Maine, from a traditional four-year program to an innovative five-year program. This program was sponsored by Unum with the understanding that, if the program were successful, it would be institutionalized when the Unum Foundation grant expired. The company hoped that ETEP would create a model within the system of an innovative new way in which to train teachers.

Moving on to New Challenges

In 1997, the Coalition needed to redefine its mission. Initially, MCEE had successfully created a plan for change. It had then redirected itself to focus on lobbying for the passage into law of the plan's goals. Now, with these goals largely accomplished, the Coalition had to address important questions about its future direction. Healey commented:

> We are now working on what the new role [of the Coalition] should be. One of the things we think we need [to do is to play] . . . an oversight role that watches for opportunities and problems and then brings them to the public's mind. . . .

Post–Lawrence–Weber:
Business and Society,
Ninth Edition

Case Studies: Unum Corp.
and the Maine Coalition for
Excellence in Education

© The McGraw–Hill
Companies, 1999

Although MCEE's plan was far from complete, Unum believed that the Coalition was capable of sustaining the effort for as long as necessary. Because it was organized on an assumption of complementary strengths rather than one sole authority in a leadership position, MCEE represented a unique working relationship among many of the state's leading businesses, education organizations, state agencies, and public and private initiatives in higher education. Its members were able to work individually and in small collaborations on issues that matched their expertise and professional responsibilities. For example, coalition members from the state's schools of education could proceed with innovations in teacher education and professional development for educators. The state Department of Education had refined the education assessment system, while the Superintendent's Association had created seminars to enhance knowledge of standards-based learning. This cooperation allowed the group's work to proceed on many fronts with minimal burdens on individual organizations and relieved members of MCEE from the need to work on activities where they had little expertise, insight, or influence.

Plotting the Future

From the company's point of view, Unum's efforts appeared to have been successful on all counts. It had worked successfully within MCEE to improve the state's education system. In the process, Unum had raised the public profile of the company and of its chief executive. Many people believed that CEO James Orr's appointment as chairman of the National Alliance of Business had resulted in large part from the favorable attention he had received through his efforts to reform education. Having achieved its initial goals, it was time for Unum to reassess its role in the education reform movement in Maine. Healey noted:

> We have been spending close to $600,000 a year [on educational reform efforts]. As in any product cycle, there comes a time when you have to ask, are there any new products that we should be focusing on. . . .

What, Healey wondered, as 1998 began and the new century loomed, should be the company's position with respect to education reform and its involvement in the MCEE?

Discussion Questions

1. What were Unum's goals in helping establish the Maine Coalition for Excellence in Education? How well did the company achieve these goals?
2. What were the most important stakeholders in this coalition? What were their underlying interests?
3. What made this coalition work? Can you make any generalizations, based on this case, about the conditions under which collaborative partnerships are likely to succeed?
4. From the perspective of Unum and the other stakeholders in this collaboration, what do you think the next steps should be, and why?

Post–Lawrence–Weber:
Business and Society,
Ninth Edition

Case Study: Personal
Ethics Dilemmas

© The McGraw–Hill
Companies, 1999

Case Study:
Personal Ethics Dilemmas

Pat Jones

Pat Jones was an engineer at the Hamilton Company, a manufacturer of power transmission products. Hamilton was a highly respected company, offering a quality product with a reputation for ethical business practices. The company had developed and widely distributed a formal code of ethics and regularly provided ethics training for its employees.

Hamilton's management recently introduced a policy of participative management. Management believed that decision-making responsibility should rest with those closest to the decision. Participative management was intended to allow the company to respond quickly to changing market conditions. It was a deliberate move toward a decentralized organizational structure.

Hamilton's sales were running 20 percent below last year's level and were expected to continue to decline. Management attributed the slump to poor economic conditions. Hamilton's president had recently sent a memo to the sales and engineering personnel. The memo expressed concern regarding incoming orders, recommending cost-cutting measures and alluding to possible layoffs. The president also pointed out market niches that Hamilton managers should pursue more aggressively and indicated that all orders should be reviewed for potential sales of additional accessory products. Most of the accessories offered attractive profit margins.

While working on a recent order, Pat Jones noticed that the order included three oil pumps. Oil pumps were not necessary for the intended application for this order. Oil pumps were normally used on variable speed or inclined drives where the standard splash lubrication system was not adequate. For this application the oil pumps offered no advantage to the customer. The oil pump accessories were sold for $5,000 each and were to be provided on each of three gearboxes.

Note: The organizations and individuals portrayed here are fictional. They are based on the author's discussions of common ethical dilemmas with corporate managers.

Post–Lawrence–Weber:
Business and Society,
Ninth Edition

Case Study: Personal
Ethics Dilemmas

© The McGraw–Hill
Companies, 1999

Pat contacted Kelly Long, the sales agent for the order. Kelly indicated that the oil pumps were included in the order because they were often needed and the customer had insisted on a quick quote. Sales agents typically did not have sufficient information to determine when oil pumps would be required.

Kelly was reluctant to approach the customer to discuss removing the oil pumps from the order. Kelly said, "Look Pat, this customer is very difficult to work with. The purchase order specified oil pumps. Unless it has a detrimental effect on the gearbox, let's give the customer what was ordered. Besides, I'd rather put my efforts toward increasing sales than reducing sales." It was Hamilton's policy to have the sales agent handle all communications with the customer.

Pat discussed the matter with two colleagues at Hamilton. One coworker indicated that the oil pumps should be provided as ordered. The other coworker suggested that oil filters should be included with the oil pumps in the order. The oil filters would provide additional value-added to the customer by providing an oil filtration system ordinarily not furnished, although it was not clear that this additional system was essential for the customer's needs.

Discussion Questions

1. Since the Hamilton Company has introduced a participative style of management, decision-making responsibility rests with Pat Jones. In light of the firm's economic troubles, should Pat approve the order for the oil pumps? What is Pat's responsibility to Hamilton? To the customer? To the sales agent?

2. Is Hamilton's reputation as an ethical business compromised by the sales agent including oil pumps in the order, or by Pat approving the order? What ethical safeguards at Hamilton are being challenged in the case or should be developed by Hamilton to ensure ethical behavior by its employees?

3. The oil pumps provide an additional, although unnecessary, function for the customer. Is it wrong to provide this benefit to the customer? One of Pat's coworkers suggested an additional accessory: oil filters. Should they be added to the order as well?

4. Using the ethical decision-making framework presented in "Ethical Dilemmas in Business," what is the proper ethical response to the question confronting Pat? Which is a better guide for ethical conduct in this situation: utilitarianism, rights, or justice?

Chris Brown

Lee Samson and Chris Brown had worked for 15 years as entry-level system programmers for Runner Manufacturing, a leading manufacturer of automotive ride control products. Runner was a large, centralized firm with a traditional, formal hierarchy marked by multiple levels of supervision. Typically, important decisions were made by top management. Respect for authority and being a team player were highly valued by the organization's senior management team.

While working at Runner's corporate headquarters, Lee and Chris slowly worked up through the ranks of the large systems department. In the process, they developed a close friendship. As system analysts, Lee and Chris designed, tested, and brought to operational status software that automated payroll, inventory, finance, and operations management.

Eight months earlier, both had been promoted to a supervisory level upon the retirement of their predecessors. Lee became supervisor of the systems group responsible for operations (inventory controls and product plans), while Chris became supervisor of the functional systems group responsible for program maintenance and development for administration and finance areas. Although both were pleased with their promotions, they

Post–Lawrence–Weber:
Business and Society,
Ninth Edition

Case Study: Personal
Ethics Dilemmas

© The McGraw–Hill
Companies, 1999

both felt uneasy at giving up hands-on work with software. They also believed that they had reached the upper limit of career growth given the rigid cultural climate at Runner.

It was Lee Samson who broached the topic of going off on their own. At first, it was simply a little off-duty talk. Eventually, both Lee and Chris recognized they had skills in software programming that could have a real outside demand. The idea took shape of starting an information systems storage and consulting service for small and medium-sized firms. They decided to take the plunge and resign from the firm as soon as they had acquired the necessary hardware.

The new venture required Lee and Chris to convert space in Lee's home into an office for their computer. While recently inspecting new file servers (data storage equipment), Chris was surprised to find sophisticated software already loaded onto their personal systems at the new office. Closer scrutiny proved the software was similar to the operations, payroll, and accounting systems currently in use at Runner's corporate headquarters. When questioned, Lee at first tried to hedge but finally admitted to systematically copying Runner's system programs and routines that would be useful in their new business. Copying was a simple matter since the office in Lee's home was connected by a modem to the company's mainframe computer. Lee assured Chris that great care had been taken to avoid copying any actual data, as this would have been theft of company proprietary information and a violation of Runner's code of ethics. Seeing Chris's dismayed look, Lee said, "Look Chris, we've worked our tails off for 15 years installing, testing and making every one of these systems run. If anyone 'owns' these systems and the right to their use, it's you and me. Runner loses nothing in this, no product or customer data, absolutely nothing."

Discussion Questions

1. From an ethical perspective, who owns the computer software—the developers of the software (Lee and Chris), or the firm that hired the developers (Runner Manufacturing)? What ethical principles support your position?
2. Using Figure 1, why did this ethical problem occur for Chris?
3. What action alternatives are available to Chris in this case? Using each of the six stages of moral development and ethical reasoning discussed in "Ethical Dilemmas in Business," what action do you think Chris will select? What is the best action for Chris?

Figure 1

Why ethical problems occur in business.

Reason	Nature of Ethical Problem	Typical Approach	Attitude
Personal gain and selfish interest	Selfish interest vs. others' interests	Egoistical mentality	"I want it!"
Competitive Pressures on Profits	Firm's interest vs. others' interests	Bottom–line mentality	"We have to beat the others at all costs!"
Business Goals vs. Personal Values	Boss's interests vs. subordinates' values	Authoritarian mentality	"Do as I say, or else!"
Cross-Cultural Contradictions	Company's interests vs. diverse cultural traditions and values	Ethnocentric mentality	"Foreigners have a funny notion of what's right and wrong"

Post–Lawrence–Weber:
Business and Society,
Ninth Edition

Case Study: Personal
Ethics Dilemmas

© The McGraw–Hill
Companies, 1999

Jesse Green

Jesse Green worked in the accounting department for Premier Jewelry, Incorporated. Premier Jewelry had been in existence for over 100 years. The company had a written mission statement that emphasized the value of respecting its employees. The company was highly regarded throughout the industry, operating stores in 17 states.

Jesse Green had worked with the company for five years and had been quite successful. The company was going through a time of change in the past three years with many departments downsizing and restructuring to cut costs. It was increasingly important for Premier Jewelry to manage expenses so that profit margins were equivalent or better than other similar companies in the jewelry industry. The accounting function for the company recently had been decentralized and Jesse was in charge of the accounting area for a business unit of Premier Jewelry.

Jesse was given a specific personnel target size during an interim reorganization period. Several permanent positions were decided, but it was determined that several positions should be filled with temporary employees until the organization would know definitely its long-term needs for permanent staffing.

Premier Jewelry had stated in its policy manual that it would hire people permanently or let them go after one year. This policy had generally not been in conflict with everyday business practices in the past, as temporary employees were usually able to complete their work in less than a year. Temporary employees were not typically told that they had no chance of permanent employment with the company.

Jesse's department had two temporary employees. Alex, a secretary, had been an employee for just over one year. Leslie, an accounting clerk, had been employed for just under a year. Both contracts had been extended for an additional six months by the controller for Jesse's business and the director of finance for Jesse's division. The controller told Jesse that making a personnel hiring decision was a million dollar decision for every employee. The controller and director were in favor of limiting the number of permanent employees for cost reasons. Jesse was told that managing division expenses was something considered in the annual employee performance review.

Jesse felt that the current situation was in violation of the company's stated policy not to hire temporary employees for extended periods of time. Additionally, Jesse felt the company was being unfair and deceptive to the individuals involved, as they had not been told they had no opportunity for long-term employment.

Jesse worked with two other managers in the financial accounting area. Both had been in similar situations and suggested that if Jesse wanted to continue on a successful career path that the two temporary employees should be hired for an additional six months and Jesse should not worry about it. "Besides," they said, "everybody is doing it."

Discussion Questions

1. Assess the ethical basis for Premier Jewelry's policy regarding the hiring of temporary employees. Is the policy fair? Does it respect the employees' rights? Does it achieve the greatest good for the greatest number affected?
2. Which of the nine ethical climates, discussed in "Ethical Dilemmas in Business," reflects Premier Jewelry's ethical climate? Is this climate ethically acceptable? If not, how could it be improved?
3. Assume that Jesse finds it ethically objectionable to extend Alex and Leslie's contracts for an additional six months. What company ethical safeguards could Jesse use or create to avoid taking this action?

Post–Lawrence–Weber:
Business and Society,
Ninth Edition

Case Study: Shell Oil in
Nigeria

© The McGraw–Hill
Companies, 1999

Case Study:
Shell Oil in Nigeria

On November 10, 1995, world-renowned Nigerian novelist and environmental activist Ken Saro-Wiwa was executed by hanging in a prison courtyard. Just eight days earlier, he had been convicted by a military tribunal on charges that he had ordered the murder of political opponents. Throughout his trial, Saro-Wiwa had vigorously maintained his innocence. Despite protests by many world leaders and human rights organizations, the Nigerian military regime had quickly carried out the death sentence.

Saro-Wiwa's execution provoked a profound crisis for the Royal Dutch/Shell Group of Companies. In its wake, some environmentalists and political leaders called for an international boycott of Shell's gasoline and other products. The World Bank announced it would not provide funding for Shell's liquefied natural gas project in Nigeria. Several groups, including the London Royal Geographic Society, voted to reject the company's charitable contributions. In Canada, the Toronto provincial government refused a major gasoline contract to Shell Canada, despite its low bid. Some even called for the oil company to pull out of Nigeria altogether.

Note: This is an abridged version of a longer case: Anne T. Lawrence, "Shell Oil in Nigeria," *Case Research Journal* 17, no. 4 (Fall/Winter 1997). Abridged by the author by permission of the *Case Research Journal.* Sources include articles appearing in *The Wall Street Journal, New York Times, Economist, Fortune, Guardian* (London), *Independent,* and *Village Voice;* U.S. congressional hearings, reports by Amnesty International, Greenpeace, and the World Bank; and material posted by Shell Nigeria on its Web site at http://www.shellnigeria.com. The history of Royal Dutch/Shell is based on Adele Hast, ed., *International Directory of Company Histories* (Detroit, MI: St. James Press, 1991); and *World Class Business: A Guide to the 100 Most Powerful Global Corporations* (New York, NY: Henry Holt, 1992). Ken Saro-Wiwa's story is drawn primarily from his memoir, *A Month and a Day: A Prison Diary* (New York: Penguin Books, 1995), and other writings. A full set of footnotes is available in the *Case Research Journal* version. Copyright © 1997 by the *Case Research Journal* and Anne T. Lawrence. All rights reserved.

Post–Lawrence–Weber:
Business and Society,
Ninth Edition

Case Study: Shell Oil in
Nigeria

© The McGraw–Hill
Companies, 1999

Alan Detheridge, Shell's coordinator for West Africa, told a reporter in February 1996, "Saro-Wiwa's execution was a disaster for us."

Just what was the connection between Saro-Wiwa's execution and Shell Oil? Why did the company find itself suddenly, in the words of the *New York Times,* "on trial in the court of public opinion?" Had the company done anything wrong? And what, if anything, could or should it do in the face of an escalating chorus of international criticism?

The Group

The Royal Dutch/Shell Group was the world's largest fully integrated petroleum company. Upstream, the conglomerate controlled oil and gas exploration and production; midstream, the pipelines and tankers that carried oil and gas; and downstream, the refining, marketing, and distribution of the final product. The company also had interests in coal mining, metal mining, forestry, solar energy, and biotechnology. In all, the Anglo-Dutch conglomerate comprised over 2,000 separate entities, with exploration and production operations, refineries, and marketing in scores of countries. Royal Dutch/Shell was, in both its ownership and scope, perhaps the world's most truly transnational corporation.

In 1994, Royal Dutch/Shell made more money than any other company in the world, reporting astonishing annual profits of $6.2 billion. The same year, the company reported revenues of $94.9 billion, placing it tenth on *Fortune*'s Global 500 list. Assets were reported at $108.3 billion, and stockholders' equity at $56.4 billion. With 106,000 employees worldwide, it had the largest workforce of any oil company in the world.

This highly successful global corporation traced its history back over more than a century and a half. In the 1830s, British entrepreneur Marcus Samuel founded a trading company to export manufactured goods from England and to import products, including polished sea shells (hence, the name "Shell"), from the Orient. In the early 1890s, Samuel's sons steered the company into the kerosene business, assembling a fleet of tankers to ply the fuel through the Suez Canal to Far Eastern ports. At about the same time, a group of Dutch businessmen launched the Royal Dutch Company to drill for oil in the Dutch East Indies. In 1907, Royal Dutch and Shell merged, with Royal Dutch retaining a 60 percent interest and Shell, 40 percent. The resulting organization came to be known as the Royal Dutch/Shell Group of Companies, or simply the Group.

Over the years, Royal Dutch/Shell had developed a highly decentralized management style, with its far-flung subsidiaries exercising considerable autonomy. The company believed that vesting authority in nationally based, integrated operating companies—each with its own distinctive identity—gave it the strategic flexibility to respond swiftly to local opportunities and conditions. The corporation was governed by a six-person board of directors. Reflecting its dual parentage, the Group maintained headquarters in both London and The Hague. The chairmanship rotated periodically between the president of Shell and the president of Royal Dutch. Decision making was by consensus, with no dominant personality.

Shell Nigeria

The Shell Petroleum and Development Company of Nigeria—usually called Shell Nigeria—stated its corporate objective simply. It was "to find, produce, and deliver hydrocarbons safely, responsibly, and economically for the benefit of our stakeholders."

The Royal Dutch/Shell Group had begun exploring for oil in West Africa in the 1930s, but it was not until 1956 that oil was discovered in the Niger River delta in southeastern Nigeria. In 1958, two years before Nigeria's independence from Britain, Shell was the first major oil company to commence operations there. Nigerian oil was of very high quality by world standards; in the industry, it was referred to as "sweet crude," meaning that only minimal refining was required to turn it into gasoline and other products.

Post–Lawrence–Weber:
Business and Society,
Ninth Edition

Case Study: Shell Oil in
Nigeria

© The McGraw–Hill
Companies, 1999

In 1995, Shell Nigeria was the largest oil company in the country. The company itself was actually a joint venture with the Nigerian federal government, which owned a 55 percent stake. Royal Dutch/Shell owned a 30 percent stake in the joint venture; the remaining 15 percent was owned by two European oil companies strategically aligned with Shell. Although the Nigerian government was the majority owner in the joint venture, its role was confined mainly to providing mineral rights; Shell built and managed the lion's share of the oil operations on the ground. Other players in the Nigerian oil industry, including Mobil and Chevron, mainly operated offshore. Of all the multinational oil companies in Nigeria, Shell had by far the most visibility.

Shell Nigeria's operations were huge, not only by Nigerian standards, but even by those of its parent firm. In 1995, Shell Nigeria produced an average of almost one million barrels of crude oil a day—about half of Nigeria's total output—in 94 separate fields spread over 31,000 square kilometers. It owned 6200 kilometers of pipelines and flow lines, much of it running through swamps and flood zones in the Niger delta. In addition, the company operated two coastal export terminals. The Nigerian operation provided about 14 percent of Royal Dutch/Shell's total world oil production—and probably a larger share of its profits, although financial data for Shell's subsidiaries were not separately reported.

Shell Nigeria employed about 2,000 people. Ninety-four percent of all employees, and about half of senior managers, were Nigerian. Few employees, however, were drawn from the impoverished delta communities where most oil facilities were located. For example, by one estimate, less than 2 percent of Shell Nigeria's employees were Ogoni, the delta ethnic group of which Saro-Wiwa was a member. The percentage of local people was higher—20 to 50 percent—on Shell's seismic crews, which did the dirty and dangerous work of drilling and blasting during oil exploration.

The company's financial arrangements with its host country were highly beneficial to the Nigerian government. For every barrel of oil sold by Shell Nigeria, 90 percent of net revenues (after expenses) went to the federal government, in the form of taxes and royalties. Shell and its aligned companies split the remaining 10 percent. Although Shell and the Nigerian government worked hand in glove in the oil industry, relations between the two were often strained. Although usually unwilling to comment publicly, Shell seemed to resent the Nigerian government's large take and was frustrated by its frequent failure to pay revenues due its corporate partners.

The Giant of West Africa

Nigeria, the Group's sometimes troublesome partner, has been called the "giant of West Africa." Located on the North Atlantic coast between Benin and Cameroon, Nigeria was slightly more than twice the size of California, and—with 98 million people—the most populous country on the continent. Nigeria's gross domestic product of $95 billion placed its economy second, smaller only than South Africa's. The economy was heavily dependent on petroleum; oil and natural gas sales produced 80 percent of the federal government's revenue, and over 90 percent of the country's foreign exchange. Thirty-seven percent of all exports—and 50 percent of oil exports—went to the United States, more than to any other single country.

Nigeria was a land of stark socioeconomic contrasts. The nation's military and business elites had grown wealthy from oil revenues. Yet, most Nigerians lived in poverty. The annual per capita income was $250, less than that of Haiti or China, and in the mid-1990s, economic distress in many parts of Nigeria was deepening.

Post–Lawrence–Weber:
Business and Society,
Ninth Edition

Case Study: Shell Oil in
Nigeria

© The McGraw–Hill
Companies, 1999

A legacy of colonialism, in Nigeria as elsewhere in Africa, was the formation of states that had little historical basis other than common colonial governance. In the Nigerian case, the modern nation was formed from what had been no less than 250 disparate ethnic groups, many with few cultural or linguistic ties. The nation was comprised of three main ethnic groups: the Hausa-Fulani, the Yoruba, and the Ibo. Together, these three groups made up 65 percent of the population; the remaining 35 percent was made up of scores of smaller ethnic groups, including the Ogoni.

Since its independence from Britain in 1960, Nigeria had been ruled by military governments for all but nine years. Several efforts—all eventually unsuccessful—had been made to effect a transition to permanent civilian rule. In June 1993, military dictator Ibrahim Babangida annulled the presidential election, suspended the newly created national assembly, and outlawed two fledgling political parties. Just five months later, yet another military man, General Sani Abacha, took power in a coup. The Abacha regime quickly developed a reputation as "indisputably the cruelest and most corrupt" government in Nigeria since independence. A specialist in African politics summarized the situation in Nigeria before the Senate Foreign Relations Committee in 1995:

> [The] current government appears indifferent to international standards of conduct, while dragging the country into a downward spiral of disarray, economic stagnation, and ethnic animosity. . . . [It] has curtailed political and civil rights to an unprecedented degree in Nigerian history, magnified corruption and malfeasance in an endemically corrupt system, and substantially abandoned responsible economic management.

In 1993, inflation was running close to 60 percent annually, foreign debt was growing, and the country's balance of payments was worsening. Corruption was so rampant in Nigeria, the *Economist* concluded in an editorial, that "the parasite . . . has almost eaten the host."

The Ogoni People

The Ogoni people, Saro-Wiwa's ethnic group, lived in the heart of the Nigerian oil fields. Numbering about half a million in the mid-1990s, the Ogoni spoke four related languages and shared a common animistic religion. Prior to the arrival of the British in 1901, a stable Ogoni society based on fishing and farming had existed for centuries in a small area (a mere 12 by 32 miles) in the delta region near the mouth of the Niger River. It was here that Shell had discovered oil.

Although Ogoniland was the site of tremendous mineral wealth, the Ogoni people had received virtually no revenue from its development. Somewhere on the order of $30 billion worth of oil was extracted from Ogoniland's five major oil fields between 1958 and 1994. Yet, under revenue sharing arrangements between the Nigerian federal government and the states, only 1.5 percent of oil taxes and royalties was returned to the delta communities for economic development, and most of this went to line the pockets of local officials.

The Rivers State, that included Ogoniland, was among the poorest in Nigeria. No modern sanitation systems were in place, even in the provincial capital. Raw sewage was 'simply buried or discharged into rivers or lakes. Drinking water was often contaminated, and water-related diseases such as cholera, malaria, and gastroenteritis were common. Ogoniland's population density was among the highest of any rural area in the world. Housing was typically constructed with corrugated tin roofs and cement or, more com-

Post–Lawrence–Weber:
Business and Society,
Ninth Edition

Case Study: Shell Oil in
Nigeria

© The McGraw–Hill
Companies, 1999

monly, dirt floors. Approximately 30–40 percent of delta children attended primary school, compared with about three-quarters in Nigeria as a whole; three-quarters of adults were illiterate. Unemployment was estimated at 30 percent. A British engineer who later returned to the delta village where oil was first discovered commented, "I have explored for oil in Venezuela, I have explored for oil in Kuwait, [but] I have never seen an oil-rich town as completely impoverished as Olobiri."

In 1992, in response to pressure from the Ogoni and other delta peoples, the Nigerian government established a commission, funded with 3 percent of oil revenues, to promote infrastructure development in the oil-producing regions. In 1993, the group spent $94 million, with about 40 percent going to the Rivers State. Shell Nigeria also gave some direct assistance to the oil-producing regions. In 1995, for example, the company's community development program in Nigeria spent about $20 million. Projects included building classrooms and community hospitals, paying teacher salaries, funding scholarships for Nigerian youth, and operating an agricultural station. According to one study, however, almost two-thirds of Shell's community development budget was allocated to building and maintaining roads to and from oil installations. Although open to the public, these roads were of little use to most delta residents, who did not own cars. Moreover, Shell made little effort to involve local residents in determining how its community development funds would be spent.

Ken Saro-Wiwa: Writer and Activist

Ken Saro-Wiwa, who became a leader of the Ogoni insurgency, was in many respects an unlikely activist. A businessman who later became a highly successful writer and television producer, he had a taste for gourmet food, sophisticated humor, and international travel. Yet, in the final years of his life he emerged as a world famous advocate for sustainable development and for the rights of indigenous peoples who was honored by a Nobel peace prize nomination and the Goldman Environmental Prize.

Saro-Wiwa was born in 1941 in an Ogoni village. A brilliant student, he was educated first at missionary-run schools and later, with the aid of a scholarship, at the University of Ibadan, where he studied literature. After a brief stint as a government administrator, Saro-Wiwa left public service to launch his own business. After four years as a successful grocer and trader, he took the proceeds and began investing in real estate, buying office buildings, shops, and homes. In 1983, with sufficient property to live comfortably, Saro-Wiwa turned to what he called his first love, writing and publishing. He proved to be a gifted and prolific writer, producing in short order a critically acclaimed novel, a volume of poetry, and a collection of short stories.

In 1985, Saro-Wiwa was approached by a university friend who had become program director for the state-run Nigerian television authority. The friend asked him to develop a comedy series. The result, "Basi & Co.," ran for five years and became the most widely watched television show in Africa. Reflecting Saro-Wiwa's political views, the program satirized Nigerians' desire to get rich with little effort. The show's comic protagonist was Basi, "a witty rogue [who] hustled on the streets of Lagos and was willing to do anything to make money, short of working for it."

By the late 1980s, Saro-Wiwa had become a wealthy and internationally known novelist and television scriptwriter. His wife and four children moved to London, where his children enrolled in British private schools. Saro-Wiwa joined his family often, making many friends in the London literary community who would later work doggedly, although unsuccessfully, for his release.

297

Post–Lawrence–Weber:
Business and Society,
Ninth Edition

Case Study: Shell Oil in
Nigeria

© The McGraw–Hill
Companies, 1999

In 1988, Saro-Wiwa undertook a nonfiction study of Nigerian history, later published under the title, *On a Darkling Plain.* This work reawakened his interest in politics and in the plight of his own Ogoni people. In a speech in March 1990, marking the study's publication, Saro-Wiwa laid out a theme from the book that was to become central to the rest of his life's work:

> The notion that the oil-bearing areas can provide the revenue of the country and yet be denied a proper share of that revenue because it is perceived that the inhabitants of the area are few in number is unjust, immoral, unnatural and ungodly.

On a Darkling Plain, not surprisingly, ignited a storm of controversy in Nigeria, and "Basi & Co." was canceled shortly after its publication, as was a column Saro-Wiwa had been writing for the government-owned weekly *Sunday Times.*

Movement for the Survival of the Ogoni People

The cancellation of his TV series and newspaper column seemed to propel Saro-Wiwa further into political activism. In August 1990, he met with a group of Ogoni tribal chiefs and intellectuals to draft an Ogoni Bill of Rights. This document called for political autonomy; cultural, religious, and linguistic freedom; the right to control a "fair proportion" of the region's economic resources; and higher standards of environmental protection for the Ogoni people.

Shortly thereafter, drafters of the bill of rights met to form an organization to press their demands. The group chose the name Movement for the Survival of the Ogoni People (MOSOP). From its inception, MOSOP adopted a philosophy of nonviolent mass mobilization. The group's earliest organizational efforts focused on educational work and appeals to the military government and the oil companies. The organization published the Ogoni Bill of Rights and organized a speaking tour of the region to present it to the Ogoni. Saro-Wiwa traveled abroad—to the United States, Switzerland, England, the Netherlands, and Russia—where he met with human rights and environmentalist groups and government officials to build support for the Ogoni cause. MOSOP also issued a propagandistic "demand notice" calling on Shell and its Nigerian partners to pay damages of $4 billion for "destroying the environment" and $6 billion in "unpaid rents and royalties" to the Ogoni people.

Environmental Issues

A central plank in the MOSOP platform was that the oil companies, particularly Shell, were responsible for serious environmental degradation. In a speech given in 1992 to the Unrepresented Nations and Peoples Organization (UNPO), Saro-Wiwa stated MOSOP's case:

> Oil exploration has turned Ogoni into a wasteland: lands, streams, and creeks are totally and continually polluted; the atmosphere has been poisoned, charged as it is with hydrocarbon vapors, methane, carbon monoxide, carbon dioxide, and soot. . . . Acid rain, oil spillages and oil blowouts have devastated Ogoni territory. High-pressure oil pipelines crisscross the surface of Ogoni farmlands and villages dangerously. The results of such unchecked environmental pollution and degradation include the complete destruction of the ecosystem.

Shell disputed these charges, saying that they had been "dramatized out of all proportion." Shell argued that the land it had acquired for operations comprised only 0.3 percent of

Post–Lawrence–Weber:
Business and Society,
Ninth Edition

Case Study: Shell Oil in
Nigeria

© The McGraw–Hill
Companies, 1999

the Niger delta. Moreover, Shell charged, many of the oil spills in the area had been caused by sabotage, for which they could not be held responsible.

The Niger delta was one of the world's largest wetlands, a vast floodplain built up by sedimentary deposits at the mouths of the Niger and Benue Rivers. In a comprehensive study of environmental conditions in the Niger delta completed in 1995, the World Bank found evidence of significant environmental problems, including land degradation, overfishing, deforestation, loss of biodiversity, and water contamination. The study did find evidence of air pollution from refineries and petrochemical facilities and of oil spills and poor waste management practices at and around pipelines, terminals, and offshore platforms. Most of the delta's environmental problems, however, the World Bank concluded, were the result not of oil pollution but rather of overpopulation coupled with poverty and weak environmental regulation.

Of the environmental problems associated with the oil industry, the World Bank reported, the worst was gas flaring. Natural gas is often produced as a by-product of oil drilling. In most oil-producing regions of the world, this ancillary gas is captured and sold. In Nigeria, however, gas was routinely simply burned off, or flared, in the production fields. In 1991, over three-quarters of natural gas production in Nigeria was flared—compared with, say, less than 1 percent in the United States or a world average of less than 5 percent. In 1993, Nigeria flared more natural gas than any nation on earth.

Gas flaring had several adverse environmental consequences. The flares produced large amounts of carbon dioxide and methane, both greenhouse gases and contributors to global warming. Residents in the immediate vicinity of the flares experienced constant noise, heat, and soot contamination. The flares, which burned continuously, lit up the night sky in much of the delta with an eerie orange glow. One British environmentalist commented poignantly after a fact-finding visit to the delta that "some children have never known a dark night, even though they have no electricity."

During the early 1990s, Shell Nigeria was involved in a joint venture known as the Nigeria Liquefied Natural Gas project. The aim of this scheme, in which Shell was a 24 percent shareholder, was to pipe natural gas to ocean terminals, liquefy it, and ship it abroad in special ships at supercooled temperatures. In late 1995, the fate of this venture was still unclear.

Contrary to charges made by some of Shell's critics, Nigeria did have some environmental regulations in place, dating from the late 1980s. These laws, which were enforced by the federal Department of Petroleum Resources, required industry to install pollution abatement devices, restricted toxic discharges, required permits for handling toxic wastes, and mandated environmental impact studies for major industrial developments.

Civil Disturbances in Ogoniland

During the early 1990s, civil disturbances in Ogoniland and nearby delta communities, many directed at Shell, escalated. Shell later posted on the Internet descriptions of some of these incidents. Two examples of Shell's posted accounts follow:

> [This] incident happened when armed youths invaded and occupied a rig location and nearby flow station, chasing off staff who were not given the opportunity to make the location safe. The youths demanded N100 million [*naira,* the Nigerian currency, at that time worth about $12.5 million], a new road, and a water scheme. Attempts to talk with the youths, who were armed with guns and machetes, failed.

Post–Lawrence–Weber:
Business and Society,
Ninth Edition

Case Study: Shell Oil in
Nigeria

© The McGraw–Hill
Companies, 1999

In response, Shell staff called the Nigerian police, which sent in mobile units. In the ensuing riot, at least one policeman and seven civilians in the local village were killed. Shell concluded its posting, "The Shell response to the threatening situation was made with the best intentions and what happened was a shock to staff, many of whom had friends [in the village]."

In the second incident, as reported by Shell:

A gang of youths . . . stormed . . . a drilling rig in the Ahia oil field . . . looting and vandalizing the facility and rig camp. Rig workers were held hostage for most of the first day while property worth $6 million was destroyed or stolen. The rig was shut down for 10 days and the Ahia flow station was also shut down. . . . [A protest leader] raised the issue of [distribution] . . . of oil revenues to the oil producing communities by the government, the need for a new road, and rumours of bribery by Shell of a [local] chief.

In this incident as well, Shell called the police; this time, no injuries resulted.

Most of the civil disturbances followed a similar pattern, as these examples suggest. A group of young men, armed with whatever weapons were readily available, would attack one of Shell's many far-flung oil installations in the delta. Employees would be attacked, equipment would be sabotaged, and the group would make demands. The demands would be denied, and the company would call in police. Violence against civilians sometimes followed.

Shell's own data on patterns of community disturbances in the Niger delta, posted on the Internet, revealed a pattern of escalating violence throughout the early 1990s, peaking in 1993. Shell estimated that the company sustained $42 million in damage to its installations in Ogoniland between 1993 and the end of 1995, as a direct result of sabotage.

The relationship between these incidents and MOSOP was complex. Saro-Wiwa's group explicitly rejected violence and repeatedly disavowed vigilante attacks on Shell or other companies, and Saro-Wiwa himself frequently toured Ogoniland to restore calm. Yet, publication of the Bill of Rights and MOSOP campaigns focusing attention on injustices suffered by the Ogoni clearly had the effect of escalating expectations within Ogoni society. In this context, many young unemployed Ogoni men simply took matters into their own hands.

On January 3, 1993, MOSOP held a massive rally to mark the start of the Year of the Indigenous Peoples. Held at successive locations across Ogoniland, the rally was attended by as many as 300,000 people, three-fifths of the Ogoni population. Protesters carried twigs, a symbol of environmental regeneration. Two weeks later, Shell abruptly announced that it would withdraw from Ogoniland. It evacuated all employees and shut down its operations. Company officials gave a terse explanation: "There is no question of our staff working in areas where their safety may be at risk."

The Militarization of Commerce

As civil unrest escalated in Ogoniland, Shell began to work more and more closely with the Nigerian police. Shell defended this practice, saying that it was normal in Nigeria to request police protection in areas where crime rates were high. Shell acknowledged that it provided firearms to police protecting its facilities. Several human rights organizations claimed that Shell provided more than handguns. The Nigerian Civil Liberties Organization reported that Shell-owned cars, buses, speedboats, and helicopters were regularly used to transport po-

Post–Lawrence–Weber:
Business and Society,
Ninth Edition

Case Study: Shell Oil in
Nigeria

© The McGraw–Hill
Companies, 1999

lice and military personnel to the site of civil disturbances. Human Rights Watch reported that Shell met regularly with representatives of the Rivers State police to plan security operations.

After General Abacha took power in November 1993, he apparently decided to take a hard line with the Ogoni insurgency in an effort to induce Shell to resume operations. One of his first acts as chief of state was to assemble a special paramilitary force, comprised of selected personnel from the army, navy, air force, and police, to restore order in Ogoniland. According to internal memos, later revealed, the purpose of this force was to ensure that those "carrying out business ventures in Ogoniland are not molested." A memo dated May 12, 1994, read in part: "Shell operations still impossible unless ruthless military operations are undertaken for smooth economic activities to commence." It advised the governor of Rivers State to put "pressure on oil companies for prompt regular inputs as discussed."

In May and June 1994, intense violence erupted in Ogoniland. Amnesty International, which collected eyewitness accounts, reported that the government's paramilitary force entered Ogoniland, where it "instigated and assisted" interethnic clashes between previously peaceful neighboring groups. The units then "followed the attackers into Ogoni villages, destroying houses and detaining people." In May and June, the force attacked 30 towns and villages, where its members "fired at random, destroyed and set fires to homes, killing, assaulting, and raping, and looting and extorting money, livestock, and food," according to the Amnesty International report. As many as 2,000 civilians may have been killed.

In 1995, despite the government's efforts to make the area safe for business, Shell had still not returned to Ogoniland. All its other oil production operations in the Niger delta were being conducted under round-the-clock military protection. Claude Ake, a well-known Nigerian political economist, described the situation in a chilling phrase: "This is a process," he wrote, "of the militarization of commerce."

The Arrest, Trial, and Execution of a Martyr

On May 21, 1994, just over a week after the "smooth economic activities" memo, Saro-Wiwa was en route to a MOSOP rally where he was scheduled to speak. On the way, his car was stopped at a military roadblock, and he was ordered to return home. He never attended the rally. Later that same day, a group of Ogoni chiefs, who were political opponents of Saro-Wiwa, held a meeting. Their gathering was interrupted by a crowd of several hundred youths, who denounced the men as vultures who had collaborated with the military government. Four of the chiefs were assaulted and bludgeoned to death.

The following day, Saro-Wiwa and several other leaders of MOSOP were arrested. In a televised press conference, the governor of Rivers State blamed the MOSOP leaders for the murders. Saro-Wiwa and his colleagues were detained in a secret military camp, where they were chained in leg irons and denied access to medical care. It would be eight months before they were formally charged.

During Saro-Wiwa's imprisonment, his brother, Owens Wiwa, met on three occasions with Shell Nigeria's managing director Brian Anderson to seek his help in securing Ken's release. Wiwa later gave an account of these meetings that was posted on the Internet. Anderson told him, Wiwa reported, that it would be "difficult but not impossible" to get his brother out of prison. Anderson allegedly said, "if [MOSOP] can stop the campaign [against Shell] we might be able to do something." Wiwa refused. Wiwa also re-

Post–Lawrence–Weber:
Business and Society,
Ninth Edition

Case Study: Shell Oil in
Nigeria

© The McGraw–Hill
Companies, 1999

ported that he had asked Anderson if the company had made payments to the government's paramilitary force. "The answer he gave is that '*I* [emphasis added] have never approved payment to [the force].' He did not deny that Shell was paying. . . . I think he knew about it, and the people in London knew about it." While later acknowledging that meetings between Anderson and Wiwa had taken place as part of an effort at "quiet diplomacy," Shell denied Wiwa's specific allegations as "false and reprehensible."

In November, General Abacha appointed a Civil Disturbances Special Tribunal to try the case of the MOSOP leaders. Established by special decree, this tribunal was empowered to impose the death penalty in cases involving civil disturbances. The decision of the court could be confirmed or disallowed by the military government, but defendants had no right of judicial appeal. Amnesty International and many other human rights organizations denounced the tribunal for violating standards of due process guaranteed by Nigeria's own constitution and by international treaties.

Saro-Wiwa's trial for murder began in February 1995. Government witnesses testified that Saro-Wiwa had relayed a message to his youthful supporters, after the roadblock incident, to "deal with" his opponents. Saro-Wiwa's defense attorneys countered that Saro-Wiwa had been at home at the time and had had nothing to do with the killings. The defense team also presented evidence that two key prosecution witnesses had been bribed by the government with Shell contracts and cash in exchange for their statements implicating Saro-Wiwa. Shell adamantly denied bribing witnesses.

On November 2, the tribunal found Saro-Wiwa and eight other MOSOP leaders guilty of murder and sentenced them to death. Six defendants were acquitted. On November 8, Shell issued this statement, in response to international appeals that it seek a commutation of the sentence:

> We believe that to interfere in the processes, either political or legal, here in Nigeria would be wrong. A large multinational company such as Shell cannot and must not interfere with the affairs of any sovereign state.

Two days later, Saro-Wiwa and eight MOSOP associates were hanged in prison. His last words on the gallows were: "Lord, take my soul, but the struggle continues."

With Deep Regret

Shell issued a statement on the executions that read, in part, "It is with deep regret that we hear this news. From the violence that led to the murder of the four Ogoni leaders in May last year through to the death penalty having been carried out, the human cost has been too high." Shell told reporters that it had approached the government privately after Saro-Wiwa's conviction to appeal for clemency on humanitarian grounds. It would have been inappropriate, however, the company said, to have intervened in the criminal trial. The company also declined to comment further regarding human rights in Nigeria. A spokesperson said, "We can't issue a bold statement about human rights because . . . it could be considered treasonous by the regime and [our] employees could come under attack."

The company also defended its actions in the months leading up to Saro-Wiwa's arrest and trial. Shell representatives stated that it would have been wrong to have tried to influence government policy on environmental protection, Ogoni autonomy, or other issues of concern to MOSOP. With respect to the actions of the Nigerian police, the company argued that it would have been improper to provide its own armed security. An executive told the news media, "Our responsibility is very clear. We pay taxes and [abide

Post-Lawrence-Weber:
Business and Society,
Ninth Edition

Case Study: Shell Oil in
Nigeria

© The McGraw-Hill
Companies, 1999

by] regulation. We don't run the government." Shell also vigorously resisted demands by some human rights activists and environmentalists that the company withdraw from Nigeria. If it left, the company argued, whatever organization took over its operations would probably operate with lower environmental and safety standards, and the jobs of its Nigerian employees would be imperiled.

Shell's public disclaimers did little to slow down the controversy swirling around the company. By mid-1996, the company was facing a growing international boycott, the possibility that it would have to abandon plans to proceed with its liquefied natural gas project, and persistent demands that it withdraw from Nigeria altogether. The crisis threatened the company's shareholders, employees, franchisees, and customers—not only in Nigeria, but throughout the world.

Discussion Questions

1. What arguments did Shell make in defending its actions in Nigeria? How would Shell's critics counter these arguments? Do you believe Shell could or should have done anything differently in Nigeria?

2. What internal or external factors contributed to the emergence of this crisis for Shell?

3. What, if anything, should Shell do now?

4. Evaluate Shell's actions in Nigeria in reference to an existing code of conduct for multinational organizations. Do you believe that Shell was in compliance with the code you have selected? If not, how not? Do you believe the code you have selected is appropriate and adequate?

5. In your opinion, is it possible to develop a universal set of ethical standards for business, or do cultural differences make universal standards impractical, if not impossible?

Post−Lawrence−Weber:
Business and Society,
Ninth Edition

Case Study: The Tobacco
Deal

© The McGraw−Hill
Companies, 1999

Case Study:
The Tobacco Deal

On June 20, 1997, at a little after three in the afternoon, tobacco industry attorney Phil Carlton and Arizona attorney general Grant Woods emerged exhausted from a meeting room at the Park Hyatt Hotel in Washington, D.C. From inside the room—where negotiators for the tobacco industry, public health organizations, and state attorneys general had been engaged in days of nearly around-the-clock talks—reporters waiting in the hall could hear applause, then whooping and whistling. Woods flashed a thumbs-up sign to the press corps. "We've got a deal," he announced.

For weeks, the outcome of the delicate tobacco negotiations had been in doubt. Observers had called the talks chaotic and fractious. The talks had nearly broken down several times during the final few days, as negotiations foundered on the issues of document disclosure, government regulation, and whistle-blower protection. At one point, the attorney representing 20 of the 32 states at the table had simply walked out and flown off in his Lear jet. But at the last moment, both sides had made key concessions, and an agreement was reached.

Note: An earlier version of this case, Anne T. Lawrence, "The Tobacco Deal," was presented at the Western Casewriters Association Annual Meeting, Portland, Oregon, March 26, 1998. The author would like to thank Carol Anderson, an MBA student at San Jose State University, for research assistance. This case was prepared from publicly available materials, including newspaper stories appearing in the *New York Times, The Wall Street Journal, Washington Post, Arizona Republic, Louisville Courier-Journal, Business Week, U.S. News & World Report,* and *USA Today;* material published on the Internet by Center for Responsive Politics; a special issue of *Mother Jones* magazine (May 1996); and two book-length studies, Philip J. Hilts, *Smokescreen: The Truth behind the Tobacco Industry Cover-up* (Reading, MA: Addison-Wesley, 1996); and Stanton E. Glantz, John Slade, Lisa A. Bero, Peter Hanauer, and Deborah A. Barnes, *The Cigarette Papers* (Berkeley, CA: University of California Press, 1996). The Brown & Williamson papers are available on the Internet at http://www.library.ucsf.edu/tobacco.

Post–Lawrence–Weber:
Business and Society,
Ninth Edition

Case Study: The Tobacco
Deal

© The McGraw–Hill
Companies, 1999

In many respects, the deal struck at the Park Hyatt was astonishing. The big tobacco companies had agreed to pay *369 billion* dollars over the next quarter century and to submit to federal regulations and broad restrictions on cigarette advertising. In exchange, many state lawsuits would be settled, and the industry would be protected from most future litigation.

Never before had the tobacco giants been willing to make such vast concessions to their opponents. And never before had prominent public health advocates been willing to endorse limits on how much money smokers with lung cancer and heart disease could recover from the tobacco industry. The tobacco deal, said Mike Moore, Mississippi attorney general and a lead negotiator—with a bit of enthusiastic redundancy—was "the most historic public health achievement in history."

Many thought the agreement could herald a new era in the relationship between the tobacco industry and its critics in government and the public health community, as well as a model for the settlement of mass liability cases. On the other hand, the agreement itself was just the first step. In order to become law, the tobacco deal required congressional support. For this to happen, it would likely need the backing of the president, several federal agencies, and the many stakeholder groups it affected. None were assured. The historic tobacco deal could easily go up in smoke.

The U.S. Tobacco Industry

In 1997, tobacco was one of the United States' most profitable businesses, as well as one of its most controversial.

The U.S. cigarette industry was dominated by five companies, as shown in Table 1. The industry leader was Philip Morris Companies, Inc. The world's largest tobacco company, Philip Morris controlled almost half of the U.S. market for cigarettes and owned the world's second most valuable brand, Marlboro (the most valuable brand was Coca-Cola). The company's market value in 1996 was slightly under $107 billion. Although over half

Table 1   *The big five tobacco companies, 1997, ranked by U.S. market share*

Company	Subsidiary	Key Brands	Market Share (percent U.S./ percent global)	Market Value	Sales	Profits	Assets
Philip Morris	—	Marlboro, Virginia Slims	43/16	$106,580	$54,553	$6,303	$54,871
RJR Nabisco	RJ Reynolds	Camel, Winston	28/6	8,758	17,063	611	31,289
BAT Industries	Brown & Williamson	Lucky Strike, Kool	18/13	27,767	25,721	2,536	76,630
Loews Corp.	Lorillard	Kent, Newport	7	11,188	19,964	1,384	67,683
Brooke Group	Liggett	L&M, Chesterfield	2	93	414	196	135

Note: Market value is the share price on May 30, 1997, multiplied by the latest available number of shares outstanding. Sales is annual net sales reported by the company. Profits is latest after-tax earnings available to common shareholders. Market value, sales, profits, and assets are worldwide.
Sources: "The Business Week Global 1000," *Business Week,* July 7, 1997, pp. 55–92; http://www.hoovers.com/quarterlies/; http://www.sec.gov/archives/edgar/data/.

Post–Lawrence–Weber:
Business and Society,
Ninth Edition

Case Study: The Tobacco
Deal

© The McGraw–Hill
Companies, 1999

the company's revenue came from the sale of tobacco products, Philip Morris also owned profitable real estate, financial services, and food and beverage businesses, including Kraft and Miller Brewing.

Second, ranked by U.S. market share, was RJR Nabisco Holdings Corp. The company's tobacco subsidiary, R.J. Reynolds, produced Camel, Winston, and Salem cigarettes, among others. The company's food subsidiary, Nabisco, was a major producer of cereals, crackers, cookies, candy, gum, and other packaged food products. Although sales were split about evenly between tobacco and food products, most of the company's profits came from cigarettes.

Bringing up the rear were three companies with smaller market shares. BAT Industries (formerly, British American Tobacco), based in Britain, was the owner of Brown & Williamson, maker of Lucky Strike and Kool cigarettes, with an 18 percent share. (BAT had acquired another U.S. company, American Tobacco, in 1995.) Loews Corporation, controlled by billionaire brothers Laurence and Robert Tisch, was a holding company that included CNA Financial (an insurance company) and the Loews Hotels. One of Loews' smaller holdings was the Lorillard Tobacco Company, maker of Kent, Newport, and True cigarettes.

The smallest of the big five was Brooke Group Ltd. Brooke's Liggett division (formerly Liggett & Myers) held about 2 percent of the U.S. market with its Chesterfield, L&M, Lark, and some discount varieties of cigarettes. Brooke's chairman and CEO, Bennett LeBow, owned 57 percent of the company. (UST Holdings, formerly U.S. Tobacco, was normally not included in the big five because it manufactured chewing tobacco and snuff, rather than cigarettes.)

In the United States in 1997, 26 percent of adults smoked. Slightly more men (28 percent) than women (23 percent) used cigarettes.

Domestic sales, however, were slipping, as they had for some time. At the peak of cigarette consumption in the United States in the early 1950s, fully half of American adults smoked; this percentage had been nearly halved in 40 years. All major tobacco companies had responded by moving aggressively to expand overseas sales, especially in the booming overseas markets of Asia, Eastern Europe, South America, Africa, and the Middle East, where American brands had status and consumption was rising. This strategy was to a large degree successful; in 1996, total international tobacco sales were $296 billion (the U.S. accounted for less than 40 percent).

The cigarette industry was phenomenally profitable. Warren Buffett, the well-known investor, explained the matter simply. "I'll tell you why I like the cigarette business," he said. "It costs a penny to make. Sell it for a dollar. It's addictive. And there's fantastic brand loyalty."

The tobacco industry was a major contributor to the U.S. economy. It added over $55 billion annually to the gross domestic product. Federal, state, and local taxes collected from the sale of cigarettes and other tobacco products in the United States totaled $13.1 billion in 1996. The industry was also a major employer in some states. Of the approximately 700,000 people employed in growing, processing, transporting, marketing, and retailing tobacco and its products, most were concentrated in the southeastern states. These workers, of course, contributed to the economy through their spending and income taxes. Tobacco products, a major export, significantly improved the U.S. balance of trade. The industry spent $6.2 billion a year for advertising, a big boost to Madison Avenue, and kept legions of attorneys and public relations people employed.

Post–Lawrence–Weber:
Business and Society,
Ninth Edition

Case Study: The Tobacco
Deal

© The McGraw–Hill
Companies, 1999

The tobacco industry also imposed significant economic costs. The total annual costs of smoking-related illnesses were estimated by the Centers for Disease Control in 1996 to run around $50 billion. These costs included health care for persons with emphysema, lung cancer, heart failure, and other tobacco-related illnesses, and lost work time and reduced productivity of smokers. Some of these costs were borne by the federal government, and hence, indirectly, taxpayers, through Medicare and Medicaid. Annual state spending (through various state medical plans) on smoking-related health care varied by population, of course; to cite a few examples, the yearly tab was $250 million in Florida, $240 million in Massachusetts, and $500 million in West Virginia. Individuals also paid, both directly and through their insurance premiums. These figures did not include, of course, the incalculable costs of pain and grief suffered by victims and their families. On the other hand, one study—funded by the tobacco industry—argued that smoking actually *saved* the U.S. health-care system money, for the simple reason that many smokers died early, sparing the system the cost of caring for them in old age.

Public Health Issues

The adverse health effects of cigarettes had been well-known in the public health community since the early 1950s. Smokers are 10 to 20 times more likely to suffer from lung cancer than are persons who do not smoke. Among smokers, the number of cancers rise with the number of cigarettes smoked. Cigarette smoke has been linked with cancer in animal studies, and a specific chemical agent in tobacco tar, *benzo(a)pyrene,* has been found in experiments to cause cancerous mutations in human lung cells. In addition to causing lung cancer, cigarette smoking also causes a number of other ailments. Smokers are at higher risk for coronary heart disease, stroke, throat and bladder cancer, chronic bronchitis, and emphysema. Smoking by pregnant women retards fetal growth. Secondhand smoke can cause lung cancer and heart disease in healthy nonsmokers.

Smoking is the leading preventative cause of death in the United States. Each year, about 420,000 smokers and 53,000 nonsmokers die from tobacco-related illnesses, many more times as many as die from all other preventable causes of death (alcohol, auto accidents, AIDS, suicide, homicide, and illegal drugs) combined.

Nicotine, the pharmacologically active component of tobacco, is highly addictive. A member of the alkaloid family, nicotine is chemically related to other well-known addictive substances, including cocaine, heroin, and morphine. In any given year, about a third of smokers try to quit; only about 10 percent succeed, mainly because of the effects of nicotine addiction.

Smoking as a Pediatric Disease

Dr. David Kessler, commissioner of the Food and Drug Administration, frequently referred to smoking as a pediatric disease, that is, a disease of children.

The reasons for Kessler's somewhat startling assertion is that most people take up the cigarette habit in their teens. Among lifelong smokers, 90 percent began smoking by the time they were 18 and over half by the age of 14. The percentage of U.S. high-school students in 1995 who said they had smoked in the past month was 35 percent, up from 28 percent in 1991.

The reasons that smokers start in their teens are complex. Although nicotine is highly addictive, it does not promote an immediate physiologic dependence as do heroin and some other drugs. Rather, nicotine addiction takes on average one or two years of smoking to become fully established. At the same time, the act of smoking itself, for many people, is not particularly pleasurable initially; beginning smokers report that cigarettes burn their throats, make them cough, and don't taste particularly good. Who, then, sticks with the habit long enough to become hooked? The answer is: People in situations where peer pressures to smoke are strong and for whom peer influence is particularly compelling. Study after study has come to the same conclusion: Teens start smoking because their friends do. Once they've smoked regularly for a year or two, many find it extraordinarily difficult to quit, even if they want to.

Every day in the United States, 3,000 new young people take up the smoking habit. One out of three of them will die from tobacco-related illnesses, many in middle-age.

From the perspective of the tobacco companies, these facts about how people start smoking present a vexing problem. Sales of cigarettes to minors are illegal, and tobacco companies would prefer not to break the law or to face the public disapproval caused by peddling an addictive substance to youngsters. However, the industry is also well aware that it loses customers all the time; 1.3 million smokers quit every year, and 420,000 die. Most replacement smokers will be recruited, if they are recruited at all, from the ranks of the young.

Moreover, brand loyalty is exceptionally high among smokers, so the cigarette a smoker begins with often remains his or her brand for life. Cigarette makers thus have a strong financial incentive to market their products to teens, even though it is publicly awkward—not to mention illegal—to do so.

Lines of Defense

Although smoking was well known to cause death and disease, for many years the tobacco industry maintained a remarkable record of defending itself against both lawsuits and government regulation.

Until 1996, the tobacco industry never lost a lawsuit brought by a smoker. The tobacco companies were well funded, hired top attorneys, and defended all lawsuits extremely vigorously. The industry consistently maintained that tobacco had not been proven to cause cancer or other diseases. After warning labels were introduced in 1965, the industry was also able to argue that smokers had been informed of the risk and had assumed those risks and the consequences. Most juries blamed the smoker for not having the willpower to quit. "The American people know smokers can and do quit, and they still believe in individual responsibility," contended a press release distributed by R.J. Reynolds.

Moreover, the tobacco industry successfully used a variety of political strategies to block antismoking legislation and to thwart efforts to impose government regulation. The big five and their political organization, the Tobacco Institute, consistently donated large sums of money both to political parties and, through their political action committees, to individual candidates. Historically, the industry had funneled funds more or less equally to both major parties, but in the mid-1990s—following the Clinton administration's stepped-up efforts to impose regulations on the industry—its support shifted notably to the Republicans. The industry's 1996 contributions to political parties are shown in Table 2. That year, Philip Morris was the top donor of soft money among *all* contributors. Collectively, the tobacco industry was responsible for $6.6 million to both parties, out of the $263 million total for soft-money contributions that year.

In addition, the industry provided financial support to a variety of advocacy groups and think tanks with interests allied to its own—for example, those opposing FDA regu-

Post–Lawrence–Weber:
Business and Society,
Ninth Edition

Case Study: The Tobacco
Deal

© The McGraw–Hill
Companies, 1999

Table 2   *Tobacco industry soft-money political contributions,
1996 election year*

Company	Republican	Democrat	Total
Philip Morris	$2,520,518	$496,518	$3,017,036
RJR Nabisco	1,442,931	254,754	1,697,685
Brown & Williamson	635,000	7,500	642,500
U.S. Tobacco	556,603	118,362	674,965
Tobacco Institute	424,790	106,044	530,834
Total	$5,579,842	$983,178	$6,563,020

Note: Soft money refers to funds donated directly to political parties to support party-building efforts such as televised campaign commercials that do not support a specific candidate, get-out-the-vote drives, and other activities in connection with presidential and congressional races. Soft money was legal under U.S. election laws in 1996. Limiting, or banning, soft-money contributions has been a key element of many campaign finance reform proposals.
Source: Center for Responsive Politics, from Federal Election Commission data, based on year-end reports filed by political parties, January 31, 1997.

latory authority, promoting smoker's rights, and supporting free-speech rights for advertisers. The industry's powerful corporate lobby, The Tobacco Institute, vigorously promoted its point of view. Individual firms also maintained their own lobbying efforts; in 1996, for example, Philip Morris spent $19.6 million on its Washington, DC, lobbying operation.

The industry-funded Council for Tobacco Research (founded in 1954 as the Tobacco Industry Research Committee) sponsored partisan research and publicized the industry's contention that there was no proof that smoking caused cancer and heart disease. Commented the attorney for the National Center for Tobacco-Free Kids, "While [the industry's] PR campaigns were a failure with the public, they accomplished something more important: They gave politicians cover for failing to act."

Tobacco's political and public relations efforts were remarkably successful. For many years, the industry succeeded in avoiding the regulation of nicotine, holding cigarette taxes to a moderate level, blocking many local antismoking ordinances, and retaining mildly worded warning labels. In instance after instance, the tobacco industry actually managed to turn apparent setbacks to its advantage. When Congress banned television advertising of cigarettes, it benefited existing brands because, without television, introducing new brands was prohibitively expensive. The TV ban also meant the end of mandated public interest antismoking television spots, ones that had been hurting sales. When Congress required warning labels on cigarette packs, the industry won a clause in the law that effectively blocked lawsuits, on the grounds consumers had been warned of the risks. When the government has levied taxes on cigarettes, tobacco companies have often raised prices and then blamed government intrusion.

"Without exception, federal legislation designed to favor the public health has worked to the advantage of the industry," commented tobacco policy expert Kenneth E. Warner.

Chinks in the Industry's Armor

By the mid-1990s, however, tobacco's invincibility was weakening, leading some of its key strategists to consider negotiating an agreement with its adversaries. Several factors contributed to the industry's deteriorating position.

310

Post–Lawrence–Weber:
Business and Society,
Ninth Edition

Case Study: The Tobacco
Deal

© The McGraw–Hill
Companies, 1999

Congress Holds Hearings

In April 1994, the Democratic-controlled House of Representatives opened hearings on the health effects of tobacco. In testimony under oath, top executives of the tobacco industry assured Congress that their companies did not manipulate nor independently control the level of nicotine in cigarettes, and that cigarettes did not cause cancer or other illnesses. The hearings served to focus public attention on the industry. The tobacco industry executives' testimony was widely ridiculed; one survey later found that, when shown to the public, videotape of the tobacco chieftains swearing to tell the truth elicited "instant recognition and instant laughter." Grand juries later considered whether tobacco executives illegally conspired to obstruct a Congressional investigation.

Industry Whistle-Blowers Come Forward

Just a few weeks later, an industry whistle-blower made public some highly damaging internal company documents. Merrell Williams was a paralegal working for a law firm in Louisville, Kentucky, that had been hired by Brown & Williamson to review thousands of pages of company documents in connection with its legal defense. Williams, a long-time smoker of Kools who was suffering from heart disease, was shocked at what he saw. Over a several-month period, Williams smuggled documents out of the office and secretly copied them before returning the originals.

In May 1994, Williams mailed these documents to a prominent antitobacco researcher at the University of California–San Francisco, Dr. Stanton Glantz. Glantz subsequently posted the documents on the Internet. In July 1995, Glantz and his colleagues published an initial review of the B&W documents that provided strong evidence that Brown & Williamson was aware of the addictive nature of nicotine and of the health hazards of tobacco.

FDA commissioner Kessler later stated that the publication of the B&W documents was "a major moment, beyond which all went in one direction. It was the first time we had anyone saying, 'We are in the business of selling nicotine, which is an addictive drug.' Before that, it was all indirect evidence."

In November 1995, a second whistle-blower came forward. Dr. Jeffrey Wigand, chief of research for B&W from 1989–1993, gave a deposition in which he confirmed that the company had known that nicotine was addictive and had actively manipulated its levels in the final product.

FDA Moves to Regulate Tobacco

The B&W documents supplied the FDA with a new and powerful rationale for regulation. Under the Food, Drug, and Cosmetics Act, an article or substance is subject to regulation if it "affects the structure or function of the body." The industry had always maintained that, as a natural product—not a drug or device—tobacco should not be controlled by the FDA. The industry's apparent intent to cause addiction through the active manipulation of nicotine levels, however, seemed to qualify cigarettes as a drug-delivery device and hence subject to regulation.

In August 1995, using this reasoning, the FDA proposed far-reaching new rules that called for eliminating cigarette vending machines, billboard advertising near schools, and many forms of promotion aimed at young people, such as ads in youth-oriented magazines. The proposed rules also banned brand-name sponsorship of sporting events, the sale of tobacco-branded merchandise, and the distribution of free samples.

Within days, the tobacco industry and its allies in the advertising industry filed suit in North Carolina, claiming the FDA had no legal authority to regulate tobacco and that the proposed restrictions on cigarette advertising violated First Amendment rights.

Post–Lawrence–Weber:
Business and Society,
Ninth Edition

Case Study: The Tobacco
Deal

© The McGraw–Hill
Companies, 1999

State Lawsuits Progress

Several states brought lawsuits against the tobacco companies to recover the costs of health care for citizens with smoking-related illnesses. Mississippi was the first in 1994; it was quickly followed by a slew of others. Eventually, 29 states mounted lawsuits. These cases gradually worked their way through the system, threatening the tobacco companies with the possibility of massive judgments and bad publicity. The Mississippi case was scheduled to go to trial in June 1997.

Brown & Williamson Found Liable

In August 1996, for the first time ever, the tobacco industry lost in court. Brown & Williamson Tobacco Corp. was ordered to pay a landmark $750,000 in a personal-injury case in Florida brought by a man who had contracted lung cancer after 25 years of smoking. The suit charged the tobacco industry with marketing a defective and dangerous product. Invoking the doctrine of strict liability, plaintiff's attorneys had argued that the company should be held liable for damage done by its products whether or not they were aware of the potential dangers. This landmark decision threatened the tobacco industry, for the first time, with a flood of personal-injury lawsuits.

Liggett Breaks Ranks

In March 1996, the Liggett Group Inc.—the smallest and financially weakest of the major tobacco companies—broke ranks, destroying the industry's long-standing united front. As part of an effort to make Liggett more attractive as a possible acquisition, Bennet LeBow, CEO of Liggett's owner, the Brooke Group, cut separate deals with class-action lawyers and states then suing the tobacco companies. As part of the settlement, LeBow acknowledged that cigarettes were addictive and carcinogenic and said manufacturers had targeted youths under age 18 in their marketing. He also agreed to drop opposition to FDA regulation and to turn over documents that the state attorneys general believed would assist them in their litigation against the tobacco industry.

Tobacco Becomes an Issue in the Campaign

In the 1996 presidential campaign, tobacco regulation became a campaign issue. The Clinton administration focused on protecting children from the dangers of smoking. Senator Robert Dole, the Republican nominee, committed an apparent gaff when he stated during an interview that he did not believe nicotine was addictive. By some accounts, the tobacco issue helped the Democrats win the presidential election.

More Whistle-blowers Come Forward

In March 1997, the FDA released affidavits from three former Philip Morris employees that confirmed earlier allegations that their employer had deliberately manipulated nicotine levels in its cigarettes to ensure smokers got a nicotine jolt. One former scientist for the company stated that, "Nicotine levels were routinely targeted and adjusted by Philip Morris. . . . Knowledge about the optimum range for nicotine in a cigarette was developed as a result of a great many years of investigation." A former shift manager at a cigarette manufacturing plant in Richmond, Virginia, outlined for the FDA how Philip Morris carefully calibrated nicotine levels in a key production process.

Post-Lawrence-Weber:
Business and Society,
Ninth Edition

Case Study: The Tobacco
Deal

© The McGraw-Hill
Companies, 1999

Philip Morris responded to these allegations by denying that it manipulated the levels of nicotine in its tobacco products. To the contrary, the tobacco company described nicotine as a key component of taste. "At Philip Morris USA, we work hard to ensure the consistency and quality of our products—and quality control, no matter what the product or service, does not constitute 'manipulation.'"

FDA Jurisdiction Upheld

On April 25, 1997, a federal judge in North Carolina, acting in the industry's lawsuit, upheld the FDA's jurisdiction over tobacco. However, the court also ruled that the FDA had exceeded its authority when it banned certain forms of cigarette advertising, including billboard ads.

The Negotiations

The emergence of whistle-blowers and damaging internal documents, encroaching FDA regulation, successful smoker lawsuits, shifting public opinion, and a break in their own ranks combined to put great pressure on the tobacco companies. The industry was plainly concerned about the extent, and uncontrollability, of their liability for tobacco-related illnesses. For the first time, top executives of the leading tobacco companies began talking about a possible settlement. Cigarette makers "can't continue in public as kind of an outlaw industry," declared RJR Nabisco CEO Steven F. Goldstone. "A lot of forces are at work" favoring some broad settlement with industry adversaries, he noted. "In 1997, the most meaningful thing I can do is come to some solution [to] this problem."

From the industry's standpoint, a settlement held some attractions. Although any agreement would be extremely expensive, at least some of the costs could be passed on to consumers through higher prices. A deal would reduce the industry's legal fees, then running around $600 million a year. Stock prices could rise as tobacco shares, long depressed by investor concern over potential liability, emerged from under a cloud of uncertainty. And, in the United States at least, a public admission of the hazards of tobacco would free the industry to produce a new range of "safer" products, such as smoke-free or low-smoke cigarettes, those with lower concentrations of carcinogens, or even those designed to help smokers quit.

In April 1997, a group of state attorneys general, plaintiff attorneys, and representatives of all of the big five (except for Liggett, which had already settled) began the negotiations that led to the June 1997 deal. Also included in the talks were a few representatives of the public health community, including Matthew Myers, general counsel for the National Center for Tobacco-Free Kids. The White House was not directly involved, but Bruce Lindsey, a key presidential aide, monitored the talks closely as they proceeded.

Terms of the Deal

The June 20, 1997, settlement included the following provisions:

- **Tobacco industry payments.** The tobacco industry would be required to pay $368.5 billion for the first 25 years and then $15 billion a year indefinitely. Most of this money would go to the states, to compensate them for the cost of health care for persons with tobacco-related illness. $25 billion would go toward health care for uninsured children. Some funds would also finance antismoking education and advertising and enforcement of the settlement. Some (the percentage was

Post–Lawrence–Weber:
Business and Society,
Ninth Edition

Case Study: The Tobacco
Deal

© The McGraw–Hill
Companies, 1999

not specified) would pay the fees of attorneys who negotiated the settlement. Passing these costs along to consumers would, by some estimates, result in a 62-cents-a-pack increase in the price of cigarettes.

- **Advertising.** All billboard and outdoor advertising of tobacco products, the use of human and cartoon figures (such as "Joe Camel") in ads, Internet advertising, product placements in movies and TV, and brand-name sponsorship of sporting events and brand-name promotional merchandise would be banned. Tobacco companies would be required to change their advertising to make it less appealing to children.

- **Warning labels.** Warning labels on cigarette packs would include the statements "Cigarettes Are Addictive," "Cigarettes Cause Cancer," "Smoking Can Kill You," and "Tobacco Smoke Causes Fatal Lung Disease in Nonsmokers" in white lettering on a black background over 25 percent of the top front of cigarette packs.

- **Government regulation of nicotine.** The Food and Drug Administration would be allowed to regulate the *quantity* of nicotine in cigarettes. However, the FDA could not *ban* nicotine from cigarettes until 2009. Even then, in order to reduce nicotine yield, the FDA would have to prove its action would result in a significant overall reduction of health risks, was technologically feasible, and would not create a significant demand for more potent black market cigarettes.

- **Cap on liability.** Tobacco companies would be protected from future litigation by a ban on punitive damages, class-action lawsuits, and consolidated litigation. The agreement would also settle the suits of 40 states and Puerto Rico, one class-action suit against the tobacco industry, and 16 others seeking certification. No money was given to plaintiffs in the 17 class-action suits. The agreement would ban class-action suits, consolidation of multiple suits, and punitive damages for past conduct. Medical bills and lost wages of individual claims would be paid from an annual $5 billion tobacco-company fund. Lawsuits by insurers to recover health-care payouts linked to smoking would be restricted. Also, there would be a yearly cap on payments for settlements and judgments.

- **Access to children.** Sale of cigarettes through vending machines would be outlawed, and a nationwide licensing system for tobacco retailers would be required to enable regulators to enforce the prohibition on access to minors.

- **Youth smoking.** The tobacco industry would be subjected to fines if youth smoking did not drop 30 percent in five years, 50 percent in seven years, and 60 percent in 10 years. There would be a penalty of $80 million per percentage point by which the target was missed. The annual fines would begin in 2002. The industry could petition for a 75 percent refund of a fine if it could show it had acted in good faith and in full compliance with the agreement, pursued all reasonable measures, and did nothing to "undermine achievement of required results."

- **Public smoking.** Smoking in public places and most workplaces without separately ventilated smoking areas would be prohibited. However, restaurants, bars, casinos, and bingo parlors would be exempt.

- **Smoker assistance.** Smokers would received modest payments for smoking-cessation treatment and monitoring smoking-related illnesses.

Post–Lawrence–Weber:
Business and Society,
Ninth Edition

Case Study: The Tobacco
Deal

© The McGraw–Hill
Companies, 1999

An Agreement under Fire

The tobacco deal was immediately under fire from several quarters. The Advocacy Committee on Tobacco Policy and Public Health, a panel of experts headed by C. Everett Koop, a former surgeon general, rejected the deal as unacceptable. The panel criticized the proposed penalties for failing to reduce teen smoking as too small and also said that the pact would undercut the FDA's ability to regulate nicotine. Dr. David Kessler, who had recently left his post as FDA chief—and who also served on the Advocacy Committee—argued that the government's right to regulate nicotine as a drug had already been upheld by the courts. Therefore, any rules that would require the agency to "give up authority or jump through a lot of hoops" would be a major step backward, he said.

Some antismoking and public health organizations that had not participated in the negotiations criticized the proposed plan as a sellout to industry. "The public health community has been locked out of this negotiation," charged the director of SmokeFree Pennsylvania. The American Lung Association, which had opposed negotiations in the first place, said that the agreement was not sufficiently punitive to the industry. An ALA representative pointed out that all payments made by the tobacco companies, under the deal, would be tax deductible, costing the federal treasury some $125 billion. "In terms of holding this industry accountable, it's a free ride," she said.

Some thought that the government should simply stay out of the whole business. "Don't you think there are enough regulations out there?" asked Representative Henry Bonilla of Texas. He questioned whether it was wise "to substitute the federal government for the responsibility of a mother and a father to stop kids from smoking."

And while many state attorneys general had been party to the deal, others opposed it. Minnesota attorney general Hubert H. Humphrey III, who had declined the sign the pact, prepared to move forward with a separate trial against the tobacco companies. He believed that new evidence, including thousands of internal industry documents, could produce a much bigger settlement than his colleagues had negotiated.

Others prepared to mount constitutional challenges to the agreement, should it be approved by Congress. Some legal experts believed that the pact's provisions forcing settlement of existing class-action lawsuits and restricting future rights of smokers to sue violated constitutional rights to due process. The pact's limits on advertising might violate free-speech protections. Finally, the pact would override some state laws, for example, those governing retail licensing, potentially violating states' rights. The agreement was a "constitutional minefield," commented the president of the Association of Trial Lawyers of America.

But the tobacco industry and the state attorneys general vigorously defended the agreement. Massachusetts attorney general Scott Harshbarger said, "I am baffled by [the] criticism. . . . [Under the negotiated settlement], the FDA will for the first time have the money, the resources, and the power to control fully the nature and marketing of tobacco." And a representative of the tobacco industry argued, "People should look upon the settlement as a whole package. They should be aware of the enormous compromises made by the industry which will deliver significant progress in public health, especially in the area of reducing smoking by people who are underage."

Before going into effect, the settlement had to pass the scrutiny of several federal agencies including the Department of Health and Human Services, the Justice Department, and the Agriculture Department. It required presidential approval. And, of course, it had to be approved by Congress. The future of the tobacco deal was all but certain.

315

Post–Lawrence–Weber:
Business and Society,
Ninth Edition

Case Study: The Tobacco
Deal

© The McGraw–Hill
Companies, 1999

Discussion Questions

1. Who were the key stakeholders involved in, or affected by, the negotiations for a tobacco deal, and what were their central interests? To what degree were the interests of the various stakeholders met by the negotiated settlement?

2. Should the FDA regulate tobacco? What are the key arguments for and against involvement of the FDA in restricting or banning the sale or promotion of tobacco products?

3. What mechanisms of political influence had the tobacco industry historically used? Do you believe that the tobacco industry influenced the public policy process legitimately, or did it have too much influence?

4. Do you think it was ethical for the tobacco industry to continue to market cigarettes, even after evidence emerged that smoking caused lung cancer and other illnesses? Why or why not? In your answer, please refer to the three main methods of ethical analysis: utilitarianism, rights, and justice.

5. Do you support the tobacco deal? Why or why not? If not, what changes in the agreement, if any, would lead you to support it?

Post−Lawrence−Weber:
Business and Society,
Ninth Edition

Case Study: The Spotted
Owl, the Forest Products
Industry, and the Public
Policy

Case Study:
The Spotted Owl,
The Forest Products Industry,
and the
Public Policy Process

On April 2, 1993, an extraordinary day-long conference opened at the Portland Convention Center in Portland, Oregon. Convened and chaired by President Bill Clinton, the conference was designed—as Clinton had promised during his campaign—to bring together key parties to a long-running dispute over protection of the threatened spotted owl and the logging of old-growth forest in the Pacific Northwest. The conference represented a key, early test of Clinton's position that economic growth and environmental protection are compatible and of his administration's ability to solve difficult problems through open, multiparty discussions.

Note: This is an edited version of a case presented at the North American Case Research Association (NACRA) annual meeting, New Orleans, Louisiana, November 2, 1994: Anne T. Lawrence, "The Forest Conference: The Pacific Northwest Forest Products Industry, the Spotted Owl, and the Public Policy Process." The case is based on articles appearing in the *New York Times, Washington Post, Seattle Post-Intelligencer,* and other daily newspapers. A full account of the events leading up to the Forest Conference may be found in William Dietrich, *The Final Forest: The Battle for the Last Great Trees of the Pacific Northwest* (New York: Penguin Books, 1992); an analysis of the public policy aspects of the spotted owl controversy may be found in Steven Lewis Yaffee, *The Wisdom of the Spotted Owl: Policy Lessons for a New Century* (Washington, D.C.: Island Press, 1994).

Post–Lawrence–Weber:
Business and Society,
Ninth Edition

Case Study: The Spotted
Owl, the Forest Products
Industry, and the Public
Policy

© The McGraw–Hill
Companies, 1999

The importance of the event was underscored by the many top government officials in attendance, including the vice president; the secretaries of Commerce, Labor, Agriculture, and the Interior; the administrator of the Environmental Protection Agency; and the governors of the states of Oregon, Washington, California, Idaho, and Alaska. Arrayed at three roundtables were some 50 invited speakers—scientists, industry officials, timber workers, and environmentalists—many of them longtime antagonists in the controversy.

In addition to the hundreds of observers in the convention center itself, perhaps thousands more rallied noisily outside, where industry groups passed out tree seedlings, environmentalists demonstrated to rock music, and loggers rumbled down the street in their trucks. Although some expressed apprehension about the potentially volatile mixture of groups gathered face to face, expectations ran high that the conference might break the gridlock that had gripped the Pacific Northwest since the late 1980s.

The Spotted Owl and Old-Growth Forest

At the center of the controversy was the survival of a reclusive bird that few present at the conference had ever seen: the northern spotted owl. This small, brown and white predator—just 22 ounces when full-grown—lives mainly in old-growth forests west of the Cascade Mountains from British Columbia to Northern California. As once vast, ancient forests were logged from the Pacific Northwest, the spotted owl's habitat declined; by 1993, only about 3,600 breeding pairs of spotted owls remained, scientists estimated.

The survival of the northern spotted owl is closely linked with the fate of the Pacific Northwest's old-growth forest. Old-growth forest is one in which trees are at least 150 to 200 years old. The majestic stands of old growth in the Pacific Northwest are typically dominated by mature Douglas fir and coastal redwood, often spanning 15 feet in diameter at the base and towering as high as 300 feet. Below these "climax" species grow smaller trees, creating a dense, multilayered canopy in which a great diversity of plant and animal species thrives.

Old-growth forest provides an ideal habitat for the northern spotted owl. The bird typically nests in snags, trees with broken tops. Fallen, decaying logs on the forest floor support abundant prey; and the multilayered canopy protects the spotted owl from extreme temperatures and from its own predators such as the goshawk and the great horned owl. Because of its close association with old-growth forest, ecologists refer to the northern spotted owl as an *indicator species,* meaning that its survival is a kind of warning light for the survival of the old-growth ecosystem as a whole and for numerous less well-known species of plants and animals that flourish there.

The Forest Products Industry

The old-growth forest on which the spotted owl depends is also a critical resource to a large and powerful industry: the Pacific Northwest forest products industry.

When pioneers first settled the Pacific Northwest in the mid-1800s, somewhere between 17 and 19 million acres of old-growth forest covered the landscape. Much of this land was eventually accumulated by big timber companies such as Weyerhaeuser, Georgia-Pacific, Boise-Cascade, and International Paper, and by holding companies such as railroads and insurance firms.

Throughout the twentieth century and accelerating in the postwar years, old-growth forests were harvested for their high-quality wood. By the 1980s, somewhere between 80 and 90 percent of the ancient forest had been logged. Virtually all privately owned timber, and most on state-owned lands, had been cut; fully 86 percent of remaining spotted owl habitat was in federally owned national forests and 8 percent on the national parks.

318

Post–Lawrence–Weber:
Business and Society,
Ninth Edition

Case Study: The Spotted
Owl, the Forest Products
Industry, and the Public
Policy

© The McGraw–Hill
Companies, 1999

Just a few patches of private old growth remained, including some owned by Plum Creek Timber Company, a firm divested by Burlington Northern Railroad during a reorganization in the late 1980s.

Beginning in the 1960s, many of the bigger timber companies, led by Weyerhaeuser, began a transition to *managed forestry,* the practice of growing genetically superior seedlings on massive tree farms carved from previously clear-cut forest. These firms introduced mechanical harvesting machines and developed new, high-tech mills designed to process the much smaller second-growth logs. They also pursued strategies of vertical integration, building or acquiring facilities for making pulp and paper and manufactured wood products.

A second segment of the forest products industry consisted of independent sawmills and manufacturers that processed old-growth logs and fashioned them into various finished wood products. In the early years, the independents were supplied mainly by private landowners. Later, as private reserves were exhausted, they turned to national forests as their main source of old-growth logs. Although prohibited from selling timber from *national parks,* the U.S. Forest Service was permitted—in fact, encouraged—to sell timber from *national forests,* since these sales provided revenue to the U.S. Treasury. Although some independents switched to processing second-growth timber, capital costs of this transition were high, and many remained dependent on federal old growth for their timber supplies.

The Environmentalists' Campaign to Protect the Ancient Forest

Environmentalists seeking to preserve remaining ancient forests were quick to seize on the potential value of the spotted owl. "The northern spotted owl is the wildlife species of choice to act as a surrogate for old growth protection," one environmentalist observed. "I've often thought that thank goodness the spotted owl evolved in the Northwest, because if it hadn't, we'd have to genetically engineer it."

In 1986, environmentalists petitioned the Department of the Interior to list the spotted owl as an endangered species.[1] The petition was initially refused, but in 1990 the department reversed its position, listing the spotted owl as threatened.

In May 1991, in response to further lawsuits brought by environmentalists, U.S. District Court Judge William Dwyer ruled that the evidence revealed "a deliberate and systematic refusal by the [U.S.] Forest Service and the Fish and Wildlife Service to comply with the laws protecting wildlife." Judge Dwyer issued an injunction blocking timber sales in spotted owl habitat in 17 national forests in Washington, Oregon, and Northern California until the Forest Service could develop an acceptable plan for protecting the threatened species.

Impact on the Economy of the Pacific Northwest

The injunction effectively brought federal timber sales to a halt. In 1992, only 0.7 million board feet of timber were sold from national forest lands in the Pacific Northwest (down from a peak of 5 *billion* board feet during the peak year of 1987). (A board foot is equal to one foot square by one inch thick; a typical single-family house uses about 10,000 board feet of lumber.)

[1]The Endangered Species Act (ESA) is the most recent of a series of laws protecting wildlife dating back to 1890. Enacted in 1973, the ESA aims to conserve species of animals and plants whose survival is endangered or threatened. The government is required to make a list of such species and to designate critical habitat. Federal agencies must develop programs to conserve listed species and must not do anything that would destroy or modify critical habitat. One of the most important features of the ESA is that, once a species is listed, economic factors may not be considered in deciding what action to take—or not to take. In their lawsuits, environmentalists also relied on the National Forest Management Act of 1976, which requires that national forests be managed as total ecosystems.

Post–Lawrence–Weber:
Business and Society,
Ninth Edition

Case Study: The Spotted
Owl, the Forest Products
Industry, and the Public
Policy

© The McGraw–Hill
Companies, 1999

The consequences for the rural economy in many areas of the Pacific Northwest were devastating. By 1993, as many as 135 mills had closed, pushing unemployment up to 25 percent in some small communities. Cutters, loggers, truck drivers, and those in businesses serving them were thrown out of work. Tax receipts declined, affecting social services; the incidence of family problems, alcoholism, and other social problems increased. The intense frustration felt by many in rural Washington and Oregon was reflected in such slogans as "Support your local spotted owl—from a rope" and "Save a logger, shoot an owl."

President Clinton appeared fully aware of the intense controversy that had preceded the Forest Conference as he opened the event—and of the difficulty of reaching a resolution. "The process we begin today will not be easy," he observed. "Its outcome cannot possibly make everyone happy. Perhaps it won't make anyone completely happy. But the worst thing we can do is nothing."

Testimony before the Forest Conference, April 2, 1993[2]

Participants were seated at three large roundtables. As the conference proceeded, each roundtable was addressed in turn. Participants were asked to make a three-minute statement; the table was then opened for questions and discussion among those seated at the table and officials in attendance.

The First Roundtable

The first roundtable was designed to give, in President Clinton's words, a "diverse, but . . . representative group of people in the Pacific Northwest the chance to say what they have seen or experienced personally about the impact of the present set of conditions."

Diana Wales, attorney (family law), Roseburg, Oregon

"Historically, federal forests in the Northwest have been managed essentially as though they were an inexhaustible raw material stockpile. The result is an ecosystem on the verge of collapse. It strikes me that past policies have been like buying a car and then never changing the oil, checking the water, or replacing the tires. Sooner or later, there's going to be a major problem.

"The environmental protection laws we have, such as the Endangered Species Act, are like the red idiot lights going on simultaneous with something terrible happening to your car. The spotted owl, marbled murrelet, and numerous wild fish stocks now at risk are the equivalent of all the lights coming on at once.

"When that happens, it's too late to think about a tune-up. You simply have to stop. And the answer is not disconnecting the idiot lights, just as the answer to the forest management dilemma is not suspending or disobeying the laws that let us know we have a serious problem. . . .

"The bottom line is that the 'who' most affected by environmental decisions of this decade will be the grandchildren of our grandchildren. Difficult as it may be, it is vital that all of our vision extends significantly beyond our own lifetimes. We must also recognize that we are simply a part of and dependent upon an ecosystem we do not fully comprehend, but are systematically destroying."

Ken Marson, Marson & Marson Lumber Company

"I'm speaking here on behalf of 9,000 lumber dealers, . . . the lumber prices have gone up substantially since last October, nearly have doubled, and a $5,000 increase or more

[2]The balance of this case consists of edited excerpts from the verbatim transcript of the Forest Conference, held at the Portland Convention Center, Portland, Oregon, April 2, 1993. Not all speakers are included; however, the speakers represented here appear in the same order in which they spoke at the conference. The original transcript runs 123 pages, single spaced, and is available from the library of the University of Oregon, Eugene, Oregon.

Post–Lawrence–Weber:
Business and Society,
Ninth Edition

Case Study: The Spotted
Owl, the Forest Products
Industry, and the Public
Policy

in the cost of a house eliminates approximately 127,000 people from the housing market every year. In many cases, the increases in prices have gone up much more substantially than just $5,000.

"Housing . . . is an essential component of the economic development and growth of this country, and we're really concerned that we're starting to see areas of the country have a slowdown in housing because the builders can't afford it. . . . I really think lumber is truly the most compatible building material we have with the environment. Aluminum, steel, even masonry, they're never going to be renewable."

Buzz Eades, Eades Forest Products

"I cut trees for a living, just like my father did before me, and my grandfather. I represent a family that has been working actively in the logging and lumbering business for almost 200 years.

"Two hundred years is a long time. . . . That's how long it takes one of these trees to reach that point we call old growth. I like to think that some of those trees that started life when my ancestor first worked in the timber might be old growth someday, and the trees I am so careful to leave might be my grandchildren's old growth. . . . We're getting old growth, some every day."

Bill Arthur, Sierra Club

"It's not an accident that this conference is taking place on the edge of the Pacific Ocean. We have cut our way west from the Atlantic to the Pacific. It took a little bit over a generation to wipe out the great woods of Wisconsin and Michigan and for the logging to move west.

"We are blessed with bigger, larger, vaster forests here in the Northwest. It took a couple of generations to eliminate 90 percent of the once vast ancient forests that we have here. We have only 10 percent left. We're at the edge of the Pacific Ocean, and the timber frontier is over. We have to learn to protect and work with and revive what we have.

"Balance is important, and that's something that we should strive for. But balance means saving the 10 percent we have left. . . . We don't hunt buffalo, we no longer kill whales, and we can't sacrifice the last 10 percent of a remaining ancient forest for the future."

Nat Bingham, commercial fisherman

"This problem is more than just spotted owls. . . . There is another industry that is dependent on a healthy forest, the salmon fishing industry. . . . If we don't do something right now to protect the remaining habitats, we're going to see listings of salmon that will be of an order of magnitude under the Endangered Species Act that will make the spotted owl situation pale by comparison. I don't think that's something any of us want to see happen."

Meca Wawona, New Growth Forestry

"I founded New Growth Forest in 1976 because I was so appalled at the destruction of the magnificent redwood forests in northern California. . . . I thought then that . . . if we figured out a way to make a second-growth forestry sustainable, that would extend the nation's wood supply. So we started the company with a vision of helping small, private landowners practice sustainable forestry.

"Sustainable forestry is guided by natural selection and biological criteria, not short-term profiteering. . . . We've discovered over the years that we're up against a number of

Post–Lawrence–Weber:
Business and Society,
Ninth Edition

Case Study: The Spotted
Owl, the Forest Products
Industry, and the Public
Policy

© The McGraw–Hill
Companies, 1999

economic disincentives. For example, sustainable forestry requires more skills and time in the woods to get the wood out. This means it's more job-intensive, so there's more costs. Since the majority of logging operations on corporate timberlands are quick and dirty extractions, the playing field for sustainable forestry is not level. . . . Wood is simply too cheap, even at today's prices, to afford the practice of sustainable forestry."

John Hampton, Willamina Lumber Company
"I . . . have experience in second-growth forests. . . . Our company hasn't cut an old-growth log since 1950. We have high technology. . . . The cost of modern technology is extraordinary. It takes a leap of faith, under these conditions, to invest the kind of money that one does to modernize a plant. Last year, at our Tillamook Lumber Company plant alone, we invested 5 million private dollars in the renovation of that plant, which was in pretty good shape before that, to get the highest value and quality and volume out of those second-growth logs. It's laser technology; it's scanning; it's computerized positioning, all run by skilled workers who make [an average wage of] $39,000 a year."

Larry Mason, Western Commercial Forest Action Committee
"I can speak as an individual who owned a small sawmill. . . . Our mill was an old-growth mill. The reason it was an old-growth mill was because the only available timber supply that was accessible to us was off of federal lands, and the federal lands where I live, on the Olympic Peninsula [in Washington], are managed on a 100-year rotation, much longer than on some [privately owned land]. And we were 50 years into that rotation. . . . What would have happened . . . was a gradually declining volume of old-growth timber access and a gradually increasing volume of second growth. And we built our mill to make that transition.

"But you don't make those transitions overnight when your timber supply is disrupted by a court injunction. You don't make those transitions overnight when your American dream has turned into a nightmare."

Unidentified participant
"Stop looking at it as a little loaf of bread that can be neatly sliced and passed out to special interest groups, one piece for the spotted owl, one piece for the salmon, one piece for the marbled murrelet, and one piece for the people. That doesn't work. That's like drawing lines on maps with arbitrary disregard for what's really best for the forest.

"How about taking a step back and concentrating on overall forest health? How do the forest ecosystems work best? . . . That's a comprehensive approach that will take us to a road where the future will be more stable."

Phyllis Strauger, mayor of Hoquiam, Washington
"This conference is too late for my city. My city got hit on November 12th with the closure of a three-unit mill, and our unemployment rate is now 19.5 percent and climbing. We expect it to go over 20 percent."

Margaret Powell, Hoopa Valley Indian Tribe
"I . . . serve as a member of the tribe's Integrated Resources Management Committee. It seems ironic that we are required to manage within the parameters of a complex federal legal and regulatory management scheme that [is] intended to protect the environment when, in reality, we have practiced the principles of conservation for thousands of years. In fact, even before the present-day environmental regulations on timber and related de-

Post–Lawrence–Weber:
Business and Society,
Ninth Edition

Case Study: The Spotted
Owl, the Forest Products
Industry, and the Public
Policy

© The McGraw-Hill
Companies, 1999

velopment, our tribe imposed similar restrictions on ourselves as a matter of tribal law. . . .
I respectfully submit that Indian tribes such as Hoopa may serve as useful models of the
problems confronting this conference."

The Second Roundtable

The second roundtable was designed, President Clinton stated, to present "the range of
scientific opinions about where we are and where we might go."

John Gordon, Yale University

"Ecosystem management, based on sound integrated knowledge of the whole forest, allows us to do many things at the same time, rather than saving one or two species at a
time, and has the potential, I think, to remedy this old-growth deficit.

"It focuses on maintaining the health and productivity of the entire forest asset,
rather than on isolating parts of processes. But it's important to recognize that it will probably not anywhere result in the optimization of yield of any single resource commodity
or species. . . .

"When we talk about vision, foresters and other professionals can't do a good job
unless we have a clear idea of what our clients want. . . . What does society want for and
from their forests? How do they want to make a living? How do they want the Pacific
Northwest to look? How much assurance do they want that endangered species will survive and flourish?"

Lorin Hicks, Plum Creek Timber Company

"We are applying new forestry techniques to spotted owl habitat. For example, at the Frost
Meadows site on the east side of the Cascades in Washington, I have worked with our
foresters to design a timber sale that would maintain spotted owl habitat after harvest. We
harvested 55 percent of merchantable timber in this unit, while retaining 80 percent of the
trees and maintaining functional old-growth habitat characteristics such as snags, large
down-logs, and healthy green trees representative of the original stands. Our radio tracking data revealed that owls continue using the Frost Meadows unit following the harvest."

Charles Meslow, U.S. Department of the Interior, Fish and Wildlife Service

"During the course of developing a recovery plan for the northern spotted owl, biologists
determined that some 480 other species of plants and animals were importantly associated with old forests. The recovery team identified 36 other species of birds associated
with old forests, 22 species of mammals, 17 amphibians, 43 mollusks.

"In addition, more than 200 stocks of fish are considered at risk within the range of
the owl. Thus, the northern spotted owl and marbled murrelet are perhaps only the tip of
the iceberg. At least 480 other species may be following in their wake."

Jerry Franklin, University of Washington

"What I've been trying to do during the last decade is . . . to try to produce approaches
that do a better job of integrating both ecological and economic values. That's fundamentally what new forestry is all about. . . . We can, with the new forestry, grow struc-
turally complex forests. We probably can grow spotted owl habitat. But we do not know,
and it's unlikely we're going to know anytime soon, how to grow old-growth forest, because the complexity of these systems is beyond imagination."

Unidentified participant

"My understanding is that folks who deal in mediation say that sometimes when you're
dealing with a can of worms, the trick is to open a larger can of worms. Maybe that's
what we need to do with this issue, is start taking the big picture, take our focus off the
remaining old growth and really start dealing with the forest landscape."

Post–Lawrence–Weber:
Business and Society,
Ninth Edition

Case Study: The Spotted
Owl, the Forest Products
Industry, and the Public
Policy

© The McGraw–Hill
Companies, 1999

Louise Fortman, University of California, Berkeley

"We need community-initiated and locality-based planning and management units that make ecological sense and social sense. Locally based management will involve local people and others of their choosing in gathering scientific evidence about local social and economic conditions and about local ecosystems. It will involve community members and others meeting to establish community goals and planning and implementing actions to achieve them. . . .

"Two examples from Northern California: the Plumas Corporation in Plumas County has organized an ecosystem restoration and is working on an economic transition strategy. Trinity Alps Botanicals produces nontimber forest products for export and is developing a forest stewardship program. . . .

"I think that the success of . . . community-based experiments in change tell us that facilitating local process is going to be the most important product of this conference."

Bob Lee, University of Washington

"We're moving into a process which looks an awful lot like what happened to the inner city. We're seeing the collapse of families, disintegration of families, disintegration of communities, loss of morale, homelessness, stranded elderly people, people whose lives are in disarray because of substance abuse. It's a very difficult situation."

Ed Whitelaw, University of Oregon

"Timber [is] no longer driving the Northwest economies. . . . We have accumulating evidence . . . that many of those jobs—including jobs in manufacturing that are paying substantially higher than the timber industry is paying—many of those jobs are quite sensitive to the environmental amenities here in the Northwest."

The Third Roundtable

The third roundtable was designed, President Clinton said, "to lay out some very specific suggestions about what we ought to do."

Julie Norman, Headwaters

"We must disturb no more of the last remaining centers of biodiversity. These are the refuges and the seed sources for tomorrow's forests, tomorrow's wildlife, and tomorrow's economy. Therefore, we must establish a permanent forest and watershed reserve system based on the best scientific knowledge.

"We must also establish interim protection for additional areas to preserve our options, while thorough scientific studies are completed. All suitable habitat for threatened species, all roadless areas, key watersheds for salmon, riparian zones, and large blocs of intact forest must serve as our scientific controls during this research period."

Unidentified Participant

"When I come to this issue of [log] exports, I always feel there's something fundamentally wrong if we're hauling items of that magnitude and weight across the Pacific."

Jim Geisinger, Northwest Forest Association

"The first step is to break the legal gridlock that has essentially kept our federal forest agencies from selling any timber during the last two years. If we don't reinstate some federal timber sale program this year, our industry is going to be forced to lay off thousands of workers and curtail production very significantly. Some type of interim ecosystem protection and timber production plan is essential to try to get us from where we are today to when Congress can act on a long-term solution. The alternative is to do nothing and experience economic catastrophe in the Pacific Northwest. . . ."

324

Post–Lawrence–Weber:
Business and Society,
Ninth Edition

Case Study: The Spotted
Owl, the Forest Products
Industry, and the Public
Policy

© The McGraw–Hill
Companies, 1999

"I want to make one final comment about the allegation that . . . only 10 percent is left. . . . [T]he Forest Service, the Bureau of Land Management, and the National Park Service say that they have about eight million acres of old-growth forest on their ownerships today. Mathematics would tell you then that at some point in time there was 80 million acres of old-growth in existence. Yet I have to tell you there's only 42 million acres of commercial forest in all of Washington and Oregon. So we don't buy that figure."

Gus Kostopulos, Woodnet

"Woodnet is a nonprofit organization . . . it's a network of over 300 very independent wood products manufacturers. . . . Our goal is to get our members to work together in loosely formed networks. They are sometimes called flexible manufacturing networks, and they engage in activities that, by their nature, can be done better in larger groups than they can undertake on their own. It gives them economies of scale that they otherwise wouldn't have."

Roslyn Heffner, vocational counselor

"I found that these workers [unemployed loggers and millworkers] were rugged individuals and proud of their skills and livelihood. . . . [I]n my professional opinion, . . . formal schooling—I'm going to get some flak for this—even in a community college setting does not work well with this group of people. They're not used to sitting in a classroom, and they haven't done it in years. . . . So that in my opinion, [we should be] giving them on-the-job training, even in a new skill, but placing them at the work-site, giving lots of incentives, including targeted jobs [and] tax credit for the employer."

Rich Nafziger, deputy insurance commissioner, State of Washington

"[W]e must adjust our trade policies. Landowners cannot be expected to stop exporting logs when our trading partners put up barriers to finished products but not to raw logs."

Charles W. Bingham, Weyerhaeuser Corporation

"Weyerhaeuser [has] been in business for 93 years. I think if there's one thing that we have learned, it is that we must manage large-scale change. . . . And I would suggest—and this is the big dilemma we're all engaged in—we're going to have to ride the bicycle here for a while, while we repair the tire. We can't just throw everybody out of work."

Andy Kerr, Oregon Natural Resources

"[E]nvironmentalists such as myself were very wary about this event today because, in a situation like this, all the parties are often called upon to compromise a little and give and take something like that, like a labor-management negotiation, and then everybody splits the difference and says there's a deal. But when so little of the virgin forest is left—that 10 percent—environmentalists are not in a position to compromise that, compromise the forest any further . . . the forest has been compromised all it can stand.

"[P]eople do make money off of forests without cutting them down. My organization has appealed a few timber sales in its day, and one of the timber sales that we appealed is a sale where we tried to show the Forest Service that . . . the annual harvest of gourmet mushrooms from that stand of trees each year was worth more than the standing value of the timber."

Irv Fletcher, Oregon AFL-CIO

"We . . . need . . . adequate assistance for displaced workers . . . both wood products workers and those workers that are going to be displaced because of the wood products jobs that are gone. . . . [W]e also need some guaranteed level in place of the timber receipts . . . [and we need] a release of timber now."

Post–Lawrence–Weber:
Business and Society,
Ninth Edition

Case Study: The Spotted
Owl, the Forest Products
Industry, and the Public
Policy

© The McGraw–Hill
Companies, 1999

Bob Dopplet, Pacific Rivers Council
"[Programs to protect and restore rivers will create] jobs back up in the woods doing things that many of the rural community people have done in the past, like use bulldozers and excavators to treat road systems."

Jack Ward Thomas, U.S. Department of Agriculture Forest Service
"[T]he first paragraph in the Endangered Species Act says it's not the species that's listed, it's the ecosystem on which it depends. . . . [I]t appears, to me at least, that we have a de facto policy of biodiversity protection, particularly for national forest lands. It becomes an overriding objective."

Walter Minnick, TJ International
"We've worked very hard on these reconstituted wood products. This is an example. This is a product that is made out of laminated veneer lumber. . . . [T]he wood fiber can come out of second-growth trees and, because it's got a very high labor content, probably creates twice as many jobs as sawing a round log into rectangular lumber. . . . Essentially, what we need the government to do is to get out of the way, let the market system work, because we don't know whether to build another plant here or to go to Canada or even whether we should be hiring folk for a month from now, because we can't be assured that our veneer supplies are going to have the raw material we're going to need. . . .

"[T]here is a pretty straightforward and simple answer conceptually. . . . [W]e've got to set aside . . . some forest preserves. . . . We've got to surround these areas with some buffer areas that are managed with Jerry Franklin's new forestry. . . . Then, we've got to release the balance—and some of it's old growth—into the commercial timber base."

Jim Coates, International Woodworkers of America
"I represent the voice of those who haven't been heard through most of this, and that's the workers—those of the unemployed. . . . I hear Andy and some of the other talking about the beauty of the forest. When I go into the beauty of the forest in the Capital Forest and in the Park Service and in the rock quarries, we have people living there. They have no home; they have no water; they have no power. If I was to divulge where these people were, they wouldn't have their children either."

Ted Strong, Columbia River Inter-Tribal Fish Commission
"In actuality, tomorrow we go out and build coalitions across all ideological lines. We unite as a family, and we begin to do the work that lets us leave behind a legacy of love for our natural resources, to be enjoyed in perpetuity by all humans yet to walk this earth."

Bill Clinton, President of the United States
"One of the things that has come out of this meeting to me, loud and clear, is that you want us to try to break the paralysis that presently controls the situation—to move and to act. I hope that, as we leave here, we are more committed to working together to move forward than perhaps we were when we came. . . .

"I intend to direct the cabinet and the entire administration to begin to work immediately to craft a balanced, a comprehensive, a long-term policy; and I will direct the cabinet to report back to me within 60 days to have a plan to end this stalemate."

Post–Lawrence–Weber:
Business and Society,
Ninth Edition

Case Study: The Spotted
Owl, the Forest Products
Industry, and the Public
Policy

© The McGraw–Hill
Companies, 1999

Discussion Questions

1. Conduct a stakeholder analysis of this case. Who are the primary and secondary stakeholders, and what are the major concerns of each? Draw a stakeholder map, showing the major lines of expected coalition formation.

2. If you were a member of the interagency task force assembled by the president to devise a solution to this problem, what *goals* or *principles* would you establish to guide development of a plan?

3. What key ideas mentioned by participants in the conference provide a basis for an integrative solution to the controversy faced by public policymakers in this case—a solution that would address both economic and ecological concerns? Do you support these ideas? Why or why not?

4. The Endangered Species Act has been criticized for being too extreme and for not permitting policymakers to balance ecological and economic considerations. Do you agree? If so, in your opinion, what other approach to species protection would work better?

Post–Lawrence–Weber:
Business and Society,
Ninth Edition

Case Study: Doing
Business in the
Maquiladoras: A
Shareholder Challenge

© The McGraw–Hill
Companies, 1999

Case Study:
Doing Business in the
Maquiladoras:
A Shareholder Challenge

In the early 1990s, the Coalition for Justice in the Maquiladoras, an international association of more than 60 environmental, religious, community, labor, women's, and Latino organizations, emerged as an important shareholder activist group. The coalition's goal was to convince U.S. multinational corporations to adopt socially responsible business practices in their factories along the northern Mexican border. Many large U.S. corporations had plants in this region, including AlliedSignal, Chrysler, Du Pont, Eastman Kodak, IBM, and Xerox. Both the region and the factories in the Mexican border area were known as the *Maquiladoras*.

Specifically, the coalition urged the adoption of standards of conduct for firms operating in the Maquiladoras region. These standards emphasized responsible practices for hazardous-waste handling, environmental protection, worker health and safety, fair employment practices, and a concern for the impact of the Maquiladoras factories on the surrounding communities. These standards were addressed in a number of social activist shareholder resolutions voted on by company stockholders on annual proxy ballots or at companies' annual stockholder meetings. The resolutions called for comprehensive investigation of companies' Maquiladoras operations, public reporting of the findings of the investigations, and correction of unacceptable company practices if discovered. "We want

Post–Lawrence–Weber:
Business and Society,
Ninth Edition

Case Study: Doing
Business in the
Maquiladoras: A
Shareholder Challenge

© The McGraw–Hill
Companies, 1999

to send a message into corporate boardrooms," explained Sister Susan Mika, president of the Benedictine Sisters and of the Coalition for Justice in the Maquiladoras. "Moral behavior knows no borders. What is wrong in the United States is wrong in Mexico, too."[1]

Economic and Social Conditions along the Border

The Maquiladoras development represents the fruits of a Mexican government program begun in 1965. To attract capital investment and address high unemployment in the northern border towns, the Mexican government offered lucrative incentives such as preferential tariffs and tax breaks for foreign firms operating plants there. Maquiladoras factories would pay no tariffs on materials and semifinished products imported into Mexico. When Maquiladoras plants shipped finished products out of Mexico, they would pay tariffs only on the value added in Mexico, not on the value of the entire product. Since the 1980s, companies have flooded to this region, establishing factories that produced a variety of goods. By 1996, more than 2,350 factories were located along the northern Mexican border, over 50 percent of them owned by U.S. corporations or part of a U.S.– Mexican joint venture. These plants produced electronic goods, auto parts, chemicals, furniture, machinery, and clothing and employed nearly 750,000 workers.[2]

The Mexican government saw the development project as an economic success. In 1992, it is estimated that the Maquiladoras industries contributed $4.74 billion in value-added worth to the products manufactured or assembled in these factories. The Maquiladoras region became identified as an attractive site for manufacturing facilities, particularly for companies whose products required labor-intensive assembly. Various businesses associated with the construction and maintenance of manufacturing plants—raw materials suppliers, eateries, grocery stores, and so on—provided an additional boost to the region's economy. In addition to the employment of more than a half million people, billions of dollars of investment capital gave the Mexican government a stronger bargaining position when negotiating trade agreements with the United States, Canada, and other trade partners.

Some believed that the benefits of the Maquiladoras development did not justify the costs incurred by Mexican workers, local communities, and the natural environment, however. Timothy Smith, executive director of the Interfaith Center on Corporate Responsibility explained,

> We find a range of corporate behavior in the Maquiladoras . . . from the irresponsible polluter and exploiter of labor to companies which are working to live up to standards of fairness. Though many company and plant officials proudly point to their high standards for wages, health and safety, and environment, until now [1991] most companies seem to be involved in a race to the bottom.

Social watchdog organizations documented abhorrent conditions in the Maquiladoras area. For example, contamination of the water supply affected both U.S. and Mexican

---

[1] All quotations are from "Environmental, Religious and Labor Organizations Promote Corporate Social Responsibility in the Maquiladora Industry," *The Corporate Examiner* 20, no. 1 (1991), pp. 1–8.

[2] Pamela Varley, Peter DeSimone, and Heidi Welsh, "U.S. Business in Mexico," IRRC Social Issue Service, 1997 Background Report D, January 22, 1997.

Post–Lawrence–Weber:
Business and Society,
Ninth Edition

Case Study: Doing
Business in the
Maquiladoras: A
Shareholder Challenge

© The McGraw-Hill
Companies, 1999

residents. Raw sewage from plants located in Mexicali, Mexico, was dumped into the New River, a waterway extending 120 miles into California. In the early 1990s, more than 20 viruses and bacteria were identified in the river along with over 100 industrial chemicals. People in San Elizario, Texas, were at risk of exposure to hepatitis. Ninety percent of 30-year-olds in this border town had contracted the disease. On the Mexican side of the border, the 85,000 residents of the town of Juarez had no running water and stored their water supply in 55-gallon drums that previously contained dangerous chemical compounds used at Maquiladoras plants. As little as 20 percent of the toxic wastes generated by Maquiladoras plants were returned to the United States for proper disposal as required by U.S. and Mexican law.[3]

The Coalition for Justice in the Maquiladoras charged that multinational corporate owners of Maquiladoras factories had failed to improve the living standards of their workers, often migrants from the inland regions of Mexico. According to a 1997 report, the average hourly wage for Maquiladoras workers was $.74 per hour. It would take a Maquiladoras worker more than 2 hours to earn enough to purchase a dozen eggs, 3 hours for a chicken, and nearly 12 hours to buy a box of 30 diapers![4]

Hazardous working conditions in Maquiladoras plants were blamed for a 300 percent increase in the annual low birth weight of babies born to female workers in the early 1990s. Medical records showed that children of mothers who worked at an electronics plant were more vulnerable to being born mentally retarded than other Mexican children. Those women were exposed to highly toxic polychlorinated biphenyl (PCB) compounds for long hours, often reaching into deep vats of the chemicals wearing only rubber gloves for protection.

Since Maquiladoras plants paid virtually no taxes in Mexico, local governments did not receive sufficient revenue from the corporations to defray the costs for city roads, sewer systems, utility lines, and other public services incurred from the plants' operations. Corporations operating Maquiladoras were accused of ignoring the deteriorating public services in border towns from Matamoros, Mexico (near Brownsville, Texas) to Tijuana (across the border from San Diego, California). Although plants in the region had electricity, water, sewage disposal, and green grass, only a short distance away, residents in nearby towns had, at best, limited access to such basic services and amenities. The U.S. National Toxics Campaign conducted research in the early 1990s to investigate accusations of careless or illegal transportation or disposal of hazardous waste by-products by the Maquiladoras factories. The investigation found a "clear and consistent pattern . . . of widespread and serious contamination [of the Maquiladoras region] by U.S.-owned firms. They are turning the border into a 2,000-mile long Love Canal [an area in New York contaminated by long-term underground disposal of toxic wastes]."

Social Issues Enter Corporate Boardrooms

In 1990 the Coalition for Justice initiated the Maquiladoras campaign by sponsoring social responsibility shareholder resolutions. These resolutions called on 12 U.S. corporations to describe in detail their environmental practices, health and safety standards, and

[3]Roberto A. Sanchez, "In the Maquiladora Industry, Health Is Also at Risk: Maquiladora Masquerade," *Business Mexico* 3, no. 1 (1993), pp. 13 – 15; and "A Maquiladora Case Study: Hazardous Waste Issues," *IRRC News for Investors*, November 1994, pp. 20 – 23.
[4]"Maquiladora Worker Demands Living Wage," *Cross Border Connection*, October 1996, http:www.pctvi.com/laamn/maquiladora.html.

workers' standard of living in and around their Maquiladoras plants. Ten companies, including AT&T, Ford Motor, Johnson & Johnson, and PepsiCo, agreed to provide the information or allow inspection of their facilities by interested investors. The shareholder resolutions were then withdrawn.

The campaign escalated a year later when the coalition proposed that corporations operating in the Maquiladoras region adopt the Maquiladora Standards of Conduct. These standards called for companies operating Maquiladoras plants to comply with Mexican and U.S. environmental regulations; to observe fundamental workers' rights, including fair wages, a safe and healthy workplace, reasonable hours of work, and decent living conditions; and to support community public service needs, including a commitment to community economic development. The filing of shareholder resolutions targeting Maquiladoras operations continued throughout the 1990s. The coalition's philosophy and an excerpt from a sample shareholder resolution are presented later in this case study.

Companies Respond to the Shareholders

Some U.S. corporations were quick to respond to the shareholder resolutions filed by coalition members. These firms were already in compliance with or exceeded Mexican laws and regulations. Some firms were committed to applying environmental and employee policies and practices worldwide. The same policies governing U.S. operations were used at the Maquiladoras plants. Therefore, some firms already were addressing the various issues emphasized in the shareholder resolutions. A number of these firms drafted statements in response to the shareholder challenges and made these documents available to interested company stakeholders. Highlights from these documents are presented next.

AT&T's Report on their Mexican Operations

AT&T compiled "A Report for AT&T Shareowners: Manufacturing in Mexico." The report, made available to all interested company stakeholders, addressed numerous issues raised by the coalition, such as human resource, environmental, and worker safety policies and practices.

AT&T was committed to "maintain[ing] consistent, equitable and fair human resources policies at all its locations worldwide." The company policies included paying a competitive wage to all employees, participating in salary surveys in each country where it operated to determine what was a "fair wage," and providing each employee with benefits comparable to what other companies in that country were offering their employees.

AT&T complied with the legal expectations in Mexico regarding the maximum number of hours an employee could work in a week, scheduled rest periods within each workday, and vacation benefits provided for employees. For example, AT&T workers at the Maquiladoras plant were paid for 56 hours per week, although the workweek consisted of only 48 hours or less. In addition, the company provided quality of work benefits and programs for its workers. Comprehensive medical care available to AT&T employees exceeded Mexico's legal requirements. Employees were offered educational assistance programs, sports programs, and, in some locations, subsidized plant cafeterias, food and clothing allowances, and free transportation.

AT&T pledged its commitment to support the Mexican government's efforts toward environmental responsibility. The corporation established the following goals for its Maquiladoras operations: reducing manufacturing emissions of chlorofluorocarbons (CFCs), reducing toxic air emissions, reducing amounts of manufacturing process waste sent for disposal, reducing paper use, and increasing recycling efforts.

The company was actively involved in various environmental initiatives, such as the Industry Cooperative for Ozone Layer Protection, Global Environmental Management Initiative, and International Environmental Health and Safety Conference, which was held in 1992. AT&T went beyond legal requirements in Mexico when it established a self-contained water supply and waste-water systems at its Guadalajara plant.

Worker safety was also a key emphasis for AT&T at its Maquiladoras operations. In compliance with Mexican regulation, each manufacturing unit formed a safety committee with representation from the workers' union, management, production, and medical departments. New workers at AT&T's Maquiladoras plants participated in an orientation program that focused on safety procedures, in compliance with Mexican law.

Ford Motor Company's Maquiladoras Facilities Report

Ford Motor Company's report, "Environmental Practices, Health and Safety Standards and Employee Welfare at Ford Motor Company's Maquiladora Facilities in Mexico," was issued on March 19, 1991, and responded to many of the coalition's various concerns. The report stated that Ford required its Maquiladoras operations to meet high standards for responsible environmental, health, safety, personnel, and community relations policies and, whenever possible, to follow the same policies and practices as did Ford operations in the United States.

For example, although not required by Mexican law or regulation, Ford applied its U.S. environmental policies to the Maquiladoras facilities. These policies required the plants to monitor the handling and disposal of any hazardous materials used in manufacturing processes, which included solvents, cleaners, lubricants, and various metals. The Waste Management Program, launched in 1985 and strengthened in 1990 at Ford's U.S. plants, was applied to its Maquiladoras operations. Cross-functional teams within manufacturing, plant engineering, environmental quality, research, occupational safety and health, and others met regularly to explore safety issues and recommend solutions if necessary. In compliance with Mexican regulation, enforced by SEDUE (the Mexican equivalent to OSHA) and the Mexican Department of Labor, random audits of Ford's Maquiladoras facilities were conducted. In addition, self-audits were often conducted at the plants to ensure compliance with Mexican law as well as company policies.

One of Ford Motor Company's basic values is embodied in the statement: Our people are the source of our strength. This value was manifested in the policies and practices affecting the employees at Ford's Maquiladoras plants. To establish a fair wage scale for its employees, Ford utilized the services of two international compensation consultants who advised the company regarding competitive wages and fringe benefits for each plant location. The company took pride in being able to offer employment to over 10,000 Mexican citizens, providing them with competitive wages and benefits that they could not receive elsewhere, according to the company's report on its Maquiladoras operations. Ford had been a part of Mexico and the Mexican people for over 65 years. According to the Maquiladoras facilities report, "Ford has actively participated in the economic, social, and cultural growth of Mexico in many ways. Our active cultural, educational and community participation is a matter of public record of which we are proud."

PepsiCo's Maquiladoras Report

Evidence of corporate social responsiveness to the social activist shareholder resolutions was reflected in PepsiCo's report:

Post–Lawrence–Weber:
Business and Society,
Ninth Edition

Case Study: Doing
Business in the
Maquiladoras: A
Shareholder Challenge

© The McGraw–Hill
Companies, 1999

PepsiCo is committed to making a real contribution to Mexican economic, technological and social development. PepsiCo operations are guided by these basic principles.

- PepsiCo companies are committed to the communities they serve, in terms of providing employment opportunity, fair and equitable working conditions and working with local industry suppliers.
- PepsiCo businesses believe in investing in the future, including establishing employee training and research programs and supporting educational and charitable organizations.
- PepsiCo believes in full cooperation with the Mexican government, to ensure that our objectives are in the nation's best interest.
- Finally, PepsiCo is committed to Mexico for the long term and we are projecting continued expansion.[5]

The Future for the Maquiladoras

With the signing of the North America Free Trade Agreement by the United States and Mexico in 1994, Maquiladoras lost some of their privileges—for example, wholesale relief from import duties on components—but they also gained some advantages—for example, freedom to sell products domestically in Mexico and general tariff relief on exports to the United States and Canada. Nonetheless, the Coalition for Justice in the Maquiladoras remained committed to challenging U.S. companies to establish safe, healthy, and environmentally sound business operations in the Maquiladoras region. The number of companies receiving shareholder resolutions and requests for entering into dialogue with the coalition doubled from 1992 to 1993. In 1993 and 1994, the Coalition requested adherence to their standards of conduct or disclosure reports from 38 companies with Maquiladoras operations. In 1997, six companies—AlliedSignal, ALCOA, Becton Dickerson, General Electric, Johnson & Johnson, and United Technologies—were asked by religious-affiliated stockholders to initiate a review of their company's Maquiladoras operations. In addition, AlliedSignal, Chrysler, General Electric, and Johnson & Johnson were requested via a shareholder resolution to review or amend their codes or standards governing all international operations, which included Maquiladoras.

Mission Statement and Standards of Conduct of the Coalition for Justice in the Maquiladoras

The Coalition for Justice in the Maquiladoras adopted the following mission statement:

We are a tri-national coalition of religious, environmental, labor, Latino and women's organizations that seek to pressure U.S. transnational corporations to adopt socially responsible practices within the maquiladora industry, to ensure a safe environment along the U.S./Mexican border, safe work conditions inside the maquila plants and a fair standard of living for the industries workers.

A central vehicle for achieving these goals is the establishment of the "MAQUILADORA STANDARDS OF CONDUCT." This document provides a code

---

[5] "Maquiladoras PepsiCo, Inc.," reprinted courtesy, © PepsiCo, Inc.

Post–Lawrence–Weber:
Business and Society,
Ninth Edition

Case Study: Doing
Business in the
Maquiladoras: A
Shareholder Challenge

© The McGraw–Hill
Companies, 1999

through which we demand that corporations alleviate critical problems created by the industry.

Our efforts are grounded in supporting worker and community struggles for social, economic and environmental justice in the maquiladora industry. Moreover, by supporting these struggles, we believe our efforts will serve the interests of workers and communities along the U.S./Mexican border.

We dedicate ourselves to democratic process and unity of action maintaining sensitivity to the diverse representation within our coalition.

The following is a summary of the issues proposed in the Maquiladora Standards of Conduct.[6]

Introduction: Purpose and Scope of the Standards of Conduct

The "MAQUILADORA STANDARDS OF CONDUCT" are addressed to all U.S. corporations which operate subsidiaries, have affiliates, or utilize contractors or shelter plants in Mexico. The objective of these Standards is to promote socially responsible practices, which ensure a safe environment on both sides of the border, safe work conditions inside Maquiladora plants and an adequate standard of living for Maquiladora employees.

United States citizens, who urge U.S. transnational corporations to adhere to these standards, recognize that both Mexico and the U.S. have the inherent right to regulate commerce within their own boundaries. These Standards are designed to help promote international efforts to secure a safe workplace for Maquiladora employees, the protection of the environment and the promotion of human rights and economic justice on both sides of the border.

All company disclosures associated with these Standards should be provided in Spanish and English.

Section I: Responsible Practices for Handling Hazardous Wastes and Protecting the Environment

Pollution from the Maquiladora industry is a binational problem which threatens the health of citizens both in Mexico and the United States. Illegal dumping of hazardous wastes pollutes rivers and aquifers and contaminates drinking water on both sides of the border. In addition, accidental chemical leaks from plants or transportation vehicles carrying hazardous materials impact both sides of the border.
In general, corporations operating Maquiladoras will be guided by the principle that they will follow Mexican and United States environmental protection regulations as established by SEDESOL and EPA [the Mexican and United States' environmental regulatory agencies. . . . Corporations operating Maquiladoras, including corporations which utilize contractors or shelter plants, will: (1) Act promptly to comply with Mexican environmental laws (*Ley General del Equilibrio Ecológico y la Protección al Ambiente.* . . . . (2) Annually, provide full public disclosure of toxic chemical discharges and releases into the air, water and land and amounts of hazardous

[6] The "Maquiladora Standard of Conduct" is reprinted in a condensed form by permission of the Coalition for Justice in the Maquiladoras, San Antonio, Texas.

Post–Lawrence–Weber:
Business and Society,
Ninth Edition

Case Study: Doing
Business in the
Maquiladoras: A
Shareholder Challenge

© The McGraw–Hill
Companies, 1999

materials stored and utilized. . . . (3) Provide full public disclosure of hazardous waste disposal methods, including the final location of waste disposal. . . . (4) Use state-of-the-art toxics use reduction, chemical accident prevention and pollution control technologies. . . . (5) Ensure safe and responsible transportation of all hazardous materials in Mexico and the United States. . . . (6) Provide public verification of all hazardous materials being returned to the country of origin. . . . (7) Ensure proper disposal of all spent containers used for chemicals and take necessary initiatives to assure that these containers are not used for the storage of drinking water. . . .
(8) Take remedial action to clean up any past dumping which threatens to release hazardous materials into the environment. . . . (9) Provide fair damage compensation to any community or individual, which has been harmed by pollution caused by the corporation or its subsidiary. . . . (10) Discuss environmental concerns with the community . . . .

Section II: Health and Safety Practices

In general, corporations operating Maquiladoras will be guided by the principle that they will follow regulations established by the *Secretaria del Trabajo y Previsión Social* [Secretary of Labor and Social Provision] and the U.S. Occupational Safety and Health Administration (OSHA).

Corporations operating Maquiladoras will: (1) Disclose to employees, their designated representatives and the public the chemical identity of all chemicals used, as well as amounts of chemical materials and wastes stored on premises. Ensure that all chemical containers will have appropriate warning labels in Spanish as well as English. . . . (2) In accordance with Mexican law, provide employees with written explanation of risks associated with the use of toxic materials. . . . (3) Use chemicals that are the safest and least toxic for employees. . . . (4) Design work operations and tasks to limit repetitive strain injuries and other ergonomic problems. . . . (5) As required by Mexican law, each plant will establish worker/management health and safety commissions. . . . (6) Provide all employees with health and safety training using a qualified instructor approved by the Joint Health and Safety Commission. . . .
(7) Provide an adequate ventilation system including local exhaust for all point sources of air contamination, as well as provide employees with appropriate protective equipment and clothing. . . . (8) Arrange health and safety inspections by qualified outside consultants (approved by the Joint Health and Safety Commission) at least once every six months and provide public disclosure of inspection reports. . . .
(9) Provide fair damage compensation to any worker who suffers an occupational injury or illness. . . . (10) In accordance with Mexican law and the OSHA Medical Records Rule, provide all employees and their designated representatives access to medical records. . . .

Section III: Fair Employment Practices and Standard of Living

U.S. corporations will respect basic workers' rights and human dignity. (1) U.S. corporations will not engage in employment discrimination based on sex, age, race, religious creed or political beliefs. Equal pay will be provided for equal work, regardless of sex, age, race, religious creed or political beliefs. . . . (2) In general, workers

336

Post–Lawrence–Weber:
Business and Society,
Ninth Edition

Case Study: Doing
Business in the
Maquiladoras: A
Shareholder Challenge

© The McGraw–Hill
Companies, 1999

will be provided with a fair and just wage, reasonable hours of work and decent working conditions. . . . (3) U.S. corporations will not interfere with workers' rights to organize and to reach collective bargaining agreements. . . . (4) U.S. corporations will not employ or utilize child labor and will exercise good faith in ensuring that employees are of legal working age. . . . (5) U.S. corporations will distribute profit sharing to employees as required by Mexican law. . . . (6) U.S. corporations will print and distribute a written handbook on company employment policies to all employees as required by Mexican law. . . . (7) In the workplace, U.S. corporations will take positive steps to prevent sexual harassment. . . .

Section IV: Community Impact

U.S. transnational corporations recognize that they have social responsibilities to the local communities in Mexico and the United States where they locate facilities. These responsibilities include a commitment to community economic development, and improvements in the quality of life. Facilities will not be abandoned to avoid these responsibilities. (1) U.S. corporations will not promote barracks-style living arrangements for employees. Where these living arrangements already exist, U.S. corporations will take immediate action to improve living conditions and ensure that workers are provided with basic human rights. . . . (2) Corporations operating Maquiladoras will work to establish special trust funds to finance infrastructure improvements in communities near Maquiladora plants.

Discussion Questions

1. Assume that the Coalition for Justice in the Maquiladoras has introduced a shareholder resolution at a firm where you are on the board of directors. Would you recommend that your firm adopt the practices outlined in the Maquiladora Standards of Conduct? What values or reasons underlie your recommendation? What is your firm's responsibility to your shareholders?

2. The Maquiladora Standards of Conduct also ask companies to disclose operations information. Should your firm agree to make public information about your Maquiladora operations, as requested by the coalition? Why or why not?

3. If you were a shareholder, would you vote for or against the resolution? Why?

4. Some believe that the SEC should permit stockholders to vote on social as well as economic questions related to the business of the corporation; others do not. Do you believe that the issues raised by the Maquiladora Standards of Conduct are appropriate ones for stockholders to consider, or should these issues be better left up to management or public officials?

5. Laws governing such matters as environmental policy, labor standards, and gender and race discrimination often differ among nations. Do you believe that multinational corporations have an obligation to apply standards consistently among all their operations or simply to follow the law in the country or countries in which they are operating?

Post–Lawrence–Weber:
Business and Society,
Ninth Edition

Case Study: Dow Corning
and the Silicone Breast
Implant Controversy

© The McGraw–Hill
Companies, 1999

Case Study:
Dow Corning and the
Silicone Breast Implant
Controversy

The corporate jet lifted off from Washington's National Airport, en route to Dow Corning Corporation's headquarters in Midland, Michigan. February 19, 1992, had been a grueling day for Keith R. McKennon. Named chairman and chief executive officer of Dow Corning less than two weeks earlier, McKennon had just testified before the Food and Drug Administration's Advisory Committee on the safety of the company's silicone gel breast implants. Although not the only manufacturer of breast implants, Dow Corning had invented the devices in the early 1960s and had been responsible for most of their medical testing. Now, the company was faced with the task of defending the product against

Note: This is an abridged version of a longer case: Anne T. Lawrence, "Dow Corning and the Silicone Breast Implant Controversy," *Case Research Journal* 13, no. 4 (Winter 1993), pp. 87–112. Abridged by the author by permission of the *Case Research Journal.* Sources include articles appearing in the *New York Times, The Wall Street Journal, Business Week, Newsweek, Time, Chemical and Engineering News, American Bar Association Journal, Journal of the American Medical Association, New England Journal of Medicine,* the Public Citizen Health Research Group *Health Letter,* the Command Trust Network *Newsletter,* press reports of the *Federal News Service,* and U.S. congressional hearings. The history of Dow Corning and the development of silicones is based on Don Whitehead, *The Dow Story: The History of the Dow Chemical Company* (New York: McGraw-Hill, 1968); and Eugene G. Rochow, *Silcon and Silicones* (Berlin: Springer-Verlag, 1987). The case also draws on internal Dow Corning documents released to the public in February 1992. A full set of footnotes is available in the *Case Research Journal* version.

Post–Lawrence–Weber:
Business and Society,
Ninth Edition

Case Study: Dow Corning
and the Silicone Breast
Implant Controversy

© The McGraw–Hill
Companies, 1999

numerous lawsuits and a rising tide of criticism from the FDA, Congress, the media, and many women's advocacy organizations.

The company's potential liability was large: as many as two million American women had received implants over the past three decades, perhaps 35 percent of them made by Dow Corning. In December 1991, a San Francisco jury had awarded a woman who claimed injuries from her Dow Corning implants an unprecedented $7.3 million in damages. Although the company believed its $250 million in product liability insurance was adequate to meet any possible claims, some felt that the company's liability exposure could be much, much larger.

The hearings had been contentious. Critics had repeated their allegations, heard often in the press in recent weeks, that the implants could leak silicone into the body, causing pain, scarring, and—most seriously—debilitating autoimmune diseases such as rheumatoid arthritis and scleroderma. The silicone prostheses could also interfere with detection of breast cancer by mammography, they charged. In response, McKennon had testified that implants served an important public health need and did not pose an unreasonable risk to users. On the job less than a month, however, McKennon had had little time to sort through the thousands of pages of relevant documents or to talk with the many managers who had been involved with the product's development over the past 30 years.

The breast implant controversy would surely be a litmus test of McKennon's crisis management skills. Recruited from Dow Chemical Corporation, where he had been executive vice president and head of domestic operations, McKennon came to his new position with a reputation as a seasoned troubleshooter. At Dow Chemical (which owned 50 percent of Dow Corning), McKennon had earlier managed his firm's response to charges that its product Agent Orange, a defoliant widely used during the Vietnam War, had caused lingering health problems for veterans. Later, he had managed Dow Chemical's problems with Bendectin, an antinausea drug alleged to cause birth defects. At the time of his appointment as chairman and CEO, McKennon had served on Dow Corning's board of directors for nearly six years.

The unfolding breast implant crisis showed every sign of being just as difficult—and potentially damaging—as any McKennon had confronted in his long career. Would Dow Corning become known as another Johnson & Johnson, renowned for its skillful handing of the Tylenol poisonings in the 1980s? Or would it become another Manville or A. H. Robins, companies that had declared bankruptcy in the wake of major product liability crises? McKennon was well aware that the future of the company, as well as his own reputation, might well hinge on decisions he and his top managers would make within the next weeks and days.

Dow Corning, Inc.

Dow Corning was founded in 1943 as an equal joint venture of Dow Chemical Company and Corning Glass Works (later known as Corning, Inc.) to produce silicones for commercial applications. The term *silicone* was coined to describe synthetic compounds derived from silicon, an abundant element commonly found in sand. In the 1930s, Corning researchers working on possible applications of silicone in glassmaking developed a number of resins, fluids, and rubbers that could withstand extremes of hot and cold. In 1940, Corning approached Dow Chemical with a proposal for a joint venture, and by 1942 a small plant in Midland, Michigan (Dow's hometown), had begun production of silicones for military applications. At the close of World War II, Dow Corning moved successfully to develop multiple commercial applications for silicone. Within a decade, the company had introduced more than 600 products and doubled in size three times, making it one of the fastest-growing firms in the booming chemical industry. Its varied product line included specialty lubricants, sealants, and resins as well as a variety of consumer items—ranging from construction caulk, to adhesive labels, to Silly Putty.

Although most uses of silicone were industrial, by the mid-1950s Dow Corning scientists had become interested in possible medical applications and developed several implantable devices. In the early 1960s, Dow Corning engineers developed the first prototype of a breast implant by encapsulating a firm-density silicone gel within a silicone rubber bag. First marketed in 1963, this device—known as the Cronin implant—was used initially almost exclusively in reconstructive surgery performed on breast cancer patients following mastectomies (surgical removal of the breast).

When Dow Corning first developed and marketed breast implants (as well as its other medical products), the company was operating with virtually no government oversight. Unlike pharmaceutical drugs, regulations since 1906 under the Pure Food and Drug Act and its several amendments, medical devices—even those designed for implantation in the body—were for all practical purposes unregulated. Under the Food, Drug, and Cosmetics Act of 1938, the FDA had the authority to inspect sites where medical devices were made and could seize adulterated or misbranded devices. The agency could not require premarket approval for the safety or effectiveness, however, and could remove a product from the market only if it could demonstrate that the manufacturer had broken the law.

Although not required to prove its implants safe by law, Dow Corning—in accord with standard "good manufacturing" practices at the time—attempted to determine the safety of its own medical products before releasing them for sale. In 1964, Dow Corning hired an independent laboratory to undertake several studies of the safety of medical-grade silicones, including those used in breast implants. No evidence was found that silicones caused cancer, but two studies found that silicone fluid injected in experimental animals spread widely—becoming lodged in the lymph nodes, liver, spleen, pancreas, and other organs—and created persistent chronic inflammation. The company appeared unconcerned, noting that it did not advocate the direct injection of silicone fluid.

In the early 1970s, Dow Corning's breast implant business for the first time experienced a serious competitive threat. In 1972, five young men—all scientists or salesmen at Dow Corning—left the company to work for Heyer-Schulte, a small medical devices company in California, where they used their experience with silicones to develop a competing breast implant. Two years later, the group left Heyer-Schulte to form their own company, McGhan Medical Corporation. Their idea was to modify the basic technology developed over the past decade by Dow Corning to make a softer, more responsive implant that more closely resembled the natural breast. By 1974, both Heyer-Schulte and McGhan Medical had competing products on the market.

The Heyer-Schulte and McGhan implants quickly gained favor with plastic surgeons, and Dow Corning's market share began to erode. By 1975, Dow Corning estimated its market share had declined to around 35 percent, as plastic surgeons switched allegiance to products offered by the small company start-ups. Dow Corning managers became alarmed.

The Mammary Task Force

In January 1975—responding to the challenge from its California competitors—Dow Corning dedicated a special cross-functional team, known as the mammary task force, to develop, test, and bring to market a new generation of breast implants. The group's main goal was to reformulate the silicone gel to create a softer, more pliable implant competitive with the new products recently marketed

Post–Lawrence–Weber:
Business and Society,
Ninth Edition

Case Study: Dow Corning
and the Silicone Breast
Implant Controversy

© The McGraw–Hill
Companies, 1999

by McGhan and Heyer-Schulte. The group of about 20—all men—hoped to have the new implants ready for shipment by June 1975. The company believed it was justified in bringing the new implant to market quickly, without extensive medical testing, because the new product would be based on materials substantially similar to those used in the older Cronin implants. The safety of the existing line, management maintained, had already been satisfactorily documented on the basis of earlier studies and the history of their use.

One of the questions that quickly arose in the task force's deliberations—as reported in the minutes of its January 21, 1975, meeting—was: "Will the new gel . . . cause a *bleed through* which will make these products unacceptable?" (emphasis in original). Dow Corning scientists clearly recognized that a more watery gel (dubbed *flo-gel*), while softer to the touch, might also be more likely to permeate its envelope and bleed into surrounding tissue. Two product engineers were assigned to investigate this issue. Three weeks later they reported that their experiments "*to date* indicate that the bleed with new gel is no greater than what we measure from old gel controls." They also added, however, that they viewed their earlier results as inconclusive, and they remained concerned about "a possible bleed situation."

Biomedical tests were contracted out to an independent laboratory, which proceeded with tests in which the new gel was injected into experimental rabbits. Earlier reports back from the lab on February 26 showed "mild to occasionally moderate acute inflammatory reaction" in the test animals around the injected gel, but the pathologist concluded it was probably due to the trauma of insertion, not the product itself. The task force also ordered biomedical testing of migration of gel into the vital organs of monkeys. The laboratory results showed "some migration of the [flo-gel] formulation." However, the task force agreed that the bleed was still not any more or less than standard gel.

Development proceeded so rapidly that, by March 31, 10,000 new flo-gel mammaries were ready for packaging. The task force minutes reported that the products were "beautiful, the best we have ever made." Now six weeks ahead of schedule, the company was able to ship some samples of the new product to the West Coast in time for the California Plastic Surgeons meeting on April 21. However, earlier demonstrations did not go flawlessly. The task force got back the following report: "In Vancouver, and elsewhere on the West Coast introduction, it was noted that after the mammaries had been handled for awhile, the surface became oily. Also, some were bleeding on the velvet in the showcase." The task force ordered samples from the West Coast for examination, but no further discussion of this issue appeared in the subsequent minutes.

As the flo-gel implants came on line, the focus of the task force's discussion shifted from production issues to marketing strategy. The task force debated various aggressive marketing approaches, such as rebates, distribution by consignment, price breaks for big users, and free samples for surgeons known to perform breast enlargement operations. Noting that June and July were the peak months of the "mammary season," managers called for a big push to regain some of Dow Corning's eroding market share. The group felt that their market share, which they estimated had eroded to around 35 percent, could be lifted back to the 50 to 60 percent range if they moved aggressively.

By September, Dow Corning was producing 6,000 to 7,000 units per month and aimed to phase out the older models by early 1976. However, many bugs in the production process remained to be ironed out. The reject rate at inspection was high, as high as 50 percent on some lots. Among the problems: floating dirt, weak bags, and thin spots in the envelopes. Doctors had returned some unused mammaries, citing breakage and contamination. Overall, however, plastic surgeons liked the product. One task force member

342

Post–Lawrence–Weber:
Business and Society,
Ninth Edition

Case Study: Dow Corning
and the Silicone Breast
Implant Controversy

© The McGraw–Hill
Companies, 1999

later recalled that when plastic surgeons saw and felt the new material, "their eyes got big as saucers." Besides feeling more natural to the touch, the new softer devices were easier to insert and were more suitable for small-incision, low-trauma cosmetic procedures.

A Boom in Busts

Although breast implants first became available in the 1960s, it was only in the late 1970s and 1980s that the rate of implant surgery took off. The increase was due entirely to a fast rise in the number of so-called cosmetic procedures; by 1990, fully 80 percent of all implant surgeries performed in the United States were to increase the size of normal, healthy breasts, rather than for reconstruction following mastectomy.

One cause of the rise in cosmetic augmentations, of course, was the availability of the softer, more pliable implants, which could be inserted through smaller incisions with less trauma to the patient in less expensive outpatient procedures. In 1990, 82 percent of all breast augmentation procedures were performed on an outpatient basis. Other, broader trends within the medical profession and the wider culture also played important roles, however.

One factor behind the boom in breast augmentation surgery was the growth of the plastic surgery profession. Although procedures to graft tissue from a healthy part of the body to another that had been damaged or mutilated were developed early in the century, plastic surgery as a distinct subdiscipline within surgery did not emerge until the 1940s. During World War II, military surgeons struggling to repair the wounds of injured soldiers returning from the front pioneered many valuable reconstructive techniques. Many of these surgeons reentered civilian life to start plastic surgery programs in their home communities. Within a couple of decades, plastic surgery had become the fastest-growing specialty within American medicine. Between 1960 and 1983, the number of board-certified plastic surgeons quintupled, during a period when most other medical specialties were growing much less quickly (and the U.S. population as a whole grew by just 31 percent). The draw for the newly minted MDs was regular hours, affluent customers, and high incomes, averaging $180,000 per year after all expenses in 1987.

As their numbers soared, plastic surgeons faced an obvious problem—developing a market for their services. Demand for reconstructive surgery was not fast growing, and cosmetic procedures were often elective and typically not fully covered by medical insurance. In 1983, following approval by the Federal Trade Commission, the American Society for Plastic and Reconstructive Surgery (ASPRS), a professional association representing 97 percent of all board-certified plastic surgeons, launched a major advertising (or, as the society called it, "practice enhancement") campaign. Other ads were placed by individual surgeons. In one appearing in *Los Angeles* magazine, a seductive, well-endowed model was shown leaning against a sports car. The tag line: "Automobile by Ferrari, Body by [a prominent plastic surgeon]."

Plastic surgeons also campaigned to redefine female flat-chestedness (dubbed *micromastia* by the medical community) as a medical disease requiring treatment. In July 1982, the ASPRS filed a formal comment with the FDA that argued:

> There is a substantial and enlarging body of medical opinion to the effect that these deformities [small breasts] are really a disease which in most patients results in feelings of inadequacy, lack of self-confidence, distortion of body image and a total lack of well-being due to a lack of self-perceived femininity. The enlargement of the under-developed female breast is, therefore, often very necessary to insure an improved quality of life for the patient.

Post–Lawrence–Weber:
Business and Society,
Ninth Edition

Case Study: Dow Corning
and the Silicone Breast
Implant Controversy

© The McGraw–Hill
Companies, 1999

The ASPRS later officially repudiated this view.

By 1990, breast augmentation had become the second most common cosmetic procedure performed by plastic surgeons, exceeded only by liposuction (fat removal). Since it was a more expensive procedure, however, breast augmentation was the top money maker for plastic surgeons in 1990. That year, ASPRS members collected almost $215 million in fees from women for breast implant surgery.

Another factor contributing to the rise in cosmetic augmentation may have been changing cultural standards of feminine beauty in the 1980s, a decade characterized by social conservatism and, according to some commentators, by a backlash against feminism and female liberation. In the 1970s, women appearing in the glossy pages of fashion magazines were often tall and lanky, with long, straight hair tied at the nape of the neck, menswear dress-for-success suits, and distinctly boyish figures. The 1980s ideal woman was very different: the typical fashion model by this time was more likely to sport 1940s retro-look fashions, thick, full curls, sweetheart lips—and lots of bosom. In a special 100th anniversary edition, published April 1992, *Vogue* magazine summed up current standards of female beauty in this sentence:

And in women's bodies, the fashion now is a combination of hard, muscular stomach and shapely breasts. Increasingly, women are willing to regard their bodies as photographic images, unpublishable until retouched and perfected at the hands of surgeons.

Ironically, the same issue also ran an ad, placed by trial attorneys, in which "silicone breast implant sufferers" were invited to come forward with legal claims.

A Stream of Sick and Injured

As the rate of implant surgeries rose in the 1980s, so did the number of women who were sick, injured, and in pain from their breast surgery. Their stories began to be told at medical conferences, in legal briefs, and by women's and consumer's advocacy organizations. As they were, Dow Corning and other implant makers were forced to respond to a growing crisis of confidence in their products.

The most common adverse side effect of implant surgery was a phenomenon known as *capsular contracture,* a painful hardening of the breast that occurs when the body reacts to the implant by forming a wall of fibrous scar tissue around it. The FDA estimated that severe contracture occurred in about 25 percent of all patients; some hardening may have occurred in up to 70 percent. Implants could also rupture, spilling silicone gel into the body and often necessitating repeat surgery to replace the damaged implants. Dow Corning's data, based on voluntary reporting by surgeons, showed a rupture rate of only 1 percent. These figures were challenged by researchers who pointed out that ruptures often did not show up on mammograms; some individual doctors reported rupture rate as high as 32 percent. Once the device had broken, silicone could and did travel via the lymphatic system throughout the body, lodging in a woman's spleen, liver, and other internal organs. Also worrisome was the tendency of silicone implants to obscure cancerous tumors that otherwise would be revealed by mammography.

More controversial and less-well documented were allegations that silicone implants could lead to so-called autoimmune disorders—diseases in which the body's immune system attacks its own connective tissues. According to the FDA, by 1991 around 600 cases of autoimmune disorders, such as rheumatoid arthritis, scleroderma, and lupus erythematosus, had been reported in women with implants. Some scientists speculated that some

344

Post–Lawrence–Weber:
Business and Society,
Ninth Edition

Case Study: Dow Corning
and the Silicone Breast
Implant Controversy

© The McGraw–Hill
Companies, 1999

women were, in effect, allergic to silicone, and that their bodies had attacked their own tissues in an attempt to rid itself of the substance. Such reactions were most likely in the presence of ruptures, but even small amounts of gel bleeding through the envelope, or silicone in the envelope itself, could provoke an autoimmune response.

Other physicians believed, however, that the appearance of autoimmune disorders in women with implants was wholly coincidental. In any substantial population—and 2 million women with implants was clearly substantial—a certain number would develop autoimmune disease purely by chance. In an interview published in the *Journal of the American Medical Association,* one prominent plastic surgeon called the association between autoimmune disorders and breast implants a "crock of baloney. . . . People get immunological diseases and they just happen to have breast implants."

Unfortunately, no long-term controlled studies of the incidence of autoimmune disorders in populations of women with and without implants were initiated or even contemplated until 1991. In fact, no comprehensive registries of women with implants existed. The question about the relationship between implants and autoimmune disease was, on the basis of existing data, wholly unanswerable. Representative Ted Weiss (Democrat-New York), who reviewed data submitted to the FDA in 1991, later angrily concluded: "For 30 years, more than one million women have been subjects in a massive, uncontrolled study, without their knowledge or consent."

Victims Seek Redress

Some women who had suffered from breast implants sued. In 1984, a Nevada woman was awarded $1.5 million by jurors in a San Francisco court, who concluded that Dow Corning had committed fraud in marketing its implant as safe; the case was later settled for an undisclosed amount while on appeal, and the court records were sealed. In a post-trial ruling, a federal judge who had reviewed the case records called Dow Corning's actions "highly reprehensible." In the wake of this case, Dow Corning changed its package insert to include a warning that mentioned the possibility of capsular contracture, silicone migration following rupture, and immune system sensitivity.

As other cases slowly made their way through the courts, victims began to speak out publicly and to organize. Sybil Goldrich and Kathleen Anneken founded the Command Trust Network, an advocacy organization that became instrumental in providing information, support, and legal and medical referrals to implant victims. Other women's and public health advocacy groups also played a role in publicizing the risks of breast implants. One of the most active was the Health Research Group (HRG), a Washington, D.C.–based spin-off of Ralph Nader's Public Citizen. The HRG in 1988 began a systematic effort to pressure the FDA to ban silicone breast implants. The group petitioned the FDA, testified before Congress and other government agencies, issued regular press releases, and distributed information to consumers. The HRG also initiated an information clearinghouse for plaintiffs' attorneys. Another active advocacy organization was the National Women's Health Network, a public-interest group that widely distributed information on silicone-related issues.

Devising Regulation for Devices

The agency in charge of regulating implants—and thus the object of these and other advocacy organizations' pressure—was the Food and Drug Administration. In 1976, the year after Dow Corning's mammary task force developed its new generation of flo-gel implants, Congress passed

Post–Lawrence–Weber:
Business and Society,
Ninth Edition

Case Study: Dow Corning
and the Silicone Breast
Implant Controversy

© The McGraw–Hill
Companies, 1999

the Medical Amendments Act to the Food and Drug Act. Enacted in the wake of the Dalkon Shield controversy, in which thousands of women claimed they had been injured by a poorly designed intrauterine device, the amendments for the first time required that manufacturers of new, implantable medical devices be required to prove their products safe and effective before release to the public. Devices already on the market were ranked by risk, with the riskiest ones—designated Class III—being required to meet the same standards of safety and effectiveness as new devices.

In January 1989, after an extensive internal debate, the FDA identified silicone breast implants as Class III devices and gave their manufacturers 30 months, until January 1991, to submit safety and effectiveness data to the agency. Four breast implant manufacturers submitted the required documents to the FDA: Dow Corning, INAMED (formerly McGhan Medical), Mentor (formerly Heyer-Schulte), and Bioplasty. Surgitek, a unit of Bristol-Myers Squibb, withdrew from the implant business, saying it was unable to meet the FDA's deadline. On August 12, the head of the FDA Breast Prosthesis task force submitted a review of Dow Corning's studies, stating that they were "so weak that they cannot provide a reasonable assurance of the safety and effectiveness of these devices."

Finally, on November 13, the FDA convened an advisory panel of professionals to consider the most recent evidence and to take further testimony. The hearings were highly contentious. The panel heard, once again, arguments concerning the dangers of implants. But the hearings also generated intense support for implants from plastic surgeons, satisfied implant recipients, and breast cancer support and advocacy organizations. Among the most vocal defenders of the implants were women who had experienced successful reconstruction following mastectomies, including representatives of such peer support organizations as Y-Me and My Image after Breast Cancer. Several spoke of the positive psychological benefits of reconstruction and warned that if the FDA took implants off the market, some women, knowing that reconstructive surgery was unavailable, would delay regular checkups for breast cancer, endangering their lives. Other witnesses argued that women should be free to choose implants, so long as they were fully informed of the benefits and risks of the devices.

The advisory panel debate was, by all accounts, heated. In the final analysis, the panel split hairs: it voted that although breast implants "did not pose a major threat to the health of users," the data submitted by manufacturers was "insufficient to prove safety." However, citing "a public health need," the panel recommended that the devices be left on the market.

The regulatory decision, at this point, passed to the FDA commissioner, Dr. David A. Kessler. Appointed just a few months earlier, Kessler had brought a new commitment to regulatory activism to an agency marked by what some viewed as a pattern of weak government oversight during the Reagan administration. Now, the fledgling commissioner had two months, until mid-January, to rule on the panel's recommendation on breast implants.

Unauthorized Leaks

Unfolding events, however, forced Kessler's hand sooner. In December, a San Francisco jury returned a verdict in *Hopkins* v. *Dow Corning,* awarding Mariann Hopkins $7.3 million, by far the largest victory ever for a plaintiff in a breast implant suit. Hopkins' attorney claimed that his client's implants (made by Dow Corning in 1976) had ruptured and spilled silicone gel—causing severe joint aches, muscle pain, fatigue, and weight loss—and told the jury that "this case is about corporate greed and outright fraud." Dow Corning immediately moved to have the legal records in the case—which included hundreds of pages of internal company memos Hopkins' attorney had subpoenaed—sealed.

Post–Lawrence–Weber:
Business and Society,
Ninth Edition

Case Study: Dow Corning
and the Silicone Breast
Implant Controversy

© The McGraw–Hill
Companies, 1999

Somehow, however, the documents from the Hopkins trial ended up in Commissioner Kessler's hands. Their contents evidently alarmed him. On January 6, 1992, Kessler abruptly reversed the FDA's November decision and called for a 45-day moratorium on all sales of silicone gel breast implants, pending further study of their safety, and he recalled the advisory panel to consider "new evidence." Both the plastic surgeons and Dow Corning were furious. The president of the American Society of Plastic and Reconstructive Surgeons took the unusual step of calling a press conference to brand Kessler's action as "unconscionable—an outrage" and called on Kessler to reconstitute the advisory panel, which he called unqualified to judge the safety of the devices. For its part, Dow Corning demanded publicly to know what new evidence Kessler had obtained and restated the company's intention to block any release of "non-scientific" internal memoranda. The chief of Dow Corning's health-care business called a press conference to repeat the company's contention that "the cumulative body of credible scientific evidence shows that the implants are safe and effective."

Dow Corning's efforts to block release of the Hopkins documents, however, failed. On January 13, *New York Times* reporter Philip J. Hilts—saying only that he had obtained the material from several sources—broke the Hopkins case memos in a page-one article, under the headline "Make Is Depicted as Fighting Tests on Implant Safety." In a summary of the contents of several hundred internal company memos, Hilts charged that Dow Corning's safety studies were inadequate and that serious questions raised by its own scientific research and by doctors' complaints had not been answered.

More damaging revelations were yet to come. Over the next several weeks, newspaper readers learned of the following incidents, drawn from the company's internal documents:

- In a 1980 memo, a Dow Corning sales representative had reported to his marketing manager that he had received complaints from a California plastic surgeon who was "downright indignant" because the implant envelopes were "greasy" and had experienced "excessive gel bleed." "The thing that is really galling is that I feel like I have been beaten by my own company instead of the competition. To put a questionable lot of mammaries on the market is inexcusable," the sales representative wrote his manager. "It has to rank right up there with the Pinto gas tank."

- A marketing manager had reported in a memo that he had "assured [a group of doctors], with crossed fingers, that Dow Corning had an active study [of safety issues] under way." (The marketing manager later angrily disputed the interpretation given his remarks by the media, saying in a letter to the Associated Press that he had meant the term *crossed fingers* in a "hopeful" rather than a "lying" sense.)

- A Las Vegas plastic surgeon had had an extensive correspondence with the company reporting his dissatisfactions with the product. In one letter, he charged that he felt "like a broken record" and told of an incident in which an implant had ruptured and spilled its contents—which he described as having the "consistency of 50 weight motor oil"—onto the operating room floor.

Whether wholly justified or not, the memos created a strong impression that Dow Corning had been aware of safety concerns about its implants for many years and had failed to act on this knowledge. The press moved in aggressively, attacking Dow Corning for its "moral evasions"; a widely reprinted cartoon depicted a Dow Corning executive apparently deflating as silicone gel oozed from his body.

A Model Ethical Citizen

That Dow Corning was being labeled publicly as "a company adrift without a moral compass"—as one *New York Times* columnist put it several days after the internal memos broke in the press—struck many in and around the company as deeply unjust. Ironically, Dow Corning Corporation was widely regarded in the business community as a model for its efforts to institutionalize ethical behavior.

At the center of Dow Corning's efforts was a formal code of conduct and an unusual procedure for monitoring compliance. In 1976, the first full year of sales for its new generation of breast implants, the company's board of directors had appointed a three-person Audit and Social Responsibility Committee and charged it with developing a corporate code of ethical conduct. Top managers were motivated, in part, by a breaking scandal at that time in which several large companies had been accused of questionable payments to foreign heads of state to secure contracts. With a substantial portion of its operations overseas, Dow Corning wanted its behavior to be above reproach.

In 1977, the company published its first corporate code of conduct, laying out a comprehensive statement of ethical standards. In order to ensure compliance, the company initiated a series of annual audits, in which top managers would visit various cities around the globe to evaluate corporate performance against code standards. In addition, the company held training programs on the code, and its semi-annual employee opinion survey included a second on business ethics.

Yet, for whatever reason, the company's widely admired procedures had failed to flag the safety of breast implants as an ethical concern. A routine 1990 ethics audit of the Arlington, Tennessee, plant that manufactured silicone implants, for example, did not reveal any concerns about the product's safety. When later questioned about the apparent failure of the audit procedure, the chairperson of the conduct committee pointed out that normally product safety issues would come before the relevant management group, not the ethics review.

A Hardball Strategy

As the controversy widened, Dow Corning's response, in the words of one *Wall Street Journal* reporter, was to "play hardball." On January 14, eight days after the FDA had announced its moratorium on implant sales and one day after the first leaked documents appeared in the press, Dow Corning took a $25 million charge against fourth quarter, 1991, earnings to cover costs of its legal liability, unused inventory, and efforts to prove implants safe. The company also suspended implant production and placed workers at the company's manufacturing facilities on temporary layoff, with full pay and benefits. Investors, apparently alarmed by this turn of events, knocked down the stock price of both Corning, Inc., and Dow Chemical as they contemplated the parent firms' potential liability.

Implant recipients and trial lawyers also were contemplating the liability question. By March, as many as 600 lawsuits had been filed against Dow Corning and other breast implant makers, according to a representative of the Association of Trial Lawyers of America. The National Products Liability Database estimated that Dow Corning had been sued at least 54 times in federal court and possibly more than 100 times in state courts. Dow Corning's attorney disputed these figures, saying that there were far fewer than 200 cases pending against his client.

The unauthorized leaks created tremendous pressure on Dow Corning to release its own documents to the public. The FDA publicly called on the company on January 20 to

Post–Lawrence–Weber:
Business and Society,
Ninth Edition

Case Study: Dow Corning
and the Silicone Breast
Implant Controversy

© The McGraw–Hill
Companies, 1999

release the material so that women and their doctors could evaluate the new evidence for themselves, rather than simply relying on news reports. (The agency, although in possession of the documents, could not release them because they were still protected under court order.) The company responded two days later by releasing a group of scientific studies—but not the infamous Pinto memo and other internal materials that the company dubbed unscientific.

Suspension of breast implant sales and release of the scientific studies did not slow down the crisis engulfing the company. On January 29, in an apparent acknowledgment of the severity of the situation, the company hired former attorney general Griffin B. Bell—who had performed a similar role at Exxon Corporation following the *Valdez* oil spill and at E.F. Hutton following the check-kiting scandal—to investigate its behavior in making implants.

Finally, on February 10, following a top-level intervention by the chairmen of Corning, Inc., and Dow Chemical, both of whom sat on Dow Corning's board, the board of directors executed a stunning management shakeup. Dow Corning demoted Chief Executive Lawrence A. Reed to the position of chief operating officer and forced longtime board chairman John S. Ludington to retire. Keith R. McKennon was named chairman and CEO. Simultaneously, the board announced that it would release to the public 15 scientific reports and 94 nonscientific memos or letters from company files, including the Pinto and "crossed fingers" memos, as well as other potentially damaging materials that had not yet been reported by the media.

Several top executives of Dow Corning met the press the same day to present the company's perspective. One defended the company's decision not to release the documents earlier, saying:

> Our motives are simple. First and foremost, these memos do not answer fundamental questions and concerns that women have about breast implants. And by focusing attention on the memos rather than the science that supports the device, we do nothing but further raise the anxiety level of women and physicians and scientists.

He added that "while we are not happy with the memos, we have nothing to hide, and we believe that each memo put in its proper context can be understood and explained." Many of the memos, he said, were best understood as part of the normal give and take that occurs within a technical organization, "one part of a multifaceted dialogue or communication or discussion that goes on," and did not reflect fundamental problems. By pulling various statements out of context, he implied, the press had misrepresented questions scientists might legitimately raise in the course of their inquiry as final conclusions. The Dow Corning executives closed the press conference by denying categorically that implants could cause autoimmune disease or cancer.

Facing a Crucial Decision

On February 20, the day after his testimony before the FDA, McKennon received word from Washington. After three hours of tense debate, the FDA advisory panel had voted just after 5:00 P.M. to recommend that implants be taken off the market, except for women needing reconstruction following mastectomies or to correct serious deformities. All implant recipients would be required to enroll in clinical studies. Cosmetic augmentations would be strictly limited to those required by the design of the clinical trials. Commissioner Kessler would have sixty days to rule on the panel's recommendation.

Post–Lawrence–Weber:
Business and Society,
Ninth Edition

Case Study: Dow Corning
and the Silicone Breast
Implant Controversy

© The McGraw–Hill
Companies, 1999

McKennon would have to lay a plan of action before his board soon—he certainly could not wait another two months for the FDA's next move. The breast implant business, he had learned, had not made any money for Dow Corning for the past five years. Even in its heyday, it had contributed no more than 1 percent of the company's total revenues. Some of his top executives had urged him just to get out of the implant business altogether and let the attorneys mop up the liability problems. Many in the company felt that the huge settlement in the Hopkins case would be greatly reduced on appeal, and the company's $250 million in insurance would be sufficient to cover their liability. McKennon reflected on these issues as he contemplated his next actions. Certainly, he needed to act decisively to stem Dow Corning's financial losses. But, he pondered, did the company not also have, as he had put it to a reporter a few days earlier, an "overriding responsibility . . . to the women who have our implants"? And what of the company's reputation, so carefully nurtured, for always upholding the highest standards of ethical behavior?

Discussion Questions

1. What internal and external factors contributed to the emergence of the silicone breast implant crisis for Dow Corning?
2. What should CEO McKennon do as of February 20, 1992?
3. What steps can Dow Corning, or other companies, take to prevent this kind of situation from occurring in the future?

Post–Lawrence–Weber:
Business and Society,
Ninth Edition

Case Study: Save Our
Cities: Business and the
Community

© The McGraw-Hill
Companies, 1999

Case Study:
Save Our Cities: Business
and the Community

The portrait of urban violence, crime, drugs, and poverty displayed in newspapers and on television reflects a frightening reality for millions of Americans. Myriad social problems afflict thousands of neighborhoods in hundreds of American communities. To many observers, these problems have worsened considerably in the past 20 years. Despite millions of dollars and endless political rhetoric, the problems of America's cities seem to be escalating. Many efforts have been launched to save our cities. Often, they have failed; some may have even made the situation worse.

Fear grows as reality worsens. The city has become an even more fearful place as media attention highlights the bizarre, the insane, the dangerous. Perception often is reality, and some who can avoid the city do so, in an effort to immunize themselves from society's problems. But some people fight back, continuing to find new ways of combat-

Note: Sources for discussion of The Atlanta Project include Archie B. Carroll and Gerald T. Horton, "Do Joint Corporate Social Responsibility Programs Work?" *Business and Society Review,* Summer 1994, pp. 24 – 28; and Archie B. Carroll and Gerald T. Horton, "The Atlanta Project: Corporate Social Responsibility on a Mega Scale," in Steven Wartick and Denis Collins, eds., *1994 Proceedings of Fifth Annual Conference, International Association for Business and Society* (Hilton Head, NC, March 17 – 20, 1994), pp. 261 – 266. Primary sources include *The Atlanta Project* (Atlanta, GA: The Carter Center, 1992); *Improving the Quality of Life in Our Neighborhoods: The Atlanta Project, Strategic Plan* (Atlanta, GA: The Carter Center, March 1992); and J. Carter, "Preface," in *Because There Is Hope: Gearing Up to Renew Urban America* (Atlanta, GA: The Carter Center, 1993). Additional data provided by The Atlanta Project. We are grateful for the assistance of Richard Watson and Jason Foss of TAP.

Post–Lawrence–Weber:
Business and Society,
Ninth Edition

Case Study: Save Our
Cities: Business and the
Community

© The McGraw–Hill
Companies, 1999

ing the terror of fear. In many cities, volunteer community groups, local government, and law enforcement continue the struggle to make cities safe for citizens.

Businesses are also involved in the struggle to save America's cities. Most businesses do not have the luxury of relocating to "safe harbor" locations where crime does not happen and social ills do not exist. Most businesses, like most people, have to find ways to cope with their problems, face challenges, and continue their daily activities.

Law enforcement, vigilant neighbors, active community groups, and economic development are all needed if communities are to win the fight to save our cities. Big cities like Atlanta, Cleveland, and Boston, as well as small and medium-sized cities and towns, are undertaking new experiments and forging new approaches. Business is a critical part of these efforts. Although it is too early to know if there are best practices that can be imitated in every community, there is reason to believe that some of the new efforts being undertaken are making an impact.

How Businesses Are Involved

The Urban Institute, a research think tank based in Washington, DC, has studied business involvement in cities and concluded that while individual companies are involved in a wide variety of community activities in cities across the nation, three distinct strategic approaches have dominated corporate involvement in rebuilding and strengthening urban communities.

Direct Involvement

The concept of hands-on business activities with neighborhoods is a relatively new form of direct involvement. Traditionally, business has made somewhat passive charitable contributions to arts, educational, and community groups. Investments have rarely been neighborhood-focused, except for those in downtown redevelopment projects. Increasingly, however, businesses have made direct investments in urban neighborhoods for the purpose of stabilizing, even reclaiming, areas that were once thought to be in hopeless decline. There are a few models worth studying. One is a landmark effort, the Crown Center Redevelopment Project in Kansas City. The neighborhood around its corporate headquarters was becoming surrounded by abandoned buildings and empty lots when Hallmark Cards Inc. began a neighborhood redevelopment effort. Twenty-five years after the initiative began, Hallmark has invested more than $500 million in what is considered a jewel in Kansas City's development.

In the 1990s, neighborhood needs are being addressed in a more complete or holistic manner. This has led to direct investments that attack a range of community-based problems. Upjohn, a pharmaceutical company based in Kalamazoo, Michigan, recognized the importance of housing as a stabilizing force in the local community. Citizen ownership of a community begins with home ownership, which is seen as critical to convincing residents that they have a stake in the neighborhood. To restore housing and improve home ownership in neighborhoods near its facilities, Upjohn recruited and supported the Local Initiative Support Corporation (LISC), a nonprofit development corporation, to help build home ownership by making mortgage loans to local residents in Kalamazoo. The long-term effect of Upjohn's efforts appears favorable: home ownership has increased in the target neighborhoods, and other social indicators—crime rates, drug use—have declined.

Community Partnership around a Business Core

Some companies have found it possible to integrate community development objectives into their normal business operations. The company pursues its profit-making business but takes on as a partner a comprehensive community organization. For example, Ben & Jerry's

Post–Lawrence–Weber:
Business and Society,
Ninth Edition

Case Study: Save Our
Cities: Business and the
Community

© The McGraw–Hill
Companies, 1999

Homemade Inc. has collaborated with Larkin Street Youth Center in San Francisco to open an ice cream shop that provides job training to youths (ages 12 to 17) who are mostly runaways. The company helps meet the education, training, and self-esteem needs of youth with the center's staff. Profits from the ice cream store are shared with the Larkin Center.

Ben & Jerry's has expanded this partnership concept to many other cities and locations. In New York City, for example, the company has partnered with the Harlem Ark of Freedom. The organization runs a homeless shelter and is engaged in a range of community development activities. Again, the store partnership helps to train people who lack education and job skills, to stabilize the neighborhood, and to attract additional businesses.

Some retail businesses with large workforces and connections to the community lend themselves to this approach. A number of supermarkets such as Pathmark, Kroger, and First National have created similar community anchors by building stores, employing previously unemployed people, and serving as a magnet for other economic investment.

Use of Intermediary Institutions

In some cities, community leaders have created a separate institution to serve as an umbrella vehicle for development efforts. In Cleveland, for example, the Cleveland Foundation convened a Commission on Poverty in 1990 to devise a long-term comprehensive strategy for bringing together business, government, and community resources to connect the city's poor neighborhoods to mainstream economic opportunity.

Business leaders were recruited to work with the commission, to study its findings, and to devise alternative responses to the problems. Leaders from Cleveland-based businesses such as White Consolidated Industries, The Higbee Company, Reliance Electric, and several leading law firms participated and saw the linkage between altruism and self-interest. Economic revitalization was critical to community improvement and to building Cleveland into a community that could support a modern base of service and manufacturing industries. It required that action be taken in school reform, housing, and community services. In short, a long-term business goal—a well-trained workforce—was intimately connected to comprehensive community involvement. The Cleveland Foundation has played a central role in aligning projects, sponsors, and corporate participation in what are called *villages* or neighborhoods in the city. Four core areas of community need were defined: education, investment, family development, and health. The foundation, and its Community-Building Initiative Council, helped to coordinate the focusing, funding, and delivery of programs to address these needs in each village. In the course of five years, the entire project has begun to achieve measurable improvement in meeting these core needs using a variety of social and economic indicators.

Building Better Communities: Contrasting Approaches

Businesses often become involved in the social issues affecting cities because they are asked to play a role or work with others to tackle a critical problem. Two examples of corporate involvement are discussed next. One is The Atlanta Project, a broad sweeping approach to Atlanta's complex social issues. The macro or comprehensive approach developed in Atlanta contrasts with the narrower, more selective (micro) approach of Boston Against Drugs, which has enlisted companies to tackle drug issues throughout that city.

Post–Lawrence–Weber:
Business and Society,
Ninth Edition

Case Study: Save Our
Cities: Business and the
Community

© The McGraw–Hill
Companies, 1999

The Atlanta Project: A Macro Approach to Social Issues

The Atlanta Project (TAP) is one of the best-known and widely studied recent efforts to save America's cities. Atlanta, like many other American cities, displays contrasting faces: one is the face of wealth, prosperity, a positive spirit, and an optimistic view of life; the other is a face of despair, poverty, and fear. Dr. Johnetta Cole, president of Spelman College in Atlanta, said it this way: "We have two cities . . . one rich, one poor." In Atlanta, civic leaders such as Dr. Cole are in the vanguard of a broad effort to turn two cities into a single, prosperous, safe community for all. The Atlanta Project is a coalition of Atlanta-based organizations—businesses, churches, community groups, government agencies, universities—formed to attack the poverty, crime, and community conditions that contribute to the "second city."

The Atlanta Project was launched on October 25, 1991, by a former president of the United States, Jimmy Carter. Carter, a Georgia native, whose presidential library and home base for continuing activities—the Carter Center at Emory University—are located in Atlanta, had been persuaded by Atlanta's civic leaders to lead the campaign to address the city's poverty and related social problems. Carter's natural interest in such an effort was coupled with his own action theory of how social change occurs in any community: *through the full participation of those affected.* It is an approach Carter has put into practice in global affairs as well: his mediation in Haiti helped to peacefully remove General Cedras and restore President Aristide to power; his efforts helped defuse a crisis over North Korea's nuclear capability; and his efforts helped to negotiate a cease-fire agreement to slow ethnic warfare in Bosnia. Carter has called The Atlanta Project the domestic centerpiece of the Carter Center's work. And, as in his international mediation efforts, fear of failure does not deter the former president. "The real failure, for Atlanta and cities like it, would be not to try," according to Carter.

Collaborative Empowerment

Atlanta has a large, successful professional population. But the city also has a much larger (500,000) inner-city population that suffers the problems of chronic poverty, crime, drugs, joblessness, illiteracy, teenage pregnancy, and substandard housing. To tackle these problems, Carter was determined to engage a broad cross-section of community resources. The former president called together leaders from business, local government, and community organizations and created a consortium to engage the issues. The leaders pledged their cooperation and the involvement of their organizations. As one executive said, "Mr. Carter is very persuasive and a good arm-twister." The former president solicited substantial pledges from such Atlanta-headquartered businesses as Marriott, Coca Cola, Delta Airlines, and BellSouth. Each would become an important partner in TAP. As of 1994, Atlanta businesses had contributed more than $30 million.

TAP was organized around Atlanta's local neighborhoods. The idea was to find a natural community around which an integrated approach to social services and economic assistance could be built. The focus turned to Atlanta's high schools which, it was discovered, served as natural focal points for Atlanta's neighborhoods. Each area was designated a *cluster community.* These 20 clusters became the unit of analysis and action for the project, although they often span political boundaries (e.g., parts of three counties are included in TAP's clusters).

354

Post–Lawrence–Weber:
Business and Society,
Ninth Edition

Case Study: Save Our
Cities: Business and the
Community

© The McGraw–Hill
Companies, 1999

The concept of local empowerment is vital to every aspect of TAP. Within each TAP cluster, for example, is a cluster coordinator and assistant coordinator who live in the neighborhood they represent. These coordinators are employed by TAP to work with a cluster steering committee composed of residents, service providers, and representatives from cluster schools, churches, businesses, and community groups. Cluster coordinators are not bosses in this process; rather, they are facilitators who help the community identify its needs, find the tools for tackling the issues, and create possible solutions to the cluster's problems. TAP has a central resource center to which all coordinators can turn for help, but the emphasis is on community-based solutions to community needs. Each cluster coordinator has to be skillful at using corporate partners, local government agencies, and other community resources to address the agenda of issues, needs, and concerns that the cluster community shares. Imagination is crucial to achieving success.

Business involvement in TAP operates at several levels. The chief executives of Atlanta companies met with former president Carter and leaders of other Atlanta organizations to map out strategies and initiatives in broad terms. Individual companies have been paired with one of the clusters, assigning at least one full-time manager to work with the cluster coordinator and his or her team. (TAP requested that the companies commit a full-time manager for up to *five* years in order to build real expertise at community problem solving.) Some companies have taken the lead in specific citywide projects that span the clusters: BellSouth, for example, has had a companywide commitment to improving adult literacy. The company took the lead in creating a program to bring thousands of books to Atlanta's clusters, coupling the book donations with a volunteer program to teach reading throughout the city. Hundreds of BellSouth employees have participated in this adult literacy education effort.

Thousands of employees in TAP companies have volunteered to help in the clusters, undertaking tasks as diverse as providing computer instruction for teachers and students in local schools; offering small business forums to help residents turn ideas into community enterprises; organizing basketball camps; helping students prepare college financial aid applications; and providing local residents with technical training in electrical wiring, plumbing, secretarial skills, and how to meet commercial driver's license requirements.

Collaboration among all of Atlanta's racial, demographic, and economic segments is the essence of the process. That doesn't happen immediately in most situations because trust must be built, a common vision must be developed, and an understanding of how to work together needs to emerge. Once a diverse community starts to work together, however, new ideas emerge, action follows ideas, and visible progress begins to occur. That is the essence of former president Carter's notion of collaborative empowerment.

Problems

The Atlanta Project is not without its problems and its detractors. Some say the project is too ambitious, too costly, and too closely tied to Carter's unique vision of empowerment. Most observers, however, point to Carter's role as one of being a *catalyst,* not a director. TAP's problems, in their view, have to do with the day-to-day challenges of getting people, who may have never been involved in community processes, to participate and trust the cluster approach. There are also the problems of sustaining the "fire" in cluster coordinators and others who show signs of physical and emotional burn-out after several years of hard work and of continuing to find new ways to leverage limited resources against a very

355

Post–Lawrence–Weber:
Business and Society,
Ninth Edition

Case Study: Save Our
Cities: Business and the
Community

© The McGraw–Hill
Companies, 1999

formidable list of community issues and needs. In early 1995, as the fifth year of the five-year TAP program began, several clusters were still operating with acting coordinators.

Business involvement has also suffered some problems. Loaned executives from Atlanta companies, for example, have sometimes sought to return to their companies for personal career reasons. Five years on leave in a community job may be too long away from the mainstream of a telecommunications or banking career. And business representatives have sometimes been frustrated by the slow decision-making processes that accompany the empowerment approach. Discussion takes time, and endless meetings of community representatives may be necessary before a consensus is reached on what to do and how to do it. Still, this is an investment in community decision making that supporters believe will be repaid many times over as more complex problems are tackled by the clusters.

Atlanta's businesses seem likely to stay involved for several reasons. First, former president Carter has made it quite clear that he will not let them walk away from so vital a process. The Atlanta Project is scheduled to continue for a full five years, through 1996, and it has drawn such interest from other cities that Carter announced a national rollout of the concept to other cities starting in 1995. Second, the presence of the 1996 Olympic Summer Games in Atlanta has meant that businesses, government agencies, and community groups have to cooperate to meet the city's commitments as host city. TAP objectives and needs mesh nicely into some aspects of Atlanta's Olympic planning efforts. Third, the entire process is reinforcing an ethic in the Atlanta business community that was summarized by former Atlanta mayor and United Nations ambassador, Andrew Young, in this way: "At the end of the day, the success of business depends not on profit and loss, but on the quality of life." Quality of life cannot mean two cities, one rich and one poor; it must mean one community, with opportunity and hope for all.

Boston Against Drugs: A Micro Approach to Social Issues

Illegal drugs have been a part of America's social problems for many years. Since the 1970s, federal, state, and local governments have tried to combat drug distribution and sale through vigorous enforcement efforts. Many experts believe the nation is still losing its battle against drugs and that renewed efforts must be made to address drug sale and use.

Private sector initiatives have also been undertaken to deal with drugs. Many companies have instituted drug testing programs in the workplace to identify workers whose drug abuse may be harmful to others. To the extent drugs undermine workforce productivity, they threaten the competitiveness of companies. Worse, by far, drugs impair a person's judgment and physical actions. This can be fatal for coworkers and innocent bystanders if the impaired employee is operating mechanical equipment, motor vehicles, or airplanes. Public safety and workplace safety considerations have made drug testing and substance-abuse education common among many companies.

A second type of private sector antidrug effort has involved public education campaigns to persuade people, especially young adults, not to experiment with illegal substances. One of the best-known programs is the advertising campaign sponsored by Partnership for a Drug-Free America. Media companies, advertisers, and advertising agencies have teamed up to raise millions of dollars to broadcast the creative, sometimes shocking Partnership ads. (In one, the camera focuses on an egg as a voice says, "This is your brain." The next scene shows a cracked egg frying on a hot griddle as the voice says, "This is your brain on drugs.") The object is to deter people from ever trying drugs.

Post–Lawrence–Weber:
Business and Society,
Ninth Edition

Case Study: Save Our
Cities: Business and the
Community

© The McGraw–Hill
Companies, 1999

Business has also become involved in grassroots, community-based efforts to tackle drug use. In Boston, such a program is called Boston Against Drugs (BAD). BAD is a partnership of businesses, nonprofit organizations, and government agencies formed in 1987 when former mayor Ray Flynn called on local businesses to assist in dealing with the city's drug and substance abuse issues. A number of corporate chief executives were willing to become involved because they believed drugs to be a social scourge which their companies were already addressing through drug testing, education, and prevention programs. Others concluded it was not politically smart to say no to a popular mayor who seemed likely to hold political office for years to come.[1]

As in The Atlanta Project, Boston Against Drugs adopted a neighborhood focus. The city was divided into 16 neighborhoods. For each, a team was formed consisting of government officials, community leaders, and a business that had connections to the area. For example, in South Boston, Gillette, the consumer products giant, signed on as the corporate team member. Among the other companies were Bank of Boston; New England Telephone (NYNEX); Group Bull, a computer manufacturer; Boston Edison, an electric utility; and Blue Cross and Blue Shield, a health insurer. *The Boston Herald* (daily newspaper), MassPort (public authority that operates the airport and harbor), the MBTA (subway and bus system), and several law firms also were involved.

Business leadership was key to BAD's activities. The first challenge was to get the cooperation of community groups, government officials, and businesses to actually form the community teams. Because each of these organizations faces many demands on their time, considerable persuasion was necessary to get the proper players on board. An even greater challenge was to get the team members talking in a constructive and positive way. What were the problems in each neighborhood? What could and should be done? How could obstacles be overcome? Would any of their efforts really make a difference? Months passed before the teams developed enough trust and sense of common purpose for initiatives to begin taking shape. Once they did, however, things began to change in the community. In one neighborhood, the need was for a basketball program; in another, classes were offered at a community center; in yet another, a job counseling project was started. By the end of a year, there were signs of progress.

Boston Against Drugs started small but had potential. In 1990, the program received a federal grant to expand the program to all of the city's neighborhoods and to begin a systematic evaluation process to see whether such efforts ultimately influenced drug use by the population of a neighborhood. An evaluation team was created to work with neighborhood teams, to track results, neighborhood by neighborhood, and to facilitate sharing lessons learned. Boston became a model for other antidrug programs throughout the United States.

A Narrow Focus

Drugs are often at the center of a city's social problems. Many experts believe that by focusing sharply on antidrug activities, leverage can be created for addressing issues such as crime, education, and poverty. Some BAD leaders believe it is crucial to keep a clear

[1]Victor Forlani, "Boston Against Drugs: An Analysis of Business in the Community," in Steven Wartick and Denis Collins, eds., *1994 Proceedings of Fifth Annual Conference, International Association for Business and Society* (Hilton Head, NC, March 17–20, 1994), pp. 300–4; Boston Against Drugs, *Annual Report* (Boston: Office of The Mayor, 1994).

Post–Lawrence–Weber:
Business and Society,
Ninth Edition

Case Study: Save Our
Cities: Business and the
Community

© The McGraw–Hill
Companies, 1999

focus on drugs if anything is to be accomplished. These people fear a loss of focus if other community problems are added to the agenda.

Business played an important role in Boston Against Drugs. By providing leadership, human resources, financial leverage, and demonstrated commitment, the business community has helped make the program an important part of the city's commitment to saving its neighborhoods. When Mayor Flynn resigned in 1993 to assume the position of U.S. ambassador to the Vatican, a city council member named Thomas Menino became acting mayor. Several months later, Menino was elected to a full term as mayor of Boston. Among his early actions, the new mayor endorsed the concept and reinforced the importance of the Boston Against Drugs partnership: "If we are to build a safe city that serves all of our people, we need partnerships like BAD."

The Future

Not all public–private partnerships succeed in solving the problems of America's cities. Some observers believe that many of these efforts fall short of their goals and objectives. Since program evaluation is often weak, however, the truth is hidden.

Given the complexity of the social ills being addressed, and the challenge of coordinating private sector, public sector, and voluntary sector organizations, it is not surprising that saving the cities is a very difficult task. One role business can play is to insist on careful evaluation of programs in a continuing effort to figure out what works best and what works least well. The business community knows a great deal about program evaluation, total quality management concepts, benchmarking, and quantifying the costs, benefits, and value-added of activities. This expertise needs to be brought to bear on saving our cities. As the authors of the Urban Institute report state:

> The difficulty of measuring such abstract concepts as "improved community spirit" and "increased leadership potential," coupled with the fact that many grassroots organizations do not have access to measurement tools, has made comprehensive evaluation infrequent. However, this trend is slowly changing, partly as a result of increased corporate involvement in distressed communities. As corporations move away from pure philanthropic donations and look at their contributions as investments, they are demanding to see some return on that investment and have increased the demand for measurement of outcomes.[2]

Discussion Questions

1. What factors have helped to make The Atlanta Project a success? Which are unique to Atlanta and which are common to all communities?
2. What factors have helped to make Boston Against Drugs a success? Which are unique to Boston and which are common to all communities?
3. Consider the problems in your own community. Compare the *comprehensive* approach suggested by The Atlanta Project with the *selective* approach of Boston Against Drugs. Which approach has the best potential for success in your community?

[2]George Peterson and Dana Sundblad, *Corporations as Partners in Strengthening Urban Communities,* Research Report 1079–94 (New York: The Conference Board, 1994), p. 43.

Post–Lawrence–Weber:
Business and Society,
Ninth Edition

Case Study: Save Our
Cities: Business and the
Community

© The McGraw–Hill
Companies, 1999

4. Dr. Johnetta Cole, president of Spelman College, has been an active participant in TAP. She has said, "If we focus, if we cooperate, if we sacrifice, . . . we can do it." Are focus, cooperation, and sacrifice enough to save our cities? What else is needed? Is there a role for the federal government? the state government?

5. In some states, there are one or two large cities and many small and medium-sized communities. Should businesses that are located in the large cities, but draw employees and customers from smaller communities as well, participate in projects to strengthen all of these communities? How can they decide which ones not to support?

6. Consider the community in which your college or university is located. What kinds of community involvements does it have? How does it participate in projects to improve the community? What organizations provide the leadership?

TRIBAL WISDOM

Is it too late for us to reclaim the benefits of tribal living?

DAVID MAYBURY-LEWIS

Tribal people hold endless fascination for us moderns. We imagine them as exotica trapped in a lyrical past, or as charming anachronisms embarking on the inevitable course toward modernity. What few of us realize is that tribal peoples have not tried (and failed) to be like us, but have actually chosen to live differently. It is critical that we examine the roads they took that we did not; only then can we get a clear insight into the choices we ourselves make and the price we pay for them—alienation, loneliness, disintegrating families, ecological destruction, spiritual famishment. Only then can we consider the possibility of modifying some of those choices to enrich our lives.

In studying tribal societies, as I have for 30 years, we learn that there is no single "tribal" way of life—I use the word here as a kind of shorthand to refer to small-scale, preindustrial societies that live in comparative isolation and manage their affairs without a central authority such as the state. But however diverse, such societies do share certain characteristics that make them different from "modern" societies. By studying the dramatic contrasts between these two kinds of societies, we see vividly the consequences of modernization and industrialization. Modernization has changed our thinking about every facet of our lives, from family relationships to spirituality to our importance as individuals. Has ours been the road best traveled?

Strange relations

The heart of the difference between the modern world and the traditional one is that in traditional societies people are a valuable resource and the interrelations between them are carefully tended; in modern society things are the valuables and people are all too often treated as disposable.

In the modern world we shroud our interdependency in an ideology of independence. We focus on individuals, going it alone in the economic sphere, rather than persons, interconnected in the social sphere. As French anthropologist Marcel Mauss put it, "It is our Western societies that have recently turned man into an economic animal." What happened?

A truly revolutionary change—a social revolution centering on the rights of the individual—swept Western Europe during the Renaissance and eventually came to dominate and define the modern world. While traditional societies had denounced individualism as anti-social, in Western Europe a belief in the rights and dignity of the individual slowly came to be regarded as the most important aspect of society itself.

The glorification of the individual, this focus on the dignity and rights of the individual, this severing of the obligations to kin and community that support and constrain the individual in traditional societies—all this was the sociological equivalent of splitting the atom. It unleashed the human energy and creativity that enabled people to make extraordinary technical advances and to accumulate undreamed-of wealth.

But we have paid a price for our success. The ever-expanding modern economy is a driven economy, one that survives by creating new needs so that people will consume more. Ideally, under the mechanics of this system, people should have unlimited needs so that the economy can expand forever, and advertising exists to convince them of just that.

The driven economy is accompanied by a restless and driven society. In the United States, for example, the educational system teaches children to be competitive and tries to instill in them the hunger for personal achievement. As adults, the most driven people are rewarded by status. Other human capabilities—for kindness, generosity, patience, tolerance, cooperation, compassion—all the qualities one might wish for in one's family and friends, are literally undervalued: Any job that requires such talents usually has poor pay and low prestige.

The tendency of modern society to isolate the individual is nowhere more clearly evident than in the modern family. In the West we speak of young people growing up, leaving their parents, and "starting a family." To most of the world, including parts of Europe, this notion seems strange. Individuals do not start families, they are born into them and stay in them until death or even beyond. In those societies you cannot leave your family without becoming a social misfit, a person of no account.

When the modern system works, it provides a marvelous release for individual creativity and emotion; when it does not, it causes a lot of personal pain and social stress. It is, characteristically, an optimistic system, hoping for and betting on the best. In contrast, traditional societies have settled for more cautious systems, designed to make life tolerable and to avoid the worst. Americans, in their version of the modern family, are free to be themselves at the risk of ultimate loneliness. In traditional family systems the individual may be suffocated but is never unsupported. Is there a middle way?

Finding that middle way is not a problem that tribal societies have to face, at least not unless they find their way of life overwhelmed by the outside world. They normally get on with the business of bringing up children against a background of consensus about what should be done and how, which means that they can also be more relaxed about who does the bringing up. Chil-

From *Utne Reader,* July/August 1992, pp. 68-79. Excerpted from *Millennium* by David Maybury-Lewis. © 1992 by Meech Grant Productions, Ltd., David Maybury-Lewis, and The Body Shop International PLC. Reprinted by permission of Viking Penguin, a division of Penguin Books USA, Inc.

dren may spend as much time with other adults as they do with their parents, or, as in the Xavante tribe of central Brazil, they may wander around in a flock that is vaguely supervised by whichever adults happen to be nearby. As soon as Xavante babies are old enough to toddle, they attach themselves to one of the eddies of children that come and go in the village. There they are socialized by their peers. The older kids keep an eye on the younger ones and teach them their place in the pecking order. Of course there are squabbles and scraps, and one often sees a little child who has gotten the worst of it wobbling home and yelling furiously. The child's parents never do what parents in our society often do—go out and remonstrate with the children in an attempt to impose some kind of adult justice (often leaving the children with a burning sense of unfairness). Instead they simply comfort the child and let her return to the fold as soon as her bruised knee or battered ego permits. At the same time, there is never any bullying among the Xavante children who are left to police themselves.

In traditional societies, people are valuable; in modern society, things are the valuables.

The Xavante system represents as informal dilution of parents' everyday responsibilities. In many societies these responsibilities are formally transferred to other relatives. In the Pacific Islands, for example, it is quite common for children to be raised by their parents' kin. Among the Trobriand Islanders, this is seen as useful for the child, since it expands his or her network of active kin relationships without severing ties to the biological parents. If children are unhappy, they can return to their true parents. If they are contented, they remain with their adoptive parents until adulthood.

Tribal societies also differ from the modern in their approach to raising teenagers. The tribal transition to maturity is made cleanly and is marked with great ceremony. In Western societies families dither over their often resentful young, suggesting that they may be old enough but not yet mature enough, mature enough but not yet secure enough, equivocating and putting adoles-

cents through an obstacle course that keeps being prolonged.

Tribal initiation rites have always held a special interest for outside observers, who have been fascinated by their exotic and especially by their sexual aspects. It is the pain and terror of such initiations that make the deepest impression, and these are most frequently inflicted on boys, who are in the process of being taken out of the women's world and brought into that of the men. Some Australian Aboriginal groups peel the penis like a banana and cut into the flesh beneath the foreskin. Some African groups cut the face and forehead of the initiate in such a way as to leave deep scars.

Circumcision is, of course, the commonest of all initiation procedures. Its effect on the boy is, however, intensified in some places by an elaborate concern with his fortitude during the operation. The Maasai of East Africa, whose *moran* or warriors are world famous as epitomes of courage and bravado, closely watch a boy who is being circumcised for the slightest sign of cowardice. Even an involuntary twitch could make him an object of condemnation and scorn.

Initiation rituals are intended to provoke anxiety. They act out the death and rebirth of the initiate. His old self dies, and while he is in limbo he learns the mysteries of his society—instruction that is enhanced by fear and deprivation and by the atmosphere of awe that his teachers seek to create. In some societies that atmosphere is enhanced by the fact that the teachers are anonymous, masked figures representing the spirits. The lesson is often inscribed unforgettably on his body as well as in his mind. Later (the full cycle of ceremonies may last weeks or even months) he is reborn as an adult, often literally crawling between the legs of his sponsor to be reborn of man into the world of men.

Girls' initiation ceremonies are as dramatically marked in some societies as those of boys. Audrey Richards' account of the *chisungu*, a month-long initiation ceremony among the Bemba of Zambia, describes the complex ritual that does not so much add to the girl's practical knowledge as inculcate certain attitudes—a respect for age, for senior women and men, for the mystical bonds between husband and wife, for what the Bemba believe to be the dangerous potentials of sex, fire, and blood. The initiate learns the secret names of things and the songs and dances known only to women. She is incorporated into the group of women who form her immediate community, since this is a society that traces descent in the female line and a husband moves to his wife's village when they marry. Western writers tend to assume that it is more important for boys to undergo separation from their mothers as they mature than it is for girls. But the Bemba stress that mothers must surrender their daughters in the *chisungu* to the community at large (and to the

venerable mistress of ceremonies in particular) as part of a process through which they will eventually gain sons-in-law.

The ceremony Richards observed for the initiation of three girls included 18 separate events, some 40 different pottery models (shaped for the occasion and destroyed immediately afterward), nearly a hundred songs, and numerous wall paintings and dances, all used to instruct the girls in their new status. All of this represents a large investment of time and resources. The initiation gives girls a strong sense of the solidarity and powers of women in a society that also stresses male authority and female submissiveness.

The tribal initiation gives girls a strong sense of the powers of women.

Ever since the influential work of Margaret Mead, there has been a tendency in the West to assume that, if growing up is less stressful in tribal societies, it is because they are less puritanical about sex. The modern world has, however, undergone a sexual revolution since Mead was writing in the 1930s and 1940s, and it does not seem to have made growing up much easier. I think that, in our preoccupation with sex, we miss the point. Take the case of tribal initiations. They not only make it clear to the initiates (and to the world at large) that they are now mature enough to have sex and to have children; the clarity also serves to enable the individual to move with a fair degree of certainty through clearly demarcated stages of life.

A moral economy

Since earliest times, the exchange of gifts has been the central mechanism through which human beings relate to one another. The reason is that the essence of a gift is obligation. A person who gives a gift compels the recipient either to make a return gift or to reciprocate in some other way. Obligation affects the givers as well. It is not entirely up to them whether or when to bestow a gift. Even in the modern world, which prides itself on its pragmatism, people are expected to give gifts on certain occasions— at weddings, at childbirth, at Christmas, and so on. People are expected to invite others to receive food and drink in their houses and those so invited are expected to return the favor.

In traditional societies, it is gifts that bond people to one another and make society work. It follows that in such societies a rich person is not somebody who accumulates wealth in money and goods but rather somebody who has a large network of people beholden to him. Such networks are the instrument through which prominent people can demonstrate their prestige. They are also the safety net that sees an individual through the crises of life.

In modern societies these networks have shrunk, just as the family continues to shrink. There are fewer and fewer people to whom we feel obligated and, more ominously, fewer and fewer who feel obligated to us. When we think of a safety net, when our politicians speak of it, we refer to arrangements made by abstract entities—the state, the corporation, the insurance company, the pension fund—entities we would not dream of giving presents to; entities we hope will provide for us (and fear they will not).

Gift exchanges form the safety net that sees an individual through life's crises.

Traditional societies operate a moral economy, that is, an economy permeated by personal and moral considerations. In such a system, exchanges of goods in the "market" are not divorced from the personal relationships between those who exchange. On the contrary, the exchanges define those relationships. People who engage in such transactions select exchange partners who display integrity and reliability so that they can go back to them again and again. Even when cash enters such an economy, it does not automatically transform it. People still look for just prices, not bargain prices, and the system depends on trust and interdependence. In traditional societies the motto is "seller beware," for a person who gouges or shortchanges will become a moral outcast, excluded from social interaction with other people.

An ecology of mind

The sense of disconnection so characteristic of modern life affects not only the relations between people but equally importantly the relations between people and their environment. As a result, we may be gradually making the planet uninhabitable. The globe is warming up and is increasingly polluted. We cannot take fresh air or clean water for granted anymore. Even our vast oceans are starting to choke on human garbage. The rain forests are burning. The ozone layer is being depleted at rates that constantly exceed our estimates.

How have we come to this? A hundred years ago science seemed to hold such promising possibilities. But the scientific advances of the 19th century were built on the notion that human beings would master nature and make it produce more easily and plentifully for them. Medieval Christianity also taught that human beings, although they might be sinners, were created in God's image to have dominion over this earth. Whether human dominion was guaranteed by the Bible or by science, the result was the same—the natural world was ours to exploit.

Tribal societies, by contrast, have always had a strong sense of the interconnectedness of things on this earth and beyond. For example, human beings have, for the greater part of the history of our species on this earth, lived by hunting and gathering. Yet peoples who lived by hunting and gathering did not—and do not to this day—consider themselves the lords of creation. On the contrary, they are more likely to believe in (and work hard to maintain) a kind of reciprocity between human beings and the species they are obliged to hunt for food.

The reciprocity between hunter and hunted is elaborately expressed in the ideas of the Makuna Indians of southeastern Colombia. The Makuna believe that human beings, animals, and all of nature are parts of the same One. Their ancestors were fish people who came ashore along the rivers and turned into people. Out of their bodies or by their actions these ancestors created everything in the world, the hills and forests, the animals and the people. They carved out river valleys by pushing their sacred musical instruments in front of them.

People, animals, and fish all share the same spiritual essence and so, the Makuna say, animals and fish live in their own communities, which are just like human communities. They have their chiefs, their shamans, their dance houses, birth houses, and "waking up houses" (places where they originally came into being as species). They have their songs and dances and their material possessions. Above all, animals and fish are just like humans because they wear ritual ornaments, consume spirit foods—coca, snuff, and the hallucinogenic brew called *yage*—and use the sacred *yurupari* instruments in their ceremonies. When shamans blow over coca, snuff, and other spirit foods during human ceremonies, they are offering them to the animal people. When human beings

dance in this world, the shaman invites the animal people to dance in theirs. If humans do not dance and shamans do not offer spirit food to the animal people, the animals will die out and there will be no more game left in this world.

Thus when the fish are spawning, they are actually dancing in their birth houses. That is why it is particularly dangerous to eat fish that have been caught at the spawning places, for then one eats a person who is ceremonially painted and in full dance regalia. A human being who does this or enters a fish house by mistake will sicken and die, for his soul will be carried away to the

---

Tribal people maintain a reciprocity with the species they must hunt for food.

---

houses of the fish people.

It is clear that Makuna beliefs have specific ecological consequences. The sacredness of salt licks and fish-spawning places, the careful reciprocity between humans and their fellow animals and fish, all mediated by respected shamans, guarantee that the Makuna manage their environment and do not plunder it. The Swedish anthropologist Kaj Arhem, an authority on the Makuna, describes their ecological practices and cosmological speculations as an "ecosophy," where the radical division between nature and culture, humans and animals—so characteristic of Western thought—dissolves.

Arhem suggests that we need an ecosophy of our own, imbued with moral commitment and emotional power, if we are to protect the resources on which we depend and ensure not only our own survival but also that of our fellow creatures on this earth.

We, on the other hand, tend to forget our environment except when we want to extract wealth from it or use it as the backdrop for a scenic expedition. Then we take what we want. There is no compact, none of the reciprocity so characteristic of tribal societies. For the most part we mine the earth and leave it, for we do not feel we belong to it. It belongs to us. This rootlessness and the waste that goes with it are particularly shocking to traditional societies.

The Indians of the western United States were outraged by the way in which the invaders of their territories squandered the resources that they themselves used so sparingly. The Indians on the plains lived off the buffalo, killing only as many as they needed and using every bit of the dead animals. They ate the meat, made tents and clothes from the hides, and used the bones to make arrow straighteners, bows, mallets, even splints for setting fractures. They made butter from the marrow fat and cords from the sinews. When the white buffalo hunters came, it was more than an invasion. It was a sacrilege. These men slaughtered the herds with their powerful rifles, often taking only the tongue to eat and leaving the rest of the animal to rot.

The deep sadness of the Indians over this slaughter was expressed in a speech attributed to Chief Seattle, after whom the city of Seattle is named, believed to have been delivered in 1854 to an assembly of tribes preparing to sign away their lands under duress to the white man. Some contend the speech was actually written by a Texas speechwriter in 1971. Whatever their origin, these moving words convey an environmental and spiritual ethic that most tribal people share. They speak as much to us about our own predicament as they did to Chief Seattle's fellow chiefs about their defeated civilization. "What is man without the beasts?" he asked. "If all the beasts were gone, man would die from a great loneliness of spirit. For whatever happens to the beasts, soon happens to man. All things are connected. . . . We know that the white man does not understand our ways. One portion of the land is the same to him as the next, for he is a stranger who comes in the night and takes from the land whatever he needs. The earth is not his brother, but his enemy, and when he has conquered it, he moves on. He leaves his fathers' graves behind, and he does not care. He kidnaps the earth from his children. He does not care. His fathers' graves and his children's birthright are forgotten. He treats his mother, the earth, and his brother, the sky, as things to be bought, plundered, sold like sheep or bright beads. His appetite will devour the earth and leave behind only a desert."

Touching the timeless

Modern society is intensely secular. Even those who regret this admit it. Social theorists tend to assume that modernization is itself a process of secularization that has not only undermined people's religious beliefs but has also deprived them of their spirituality. In the industrial nations of the West many of the people who believe in God do not expect to come into close contact with the divine, except after death—and some of them are not too sure about it even then.

Indeed, it seems that those who live in the secular and industrialized West are already searching for ways to fill the vacuum in their lives left by "organized" religion and the numbing delights of mass society. We live in a world that prides itself on its modernity yet is hungry for wholeness, hungry for meaning. At the same time it is a world that marginalizes the very impulses that might fill this void. The pilgrimage toward the divine, the openness to knowledge that transcends ordinary experience, the very idea of feeling at one with the universe are impulses we tolerate only at the fringes of our society.

It seems that we denigrate our capacity to dream and so condemn ourselves to live in a disenchanted world. Shorn of the knowledge that we are part of something greater than ourselves, we also lose the sense of responsibility that comes with it. It is this connectedness that tribal societies cherish. Yet for modern society, this is a bond we cannot bring ourselves to seek. But if we do not listen to other traditions, do not even listen to our inner selves, then what will the future hold for our stunted and overconfident civilization?

The tightrope of power

Meanwhile, this civilization of ours, at once so powerful and so insecure, rolls like a juggernaut over societies that have explored the very solutions that might help us save ourselves. We do so in the name of progress, insisting all too often that we offer science, truth, plenty, and social order to peoples who lack these things. Yet the contrast between tribal societies and the centralized states that prey on them is not one of order and disorder, violence and peace. It is instead a contrast between societies in which no one has a monopoly on the legitimate use of force and others in which those rights are vested in a state. The 20th century has been one of the bloodiest in history, not only because of the wars between countries employing weapons of mass destruction but also because modern technology has been used by ruthless rulers to cow their own subjects. Hitler and Stalin are only the most notorious examples of dictators who directed violence against their own people in the name of the state. There are literally scores of shooting wars going on at this moment, most of them between states and their own subjects.

The state guarantees order, or is supposed to. Force, the monopoly of the government, is applied massively but, once the system is in place, relatively invisibly. Its victims are hidden in concentration camps or banished to Siberias. In many places today, the victims simply disappear.

It seems that people will often acquiesce in despotism for fear of anarchy. Recent history seems to indicate that the most advanced countries are more afraid of anarchy than they are of oppression. The Russians, whose whole history is a struggle to create order on the open steppes of Eurasia, have a fear of disorder (which they call *besporyadok,* the condition of not being "lined up") that has frequently led them to accept tyranny. At the other extreme, the United States, whose whole history is a determination to avoid despotism, allows more internal chaos than most other industrial nations. It values individual freedom to the point of allowing private citizens to own arsenals of weapons and puts up with a rate of interpersonal violence that would be considered catastrophic in other countries.

It seems that human beings are everywhere searching for the right balance between the mob and the dictator, between chaos and tyranny, between the individual and society. Industrial societies give a monopoly of power to the state in exchange for a guarantee of peace. We take this social order for granted to the extent that we tend to assume that there is anarchy and perpetual warfare in tribal societies. What we do not realize is that such societies are acutely conscious of the fragility of the social order and of the constant effort needed to maintain it. Paradoxically, the people who live in societies that do not have formal political institutions are more political than those who do since it is up to each individual to make sure that the system works, indeed to ensure that the system continues to exist at all. Tribal people avoid the perils of anarchy only through constant and unremitting effort.

Elijah Harper, an Ojibwa-Cree who is a member of parliament in the Canadian providence of Manitoba, contrasted the democratic procedures of the native Canadians he represented with those of the Canadian government that was trying to push through a revision of Canada's constitution. The new constitution was designed to respond to Quebec's demand to be considered a distinct society within Canada, with appropriate protection for its own language and culture. Harper used parliamentary procedure to block the constitutional change, on the grounds that native Canadians had been asking for similar consideration for years without getting a hearing. A new round of discussions concerning the revision of Canada's constitution is now taking place and this time the rights of Canada's "first nations," the aboriginal peoples, are also on the agenda.

The Canadian crisis makes clear what is only dimly perceived in other countries, namely that the destiny of the majority in any state is intimately linked to the fate of its minorities. The failure of the first attempt to change their constitution has forced Canadians to think about what kind of society they want theirs to be. These are the same questions that the Aborigines are trying to put on the Australian agenda and that the Indians are forcing Brazilians to think about as they protest against the rape of Amazonian regions.

It is not only in authoritarian states that questions arise about how people within a state are allowed to go about their business. The dramatic events in Eastern Europe, however, have led some people to think so. Once the heavy hand of Communist dictatorship was lifted, the nations of Eastern Europe started to unravel. Old ethnic loyalties surfaced and ethnic rivalries threaten to dismember one nation after another. The problem in Eastern Europe is not that it is made up of more peoples than states, but rather that the states have not been successful in working out political solutions that could enable those peoples to live together amicably. But neither do democratic regimes find it easy to create more imaginative solutions that allow diverse groups of people to live together.

The reason for this failure is that such solutions require us to have a different idea of the state, a kind of new federalism which, after the manner of the League of the Iroquois, permits each people in the nation to keep its council fire alight. This requires more than rules; it requires commitment. The Great Law of the Iroquois was remarkable because it was a constitution that had the force of a religion. People were willing, indeed eager, to subscribe to it because they saw it and revered it as the source of peace. Is it too much to hope that in a world riven with ethnic conflict we might search for political solutions more energetically than we have in the past? That we will not continue to expect strong states to iron out ethnicity, even if it means wiping out the "ethnics"? A new federalism is in our own interest, for it offers the hope of peace and the prospect of justice. Nations that trample on the rights of the weak are likely to end up trampling on everybody's rights. As we wring our hands over the fate of tribal peoples in the modern world, we would do well to remember John Donne's words: "Never send to know for whom the bell tolls; it tolls for thee."

Serious consideration of tribal ways of life should lead us to think carefully and critically about our own. What would it take for us to try to live in harmony with nature or to rehumanize our economic systems? How can we mediate between the individual and the family, between genders and generations? Should we strive for a less fragmented view of physical reality or of our place in the scheme of things? These questions revolve around wholeness and harmony, around tolerance and pluralism. The answers are still emerging, but they too are variations on a grand theme that can be summed up in E. M. Forster's famous phrase: "Only connect." The project for the new millennium will be to re-energize civil society, the space between the state and the individual where these habits of the heart that socialize the individual and humanize the state flourish.

CULTURAL REVOLUTION AND CHARACTER FORMATION

William R. Garrett

Popular wisdom holds that during the sixties the youth peer culture transformed American life by becoming a counterculture. The immediate upshot was to introduce a whole succession of changes in social life. These changes included an upswing in drug use; long hair for men; premarital cohabitation; increased use of obscenity and profanity; heightened violence; alienation from the basic institutions of American society including the family, education, religion, government, and corporate capitalism; opposition to the war in Vietnam; women's liberation; a greater tolerance for homosexuals; and a demand for a wider range of discretionary freedoms for individuals.

Social scientists have been puzzled about the timing of this explosion of radical changes. Why was the rather quiescent and conservative era of the fifties succeeded by the rebellious sixties? What were the triggering mechanisms that fostered such a broad range of criticism and revolution? In this article I will attempt an explanation by looking at the transformation of the youth peer group into a counterculture, using globalization theory and couching the sixties within an extensive matrix of cultural forces. The approach to globalization that I will use here stresses the formidable significance of cultural influences in the creation of a global order, alongside economic, technological, and political factors.

William R. Garrett is professor of sociology at Saint Michael's College, Colchester, Vermont.
This paper is adapted from one presented at the Professors World Peace Academy conference on "Identity and Character," held in Washington, D.C., November 24–29, 1997.

This article originally appeared in *The World & I*, May 1998, pp. 289-307. Reprinted by permission of *The World & I*, a publication of the Washington Times Corporation. © 1998.

What stands out as abnormal and in need of explanation is the fifties, not the sixties.

Actually, what stands out as abnormal and in need of explanation is the fifties, not the sixties. The radical innovations of the sixties were in a profound sense a return to cultural normality, as we will explain later, and, therefore, should have occurred after the end of World War II. Sociocultural forces conspired, instead, to produce the aberrant fifties—a period that roughly ranged from 1946 to 1964—and the conventional wisdom swiftly emerged among most social commentators that the fifties constituted normality, thereby rendering the sixties abnormal.

My argument here will reverse that judgment and give a wholly different assessment of the broad range of radical changes introduced in the sixties and continuing in slightly modified form until the present day. If my interpretative framework is credible, it will permit construction of a more nuanced assessment of the processes of identity and character formation than has been devised previously.

A SCHEMATIC ACCOUNT: THE LAST CENTURY IN GLOBAL PERSPECTIVE

The century from 1890 to 1990 can be partitioned into four relatively distinct periods: 1890–1929, the period of the takeoff of global dynamics; 1930–1945, the era of worldwide economic depression and World War II; 1946–1964, the aberrant fifties; and 1965–1990 (parenthetically, this one can be extended to the present day), an era that we can appropriately designate as the time of resurgent globalizing forces, including cultural as well as material, economic, and technological changes. I will argue that the periods 1890–1929 and 1965 to the present represent smooth curve development, interrupted by the historically disjunctive periods of depression-world war and the aberrant fifties.

It can be argued that contemporary globalization dynamics had their origin during the period when the modern nation-state was coming into existence and Victorian culture was almost everywhere under attack. Also significant is the recognition that the changes introduced after the mid-1960s continue to influence patterns of thought and behavior to the present time. While there have been some modifications—opposition to the Vietnam War no longer persists, for example—the major cultural innovations related to individual conduct remain enduring features of the societal landscape of the late twentieth century.

We can delineate, alongside the account of globalization as a historical process, four major components that constitute the global human condition, namely: individual selves or selfhood; nation-states; world systems of societies (such as the UN, NATO, the EU, etc.); and humanity. Each of these components merits brief explication.

Selfhood. Under the conditions of globality, an individual's consciousness as a self and his freedom of discretionary action are significantly intensified. This results in a sharp decline in the number of ascribed roles imposed upon the individual based on such characteristics as gender, race, ethnicity, social class, and the like. This intensified fixation on the self results in two things: Individuals are afforded greater latitude in their discretionary behaviors, and they are compelled to take greater responsibility for determining who they are. Reducing the characteristics imposed on individuals means that greater emphasis is put on the statuses and roles—even sexual roles—they select for themselves.

Nation-states. The modern nation-state emerged between 1870 and 1890, occasioned by the expanding political participation by rank-and-file members of society and the growth of their conscious attachment as a nation to the body politic. Throughout much of the world prior to this, affairs of state were almost exclusively the prerogative of the elite classes, while most ordinary folk identified with their village or region rather than with the central government. The modern, unitary nation-state has assumed an interventionist role in human affairs, based on the claim that "it alone can raise the living standards of the population, educate them, unify them, give them a sense of pride and well-being, and administer public affairs in a 'rational' and calculative manner."[1]

So the modern nation-state has become something more than an empirical functioning unit or "political entity with specific self-interests"; it has become at once an "ultimate symbol and an institutionalized global norm" with the features of "a moral community to which members of society can become subjectively attached."[2] After having been brought into existence, societies are accorded a kind of sanctity that guarantees their right to existence and legitimates not only national self-defense but the obligation of citizens to give their "last full measure of devotion" so that the nation will not perish. The substantive content and identity of na-

tion-states in the global order varies quite considerably, depending on the values, rights, governance structure, and unique history associated with each society.

Systems of nation-states. Nation-states and systems of nation-states were both born in the late nineteenth and early twentieth centuries, for as soon as nation-states emerged they formed coalitions based on economic, political, cultural, or social activities. Some of the more immediate political alliances included the Allied and Axis powers, the League of Nations (followed soon after by the United Nations), NATO, the Warsaw Pact, SEATO, the Francophone nations, and so forth. Among the economic alliances were the EU, NAFTA, GATT, and myriad more, as well as cultural, communication, transportation, business, athletic, legal (such as the World Court), human rights, and other international groupings.

The immediate upshot of these global systems of societies was to relativize the status of nation-states by imposing extra societal demands on them that they had to confront and either accept or else weather the sanctions of other, collective nation-states or various international nongovernmental organizations. The notion of nation-state sovereignty remains a formidable obstacle to achieving the aims of many international governmental and nongovernmental organizations. Nonetheless, the state-centric model is gradually being supplanted by a growing recognition of the limitations to the power of discrete nations by virtue of their necessary involvement in various systems of nation-states.

Citizens of the world are coming to a greater consciousness of their common unity with the rest of the human race.

Humanity. Citizens of the world are coming to a greater consciousness of their common unity with the rest of the human race. This affirmation is made despite such inhumane actions as the Holocaust, the ethnic cleansing of Bosnia, the tribal fratricide in Rwanda, and numerous other atrocities. Indeed, the almost universal repugnance with which such acts of violence against members of the human community are greeted provides evidence for the emergent status of humanity as a vibrant construct in geopolitical consciousness.

The substantive meaning given to the concept of humanity has been thematized

1. A.D. Smith, *Theories of Nationalism,* 2nd ed. (London: Duckworth, 1993), 231–32.
2. Frank Lechner, "Cultural Aspects of the Modern World-System," in William Swatos Jr., ed., *Religious Politics in Global and Comparative Perspective* (Westport, Conn.: Greenwood Press, 1989), 16–21.

most concretely in various human rights instruments. Although the first efforts to articulate a human rights position occurred in the late eighteenth century with France's Declaration of the Rights of Man and Citizen (1789) and the United States' Bill of Rights (1791), the globalization of the human rights tradition did not really commence until after World War II when the United Nations enacted the Universal Declaration of Human Rights (1948) as well as the subsequent International Covenant on Economic, Social and Cultural Rights (1966) and the International Covenant on Civil and Political Rights (1966). These statements, as well as myriad others pertaining to the specific rights of children, women, refugees, ethnic groups, and the like, further specify in substantive detail what humanity means in a fashion that lends practical signification to the concept.

One result of the rising notion of humanity has been to relativize the nation-state even more. Accordingly, regimes can no longer argue with impunity that how they treat their citizens is exclusively their own business and not a legitimate matter of concern for watchdog groups, systems of nation-states, or activists beyond their borders. The result has been a spiraling criticism of such nations as Sudan for permitting female genital mutilation, China for its repression of students on Tiananmen Square, India for its maltreatment of Muslim and Sikh minorities, and the United States for its frequent recourse to the death penalty.

In each instance, the charge is raised that it is an act of violence against all of us, since we all participate in that larger collectivity known as humanity. Moreover, a similar justification is put forward relative to saving the whales and protecting the rain forest, on the ground that the few remaining whales do not belong to the Norwegians or the Japanese who send out trawlers to find them, nor does the rain forest belong exclusively to Brazil. The claim is that the whales and the rain forest constitute resources for humanity, so we all have a right to seek their protection, a right that transcends the national interest of particular societies. To be sure, the legal guarantees to sustain these claims have not yet been fully institutionalized, but global public opinion has become an increasingly potent weapon in the arsenal of those who promote the interests of humanity vis-à-vis the more particularistic claims of nation-states.

SOCIOCULTURAL EVENTS

The take-off period: 1890–1930. Despite the often brash self-confidence of leaders in both North America and Europe at the outset of the 1890s, the Gilded Age manifested an increasing cacophony of discordant trends. Intellectually, a revolt began against Enlightenment rationality. Economically, the robber barons reached their pinnacle of power, and muckraking exposures prompted reforms of large corporations. Politically, nationalism emerged, leading to schemes of imperialistic expansion, while populist dissent challenged the hegemony of established party and machine politicians.

Religiously, American Protestants vacillated between evangelical revivalism and liberal theology. There was an effort to accommodate modern thought forms and—through the social gospel movement—to deal with the problems of rapid industrialization, urbanization, unionization, and immigrant assimilation. Roman Catholicism wrestled with the question of whether it was better to enter into a passive accommodation to or a full acceptance of American culture.

Demographically, American society experienced a spurt of rapid urbanization, based on many native rural folk flooding into the cities and a massive influx of immigrants. Ethnically, assimilation processing instilled in foreign-born citizens a new identity as Americans in ever-increasing numbers and fostering the formation of powerful ethnic subcommunities. Educationally, the American collegiate population increased by a staggering 38.4 percent between 1890 and 1895, and reached one million by 1930. There was a corresponding relaxation of administrative controls over the lifestyles and moral attitudes of the student peer group and an explosion of extracurricular diversions—ranging from sporting events to the expansion of the sorority-fraternity system, debating clubs, student government, and YMCA/YWCAs.

For families, the 1890s marked the beginning of the end of that distinctly Victorian pattern of the husband-dominant power structure within the nuclear family. This occurred especially as women began to slough off the virtuous woman ideal that had effectively defined a woman's proper place as a subservient housewife, mother, and wife, isolated from the workplace, from political power structures, and from leadership roles within the church, and granted only limited access to educational opportunities.

Collectively, these changes challenged the foundations of the reigning Victorian social order and redirected the cultural and structural features of American social life. The efforts of many—the labor movement, feminist vanguards, politicians of the progressive era, ethnic community lobbyists, religious reformers, and student activists—served to empower more people to behave as they wished.

The overriding trend was to emphasize a set of identities formed around class, ethnic, religious, gender, and political interests. Each of these was sharply opposed to the conservative sociocultural order of the nineteenth century. Although the role of the student peer group was not nearly so

Participants in the subculture that blossomed forth after 1910 were excited about ideas and hedonistic, but they also recognized that beyond campus there existed a world of economics, politics, labor unrest, and the arts.

pronounced then as it was during the mid-1960s, it was nonetheless a formidable influence in delegitimating Establishment authorities, ideologies, and institutions.

The trends pertaining to student peer groups' lifestyles and behavioral codes prefigured the subsequent ideological and generational conflicts. Participants in the rebel or bohemian subculture that blossomed forth after 1910 were at once excited about ideas and hedonistic—like their fraternity-sorority counterparts—but they also recognized that beyond campus there existed a world of economics, politics, labor unrest, and the arts. So the trends launched by members of the student subculture quickly began to penetrate into the larger social order as bohemian enclaves like Greenwich Village sprang up as a direct challenge to the dominant culture, movements that soon exercised influence far in excess of their actual numbers.

The interregnum years: 1930–1945. The inroads achieved by the student movement against the stultifying intellectual-moral forms of Victorian culture—combined with the deep structural changes brought about by industrial growth, ethnic assimilation, political reforms, and familial transformations—were all effectively immobilized by the worsening effects of the Depression. Even World War I had not produced so drastic a consequence.

The Depression also rekindled isolationist and antiglobal sentiments among the American populace. Historian Paul Kennedy has claimed that, had the American response to the economic crisis of world capitalism been less parochial, the Depression in the United States would have been less severe and of shorter duration. But with a large portion of our productive capacity standing idle, we reacted defensively by erecting tariff barriers to protect indigenous industries. Thus, at precisely the wrong time, access to foreign markets was cut off, causing the Depression to intensify.

This experience was emblematic for the whole decade of the 1930s. Emerging international contacts for the United States were summarily cut by the rise of isolationist ideologies based on a wide range of economic, political, cultural, or antimilitaristic views. International relations shriveled in the face of U.S. efforts to limit its foreign commitments—especially after a succession of ill-conceived attempts to manipulate currency and exchange agreements designed to promote American interests. Abroad, similar movements for student, religious, intellectual, and ethnic contacts were curtailed because of bad economic conditions. Only the labor movement enjoyed something of a resurgence of international relations as advocates of socialist and communist ideologies streamed into the nation to urge unionists to forsake the bread-and-butter orientation of market unionism in favor of a more aggressive stance that sought a role for workers in management. Ultimately, even this effort failed as Americans circled the wagons and turned inward for the resources to weather out the storm of the Depression.

The culture of American society after the mid-1940s did not return to normal.

Perhaps nowhere was the stubborn resistance to globalizing tendencies more pronounced than in the response of rank-and-file American citizens to the gathering storm of fascism in Europe and Asia that would eventually usher in World War II. The rise of totalitarian regimes—often out of soil where liberal democratic experiments had previously begun to germinate—readily awakened in the American people a sense of political revulsion. Yet disdain for fascism could not be translated into aggressive opposition; Americans blithely acquiesced to voracious gains recorded abroad on the extreme right of the political spectrum. Mounting a vigorous critique against totalitarianism seemed all but futile, given the collapse of liberal, capitalist economies and the demise of modernism's dream of evolutionary progress.

The crises of the Depression and of fascism convinced much of the American public that the only reasonable response was a defensive retreat from the global arena. That stance proved impossible to maintain, of course, after the attack on Pearl Harbor. Against its will, the United States was forced back into the global arena as a principal player in geopolitical and military affairs, a role that it found impossible to slough off after the war had ended, even though some iso-

lationist sentiment persisted and continued to manifest itself periodically all through the Cold War and into the present day. Thus, while the Depression intensified American isolationism, World War II ended any serious consideration of withdrawal from global involvements.

The aberrant fifties: 1946–1964. With the successful prosecution of the war and with the American economy spiraling to new levels of affluence thereafter, it could reasonably be expected that the liberalizing cultural patterns put on hold after the 1930s would resurface with a vengeance in the late '40s or early '50s. Instead, America experienced an elongated decade of social conservatism (1946–1964) that can best be described as the aberrant fifties. The culture of American society after the mid-1940s did not return to normal; rather, we were visited by a period of political conservatism, familism, religiosity, renewed patriotism, a passion for a sense of belonging, a quest for economic security, and a commitment to traditional gender roles. What needs to be explained relative to the postwar period is not why we experienced the radical sixties but why we entered into the conservative fifties prior to returning to the liberalizing agenda of the early part of the century.

The powerful influence of middle America, or the working class, was, in part, a direct but hidden consequence of governmental policies initiated following World War II. The GI Bill placed an otherwise inaccessible university education within the reach of a substantial segment of the lower middle-class population. The overriding ambition among these returning veterans (and later the Korean contingent as well), who were understandably anxious about time lost, was to convert higher education into better-paying occupations and, in turn, realize upward mobility. Accordingly, the size of the university population doubled twice between 1945 and 1965, creating a critical mass for the support of an independent youth peer group by the mid-1960s. Simultaneously, liberal loan programs administered through the FHA and VHA permitted blue-collar workers to emigrate en masse to the suburbs after World War II, creating in the process one of the major demographic shifts in American history, rivaled only by the movement of Afro-Americans from the South into the urbanized North and West.

A college degree, material success, and the crowning achievement of owning "a home of one's own" in the greenbelt suburbs, along with the ancillary accoutrements, were simply not the sort of aspirations that could ignite a new round of cultural innovations along the lines of the Roaring Twenties. Moreover, the sheer numbers of those in the working class who were moving through the process of becoming middle class help account for part of their influence.

The rest of the story is that this rising class group was discovered by merchandisers, manufacturers, media programmers, politicians, and a whole succession of service-sector entrepreneurs. Although individual family earnings remained relatively modest during the fifties, collectively the accelerating affluence of the working class represented a vast reservoir of wealth waiting to be tapped. The American dream of success—for producers and consumers—now appeared closer at hand than at perhaps any time in our relatively short history.

One of the enduring ironies of the fifties was that not only was the avant-garde—the members of the rising blue-collar class—socially conservative but so, too, were the leading critics of the era. The most widely read among the critics were Will Herberg, William H. Whyte Jr., and David Reisman. Herberg denounced the upsurge in religious participation in the fifties on the basis that ethnic assimilation had created a situation whereby each of the major religious traditions—Protestant, Catholic, and Jewish—was transformed into a means for identifying oneself as an American. The very fact of belonging to one of these religious traditions displaced in importance any substantive commitment to biblical faith. Thus, the widely heralded religious revival of the fifties was, in Herberg's assessment, a colossal expression of apostasy.

Similar critiques of secular culture were given by Whyte and Reisman. Although the ostensible target of Whyte's excoriating commentary was the bureaucratic environment of corporations, the real locus of the dominant social perspective of the fifties was suburbia. Corporations rewarded conformity, belongingness, and skill in manipulating social relationships, but in suburban institutions and communities one could pursue with a vengeance the norms of togetherness, inconspicuous consumption, the web of friendship, spirituality without intellectual substance, child-centered socialization, gemütlichkeit among transients, and education designed for the reproduction of the next generation's conforming consumers.

Riesman's critique dealt less with an appraisal of the institutional sectors responsible for framing the mind-set of the fifties and more with the transformation of American character structure from an "inner-directed" to an "other-directed" orientation. The shallow, conformist, and enervating style of other-directedness did not originate in the fifties, to be sure, but Riesman was convinced that this decade witnessed its maturation to full flower and—more importantly from his point of view—with the full approval of the body politic.

Although none of these critics expressed it in precisely these terms at the time, collectively they perceived that what was at stake was the emergence of a dominant ideology grounded in working-class values and

One of the enduring ironies of the fifties was that not only was the avant-garde—the members of the rising blue-collar class—socially conservative but so, too, were the leading critics of the era.

normative commitments, an ideology whose very seductiveness and vacuity threatened to lead the social-moral culture of American society into decline. But the alternatives prescribed in slightly different terms by Herberg, Whyte, and Reisman did not suggest picking up the modern, liberalization project that had lain in repose since the 1930s. Rather, their conservative proposal was to return to the rugged individualism, self-reliance, and fervent faith of nostalgic imagination in the American past.

Thus, both the working class's trend toward becoming bourgeois and the countertrend advanced by Herberg, Whyte, and Reisman were conservative and remained distinct from what had prompted a whole series of modernizing tendencies before 1930. There was, therefore, scant opportunity for rekindling the liberalizing program of social transformation dormant since the thirties.

The radical sixties: 1965–1998. The fifties ended not with a whimper but a bang. Rarely has there been a break in sociocultural continuity so abrupt and incontestable as the one that appeared in the mid-1960s. In rapid order, the Berkeley student revolt (the Free Speech Movement) of 1964 was followed by an upsurge in SDS (Students for a Democratic Society) demonstrations against the Vietnam War in 1965, the sexual revolution, and the emergence of the drug subculture with widespread experimentation with marijuana and hallucinogens. This was accompanied by revolutions in lifestyle, language usage (with a dramatic rise in profane and obscene words), musical taste (with the popularity of hard rock), dress codes and hair styles, and rebelliousness in public behavior.

The incredibly swift transformation of the youth peer group into a counterculture could lead to the inference that the movement was an ex nihilo creation of American youth between 1964 and 1965. But preparatory stirrings on the left had appeared with

increasing frequency since the late 1950s. Before his untimely death, C. Wright Mills devoted considerable energy to the task of awakening the fifties generation from what he saw as its moral-intellectual lethargy. Meanwhile, the civil rights movement inflamed youthful passions with an idealist sense of moral outrage and an activist zeal to eradicate injustice. Finally, there may well be something to Kenneth Keniston's observation that sixties youth were the first generation to relate to the American dream, not as a utopian vision, but as a reality.

Structural conditions were also a factor. By the mid-1960s, the United States had experienced almost twenty years of unprecedented economic growth and an increase in affluence unmatched in its history. Moreover, the university population more than doubled in less than a decade during the early sixties, throwing extraordinarily large numbers of youth into the most liberal and benign institution of American society, where they could interact freely as well as control the mechanisms for their own socialization. Like all unplanned groups, however, the youth peer group was largely a self-regulating entity. The matter of setting standards—moral, intellectual, aesthetic— was a collective endeavor undertaken frequently in an environment lacking overt leaders, although Todd Gitlin suggested that politicized members of the "early New Left" were "the small motor that later turned the larger motor of the mass student movement of the late Sixties."

The Vietnam War had the strongest symbolic significance. The prospect of being drafted and subsequently killed or wounded in a military conflict many regarded as unwise and unjust was sufficient to drive endless numbers of otherwise quiescent youth into the ranks of the war-opposing counterculture. While this explanation may appear to some to be merely manifesting self-interested motivations for the antiwar movement, which necessarily denigrate the moral integrity of sixties youth, this is not necessarily the case. It leaves the larger problem that it does not account for why young men in the fifties did not react in a similar manner to the Korean War.

To respond by asserting that fifties youth went obsequiously to their fate after being drafted because "times were different then" is at once both a tautological and a profoundly discerning statement. The cultural mores of the fifties would almost certainly not have tolerated the sort of virulent social critique of American democratic ideology, social institutions, military activity, and socially prescribed behavior patterns given by youth of the sixties. Yet, the question remains: What brought about the sudden delegitimation of the dominant conservative ideology of the fifties?

One place to begin an answer is with the class composition of those students who first

comprised the hard-core leadership cadre of the New Student Left. Disproportionately large numbers of the original student activists were drawn from the ranks of the upper middle class. Many of the early leadership were "red diaper babies," that is, the offspring of Old Left parents, while others were merely the children of liberal, well-to-do parents whose overprivileged backgrounds placed them in line to inherit comfortable places in American social life. These youth were, in effect, reclaiming the reins controlling the cultural apparatus of the youth peer culture as rightful heirs to the liberalizing tradition all but abandoned since the early 1930s.

The New Left rejected the technological, bureaucratic, materialistic world of nouveau affluence in which most of its adherents had spent their adolescence.

The New Left's rejection of the technological, bureaucratic, materialistic world of nouveau affluence in which most of its adherents had spent their adolescence was typically couched in terms that accentuated their alienation from many of the strategies of the Old Left. Therefore, although their rejection of labor unions, higher education, liberal religion, and even organized political parties as viable instruments for social change launched them early on toward goals not markedly different culturally from those of the Old Left, their strategies were quite different. The peaceful nonviolence of Martin Luther King and the civil rights movement swiftly gave way to the confrontational tactics of the SDS and the Black Power movement, followed in short order by the violence of the Weathermen faction. Fewer and fewer members of the New Left found themselves in sympathy with this level of orchestrated violence. Over time, in fact, the whole matter of institutional reform faded perceptively from the New Left agenda as cultural matters pertaining to self-fulfillment and lifestyle behaviors loomed ever larger as the focus point of concern.

Indeed, according to historian Terry Anderson, sixties radicalism evolved through two distinct stages: The first wave, from the early 1960s through about 1968, focused on civil rights, free speech in the university, antiwar demonstrations, feminist liberation, and lifestyle changes, all under the leadership of red diaper babies and their liberal cohorts. The second wave, from 1968 into the early 1970s, represented the dramatic popularization of the cultural trends introduced by the first wave, especially lifestyle behaviors. The early movement (which was really several distinct yet overlapping reform efforts) was transformed into a broad-based counterculture among the sixties generation.

The counterculture movement of the sixties was a global, and not simply an American, phenomenon.

The new lifestyle and moral norms introduced by college youth in the sixties had, by the early seventies, trickled down to inform the social outlook of blue-collar youth as well. Long hair, drug use, premarital sexual experimentation, language replete with four-letter words, rock music, cohabitation, and other features of the counterculture lifestyle were assimilated rapidly by working-class adolescents and young adults.

Furthermore, from a cultural perspective, the sixties have not ended. That is to say, while the confrontational political style and antiwar demonstrations abated in the early seventies, other campaigns for societal reform—the ecology, feminist, gay rights, and multicultural movements—have persisted along with the cultural trends and lifestyle experiments introduced by the sixties generation. Although some opponents of these countercultural trends sought refuge in new religious movements or antiglobal, right-wing groups, the fact is that American society generally has yet to be saved from the sixties.

MAKING SENSE OF THE SIXTIES

One of the leading claims of this analysis holds that the sixties represent the reclamation of that liberalization project first launched nearly a century earlier as the opening dynamics toward the realization of a global order. Contemporary assessments of what the sixties meant and what they accomplished vary widely and dramatically. Some participants of the generation that celebrated drugs, sex, and rock and roll are now having second thoughts, while others have aptly been described by pollster Peter Hart: "These people did a lot, regret very little, and don't want their kids to do any of it." Certainly, there were casualties along the way toward self-liberation, with many youths succumbing to drug addiction, limiting their life opportunities by dropping out

of higher education, experiencing premarital pregnancy, becoming fugitives from legal authorities and draft boards, and enduring alienation from family and friends.

Offsetting these personal costs were broader cultural gains, including more freedom for individual behavior and relaxation of previously prescribed statuses and roles. This led to a fuller enfranchisement of the self and to a fuller expansion of our understanding of the meaning of humanity in terms of the global order.

Two observations are in order. The first is that the counterculture movement of the sixties was a global, and not simply an American, phenomenon. Although the American case has been emphasized here, France, the Netherlands, Germany, Japan, Australia, Italy, and, indeed, most industrialized nations—which had also enjoyed prolonged economic prosperity, industrial development, a substantial university population, political stability, extensive media exposure, and rapid rates of upward social mobility—also experienced youth revolts. The leftist political agendas of the student radicals failed to gain popular support almost everywhere—although student protesters did contribute to the resignation of de Gaulle in France in 1969—but the lifestyle and cultural changes persisted into the seventies and after in a similar to that in the United States.

A second observation pertains to the linkage between the 1890--1930 era and the period from the mid-1960s to the present. Numerous analysts have indicated the generational continuity between the 1920–30s leftists and the leadership of the early New Student Left. Few have lingered, however, to contemplate the larger cultural significance of that continuity, for the demographic linkage actually serves as a kind of exterior index to deeper cultural processes.

Family sociologist Andrew Cherlin was one of the first scholars to assert that the sixties represented a return to normal insofar as family patterns were concerned, after the abnormal trends precipitated by the Depression, World War II, and the fifties. Early in this century, he argues, the age at which people entered their first marriage was relatively high, the number of children per household was dropping, the divorce rate was rising rapidly (as was the remarriage rate after marital dissolution), and women were beginning to enter the workforce in increasing numbers.

During the fifties almost all these trends were reversed or retarded in their growth rates: The age at first marriage declined sharply for both men and women, the birthrate increased to produce the baby boom, the divorce rate held relatively steady, and movement of women into the paid labor force outside the home rose only moderately. Indeed, Cherlin contended that, if one took a measure like the divorce rate and compared 1890–1930 with 1960–1980—omitting in

the process the 1930 to 1960 period—what one observed was smooth curve development; hence, the claim that the sixties represented a return to normal. By extension, what is being suggested here is that smooth curve development obtains for more than the divorce rate and that, in fact, trends in cultural liberation between 1890–1930 and 1965 to the present follow a similar trajectory.

The enfranchisement of the self. Although globalization theory is still being developed, considerable consensus appears to be forming around the proposition that the self, under conditions of globality, is emerging as an active, stable unit that is being called upon to define itself against the otherness of the nation-state, global collectivities, and humanity. Moreover, the production and reproduction of selfhood occurs in a situation of reflexivity wherein statuses, roles, and collective norms are constantly examined and reformed in light of the infusion of new information attained from others.

Self-determination is regarded more and more as a personal prerogative that others ought to respect as a matter of principle.

Unlike earlier selves—whose identity was largely framed by the heavy hand of tradition, extended family, and village groups or by age and gender cohorts—the modern self under conditions of globality finds that his challenge to discover his identity as a mature individual is thrust upon him as a personal responsibility. No longer, for example, is being female a justification for not aspiring to become a physician, dock worker, master plumber, mathematician, or astronaut.

Moreover, the responsibility for defining one's own identity has emerged as not simply a necessity but also a right. Self-determination is regarded more and more as a personal prerogative that others ought to respect as a matter of principle. This perspective was an intimate theme of youth subcultures in both the early twentieth century and in the sixties revolution.

Critics on both occasions frequently interpreted such claims as merely flagrant attempts to legitimate bohemian hedonism and pursue a range of narcissistic experiences that were, no doubt, pleasurable but also illegal or immoral, and often both. Certainly, it is often difficult to discern the difference between self-indulgent and self-fulfilling

> *The slogan "make love, not war" may have done little to end the Vietnam conflict, but it did symbolize a markedly altered style for doing selfhood as well as a markedly different view of appropriate behavior.*

conduct, but it would be a serious mistake to dismiss the campaign of the counterculture as simply an exercise in promulgating permissiveness. Real gains were made in giving the individual self the responsibility for his own identity formation, even to the point of now making gender orientation a matter of personal election. If nothing else, the youth peer groups in both eras constituted an avant-garde for creating a new, proactive conception of the self and empowering people to explore new roles and experiences in the process of constructing their own identities.

The strength of humanity. The emergence of the importance of humanity in the global field enjoys intricate analytical connections to the renovated conceptions of selfhood. The "movement" in the sixties was concerned not only with lifestyle changes but also with equality, justice, freedom, and self-determination for all humankind. That students enter colleges and universities today with a potent belief in equality and a firm commitment to fairness is to a large extent a testament to the success of the sixties generation in promoting the recognition that no one can be rightfully excluded from, or their privileges limited in, the global community. While empirically the sixties revolution achieved more in the acceptance of civil rights than it attained in terms of equality, nonetheless, the premise was firmly institutionalized that no one should be denied full participation in the various domains of social life on the basis of such ascribed characteristics as race, ethnicity, gender, national origin, sexual orientation, and so forth.

Implicitly, meanwhile, the emerging significance of the notion of humanity as a constellation of rights collides against another deeply held commitment among contemporary college students: the strong conviction that ethnocentrism constitutes the worst of intellectual sins. When confronted with the ongoing practice of female genital mutilation

(FGM) in Africa, for example, students are outraged, but they are also loath to condemn what is a cultural tradition of long standing in the indigenous societies in question. The growing chorus of individuals, nation-states, and international nongovernmental organizations that condemn what are taken to be inhumane practices—FGM, ethnic cleansing, the repression of religious or ethnic minorities, the exploitative use of child labor, and myriad other inhumane practices around the globe—is indicative of the emerging worldwide consciousness that we participate in a common destiny as a part of humanity.

One notable consequence of the increasing solidarity of selves around the notion of humanity has been the relativization of the nation-state. No longer can regimes declare that they alone are responsible for what transpires within their boundaries. Now noncitizens feel perfectly justified in condemning abuses on the grounds that to harm another is the legitimate concern of everyone on earth. Moreover, this conclusion is the rational outcome of trends toward inclusion and equality that initially took on form and substance in the countercultural movements of the sixties, where the rights to freedom, self-determination, gender equity, fairness, and more found renewed support.

A caveat is in order, lest the impression be created that all things bright and beautiful arose full-blossom out of the sixties revolution. I am making a much more modest and circumspect claim here: Lifestyle experimentation, for example, signified not merely a search for pleasure but also a search for authentic identity. While there were casualties in the drug subculture, spoiled academic careers, alienation of parents from children, and the like, nonetheless, the groundwork was laid for addressing such impediments to full self-development as gender repression, racial discrimination, unfulfilling marriages, educational irrelevance, and class barriers, which resulted in stultified lives. Thus, despite its often raucous, irreverent, and sometimes violent demeanor, the youth peer culture provided, on balance, an impetus toward the realization of a new solidarity grounded in the notion of humanity.

IMPLICATIONS FOR CHARACTER AND IDENTITY FORMATION

Assessing the implications of the sixties revolution on the processes of character and identity formation today is a task of considerable complexity; the findings of social scientists in numerous studies have often been at odds with one another—a not unusual state of affairs. While it may not be possible to reconcile the contradictory findings of various studies, some areas of consensus are perti-

nent to the matter of character and identity formation.

One is that the sixties did represent a watershed period wherein the context for character and identity formation was fundamentally altered. We have described this in terms of the rubrics of globalization theory as an enhanced consciousness of the self. At issue was not only individuals' desire to broaden their range of experience and to explore new lifestyle possibilities but also their need to play a larger role in defining their own identity and the substantive, moral features of their character structure. For this to occur, a whole range of previously ascribed roles and identities had to be challenged and delegitimated.

The process has not been without its pitfalls. Structural constraints limiting the exercise of free choice still persist, and not everyone has elected to participate in the more exuberant alternatives. Nonetheless, in relative terms, the context for character and identity formation has experienced considerable liberalization under the conditions of globality.

Another significant area of consensus pertains to our extended ability to identify with others on a global scale. This relates not only to the growing recognition of our common participation in humanity but also to other and more limited features of our autobiography, such as the networking on a worldwide scale of people concerned with gender issues, the environment, ethnic affiliation, peace, human rights, sexual orientation, religious persuasion, and a host of other causes and movements. Many people nowadays are convinced that, while the social environment is not completely malleable, their efforts can make a difference in reforming the world according to designs of their own creation. Put simply, the self has been empowered through the emergent notion that a person can exercise some mastery over his fate. But mastery over one's own fate necessarily entails interaction between and social relations with others from a local to a global arena.

The thematization of selfhood remains a task barely under way among contemporary social theorists because the conditions of selfhood, character formation, and identity construction are all drastically transformed under the conditions of globality. The point of this exercise has been to suggest that the current attempt to understand selfhood has some crucial roots in the social tumult and revolution that took place during the radical sixties. Our contemporary processes of character and identity formation might not have been possible without the introduction of a new discourse, a new orientation to the world, that grew out of the themes popularized by the counterculture. The slogan "make love, not war" may have done little to end the Vietnam conflict, but it did symbolize a markedly altered style for doing selfhood as well as a markedly different view of appropriate behavior.

Born to be good?

What motivates us to be good, bad or indifferent towards others? Celia Kitzinger examines the psychology of morality.

Celia Kitzinger teaches psychology at the University of Loughborough, England.

MANY of us, much of the time, act to benefit others. There are small kindnesses of everyday life—like holding open a door, sharing food or expressing compassion for someone in distress. Things so ordinary that we simply take them for granted.

We are pleased, but not particularly surprised that people commonly care for sick relatives, give money to help famine victims, donate blood to hospitals, or volunteer to assist at hospices. At times what people do for others is truly spectacular. In the US, Lenny Skutnik risked his life diving into the icy waters of the Potomac River to save an airline crash victim; in Nazi Europe many people risked their lives in offering protection to Jews. In both mundane and exceptional ways people often act to help others—which is why psychologists describe human beings not just as 'social' but also as 'pro-social' animals.

But why do people spend so much time and money and effort on others, when we could keep it all for ourselves? One argument is that self-interest lies at the root of all superficially 'moral' behaviour. According to sociobiologists, we are biologically driven towards those forms of altruism—caring for our families, for example—which improve the survival of our genes.[1] Moral actions are simply automatic and instinctive, of no greater or lesser significance than the behaviour of a mother bird putting her own life at risk leading a predator away from her chicks. Helping people who are not genetically related to us can also be in the best interest of our genes if it sets up the expectation that we—or those who share our genes—will be helped in turn.

There are many subtle ways in which helping others can offer rewards which serve our self-interest. These include the praise of onlookers; gratitude from the person being helped; the warm glow of knowing we have done a good deed; and the benefit of avoiding guilt, shame or punishment. Most people agree that some good behaviour can be attributed to self-interest. But is that all there is?

In an ingenious set of experiments, a group of psychologists set out to test the idea that empathy—the ability to imagine ourselves in the place of another and to feel their emotions—can result in genuine altruism.[2] Subjects were encouraged to be empathetic while watching a 'worker' who they believed was reacting badly to a series of uncomfortable electric shocks. They were then given a chance to help the worker by receiving the shocks themselves. If helping were only self-serving egoism, then people who felt empathy for the victim would simply want to escape from the upsetting experience. But researchers found that those with strong empathetic feelings volunteered to take the worker's place, even when told they that they could leave immediately if they refused. The researchers also found that high-empathy people, who were deprived of the opportunity to help, felt just as good when someone else helped instead. This suggests that the offer to help reflected a genuine wish to relieve the victim's suffering, rather than a desire for praise from other people. So it looks as if the cynical view that even good actions have selfish motives may well be wrong. Empathy is common in very small children who often respond to another's distress with crying and sadness, and may attempt to comfort them with a hug or a cuddly toy. Some psychologists believe that behaviour like this signals the start of moral development.[3]

Although empathy may be an important component of moral behaviour, morality cannot rely on empathy alone because this emotion is too circumscribed and partial. It can also lead us to make unfair decisions—taking sides in a dispute, for example. Another explanation for why people behave well is that they are motivated not by emotions but by reasoned moral principles. This is what Lawrence Kohlberg proposes in his 'cognitive-development model' theory.[4] Children, he says, begin at a 'preconventional' level in which they see morality in relation to obedience and punishments from adults. At the second, 'conventional' level, reached in late childhood or early adolescence, they are oriented first to pleasing and helping others and later to maintaining the existing social order. At the third and highest stage of moral development—reached by only a small proportion of adults—people begin to define moral values and principles such as human dignity, justice, universal human rights. According to this theory, morality is a matter of cognitive (not emotional) development: it matters not one whit whether we care about or empathize with other people so long as we respect their rights as human beings.

Some critics, notably feminist psychologist Carol Gilligan, have challenged the theory as sexist: men may favour abstract theoretical notions of rights and justice, but women, she says, are more likely to construct morality rooted in their sense of connection with other people, a morality of care and empathy.[5] Others criticize the ethnocentrism of the model, pointing out that Kohlberg has elevated to the highest stage of moral development precisely those views most likely to be held by white, middle-class, educated North Americans.[6]

It's more likely that moral behaviour comes about in a variety of ways: sometimes we may act well in the hope of rewards; other times good behaviour may be motivated by empathy; sometimes it is the outcome of reasoned moral arguments. Crucially, though, neither strong feelings of empathy nor high moral principles guarantee that people will behave well. There is often a gap between moral beliefs and moral action—between how people think and hope they would behave in a situation and how they actually do behave. Some of the classic studies of psychology were prompted by

From *New Internationalist*, April 1997, pp. 15-17. © 1997 by New Internationalist Publications, Ltd. Reprinted by permission.

situations in which people failed to act in accordance with their moral values.

In the 1960s a young woman named Kitty Genovese was murdered by a man who raped and stabbed her repeatedly for half an

These people were not sadists or psychopaths. They were ordinary people

hour in front of 38 residents of a respectable New York City neighbourhood. Nobody went to help her. Only one person finally called the police, after she was dead. This incident prompted a flood of research into what became known as the 'bystander effect' which examined why people don't intervene when others are in pain or in danger.[7] Sometimes people fail to intervene out of callousness or indifference. But more often they fail to act in spite of what they feel they should do, and then feel ashamed afterwards. Why is this?

A common finding is that people are uncertain how to behave because, unsure about what they are seeing, they conform with the behaviour of others, who are equally unsure. Emergencies are rare events which happen suddenly and unexpectedly. How can we know that an emergency is real and is not a prank, a game, or a film being produced? The safest thing is to sit tight and wait to see how others react. If nobody else does anything, then people worry about making fools of themselves. A large group can stand by and do nothing, each lulled into thinking that there is no need to act, each waiting for someone else to make the first move. What looks like callous indifference is actually fear of what other people will think if they make an inappropriate response in an ambiguous situation.

Someone in Kitty Genovese's situation is less likely to be helped if many people are watching than if only one person witnesses the attack. For example, subjects asked to wait in a room before being interviewed heard a woman in the next room apparently fall, hurt herself, and cry out in distress. Of those waiting alone, 70 per cent went to help her, compared with only 7 per cent of those waiting with a stranger who did nothing. Today's altruist may be tomorrow's passive bystander; it all depends on the social situation because people tend to behave in accordance with socially prescribed roles rather than as individuals.

In a well-known study by Stanley Milgram, subjects were recruited through newspaper advertisements for what was described as 'an experiment in learning'. They were seated in front of a shock machine that could administer up 450 volts to the 'learner', a man strapped into a chair.[8] Each time the 'learner' made a mistake the subject had to pull a lever to give him an electric shock, increasing the voltage each time. (In fact, the lever was a dummy, and the 'learner' was acting out his response). At 150 volts the learner started shouting. At 180 volts, he cried out in pain and pleaded to be released. At 300 volts he screamed with pain and yelled about his heart condition. Later still there was only deathly silence. If subjects wanted to stop giving shocks, the experimenter said only 'the experiment requires that you continue'. No threats, no incentives to go on, just the order. Under these conditions—and contrary to the predictions of psychiatrists who had guessed that virtually no-one would obey to the end—nearly two-thirds of subjects delivered the full range of shocks, proceeding beyond the levers marked 'Danger: Severe Shock' to the ones marked 'XXX'.

These people were not sadists or psychopaths. They were ordinary people who believed that you shouldn't hurt others, who often showed empathy for the learner, and who disliked what they were ordered to do. Virtually all of them complained to the experimenter and asked for permission to stop giving shocks. But when ordered to continue the majority did as they were told. As Milgram says: 'With numbing regularity, good people were seen to knuckle under the demands of authority and perform actions that were callous and severe.' Women were as likely as men to deliver shocks to maximum intensity.

What all these studies illustrate is the extent to which moral behaviour is a social,
not an individual issue. In thinking about why people fail to offer help, why they behave punitively, or why they inflict pain on others, we often resort to explanations which depend on individual characteristics—their personal religious beliefs, their capacity for empathy, their understanding of moral principles, or the kind of upbringing they had. But these explanations overlook the key role of social context. The frightening truth uncovered by these classic psychological studies is that it is not too difficult to set up situations in which most of us behave worse than we could have thought possible, out of conformity, fear of what others might think, loss of individual identity or obedience to authority.

The traditional view of moral behaviour is that people are intrinsically selfish beings whose natural anti-social impulses have been curbed by social structures designed to promote obedience to authority, law and order. An alternative possibility is that people are fundamentally pro-social beings, whose ability to act on altruistic impulses and moral principles is sometimes inhibited by precisely these social pressures. At the very least it is obvious that this is sometimes true, and that we need to develop ways of recognizing and challenging those social pressures which result in apathetic or cruel behaviour in our everyday lives.

Notes

1. Richard Dawkins, *The Selfish Gene*, OUP 1976.
2. CD Batson, *The Altruism Question*, Erlbaum Associates 1991.
3. C Zahn-Waxler & M Radke-Yarrow, 'The Development of Altruism' in N Eisenberg-Berg (ed.) *The Development of Prosocial Behaviour*, Academic Press 1986.
4. L Kohlberg, *The Philosophy of Moral Development*, Harper and Row 1981.
5. C Gilligan, *In a Different Voice*, Harvard University Press 1982.
6. EEL Simpson, 'Moral Development Research: A Case Study of Scientific Cultural Bias', *Human Development 17*, 1974.
7. B Latané & JM Draley, *The Unresponsive Bystander. Why doesn't he help?* Appleton-Century-Croft 1970.
8. S Milgram, 'Some Conditions of Obedience and Disobedience to Authority', *Human Relations 18*, 1965.

THE WAY WE REALLY ARE:

Coming to Terms with America's Changing Families

Stephanie Coontz

Introduction

Five years ago I wrote a book called *The Way We Never Were: American Families and the Nostalgia Trap.* As a family historian bothered by widespread misconceptions in the popular press about "traditional" families, I hoped to get people to look more realistically at the strengths, weaknesses, and surprising variability of family life in the past.

My book went to press just as Dan Quayle issued his famous condemnation of Murphy Brown, the fictional television character who decided to bear her child out of wedlock. The ensuing polemics over whether Murphy Brown was setting a bad example for our nation's youth were followed by an all-out war over family values as the 1992 election approached. Since much of the discussion focused on the contrast between today's families and "the way things used to be," I began to get calls from congressional committees, reporters, and television producers asking me for a historical perspective on these issues. Soon I found myself in the thick of a national debate over what was happening to the American family....

In my last book, I demonstrated the tremendous variety of family types that have worked—and not worked—in American history. When families succeeded, it was often for reasons quite different than stereotypes about the past suggest—because they were flexible in their living arrangements, for example, or could call on people and institutions beyond the family for assistance or support. And when families failed, the results were often devastating. There never was a golden age of family life, a time when all families were capable of meeting the needs of their members and protecting them from poverty, violence, or sexual exploitation.

The "traditional" sexual double standard, for example, may have led more middle-class girls to delay sex at the end of the nineteenth century than today, but it also created higher proportions of young female prostitutes. Respect for elders may have received more lip service in the past, but elders were until very recently the segment of the population most likely to be destitute.

Yet knowing there was no golden age in history does not satisfy most people. Okay, they say, so the past wasn't great, and people have been lamenting the "breakdown of the family" or the "crisis of modern youth" since colonial days. It may be entertaining to know that John Watson, the most famous child psychiatrist of the early twentieth century, predicted in 1928 that marriage would be dead by 1977, and that in 1977, noted sociologist Amitai Etzioni announced that "by mid-1990 not one American family will be left." But even a stopped clock is right twice a day. What if these fears are finally coming true? Am I claiming that the more things change, the more they remain the same? Do I think people are crazy to feel anxious about recent trends in family life?

"Perhaps it's good to have our illusions about the past shattered," people often say, "but once we reject the lies and the myths, what do we put in their place?" Are the only lessons from history negative? Isn't there anything positive families can learn from history and sociology? . . .

Boosting Our Social Intelligence: Putting Family and Personal Trends in Context

Understanding the history of families and the structural constraints under which they operate can prevent our emotional and social IQs from being stunted by what sometimes seems like a national campaign to "dumb us down." Politicians have become experts in squeezing the complexity out of issues to produce compressed, thirteen-second sound bites. Think-tank publicists bombard us with the out-of-context snippets of information sometimes called "factoids." . . .

Care must be taken in interpreting headlines about the explosion of unwed motherhood. Unwed motherhood has increased dramatically since 1970, but it's easy to overstate *how* dramatically, because much illegitimacy was covered up in the past and reporting methods have recently become much more sophisticated. In the past, notes Sam Roberts, many unwed mothers would tell census workers that they were separated, "resulting in the anomaly of many more 'separated' women than men." At least 80 percent of the increase in unwed motherhood reported between 1981 and 1983, explains Steve Rawlings of the Census Bureau, came from "refinements in survey procedures that were introduced early in the 1980s. This represents 10 to 15 percent of the total increase between 1970 and 1993 (or 20 to 25 percent of the increase since 1980)." And though newspapers routinely use unwed motherhood and single parenthood interchangeably, many unwed mothers are part of cohabiting couples. Five states, including California, further distort the statistics by assuming a woman is unmarried if she has a different last name than the father listed on the birth certificate!

It's also important to distinguish between the ratio of unmarried to married births and the rate of births to unmarried women. Between 1960 and 1990, the nonmarital birth ratio increased by more than 500 percent, from 5.3 percent of all births to 28 percent. But birth rates to unmarried women only increased by a factor of 1.73, not quite twofold. What explains the larger figure is that births to unmarried women rose while births to married women fell, increasing the *relative* proportion of unmarried births much more than their *absolute* numbers. In some cases, a fall in marital fertility may be so large that unwed births become a larger proportion of all births even when rates of unwed childbearing are flat or falling. The probability that an unmarried African-American woman would have a child actually fell from 9.8 to 9.0 percent between 1960 and 1990, for example; but because married-couple childbearing decreased

among African Americans even more sharply, the proportion of black children born to unwed mothers rose.

I'm not saying that the media intend to mislead. But in many cases, lack of historical perspective makes intelligent, dedicated reporters vulnerable to manipulation by people who wish to magnify one particular set of the factoids that continuously streak across our information horizon. . . .

The result is that many pronouncements about the family, often by the same commentators, have a peculiarly manic-depressive quality. On the one hand, there are the doomsday predictions. New consensus spokesman David Popenoe warns that the decay of family life is "unique and unprecedented" and that the final collapse of "the last vestige of the traditional family unit" is imminent. "Marriage is dying," says Robert Rector of the Heritage Foundation; the next ten years will "decide whether or not marriage and family survive in this nation." Our failure to halt the decay of marriage, says the Council on Families in America, is "nothing less than an act of cultural suicide."

On the other hand, these catastrophic assertions are periodically interspersed with cheerful assurances that things may be turning around. Popenoe sees hopeful signs of a "new familism" in "the nation as a whole." Charles Murray of the American Enterprise Institute thinks we may be moving toward "the restoration of a culture in which family, parenthood, . . . morality, and the virtues are all perceived and valued in ways that our grandparents would find familiar."

Such wild fluctuations in assessments result from a lack of historical context. By contrast, once people understand the complicated *mix* of long-term changes in family trends, social institutions, and cultural mores, they are less likely to think that any one-size-fits-all quick fix can turn everything around, for better or for worse. They're more likely to be realistic about what can and can't be changed, what we need to adjust to and what we may be able to resist.

For example, take the question of whether marriage is a dying institution. In 1867 there were 9.6 marriages per 1,000 people. A hundred years later, in 1967, there were 9.7. The rate reached a low of 7.9 in 1932 and an all-time high of 16.4 in 1946, a peak quickly followed by a brief but huge surge in divorce. Marriage rates fell again from the early 1950s to 1958, rose slowly until the end of the 1960s, and then began to decline again. But the proportion of women who remain single all their lives is *lower* today than at the turn of the century, and fewer women now feel they have to forgo marriage entirely in order to do anything else in their lives. Periodic predictions to the contrary, it is unlikely that we will someday record the demise of the last married couple in America.

Nevertheless, marriage is certainly a *transformed* institution, and it plays a smaller role than ever before in organizing social and personal life. One reason is that marriage comes much later, for most people, than in the past. Men's average age at first marriage today is not unprecedented, though it has now regained the previous record high of 1890. But the average age of marriage for contemporary women is two years higher than its historical peak in 1890 and almost four years higher than in the 1950s. This figure approaches the highest age ever recorded for Western Europe, a region where marriage has always taken place later than almost anywhere else in the world. And although fewer women stay single all their lives than in 1900, a higher proportion of women than ever before experience a period of independent living and employment before marriage. Women's expectations of both marriage and work are unlikely to ever be the same as in the past.

The second reason for marriage's more limited role in people's lives is that it is no longer expected to last "until death do us part." Divorce rates in America rose steadily until World War II, fell briefly during the 1950s, and took off again during the late 1960s. The divorce rate crested near the end of the 1970s, leveled off in the 1980s, and very slightly receded from 1988 to 1993. This last trend was heralded by many commentators

as a "real turnaround," a sign that Americans "are turning conservative, pro-family." But while demographers now say that only 40 percent, rather than 50 percent, of marriages will end in divorce, these remain among the highest divorce rates ever recorded. Furthermore, the cumulative effects of past divorces continue to mount. In 1960 there were 35 divorced men and women for every 1,000 married ones. By 1990 there were 140 divorced individuals for every 1,000 married ones.

People often misunderstand what statisticians mean when they estimate that one in every two or three marriages will end in divorce. The calculations refer to the chances of a marriage ending in divorce within 40 years. While rising divorce rates have increased the number of marriages at risk for dissolution, the gradual extension of life spans ensures that a marriage today has the potential to last three times longer than one of 200 years ago. Thus while the number of people who divorce is certainly unprecedented, so is the number of couples who celebrate their fortieth wedding anniversaries. In fact, the chances of doing so have never been better.

On the other hand, the average marriage that ends in divorce lasts only 6.3 years. We may be seeing more marriages that last longer and are more fulfilling than at any time in our history. But we are also seeing more marriages that are *less* committed and of shorter duration than in the past. Sociologist Valerie Oppenheimer suggests we are experiencing growing polarization between increasing numbers of very "high-quality," long-lasting marriages *and* increasing numbers of short-lived, medium- to "low-quality" ones where the partners are not committed enough to stay and work things through. Understanding this polarization helps explain some of the ambivalence Americans have about modern families. Very few people in a modern high-quality marriage would trade it for an older model where limited communication and a high degree of sexual dissatisfaction were taken for granted. And few adults in a very low-quality marriage, or their children, want to

be trapped there for life. But the commitments and consequences of "medium-quality" marriages are more ambiguous, especially for kids, and this worries many Americans.

Often their worry takes the form of a debate over whether we should return to the family forms and values of the 1950s. That decade is still close enough that many people derive their political position on the issue from personal experience. At forums I've conducted across the country, some people raised in 1950s families tell of tormented childhoods in alcoholic, abusive, or conflict-ridden families. They cannot understand, they say vehemently, why anyone would regret the passing of the 1950s for a single moment. My research validates their experience. These individuals were not alone.

But other people remember 1950s families that shielded them from adult problems and disputes. Many had unmistakably happy parents. Others had secure childhoods but learned later that one or both of their parents were miserable. Some of these individuals are now sorry that their parents stayed together, but many more say they are glad not to have known about their parents' problems and grateful for whatever kept their families together. They are also thankful that the media did not expose them to many adult realities that today's children see or read about every day. My research validates their experience too.

The only way to get past the polarized personal testimonies for and against 1950s families is to put their strengths and weaknesses into historical perspective. This permits a more balanced assessment of what we have gained and lost since then. It also helps us distinguish historical precedents we may be able to draw on from new issues requiring new responses....

Why Working Mothers Are Here to Stay

The 1950s was clearly out of balance in one direction, with almost half the adult population restricted in their access to economic and political roles beyond the family. But the last few decades have been out of balance in the opposite direction. Many of us now feel that our expanding roles beyond the family have restricted our access to family life.

At first glance, it appears that the new imbalance results from women, especially mothers, entering the workforce. Certainly, that trend has produced a dramatic change in relation to the decade that most people use as their measure of "traditional" family life. In 1950, only a quarter of all wives were in the paid labor force, and just 16 percent of all children had mothers who worked outside the home. By 1991, more than 58 percent of all married women, and nearly two-thirds of all married women with children, were in the labor force. Of the total number of children in the country, 59 percent, including a majority of preschoolers, had mothers who worked outside the home.

But to analyze today's family imbalance as a conflict between work and mothering is to misread family history and to misdirect future family policy. Historically, productive work by mothers as well as fathers (and by young people) has not only been compatible with family life but has also strengthened family relationships. What's really out of balance is the relationship between market activities and nonmarket ones (including community as well as family ties). Our jobs don't make room for family obligations. The purchase of goods and services often substitutes for family or neighborhood activities. Phone calls, beepers, faxes and e-mail constantly intrude into family time. To correct this imbalance, we need to reorganize work to make it more compatible with family life. We need to reorganize family life to make sure that all members share in the work needed to sustain it. We need to redirect technology so that it serves rather than dominates our social and interpersonal relationships.

Instead, however, the family consensus brokers encourage us to cobble together personal marital arrangements that combine what they consider to be the best family features from both

the 1950s and the 1990s. They reason that if we could convince women to take time off from work while their children are young, bolster male wages enough that more families could afford to make this choice, increase the incentives for marriage, and combat the excesses of individualism that lead to divorce or unwed motherhood, then surely we could solve the conflicts that parents now experience in balancing work and family. While recommending that men should help out more at home and expressing abstract support for equal pay and promotion opportunities for women on the job, the family values think tanks nevertheless propose that parents revive "relatively traditional marital gender roles" for the period "when children are young," cutting back on mothers' paid work.

In the absence of wider social change in work policies and family support systems, this is the individual solution that many men and women try to work out. And it may be a reasonable stopgap measure for parents who can afford it. But when such personal accommodations are put forward as an overarching political program for family life, they cease to sound quite so reasonable. . . .

Women, the argument goes, are happy to care for children, but men's biological drives point them in a different direction. Men have to be coaxed and guided into responsible fatherhood, and societies have historically achieved this by granting husbands special status as moral educators, family authority figures, and breadwinners. When society stops viewing breadwinning "as a father's special task," we lose our most powerful way "to motivate fathers to provide for their children."

The family values crusaders believe that all men and women, at least during their parenting years, should organize their families with the man as primary provider and protector and the wife as primary nurturer. Before and after child rearing, a woman is welcome to work; but unless she has no other option, she should engage in "sequencing"–alternating work and child raising rather than trying to combine them. Popenoe pro-

poses the wife take "at least a year" off work, then work part-time until her children are in their early to mid-teens. Even when both husband and wife are employed, the woman should remain primarily responsible for nurturing, with the man as "junior partner" at home. Husbands should help out more than in the past, but anything that smacks of "androgyny" is to be avoided like the plague. Society, he argues, must "disavow the popular notion of radical feminists that 'daddies can make good mommies.' "

Hostility to women's economic independence is a consistent subtext in "new consensus" writing. "Policies that encourage mothers to work instead of marry" are a large part of America's social problem, says Wade Horn of the National Fatherhood Initiative. Without providing any evidence, Dan Quayle claims studies show "that children whose parents work are *less likely* to have Mommy's undivided attention than children whose mothers stay home." Isn't it odd how quickly a discussion of working *parents* becomes an indictment of *Mommy*? According to this agenda, a male breadwinner–female homemaker division of labor is not an individual family choice but the correct model for every family. Women are told that there are compensations for giving up their aspirations to economic equality: "Even though the man is the head of the family, the woman is the neck, and she turns the head any way she wants." But if women are not willing to "give back" family leadership, groups such as the Promise Keepers advise men to "take it back. . . . Be sensitive. Treat the lady gently and lovingly. But lead!"

While we can debate the *merits* of these proposals for America's families, I am more interested in examining their *practicality*. How likely is it that a majority of mothers will once more withdraw from paid employment during the early years of child rearing? What can historical and sociological analysis teach us about how realistic it is to propose that we revive the breadwinner identity as the basis for men's commitment to marriage and child raising?

The Late Birth and Short Life of the Male Breadwinner Family

One of the most common misconceptions about modern marriage is the notion that coprovider families are a new invention in human history. In fact, today's dual-earner family represents a return to older norms, after a very short interlude that people mistakenly identify as "traditional."

Throughout most of humanity's history women as well as men were family breadwinners. Contrary to cartoons of cavemen dragging home food to a wife waiting at the campfire, in the distant past of early gathering and hunting societies women contributed as much or more to family subsistence as men. Mothers left the hearth to forage for food, hunt small animals, trade with other groups, or tend crops.

On this continent, neither Native American, African-American, nor white women were originally seen as economic dependents. Among European colonists, men dominated women, but their authority was based on legal, political, and religious coercion, not on men's greater economic importance. The most common words for wives in seventeenth- and eighteenth-century colonial America were "yoke-mates" or "meet-helps," labels that indicated women's economic partnership with men. Until the early nineteenth century, men and women worked together on farms or in small household businesses, alongside other family members. Responsibility for family life and responsibility for breadwinning were not two different, specialized jobs.

But in the early 1800s, as capitalist production for the market replaced home-based production for local exchange and a wage-labor system supplanted widespread self-employment and farming, more and more work was conducted in centralized workplaces removed from the farm or home. A new division of labor then grew up within many families. Men (and older children) began to specialize in work outside the home, withdrawing from their traditional child-raising responsibilities. Household work and child care were delegated to wives, who gave up their older roles in production and barter. While slaves and free blacks continued to have high labor force participation by women, wives in most other ethnic and racial groups were increasingly likely to quit paid work outside the home after marriage.

But it's important to remember that this new division of work between husbands and wives came out of a *temporary* stage in the history of wage labor and industrialization. It corresponded to a transitional period when households could no longer get by primarily on things they made, grew, or bartered, but could not yet rely on purchased consumer goods. For example, families no longer produced their own homespun cotton, but ready-made clothing was not yet available at prices most families could afford. Women still had to sew clothes from cloth that men purchased with their pay. Most families still had to grow part of their food and bake their own bread. Food preparation and laundering required hours of work each day. Water often had to be hauled and heated.

Somebody had to go out to earn money in order to buy the things the family needed; but somebody else had to stay home and turn the things they bought into things they could actually use. Given the preexisting legal, political, and religious tradition of patriarchal dominance, husbands (and youths of both sexes) were assigned to work outside the home. Wives assumed exclusive responsibility for domestic matters that they had formerly shared with husbands or delegated to older children and apprentices. Many women supplemented their household labor with income-generating work that could be done at or around home—taking in boarders, doing extra sewing or laundering, keeping a few animals, or selling garden products. But this often arduous work was increasingly seen as secondary to wives' primary role of keeping house, raising the children, and getting dinner on the table.

The resulting identification of masculinity with economic activities and femininity with nurturing care, now often seen as the "natural" way of organizing the nuclear family, was in fact a historical product of this nineteenth-century transition from an agricultural household economy to an industrial wage economy. So even as an ideal, the male breadwinner family was a comparatively late arrival onto the historical scene. As a reality—a family form in which most people actually lived—it came about even later....

The Revival of Women's Role as Family Coprovider

...For approximately 50 years, from the 1920s through the 1960s, the growth in married women's work outside the home was smaller than the decline in child labor, so that the male breadwinner family became increasingly dominant. But even at its high point in the 1950s, less than 60 percent of American children spent their youth in an Ozzie and Harriet-type family where dad went to work and mom stayed home. And by the 1970s the fifty-year reign of this family form was definitely over....

After 1973, real wages for young men began falling, creating a larger proportion of families where the mother worked just to keep the family afloat. Housing inflation meant that families with young children were especially likely to need the wife to work, in order to afford the new home that their growing family motivated them to buy. By 1989, almost 80 percent of all home buyers came from two-income households. Another incentive was the rising cost of higher education, which increased nearly three times faster than household income between 1980 and 1994.

Today most families can no longer think of the earnings that wives and mothers bring home as a bonus that can be put aside when family needs call. Nor, increasingly, do the jobs women hold allow them the luxury of choosing to cut back or quit when family priorities change, any more than their husbands' jobs would. By 1993, married women working full-time contributed 41 percent of their families' incomes. Indeed, in 23 percent of two-earner couples, the wives earned *more* than their husbands.

The sequencing of mothering and paid employment that characterized many women's activities over the past 100 years is becoming a thing of the past. Through most of this century, even though labor participation rates for women rose steadily, they dropped significantly when women were in their twenties and thirties. By 1990, however, labor-force participation rates no longer dipped for women in their child-raising years. Today, fewer and fewer women leave their jobs while their children are very young.

Proponents of the modified male breadwinner family believe that if we could drastically reduce the number of single-mother households, raise wages for men, and convince families to get by on a little less, we might be able to get wives to quit work during their child-raising years. Polls consistently show that many women would like to cut back on work hours, though not quit entirely (and it's interesting that an almost equal number of men would also like to cut back their hours). But a return to the norm of male breadwinner families is simply not feasible for most Americans.

Why Wives and Mothers Will Continue to Work Outside the Home

It's not just a dollars-and-cents issue. Most women would not give up the satisfactions of their jobs even if they could afford to quit. They consistently tell interviewers they like the social respect, self-esteem, and friendship networks they gain from the job, despite the stress they may face finding acceptable child care and negotiating household chores with their husbands. In a 1995 survey by Louis Harris & Associates, for example, less than a third of working women said they would prefer to stay home even if money were no object.

Another reason women do not want to quit work is that they are not willing to surrender the increased leverage it gives them in the family. The simple truth is that women who do not earn income have much less decision-making power in marital relations than women who do. And no amount of goodwill on the part of husbands seems to lessen this imbalance. In one in-depth study of American families, researchers found that the primary determinant of power in all couples was who brings in the money. The only exception was among lesbians. Lesbian couples might be persuaded to have one partner stay home with the kids and the other earn the money, but I doubt that the Institute for American Values would consider this a positive step in the direction of "marital role complementarity."

Aside from women's own motivations to remain at work, the issue of whether a family can afford to have the wife stay home is quite debatable. One of the most longstanding American traditions, much older than the ideal of the male breadwinner, is the search for socioeconomic mobility. That's why many families came to America in the first place. It's what people were seeking when they crossed the plains in covered wagons, why farmers switched from diversified family crops to specialized market production, what parents have expected education to provide for their children.

From the mid-nineteenth to the mid-twentieth century, there were three main routes to family economic advancement. One was child labor, allowing parents to accumulate enough to buy a house and possibly send a later generation to school. Another was the move from farm to city, to take advantage of higher wage rates in urban areas. The third was investment in increased training and education for male members of the family.

But child labor was abolished in the early twentieth century, and even before 1950 most men had already obtained nonfarm jobs. By the mid-1960s there were diminishing returns to the gains families could expect from further education or training for men. As these older strategies ceased to guarantee continued mobility, women's employment became so central to family economic advancement that it could less and less often be postponed or interrupted for full-time child raising.

In other words, even for families where the uninterrupted work of wives isn't essential for minimum family subsistence, it is now the main route to even a modest amount of upward mobility. Those who tell women who "don't need to work" that they should go back to full-time child rearing are contradicting many of the other ideals most Americans hold dear. We're talking about abandoning the American dream here. The only way to get a significant number of families to make this choice would be to foster a thoroughly untraditional—some might even say un-American—acceptance of a stationary standard of living, a no-growth family economy. Some families may harbor such subversive ideals; yet the chances are slim that this will become a mass movement any time soon.

LONG LIVE COMMUNITY

SOCIAL CAPITAL AS PUBLIC HEALTH

BY ICHIRO KAWACHI, BRUCE P. KENNEDY, AND KIMBERLY LOCHNER

Americans now understand that their health is at risk if they smoke, overeat, and fail to exercise. But a growing body of evidence suggests that public health also depends on a less widely understood influence—social cohesion. And while many Americans have stopped smoking, gone on diets, and put on jogging shoes, American society has become, if anything, less cohesive.

Consider what happened in Roseto, a small Italian-American community in eastern Pennsylvania. During the 1950s, when the town first caught the attention of medical researchers Stewart Wolf and J. G. Bruhn, Roseto posed something of a mystery. Death rates in the small town of about 1,600 people were substantially lower than in neighboring communities. In particular, the rate of heart attacks was about 40 percent lower than expected and could not be explained by the prevalence of factors known to increase the risk of the disease. Citizens of Roseto smoked at the same rate as neighboring towns, they were just as overweight and sedentary, and their diet consisted of about the same amount of animal fat. But the one feature that stood out was the close-knit relations among residents in the community. The town had been originally settled by immigrants during the 1880s, who all came from the same village in rural Italy. The researchers noticed the social cohesiveness and ethos of egalitarianism that characterized the community:

> Proper behavior by those Rosetans who have achieved material wealth or occupational prestige requires attention to the delicate balance between ostentation and reserve, ambition and restraint, modesty and dignity. . . . The local priest emphasized that when preoccupation with earning money exceeded the unmarked boundary it became a basis for social rejection. . . . Rosetan culture thus provided a set of checks and balances to ensure that neither success nor failure got out of hand. . . . During the first five years of our study it was difficult to distinguish, on the basis of dress or behavior, the wealthy from the impecunious in Roseto. . . . Despite the affluence of many, there was no atmosphere of "keeping up with the Joneses" in Roseto.

But as young people began to move away to seek jobs in neighboring towns and the community entered the mainstream of American life, the social taboos against conspicuous consumption began to weaken, as did the community bonds that once maintained the town's egalitarian values. About a decade into the study, the researchers noted:

> For many years the more affluent Rosetans restrained their inclination toward material indulgence and maintained in their town the image of a relatively classless society. When a few began to display their wealth, however, many others followed. By 1965 families had begun to join country clubs, drive expensive automobiles, take luxury cruises, and make flights to Las Vegas.

The unforeseen consequence of improved material well-being and, probably more important, rising socioeconomic disparities was that the incidence of heart attack in Roseto caught up with neighboring towns within a span of a decade.

The notion that social cohesion is related to the health of a population is hardly new. One hundred years ago, Emile Durkheim demonstrated that suicide rates were higher among populations that were less cohesive. In 1979, after a nine-year study of 6,928 adults living in Alameda County, California, epidemiologists Lisa Berkman and S. Leonard Syme reported that people with few social ties were two to three times more likely to die of all causes than were those with more extensive contacts. This relationship persisted even after controlling for such characteristics as age and health practices, including cigarette smoking, drinking, exercise, and the use of medical services. The basic findings of the Alameda County Study have since been confirmed in more than a half dozen epidemiological studies in different communities.

These findings have ominous implications if the political scientist Robert Putnam is right that social capital is declining in America [see "The Strange Disappearance of Civic America," *TAP*, Winter 1996]. Putnam's memorable metaphor for this change is bowling league membership, which has declined while bowling overall has increased. By social capital Putnam means the invisible glue that holds society together—the social networks, norms, and trust that enable groups of individuals to cooperate in pursuing shared objectives. On the basis of research in Italy and elsewhere, Putnam argues that social capital is a major contributing factor in economic growth [see "The Prosperous Community: Social Capital and Public Life," *TAP*, Spring 1993]. In fact, as the public health research shows, the harm from weakening social cohesion may not only be civic and economic—it may also be physical.

IT DOES HURT TO BE ALONE

To explore this question, we set out to test the relationship between social capital and public health at the state level. In fact, there are quite marked geographical variations in civic trust and association membership across the United States, and when these indicators of social capital are arrayed against regional differences in mortality and morbidity, the resulting correlations are striking. The chart "Social Capital and Mortality Rates" (above) shows the relationship between the level of civic trust and the age-adjusted rate of death

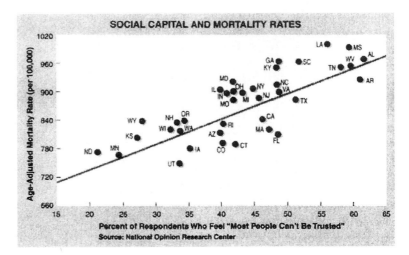

from all causes for the 39 states for which data were available in the National Opinion Research Center's General Social Surveys. The lower the trust between citizens—as indicated by the proportion of respondents in each state who believed that "most people cannot be trusted"—the higher is the average mortality rate.

A similar relationship with mortality prevails for the per capita membership of state residents in voluntary associations. These relationships between social cohesion and mortality hold among both whites and African Americans, as well as among men and women, and they persist after statistical adjustment for state variations in median household income and proportion of households living below the federal poverty threshold.

The figure on the next page, "Social Trust and Quality of Life," displays the correlation between level of civic trust and a measure of self-reported well-being. The National Center for Chronic Disease Prevention and Health Promotion employed the Behavioral Risk Factor Surveillance System (BRFSS) to ascertain the proportion of residents in each state reporting that their health was only fair or poor as opposed to good or excellent. (The BRFSS is a representative, random telephone survey that sampled more than 350,000 community-dwelling American adults between 1993 and 1996.) Again, there is a striking correlation between social capital and quality of life.

But does "bowling alone" really increase the likelihood that you'll get sick? Putnam's reference to the decline in bowling leagues evinced skepticism from some critics. Katha Pollitt, for example, pointed out that the popularity of bowling leagues emerged from a particular period in American blue-collar culture that permitted husbands plenty of boys' nights out (think of the memorable first glimpses of Marlon Brando in *A Streetcar Named*

384

Desire). Other critics have pointed out that declining bowling league memberships may be offset by increased participation of other kinds, such as coaching and playing in youth soccer leagues.

Nonetheless, bowling league membership turns out to correlate rather well with who lives or dies (see "Bowling League Membership and Mortality," below). To paraphrase John Donne, no man or woman is an island entire of itself—therefore we should never send to ask from whom the ball rolls.

INEQUALITY AND PUBLIC HEALTH

Another feature of a society that may influence both its cohesiveness and its members' health is the level of economic inequality. In many countries, notably America, income and wealth are becoming more concentrated. According to a Census Bureau report released last year, the share of total income going to the top fifth of American households increased from 40.5 percent to 46.9 percent between 1968 and 1994. By contrast, the shares of the bottom 80 percent either declined or stagnated. The biggest income gains went to the top 5 percent of households, whose share of the economic pie increased from 16.6 percent to 21 percent. In 1994, the average income among the top 5 percent of households was more than 19 times that of the bottom 20 percent.

Might this polarization of incomes be loosening the social cement? In a forthcoming article in the *American Journal of Public Health,* we argue that this

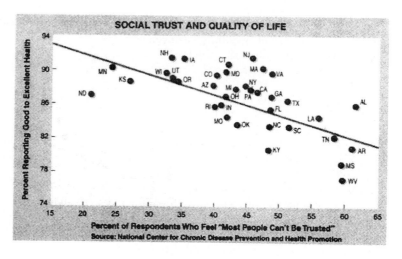

SOCIAL TRUST AND QUALITY OF LIFE

Source: National Center for Chronic Disease Prevention and Health Promotion

is the case. "Income Inequality (Robin Hood Index) and Social Trust" (next page) shows the rising trend in income inequality plotted against the steady decline in civic trust, as tracked by the General Social Surveys. The measure of income inequality we used is the Robin Hood Index, which equals the proportion of aggregate income that would have to be redistributed from households with disproportionate earnings to those earning less, if incomes were to be level. The higher the Robin Hood Index, the bigger the income gap. As "Income Inequality and Social Trust" shows, the larger the income gap, the lower is citizens' trust in each other. Nearly identical results are obtained when we plot income disparity against per capita participation in voluntary associations.

Comparing public health and income distribution across countries lends further credence to the notion that income distribution plays a greater role in the quality of public health than more traditional indices do. In his recent book, *Unhealthy Societies: The Afflictions of Inequality,* economic historian Richard Wilkinson argues forcefully that the life expectancy in developed countries cannot be explained by differences in their absolute standard of living as measured, for example, by per capita income. Rather, a population's health depends more on the level of economic inequality.

The United States, despite having one of the highest living standards in the world (the real gross domestic product [GDP] per capita was $24,680 in 1993), has a lower life expectancy (76.1 years in 1993) than less affluent but more egalitarian countries like the Netherlands (GDP, $17,340; life expectancy, 77.5 years); Israel (GDP, $15,130; life expectancy, 76.6 years); or Spain (GDP, $13,660; life expectancy, 77.7 years). In fact, societies with the smallest income differences between rich and poor, such as Sweden and Japan, tend to enjoy the highest life expec-

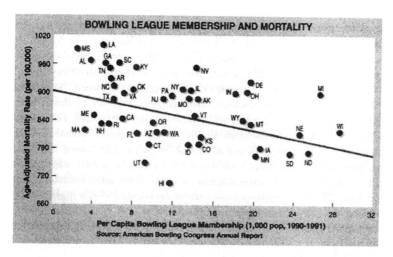

BOWLING LEAGUE MEMBERSHIP AND MORTALITY

Source: American Bowling Congress Annual Report

tancy (78.3 and 79.6 years, respectively). An egalitarian distribution of wealth and income seems to imply a more cohesive, harmonious society. The quality of social relations, Wilkinson concludes, is the prime determinant of a country's human welfare and quality of life.

What does this imply for our future quality of life in this country? Is what has been happening to American society simply a case of Roseto writ large? Two studies published simultaneously in the April 20, 1996, issue of the *British Medical Journal,* including one we conducted, found that differences in income distribution across the 50 states were highly correlated with mortality rates, including deaths from heart disease, homicides, and infant mortality. To be sure, overall life expectancy in the United States has been steadily improving due to advances in medical treatment and the prevention of disease through lifestyle changes. But mortality might have declined more if income inequality had not risen. Our model suggests that for every percent increase in income inequality, the overall death rate is 2 to 3 percent higher than it needed to have been. By any definition, this is an important public health problem.

In recent years, unfortunately, government policy has tended to reinforce growing inequality, which is

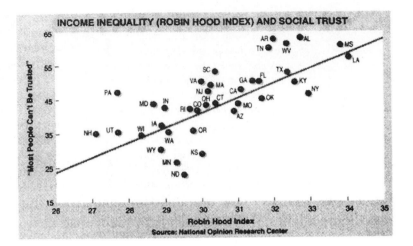

unsurprising in view of the disproportionate political weight that the well-off carry [see Sidney Verba, Kay Lehman Schlozman, and Henry E. Brady, "The Big Tilt: Participatory Inequality in America," *TAP,* May-June 1997]. The danger is a self-perpetuating cycle of growing income inequality, growing political inequality, and diminishing social capital. And because health too is at stake, it is no exaggeration to say that breaking that cycle will affect the body politic in every sense.

The Inequality Express

Barry Bluestone

In his 1958 book, *The Rise of the Meritocracy, 1870–2033,* British sociologist Michael Young predicted that growing inequality in Britain's income distribution would spark a great populist rebellion in the year 2034. As British society moved closer to realizing the ideal of equal opportunity, Young wrote, it would also abandon any pretense of equal outcome: Each individual's socioeconomic status would depend less on lineage, family connections, and political influence, and more on intelligence, education, experience, and effort. Outright racial and gender discrimination and iniquitous privilege would be gone; inequality based on merit would take their place. The victims of this new inequality—those who were once protected by good union wages, civil service status, or seniority—would then take to the barricades.

We haven't seen any such revolution yet, but the rest of Young's prophecy today seems uncomfortably prescient. Virtually every number cruncher who has perused contemporary income data from the United States and the United Kingdom reports three clearly defined trends, each consistent with Young's forecast. First, the distribution of earnings in both countries increasingly reflects the distribution of formal education in the workforce. Second, the gap in earnings between the well educated and the not-so-well educated is steadily increasing. And finally, the real standard of living of a large proportion of the workforce—particularly those with less than a college degree—has steadily and sharply declined.

From *Ticking Time Bombs,* edited by Robert Kuttner, 1996, Part II, pp. 58-73. Published by The New Press, New York, NY. © 1996 by American Prospect. Reprinted by permission.

Universal acceptance of these trends has not, however, led to any agreement about their source. Some scholars emphasize increasing demand for skills in a high-technology economy. Others claim globalization of the economy has thrown workers in high-wage countries into competition with workers in low-wage ones. Still others indict deindustrialization, the decline of unions, rising immigration, and the proliferation of winner-take-all labor markets. This lack of consensus about causes has produced a lack of consensus about remedies.

Here we will attempt to solve the mystery of rising wage inequality, and in so doing consider what might be done to stymie it. The best primer for this exercise is Agatha Christie's *Murder on the Orient Express.*

MERIT OR MARKET?

When Young penned his satire, there appeared little reason to heed his warning. In the immediate postwar period, while Europe and the United States were enjoying the heady days of rapid growth, economic expansion almost always spawned greater equality. Class warfare was giving way to an implicit and generally peaceful social contract. The big trade-off between equality and growth so elegantly detailed by the American economist Arthur Okun seemed to hold more true in theory than in practice. In the U.S., real average weekly earnings would grow by 60 percent between 1947 and 1973. Median family income literally doubled. And over the same period, personal wages and family incomes became tangibly more equal, not less. Along with growth and greater equality, poverty declined across the nation. Those at the bottom of the distribution gained more—on a percentage basis—than those at the top. The higher wages of unionized workers did not come at the expense of other workers' living standards. If anything, the rising wages of higher-paid labor were extracted from the profits that traditionally went to the wealthy.

There is little dispute that by 1973 this trend had come to an end. Inequality actually rose, especially during the 1980s. Many initially blamed a slowdown in overall economic growth. But the expansion of the economy after the 1980–82 recession suggested a new dynamic at work: Faster growth no longer reduced inequality or did much to increase the earnings of those at the bottom of the skill ladder. Wage dispersion returned to levels not seen since before the 1960s. By the late 1980s, family income inequality was higher than at the end of World War II.

Wage dispersion, of course, is not the only source of economic inequality. Another source is demographic trends, such as the simultaneous rise in the number of dual income couples and single-parent families. The tremendous increase during the 1980s in non-wage sources of income for the well-to-do—interest, dividends, rent, and capital gains—plays an important role as well. But whatever role these other causes may play, changes in the distribution of wages and salaries are clearly a primary factor in rising inequality.

Racial and gender discrimination continue to be the basis of large earnings differences. However, as the influence of more virulent prejudices has declined in the labor market, differences in education and skill have had a greater impact on wages. One manifestation of this trend is the increasing wage ratio of college-educated workers to high school dropouts. In 1963, the mean annual earnings of those with four years of college or more stood at just over twice (2.11 times) the mean annual earnings of those who had not completed high school. By 1979, this ratio had increased to 2.39. This was but a harbinger of things to come. By 1987, the education-to-earnings ratio had skyrocketed to nearly three to one (2.91). The trend continues today.

In fact, the entire pattern of wage growth during the 1980s reflects a remarkable labor market "twist" tied to schooling. During this decade, the average real wage of male high school dropouts fell by over 18 percent, while male high school graduates suffered nearly a 13 percent real earnings loss. At the other end of the distribution, men who completed at least a master's degree emerged as the only real winners. Their earnings rose by more than 9 percent. Note that even men who had attended college without graduating saw a serious erosion in their earning power. And men who completed college discovered that their undergraduate degrees merely served to prevent a decline in inflation-adjusted wages. Women fared better than men in terms of overall wage growth, but the imprint of a labor market twist is clearly discernible here as well.

That three out of four U.S. workers have not completed college provides some indication of how large a proportion of the entire labor force has been adversely affected by the new meritocratic distribution. If we take some liberty with Robert Reich's definition of symbolic analysts—people such as research scientists, design engineers, and public relations executives whose work focuses on problem-solving, problem-identifying, and strategic brokering activities—and limit the use of this term to those with two or more years of schooling beyond the bachelor's degree, the successes in the new economy account for just 7 percent of the U. S. labor force. If we include men with the equivalent of at least a master's degree plus women with at least a bachelor's, we could say the proportion of real earnings winners includes about 15 percent of the workforce. The extreme losers in this new meritocratic society—those with no more than a high school diploma—still comprise more than half of all U.S. workers.

In economic terms, the "return" of education, or how much one earns with a given level of education, has diverged sharply from its "rate of return," or how much an additional year of education is worth. What we have seen is a reduction in the return of education—a decline in earnings for high school graduates, for example—while the increment in earnings due to a little more schooling pays off a whole lot, most notably at the high end. This is why the college degree for men has become a defensive good. It provided almost no wage growth during the entire decade of the 1980s, but at least it kept college graduates from suffering the nearly 13 percent loss sustained by those with only a high school diploma. For men, completing college during the 1980s became the equivalent of donning a brand new pair of running shoes to go bear hunting with a companion. If the bear ends up attacking you, you cannot outrun it. But in order to survive you need to outrun your friend. Anyone who has visited a vocational guidance counselor lately will recognize this as the principal underlying message. The college degree still outfits women with the equivalent of a new pair of Reeboks, but any less schooling leaves women trying to run in quicksand.

THE ECONOMISTS' LINEUP

To explain the crisis, economists have offered up ten suspects:

SUSPECT ONE: TECHNOLOGY. Robert Lawrence of Harvard's John F. Kennedy School of Government and Paul Krugman, now at Stanford University, are the leading advocates of this position. They believe that the new information technologies skew the earnings distribution by placing an extraordinary premium on skilled labor while reducing the demand, and hence the wage, for those of lesser skill. This, they contend, is about all you need to explain current earnings trends.

The problem is that no one has any direct measure of the skill content of technology. Proving this hypothesis would require proving not just skill-biased technological change but also a tremendous acceleration in new technology during the 1980s. After all, at least some level of technological change occurred in earlier decades without such an adverse impact on earnings equality. What's so different about technology in the 1980s and 1990s? According to David Howell (see "The Skills Myth," *Ticking Time Bombs* [1996]), and Lawrence Mishel and Jared Bernstein in an Economic Policy Institute working paper, there is little evidence that the pace of innovation—the speed at which new machines are brought to factories and new products are developed—was any faster than during the 1960s and 1970s. Most businesses are not introducing technology that requires vastly improved skill. Many are simply paying less for the same skills they have been using all along while others are hiring better educated workers at lower wage rates to do the work previously relegated to lesser-educated employees.

SUSPECT TWO: THE SERVICE-BASED ECONOMY. Other researchers, including George Borjas of the University of California at San Diego, have argued that a primary suspect is deindustrialization—the shift of jobs from goods-producing sectors to the service sector. In previous writings, I have estimated that between 1963 and 1987 the earnings ratio between college graduates and high school dropouts working in the goods-producing sector (mining, construction, and manufacturing) increased from 2.11 to 2.42—a jump of 15 percent. In the service sector, however, the education-to-earnings ratio mushroomed from 2.20 to 3.52—a 60 percent increase. All of the employment growth in the economy during the 1980s came in the services sector, where wages were polarizing between high school dropouts and college graduates four times faster than the goods-producing industries. Hence, this could explain at least part of the dramatic increase in earnings inequality.

SUSPECT THREE: DEREGULATION. Government deregulation of the airlines, trucking and telecommunications industries very likely has produced the same effect. In each of these industries, intense competition from new non-union, low-wage entrants, such as the short-lived People Express in the airline industry, forced existing firms to extract large wage concessions from their employees to keep from going bankrupt. How much this has contributed to overall earnings inequality remains an open question.

SUSPECT FOUR: DECLINING UNIONIZATION. Unions have historically negotiated wage packages that narrow earnings differentials. They have tended to improve wages the most for workers with modest educations. As Richard Freeman of Harvard and a number of other economists have noted, the higher rate of union membership is one of the reasons for the smaller dispersion of wages found in manufacturing. That unions have made only modest inroads into the service economy may explain in part why earnings inequality in this sector outstrips inequality in the goods-producing sector.

SUSPECT FIVE: DOWNSIZING. The restructuring of corporate enterprise toward lean production and the destruction of internal job ladders as firms rely more heavily on part-time, temporary, and leased employees is still another suspect in this mystery, according to Bennett Harrison of Carnegie Mellon. The new enterprise regime creates what labor economists call "segmented" labor force of insiders and outsiders whose job security and earnings potential can differ markedly.

SUSPECT SIX: WINNER-TAKE-ALL LABOR MARKETS. The heightened competitive market, which forces firms toward lean production, may also, according to Robert Frank and Philip Cook, be creating a whole new structure of free-agency, "winner-take-all" labor markets. As Frank has explained ("Talent and the Winner-Take-All Society," *The American Prospect,* Spring 1994, No. 17), in winner-take-all markets, "a handful of top performers walk away with the lion's share of total rewards." The difference between commercial success and failure in such markets may depend on just a few "star" performers—in movies the director and leading actor or actress; in the O. J. Simpson trial the conduct of just one or two trial attorneys. Given the high stakes involved in a multimillion dollar movie project or a murder trial involving a well-to-do client, investors are willing to pay a bundle to make sure they employ the "best in the business."

Today, the fields of law, journalism, consulting, investment banking, corporate management, design, fashion, and even academia are generating payoff structures that once were common only in the entertainment and professional sports industries. Just a handful of Alan Dershowitzes, Michael Milkens, and Michael Eisners can have a sizeable impact on the dispersion of wages in each of their occupations. There is considerable evidence that inequality is not only rising across education groups but within them, very likely reflecting such winner-take-all dynamics.

SUSPECT SEVEN: TRADE. Even more fundamental to the recent restructuring of the labor market—and a likely proximate cause of deindustrialization, deunionization, lean production, and perhaps even the free-agency syndrome—is the expansion of unfettered global trade. According to trade theory, increased trade alone is sufficient—*without* any accompanying multinational capital investment or low-wage worker immigration—to induce the wages of similarly skilled workers to equalize across trading countries. Economists call this dynamic "factor price equalization." As the global economy moves toward free trade, lower transportation costs, better communications, and the same "best practice" production techniques available to all countries, factor price equalization is likely to occur.

Unfortunately, in a world like ours where there is a plentiful supply of unskilled labor juxtaposed to a continued relative scarcity of well-educated workers, this "price equalization" *within* skill categories leads to a "wage polarization" *between* skill categories. The gap between the compensation of low-skilled workers and high-skilled workers everywhere will tend to grow. According to the well-respected trade theorist Edward Leamer of the University of California at Los Angeles, freer trade will ultimately reduce the wages of less-skilled U.S. workers by about a thousand dollars a year, partly as a result of NAFTA. If factor price equalization is a chief source of wage dispersion today, just consider the implications when China and India with their immense unskilled workforces enter fully into global markets.

SUSPECT EIGHT: CAPITAL MOBILITY. Freer trade generally provides for the unrestricted movement of investment capital across borders. This inevitably accelerates the process of growing wage inequality. Modern transportation and communications technologies, combined with fewer government restrictions on foreign capital investment, have led to increased multinational capital flows between countries. To the extent that companies move to take advantage of cheaper unskilled labor, transnational investment adds to the effective supply of low-skilled workers available to American firms, thus reinforcing factor price equalization.

SUSPECT NINE: IMMIGRATION. Increased immigration potentially has the same effect, if a disproportionate share of new immigrants enters with limited skills and schooling. This is true at least for legal immigrants. The typical legal immigrant in the U.S. today has nearly a year less schooling than native citizens. Undocumented immigrants surely have even less. As such, while many immigrants to the U.S. come here with excellent education and skills, there is little doubt that the large number of Central American, Caribbean, and Southeast Asians seeking refuge in this country has had the unfortunate side effect of at least temporarily boosting the supply of low-skill workers seeking jobs.

SUSPECT TEN: TRADE DEFICITS. The trade gap has contributed to the decline in those sectors of the economy that have in the past helped to restrain earnings inequality. Moreover, trade data indicate that the import surplus itself is disproportionately composed of products made by low-skilled and modestly skilled labor. This boosts the effective supply of workers at the bottom of the education-to-earnings distribution and thus depresses their relative wages.

WHODUNNIT?

Thus, in our rogue's gallery we have ten suspects: skill-based technological change, deindustrialization, industry deregulation, the decline of unions, lean production, winner-take-all labor markets, free trade, transnational capital mobility, immigration, and a persistent trade deficit. Quantitatively parsing out the relative impact of all of these forces on wage distribution is fraught with enormous difficulty. Still, Richard Freeman and Lawrence Katz have attempted to do something like this, at least for the wage gap between men with a college degree and those with a high school diploma.

What do these results suggest? If the Freeman and Katz estimates are in the right ballpark, the answer to our mystery is the same denouement as Agatha Christie's in *Murder on the Orient Express.* They all did it. Every major economic trend in the U.S. contributes to growing inequality largely linked to merit. None of these trends shows the least sign of weakening.

Each trend reflects the growth of market forces and the decline of institutional constraints on competition. This was Young's essential message more than 30 years ago. Increased reliance on domestic market dynamics as the sole determinant of earnings produces inequality. Heightened competition within these markets, as a consequence of fuller integration into the global economy, exacerbates this wage dispersion. While it may be sinister, there is nothing conspiratorial about this phenomenon. It is embedded in the very nature of laissez-faire market dynamics. For this reason, meritocratic inequality is much harder to remedy than overt forms of discrimination based on race and sex.

POLICY ENDGAMES

Even economists who tout the merits of the market have come to recognize the need to soften the potentially devastating social impact of current income trends. Yet given the long-standing resistance to most forms of public intervention in the marketplace, the search for solutions has been restricted to just three types of countermeasures: education and training, immigration reform, and direct tax-and-transfer policy.

In theory, education can offset the effect of skill-biased technological change and factor price equalization. If somehow we could produce a true glut of symbolic analysts in place of high school dropouts, meritocratic inequality would begin to resolve itself. Education reduces the surplus of low-skilled workers and relieves the shortage of skilled workers. If this strategy also happens to increase the overall level of education, it has the added advantage of improving overall labor productivity and ultimately real wages.

A number of education and training programs have widespread appeal. These include expanding the Head Start program for disadvantaged preschool children, levying a corporate tax to finance on-the-job training, instituting a national apprenticeship program, and converting current grant and loan programs into income-contingent loans for college and university students. Other possibilities under consideration for education reform include setting national standards for school performance, introducing merit systems to reward successful teaching, instituting voucher systems, and increasing teacher and parent control over schools.

Legal restriction of immigration is a second possible means of reducing wage inequality. Canada has a higher rate of immigration than the United States. But immigration laws in the two countries have produced very different effects on their respective labor markets. Since the 1960s, U.S. policy has stressed family reunification. Canada, in contrast, employs a point system designed to produce a more skilled immigrant labor pool. This approach has produced legal immigrants in Canada who average 1.3 more years of education than native Canadians. If we ignore the thorny ethical issues surrounding the rights of political refugees and judgments about the worthiness of individuals seeking to immigrate—a whole other debate—one could imagine tilting immigration policy toward greater use of skill-based criteria.

Finally, if immigration control and education cannot do the job, there is the old standby of progressive tax-and-transfer policy to effect greater equality after wages are paid. Traditionally, most contemporary liberal economists have favored this method,

for it entails the least interference with market forces.

On the surface, this complement of liberal policies seems germane for coping with meritocratic inequality. Not surprisingly, all three policies are at the top of the domestic agenda of the Democratic Party. Yet, given the powerful set of national and global forces at work in the economy, these policies may not be enough.

A case in point is education and training. Greater equality in schooling does not by itself produce more equal earnings. The distribution of education has become significantly more even over the past three decades. Among year-round, full-time workers, the overall variation in completed years of schooling has declined by more than 25 percent since 1963. The performance of black students and other minorities on the Scholastic Aptitude Test (SAT) is further evidence of this convergence. In 1976, the average verbal SAT score for blacks stood at the 74th percentile of whites; by 1990 the average score was up to the 80th percentile. Math SAT scores for black students improved by the same amount.

But even as education backgrounds have converged, the importance of small differences in education has increased—enough so to offset any equalizing effect education would otherwise have. Recall the distinction between the return and the rate of return of schooling. As such, no matter what other benefits might flow from increased schooling, expanded education is not, by itself, a certain cure for inequality.

Job training programs have made even less headway. While the federal government has experimented with a bevy of programs from the original Manpower Development and Training Act (MDTA) of the Great Society to the Job Training and Partnership Act (JTPA) of the 1980s, repeated evaluations suggest mixed results at best. Some programs like the Job Corps, which provide long-term training opportunities to disadvantaged youth, have been cost effective. The vast majority, however, have provided dubious returns. And even when these programs are deemed successful, the earnings advantage they give participants produces only the slightest deviation in the trend toward income inequality.

James Heckman of the University of Chicago has estimated just how small this deviation really is. Assuming a generous 10 percent rate of return on investment, he calculates that the government would need to spend a staggering $284 billion on the U.S. workforce to restore male high school dropouts to their 1979 real incomes. To restore education-based wage differentials to 1979 levels without reducing the real incomes of existing college-educated workers would take more than $2 trillion.

Future investments in human capital programs may have a somewhat better track record than past attempts, particularly if they are well targeted. But one cannot ignore the enormous increases in inequality that have already taken place. And to keep inequality from growing even more quickly, government would have to expand these programs at a frenetic pace. This is not to say that there is no role for training in solving America's labor market problems. While more training may not significantly reduce inequality, it is nevertheless useful for raising overall productivity, providing individual workers with a defense against further wage decline, and for rectifying specific skill shortages which could otherwise lead to wage-led inflation.

Immigration reform may also have a marginal impact on the earnings distribution, but any improvement will be largely limited to regions of the country where immigration flows have been disproportionately large—California, Texas, Florida, and perhaps a few states in the Northeast.

That leaves tax-and-transfer programs as the centerpiece for adjusting distributional outcomes. On paper, a suitably progressive set of tax rates combined with sufficiently generous transfer assistance could radically redistribute income after it is earned in the market. But in practice even such hard-to-win liberal measures as President Clinton's 1993 tax initiative produce relatively little redistribution. In 1977, when the federal tax system was significantly more progressive than today, the richest fifth of American families had 9.5 times the pretax total income of the poorest fifth. Federal taxes reduced the overall gap in relative shares by less than 20 percent; regressive state and local taxes wiped out this improvement. Given increased reliance on regressive payroll taxes and an aversion to any further increase in progressive income taxation, the tax system is unlikely to do much more.

The same is true of public transfer programs. Over the past 20 years, the New Deal safety net of unemployment insurance and welfare assistance has come under attack. Unemployment insurance covered more than 60 percent of the jobless during the 1961 and 1975 recessions. Despite the greater severity of the 1982 recession, only 43 percent of jobless Americans collected unemployment benefits. During the 1991 recession, coverage was down to 40 percent. While the Clinton administration implemented important reforms of the federal unemployment insurance system, the states and the federal government are unlikely to greatly expand coverage of the unemployed. As for the traditional welfare system, including Aid to Families with Dependent Children (AFDC), real benefit levels have been cut in many states and the government has imposed greater eligibility restrictions. Most of the proposed reforms of the AFDC program would change the dynamics of dependency, but do nothing to change the final distribu-

tion of income—and they could, by forcing welfare recipients off the roles after two years, make matters worse.

Education and immigration reform, as well as redistributive tax-and-transfer policy, could contribute to reducing inequality, but they are by themselves—even under the best of political scenarios—no match for the concerted forces now driving the labor market. Indeed, relying exclusively on redistributive tax-and-transfer schemes to redress the growing inequality problem would likely require tax rates and transfer sums so large that there would be not only massive political resistance but real economic costs in terms of disincentives to investment and growth.

THE END OF INEQUALITY?

There is, however, an additional policy agenda which a progressive government could embrace. This agenda would focus attention on the market forces that generate greater inequality. First, there is direct regulation of the labor market. As the empirical evidence demonstrates, the growth in earnings inequality has materialized in part because of a serious erosion in wages at the bottom of the skill distribution and a sharp decline in unionization. Higher minimum wage standards are one way government can affect the distribution of employee compensation. While raising the mandatory wage minimum theoretically entails some trade-off in the form of job loss, some recent studies prove the positive earnings impact of modest increases in the statutory minimum far outweighs any unemployment effect. Thus, the aggregate wage bill paid to less-skilled workers increases, improving the living standards of those on the bottom rungs of the earnings ladder.

Labor law reform makes it easier for unions to organize workers and provides an indirect method of accomplishing the same objective. While there are many reasons why union membership is dwindling, the recent *Fact Finding Report* of the U.S. Commission on the Future of Worker-Management Relations found undeniable evidence that the playing field is tilted heavily toward employers. Employers can permanently replace striking employees, which reduces the ability of unions to organize and to freely negotiate collective bargaining agreements. Unions do not have free access to employees during membership drives, and the penalties for employer unfair labor practices are trivial. To remedy this, government could ban permanent striker replacements, permit union organizers access to in-plant bulletin boards and public forums, impose more costly penalties on employers who violate the rights of union organizers, expedite legal remedies, and authorize binding arbitration for first contracts.

There are also industrial and trade policies to consider. Advocates of industrial policy can cite the success of the U.S. aircraft and agriculture industries, in which government purchases and research-and-development subsidies helped to create and maintain industries that now dominate world markets. The Carter administration's Chrysler loan guarantee, which provided an eleventh-hour reprieve from certain bankruptcy for the then-hapless automaker, turned around an old smokestack company and saved tens of thousands of well-paying jobs—not only at Chrysler but at hundreds of its suppliers. With a new lease on life, Chrysler has surged back as a world leader in automotive technology. There are, of course, many instances of failed industrial policy—the government's ill-fated Synfuels Corporation, for example—but there are an ample number of cases on the other side of the ledger. Maintaining the nation's manufacturing base would have a salutary effect on incomes.

The other policy that can bolster the goods-producing sector is implementation of fair-trade language in trade agreements. One way of doing this is to use tariffs and trade barriers designed to give *temporary* protection to key industries, promoting industrial revitalization and economic transition. Another form of managed trade would tie the offer of reduced protection to a trading partner's compliance with certain environmental and labor standards. Critics of NAFTA argued for side agreements that would have linked the pace of tariff reduction to the rate at which Mexican wages caught up with Mexico's rapidly rising productivity. To be sure, government-imposed limits on trade can have detrimental effects on prices and therefore reduce average real incomes from what they might be under a free trade regime. Nevertheless, a carefully crafted set of trade policies that condones temporary protection of selected domestic markets and sets minimum labor and environmental standards can soften the distributional impact of factor price equalization. The trick is to keep such protection from becoming permanent or prompting a trade war.

One last point: What about the use of macroeconomic stimulus to counteract inequality? As noted above, growth per se is no longer an antidote to increased wage dispersion. But it is important to realize that it is the sine qua non for providing the tax revenue and the political will to address inequality through government action. Hence, overzealous attacks on government deficits that reduce aggregate demand and overly restrictive monetary policies that unnecessarily boost interest rates can poison the environment for possible egalitarian reforms.

Is there any evidence that more aggressive structural policies can help? Critics like Mickey Kaus, the *New Republic* columnist and author of *The End of Equality*, think not.

In declaring that "the venerable liberal crusade for income equality is doomed," Kaus argues that

> you cannot decide to keep all the nice parts of capitalism and get rid of all the nasty ones. You cannot have capitalism without 'selfishness,' or even 'greed,' because they are what make the system work. You can't have capitalism and material equality, because capitalism is constantly generating extremes of inequality as some individuals strike it rich . . . while others fail and fall on hard times.

This may sound sensible, but it will come as remarkable news to a large number of our foreign capitalist competitors. A comparison of earnings trends across countries suggests that different institutional frameworks, all operating within a capitalist framework, produce substantially different distributional outcomes.

Kaus confuses capitalism with laissez-faire economics. All nations now face nearly identical pressures from technological change and global competition. Yet not all are experiencing the same degree of growing income inequality. Those countries with stronger unions, national wage solidarity agreements, generous social welfare programs, and more vigorously pursued industrial and trade policies have greater wage equality than countries pursuing pure free-market strategies. Relying on an extensive review of comparative statistics, Richard Freeman and Lawrence Katz conclude that while educational and occupational skill-wage differentials were growing rapidly in the United States and the United Kingdom during the 1980s, the experience elsewhere was quite different. Wage equality increased in the Netherlands; wage differentials did not change noticeably in France, Germany, and Italy; and wage dispersion increased modestly—if at all—in Australia, Canada, Japan, and Sweden.

In all of these capitalist countries, intensified global competition and technological innovation pushed the distribution of earnings and income toward greater inequality. Structural protection against this onslaught was greater in countries that did not follow the Reagan-Thatcher road to full-scale deregulation and laissez-faire trade policies.

True, the flexibility of the U.S. market may be partly responsible for lower overall unemployment rates compared with these other countries, but the price of this flexibility seems to be much higher levels of economic polarization and social inequality. Moreover, recent research by Rebecca Blank, a labor economist at Northwestern University, suggests there is little empirical evidence that social protection programs substantially affect labor market flexibility. Expansive social protection problems, then, are not the most important factor behind the high rate of unemployment in Europe, as many others suggest. Blank goes on to show that cutting back on social protection policies does not automatically reduce unemployment or increase the speed of labor market adjustment. Instead she finds that by enhancing worker well-being, social protection policies may actually permit flexibility that would not otherwise be possible. All of which means that the U.S. can adopt policies to directly redress income inequality without raising the specter of double-digit unemployment.

So can we avoid fulfilling Michael Young's prophecy for 2034? Can a society with high- and low-skill workers have a reasonably equitable distribution of income? The answer is a qualified, "yes," but it requires that we focus on equal outcome, not just equal opportunity. There is a fundamental distinction separating progressives from neoconservatives and neoliberals, and it turns largely on this point. Progressives are willing to consider a broader and more balanced array of public policies to keep the free market from perpetrating and then perpetuating socially destructive levels of inequality.

Foreword:

Making Ends Meet

How Single Mothers Survive Welfare and Low-Wage Work

Christopher Jencks

Ever since Lyndon Johnson first asked his Council of Economic Advisors to estimate how many Americans were poor, public officials, policy analysts, and journalists have relied on the Census Bureau for information about poverty. When the bureau reports that poverty has become less common among the elderly, as it has over the past generation, we congratulate ourselves. When the bureau reports that poverty has become more common among children, we wring our hands.

In *Making Ends Meet,* Kathryn Edin and Laura Lein present powerful evidence that the Census Bureau's measures of poverty are often quite misleading. The good news is that poor families have more resources than a naive reader of census statistics might think. The bad news is that the official poverty thresholds also underestimate poor people's needs. Because of these problems, the official poverty count may be either too high or too low. Fortunately, almost everyone recognizes that the line between the poor and the nonpoor is somewhat arbitrary, so it does not much matter whether we say that 10 or 20 percent of the population is "poor." What does matter is that poverty rates for different groups reflect the frequency of destitution in each group. When the poverty rate is higher among children than among the elderly, for example, we need to be confident that all children are in fact more likely to lack basic necessities. It is also important that changes in the official poverty rate mirror changes in people's ability to buy basic necessities. If the official poverty rate frequently rises while material hardship falls, or vice versa, poverty statistics are worse than useless.

Making Ends Meet focuses on the group that has traditionally had the highest poverty rate in America: unskilled single mothers and their children. Edin and Lein's findings suggest that, at least for the next few years, official poverty statistics will probably provide a quite misleading picture of how these families' economic status is changing. As the new time limits on welfare receipt begin to take effect, more and more single mothers will have to take jobs. Most of these newly employed mothers will have more income than they had on welfare, so their official poverty rate will fall. But they will also have more expenses than they had on welfare, and they will get fewer noncash benefits. Edin and Lein's findings dramatize the likely result. Between 1988 and 1992, mothers who held low-wage jobs reported substantially more income than those who collected welfare, but they also reported more hardship. If this pattern persists in the years ahead, time limits will probably bring both a decline in the official poverty rate and an increase in material hardship.

OFFICIAL STATISTICS VERSUS REAL BUDGETS

Measuring income is extraordinarily difficult. Until 1940 the Census Bureau did not even try to ask Americans about their income because the subject was considered too sensitive. Now the bureau asks people about their income all the time, but only two-thirds of the nation's households answer all the bureau's questions. Those who do answer often make mistakes. Some even provide deliberately misleading information. In general, families that get most of their income from a regular paycheck or pension check seem to report their income quite accurately. But the poor get more of their income from irregular sources, and such income is not well reported.

Sometimes the resulting data seem implausible at best. According to the Census Bureau, for example, 1.5 million single mothers had cash incomes below $5,000 in 1992. These mothers typically had two children. Most got food stamps and Medicaid, but only a minority lived in subsidized housing.[1] Taking these women's reported income at face value implies that they paid for their rent, utilities, transportation, clothing, laundry, and other expenses from a monthly budget of less than $420. Almost half appeared to be living on less than $200 a month.

One way to see whether families really live on such tiny sums is to look at the Labor Department's Consumer Expenditure Survey (CES). According to the CES, families with incomes below $5,000 in 1992 took in an average of only $180 a month.[2] Yet these families told the CES that they had spent an average of $1,100 a month. This confirms the common-sense belief that families cannot live on air. But we still need to explain how these families manage to spend six times as much as they take in.

Ask an economist this question and you will get a standard answer. Low-income families appear to live beyond their means because they are only temporarily poor. When their incomes dip, they use savings, credit cards, or loans from relatives to smooth their consumption. When their incomes rise, they repay their debts. This explanation makes sense for families in which the breadwinner has just lost a steady job or the family business is losing money. But single mothers who report incomes below $5,000 seldom have savings or credit cards, and most stay poor for a long time. How do they manage?

Making Ends Meet shows that almost all poor single mothers supplement their regular income with some combination of off-the-books employment and money from relatives, lovers, and the fathers of their children. Few keep a record of such income. Even if they knew the annual total, they would not necessarily report it to the Census Bureau, since they do not report it to the Internal Revenue Service. Secretiveness is especially common among welfare recipients, almost all of whom have non-welfare income that they conceal from the welfare department.

Taking account of irregular income has a dramatic effect on our picture of welfare mothers' economic status. Consider Illinois, a fairly typical state that Edin studied intensively from 1988 to 1990. During 1990 an Illinois mother with two children and no other income got $367 a month from Aid to Families with Dependent Children (AFDC).[3] She got another $50 a month if the father of her children made child support payments to the state. (If the father paid more than $50, the state kept the rest.) If she worked, she could keep a small part of her earnings to cover work-related expenses, but anything beyond that amount was subtracted from her AFDC check. Most Illinois welfare recipients were therefore expected to live on less than $5,000 a year in cash, plus food stamps and Medicaid.

Most Illinois welfare recipients live in the Chicago area, and most live in unsubsidized housing. Even in Chicago's worst neighborhoods, unsubsidized apartments almost always cost at least $350 a month in 1990. An optimist might think that welfare mothers somehow found unusually cheap apartments, but when Edin asked forty Chicago mothers in unsubsidized housing how much they paid, only one spent less than $300 and only five spent less than $350. Edin also interviewed frontline welfare workers who routinely checked recipients' rent stubs. These informants confirmed that when welfare recipients lived in unsubsidized apartments they usually spent about as much for rent as they got from AFDC.

Nonetheless, there was no public discussion of how welfare recipients paid their other bills. The most obvious explanation for this was political. Conservatives did not raise the question because they did not want to draw attention to the fact that AFDC benefits were too low to support a family. Liberals were equally reluctant to discuss the issue, because they did not want to admit that recipients were balancing their budgets with unreported income. This conspiracy of silence encouraged the public to imagine that welfare recipients could get by on whatever the legislature chose to give them. Once the public accepts this comforting assumption, it becomes natural to cut benefits whenever the state budget tightens.

I myself never thought seriously about how welfare recipients could live on $300 or $400 a month until Kathryn Edin forced me to do so. This happened quite fortuitously. In 1983 and 1985 Fay Cook and Susan Mayer, my colleagues at Northwestern University, and I had conducted two telephone surveys in which we asked Chicago residents whether they had recently experienced various material hardships, such as going hungry, not seeing a doctor when they thought they needed treatment, or having their utilities shut off. We found a lot of hardship. But a lot of families with very low incomes also said that they had not experienced any of the hardships we listed. Following standard economic logic, we assumed that most of these families either spent an unusually large fraction of their income on the things we had asked about or that they spent this money unusually efficiently.[4]

To see if these speculations were correct, we hired Kathryn Edin (who was then a graduate student at Northwestern) to reinterview some of our respondents. After a few weeks she reported that she was getting nowhere. When she called back low-income respondents who had not reported any hardships and asked how they managed, they were reluctant to talk with her. Many seemed to suspect that she was working for the welfare department or some other government agency. She therefore proposed a different approach. Instead of interviewing respondents who had no reason to trust her, she would ask people who worked with welfare recipients to introduce her and vouch for her trustworthiness. She would then build a "snowball" sample by asking each initial respondent to introduce her to additional welfare mothers.

Edin asked each mother in this new sample how much money she spent in an average month on different goods and services. Having established the family's average monthly expenditures, she asked mothers how they paid their bills. Piecing this story together often took many interviews spread over several months, but eventually all her respondents provided budgets that more or less balanced. None of them lived on AFDC alone, and none of them reported all their income to the welfare department. The average mother got only half her cash from AFDC. The remainder came primarily from off-the-books employment, family members, boyfriends, and absent fathers.

After interviewing fifty welfare recipients, Edin received a grant from the Russell Sage Foundation to support a comparative study of unmarried Chicago mothers who worked at regular jobs paying less than $7.50 an hour. Then she and Laura Lein proposed a collaborative study of Boston, Charleston, and San Antonio. Once again they approached respondents through trusted intermediaries. This inevitably meant that they oversampled people with a lot of friends, especially friends on welfare or with low-wage jobs. Fortunately, there is no obvious reason why that fact should distort conclusions about single mothers' budgets.

DRAWING THE LINE

Making Ends Meet describes what Edin and Lein found in Boston, Charleston, Chicago, and San Antonio. It shows that all but a handful of single mothers consumed goods and services whose value exceeded the official poverty line. This does not mean they were living well. Edin and Lein found widespread material hardship. Based on what they found, I would argue that the official poverty threshold is too low. But the evidence is not clear-cut, and not all readers will agree.

Everyone who studies these mothers' budgets will find a few items they regard as "luxuries" rather than "necessities." This is consistent with everyday experience. All of us have seen poor people buy things that we ourselves would not buy, and most of us have occasionally felt that such behavior was extravagant. One reason food stamps have become so unpopular is that millions of Americans have watched the woman ahead of them in the checkout line use stamps to pay for something they judged too expensive for their own family. Such judgments flow partly from the fact that no two people seem to agree on what constitutes a necessity. But there is also another more fundamental problem: most people find that spending all their money on necessities is unbearably depressing. The poor are as subject to this dilemma as the rest of us.

In American usage, a necessity is something essential for physical survival or a moderate level of physical comfort. Food, shelter, heat, light, warm clothing, and medical care are the standard examples. Purchases that merely generate pleasure, like a television set or a birthday present, or that generate self-respect, like attractive clothes or cosmetics, are not defined as necessities. Nonetheless, poor people in every culture occasionally forgo physical necessities in order to obtain luxuries that they value for non-material reasons. This always seems extravagant to outsiders for whom the luxuries in question have less symbolic significance. But neither morality nor common sense requires human beings to value their health and physical comfort more than their honor, pleasure, or self-respect. Once we concede that people cannot live by bread alone, we should not expect poor people to spend all their money on either bread or its equivalent.

This logic suggests that the mother who takes her children to McDonald's once a month is not necessarily being extravagant or foolish, even if her treat means that there is not enough for breakfast or dinner later in the week. Such a mother may have a better sense of what her children need than the nutritionist who tells her to buy more beans and rice. The fact that she buys occasional treats does not mean that she has more money than she needs for necessities. It just means that for most people an occasional luxury is a necessity, and that the line between the two is less clear-cut than some of my New England ancestors might have wished.

Edin and Lein's budgets also provide useful evidence about how much money a mother needs to keep her family together. The crucial clue here is that Edin and Lein found no single mothers who lived on welfare alone. In theory, this could just mean that every mother is capable of supplementing her welfare check in some way, and that every mother prefers more income to less. But this explanation stretches credulity. In order to supplement her welfare check, a mother must have either job skills that some employer values, interpersonal skills that allow her to make continuing claims on her relatives, or a capacity to trade her charms for some man's money. Many mothers lack at least one of these resources. It follows that some mothers almost surely lack them all. If such mothers cannot supplement their welfare checks, what becomes of them?

The fact that Edin and Lein did not find such mothers suggests to me that they cannot maintain their own households. Edin and Lein also interviewed welfare mothers who shared housing. They too had some supplementary income. (A mother who cannot earn any money on the side, has no boyfriend, and cannot get help from her relatives is unlikely to have the makings of a good roommate.) Some mothers who cannot supplement their check presumably live with their parents. This is especially common among teenage mothers, whom Edin and Lein did not interview. But as teenage mothers grow up, they usually move out of their parents' (or mother's) household. Some teenage mothers may leave their children with the grandmother. Others move out with their children but later find that they cannot pay their bills and move back in with their parents or other relatives, or show up in shelters. If a mother has exhausted these sources of help, she may send her children to live with her mother or some other relative. In a few cases her children end up in foster care.

How common are such family breakups? The 1992 Current Population Survey (CPS) found that 2.6 percent of children under the age of eighteen lived with neither their mother nor their father.[5] About 2 percent lived with a grandparent, aunt, sibling, or other relative. The remaining 0.6 percent lived with non-relatives (usually foster parents). Anecdotal evidence suggests that most of these children had a living mother, but statistical data is not currently available on this topic or on the reasons why children live with people other than their natural parents.

An interpretation of Edin and Lein's budgets suggests, the official poverty thresholds underestimate poor families' needs by roughly 25 percent—though there is clearly much individual variation around this (or any other) estimate. Moreover, this threshold is not the level at which families begin to experience material hardship and therefore seem "poor." Rather, the threshold represents the lowest level of resources that allows a family to live independently. When families appear to be living on significantly less than this, we are underestimating their resources, either because they do not report all their income or because they are not paying cash for a lot of what they consume.

PREDICTING THE FUTURE

In August 1996, President Clinton signed legislation abolishing AFDC and replacing it with Temporary Assistance for Needy Families (TANF). TANF's most widely publicized feature is its requirement that able-bodied welfare recipients work after two years. But the new law also gives states a lot of freedom to design their own TANF rules. A generous state that wants to get around the federal time limits can probably do so. Few states will try, however, because the new law also gives them strong financial incentives to cut their overall level of welfare spending.

Under the pre-1996 system, every dollar that a state appropriated for AFDC was matched by one to four dollars of federal money. (The matching formula was more generous for poorer states.) Under TANF, states get a block grant whose size does not depend on how much of their own money they spend.[6] If a state decides to spend more

because the number of TANF applicants has risen, because the cost of living has risen, or because recipients who hit their time limit cannot find work, it will have to pay the additional cost from its own treasury. Conversely, if states cut limit eligibility or cut benefit levels, they will be able to keep every dollar they save. Instead of paying twenty to fifty cents for a dollar's worth of charity, states will now have to pay a full dollar.

Raising the cost of altruism almost always reduces its frequency. Once legislators digest the fact that spending a dollar on welfare means that they have a full dollar less for hospitals, schools, highways, or tax cuts, welfare will almost inevitably get a smaller share of every state's budget. Most states are already setting even tighter time limits than federal law requires. Some are also cutting benefits. As time goes on, the real value of the federal block grants will fall. As a result, most states will probably let real benefit levels fall and tighten their time limits.

The combination of lower real benefits and tighter eligibility standards will push more mothers into the labor force. No one knows for sure how single mothers will fare, but the evidence assembled in *Making Ends Meet* is probably our best currently available guide to the economic impact of this change. Edin and Lein's data bear both on what is likely to happen and how we will interpret these changes. I take these issues up in reverse order.

Measuring Change

If past experience is any guide, policy analysts, journalists, and social scientists will all turn to the Census Bureau's poverty statistics for evidence about TANF's economic impact. If the poverty rate among single mothers rises, liberals will say "I told you so." If it falls, conservatives will say the same thing. Yet for reasons to which I have already alluded, official poverty statistics will almost inevitably overstate TANF's benefits or understate its costs.

When TANF pushes mothers into the labor force, they will usually earn more than they got from welfare. But newly employed mothers will also need more cash to pay their bills.

- Newly employed mothers will usually have to pay for child care. (Most mothers who can get free child care are already working, either formally or informally.)
- Most newly employed mothers will have to pay for transportation to work. In cities without efficient public transit systems, they will usually need an automobile.
- Because newly employed mothers will usually have more income, their food stamp allotment will be cut. Every $100 of extra cash income will mean $30 less in food stamps.
- If newly employed mothers have a federal housing subsidy, every extra $100 in

cash income will also raise their rent by $30.
- In most cases taking a job will mean that the mother eventually loses her Medicaid benefits. In some cases her children will also lose their benefits. Some newly employed mothers will get health insurance at work, but many will not. Working mothers will therefore have more out-of-pocket medical expenses.

The official poverty measure does not take account of such changes. The Census Bureau does publish an unofficial poverty series that incorporates the estimated value of food stamps, housing subsidies, and Medicaid, but even this series ignores work-related expenses. All the bureau's current poverty estimates will therefore exaggerate the economic benefits of TANF. In order to eliminate this bias, the bureau would have to create a new series that not only added the value of noncash benefits to income but subtracted work-related expenses.[7]

Political support for such a change may be hard to find. Both the president and Congress are now irrevocably committed to the idea that single mothers should work. Both therefore want to show that working can improve a single mother's economic status. Neither the president nor Congress wants to deal with evidence suggesting that Washington will have to spend more money if it wants to make this hope a reality. The Census Bureau is not oblivious to its political environment, and it may decide to treat the biases built into its current poverty statistics as a low priority problem.

Forecasting Change

Edin and Lein found that single mothers who earned $5 to $7 an hour between 1988 and 1992 experienced slightly more material hardship than those who relied primarily on welfare. This makes it tempting to predict that hardship will increase as TANF pushes more mothers into such jobs. But before accepting this gloomy prophecy we need to ask how closely "post-TANF" working mothers will resemble the mothers whom Edin and Lein studied. Post-TANF mothers will probably have to spend more for child care and medical care. Recent increases in the earned income tax credit (EITC) should offset some of these disadvantages, but probably not all of them.

Edin and Lein looked hard for single mothers in minimum-wage jobs. They found hardly any. This was because they did their fieldwork at a time when single mothers still had a choice between work and welfare. Minimum-wage jobs left single mothers worse off than they were on welfare, so they seldom took such jobs. Once mothers hit their TANF time limits, however, those who cannot find jobs paying $6 or $7 an hour will have to settle for whatever they can get. Post-TANF mothers are therefore likely to earn less than the working mothers whom Edin and Lein interviewed.[8] Indeed, the main goal of time limits was to push single mothers into jobs they would not otherwise take. In most cases that will mean jobs paying close to the minimum wage.

Edin and Lein did not interview working mothers who were currently unemployed, and they did not factor unemployment into working mothers' monthly budgets. This was not because single mothers never lost their jobs or always found other positions immediately. But when single mothers lost their jobs, thy could go back on AFDC while they looked for work. Under TANF, a steadily rising fraction of single mothers will lose this safety net and will have to plan on periods without income.

History suggests that the American economy can create some kind of work for almost every pair of willing hands. But history also suggests that American employers usually reserve steady work for those who are unusually reliable or have valuable firm-specific skills. If a firm can train someone to do a job in a few days, it has no incentive to keep her on the payroll when business is slow, when she misses work because her children are sick, or when she irritates her supervisor. Most employers see a former welfare recipient as a risky hire. They will hire her only if they know they can easily replace her should things not work out. As a result, the jobs open to former recipients tend to be those with high turnover and frequent layoffs.

Unskilled adults almost always have unemployment rates at least twice the national average. Since the national unemployment rate seldom falls below 5 percent, we have to assume that "post-TANF" welfare mothers will be unemployed at least 10 percent of the time when the economy is doing well and even more during recessions. In poor inner-city neighborhoods and depressed rural areas, the rate is likely to be even higher. The least skilled and least reliable mothers will often have trouble finding any kind of work.

For all these reasons, it seems unlikely that welfare mothers who hit their TANF time limit will earn as much (at least in real terms) as the mothers whom Edin and Lein interviewed. Nonetheless, their annual income may be higher because Congress has made the EITC considerably more generous since 1992. If a single mother with two children works regularly at $5.15 an hour, which will become the legal minimum wage in September 1997, the EITC will now give her an extra $2 an hour. If she works thirty-five hours a week and is unemployed 10 percent of the time, she will end up with about $12,000 for the year. If she can work forty hours a week at $6 an hour and is never laid off, she can end up with about $16,000. In real terms, that is not far from what Edin and Lein's working mothers earned.

The mothers whom TANF pushes into the labor force will, however, need to spend more on child care and medical care than Edin and Lein's mothers spent. Single moth-

ers with low-wage jobs seldom paid market rates for child care between 1988 and 1992. Some got a government subsidy. Some had a relative who watched their children. Some had older children who did not need (or at least did not get) regular supervision. Mothers who had to pay market rates for child care rarely worked. When time limits push such mothers into the labor force, their child care bills will be much higher than those of the mothers who chose to work under the old system.

Edin and Lein's working families also needed less medical care than their welfare families. Chronic illness, whether of a child or a mother, makes it hard for the mother to work. In addition, AFDC recipients got automatic Medicaid coverage, whereas low-wage workers got more limited coverage or none at all. TANF will push more mothers with high medical bills into the labor force. How they will pay these bills once they lose their Medicaid coverage remains a mystery.

Judging by Edin and Lein's data, working mothers who can earn $16,000 (including EITC) in 1997 should be close to self-sufficiency. If they get either child support or a child care subsidy and are either healthy or insured, they should be able to make ends meet. If a mother earns only $12,000, however, she will usually need a lot of outside help to balance her budget.

If these predictions are correct, implementing TANF is likely to cause a lot of hardship. The country could then respond in either of two ways. One option would be for states to make TANF's time limits more flexible. Most liberals will support this solution, but this may be a mistake. Supporting single mothers who did not work was politically defensible in an era when married mothers seldom worked, but that era is long gone. Today, few Americans believe that poor children will suffer if their mother takes a job, and most therefore think that single mothers should work.[9] A system predicated on single mothers staying home will never again win political support or provide decent benefits. And it will always treat recipients as scum.

The better option is to accept the public's judgment that no able-bodied adult should get something for nothing, assume that single mothers ought to work whenever jobs are available, and build a support system that also allows such mothers to care for their children and pay their bills. How might we do this?

Raising the Minimum Wage
The minimum wage will rise to $5.15 an hour in September 1997. This will be about 40 percent of what the average blue-collar worker earns in manufacturing. During the 1950s and 1960s, unions were stronger and the minimum wage was about 50 percent of the blue-collar average in manufacturing. One obvious way to mitigate TANF's adverse impact on single mothers would be to raise the minimum to at least $6 or perhaps even $6.50

an hour. While a $6 minimum would probably eliminate some marginal jobs, past experience suggests that the reduction would be small. The wage gain for single mothers would, in contrast, be quite large.

Child Care Subsidies
For mothers with young children, the cost of child care is the most obvious obstacle to working. While some former welfare recipients get child care subsidies, there is not enough money available to cover everyone who will need help once TANF's time limits begin to take effect. Expanding the number of subsidized child care slots would be expensive, partly because a lot of mothers who currently rely on informal care would apply for slots. But all schemes for moving single mothers into the labor force are expensive. Putting these women to work is simply not cost-effective. The rationale for TANF has to be political, social, and cultural, not economic. And while child care subsidies do not make economic sense, they are probably the most politically plausible way of ensuring that single mothers who work can also pay their bills.

Federal Housing Subsidies
The single mothers who experience the greatest economic hardship when they take minimum-wage jobs will be those in high-rent areas like Boston, California, and New York. One simple way to help these mothers would be for Congress to alter the rules governing the distribution of federal housing subsidies. If families with a full-time worker went to the head of the waiting list, and if Congress set these families' rent at 25 percent rather than 30 percent of their income, single mothers would have more incentive to find work. Increasing the proportion of working adults in public housing would also improve the social environment in the projects. Even if working mothers paid only 25 percent of their income in rent, they would usually pay more in dollars than welfare recipients do, so the cost to the taxpayer would fall.

Health Insurance
Allowing all low-income families to buy into Medicaid for 10 percent of their earnings would go a long way towards making work pay for many unskilled single mothers.

Child Support Enforcement
Some TANF enthusiasts believe that absent fathers can be forced to hand over significant amounts of money to the mothers of their children. This is probably true for fathers who hold steady, well-paid jobs. But women who end up in minimum-wage jobs have seldom had children by men who now work steadily at a good job. Such women are more likely to have had a child with a man whom they cannot identify or who is now dead, in jail, homeless, or addicted to drugs. Pursuing

absent fathers is a positive step, but it is not likely to raise much money for the single mothers who will need the most help.

A higher minimum wage plus a mix of health care subsidies, housing subsidies, and child care subsidies would allow even single mothers with unstable low-wage jobs to make ends meet. At the moment, however, Congress and the president are preoccupied with budget cutting. If they add any new federal outlays, these will probably go either to the Pentagon or to middle-income voters, not to the poor. Middle-of-the-road legislators may eventually become convinced that the country should do more to supplement the earnings of poor single mothers, but not until they have read a lot of horror stories about working mothers who end up in shelters or have to send their children away to live with their relatives. Meanwhile, a lot of women and children are likely to suffer.

WOULD HELPING SINGLE MOTHERS MAKE THEM MORE NUMEROUS?

Some conservatives oppose all efforts to help single mothers balance their budgets, even when the mother works. They argue that making life easier for single mothers will just make them more numerous. For those who see single mothers as a major cause of the nation's social problems, cutting their numbers is even more important than reducing material hardship.

Although liberals scoff publicly at these arguments, few really doubt that changing the economic consequences of single motherhood can affect its frequency. Imagine a society in which unmarried women knew that if they had a baby out of wedlock their family would turn them out, the father would never contribute to the baby's support, the government would give them no help, and no employer would hire them. Hardly anyone, liberal or conservative, doubts that unwed motherhood would be rarer in such a society than it is in the United States today. In the United States, however, traditionalists who want to discourage unwed motherhood have a limited array of policy levers to pull. They cannot prevent parents from helping out daughters who become single mothers, employers from hiring such women, or men from marrying them. Those who want to discourage single motherhood are left with only one lever: they can reduce single mothers' government benefits.

Economists have tried to estimate the effect of this strategy by studying state-to-state differences in AFDC benefits. At first glance, these look huge. In 1994, monthly cash benefits for a family of three ranged from $680 in Connecticut to $120 in Mississippi. Unfortunately for social science, these differences are more apparent than real. First, federal food stamp benefits are lower in high-benefit states. Second, rents also tend to be lower in low-benefit states. Susan

FIGURE F-1. Relationship Between the Incidence of Single Motherhood and the Relative Odds that Single Mothers and Couples Will Be Poor: Fourteen Rich Countries Circa 1990

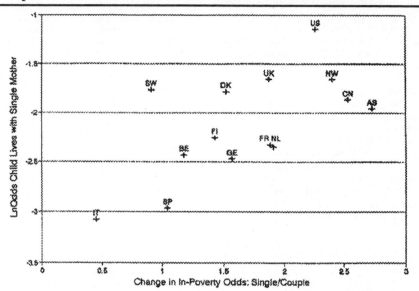

Note: AS=Australia, BE=Belgium, CN=Canada, DK=Denmark, FI=Finland, FR=France, GE=West Germany (1989), IT=Italy, NL=Netherlands, NW=Norway, SP=Spain, SW=Switzerland, UK=United Kingdom, US=United States.

Source: Tabulations by Lee Rainwater using national surveys conducted between 1989 and 1994 and available through the Luxembourg Income Study. Note: All estimates are weighted by the number of children in the household.

Mayer found that when two states' nominal 1990 benefits differed by $100, welfare recipients' disposable income (after paying for food and rent) typically differed by only $30.[10] The true difference between high- and low-benefit states thus turns out to be closer to $175 than $560. Judging by current evidence, differences of this size exert little influence on fertility decisions and only a modest influence on living arrangements.[11]

The economic consequences of becoming a single mother vary more from country to country than they do within the United States. Cross-national comparisons therefore provide a useful check on how the risk of ending up poor affects a woman's decision about whether to become (or remain) a single mother.[12] Using data from the Luxembourg Income Study (LIS), Lee Rainwater and Tim Smeeding have estimated poverty rates and living arrangements for children in fourteen rich countries during the early 1990s.[13] They define a child as poor if the child's family income (adjusted for family size) is less than half that of the median family income in the same country. They treat a mother as "single" if she did not live with either a husband or a male partner. To get a rough estimate of how costly it was to become a single mother in each of the fourteen countries, I subtracted the (logged) odds that children who lived with a married couple would be poor from the odds that children who lived with a single mother would be poor.

Among children who lived with a single mother in the early 1990s, Rainwater and

Smeeding found poverty rates ranging from a high of 56 percent in the United States and Australia to lows of 5 percent in Sweden and 7 percent in Finland. The gap between the rates for single and married mothers also varied dramatically, exceeding 40 percentage points in Australia, Canada, and the United States but falling below 10 percentage points in Denmark, Finland, Sweden, Belgium, and Italy.

If fear of poverty discouraged single motherhood, we would expect to find relatively few single mothers in English-speaking countries and far more in Scandinavia. Figure F-1 shows no such pattern. Instead, single motherhood appears to be more common in the countries where its cost is highest.[14] Single motherhood increases the odds of being poor in Australia, Canada, and the United States more than in most other countries. (The Norwegian observation reflects the near-zero probability that Norwegian couples will be poor.) But the number of single mothers is far higher in the United States than elsewhere and is as high in Australia and Canada as in Sweden and Denmark. European rates of single motherhood seem to be more influenced by proximity to the North Sea than by the risk that becoming a single mother will make you poor. These comparisons suggest that the frequency of single motherhood in rich countries depends mainly on its cultural rather than its economic cost.[15]

Both domestic and international evidence thus suggests that the United States could do substantially more than it now does to help single mothers without appreciably increasing the percentage of women who raise their children alone. But evidence of this kind is unlikely to affect many American legislators' willingness to support such policies. For conservative legislators and voters, single motherhood is a moral rather than a practical problem. They want the government to punish what they see as bad behavior, regardless of whether such punishment has any deterrent value.

Some American liberals and progressives are equally passionate in their defense of single motherhood. American feminists often see divorce and unwed motherhood as sensible responses to the defects of American men. From their vantage point, having to depend on a potentially abusive or unreliable man is even worse than having to depend on the government. Because relations between the sexes are particularly strained among African Americans, black women are especially likely to raise children on their own. Some black nationalists like to portray the two-parent family as a European invention that whites should not impose on people of color, and white multiculturalists often echo this view.

The "culture wars" between liberals and conservatives have left American children worse off than they would be if either liberalism or conservatism were hegemonic. Because so many Americans see single motherhood as a legitimate and perhaps even prudent choice, our children are unusually likely to live in households without a male breadwinner. Because so many conservatives regard single motherhood as a menace, the government does little to help, and these households are unusually likely to be poor. What really harms children, it seems to me, is America's much-vaunted diversity. What children need is consensus—any kind of consensus will do—about how they should be supported. But consensus is precisely what America seems least likely to produce.

If this argument is correct, the United States is unlikely to do much to improve single mothers' economic status in the near future. But if TANF makes single mothers significantly worse off, as seems to me likely, legislators will probably initiate some new programs for helping single mothers who work. Anyone who wants to approach that challenge realistically should read *Making Ends Meet*.

CHRISTOPHER JENCKS
Kennedy School of Government,
Harvard University

References

1. For data on both cash income and the value of noncash benefits, see U.S. Bureau of the Census (1994f) table 1.
2. The CES income questions are similar to those that the Census Bureau uses in other surveys, but the CES does not impute values to those who fail to answer one of the income questions. Instead, it excludes those who fail to report their major source of income and sets other missing amounts to zero. Excluding respondents with missing data does not, however, greatly reduce the ratio of expenditure to income among those with very low reported incomes. For 1992 data, see U.S. Bureau of Labor Statistics (1993) table 2.
3. The national median in 1990 was $364 (U.S. House of Representatives 1994, p. 377).
4. Mayer and Jencks (1989) pp. 88–114.
5. The 1992 CPS found 26.6 percent of children living with one parent (23.3 percent with their mother and 3.3 percent with their father), and 70.7 percent living with two parents (a category that includes children who live with one natural and one stepparent). All the CPS estimates exclude children in institutions and count adopted children as living with their parents. The overall percentage of all children not living with either of their natural parents is therefore more than 2.6 percent. I am indebted to David Knutson for the CPS tabulations.
6. TANF penalizes states that cut their contribution to the support of single mothers below 75 percent of its 1996 level (in nominal dollars). States can, however, count all sorts of activities besides cash transfers to the poor in meeting this "maintenance of effort" requirement. In any event, inflation will make the requirement steadily weaker as time goes on.
7. The National Research Council's panel on poverty measurement recently recommended the exclusion of work-related expenses from allowable income (Citro and Michael 1995).
8. The minimum wage will rise to $5.15 an hour in September 1997. If the Consumer Price Index (CPI) is an accurate measure of inflation, this should put its real value close to what it was after the last rise in 1991, and somewhat above its level from 1988 to 1990. Most economists think the CPI overstates inflation, but that does not necessarily mean that it overstates the increase in single mothers' need for cash. The fact that the CPI ignores qualitative improvements in medical care, for example, means that it overstates the cost of buying medical services of constant quality. But if a mother takes her child to the emergency room in 1997, buying 1990 services at 1990 prices will not be a real option. She will have to pay for 1997 services at 1997 prices. If higher prices lead to more effective treatment, she will be better off, but her need for cash will still have risen.
9. For a good review of public opinion on welfare, see Blendon et al. (1995) pp. 1065–1069.
10. Mayer (1997).
11. For a good summary of this literature, see Moffitt (1992) pp. 1–61. Charles Murray, who has staked his reputation on the idea that generous welfare benefits encourage unwed motherhood, also finds that little evidence that state-to-state differences in benefit levels have much effect (Murray 1993, pp. S224–S262). For a recent study suggesting much larger effects but making somewhat uncertain assumptions, see Rosenzweig (1995).
12. In principle, one could also ask how the risk of poverty affects the fraction of children born out of wedlock. In practice, this is difficult for two reasons. First, while household surveys usually ask who lives in the household, they do not ask whether the children were born out of wedlock. This makes it harder to ascertain the economic effect of having had a baby out of wedlock in the past than to determine the effect of current living arrangements. Second, while the rate of out-of-wedlock childbearing is higher in Scandinavia than in other rich countries, its effect on living arrangements is also different. In the United States, unmarried couples seldom live together for a protracted period after the birth of their child without marrying. In America, therefore, a woman who has a baby out of wedlock is quite likely to be the only adult with clear responsibility for its support. In Scandinavia, couples who have children out of wedlock often live together for many years, so the connection between marital status and living arrangements is weaker. For economic purposes, living arrangements are what matter.
13. Lee Rainwater and Timothy Smeeding describe their analytic framework and present their preliminary results in Rainwater and Smeeding (1995). In December 1996, Rainwater sent me corrected estimates, which I use here.
14. If one regresses the percentage of children living with a single mother (P) on the difference between the poverty rates for children living with single and married mothers (D), the equation is $D = 8.13 + .17D$ ($R^2 = .26$; $t = 2.05$). (Using logged odds ratios, R^2 rises to .44 and the $t = 2.85$.) This positive relationship can hardly be causal. An alternative hypothesis is that in countries where voters oppose single motherhood, they respond to its increase by limiting benefits for single mothers.
15. Because the LIS data come from national surveys that ask different questions, the data describing children's living arrangements may not be precisely comparable across countries, though they appear to be better than estimates from any other source. One worrisome finding is that the LIS data show 9 percent of U.S. children living in a household headed by a single woman that also includes other adults over the age of eighteen. This figure is below 3 percent in other countries. Since the percentage of children living in one-adult households headed by unmarried women is about the same in the United States, Britain, and Scandinavia, it is not clear why two-adult households headed by unmarried women should vary so much. I can see no obvious reason why children over eighteen would be less likely to live with their mother in Britain and Scandinavia than, for example, in the United States. A more rigorous analysis of the LIS data would need to use continuous rather than dichotomous measures of economic status and would control for demographic differences between single and unmarried mothers, the magnitude of which presumably varies from country to country.

AID TO DEPENDENT CORPORATIONS

EXPOSING FEDERAL HANDOUTS TO THE WEALTHY

CHUCK COLLINS

In 1992 rancher J. R. Simplot of Grandview, Idaho paid the U.S. government $87,000 for grazing rights on federal lands, about one-quarter the rate charged by private land-owners. Simplot's implicit subsidy from U.S. taxpayers, $261,000, would have covered the welfare costs of about 60 poor families. With a net worth exceeding $500 million, it's hard to argue that Simplot needed the money.

Since 1987, American Barrick Resources Corporation has pocketed $8.75 billion by extracting gold from a Nevada mine owned by the U.S. government. But Barrick has paid only minimal rent to the Department of the Interior. In 1992 Barrick's founder was rewarded for his business acumen with a $32 million annual salary.

Such discounts are only one form of corporate welfare, dubbed "wealthfare" by some activists, that U.S. taxpayers fund. At a time when Congress is attempting to slash or eliminate the meager benefits received by the poor, we are spending far more to subsidize wealthy corporations and individuals. Wealthfare comes in five main varieties: discounted user fees for public resources; direct grants; corporate tax reductions and loopholes; giveaways of publicly funded research and development (R&D) to private profit-making companies; and tax breaks for wealthy individuals.

Within the Clinton administration Secretary of Labor Robert Reich and Budget Director Alice Rivlin have attacked "welfare for the rich." Armed with a study from the Progres-

sive Policy Institute, the Democratic Leadership Council's think tank, Reich floated the notion that over $200 billion in corporate welfare could be trimmed over the next five years. In a sign of the problems with our two-party system, Clinton discouraged Reich from taking this campaign further, for fear of alienating big Democratic Party funders.

TAX AVOIDANCE

The largest, yet most invisible, part of wealthfare is tax breaks for corporations and wealthy individuals. The federal Office of Management and Budget (OMB) estimates that these credits, deductions, and exemptions, called "tax expenditures," will cost $440 billion in fiscal 1996. This compares, for example, to the $16 billion annual federal cost of child support programs.

Due both to lower basic tax rates and to myriad loopholes, corporate taxes fell from one-third of total federal revenues in 1953 to less than 10% today (see "Disappearing Corporate Taxes," *Dollars & Sense,* July 1994). Were corporations paying as much tax now as they did in the 1950s, the government would take in another $250 billion a year—more than the entire budge deficit.

The tax code is riddled with tax breaks for the natural resource, construction, corporate agri-business, and financial industries. Some serve legitimate purposes, or did at one time. Others have been distorted to create tax shelters and perpetuate bad business practices. During the 1993 budget battle, New Jersey Senator Bill Bradley attacked the "loophole writing" industry in Washington, where inserting a single sentence into the tax laws can save millions, even billions, in taxes for a corporate client.

Depreciation on equipment and buildings, for example, is a legitimate business expense. But the "accelerated depreciation" rule allows corporations to take this deduction far faster than their assets are wearing out. This simply lets businesses make billions of dollars in untaxed profits. One estimate is that this loophole will cost $164 billion over the next five years.

One particularly generous tax break is the foreign tax credit, which allows U.S.-based multinational corporations to deduct from their U.S. taxes the income taxes they pay to other nations. Donald Barlett and James Steele, authors of *America: Who Really Pays the Taxes,* say that by 1990 this writeoff was worth $25 billion a year.

While in many cases this credit is a valid method of preventing double taxation on profits earned overseas, the oil companies have used it to avoid most of their U.S. tax obligations. Until 1950, Saudi Arabia had no income tax, but charged royalties on all oil taken from their wells. Such royalties are a payment for use of a natural resource. They are a standard business expense, payable *before* a corporation calculates the profits on which it will pay taxes.

These royalties were a major cost to ARAMCO, the oil consortium operating there (consisting of Exxon, Mobil, Chevron, and Texaco). But since royalties are not income taxes, they could not be used to reduce Exxon and friends' tax bills back home.

When King Saud decided to increase the royalty payments, ARAMCO convinced him to institute a corporate income tax and to substitute this for the royalties. The tax was a sham, since it applied only to ARAMCO, not to any other business in Saudi Arabia's relatively primitive economy. The result was that the oil companies avoided hundreds of millions of dollars in their American taxes. Eventually the other oil-producing nations, including Kuwait, Iraq, and Nigeria, followed suit, at huge cost to the U.S. Treasury.

In contrast to the ARAMCO problem, many corporate executive salaries should not be counted as deductible expenses. These salaries and bonuses are often so large today that they constitute disguised profits. Twenty years ago the average top executive made 34 times the wages of the firm's lowest paid workers. Today the ratio is 140 to one. The Hospital Corporation of America, for example, paid its chairman $127 million in 1992—$61,000 an hour! In 1993 the Clinton administration capped the deductibility of salaries at $1 million, but the law has several loopholes that allow for easy evasion.

CHICKEN MCNUGGETS AND OTHER VITAL MATTERS

Taxes are but one form of wealthfare. Subsidized use of public resources, as with J. R. Simplot's grazing and American Barrick's mining, is also widespread. Barrick's profit-making was allowed by the General Mining Law of 1872. Just last year the government finally put a one-year moratorium on this resource-raiding.

In a manner similar to the mining situation, the U.S. Forest Service under-charges timber companies for the logs they take from publicly-owned land. The Forest Service also builds roads and other infrastructure needed by the timber industry, investing $140 million last year.

Many corporations also receive direct payments from the federal government. The libertarian Cato Institute argues that every cabinet department "has become a conduit for government funding of private industry. Within some cabinet agencies, such as the U.S. Department of Agriculture and the Department of Commerce, almost every spending program underwrites private business."

Agriculture subsidies typically flow in greater quantities the large is the recipient firm. Of the $1.4 billion in annual sugar price supports, for example, 40% of the money goes to the largest 1% of firms, with the largest ones receiving more than $1 million each.

The Agriculture Department also spends $110 million a year to help U.S. companies advertise abroad. In 1992 Sunkist Growers got $10 million, Gallo Wines $4.5 million, M&M/Mars $1.1 million, McDonalds $466,000 to promote Chicken McNuggets, and American Legend Fur Coats $1.2 million.

The Progressive Policy Institute estimates that taxpayers could save $1.4 billion over five years by eliminating or restricting such direct subsidies. Farm subsidies, for example, could be limited to only small farmers.

The government also pays for scientific research and development, then allows the benefits to be reaped by private firms. This occurs commonly in medical research. One product, the anti-cancer drug Taxol, cost the U.S. government $32 million to develop as part of a joint venture with private industry. But in the end the government gave its share to Bristol-Myers Squibb, which now charges cancer patients almost $1,000 for a three-week supply of the drug.

WHO IS ENTITLED?

Beyond corporate subsidies, the government also spends far more than necessary to help support the lifestyles of wealthy individuals. This largess pertains to several of the most expensive and popular "entitlements" in the federal budget, such as Social Security, Medicare, and the deductibility of interest on home mortgages. As the current budget-cutting moves in Congress demonstrate, such universal programs have much greater political strength than do programs targetted solely at low-income households.

While this broad appeal is essential to maintain, billions of dollars could be saved by restricting the degree to which the wealthy benefit from universal programs. If Social Security and Medicare payments were denied to just the richest 3% of households this would reduce federal spending by $30 to $40 billion a year—more than the total federal cost of food stamps.

Similarly, mortgage interest is currently deductible up to $1 million per home, justifying the term "mansion subsidy" for its use by the rich. The government could continue allowing everyone to use this deduction, but limit it to $250,000 per home. This would affect only the wealthiest 5% of Americans, but would save taxpayers $10 billion a year.

Progressive organizations have mounted a renewed focus on the myriad handouts to the corporate and individual rich. One effort is the Green Scissors coalition, an unusual alliance of environmental groups such as Friends of the Earth, and conservative taxcutters, such as the National Taxpayers Union. Last January Green Scissors proposed cutting $33 billion over the next ten years in subsidies that they contend are wasteful and environmentally damaging. These include boondoggle water projects, public land subsidies, highways, foreign aid projects, and agricultural programs.

Another new organization, Share the Wealth, is a coalition of labor, religious, and economic justice organizations. It recently launched the "Campaign for Wealth-Fare Reform," whose initial proposal targets over $35 billion in annual subsidies that benefit the wealthiest 3% of the population. The campaign rejects the term "corporate welfare" because it reinforces punitive anti-welfare sentiments. Welfare is something a humane society guarantees to people facing poverty, unemployment, low wages, and racism. "Wealthfare," in contrast, is the fees and subsidies extracted from the public by the wealthy and powerful—those who are least in need.

Today's Congress is not sympathetic to such arguments. But the blatant anti-poor, pro-corporate bias of the Republicans has already begun to awaken a dormant public consciousness. This will leave more openings, not less, for progressives to engage in public education around the true nature of government waste.

Resources: Green Scissors Report: Cutting Wasteful and Environmentally Harmful Spending and Subsidies, Friends of the Earth, 1995; *Killing the Sacred Cows,* Anne Crittendon, Penguin Books, 1993; *Aid to Dependent Corporations,* Janice C. Shields, Essential Information, 1994; *Cut-and-Invest to Compete and Win: A Budget Strategy for American Growth,* Robert Shapiro, Progressive Policy Institute, 1994; *America: Who Really Pays the Taxes,* Donald Barlett and James Steele, Simon and Schuster, 1994.

Chuck Collins is the Co-Coordinator of the Share the Wealth Project, and works with the Tax Equity Alliance of Massachusetts.

LET US COUNT THE WAYS

A few of the many subsidies received by the wealthy are:

- *The Mansion Subsidy.* Home mortgage interest is deductible up to $1 million per year. Reducing the limit to $250,000 would save the government $10 billion a year.
- *The Accelerated Depreciation Subsidy.* Companies get to depreciate their equipment much faster than it wears out. The cost: $32 billion a year.
- *The Advertising Subsidy.* Corporations fully deduct the cost of their advertising. If only one-fifth of advertising expenses were considered a capital cost of building brand name recognition, and so deductible gradually over time, taxpayers would save $3.5 billion a year.
- *McSubsidies.* $110 million a year goes directly to companies that advertise their products abroad. Beneficiaries include Sunkist, McDonalds, and M&M/Mars.
- *Wealthfare for Mining Companies.* The U.S. lets big mining companies pay peanuts for the use of federally-owned lands—our lands. An 8% royalty would earn $200 million a year.
- *Corporate Agri-Business Subsidy.* The federal government gives $200 million a year to corporate farms that each have income over $5 million a year.

401

The Shrinking Welfare State: The New Welfare Legislation and Families

D. STANLEY EITZEN
Colorado State University

MAXINE BACA ZINN
Michigan State University

From 1935 to 1996 the United States had a minimal welfare program for those in need. Since the Reagan administration this welfare program has gradually been dismantled. This dismemberment accelerated in 1996 when the federal government made welfare assistance to families temporary and withdrew $55 billion of federal aid to the poor. Thus, the federal safety net under the poor has been shredded especially for poor families with children (Schorr, 1997:163). This paper examines the general and family-specific consequences resulting from the recent welfare legislation.

The Personal Responsibility and Work Opportunity Reconciliation Act of 1996

The welfare system prior to 1996 needed an overhaul. Its provisions encouraged dependency since recipients leaving welfare lost medicaid. It provided disincentives to work because money earned was subtracted from welfare payments. By leaving the distribution of benefits for many programs to the states, there were wide disparities in benefits by geographical location. And, the benefits provided were never enough to lift people out of poverty. The welfare system, however, did help many on the

Paper presented at the Thematic Session "The Shrinking State: New Forms of Social Inequality" during the Annual Meetings of the American Sociological Association, San Francisco (August 21–25, 1998).

economic margins to get above the poverty line. A study by the Center on Budget and Policy Priorities found that

> without such assistance, 57.6 million people would have been poor in 1995. "But when government benefits are counted, including food stamps, housing assistance, school lunch support and benefits provided through the earned-income tax credit, *the number of poor people drop to 30.3 million*" (emphasis added). (Reported in Herbert, 1996:68A)

While this difference is certainly meaningful, the government could do much better. For example, France and the United States both would have child poverty rates of about 25 percent if it were not for government assistance. With the generous government assistance provided in France, the child poverty rate is reduced to just 6.5 percent. The minimal U.S. welfare program, on the other hand, reduces the child poverty rate to about 21 percent (Raspberry, 1997).

In 1996 the Republican-dominated Congress and a middle-of-the-road Democratic president passed a sweeping welfare law that *ended the 61-year old safety net for the poor, completing the Reagan Revolution* (Watts, 1997:409). The major provisions of this law (as later amended) include the following (much of the description of the new welfare law and its consequences are from the Children's Defense Fund, 1997: Edelman, 1997; Schorr, 1997; Watts, 1997; and Eitzen, 1996): First, states, through federal block grants, were given a fixed sum of money and considerable flexibility in how to spend it.

Second, the law insisted on work. States were required to demand that parents work within two years of receiving cash assistance, although states had the right to shorten the period before recipients must work. Third, the law mandated a five-year lifetime limit on the receipt of assistance, which states can reduce if they wish. Fourth, benefits are prohibited to unwed parents under 18 who do not live with an adult and do not attend school. Fifth, various federal assistance programs targeted for the poor were cut by $54.5 billion over six years. Included in these budget cuts were $27 billion from the food stamp program, $7 billion from the children's portion of the Supplemental Security Income program, and $3 billion over six years for child nutrition, and federal funding for social services was cut by a six-year total of $2.5 billion. Cuts were also made by tightening the qualifying criteria for being defined as a disabled child. Ironically, the narrowed eligibility requirements "result in the loss of coverage for some children who if they were adults would be considered disabled" (Edelman, 1997:48). Sixth, the welfare law denied a broad range of public benefits to legal immigrants. Concerning this last point, although there is some variation from state to state (since the states administer the programs), all legal immigrants were cut off from food stamps and those who entered the country after the welfare bill was signed were ineligible for federal programs such as Supplemental Security Income and state run programs such as temporary welfare and Medicaid. And, seventh, the federal money given to the states is now capped at $16.4 billion annually. This is significant because it means that there is no adjustment for inflation or population growth. In effect, by 2002 states will have considerably less federal money to spend on welfare than they did under the old welfare provisions.

In sum, this new welfare legislation ended the entitlement which guaranteed that states must give help to all needy families with children. Now assistance for poor families is temporary with parents required to work. Lamenting the passage of the 1996 Welfare Act, *The Nation* editorialized: "There is now a bipartisan agreement that the United States bears no responsibility for its poorest families." (*The Nation*, 1995:371)

The Conservative Assumptions Guiding Current Welfare Policy and the Progressive Response.

Assumptions from conservative ideology provide the bedrock of the 1996 Welfare Law. First, there is the assumption that welfare programs establish perverse incentives that keep the beneficiaries from working and to have babies outside of marriage. That is, welfare is so generous that it makes sense to stay on welfare, rather than go to work. Moreover, since the benefits increase with each child, women on welfare make the rational

decision to have more children. Progressives argue that this reasoning is fallacious because it ignores five facts: (1) The average monthly AFDC payment, accounting for inflation, has withered by almost 50 percent since 1970, yet the birth rate for unmarried mothers has soared during this period; (2) The average monthly AFDC payment plus food stamps provides benefits that are much below the poverty line; (3) States with low welfare benefits have higher illegitimacy rates than states with higher welfare benefits; (4) New Jersey's 1993 law that ended the practice of increasing a welfare check when a recipient had another baby did *not* drive down birth rates among women on welfare (Healy, 1997); and (5) The much more generous welfare states of Canada, western Europe, and Scandinavia have much lower out-of-wedlock birth rates than found in the United States.

A second assumption of the lawmakers is that when poor people are confronted with a "sink or swim" world they will develop the determination and the skill to stay afloat (Murray, 1984). By shoving welfare recipients off of welfare, their only recourse will be to work, resulting in productive rather than parasitic people. Progressives, however, note that under current societal conditions many of the poor will "sink" even if they wanted to "swim." There are not enough jobs and many of the jobs that are available do not lift the poor out of poverty. And, many who are being pushed "into the pool" cannot "swim" because they lack the skills and experience required.

Third, there is a moral condemnation of those on welfare because their poverty is assumed by conservatives to be the consequence of an attitude, a way of life, and a choice to reject the work ethic. Progressive argue, to the contrary, that the problem for most welfare recipients is not a lack of a work ethic but a lack of jobs that pay enough to enable them to become independent (Handler and Hasenfeld, 1997:12). Moreover, they see a tendency on the part of the conservatives to reserve this moral condemnation of the poor "for those who are not only poor but different—in terms of race, ethnicity, country of origin, or religion—or who violate patriarchal norms" (Handler and Hasenfeld, 1997:9).

Progressives argue that willingness to work on the part of the poor is not the problem. Research from a number of studies shows that most welfare recipients bring in extra money from various activities such as house cleaning, doing laundry, repairing clothing, child care, and selling items that they have made. For example, sociologist Kathleen Harris, summarizing her findings from a nationally representative sample of single mothers who received welfare, says:

I found exclusive dependence on welfare to be rare. More than half of the single mothers whom I studied worked while they were on welfare, and two-thirds left the welfare rolls when they could support themselves with jobs. However, more than half (57 percent) of the women who worked their way off public assistance later returned because their jobs ended or they still could not make ends meet. (Harris, 1996:B7)

This outside work to supplement welfare is necessary because welfare payments are insufficient to make ends meet. In 1991, for example, the average AFDC payment and food stamps averaged $565 a month, while the average monthly expenses were $876—a deficit of $311 (Koretz, 1996). This difference is made up through various strategies including income-producing work and help from family, friends, neighbors, boyfriends, and absent fathers.

A question arising from the requirement that all welfare recipients work is whether a single mother is "able" to work (McLarin, 1995). Traditionally, she was not considered so. AFDC was created in 1935 with the goal of keeping women at home with their children. The new legislation has changed that, forcing poor women with children to work, without the training, without the jobs, and without the child care. Through twisted logic, many of the same politicians who want poor mothers to work, want middle-class mothers to give up their jobs because a stay-at-home mother is positive for children.

Another issue regarding work has to do with its availability. During the Great Depression the federal government provided jobs to the poor. These jobs included the construction of roads, bridges, and buildings, clearing forests, planting trees to stop wind erosion, and the like. This government jobs program was successful. The jobs provided society with important projects and needy individuals and families with income and skill development. The situation is different now. The new legislation mandates that poor people will work but *without* providing the jobs.

> This punitive overhaul [of the welfare system] sends [welfare recipients] off on their own to secure work in a world of downsizing, layoffs and capital flight. Where are the welfare recipients going to find stable jobs? How can they pay for health insurance and child care when they earn the minimum wage? What will happen to their children? (*The Nation*, 1995:372)

Fourth, welfare dependency is assumed to be the source of poverty, illegitimacy, laziness, crime, unemployment, and other social pathologies. Progressives, however, point to the nations with a much more generous welfare system than in the United States, noting that cities in those countries are much safer, and that violent crime is very much lower than in the United States, as is the rate of teenage pregnancy. Also, from 1970 to the mid-1990s AFDC benefits declined sharply (from $792 per month in inflation-adjusted 1994 dollars in 1970 for a family of four to $435 per month in 1994. If welfare benefits affect marriage and fertility, then one would expect that the drop in welfare benefits would have made marriage more attractive and childbearing outside of marriage less attractive. "Yet divorce, cohabitation, and

the percentage of births that occurred outside of marriage all increased during this period" (Cherlin, 1998:124).

Progressives argue that when welfare is seen as the cause of societal ills, the remedy is to get rid of welfare rather than confronting the more fundamental problems of growing inequality, poverty, and a deteriorating low-wage labor market (Handler and Hasenfeld, 1997:5). The causes of poverty are complex, involving the social locations of class, race, and gender, the changing economy, the lack of good jobs, institutional racism and sexism, the maldistribution of resources for schools, and inadequate pay and benefits for low-end jobs. Thus, a cure for poverty involves much more than greater individual effort and getting rid of the welfare system. It requires structural changes in society.

Fifth, there is racial subtext in the welfare legislation. Underlying the debate on welfare were the dominant but erroneous notions about certain groups, their families, and the women who seek public funds and services to support and maintain families. The conservative ideology posits that these groups have no claim to these resources because they do not conform to traditional family values. Fueling this assumption is the false belief that Black women dominate the welfare rolls. Similarly, "negative images of Latinos and other immigrants fueled debates in the states and paved the way for denying benefits to legal immigrants nationwide" (Dill, Baca Zinn, and Patton, 1998:21).

The conservative response, in short, is that the welfare state is bad and should be eliminated. But just what is it that we are in the process of killing off? What will its death mean for society? The U.S. welfare state, which is the most modest of the industrialized nations, emerged in the 1930s as a reaction to the instability of the Great Depression and capitalism run amuck (the following is from Moberg, 1995). Motivated by a fear of radical unrest by the economically disadvantaged and disaffected and the need to save capitalism from its own self-destructive tendencies (economic instability, rape of the environment, worker exploitation, lack of worker and consumer safety), the creators of the New Deal under Roosevelt and the Great Society under Johnson instituted Social Security, the minimum wage, federal aid to education, health and nutrition programs, subsidized housing, and Aid to Families with Dependent Children. These welfare programs go too far, say the conservatives. Progressives, on the other hand, argue that they do not go far enough.

The Consequences of the 1996 Welfare Legislation for Families

Although the time is relatively short since the 1996 welfare legislation, we can examine some preliminary results and anticipate its longer term effects. As of June 1998, the welfare rolls had declined from 12.1 million to

8.4 million since the enactment of the welfare legislation. This dramatic reduction has led supporters of the new welfare law to declare that the new law was working as intended. This interpretation is much too optimistic for at least four reasons. First, those who left the welfare rolls first were likely the easiest to place in jobs, that is, they have some secondary education and job experience. The much more difficult task will be to find jobs for those who have little education, work experience, or job skills, or who are functionally disabled. Second, the welfare legislation was passed at a propitious historical moment—during an economic expansion when jobs were being created and unemployment was low. A year later the unemployment rate had dropped to 4.7 percent, the lowest rate in 24 years. Because of a growing economy the number of AFDC recipients declined by 2.1 million in the two years *before* the 1996 legislation (DeParle, 1997; Mechler, 1998).

But even with the booming economy and many still receiving welfare because their time limits had not been reached, there are reports of rising rates of homelessness and hunger. The U.S. Conference of Mayors reported average 1997 increases of 16 percent in requests for emergency food in a 29-city survey (the largest increase since 1992) (reported in Loven, 1998). Another survey by Second Harvest, the nation's largest network of food banks, found that more than 21 million people used emergency food programs in 1997, 40 percent of whom came from working households (reported in Wolf, 1998). Low-cost housing has also become more scarce because of gentrification, the housing boom, and the reduction in subsidized apartments. As a result the Department of Housing and Urban Development revealed that a record 5.3 million families with low incomes face a crisis of unaffordable rent—defined as rents exceeding 30 percent of one's income (Associated Press, 1998).

These realities raise serious questions about job availability, hunger, and homelessness, when the unemployment rate goes up to seven or eight percent, or worse, when there is an economic recession. In either situation there will be layoffs, which means that the last to be hired (the workers only recently off welfare) will be the first to be fired. If these former employees had used up their time limits for welfare, they will be on their own without a safety net with nowhere to turn for rent, utilities, food, and health care.

Third, the availability of low end jobs is distributed unevenly. Some social categories have more difficulty getting low-wage employment than others. "Not surprisingly, in the fierce competition for jobs in that sector, individuals who are young, black and non-college educated fare the worst" (Herbert, 1997:70A). When the unemployment rate was 5.2 percent in 1996, unemployment among young African American women (ages 15 to 25) with a high school diploma was 19.7 percent (Economic Policy Report, cited in Herbert, 1997).

Work by itself is not the solution. Latino women and men participate in the labor force at nearly the same rate as Whites (66.5 percent compared to 67.2 percent [U.S. Department of Labor, 1997]), yet the poverty rate in 1996 for Latinos was 29.4 percent, compared to 11.2 percent for Whites (Dill et al., 1998). Moreover, 10 percent of the poor worked year-round, full-time in 1996. Underscoring one of the above points: working for the minimum wage, which most former welfare recipients do, gives a full-time worker an annual income that is more than $2000 *below* the poverty line for a family of three. Obviously, then, it takes adequately compensated work to climb out of poverty, a provision missing from the welfare legislation.

The 1996 legislation was especially harsh to immigrant families (Cherlin, 1998), who are mostly people of color. New legal immigrants, except for those of refugee status, are now ineligible for Temporary Assistance to Needy Families (the mechanism that replaced AFDC), food stamps, and most other federally funded benefits until they become citizens, which takes a minimum of five years. Under these conditions, it seems more than reasonable to assume that hundreds of thousands of immigrant families will be pushed into poverty.

Marriage. Stephanie Aaronson and Heidi Hartmann conclude that the "preponderance of research suggests that welfare has no impact on women's marital and childbearing behavior..." (Aaronson and Hartmann, 1996:586). Poverty, on the other hand, does. After reviewing the literature, family historian Stephanie Coontz summarizes what previous research predicts:

> Poor couples are twice as likely to divorce as more affluent ones. Jobless individuals are three to four times less likely to marry. And teens who live in areas of high unemployment and inferior school systems are six to seven times more likely to become unwed parents than more fortunate teens. Dozens of research studies show that the most effective deterrent to early childbearing is access to, among other things, good schools and steady jobs. (Coontz, 1994:19)

Women and Children. The recent welfare legislation is going to put more children at risk as they and their mothers no longer receive AFDC, food stamps, and other welfare benefits. Many of their mothers will now work at minimum wage jobs with new expenses (transportation, child care, clothing), and likely no health insurance. And, we know that many who work will not escape poverty. Columbia University's National Center for Children in Poverty, reported, for example, that in 1996 some 5.5 million children lived in poverty and 63 percent of them lived in families with at least one working parent (reported in Healy, 1998). Many of their mothers are difficult to employ because they suffer disproportionately from mental health problems and they often lack quality education and work experience. Thus, many former mothers on welfare will likely be unemployed *and* without the safety net after two years. Clearly, without raising the minimum wage, providing training programs, guaranteeing work, and subsidizing child care, more children will be raised in poverty under the new welfare rules. Daniel Lichter's review of children in poverty shows that before the 1996 welfare legislation went into effect, the rate of child poverty was at a 30-year high, and the income gap between rich and poor children greater than at any time in recent memory (Lichter, 1997:141). Will the new poverty legislation increase the child poverty rate and the income inequality gap? We think so, as does the Urban Institute, which estimated that an additional 1.1 million children would become poor as a result of the 1996 legislation (The Urban Institute, 1996; see also Albelda and Tilly, 1997:127). Moreover, more than eight million families with children would lose an average of $1,300 per family (cited in Edelman, 1997:46). Thus, more children then ever will be further impoverished, which will have serious debilitating consequences for them.

We ask: It is appropriate to take $28 billion over six years in food assistance from poor women and their children? As Marian Wright Edelman has stated: "The elimination of the national guarantee to protect children is a moral outrage . . .a massive betrayal that places the lives of many of our youngest and most vulnerable citizens in grave danger" (Edelman, 1996:1).

What is Missing in the New Welfare Legislation

Foremost, the legislation ignored the conclusions of social science research (Astone, 1997). This research documents, for example, that 70 percent of ADFC recipients left welfare within two years. We also know that nearly three-fourths of those who left end up back on welfare because of inadequate pay, the lack of medical benefits, or their lack of job skills. Social science research also informs us of the detrimental effects of poverty on marriage relationships, the increased probability of spouse and child abuse, and the dismal future for many children of the poor.

Second, while focusing on the replacement of work for welfare, there is no provision for jobs and if one finds work there is no assistance for transportation (two-thirds of all new jobs are in the suburbs, while three-quarters of welfare recipients live in central cities or rural areas; just one in 20 welfare recipients owns a car, Bailey, 1997); and there is no child care subsidy or provision of high level day care for the children of working parents. Moreover, this law contains no provisions requiring the states to provide educational or job-training programs for those displaced from welfare. Especially hard hit are women. Without education:

women's wages will not grow, and without growth in their wages, welfare mothers will never be able to afford child care or health care. . . . Eliminating welfare without

improving the pay and benefits of the jobs they can get—or improving their ability to get better jobs—can have only one result: an increase in poverty among women and children. (Harris, 1996:B7)

The 1996 welfare legislation assumes that jobs are uniformly available. But the availability of low-wage, entry-level jobs depends on time and place. Some regions (the coal mining region in Appalachia), states such as California and cities such as New York City have to overcome a mismatch—huge numbers on welfare and relatively few jobs. In New York City, for example, the ratio of welfare recipients to jobs is four times the national average. From 1992 to 1996 in that city there was a net gain of only 88,000 jobs. "At that slow rate of growth, if every job gained by the local economy were given to a New Yorker now on welfare it would take 21 years for all 470,000 adults to be absorbed into the economy" (Finder, 1996:17). Similarly, by mid-1999 when most welfare recipients will be forced to find some type of work, Detroit expects a shortfall of 75,303 jobs and Philadelphia will fall 53,400 jobs short (Associated Press, 1997). There are many pockets of rural poverty where jobs are few and poverty high. In East Carroll Parish, Louisiana, for example, 55 percent of the residents live below the poverty line, the unemployment rate is three times the national average, and the median household income is less than one-third the median for the country. There is no industry other than farming (Kelly, 1996). Nearby in the eleven delta counties of Mississippi, the poverty rate is 41 percent and unemployment more than double the national rate. Frank Howell of Mississippi State University has estimated that for every 254 families leaving welfare in those countries only one new job will be created (cited in DeParle, 1997). Or consider the case of California, where the state's economy is generating 300,000 jobs a year (many of which are high tech jobs not suitable for the underschooled and undertrained), which is insufficient for the 1 million current welfare recipients who have to be moved into a job market and where 2 million people not on welfare are currently looking for jobs and another half-million part-timers want more work (USA Today, 1997).

A major concern with the welfare legislation is that by pushing the poor into an already crowded workforce, wages for low-end jobs will be driven down. This hurts those leaving welfare as well as the working poor. There are 38 million working poor who receive $7.50 or less an hour for work and usually have no health insurance. What will happen to their wages and jobs when 4 million people (50 percent of all adults on welfare assistance) are added to the workforce by 2000, as mandated by the law? Employers are prohibited from firing existing workers to hire welfare recipients whose compensation is subsidized by the state. But employers can reduce working hours, wages, and benefits for existing workers, a likely occurrence. The plight of the working poor, always mar-

407

ginal, thus becomes worse because of welfare reform. Researchers at the Economic Policy Institute estimate that with the addition of one million new low-wage workers the income of the bottom 30 percent of earners will be reduced on average by 11.9 percent. This drop in wages will be even more severe in those states and local[e]s with large numbers of people on welfare (McCrate, 1997). This has at least three additional negative consequences. First, it weakens those labor unions who organize low-pay workers such as janitors, municipal workers, and food handlers. This weakness reinforces low wages and minimal benefits for the economically marginal. Second, the anger of the working poor, most likely, will be directed at the former welfare recipients, not the economic system that limits their opportunities and exploits them. Third, and related to the second, the anger of the working poor will likely be overtly racist as the working poor perceive their economic situation reduced by racial minorities and immigrants who they believe are the majority of welfare recipients (a belief that is false, by the way, as 56 percent of first-time female-headed welfare recipients from 1990 to 1992 were White (Center on Social Welfare Policy and Law, 1996:28).

The third missing ingredient in the new welfare legislation is an understanding of the structural sources of poverty·and meeting the challenges of a rapidly changing economy.

Fourth, the legislation offers no safety net for the people who are not able to find jobs or who are not able to get into day care. When the economy slows down, as it inevitably will, many of the working poor and former welfare recipients will lose their jobs. What will happen to them when they cannot pay their rents or house payments, or their utility bills, or medical bills? Under the previous welfare system, many families were just a lost job, divorce, or medical disaster away from losing their housing. The fastest growing category of homeless during the late 1980s and early 1990s were families (Timmer, Eitzen, and Talley, 1994). Under the new welfare law, and especially when society experiences an economic downturn, increasing numbers of families will have to move into substandard housing or even into homeless shelters. According to Peter Edelman:

> There will be suffering. Some of the damage will be obvious—more homelessness, for example, with more demand on already strapped shelters and soup kitchens. The ensuing problems will also appear as increases in the incidence of other problems, directly but perhaps not provably owing to the impact of the welfare bill. There will be more malnutrition and more crime, increased infant mortality, and increased drug and alcohol abuse. There will be increased family violence and abuse against children and women, and a consequent significant spillover of the problem into the already overloaded child-welfare system and battered-women's shelters. (Edelman, 1997:53)

Fifth, there is a major concern with the abdication of federal responsibility for welfare. By turning over welfare to the states, we have fifty welfare programs. This devolution has the effect of making benefits very uneven as some states will be relatively generous and others will be much less so. Tufts University's Center on Hunger and Poverty surveyed the fifty states to study the implementation of federal welfare reform. The study found that only fourteen states had revamped their systems in such a way as to likely improve the financial condition of the poor. Two-thirds of the states actually made changes that threaten even greater poverty (reported in *The Nation*, 1998). States' rights have not always worked in the past. "States failed in the past to take the lead in trying to end racial discrimination or to alleviate unemployment and poverty. That's why the country need[s] the New Deal, civil rights legislation, and social welfare programs . . ." (Hettleman, 1997:24; see also Schlesinger, quoted in Shanker, 1995:E7).

Moreover, the federal block grants to not reflect economic reality, since they do not adjust for inflation, for economic change, or for demographics (Primus, 1997:20). This oversight ensures that the spending on the poor will not only vary by state but that the amount will be increasingly inadequate.

Sixth, the welfare legislation does not protect children of poor parents. How are they to escape poverty without adequate supports for their health and education?

Seventh, the welfare legislation did not address the real issue—ending poverty.

> Many of us had assumed that welfare reform was fueled by a desire to eliminate poverty. This is not the case. Under the new law, welfare is seen as an issue in and of itself, divorced from issues of poverty. *Ending welfare had nothing to do with addressing poverty.* (Watts, 1997:412)

The Solution

Is the answer to these poverty-related problems a more feeble welfare system or a more robust one? In our view the only way to help the poor is to spend more money, not less as the government has done since the Reagan administration. This money would be spent on helping people with child care, increasing the minimum wage, providing job training and education programs, universal health care (at present we provide some health care for the poor through Medicaid, but do not help the working poor—clearly, a perverse incentive system), guaranteeing jobs, and reducing the tax burden on the poor who are trying to work their way out of poverty. In Wisconsin, for example, the welfare rolls have been cut by 65 percent over ten years. This effort to get people working rather than on welfare has cost the state more, not less, for health care, child care, transportation, and training. In 1987, for instance, Wisconsin spent $12 million a year on child care. By 1998, it will spend $180 million annually (Dionne, 1997).

Is there a way to restructure the welfare system to apportion money and services more fairly to the needy? Is there a way to move people away from welfare dependency and toward autonomy, responsibility, and self-sufficiency? Is there a way to strengthen families on the economic margins? Is there a way to protect the children of the impoverished? Is there a way to meet the needs of the working poor as well as the poor? Is there a way to structure such a federal program so that it attacks the causes of poverty, not the symptoms? An editorial in *In These Times* provides the progressive solution to these important questions:

> Welfare as we know it should surely be ended. But it should be ended in a way that provides every person capable of working with an equal right to employment, and everyone who is employed with a living wage. In the long run, that would also require equal educational opportunity for all at all levels of instruction, universal health care and quality child care for working mothers. Such a program should be federally mandated and funded, but administered by the states or by elected community councils. And it should be available to all citizens and legal residents up to a comfortable income level, and paid for by graduated income taxes on those above that level. (*In These Times*, 1996:2; see also Edelman, 1997)

References

Aaronson, Stephanie and Heidi Hartmann. 1996. "Reform, Not Rhetoric: A Critique of Welfare Policy and Charting New Directions." *American Journal of Orthopsychiatry* 66 (October): 583–598.

Albelda, Randy and Chris Tilly. 1997. *Glass Ceilings and Bottomless Pits: Women's Work, Women's Poverty*. Boston: South End Press.

Associated Press. 1998. "Housing Costs Cripple Families." (April 29).

Astone, Nan Marie. 1997. "Review of the Personal Responsibility and Work Opportunity Reconciliation Act of 1996." *Contemporary Sociology* 26 (July): 413–415.

Center on Social Welfare Policy and Law. 1996. *Welfare Myths: Fact or Fiction? Exploring the Truth About Welfare*. New York: Center on Social Welfare Policy and Law.

Cherlin, Andrew J. 1998. "How Will the 1996 Welfare Reform Law Affect Poor Families?" *Public and Private Families*, Andrew J. Cherlin (ed.), (New York: McGraw-Hill), pp. 120–127.

Children's Defense Fund. 1997. *The State of America's Children: Yearbook 1997*. Washington, D.C.: Children's Defense Fund.

Coontz, Stephanie. 1994. "The Welfare Discussion We Really Need." *The Christian Science Monitor* (December 29): 19.

DeParle, Jason. 1997a. "A Sharp Decrease in Welfare Cases Is Gathering Speed." *New York Times* (February 2): 1A, 12A.

DeParle, Jason. 1997b. "Welfare Law Weights Heavily on Delta, Where Jobs Are Few." *New York Times* (October 16): 1A.

Dill, Bonnie Thornton, Maxine Baca Zinn, and Sandra Patton. 1998. "Valuing Families Differently: Race, Poverty and Welfare Reform." *Sage Race Relations Abstracts* 23 (Fall): 4–31.

Dionne, E. J., Jr. 1997. "Welfare Reform's Clues Are in Wisconsin." *Washington Post National Weekly Edition* (September 29): 26.

Edelman, Marian Wright. 1996. "Need for State Advocacy Intensifies." *Children's Defense Fund Reports* 17 (September): 1.

Edelman, Peter. 1997. "The Worst Thing Bill Clinton Has Done." *The Atlantic Monthly* 279 (March): 43–58.

Eitzen, D. Stanley. 1996. "Dismantling the Welfare State." *Vital Speeches of the Day* 62 (June 15): 532–536.

Finder, Alan. 1996. "Welfare Recipients in Big Cities Outnumber Jobs They Might Fill." *New York Times* (August 25): 1, 17.

Handler, Joel F. and Yeheskel Hansenfeld. 1997. *We the Poor People: Work, Poverty, and Welfare*. New Haven, CT: Yale University Press.

Harris, Kathleen Mullan. 1996. "The Reforms Will Hurt, Not Help, Poor Women and Children." *The Chronicle of Higher Education* (October 4): B7.

Healy, Melissa. 1997. "Welfare 'Family Caps' Fail Test." *Denver Post* (September 12): 23A.

Healy, Melissa. 1998. "Many Kids of Working Parents Still in Poverty." *The Denver Post* (March 13): B4.

Herbert, Bob. 1996. "Taking Scissors to the Safety Net." *Rocky Mountain News* (December 14): 68A.

Herbert, Bob. 1997. "Not All Enjoy Highs of Low Jobless Rate." *New York Times* (November 21): 70A.

Hettleman, Kalman R. 1997. "States' Rights, School Wrongs." *The Nation* (March 10): 23–24.

In These Times. 1996. "Ending the Democratic Party As We Know It." *In These Times* (August 19): 2.

Kelly, Katy. 1996. "Community in Need Cries Out to be Noticed." *USA Today* (October 18): 19A.

Koretz, Gene. 1996. "Breaking the Ties to Welfare." *Business Week* (May 20): 26.

Lichter, Daniel T. 1997. "Poverty and Inequality Among Children." *Annual Review of Sociology* 23:121–145.

Loven, Jennifer. 1998. "Evidence Links Food Stamp Cuts to More Hungry Americans." Associated Press release (January 5).

McCrate, Elaine. 1997. "Hitting Bottom: Welfare 'Reform' and Labor Markets." *Dollars and Sense*, No. 213 (September/October): 34–35.

McCrate, Elaine and Joan Smith. 1998. "When Work Doesn't Work: The Failure of Current Welfare Reform." *Gender & Society* 12 (February): 61–80.

McLarin, Kimberly J. 1995. "For the Poor, Defining Who Deserves What." *New York Times* (September 17): 4E.

Meckler, Laura. 1998. "L. A. County Gives Hope to Welfare Reform." Associated Press release (August 20).

Moberg, David. 1995. "Reviving the Public Sector." *In These Times* (October 16): 22–24.

Murray, Charles. 1984. *Losing Ground*. New York: Basic Books.

The Nation. 1995. "Welfare Cheat." *The Nation* (October 9): 371–372.

The Nation. 1998. "States' Ailing Welfare." *The Nation* (March 16): 7.

Primus, Wendell. 1997. "The Issue Is Poverty: A Conversation on Welfare Reform." *Sojourners* 26 (March/April): 18–24.

Raspberry, William. 1997. "Poor—and Different From You and Me." *Washington Post National Weekly Edition* (November 24): 26.

Schorr, Lisbeth B. 1997. *Common Purpose: Strengthening Families and Neighborhoods to Rebuild America*. New York: Anchor Books Doubleday.

Shanker, Albert. 1995. "In Defense of Government." *New York Times* (November 5): E7.

Timmer, Doug A., D. Stanley Eitzen, and Kathryn D. Talley. 1994. *Paths to Homelessness: Extreme Poverty and the Urban Housing Crisis*. Boulder, CO: Westview Press.

U.S. Bureau of the Census. 1997. "Poverty in the United States: 1996." *Current Population Reports*, P60–198. Washington, D.C.: U.S. Government Printing Office.

U.S. Department of Labor. 1997. "Women of Hispanic Origin in the Labor Force." *Facts on Working Women* (U.S. Department of Labor, Women's Bureau, No. 97–2).

Urban Institute. 1996. Http:1//www.urban.org. Washington, D.C.: Urban Institute.

USA Today. 1997. "Rush to Workfare Costs Jobs of Working Poor." *USA Today* (April 23): 14A.

Watts, Jerry. 1997. "The End of Work and the End of Welfare." *Contemporary Sociology* 26 (July): 409–412.

Wolf, Richard. 1998. "Survey: Good Economy Hasn't Helped the Poor." *USA Today* (March 10): 3A.

Supply-Side Affirmative Action

Clarence Page

Occasionally I have been asked whether I ever benefited from affirmative action in my career. Yes, I respond. You might say that my first jobs in newspapers came as a result of an affirmative action program called "urban riots."

Most newspapers and broadcast news operations in America were not much interested in hiring black reporters or photographers when I graduated from high school in 1965. Nevertheless, I asked the editor of the local daily if he had any summer jobs in his newsroom. I knew I was good. I was an honors graduate and feature editor at the local high school's student newspaper. I had a regional award already glistening on my short resume. Still, I was not picky. I would be delighted to mop floors just to get a job in a real newsroom.

And it was not as if I did not have connections. The editor had known me since I had been one of his newspaper's carriers at age twelve. Still, it was not to be. He told me the budget would not allow any summer jobs for any young folks that year. Then the very next day I found out through a friend that the newspaper did have an opening after all. The editors had hired a white girl a year younger than I, who also happened to be a reporter under my supervision at the student newspaper, to fill it.

Don't get mad, my dad advised me, just get smart. Get your education, he said. "Then someday you can get even!"

My saintly, interminably patient schoolteacher grandmother, dear old Mother Page, also helped ease my tension. "Son," she said, "just prepare yourself, for someday the doors of opportunity will open up. When they do, you must be ready to step inside."

Little did she know that that very summer, riots would erupt in the Watts section of Los Angeles. More than four hundred riots would explode across the nation over the next three years. Suddenly editors and news directors across the country were actively looking to hire at least a few reporters and photographers who could be sent into the "ghetto" without looking too conspicuous.

Many of the black journalists hired in that talent raid, much of it waged on the staffs of black publications and radio stations, would bring Pulitzers and other honors to their new bosses, dispelling the notion that they were mere "tokens" and confirming the depth of talent that had been passed over for so long. Women soon followed. So did Hispanics, some of whom had worked for years with Anglo pseudonyms to get past anti-Latino prejudices; Asians; and Native Americans.

Times have changed. Twenty-two years after it became the first newspaper to turn me down for a job, my hometown daily became the first to purchase my newly syndicated column. The advice of my elders ("Just prepare yourself") had come to fruition.

You might say that it took me only twenty years to become an "overnight success."

Yet it is significant that I and other "first blacks" hired in the nation's newsrooms felt pretty lonely through several years of "tokenism" before affirmative hiring—or, if you prefer, "diversity hiring"—policies began to take hold at the dawn of the 1970s. The message to us journalists of color was clear: White managers did not mind hiring a few of us now and then, but they didn't want to make a habit of it, not until policies came down from the top stating in military fashion that "you *will* hire more women and minorities."

So, of all the arguments I have heard various people make against affirmative action, I find the least persuasive to be the charge that it makes its recipients feel bad. Stanford law professor Barbara Babcock had the proper response to that notion when President Jimmy Carter appointed her to head the civil rights division of the Justice Department. When she was asked in a press conference how it felt to think that she had gotten the job because she was a woman, she replied that it felt a lot better than thinking that she had *not* gotten the job because she was a woman.

True enough. Most white males have not felt particularly bad about the special preferences they have received because of their race and gender for thousands of years. Why should we? Believe me, compared to the alternative, preferential treatment feels better.

Nor have I heard many express a nagging doubt about their ability to "hack it" in fair competition with others. Quite the opposite, privileged groups tend to look upon their privilege as an entitlement. Whatever guilt or misgivings they may have are assuaged by the cottage industry that has grown up around bolstering the self-esteem of white people. Books like Charles Murray and Richard J. Herrnstein's *Bell Curve* are intended, at bottom, to answer this deep yearning. Much is made in the book about how whites perform fifteen percentage points higher on average than blacks do on standardized tests and that this may easily explain why whites earn more money than blacks. Little is made of how Asian Americans perform fifteen percentage points higher than whites, yet they have hardly taken over management or ownership of American corporations.

Or, as one of my black professional friends put it, "Since we all know that hardly any of us is really all-black, I want to know how come we only got all the dumb white folks' genes?"

The notion that Babcock should feel bad about her appointment is based on the pernicious presumption that, simply and solely because she is a woman, she must be less qualified than the man who normally would be preferred simply because he was a man.

Charles Sykes, in *A Nation of Victims: The Decay of the American Character* (1993), says that those who insist on affirmative action really are arguing that "minorities" (he speaks little of women) cannot meet existing standards, and that ultimately affirmative action forces all minorities to "deal with the nagging doubt that its policies stigmatize all successful minority individuals."

Another critic of affirmative action, Dinesh D'Souza, resident scholar at the American Enterprise Institute, goes so far as to say in his inflammatory *The End of Racism: Principles for a Multiracial Society* (1995) that most of us middle-class blacks should be stigmatized because we owe our prosperity, such as it is, to affirmative action. He then speculates that middle-class blacks must suffer "intense feelings of guilt" because "they have abandoned their poor brothers and sisters, and realize that their present circumstances became possible solely because of the heart-wrenching sufferings of the underclass."

Yet nothing in affirmative action law calls for the unqualified to be hired regardless of merit. Even "special admissions" minority students are selected from among those who already have met the standards required to do the college's work.

Affirmative action calls only for "merit" standards to be more inclusive. Affirmative action, properly implemented, *widens the pool* of qualified candidates who will be considered. This often benefits qualified white males, too, who would otherwise have been bypassed because of nepotism, favoritism, and other unnecessarily narrow criteria. My favorite example is the University of Indiana Law School's decision in 1969 to broaden its acceptance criteria to open doors to bright, promising applicants who showed high potential but, for the present, had not scored as well as other applicants in a highly competitive field. The goal of the program was to offer a second chance to disadvantaged students like those who could be found in abundance in Gary and other urban centers, but the program was not limited to them. Several white students got in, too. One was a well-heeled De Pauw University graduate named J. Danforth Quayle. He later became vice president of the United States. He apparently had not scored well enough to qualify for the law school under existing criteria, but, like him or not, he did have potential. Some people are late bloomers. . . .

Arguments against affirmative action fall under the following general categories:

"We don't need it anymore."   The work of early feminists and the civil rights movement did their job, but now it is time to move on. The nation has outgrown employment and educational discrimination. Nonwhite skin may actually be an advantage in many businesses and schools. The market is ultimately color-blind and would be fair, if only those infernal lawyers and government regulators would get out of the way.

Comment: Americans hate intrusions into their marketplace, unless the intrusions benefit them. I would argue that bias is as natural as xenophobia and as common as apple pie. Until opportunities are equalized enough to encourage women and minorities to have more trust in the free marketplace, there will be a glaring demand for extraordinary measures to target what is actually only a quite modest amount of jobs, scholarships, and contracts to minorities.

"Racism has reversed." This is David Duke's claim. Whites, particularly white males, now suffer a distinct disadvantage in the workplace and in college applications. Affirmative action sets racial "quotas" that only reinforce prejudices. Besides, two wrongs do not make a right.

Comment: Not anymore. Conservative court decisions in the 1990s actually have shifted the burden of proof in hiring, promotions, publicly funded scholarships, and contract set-aside cases from whites and males to minorities and women. If women and minorities ever had a time of supremacy under the law, it is gone. Conservative court opinions have worked hastily to restore white male primacy.

"It cheats those who need help most." The biggest beneficiaries of affirmative action have been, first, middle-class women and, second, advantaged minorities. It misses the less qualified "underclass."

Comment: It is easy to criticize a program that fails to reach goals it never was intended to achieve. The argument that affirmative action benefits those who need help the least falsely presumes affirmative action to be (1) an anti-poverty program and (2) a program that forces employers and colleges to accept the unqualified. It is neither. It is an equal opportunity process that, by that definition, helps most those who are best equipped to take advantage of opportunities once they are opened. I find it ironic that many of the same critics who argue that affirmative action is anti-competitive and bad for business can so quickly spin on a dime to complain that it also is uncharitable.

For example, the biggest black beneficiaries of affirmative action have been working-class blacks who had skills but were shut out of slots for which they were fully qualified in higher-paying blue-collar semiskilled, service, craft, police, and firefighter jobs because of restrictive unions and other discriminatory policies. Before President Nixon signed an executive order in 1972 calling for vigorous affirmative action among federal contractors, few black carpenters, plumbers, and other skilled building tradesmen were allowed to receive union cards. Only when construction boomed high enough to hire all available whites were skilled black tradesmen given union cards, and then only temporary cards, on a last-hired, first-fired basis. Significantly, within months of signing the executive order, Nixon was campaigning for reelection against racial "quotas." His executive order had come not so much out of his best intentions for blacks as out of a keen desire to drive a political wedge between minorities and labor-union whites.

Other examples can be found in the southern textile industry, which, under government pressure in the middle and late 1960s, finally hired blacks into their predominantly female workforce as laborers, operatives, and service and craft workers. "As a result, these black women—many of whom had spent their working lives cleaning other people's homes for a few dollars a day—tripled their wages, an enormous improvement in the quality of their lives," Gertrude Ezorsky, a Brooklyn College philosophy professor, wrote in *Racism & Justice: The Case for Affirmative Action* (1991). "I conclude that affirmative action has not merely helped a 'few fortunate' blacks."

"Be like the model minorities." Behave more like Asians and, for that matter, hardworking immigrant African and West Indian blacks who appear to get along just fine despite racism and without affirmative action. In one notable screed, backlash journalist Jared Taylor's *Paved with Good Intentions: The Failure of Race Relations in America*, asks the question: Why do blacks continue in spite of civil rights reforms and outright preferential treatment to bring so much trouble on themselves and others with family failures, violent crimes, and drug abuse? Black leaders are no help, says Taylor, for they have become "shakedown artists" who encourage excuses, handouts, and self-pity that generate a "denial of individual responsibility." Why, oh why, asks Taylor, don't blacks simply behave more like Asian immigrants in "taking possession of their own lives"?

Comment: Opponents of affirmative action invented the "model minority" myth to stereotype

413

Asian-American success in misleading ways that don't benefit Asians or anyone else. According to the myth, Asians succeed better academically and earn higher household income than whites despite racial discrimination and without the benefit of affirmative action. Quite the contrary, goes the myth, affirmative action sets quota ceilings on Asian participation, much like those that once limited enrollment of Jews in the Ivy League. So, therefore, affirmative action actually is harmful, both to minority initiative and to Asian success.

It's an attractive myth, but reality is a bit more complicated. There is a significant difference, for example, between *household* income and *individual* income. Asian household income, like the household income of immigrant blacks from the West Indies, exceeds white household income because more individuals in the house are likely to be working. Asian individual income still lags behind whites at every income level, from the bottom, where low-income Hmongs and many Filipinos, in particular, suffer poverty not unlike that of poor blacks and Hispanics, to the upper levels of corporate management, where a new set of myths continue to stereotype Asians as "not quite American" or "good at rational skills, but not 'people skills.'" Asian-American friends whose families have been here for several generations speak of being asked routinely, "You speak such good English; how long have you been in this country?" More ominous to many Asians are the horror stories like that of Vincent Chin, a Chinese-American who was beaten to death one night in the early 1980s by two disgruntled Detroit auto workers who were angry at competition by Japanese automakers. . . .

"Give meritocracy a chance." Free market zealots like University of Chicago law professor Richard Epstein, who believes all "irrational discrimination" would disappear in an unfettered marketplace, have called for the elimination of anti-discrimination laws, saying the market will punish those who turn aside talented workers or customers with money in their pockets just because of race or ethnicity. D'Souza agrees with Epstein's bold assertion that anti-discrimination laws actually get in the way of women and minorities who would prefer to hire family members. He calls for an end to all anti-discrimination laws except those that apply solely to government.

Comment: "Merit" by whose standard? Market forces do count, but so do culture and personal prejudices. Segregation cost white businesses valuable consumer business, yet, even in the North, where it was required only by local custom, not by government, many refused to serve blacks anyway.

Any intrusions into the marketplace trouble free-market conservatives like Epstein and D'Souza, but the larger question we Americans must ask ourselves is this: What kind of country do we want? There is no neutral "color-blind" approach to the law that has for centuries been tilted against women and minorities. It either defends the status quo, which is imbalanced by race and gender, it shifts some benefits to certain groups, or it shifts benefits away from those groups. Do we want rampant irrational completely unfair discrimination reminiscent of the Jim Crow days that dehumanizes large numbers of Americans while we wait for the vagaries of the marketplace to catch up? Or do we want to shape law and social practice to encourage people to mix, get to know each other better, and ultimately reduce tensions?

"It encourages balkanization." Affirmative action opens social wedges that threatens to replace the basic American melting pot creed with a new "balkanization."

Comment: Anyone who thinks American society was *less* balkanized in the 1950s and 1960s was not only color-blind but also quite deaf to the complaints of people of color. If there were less racial or gender friction in major newsrooms, campuses, and other workplaces, it is only because there was no race or gender in them except white men.

Racism and sexism have not disappeared, it is widely agreed, they have only become more subtle—"gone underground"—making them less easy to detect, harder to root out. Most of us tend to ignore our own prejudices unless someone points them out. If individuals wish to discriminate in their private social world, that's their business. But discrimination in hiring and promotional practices is everyone's business. With the courts already jammed and the complaint mechanisms of the Equal Employment Opportunity Commission suffering backlogs of two years or worse, especially after Americans with Disabilities Act cases were layered onto its already overtaxed, underfunded enforcement mechanisms, promises of enforcement of individual complaints were simply not enough to make up for cruel realities. Even when the courts do reach guilty verdicts, they often impose racial or gender quotas onto the plaintiffs as part of the penalty and remedies. Such court-ordered mandates are, by the way, the only real "quotas" that are allowed under civil rights law and only as a last resort to remedy particularly egregious cases of historic discrimination, such as the police and fire department hiring and promotion practices in cities like Chicago, Memphis, and Birmingham. Yet even these quotas have been quite modest, used sparingly, and, beginning in the 1980s, steadily rolled back by the courts, even while the numbers showed modest progress in the face of the enormous problem.

What most people call rigid "quotas" are actually quite flexible goals and timetables, a distinction that has diminished in the public mind in recent years as conservative politicians have, with remarkable success, attacked flexible goals and timetables with as much vigor as they once reserved for attacking rigid quotas.

"Focus on class not race." In attempts to salvage some rudiments of affirmative action in the face of a conservative onslaught, some centrists have argued for programs that reach out to the most needy, regardless of race or gender. If such programs are conducted equitably, a preponderance of minorities will be brought in anyway, without the dubious air of unfairness.

The ghetto "underclass" has not benefited from affirmative action, University of Chicago sociology professor William Julius Wilson writes in *The Truly Disadvantaged* (1987) because this group is "outside the mainstream of the American occupational system." For this group, Wilson advocates macroeconomic policies aimed at promoting economic growth to replace inner-city manufacturing jobs lost since the 1950s and on-the-job training programs.

Each of these arguments has some merit and much myth. Left to our own devices, most of us unfortunately will discriminate, often in ways too subtle for us to notice even when we do it. Either way, such irrational discrimination occurs and is not healthy for a diverse society. . . .

America will not have racial equality until opportunities are equalized, beginning at the preschool level, to build up the supply of qualified applicants for the new jobs emerging in information-age America. The American ideal of equal opportunity still produces rewards, when it is given a real try. It needs to be tried more often. Affirmative action is not a perfect remedy, but it beats the alternative, if the only alternative is to do nothing.

Reinventing the Corporation

The public gives corporations their right to exist and asks very little in return.
It doesn't have to be that way

JONATHAN ROWE

When an act of simple human decency appears heroic, it's time to ask some basic questions about the culture in which that act takes place. That's what happened last December in an old mill town in Massachusetts. AT&T had just announced it was laying off 40,000 workers, even though profits and executive pay were soaring. U.S. corporations had inflicted over three million such layoffs since 1989, and there was a depressing new litany on the evening news: jobs down, stock market up. (More recently, it's been the equally revealing counterpart: jobs up, market down.) The new Republican Congress was giving these corporations the store. Yet the more they got, the less they seemed willing to give back in return.

Amidst this grim backdrop, Aaron Feuerstein's textile mill in Lawrence, Mass. burned down. Without hesitation, he announced that he wasn't going to pull up stakes and move to Mexico. He was going to rebuild the mill right there, in the state conservatives deride as "Taxachusetts." Not only that, he was going to pay his workers a month's wages to get them through the Christmas season.

Soon everyone was talking about Feuerstein. He was an ABC News "Person of the Week." He sat next to Hillary Clinton at the State of the Union address. Yet Feuerstein himself couldn't understand the fuss. "What?" he asked. "For doing the decent thing?" While his modesty may be excessive, his instinct is on the mark. By his example, he raised a pointed question: Why do we expect so little from major businesses these days?

Certainly, that thought is abroad in the land. Not since Ralph Nader's heyday in the early seventies have the words "corporate responsibility" come up so often in political debate. Because the prime messenger this time is Pat Buchanan, much of the mainstream media has dismissed the issue as the benighted economics of Bible-thumping ignorami. But the notion

that corporations have responsibilities, just like real people, touches a deep chord; and while the term "corporate responsibility" may strike jaded modern ears as oxymoronic and naive, historically it is exactly right. "The corporation is a creature of the state," the Supreme Court observed back in 1906. "It is presumed to be incorporated for the benefit of the public."

How to get back to that original intent—to traditional moral values in the economic realm—is an urgent question. Conservatives say, correctly, that government should do less and individuals and business more. But if that's so, we have to consider whether the dominant form of business is up to the job. If there is to be less top-down regulation and more voluntary well-doing, then we have to ask whether the Wall Street-oriented corporation of today is capable of such a thing.

The issue here is not the hoary ideological debate between the government and the market. Rather, it concerns the kind of entities that will comprise the market. The corporation is an artifice of government, no less than the welfare system or foreign aid. Historically, it has evolved as society has changed. The time has come to ask what the next phase of that evolution should be. In simple terms, how can we reconnect the corporation to the social and community concerns it was originally intended to serve?

The way the corporation drifted from that role is a story that has all the elements of a neoconservative morality play. Corrupt government; self-serving politicians seeking to fill the public coffers and give the voters something for nothing; elite Eastern lawyers riding roughshod over traditional moral values; liberal permissiveness, economic style, and unintended consequences galore—it's all there.

Racing to the Bottom

Today we assume that corporations exist to make money. Ideologists-qua-economists like Professor Milton Friedman of the Hoover Institution assert this as a moral imperative. Yet if we travel back in time five or six hundred years, the European

---

Jonathan Rowe is on the staff of Redefining Progress and is a contributing editor of The Washington Monthly.

corporations of that era were very different from those of to-day. They were regulatory bodies, not acquisitive ones, which served to reconcile individual behavior with larger social ends. Gilds, boroughs, monasteries, and the like—today we would call them "mediating institutions," bulwarks of the civil society that has fallen into such disrepair. "Corporations have constituted, for the most part, the framework of society subordinate to that of the state," as John P. Davis put it in his exhaustive two-volume study back in 1905.

When the British Crown was eager to claim the wealth of the New World, it required commercial ventures of enormous scale. But few investors would come forward because they could be held responsible for the enterprise as a whole. The solution was the "joint stock company," the forerunner of today's business corporation. The corporate entity became a legal buffer zone between the enterprise and the actual owners. Ownership and responsibility were severed, so that a larger enterprise could result.

This was a radical step. Individual responsibility is a bedrock principle of the common law tradition. People must stand accountable for their actions and those taken on their behalf. To compromise this principle, something had to be given in return; specifically, the enterprise that gained this exemption had to serve the public in concrete ways.

Accordingly, in the early days, corporate charters were not granted to all comers the way they are today. They were granted selectively, one by one, for ventures that seemed worthy of public promotion and support. The trading companies that served as commercial agents of British foreign policy were prime examples; in today's terms they were much like Amtrak or the Tennessee Valley Authority.

This basically was the form of corporation that existed in Adam Smith's day. When Smith called England a "nation of shopkeepers," he was speaking literally. His notion of a divine market mechanism guiding individual ambition towards the betterment of all was premised on a world of individual business people, rooted in locality and place and subject to social mores and conscience. In one of the less prescient passages in the *Wealth of Nations,* Smith contended that corporations would never amount to much in the international marketplace. They were too cumbersome and bureaucratic, he said. Individual business people, with their superior "dexterity and judgment," would run rings around them.

In other words, the notion of the invisible hand is premised on a pre-corporate world that no longer exists. So too were the founding premises of the American republic. The colonists were extremely suspicious of corporations, which were seen as oppressive agents of the Crown and potential usurpers of the public will. At the time of the Constitutional Convention, only some 40 business corporations had been chartered in all the colonies. Most of these were for bridges, toll roads, and similar public-works endeavors. So it's not surprising the Founding Fathers omitted the corporation from the scheme of checks and balances by which they hoped to keep institutional power under restraint.

Even as business corporations became more common, they stayed grounded in the premise that they were agents of a larger public good. Charters typically spelled out that the corporation in question was created to serve "the public interest and necessity." Some required shareholders to be local residents, and some even vested part ownership in the public. Before 1842, for example, the State of Maryland chose one third of the directors in the Baltimore and Ohio Railroad. There were also mandates to serve the public in specific ways: A bank charter in New Jersey, for example, required the company to help local fisheries.

As decades passed, the nation's surging commerce pushed against these restraints. Legislatures were besieged by supplicants seeking the privilege of operating as a corporation. In addition, the corporate charter process had gotten a taint of special privilege. The result was the general incorporation laws, which made the corporate form available to everyone.

This didn't mean that the suspicion of agglomerated power had died, nor the conviction that the corporate privilege was connected to a public purpose. Until 1837, for example, every state still required that corporations be chartered only for a particular kind of business. It took almost half a century for states to permit blank-check incorporation "for any lawful purpose." Restrictions on size were common too. New York, which was not unfriendly to business, limited corporations to $2 million in capital until 1881; and to $5 million until 1890.

Similarly, as late as 1903, almost half the states limited the duration of corporate charters to 20 to 50 years. Legislatures would actually revoke charters when the corporation wasn't fulfilling its responsibilities. With the rise of corporate megatrusts and the robber barons, the role of the corporation in American life became a topic of almost obsessive concern. The public wanted more accountability. They ended up with less.

The reason was an outbreak of corporate charter-mongering among the states that eventually dragged them all down to the lowest common denominator. The downward spiral actually began when John D. Rockefeller's lawyer concocted a way to evade the state charter laws. (The story is laid out in one of Ralph Nader's less-noted studies, called "Constitutionalizing the Corporation," which he wrote 20 years ago with Mark Green and Joel Seligman.) The device was the infamous secret trust agreement which enabled the Standard Oil empire to grow far beyond the size the state laws permitted. Rockefeller's conniving set off a wave of trusts—whiskey, sugar, lead, and others—which came to control much of the commerce in their industries.

Eventually these agreements came to light, and the state courts struck them down as exceeding the powers granted in the charters of the individual corporations that comprised them. The charter laws had done their job. Therefore, the charter laws would have to go, and the first to fall was New Jersey.

As Nader's study recounts, in 1890 a young New York lawyer named James B. Dill made an offer that the governor of New Jersey couldn't refuse. Enact the most liberal and permissive law in the land, Dill said. Let corporate managements do whatever they want, shareholders and public be damned. Corporations will flock to your state for new charters; revenues will pour into the treasury. Plus the clincher: Dill would form

What "Pitchfork Pat" (and You) Can Do for Workers

Rare is the Brooklyn pensioner who can say she changed the lives of thousands of workers, but Marie Walsh did just that. She didn't run for office or write articles. She merely inquired about where her pension money was invested.

In 1984, the trustees of the $70 billion New York City Comptroller pension funds were meeting to discuss the Sullivan principles, which guided corporate investment in South Africa. Walsh went to the meeting. Why, she asked the trustees, weren't they also looking at companies doing work in Northern Ireland, where Catholic workers were being heavily discriminated against? The trustees considered her question, and then investigated her charge. Soon after, they drew up the MacBride Principles, which insisted that American companies in Ireland halt discriminatory employment practices. They convinced other funds, state legislatures, and hundreds of companies to adopt the principles. Ultimately, the principles led to an anti-discrimination employment law in Britain.

What Walsh did—raising a question at a trustee meeting—is within the rights of every American with money invested in a pension fund. Yet few workers or pensioners exercise those rights; most Americans have no idea which companies they own stock in.

So American workers watch the nightly news and mutter about the layoffs from corporations; sometimes they themselves are laid off. The irony is that together, they *own* corporate America. More than 50 million Americans own stock, enough that if they exercised their rights and responsibilities as company owners, the results could be revolutionary.

The real players are the "institutional investors," such as public and private pension funds, and most workers have a stake in them. Pension funds alone owned 27 percent of all outstanding U.S. equities as of the end of 1994, according to *The Brancato Report on Institutional Investment*. Other institutional investors with ready-made constituencies among their shareholders include religious institutions such as the Catholic archdioceses; large foundations; and even some mutual funds set up specifically for stockholders in search of socially responsible investing. Most institutional investors are invested for the long haul—10 or 20 years—and their holdings are so large they can't do the "Wall Street walk" and quickly sell out. Their only hope of influence is to encourage or force a company to reform. They are long-term owners, not short-term traders.

It was the corporate raiders of the 1980s who laid the foundations for shareholder influence. Until then, institutional investors were sleeping giants—they put up money, then shut up. But suddenly, shareholders saw management using *their* money to entrench itself against hostile takeovers. Up sprang a shareholders' movement in which the owners, and not just the managers, of capital began calling the shots.

Led by the California Public Employees Retirement System (CalPERS)—which currently has $96.9 billion in its portfolio—public pension funds began targeting companies who were underperforming in comparison to their industry average. The investors would first try quiet diplomacy, then pull out the big guns: *Wall Street Journal* ads and other bad publicity, shareholder resolutions, proxy votes. They have lobbied for more responsive directors, for disclosure of executive compensation—and sometimes for new executives. As such targeting has become routine, companies from Sears to Kodak have felt investors' wrath.

By performance measures, shareholder activists have been extraordinarily successful. Companies pushed to reform by members of the Council of Institutional Investors subsequently outperformed the Standard & Poor 500 by 14 percent, according to a study by the Council. Institutional investors—particularly pension funds—essentially stopped Kirk Kerkorian's takeover attempt at Chrysler because they opposed his plan to deplete the company's cash reserves.

But the activism, to date, has been almost exclusively about shareholders' rights—specifically, the right to maximize investment return by influencing corporate governance. For those who despair at corporate callousness, the real potential of shareholder activism lies in getting shareholders to recognize their *responsibilities* as company owners.

To date, this type of activism has been limited in scope, but effective where it has weighed in. The most visible campaigns have involved human rights in countries where American companies do business, such as South Africa or Nigeria. But there have also been shareholder campaigns on everything from glass ceilings to environmental protection.

One recent, and inspiring, example came from the New York-based Jesse Smith Noyes Foundation. The foundation was heavily invested in the computer chip maker, Intel. At the same time, it was helping the Southwest Organizing Project, a community-based organization in New Mexico, battle Intel's usurpation of water and land at its New Mexico plant. The foundation decided to take an obvious step: to use its status as an Intel shareholder—meeting with management, bringing shareholder resolutions—to force Intel to negotiate with Southwest. Intel eventually agreed to the foundation's demands.

---

a company to handle the paperwork for the incorporating process, and the governor would get a cut.

Soon, Standard Oil, U.S. Steel, and other major companies were lining up for New Jersey charters. Prompted by the permissive new laws, there was an orgy of mergers and combinations, which hastened America's transition from a nation of entrepreneurs to one of corporate employees.

But politically, the New Jersey regime reaped its reward. By 1905 the state was running a surplus of almost $3 million. "Of the entire income of the government, not a penny was contributed directly by the people," the governor boasted. These revenues enabled him to push a rash of new social programs and public works projects, all without burdening ordinary taxpayers. In other words, tax-and-spend liberalism was boosted by the movement that set corporations free of every vestige of social accountability and restraint.

Other states were helpless to counter New Jersey's dirty deal. So, why not get a piece of the action? Those revenues were pretty attractive, as were the other benefits that flowed to politicians more directly. West Virginia was among the first; the "Snug Harbor for roaming and piratical corporations," a contemporary legal treatise called it. Maine, Delaware, Maryland and Kentucky followed in this new race to set the lowest standards and collect the most booty. At one point, the New York legis-

Another unexpected flare of shareholder activism came in 1992, when Sire/Time Warner released rapper Ice-T's "Body Count" album, with the song "Cop Killer." There was a national outcry, but the most intense pressure came from Time Warner shareholders—particularly police pension funds. Some divested; others protested at the annual meeting. Distribution of "Cop Killer" was stopped; Ice-T and Time Warner later parted ways.

Labor unions, meanwhile, have brought the spirit of labor organizing to their status as major investors. The carpenters' union pension funds, for example, pressed Dow Chemical to improve workplace safety, and even visited plants to check on conditions. Several years ago, the AFL-CIO adopted a set of proxy guidelines that are a model for shareholder responsibility. They advocate the consideration of employee security and compensation in proxy voting; and they encourage funds to prioritize domestic over foreign investment.

In their concern for American workers and communities, though, labor unions too often are the exception. Socially responsible institutional investors are reluctant to confront corporate management on bread-and-butter issues relating to American workers. Shareholders can't—and shouldn't—micromanage the companies they invest in. But they could push for a set of guiding principles, such as avoiding cataclysmic layoffs or investing in retraining, that make clear their commitment to balancing the interest of other corporate stakeholders, from employees to the local community, with profitability.

Larger numbers of institutional investors aren't more active in part because of political dynamics in the investment community. Private pension funds are the largest institutional investors out there (they own 16 percent of all outstanding equity), and they are supposed to be independent of company management. Clubby corporate culture ensures that's rarely the case. Few private pension funds ever attempt to influence the corporate governance of the companies they hold stock in. And at public pension funds, the state or local politicians who sit on the board—or control who does—tend to dissuade activism that might alienate corporations. When one Wisconsin state pension fund targeted T. Boone Pickens, it got an angry call from Gov. Tommy Thompson saying "lay off"—he was trying to lure Pickens to do business in the state.

Other barriers to shareholder activism are regulatory. In 1992, for example, under pressure from the Business Roundtable, the Securities and Exchange Commission ruled that *all* issues pertaining to the general workforce (any worker below top management, in other words) were "ordinary business," and therefore beyond shareholder domain under SEC regulations; that means everything from whether a company discriminates in hiring to issues of fair compensation and safe working conditions. The ruling seemed designed to muzzle investors who *should* monitor a company's employment principles—because as owners they are responsible for the welfare of employees and communities.

Under President Clinton, the SEC has not reversed the 1992 ruling. "The SEC [is] bending over to encourage companies to dodge the scrutiny of their own shareholders on policies and responsibilities the administration is encouraging," says Diane Bratcher of the Interfaith Center on Corporate Responsibility, which represents 275 religious institutional investors. She's referring to Robert Reich's support for tax-code carrots and sticks to make corporations behave responsibly. As Bratcher suggests, doesn't it make more economic and political sense to encourage shareholders to wield the sticks themselves?

Wary money managers and trustees tend to portray such activism as a threat to profits; it's either social responsibility or maximum profitability, they think, and a fund manager's duty is to the latter. That dichotomy, though, is a false one: In the long run, how a company treats its workforce has direct impact on the value of its stock. A company that's managed well should never have to resort to the draconian layoffs that AT&T enacted. And insecure, underpaid, or undertrained employees aren't going to be the most productive.

Edward Durkin of the United Brotherhood of Carpenters and Joiners of America notes that when his funds look at a company's health and safety activities, they are acting as a representative of labor, but also as investors: They don't want to absorb liability for regulatory violations or workplace accidents. (The same concern, incidentally, may shake up the tobacco industry; worried about a massing stormfront of anti-tobacco litigation, some institutional investors are beginning to rethink their investments, or press conglomerates to spin off tobacco units or eliminate marketing practices that seem to target underage smokers.) Corporate accounting procedures, unfortunately, are geared to short-term, quantifiable measures—investment in labor is a cost, not an asset. Reforming those methods could help; so could AFL-CIO efforts to survey companies on issues like employee training.

Individual investors, of course, have far fewer shares, and therefore less clout. But they can still make a difference; any shareholder can bring a resolution or attend an annual meeting. Indeed, as the spring season of annual meetings approaches, who better than "Pitchfork Pat" Buchanan—who owns stock in AT&T and other companies whose labor policies he's deplored—to lead stockholding peasants in storming corporate castles?

—*Amy Waldman*

---

lature enacted a special charter for the General Electric Company, based on the lax New Jersey standards, to prevent the company from absconding across the Hudson River. The Commission on Uniform Incorporation Law declared that the evolving system ensured "the maximum protection of fraud" and "the minimum of protection and cover . . . for honest dealing."

There was a brief flurry of rectitude in New Jersey when Woodrow Wilson became governor in 1910. But others were only too ready to fill the temporary gap at the bottom—Delaware most of all. By the time of the Great Depression, Delaware had become home to more than one third of the industrial corporations on the New York Stock Exchange; 12,000 corporations claimed legal residence in a single office in downtown Wilmington.

When other states made their own runs for the bottom, Delaware dropped standards even further. In the 1960s, it simply turned over the drafting of a new law to a bevy of corporate lawyers. The legislature rubber stamped the results. By the mid-1970s, half the nation's largest 500 corporations were chartered in tiny Delaware. Now only directors, rather than shareholders, could propose amendments to the corporate charter. On top of that, corporate officers and directors could be indemnified for court costs and settlements of criminal and civil cases without shareholder approval.

In other words, the concept of individual responsibility for corporate management was entirely out the window. This trend had troubled the upholders of traditional morality from the very beginning. "The pernicious movement has decreased the personal responsibility on which the integrity of democratic institutions depends," Professor Davis observed seven decades earlier. William Carey, former chairman of the Securities and Exchange Commission and author of a leading textbook on corporate law, declared that the only public policy left in Delaware's corporation law was "raising revenue."

Such developments did not go unnoticed politically. Theodore Roosevelt, a Republican, actually established a Federal Bureau of Corporations to monitor the impact of these new and disruptive entities. Presidents Roosevelt, Taft, and Wilson all proposed federal chartering for large corporations, in order to stop the state charter-mongering and set minimum standards for national businesses. (Most corporations chartered in Delaware had little presence there besides a file in a lawyer's office.) These corporations "are in fact federal," Taft said, "because they are as wide as the country and are entirely unlimited in their business by state lines."

But Congress chose instead the routes of antitrust and regulation, trying to restrain what the permissive state charter laws had set loose. The first big growth of federal government came from new agencies, such as the Interstate Commerce Commission and the Federal Trade Commission, that were supposed to keep the burgeoning corporations in check.

In the New Deal-era, people like David Lillienthal, the first chairman of the TVA, tried to tilt the balance back toward individual entrepreneurs and local enterprise. But this group lost out, first to the megaplanners, and then to the new Keynesian technocrats, who reduced the economic problem to the manipulation of the valves and levers of taxation, expenditure, the money supply, and the maintenance of "consumer demand." Those who raised questions about corporate governance and the scale of enterprise were dismissed as descendants of the bumpkins and small-town nostalgics whom Richard Hofstadter ridiculed in *The American Political Tradition*.

Chartering A New Course

That is pretty much where things stand today. The Keynesian policy nostrums no longer hold, but the fixation on scientistic "macro" policy still dominates the national debate. Just get taxes right, cut federal spending, and the Red Sea will open wide. When a Robert Reich or a Pat Buchanan suggest that something more is involved—that the economic entities that do so well in America perhaps owe America something in return—they are dismissed as demagogues and know-nothings.

But Buchanan has let the genie out of the political bottle. Whether you agree with his remedies or not, he has tapped a genuine feeling of betrayal. Americans think the high and mighty as well as welfare mothers have responsibilities—and that corporate America has been obscenely derelict in this regard. *Business Week* put it well when it observed, "U.S. corporations may have to strike a new balance between the need

to cut costs to be more globally competitive, and the need to be more responsible corporate citizens."

The problem, of course, is that corporations today aren't constituted to be responsible. The large corporation whose stock is traded publicly on stock exchanges has become an extension of the Wall Street mind. A CEO who did what Aaron Feuerstein did—that is, who forsook a measure of profit for acts of decency to employees and the community—could have furious portfolio managers to contend with. Shareholders might have his or her scalp. The publicly-traded corporation does to the economic realm what the political action committee does to politics—it reduces people to the lowest common denominator of self-seeking, and subordinates their best instincts to an institutional mandate to maximize pecuniary gain.

This might have been tolerable for a period in our history. But in a global economy, with the sense of community coming apart, institutional self-interest has flown out of orbit, sweeping up even smaller companies in its centrifugal pull. Yvon Chouinard, founder of Patagonia clothing, has put the problem eloquently. The goal in the entrepreneurial world today is to "grow (your business) as quickly as you can until you cash out, and retire to the golf courses of Leisure World," he wrote. "When the company becomes the fatted calf, it's sold for a profit and its resources and holdings are often ravaged and broken apart, disrupting family ties and jeopardizing the long-term health of local communities."

Chouinard, a mountain-climber who happened into the gear-and-clothing business, has gone the opposite route. Instead of cashing out, he decided to keep the company at a scale at which it can still embody the values he seeks to live.

You can't legislate that kind of decency. But it is possible to encourage the kind of enterprise that gives it room to operate. Individual and family owners, for example, at least have the ability to temper their profit-seeking with civic and other concerns. (The Cleveland Browns' owner, Art Modell, is a good reminder that not all of them will.) Family-owned newspapers have done this for decades, which is one reason that the corporatizing of the media is a tragedy.

Local ownership also can have a salutary effect, even from a business standpoint. Consider the Green Bay Packers football team, which is owned by about 2,000 individual shareholders, most of them residents of Green Bay. The Packers have a stability that is rare in business today, let alone pro sports. Packer fans don't worry that a greedy owner will skip town—because they are the owner. The Packers won the first two Superbowls and made it to the conference championship this year. Yet NFL rules now bar franchises from Packers-style local ownership.

If community-centered ownership works in pro sports, which have become the ultimate business, then why not in other businesses? Inner cities, for example, have trouble luring supermarkets and other essential services. There's lots of money to be made, but it takes a level of patience and hands-on commitment that most major corporations aren't willing to expend when there's such easy pickings in the suburbs. Local and community-based ownership can fill in the gap.

Employee ownership works much the same way. It's not a panacea, but an employee-owned company is less likely to move jobs abroad or lay off 40,000 workers when business is booming. It is more likely to take seriously the impact of business decisions on the community at large. *The New York Times* recently highlighted this balance at United Airlines, where employee owners resisted taking over USAir because it would have caused layoffs there. But United has also found that employee owners are also willing to make sacrifices for the company, such as accepting pay freezes, in return for job security.

Unfortunately, the most common form of employee ownership is the Employee Stock Ownership Plan (ESOP), which is a passive investment scheme that often denies workers a real say in policy. Management frequently uses ESOPS as a financial ploy to fend off takeover bids. That's not good enough. Ownership and control need to go together, as they do at United.

The nation can encourage socially-cohesive forms of ownership—family, local, and employee—in any number of ways. Taxes are an obvious example. Currently, estate tax laws push heirs to sell a family business, such as a newspaper, to generate the cash to pay the tax. That's insane; it should be possible to keep family businesses—up to a certain size—in the family, as long as there's active management and ownership. Similarly, the tax laws currently encourage mobility instead of stability. If there's a deduction for moving expenses, for example, shouldn't there be one for staying expenses, as when a firm stays in the inner city when it would be less expensive to operate elsewhere? Deductions for moving expenses should not be permitted at all when a profitable company is enticed away by public subsidies offered elsewhere.

With the largest corporations, we must address the problem directly, and revisit the corporate charter laws themselves. Presidents Theodore Roosevelt, Taft, and Wilson were right. The largest corporations should be chartered at the federal level. Decentralization is great for some things, but it just doesn't work for dealing with the largest economic institutions on the planet. A Delaware charter has become the business equivalent of a Liberian flag of convenience or a Haitian divorce. At the very least there should be a minimal federal standard, as with estate taxes, so the Delawares can't drag everyone down.

That standard should include individual responsibility for corporate officials, of the kind that existed before Delaware's lax and permissive regime. Charters should specify particular kinds of business, the way they used to. And charters should expire after a given period of years, for review under fair standards that ensure renewal except for egregious bad behavior. Nothing would do more to insure a minimum level of decent conduct—without a multitude of new regulations—than the knowledge that sooner or later, the corporate charter would come up for review.

Right-wing ideologues will fume about government "tinkering." But the corporation itself is a form of tinkering; and if the government is going to establish something, shouldn't there be some built-in accountability to the people? Let's not forget: the period of American history that is most associated with rugged individualism and the frontier enterprise spirit—that is, the era of President Andrew Jackson—was one in which corporate charter restrictions were still strong. Individualism thrived when institutional economic power was held in check.

Finally, there's a need to bring back a healthy dose of good old-fashioned shame, the kind that used to operate in small-town business settings. The way to do this, for sprawling corporations, is through public information regarding their behavior. Currently, the SEC collects elaborate data on corporate finances. Now we need to add information on community involvement, treatment of workers, investment in the U.S. and the rest. One of the environmental success stories of recent years has been the toxics inventory. Corporations have made significant steps towards cleaning up their operations, simply because they had to be good neighbors and make known the chemicals they used and were emitting. This approach works without cumbersome regulations and bureaucracy, and it can work in the broader arena of social responsibility as well.

An economy can't thrive for long if the underlying social structure is falling apart. After two decades of reinventing the corporation to be more efficient, we have to ask whether the result is merely a more efficient machine for corroding the nation's social glue. If Americans were asked which they thought the nation needed more right now, more corporate profits or more social cohesion and trust, there's not much question which they would choose. Aaron Feuerstein, explaining why he chose to keep his mill in Lawrence, gave his version of the ancient Jewish teaching: "In a place where there's moral depravity and no feeling of moral responsibility, do your damnedest to be a man." Wouldn't it be something if the chairman of AT&T would say that too?

The State of American Workers

Lawrence Mishel, Jared Bernstein, and John Schmitt

This excerpt is taken from probably the best round-up on America's standard of living compiled anywhere. The conclusion is that we are still not progressing the way we once did.

B y the mid-1990s, the overall economic environment facing American workers and their families had clearly improved. By 1995 the unemployment rate had fallen to the level of the previous business cycle peak in 1989, the result of steady job growth in the recovery following an initial phase of "jobless recovery." Moreover, the disturbing shift toward part-time work and multiple job-holding that was evident in the 1980s has not continued in the 1990s.

On the other hand, the financial condition of the typical worker continued the long-term deterioration that began in the late 1970s. The real wages of the majority of workers have fallen over the current business cycle as they did in the last one (1979–89). As a result, income inequality between the richest Americans and the rest of the population is still on the rise.

The combination of falling wages and increased job loss that the blue-collar, non–college-educated workforce experienced in the 1980s has now spread upscale to higher-wage, white-collar men and to middle-wage women. Insecurity has been exacerbated by a decline in the net worth, or wealth, of middle-class families and by an erosion of good employer-provided health insurance or pension coverage. These trends indicate a disconnect between conventional measures of macroeconomic success and the actual living standards of the typical American. Our analysis suggests that wage deterioration and increased economic insecurity will continue in the near term, absent a major shift in government and management strategies.

Adapted from *The State of Working America, 1996–97* (published by M.E. Sharpe for the Economic Policy Institute, 1996).

The first part of this essay, which delineates the major income, wage, and other living-standard trends that have characterized the current business cycle from 1989 to 1995 (our latest data) and the prior business cycle

---

There is no evidence that the economic squeeze on families is part of some sacrifice that will benefit families in the future.

---

from 1979 to 1989 finds that the typical American family is facing considerable economic pain. We then look at fundamental economic trends such as productivity, competitiveness, and capital accumulation (investment) in order to ask: has the economy's overall performance and efficiency been improving, or has it improved more rapidly in the 1980s and 1990s? This examination allows us to assess whether there has been some gain for all the pain. In other words, we seek to discover whether the process that is generating widespread wage deterioration, economic insecurity, and growing inequality can also be said to be generating a "better economy" or a "bigger economic pie."

What we find is that there seems to be no overall gain or efficiency payoff associated with all of the evident pain. There is no evidence that the economic squeeze on families is part of some sacrifice that will benefit families in the future. The economic indicators that are setting records, however, are the overall profit rate, the return of all capital income (interest, profits) per dollar of assets, and the growth of executive compensation.

A different, competing view of the world states that the economy is primarily generating "good jobs" and that most families are faring well economically. If there is a problem, it is because a limited number of unskilled workers cannot keep up with the requirements of a new era of technological change and globalization or that demographic trends such as more female-headed families are generating inequality. In this view, economic forces are not creating any widespread stress on the living standards of working families.

The data compiled in this book do not support such an optimistic view.

The Income and Wage Squeeze

The relatively low 5.6 percent unemployment rate in 1995, comparable to that attained at the end of the last recovery in 1989,

was achieved through steady employment growth in the current recovery following an initial phase characterized as the "jobless recovery." Involuntary part-time work and multiple jobholding are now no higher than they were at the start of the business cycle in 1989, although greater than they were in the late 1970s. Labor-force growth has been slow, however, primarily because there has been little growth in the proportion of the working-age population that wants to work.

Incomes typically fall in recessions and grow in recoveries, a process that leaves incomes higher at the end of the business cycle than at the beginning. In the 1979–89 cycle, the typical or median family's income grew slowly and, by 1989, was only 4 percent higher than at the beginning of the cycle in 1979. Perhaps surprisingly, income problems have been even more severe in the 1990s. The current business cycle started with income declines from 1989 to 1993, the first such four-year stretch in the post-war period. Family incomes grew by $902 between 1993 and 1994, but the bottom 95 percent of families in 1994 (the latest year for which we have data) still had incomes below their 1989 level, with the median family's income down 5.2 percent, or $2,168. If the current recovery should end within the next two years or so, it is unlikely that the median family's income will have recovered its 1989 level.

The 1980s have been rightly characterized as a period in which families "worked harder for less," meaning that it took more family members more hours at jobs that paid lower real wages to create modest growth in family income. In middle-income married-couple families with children, for instance, the average wife worked 314, or 35.8 percent, more hours in 1989 than in 1979. This increased work effort offset the 7 percent decline in the husbands' annual salary. Without an increase in the earnings of wives, the bottom 60 percent of married-couple families (with children) would have had lower income in 1989 than in 1979.

In the 1989–94 period, the wage deterioration among men was both more severe and more widespread. Families were no longer able to offset the lower earnings of husbands with more work or increased earnings from wives. As a result, the income of the bottom 60 percent of married-couple families lost ground over the 1989–94 period, driven by declines in husbands' wages that occurred across the bottom 95 percent of these families. Many families lost income because both wages and hours fell, while other families worked more but still lost ground.

Income growth in the 1989–94 period was as unequal as that of the 1980s. The combination of slow and unequal growth in the 1990s, however, meant higher poverty and falling incomes for the bottom 95 percent of families. There has been, therefore,

a lack of correspondence between an economic expansion in the aggregate (more employment, more national income) and increased incomes for middle- and low-income families.

Widespread Wage Deterioration

Wage deterioration and growing wage inequality have continued from the 1980s into the 1989–95 period. For instance, wages have fallen among men, younger workers, and the 75 percent of the workforce without a four-year college degree in the 1990s as well as in the 1980s.

From the mid-1980s to the mid-1990s, however, even high-wage, white-collar, and college-educated men saw their wages fall or stagnate. Wage deterioration has been widespread over the 1989–95 period, as real wages declined among the bottom 80 percent of men. The erosion of women's wages also expanded in the 1990s: Whereas real wages fell only among the bottom 20 percent of women in the 1980s, the bottom 60 percent of women experienced declining wages over the 1989–95 period. The erosion of employer-provided health insurance and pension coverage among employed men in both the 1980s and 1990s has put extra stress on families. In the 1989–93 period, health insurance coverage also began to decline among women workers.

The character of wage inequality has changed in the 1990s. In the 1980s there was a general widening of wages as high-wage earners fared better than middle-earners, and middle-earners fared better than low-earners. Since the mid- to late 1980s, however, wage inequality has taken another form: The vast majority have lost wages at the same pace while the highest wage earners are earning slightly more.

Another shift in the 1989–95 period is that education–wage differentials—such as the well-known college–high school wage gap—have grown only modestly among men and much more slowly than in the 1980s. Consequently, a growing education–wage gap has been a much less important, if not inconsequential, force in driving up overall wage inequality among both men and women in the 1990s.

Economic Insecurity on the Rise

Each year over the 1991–93 period, 5 percent of the male workforce and 4 percent of the female workforce were permanently displaced from their jobs in a downsizing, facility closure, or permanent layoff. What is remarkable about these rates of displacement is that they occurred during an economic recovery and that they were higher than the rate of displacement during the depth of the early 1980s recession (the

1981–83 period) when unemployment was nearly 2 percent higher. White-collar workers, particularly middle managers, were significantly more likely to be displaced in the early 1990s than in the 1980s. The upscaling of displacement thus created insecurity for segments of the workforce that previously felt safe, and it required many of them to undergo the wrenching experience that was and still is relatively common among blue-collar workers.

Job loss due to downsizing, plant closings, or other reasons is often associated with a significant period of unemployment and a shift to a lower-paying job, frequently one with worse or no health-care coverage. For instance, about a fourth of displaced workers who had health insurance in their old jobs were not covered in their new jobs. In today's labor market, this shift toward a "worse" job, not simply a spell of unemployment, fuels much of the anxiety and fear over job loss.

The erosion of the wealth holdings of middle-class families in the late 1980s and early 1990s has meant that many families have fewer personal resources to fall back on when paychecks are cut or disappear entirely. This wealth erosion further adds to economic insecurity. The recent decline in middle-class wealth also confirms that the benefits of the ongoing stock market boom have not accrued to typical working-class families. This should come as no surprise, since 10 percent of families, those with the highest incomes, own two-thirds of all stock, while the bottom 75 percent of households own less than 20 percent.

All Pain, No Gain

For the vast American middle class and for low-income families, neither the 1979–89 nor the 1989–95 business cycles have brought increased prosperity. Circumstances would be worse if unemployment were high or rising and if another recession were under way. Nonetheless, American families are beset by a long-term erosion in wages, deteriorating job quality, and greater economic insecurity. To some, these are the unfortunate but unavoidable costs associated with a transition to a "new economy" or a new "global and technological age."

That there have been profound structural changes in the economy over the last two decades is beyond dispute. Whether we are making a transition to a new and better economy, however, is a matter worth examining. In the post-1979 period, economic policy has moved decisively toward creating a more laissez-faire, deregulated economy. Industries such as transportation (trucking, intercity buses, railroads, airlines) and communications have been deregulated. Management has actively pursued the weakening of union protections and the right to

organize unions and to collectively bargain, goals accommodated by policy-making bodies. Social protections such as safety and health and environmental regulations, the minimum wage, government cash assistance (Aid to Families with Dependent Children, or AFDC), and the unemployment insurance system have been weakened. Increased globalization, including greater international capital mobility and international trade, has also given greater scope to market forces and managerial discretion. Taxes on capital and the average and marginal tax rates for high-income families and business have been reduced. Plus, we have had the low inflationary environment preferred by investors, Wall Street, and the bond market. In sum, there has been a conscious, decided shift of national policy designed to unleash market forces and empower management decision-makers.

The promise of all of these policies was to raise living standards and to generate more overall income growth. As with all policies and economic transformations, there were expected to be, and there have been, losers, as the large redistribution of income since 1979 attests. The question is: Was there an overall improvement in the economy that would justify all of the social costs? In economists' terms, did the benefits outweigh the costs so that the winners could compensate the losers, at least potentially if not in practice? Or simply, was the gain worth the pain? Is there reason to believe we are making a transition to a better economy?

Our review of indicators suggests that the changes in the economy have been "all pain, no gain," that the factors causing the pain of greater dislocation, economic vulnerability, and falling wages do not seem to be making a better economy or generating a "payoff" that could potentially be redistributed to help the losers. Rather, there seems to be a large-scale redistribution of power, wealth, and income that has failed to lead to or be associated with improved economic efficiency, capital accumulation, or competitiveness.

Efficiency and Capital Accumulation

Greater economic growth can occur if there is either a faster growth in employment (or hours worked) or a faster growth in output per hour, otherwise called productivity growth. The unemployment rate in 1989 and in mid-1996 is comparable to that of 1979 (although more underemployment exists in mid-1996 than in the earlier periods), so the question of whether there was more growth boils down to whether productivity has grown more rapidly in recent years. Or, equivalently, we can ask whether the economy is becoming more efficient or productive at a faster rate than has historically been the case.

Table A presents the trends in the two main indicators of productivity for the pri-

vate nonfarm business sector. Clearly, productivity growth has been slower since 1973, and there is no evidence of any acceleration in the 1980s or 1990s. Throughout the 1979–95 period, productivity output per hour has been growing a steady 1 percent per year, while multifactor productivity growth (a measure of output growth due to a more efficient use of labor and capital together) has been miserably low. This is strong evidence, in terms of fundamental efficiency, that the economy has not become better able to generate faster growth.

Two objections to this analysis are that productivity is mismeasured or understated (particularly in "services") and that the payoff is yet to come, as we learn to exploit microelectronic/computer technologies. Productivity may or may not be mismeasured, but the only relevant issue here is whether there has been a greater understatement of productivity growth in the 1980s or 1990s relative to the 1970s or earlier periods. No analysis has shown such a trend in mismeasurement. For instance, any errors in measuring service-sector productivity have been present for decades, and the service sector's share of output (or final demand) has not grown (although the service share of employment has grown), so any particular measurement error does not have growing importance.

As to the other objection, it is not possible to know whether there is a payoff awaiting us in the future. Nevertheless, one expects that a large future payoff would have provided some initial, observable downpayment this far along in the process, but there is none anywhere in sight.

Another potential payoff might be large investments that build up our capital stock, thus providing a foundation for a larger economy in the near term and distant future. The two measures of capital accumulation in Table A do not indicate any acceleration of capital accumulation in the 1980s, and they suggest a deceleration in the 1990s. That is, the redistribution of income and wealth over the 1979–94 period and the high profitability in the 1990s have not been associated with any exceptional growth in the capital stock.

Competitiveness

We are told that the U.S. economy is the most competitive it has been in years. Certainly, such a feat is a gain for the economy. Unfortunately, it is premature to claim victory over our competitiveness problems, especially if the goal is to compete successfully in global markets while maintaining a rising standard of living.

On one measure, the U.S. economy is faring better: It contributed 12.4 percent of the world's exports in 1994, up from 11.5 percent in 1979. Less noticed by observers is that the U.S. share of world imports is

Productivity Growth and Capital Accumulation, 1948–95 (Percent)

Year	Productivity*		Capital accumulation	
	Output per hour	Multifactor	Capital services per hour*	Equipment per worker
Annual growth*				
Pre-1973				
1948–73	n.a.	1.8	2.8	n.a
1959–73	2.9	1.9	2.9	3.7
Post-1973				
1973–79	1.1	0.3	2.4	4.2
1979–89	1.0	0.0	2.4	2.8
1989–94	0.9***	0.2	1.4	2.3

*Non-farm business sector.
**Log growth rate.
***1989–95.

also at a record high, reaching a 16.5 percent share in 1994, up from 13.6 percent in 1979. It should not be surprising, then, that the United States had a merchandise trade deficit equal to 2.4 percent of GDP in 1994 (it was 1.1 percent in 1979), an indication of a still-existent competitiveness problem.

Most disturbing is that the U.S. trade balance is in the red despite the fact that U.S. manufacturing workers are the only ones among the advanced countries to suffer real wage losses. In 1994, Japanese, West European, and German manufacturing workers earned, respectively, 25 percent, 15 percent, and 60 percent higher hourly compensation (in dollars) than U.S. workers. Moreover, the lowering of the dollar's value over the 1979–95 period contributes to a lower standard of living and should have helped to eliminate the trade deficit. That is, our trade position worsened despite falling wages and a lower dollar.

One area of improvement is that manufacturing-sector productivity grew faster in the 1980s and 1990s than in the 1970s. Manufacturing productivity grew 3.1 percent annually from 1959 to 1973 and then slowed to a 2.1 percent annual growth rate in the 1973–79 period. Manufacturing productivity recovered to a 2.7 percent annual growth rate in both the 1979–89 and 1989–94 periods, but that rate was in the mid-range of what other advanced countries achieved in either the 1980s or 1990s. In sum, it is hard to find evidence that the United States has attained some competitive edge even though we achieved decent manufacturing productivity growth and reduced both wages and the value of the dollar.

More Schooling, Same Money

Last, we examine the growth in average hourly compensation, which includes both wages and benefits (health, pension, and payroll taxes). Given that no productivity acceleration took place, it should come as no surprise that hourly compensation in the private sector did not accelerate in the 1980s and 1990s relative to the 1970s (see Table B). In fact, compensation growth has been far slower since 1979, which means there would have been no improved gains in workers' pay even if wage inequality had not grown.

What has been overlooked is that compensation growth has been stagnant even though we have been steadily and rapidly upgrading the education levels of the workforce. Since 1973, for instance, there has been a 50 percent reduction in the share of workers who never attained a high school degree and a doubling of the share of workers with at least a four-year college degree, an increase to 25 percent. Table B illustrates the growth in education levels by tracking the average years of schooling in the workforce, which rose from 9.8 years in 1948 to 13.4 years in 1994. Between 1973 and 1994 the average years of education increased 1.6 years by one measure and 1.4 years by the other, significant growth in either case. Table B also presents a broader measure of labor skill, which reflects changes in the amount and economic value of experience and education levels. This skill index shows steady improvement over time and an acceleration in the 1980s and 1990s. The growth in both schooling and labor quality outpaces that of hourly compensation in the 1979–94 period.

In effect, hourly compensation has risen since 1973 only because the workforce has more years of schooling. This situation is analogous to earning a higher annual wage because one works more hours at the same hourly wage—working harder at the same pay. While it is certainly a good thing to be able to work more hours, it would be a far better situation if annual wages grew primarily because of higher hourly wages (and one might even voluntarily reduce hours). Similarly with education, it would be far more preferable if hourly compensation grew beyond the growth created by more schooling, as was the case in the early post-war period.

Profitability

One economic indicator that has accelerated in recent years is profitability, before and after taxes. After plummeting in the 1970s, the rate of return on capital, or profitability, has steadily grown since the early 1980s, paralleling a boom in the stock market. By the 1994–95 period, profitability had grown to its highest level since 1959 (the earliest year for which data are available). This rise in profitability is not the consequence of an investment boom or a surge in productivity, since none occurred.

There has also been a historic revolution in the pay levels of executives at the largest U.S. firms. The rapid growth of wages, benefits, bonuses, and other forms of compensation has greatly raised the pay of chief executive officers (CEOs) in the United States relative to the pay of average U.S. workers and even to the pay of CEOs in other countries. This fast growth of CEO pay started in the 1980s and has continued in the 1990s.

Whatever process is generating this large growth in CEO pay and profits failed to lead to any improvements in the fundamentals of the U.S. economy or to widespread income gains. Higher profitability and CEO pay may be the only payoff or concrete sign of accomplishment from sixteen years of transition to a more deregulated economy.

The Myths That Say "It's Not Really Happening"

These income, wage, employment, and wealth trends indicate that there are income problems facing a broad array of families, including upper-middle-income, middle-income, and lower-income families. This income squeeze has been ongoing since the late 1970s and has been generated primarily by the widespread deterioration of hourly wages that has occurred throughout the ups and downs of the business cycles of the 1980s and 1990s. In the late 1980s, the income squeeze moved upscale as white-collar workers, particularly men, saw their wages decline and their probability of job loss increase. Spurred by an increased public consciousness of these trends, a flurry of reports and analyses have surfaced that deny or minimize the income and wage problems discussed above.

Myth: It's Mostly Demographics

Several types of demographic shifts (changes in population characteristics) have been invoked to explain or minimize current income problems. The implicit claim is that, while the economy has been performing as well as ever for working families, current demographic trends (which are outside of our control) are problematic.

It is important to distinguish between factors that can explain why there is a level of inequality from ones that explain a trend toward growing inequality. This is easiest to illustrate with a discussion of changes in family composition, such as the decline in married-couple families and the rise in single-parent families. Since single-parent families have fewer earners, they tend to have lower incomes, leading to income disparities across families in any particular year.

Whether growth in income inequality or growth in poverty can be attributed to single-parent, or female-headed, households depends primarily upon whether there has been a significant growth of these kinds of fami-

The growth of poverty in recent years has frequently been attributed to the growth in households headed by single women.

lies in recent years. In fact, the shift toward single-parent or female-headed families was slower in the 1980s than in the 1970s, so this particular demographic shift is not a good candidate to explain the growth in either inequality or poverty that occurred in the 1980s but did not occur in the 1970s. Moreover, the shift toward single-parent households has been going on for decades,

including periods in which inequality lessened. Therefore, the important forces creating inequality are the economic trends (such as changes in the wage structure) that previously produced greater equality but now create more inequality.

Another way to make this point is to note that the income problems in the post-1979 period have occurred within every type of family, married-couple and single-parent, so any explanation must go beyond shifts in family composition.

The growth of poverty in recent years has frequently been attributed to the growth in households headed by single women, who are more vulnerable to poverty because of their low incomes. The growth of female-headed households has often been equated to the growth of households headed by black women who have had children out of wedlock. However, poverty among black female-headed households did not contribute to higher poverty among female-headed households over the 1979–89 period and marginally lowered it in the 1990s. The information missing in many discussions is that the poverty among members of black female-headed households has been declining over the entire 1973–94 period. Consequently, the proportionate increase in more black families headed by single women (and the proportionate increase in the number of female-headed families that are black) has not fueled the growth in poverty among female-headed families. All of the growth of female-headed poverty is due to the greater likelihood that white female-headed households are poor.

Another demographic factor, the decline in family size, has been invoked to suggest that income declines have been less severe in terms of declining economic well-being than is indicated by conventional trends in family income. The argument is that if two families have the same income, then the smaller family is better off since there is more income per family member.

A shrinkage in family size is not an unambiguous indicator of improved economic well-being, since families may choose to have fewer children because they have reduced incomes. In any case, taking family size into account does not significantly alter an assessment of income trends: a family size–adjusted income measure shows the same stagnation in the 1980s and declines in the 1990s as the conventional measure (it actually shows a greater growth in inequality). Moreover, the size of the average family was stable over the 1986–94 period, so this demographic shift has had no bearing on the income squeeze in the 1990s.

The increase in the number of wives entering the workforce is also said to lead to greater inequality because "like marry like," meaning that high-wage men are more likely to be married to high-wage women, thereby concentrating income at the top. The pres-

ence of working wives, however, has not led to more inequality in recent years, because the women in low- and middle-income families are more likely to work, a factor that actually helps to close the income gap. Moreover, the fastest growth in wives' work effort (hours worked per year) in the 1979–89 period was among the families in the bottom 60 percent, so increased work by wives actually dampened the growth of inequality. This pattern changed in the 1989–94 period when the increased work-time of wives came disproportionately from the upper 60 percent of families. However, because the growth of work-time by wives was small in the 1989–94 period, this factor contributed very little to the growth of inequality. Over the entire 1979–94 period, the impact of working wives was equalizing.

Myth: It's in the Benefits Package

It has been suggested that the rapid growth in benefits, or nonwage compensation, has offset the wage declines experienced by workers. The rapid growth in the costs of health insurance provided by employers lends some plausibility to this view, as does the fact that the value of benefits grew 1 percent annually from 1979 to 1994.

The bottom line, however, is that hourly compensation (which includes fringe benefits) grew, on average, just slightly more than hourly wages, on average, over the 1979–94 period, 0.5 percent versus 0.4 percent. The reason that benefits growth had such little impact on compensation growth is that benefits, defined as health insurance, pensions, and payroll taxes, make up only 19 percent of the total compensation package, a share that has changed little in fifteen years. Benefits have also increased less than is frequently thought: The costs of insuring workers for health care has risen rapidly, but so has the ability of employers to shift some of these costs onto workers or to create jobs with little or no health insurance. The average cost of health insurance per hour worked has been rising $.03 per year over the 1980s and 1990s (up to $.45 over the entire 1979–94 period), hardly enough to offset the wage declines that took place—a $.75 drop for the median worker and a $2.04 drop for the median male worker.

Myth: Inflation Is Overstated, Growth Is Understated

Some analysts have claimed that wages and incomes are growing much faster than we think and that their growth only seems slow because the conventional measure of inflation overstates the growth of prices and thereby understates the growth in family incomes. Given that the research in this area is far from complete, resting on just a few studies, the claim that inflation is significantly mismeasured must be considered un-

Table B

Hourly Compensation, Skill, and Education Growth, 1948–95 (Percent)

| Year | Real hourly compensation* (1992 = 100) | Average years of school | | Labor skill index* (1987 = 100) |
		Private sector	Non-farm business**	
1948	n.a.	n.a.	9.8	91.0
1959	61.5	n.a.	10.5	94.7
1973	88.1	11.6	12.0	96.4
1979	95.4	12.3	12.5	96.5
1989	97.7	12.8	13.1	101.2
1994	98.4	13.2	13.4	105.0
1995	98.8	13.3	n.a.	n.a.
Annual growth				
Pre-1973				
1948–73	n.a.	n.a.	0.8	0.2
1959–73	2.6	n.a.	1.0	0.1
Post-1973				
1973–79	1.3	0.9	0.7	0.0
1979–89	0.2	0.4	0.5	0.5
1989–94	0.1	0.6	0.5	0.7
1989–95	0.2	0.6	n.a.	n.a.

*Non-farm business sector.
**Log growth rate.

proved. However, whether inflation is mismeasured or not does not affect our conclusions that the inequality of incomes and wages has been growing rapidly since 1979. Nor does a mismeasured inflation negate the fact that income growth has been slower in the post-1973 period than in the earlier postwar period because, if anything, there were bigger problems with the measurement of inflation in the earlier period.

Myth: It's in Your Stock Portfolio or Pension Plan

When public attention became focused on the disparity between a booming stock market and high profits on the one hand, and faltering incomes and wages on the other, an argument has been made that workers are benefiting from the current economy through the increased value of their stockholdings, much of which is held in pension plans. That stock market gains have somehow offset wage declines is not credible, however, because the majority of households do not own any stock, either directly or indirectly through pension plans, and because half the workforce is not even covered by any employer-provided pension plan.

In 1992, the latest year for which data are available, only 28.9 percent of households owned stock valued at $2,000 or more, including stock owned through mutual funds, savings plans (401k accounts or IRAs), and defined-contribution pension plans or through direct ownership. More-

over, stock ownership is highly skewed: Half of all the stock held by U.S. households is owned by the 5 percent with the highest income. In contrast (as noted above), the bottom three-fourths of households own less than 20 percent of all stock, with the bottom half owning less than 5 percent. There may be millions of people who own stock, but the gains from a stock market boom primarily benefit the best-off families, not the typical working family.

Myth: It's Unskilled and Disadvantaged Workers

The overwhelming evidence is that declining wages are not limited to a small group of workers at "the bottom" no matter how defined. Among men, there have been declining wages since 1979 among the entire non–college-educated workforce, the three-fourths of the male workforce that includes those with junior college and high school degrees. Wages have been in decline for the bottom 90 percent of men, including white-collar and college-educated men, since the mid-1980s. Among women, wage growth was relatively widespread in the 1980s, but in the current business cycle from 1989 to 1995 wages have been stagnant or falling for the bottom 70 percent of female wage earners.

Therefore, the group experiencing wage problems can hardly be considered either small, at the bottom, or unskilled, especially when one considers that the U.S. workforce

has more years of schooling than workers in other advanced countries.

Myth: It's Big Government, High Taxes, Regulation, and Deficits

Some pundits have tried to blame recent income problems on higher taxes. The problem with this idea is that federal taxes, including all payroll, income, excise, and other taxes, do not take a larger share of incomes now than in the late 1970s. Income taxation has actually declined among the middle class, but payroll taxes, primarily for social security, have grown. The end result, however, is that the middle class is currently paying the same share of its income to the federal government that it did in 1977 or 1980. Also, there has not been any significant growth in state and local taxes that is squeezing families.

The squeeze on middle-class incomes is driven by shifts in pre-tax incomes, primarily the fall in wages. It is not what the government is taking out of paychecks but what employers are putting in that has created the income squeeze.

What about the size of government? All of the measures of government's size over the 1979–94 period show that government has been shrinking. For instance, the size of the federal workforce (especially as a share of total employment), the share of government taxes and spending in total income (or GDP), and the economic costs of regulation have all declined since 1979. It is hard to

428

see, therefore, how the "growth" of government could be associated with a deterioration of wages and a growth in inequality that began around 1979. In fact, government grew proportionately bigger in the 1950s and 1960s, a time when incomes were growing more rapidly than today.

How about the deficit? The productivity slowdown and the accompanying slower growth in average compensation and wages began about 1973, many years before the explosion of federal debt. Likewise, wage deterioration and growing inequality picked up after 1979 but large structural deficits (not related to the business cycle) did not occur until 1983. Nor could one say that the period of falling fiscal deficits from 1986 to 1995 has been a better one for the growth of workers' wages. Last, studies that analyze the impact of balancing the budget over seven years show that this will raise wages less than 0.5 percent by the end of the seven-year period, or less than 0.1 percent per year. These numbers suggest that deficits have had, at most, a small negative effect on average wages, and they provide no reason to associate deficits with wage inequality.

Myth: It's a Productivity Problem

Income problems have frequently been attributed to the fact that productivity since 1973 has grown more slowly than in the earlier post-war period. However, wage declines for large segments of the workforce took place only because there was both a productivity slowdown and a huge growth in wage inequality, with the latter being by far the most important factor. It is true that most families would almost surely be better off today if productivity had grown by 2 percent rather than 1 percent since 1973. Nevertheless, even with slow productivity growth, there was still 25 percent growth in output per hour over the 1973–95 period, an increase in the size of the economic pie that should have allowed all income groups to experience real income gains.

Myth: It's a Skills or Technology Problem

The falling wages of unskilled workers and the growth in wage inequality are sometimes attributed to technological change and the notion that workers without skills are being left behind by the "new economy." Such a claim is inherently hard to test with data be-

Table C

Median Family Income, 1947–94

Year	Median family income
1947	$19,088
1967	33,305
1973	38,910
1979	40,339
1989	42,049
1994	39,881
Total Increases	
1947–67	$14,218
1967–73	5,605
1973–79	1,428
1979–89	1,710
1989–94	−2,168

cause "technology" is hard to quantify. Although reasonable people can disagree about whether technology has had little impact (our view) or a significant impact on wage inequality, it is unlikely that technology is the predominant factor behind growing wage inequality.

The basic portrait of wage shifts does not easily fit a technology/skill explanation. First, we have already noted that the groups experiencing wage losses are not a small group readily labeled "unskilled," since in the 1990s those for whom wages fell included the bottom 80 percent of men and the bottom 60 percent of women. Many of the workers affected have high school degrees, if not two-year or four-year college degrees. Nor can one see any bidding up of the wages of "more-skilled" or "more-educated" workers, since the wages of college graduates, especially men and new college graduates, have been falling.

Second, since the mid-1980s wage inequality has taken the form of the top tier of earners pulling away from both middle- and low-wage earners to an equal degree. The lowest-wage earners have been losing ground since the mid-1980s, but only as quickly as the middle-wage group, suggesting that the economic forces creating falling wages have been affecting "low-skill" and "middle-skill" earners equally. A technological explanation focused on the inadequate or outdated skills of low-wage workers cannot explain why wages for middle- and low-wage workers have moved in tandem over the past ten years.

Third, many economists have pointed out that the technology story presumes that there has been a redeployment of skills in the workplace large enough to dramatically reduce the need for "unskilled" workers and increase the need for "skilled" workers. If so, why have we not seen a productivity boom based on this large-scale implementation of new technologies and the accompanying reorganization of work and workers?

Last, we have statistically examined whether the growth in the use of high-wage or college-educated workers and, equivalently, the shrinkage in the use of low-wage, non–college educated workers has been greatest in the industries with the most technological change. While it is true that technologically progressive industries require more "skilled" workers, it is equally true that technological change had no greater impact, and maybe less, on the need for "skills" in the 1980s or 1990s than it did in the 1970s. There has been a continuous upgrading of the education levels of the workforce over the entire post-war period so that the growth in "skill levels" has generally met any technologically driven new need for skills. Our research shows nothing different about technology's impact on skill requirements in the 1980s and 1990s than in earlier periods and no evidence of a "technology shock," or an acceleration of technology's role. If there was no technology shock in the 1980s or 1990s, then technology cannot explain why wage inequality grew in the 1980s and 1990s but did not do so earlier when technology's impact was similar.

The alien payoff

The surprising new bottom line on immigration's costs and benefits

BY PAUL GLASTRIS

In the debate over immigration, Francisco Castro could be a Rorschach test. An immigrant from Mexico, Castro supports his wife and three kids by working long hours for minimum wage at Central Market, a Los Angeles fruit and vegetable mart. "I'm always working," he says, "from 7 in the morning until 6 at night, every day but Wednesday." Those who favor immigration would see Castro as a boon to the economy. Those who oppose immigration would see him as undercutting American wages.

These two opposing economic views have played a major role in the debates about immigration for over a decade. Both pro- and anti-immigrant groups have deployed fancy econometric studies to prove that immigration is either hugely costly or hugely beneficial. But there has been no referee trusted by policy makers to decide who is right.

Last week, the respected National Academy of Sciences/National Research Council released a landmark report called *The New Americans: Economic, Demographic, and Fiscal Effects of Immigration.* Commissioned by the federal government as a guide through competing, often contradictory data, the report won't satisfy either the pro- or the anti-immigrant camps—but it does come to clear conclusions about some issues that have seemed murky. The report concludes first that for all the contentious arguments about the impact of immigration on the economy, its actual effect is not that great. "The costs to native-born

workers are small, and so are the benefits," notes economist Richard Freeman of Harvard University, one of the report's authors. Second, the report finds that immigrants do impose substantial costs on large numbers of taxpayers—in the short run. But in the long run, when the bills for baby boomers' retirement come due, immigrants are likely to prove a tax blessing.

The report also notes that while the country as a whole benefits from immigrants, a few states, California in particular, bear a steep financial burden for assimilating them.

Lower fruit prices. There is little dispute about the economic value of highly skilled immigrants. Chinese engineers, Russian physicists, and Indian computer programmers earn high wages, increase the gross domestic product, and, to the extent their skills are not easily matched by those of native-born workers, increase America's per capita income. In other words, they make native-born workers marginally richer.

There has been a great dispute, however, about the economic contribution of low-skilled immigrants like Francisco Castro. The NAS report concludes that their labor does benefit the economy. But the average gain to each native-born American is relatively small. Most of the value of Castro's labor winds up in his own pocket, in the form of the wages he takes home. Those born in this country benefit only to the extent that Castro is willing to work cheaper than someone else. His lower wage translates into

greater profit for the fruit vendor he works for, higher fees paid by the vendor to the owners of Central Market, and lower produce prices for shoppers at Central Market.

But for exactly the same reason, Castro's labor also exacts a cost. While the NAS report confirms recent studies showing that immigrants have no negative effects on the wages of most Americans, there is one exception: the very low skilled. Workers with less than a high school degree (who represent about 15 percent of the work force) earn wages that are somewhat lower (about 5 percent, according to the NAS) than they would be without competition from low-skilled immigrants. Though small, the effect contributes to one of America's more troubling social trends, the growing disparity between rich and poor.

The study found that the other losers are taxpayers in California, Florida, Texas, and a few other states where most immigrants live. The taxes many newcomers pay fall short of covering the costs of the government services they use—primarily health care and public schools for their children. In California, the average household pays an extra $1,178 in taxes because of immigrants.

But the story doesn't end there. Past studies have shown that immigrants generate a growing share of taxes the longer they are here. The NAS report confirms these findings by projecting, in a way never done before, the effects of immigrants and their descendants on tax revenues over decades. According to these

The bottom line on immigration

projections, each additional immigrant and his or her descendants will provide $80,000 in extra tax revenues over their lifetimes (chart). That's equivalent to about $80 for every American household.

Up the ladder. A good example of the pattern the study found is the Martinez family. Reginaldo Martinez was a migrant worker from Mexico who, in 1954, took a job in a candy factory in Chicago. His wife, Luz, and their six children joined him in this country in the 1960s. The whole family, plus various relatives, lived in a two-bedroom apartment. The parents slept in one bedroom, the four boys in the other, the girls and a cousin in the dining room. The children were envious of an aunt who moved into the pantry, since she had a "private" room.

As the Martinez children advanced up the ladder of affluence, the clan became a fiscal asset. Each sibling earns (with his or her spouse) between $40,000 and $60,000 yearly. Juan is a foreman at a pipe-fitting factory. Javier is a conductor for the Chicago Transit Authority. Reginaldo Jr. joined the Air Force and is now an electrical engineer. Five of the six siblings own homes within blocks of one another in the bustling Mexican-American neighborhood of Little Village in Chicago. The average annual property tax payment per home is $1,300. Each sibling pays an average of $1,705 in Social Security taxes. The family's six kids have had 18 children among them, the oldest of whom are now in college. Alejandro, Juan's eldest, is in graduate school in microbiology at the University of Illinois-Urbana-Champaign. Each generation has done better than the last, contributing that much more in taxes.

But the real tax benefits of immigration, according to the National Academy of Sciences report, won't be seen for a few decades. At that point, future wage earners will have to pay the retirement and medical costs of aging baby boomers. That burden will be split among those working and paying taxes at that time. The burden would fall more lightly on all shoulders if people born here had children at a higher rate than they do now. But if fertility rates remain low, the only way to get more future workers will be through immigration.

Impact aid. The debate over immigration will hardly end with this economic report. Noneconomic questions related to culture, values, and assimilation will play a larger role. Still, Jeff Passel, an immigration policy expert with the Urban Institute in Washington, D. C., predicts that the debate will "move away from the general 'is immigration good or bad?' question toward a focus on specific problem areas." Policy makers might try, for instance, to limit the influx of low-skilled immigrants like the Castro family while boosting the number of those with higher-level skills. That might relieve wage pressures on low-skilled Americans while increasing the overall economic and fiscal benefits of the immigrant population. Having too many high-skilled immigrants, however, might someday reduce wages for high-skilled native-born workers.

The National Academy of Sciences report might also cause Washington lawmakers to revisit a proposal that almost became law last fall: federal "impact aid" to the handful of states with large immigrant populations. These states have long griped that they have to pay for education, health care, and other government services for immigrants whose entry into the country is controlled by the federal government. The NAS report strengthens these states' claims that they lose out from immigration even as Washington stands to reap a revenue gain in the long run. Pro-immigration forces might concede some of the points made by their opponents and support putting money in places like California. Reducing the costs of immigration to those it hits hardest is the surest way to preserve the benefits to everyone else.

With Warren Cohen in Chicago and Dana Hawkins

Time to Kill

Europe and the Politics of Leisure

Steven Muller

EUROPE, NOW liberated from the Cold War, is seeking to reconstitute itself, and in doing so fulfill the lofty integrationist expectations of the early post-World War II era on a fully continental basis. Despite minority undertones of skepticism both here and in Europe, the prevailing expectation is that a new and better Europe is taking shape, one that will be united, prosperous, stable, and democratic. But such expectations mirror hopes, not reality. Europe as a whole is far more likely to face a period of acute economic stagnation, the undermining rather than the expansion of democracy, and serious social upheaval.

Conventional economic analysis and a few select sociological observations suffice to account for most of Europe's coming trouble—of these more below. But it may be, too, that what would otherwise be merely trouble will turn into a full-blown crisis for a reason that has so far received little attention: that Europe is destined to bear the initial brunt of a revolutionary change in the human condition. Such a bold assertion naturally invites skepticism if not outright rejection. Nonetheless, humanity may well be standing on the edge of a fundamental reversal of the human condition: the elevation of work into a privilege and the denigration of leisure into the burden of idleness.

Revolutionary is indeed the only way to describe the implications of such a reversal of the social functions and values of work and leisure. Throughout the ages, for all but a privileged minority that could command servants, the need to labor has been accepted as an inescapable burden. Only that same privileged minority had the luxury of true leisure, meaning not merely time free from work but discretionary time and energy uncontaminated by exhaustion or deprivation. Now we

Steven Muller is president emeritus of The Johns Hopkins University.

face a future in which the need for human labor will rapidly diminish to the point where there is no longer enough work to occupy the majority—let alone the entirety—of the human talent and energy available. Leisure will become ever more abundant, up to and indeed beyond the point of idleness and boredom. Increasingly, those with meaningful work to accomplish will constitute a privileged minority, while the majority will consist of those burdened with idle "time to kill."

The origins of this transformation go back to the beginning of the Industrial Revolution when, for the first time in history, machinery began to replace heavy human and animal labor and also to provide humanity with enormously increased mobility. The pace of that revolution itself continuously accelerated, but since the arrival of electronic technology it has been explosive. Smart machines, equipped with increasingly sophisticated virtual intelligence, now more and more perform the tasks of both production and service that human society requires. The human home as well is far along in featuring autonomously intelligent, comprehensively responsive technological enhancements of human purpose—such as programmable environmental, communications, cooking, cleaning, and security systems.

These developments are already so familiar as to require no further elaboration to those living in the technologically most advanced nations. Much of humanity, of course, finds itself in earlier stages of industrial and technological development, but the more gradual pace of the lateral extension of the industrial-technological revolution has not retarded its headlong rush in the most highly developed countries. Nor has the correlation between technological advance and the growth of material prosperity broken step as this rush has continued. Up to the present, too, the volume of work has remained sufficient to sustain more or less acceptable levels of employment—and

Reprinted with permission from *The National Interest*, Summer 1997, pp. 26-36. © 1997 by National Affairs, Inc., Washington, DC.

	U.S.	Japan	France	U.K.	Neths.	Italy	Spain	Germany
GDP growth rate (%)								
1996	2.4	3.6	1.3	2.1	2.7	0.7	2.2	1.4
1990	0.8	4.8*	2.5	0.4	3.9	2.1	3.7	5.9
Unemployment (%)								
1996	5.4	3.3	12.4	7.5	7.6	12.1	22.1	10.3
1990	5.5	2.1	9.0	5.8	4.9	11.0	16.3	7.2
1985	7.2	2.6	10.2	11.3	15.7	10.1	21.9	9.3
Gov't subsidies and transfers (% of GDP)								
1994	12.8	N/A	30.0	24.2	37.7	29.4	16.3	22.6
1980	11.9	9.9	24.5	20.2	38.6	19.2	8.1	16.7
Statutory vacation allowance (days)								
1994	10‡	10	25	22‡	20	25‡	22	24

*Figure reflects GNP growth rate.

‡Typical allowance: no statutory minimum. U.S. figures typically increase to 15 days after 5 years work, and 20 days after 15 years work.

Compiled from: *World Development Indicators* (World Bank, 1997); *International Financial Statistics Yearbook* (IMF, 1996); *Government Finance Statistics Yearbook* (IMF, 1996); *The Economist* (December 23, 1995, p. 112); Employment Benefit Research Institute (Washington, DC); Hewitt Associates (Illinois); *Main Economic Indicators* (OECD, 1988–1996); *World Economic Outlook* (IMF, May 1996).

hence the consumption levels required to keep a consumer society economically robust.

In the days ahead, however—and not so far ahead—there will be an inexorable rise in unemployment in the societies already most technologically advanced: the United States, Europe, and Japan. Much can be done, and is being done, to share jobs between two or even more people, to shorten worktime, increase holidays and vacations, and search for other means to spread out employment opportunities more widely. But despite such expedients, unemployment will increase as the need for work decreases.

Now there is a standard economic objection to this scenario, and it will be just as well that it be made explicit. It may be argued that the problem of absolute scarcity was already solved thirty or forty years ago in much of the West. Certainly, to someone living a century or two earlier it would have seemed so. But people tend progressively to transform their definition of "want" into "need", and there seems to be an infinite capacity to create new—critics would say "artificial"—demands in a consumer society. It is not self-evident that this process cannot continue indefinitely, or at least for a very long time; if people are willing to spend money on some thing or some service, there will be jobs to make whatever that thing is or that service delivers. There may be more smart machines, but there will also be more demands and hence more (if different) jobs created by that demand.

What is wrong with this argument? It vastly underestimates the revolutionary impact of information technology, which holds a future where machines can make other machines, and where the overall substitution of machine for human labor will progress exponentially. Already, smart machines have polarized the labor market in the most advanced countries. On the one hand we have the symbol manipulators and the machine-builders and caregivers, and on the other the McDonald's and hospital laundry workers. This itself is a truly explosive social issue, and one that technological dynamism is likely to make much more acute as, with the passing of time, jobs on the lower end of the sophistication scale disappear much faster than those on the upper end.

Europe's Handicaps

WHETHER ONE SEES the growth of leisure as a truly revolutionary phenomenon or as a serious but still manageable social problem, its full effects are likely to be experienced first in Western Europe. For of the three economically advanced areas of the world—North America, Northeast Asia, and Western Europe—the last will be the least able to respond effectively to it. The fundamental reason for this lies in the structures of government economic policy that the exceedingly generous welfare states of the continent have adopted. Rising unemployment increases demand for compensatory public expenditures, and the states of Western Europe are badly placed to afford such additional expenditures. Their plight is due to a combination of external and internal circumstances, both of which restrict their ability to avoid a social crisis.

As for the internal constraints, here we come to mostly conventional economic considerations. While West European states are not all alike—Britain after Thatcher, for example, has reduced the role and cost of central government more than its Continental partners—they are similar enough for present purposes. The Federal Republic of Germany represents the quintessential and most acute example of the European dilemma. The recent sharp rise in German unemployment suggests more than merely cyclical adjustments and the costs of integrating the former German Democratic Republic to the tune of nearly $2 billion per year; it is almost certainly structural in nature. The current level exceeds 11 percent, one not experienced in the Federal Republic since the 1950s. The current French unemployment level is even higher (12.8 percent) and the Spanish much higher still (21.8 percent). Indeed, comparable problems exist throughout the European Union today, suggesting not random difficulties or mismanagement, but the result of something embedded in Europe's essential way of doing business.

The economic problems generated by generous welfare states are many, but for Europe the implications for unemployment are the most graphic and serious. The core of the problem is that the added costs of assisting ever increasing numbers of unemployed require ever greater public expenditures. Something has to give. Efforts to reduce the costs of the welfare state and to increase tax revenues are predictably producing heated controversy virtually everywhere in the EU countries. Governments throughout Western Europe find themselves politically unable to cut exceedingly generous benefits, and so they turn instead to efforts to stimulate more economic growth in order to pay for it all. But stimulating growth, if it is public sector growth—and that is the easiest to bring about under current circumstances—only puts more pressure on government budgets, which makes such forms of stimulation too expensive even to contemplate for many countries today. If it is private sector growth, on the other hand, that will only advance the technological revolution that will breed still higher rates of unemployment, which, of course, the state has obligated itself to subsidize at still very generous levels. And private sector growth is harder to stimulate precisely because the burdens of the welfare state have made it prohibitively expensive to create such jobs.

Obviously, then, such "solutions" cannot work for long. Taken together they resemble a sort of social welfare Ponzi scheme, where new growth is used to pay past obligations, which in turn generates ever greater future obligations. If indeed the world is entering a new

---

Sick Leave

era in which work is becoming a privilege, then it no longer follows that increased productivity and sales will increase employment. On the contrary, gains in both productivity and sales may be dependent on greater reliance on technology and consequent reductions in the use of human labor. If European governments fail to understand this dynamic, they may manage themselves straight into economic collapse.

NONETHELESS, it is inevitable that strenuous efforts will be undertaken to find ways to avoid confronting the problem. One such effort will be to allow human labor to remain cheaper than technology in performing tasks at the lower end of a polarized labor market. At the moment, for example, it is still possible for industries headquartered in technologically advanced states to export production to parts of the world where labor is cheaper than at home. It is also possible to establish immigration policies that attract cheap labor. While both such practices are now widespread, they create many problems. The former often involves systematic violations of human rights: a vast amount of apparel worn in the technologically most advanced nations, for example, is manufactured in the Third World by child labor or prisoners. And conclusive evidence of the extraordinarily high cost of German labor—the most expensive in the world due in large part to the fact that every Deutsche Mark of wages is nearly doubled by the cost of mandatory social benefits—resides in the fact that German firms have been driven to take advantage of lower labor costs in the United States by establishing manufacturing plants there.

Exporting production is also significantly counterproductive in the short run. Apart from the fact that it represents a kind of exploitative neo-colonialism often involving human rights violations, it aggravates unemployment at home and reduces domestic investment. In the long run, economic growth and rising living standards are not only likely to raise labor costs above present levels around the world, but will result globally in continued reduction of the need for, and economic advantage of, substantial human labor in all manufacturing, maintenance, transportation, and clerical processes. There is no realistic prospect that West European states can address their problems of rising unemployment by lowering their cost of human labor sufficiently to underprice technology-driven manufacture and production.

As for the second practice, that of encouraging immigration to supply cheap labor, this is doubly injurious. The immediate effect is to displace local labor, particularly local labor in unskilled and semi-skilled jobs. Worse, as the forces of technology grind away lower level jobs, immigrants end up disproportionately on the dole—as is already the case in France, Italy, and Germany. This not only bloats government financial responsibilities, but could introduce acute social divisions, with the potential to undermine both civility and democracy itself across the continent.

As to the external sources of trouble, the burden on public expenditures is further seriously increased by the pledge to establish the single European currency. While in itself that currency requires no vast new expenditures, its adoption greatly restricts the borrowing capacity of member states. As a condition for entry, the European Monetary Union demands limits on national deficits of 3 percent of GDP and on total public debt of 60 percent of GDP. West European states are therefore left with very little discretion and face a zero-sum game: spending in relief of unemployment must come at the expense of other public spending, and vice versa.

The conditions for sharing in the euro currency are uniquely devised to achieve monetary stability, but they do not stand altogether alone. Singular as their purpose may be, they also form part of a larger—and looser—design to standardize social and economic conditions within the European Union, and to do so at a high and expensive level. Bureaucracies being what they are, it comes as no surprise that the European one in Brussels is energetically pursuing the many little, and occasionally larger, steps toward the common standards and measures that lend substance to the concept of common EU citizenship. The European bureaucracy operates formally under the authority of governmental representatives from all of the member states, but in practice the servants of the European Union possess a growing ability to play a virtually unsupervised regulatory role within member states. The odds are that this ability will complicate, inhibit, and even frustrate national governments rather than provide them with assistance or relief as they struggle with the rapidly expanding problem of unemployment.

In addition, for the near future there is the added burden that Western Europe—and particularly its main economic engine, Germany—remains committed to heading a major effort to assist the economic and social recovery of Central and Eastern Europe. This commitment also extends prudentially to the successor states of the former Soviet Union, because it is feared that their instability would adversely affect the rest of Europe. From 1990-95, the member states of the European Union contributed over $50 billion to twelve Central and Eastern European beneficiaries, and these contributions have been extended to 1999.

Europe's Social Disadvantages

ECONOMIC FACTORS alone cannot account for the fact that Western Europe is already experiencing serious unemployment while U.S. unemployment is currently at a record low: 4.9 percent, less than half the rate in France and Germany. After all, America is technologically as advanced as Europe, if not more so, and American social welfare programs are also very expensive, even if they are less comprehensive and expensive than their European counterparts. The United States too, like Western Europe, devotes public funds to overseas assistance, not only to Central and Eastern Europe and the former Soviet states, but to developing economics all over the globe. Beyond that, America maintains a costly military establishment that, while reduced from Cold War levels, dwarfs its European counterparts not only in absolute terms but proportionally. How then to explain the differences? The crucial difference between the American and Western European economies lies in three areas: the leisure industry; the service industry; and the "charitable" or, better, the not-for-profit sector. Of these, the leisure industry is the most significant.

Human leisure creates economic demands as does any other human appetite. One demand generated by leisure is perhaps best designated as diversion, that is, relief from idleness or boredom. Diversion can take many forms, among them entertainment, learning, cultural pursuits, physical exercise, substance abuse, and sexual indulgence. In response to such demand, leisure industries have already mushroomed throughout the technologically most advanced economies. Is it possible then, that employment in leisure industries can over time replace jobs lost in production and manufacture? The still multiplying profusion of fitness clubs, for instance, designed to furnish healthy exercise for those whose lives no longer demand much bodily exertion, certainly offers new employment opportunities. So does the gathering of great numbers of people at entertainment and sporting events, where audiences need food, drink, sanitary facilities, transportation, and so on. Unquestionably, leisure industries will grow along with increased leisure, and they are bound to generate new employment. The question is how much new employment, and of what kind.

It may well be that the most significant capacity of the new technology will turn out to be its ability to cater profitably to individual tastes. People who crave exercise can purchase for home use the very machines that fitness clubs deploy for their users, or perform aerobics under direction by video cassette rather than a live instructor. Fast food of limitless diversity can be machine-produced and purveyed with limited human involvement. Electronic programming of literally infinite abundance can be summoned from cyberspace to meet individual taste anywhere, anytime.

As things stand today, employed people tend to make the most use of such leisure products and services; the unemployed cannot so easily afford them. In the future, however, should a way be constituted—or, rather, as a way *is* constituted, for it will have to be done in order for society to function—to distribute wealth even to those for whom there is no necessary and meaningful work to do in an age of smart machines, this would not be the case. A greatly increased demand for leisure products and services can be anticipated, but comparable increases in employment cannot, for the same technological dynamic will apply here as elsewhere in the smart-machine economy now coming into being. Today an increasing number of people are employed making, handling, shipping, retailing, and invoicing video cassettes, computer games, and the like, but, as in other domains, much of the low-skilled employment involved in this activity is being "exported" to lower-wage economies, and in the future that sort of employment is the most vulnerable to information science-based automation.

Obviously, some new jobs will continue to be generated by such leisure products and entertainment programming, but not only will the number of such jobs be limited, the better ones will be concentrated in a particular locale—America. The capacity for individuation does not eliminate the tendency of individuals to share common taste and preference: mass enthusiasm, or rejection, is still much in evidence, and such mass reaction is of great significance to those who use telecommunications for financial or political gain. Mass appeal by definition requires vulgarization. *Vulgus* is the Latin term for the people, and accurately connotes the lowest common denominator. It follows that the software (i.e., content) of telecommunications is dominated by the United States, where from its very beginnings it has been a commercialized, as opposed to a *pro bono publico,* product and industry. The American global dominance of telecommunications software generates significant employment in the United States, and also inhibits the growth of this type of employment in Europe. The commercially driven exports of American software appeal strongly to European tastes and saturate the European mass audience to the point of virtual monopoly. In this sense, Europe has been colonized by America, and to an extent that even Jacques Servan-Schreiber did not anticipate in his 1960s description of *le défi américain.*

The service industry sector in the United States is equally characterized by aggressive commercialism. Personal services of infinite variety are part of the American market economy. Their European counterparts are in general less profuse and varied, more extensively regulated, and to great extent provided by public agencies rather than for-profit entrepreneurs. The health care sector provides just one example. Although more regulated than in the past, and dependent on tax-financed subsidies for the care of the elderly and indigent, health care in the United States continues to function as a commercial industry. The recent American fervor for cost control has not reduced commercialism, only changed its shape. For-profit health maintenance organizations now charge fees for their work to reduce the direct expenses for health care providers and products. The savings that result from lower costs for medical services themselves therefore must be balanced against the new expenditures for the middleman role of the cost containers. More generally, despite recent privatization efforts in Britain and elsewhere, whole ranges of public services, transportation, sanitation, communications, public safety, and so on tend to be public enterprises in Europe but private enterprises in the United States. Even the U.S. Postal Service has been organized since 1971 to operate on a for-profit basis, and there are many and increasing examples of business as well as residential communities policed and sanitized by commercial contract, or of prisons operated by private contractors.

While European practice in the service industries obviously generates employment, that employment is funded by government budgets. These tax-supported service activities can only sustain or increase employment at public expense. The result is disproportionate European vulnerability to conditions of scarce employment and excessive leisure. To the extent that it results in greater profit and higher employment in the commercial service industries, excess leisure in the United States is not an economic disaster but an opportunity. In Europe, however, the consequence of excess leisure is greater demand for government-operated public services, increasing the need for tax revenues, and adding to employment only at greater public cost.

The U.S. economy also contains a large "third sector" (the first being the for-profit, and the second the publicly-financed), which consists of the charitably supported component. To a very pronounced extent the religious, cultural, educational, and intellectual activities of American society are in the hands of not-for-profit organizations. These provide a great range of community social services at no direct cost to the consumer. (True, this multibillion-dollar component of the American economy is partially tax-supported: the private gifts that support it are tax-deductible for the donor, and the organizations that deliver its services are tax-exempt. Thus public support is derived from taxation—but from taxation forgone rather than from tax-funded appropriations.)

The economic significance of this third sector is very considerable. Its current annual operating expenditures, involving over a million institutions, represent roughly 8 percent of gross domestic product, and it utilizes over fifteen million people, composed of approximately ten million full- and part-time employees and more than five million volunteer equivalents of full-time employees. The sector's share of national income is nearly 7 percent, just under half the 15 percent share of government. (The share of national income for for-profit business is 78 percent.) A European counterpart of this not-for-profit sector exists, but on a much reduced scale compared to the United States.

The Political Implications of Europe's Troubles

THE PURPOSE OF these observations is not to compare the American and European economies overall, but to identify specific economic circumstances that to some degree delay and cushion both the rise and cost of unemployment in the United States, while causing Europe to be more immediately and severely exposed to them. But on both sides of the Atlantic, these are early days.

The impact of the increasing lack of work and the concomitant growth of demand for tax-supported relief on advanced societies will greatly strain the fabric of European society, and do so sooner than in the United States. No one can forecast how Europe will respond to the unprecedented challenge that it is still only beginning to face, but experience suggests that its response may pass through four phases: denial, amelioration, crisis, and resolution.

Denial is the typical initial human reaction to an unexpected confrontation with threatening circumstances that defy easy comprehension. Individuals as well as societies cling to the familiar, and deny that it may no longer apply. Policymakers are of necessity focused on the issues of today and tomorrow—on the "in" tray, as the saying goes—and thus tend naturally to reject the prospect that the day after tomorrow will present radical change. At any given time politicians in Europe's democratic states, no less than those in America, keep at least one eye trained on the next election, and incline to defer identifying new problems so long as current ones provide sufficient challenge. The press and the public refer indications of trouble to traditional experts who prescribe traditional remedies. Any analysis forecasting radical change is likely to meet not only rejection, but irritated denial.

But contemporary Western Europe is approaching a degree of discomfort that already renders denial difficult to sustain. The triple burden of rising unemployment, assisting Central and Eastern Europe, and adjusting to the harsh requirements of the euro currency is directing attention to the early warning signals of a new economic and social era. Thus the second phase of response, amelioration— the effort to improve the situation by making the necessary adjustments—already seems to be in the infant stage. The issue of whether or how best to proceed with the single currency is not universally regarded as definitively settled; even the German government now suggests that the 3 percent debt figure is not holy writ, but only a general target. There is a rising European chorus urging belt-tightening and drastic measures to reduce unemployment—witness the French effort over the past two years to rein in labor benefits. But the effort to ameliorate unavoidably produces a clash between the emerging new era of work as privilege and the deeply rooted European commitment to social justice—hence, not incidentally, the long and bitter strikes that the French government's efforts have occasioned. Unless dramatically new methods are established to distribute an abundance produced by a minority of able-bodied adults in society, that clash seems bound to produce a general and mounting crisis.

On the surface, the technologically advanced societies of Western Europe and the United States are much alike. Both exhibit the dominance of an urbanized middle class whose value system sustains an essentially free-market economy, as well as political democracy. Both prefer to operate by compromise rather than command. Below the surface, however, the legacy of centuries of class consciousness and class conflict still remains part of the European social fabric. The open frontier spirit of American society, ever optimistic and individualistic rather than disciplined, ruthlessly self-centered and mobile rather than embedded in a static communitarianism, sharply contrasts with the European mentality. The sense that options are closed and that gain by one group is made possible only by loss on the part of others, that expectations should be restrained in the face of centuries of disappointment, still prevails in European thinking.

One result of these differences is that political divisions in Europe are far more deeply rooted than in the United States. The concept of social justice, while wholly accepted in America as well as in Europe, has connotations that are widely divergent from one side of the Atlantic to the other. In the United States, it brings to mind human rights, the individual freedoms of the Bill of Rights, a pragmatic need to protect the public sensibility from intolerable affront, and a keen awareness that even the indigent have economic potential. In Europe, however, social justice has echoes of revolutionary struggle, of triumph over past oppression, and of the ever-present threat to "us"—who do the work—by "them"—who rapaciously reap the profit. The fundamental difference between the European welfare state and the American version lies in the European conviction that it is the indispensable and desirable role of the democratic state to promote and preserve social justice, while for most Americans the state is at best a necessary but dubious last resort. In theory at least, they continue to subscribe to the Jeffersonian dictum that that government is best which governs least.

Differences as to the meaning of social justice between Europe and the United States are further complicated by divergences in the role of religion. As Peter Berger has shown in these pages, church membership has declined throughout the technologically most advanced nations of Europe.[1] But in the United States religion survives as a serious force, and in recent years a significant conservative religious Christian movement with important political implications has arisen. What is commonly called the "religious right" is explicitly committed to traditional Christian values, but it is also vigorously and explicitly hostile to "big government" and what its leaders decry as godless betrayal of the sacred—such as the right to life when abridged by legalized abortion.

The American religious right has been evoked by an opposition to the dominant secular religion of the day—that stream of American social and political liberalism that gained great strength from the mid–1950s to the mid–1970s. As in Europe, American liberals maintained, and still maintain, that it should be a primary obligation of government to promote social justice. Clearly it would be impossible to explain the origins of the American civil rights movement without reference to such a phenomenon. On both sides of the Atlantic, this obligation has become a canonic element in the Western civil religion—both in its diluted Christian form, and in the do-goodism into which the once proud tradition of classical liberalism has now degenerated.

The key difference between Europe and the United States in this regard is twofold: nothing comparable to the American religious right is in evidence in Europe nowadays; and the liberal orthodoxy is institutionalized far deeper in the structures of the welfare state—and even inside the churches—in Europe than

it is in America. This lay orthodoxy is under attack in America; in Europe, with the partial exception of Britain, it really is not.

These differences suggest that the outcome of large-scale enforced leisure will be a new form of social conflict in Europe. One could envisage in addition to classical "proletariat" style social upheaval a kind of cultural chaos. Masses of basically sated but bored people are less likely to man barricades than to debauch society generally. The lack of self-definition and self-respect, and the consequent demoralization that is bound to afflict so many, is likely to lead to a sense of alienation and purposelessness so acute as to touch off any number of morbid cultural trends. Indeed, we already see the beginnings of such phenomena among unemployed and underemployed youth all over the continent—and here urban North America is no exception—from self-styled anarchists in Germany to skinheads and assorted "punks" in Britain, France, Italy, the Netherlands, and beyond.

The growth of such essentially antisocial forces could be as corrosive to normal life as any amount of proto-Marxist rabble-raising. Those who believe that they are denied the right to work, as well as those who fear losing the work they still have, are likely to perceive themselves as an oppressed lower class—again, some in proletariat terms that we would recognize from the past, but others in terms of an underclass characterized by an angry cultural anomie rather than a specific political ideology. The crisis of work is already a likely source of the "many factors encouraging populist politics in Europe today", as Anthony Hartley described it. "Economic despair and xenophobia bring violence in their wake. . . . All countries need totems. Their destruction by . . . a corrosive skepticism confuses peoples who require national landmarks by which to navigate."[2] And surely national social landmarks will be destroyed wholesale when those who have work and intend to retain it behave as an upper class committed to the preservation of its privileges.

> FROM 1980 TO 1992, PER CAPITA GOVERNMENT SPENDING (AT CONSTANT PRICES) ON SOCIAL BENEFITS IN THE EUROPEAN UNION MEMBER STATES INCREASED 40.6 PERCENT.
>
> FROM 1980 TO 1990, THE SIX EU MEMBER STATES WITH THE LOWEST PER CAPITA GOVERNMENT EXPENDITURES ON SOCIAL BENEFITS RECORDED A REAL GROWTH IN SUCH EXPENDITURES OF 68.2 PERCENT; FOR THE REMAINING SIX MEMBER STATES, THAT GROWTH WAS 31.7 PERCENT.
>
> Source: *Europe in Figures*, 4th Edition (Brussels: Eurostat, 1995).

[1]Peter Berger, "Secularism in Retreat", *The National Interest* (Winter 1996/97).
[2]Anthony Hartley, "Europe's New Populism", *The National Interest* (Winter 1992/93).

As Hartley's reference to xenophobia intimates, racism will also inevitably play a role in future crises. Here, too, the European experience may be more severe than that of the United States. That may at first seem paradoxical, because the legacy of slavery, the partial extermination and subsequent segregation of Native Americans, and continuing eruptions of racial conflict are such well known aspects of American society. However, despite all the problems involved, the United States is well on the way to becoming a multiracial nation in which Americans of European descent will—within the next century—become the largest minority rather than, as in the past, the absolute majority of the population. In the much more homogenous nations of Europe, however, where the new era of work as a privilege will arrive first in full severity, the priority certain to be claimed by the indigenous majority in every country will inevitably produce racially discriminatory treatment of foreign immigrants and residents, including demands for the expulsion of foreigners. Already anti-immigration parties—the Italian neo-fascist movement, Le Pen's National Front in France, and especially Jörg Haider's Freedom Party in Austria—are gaining ground all over Europe. At present, while the world in general and Europe in particular have yet to recognize the key challenge lying ahead, and are busy treating seemingly disconnected symptoms in lieu of recognizing their common cause, it is impossible to be certain how the Continent will ultimately react to the coming crisis. But there are reasons for believing that the responses to the challenge are more likely to be authoritarian than democratic in nature. Human beings are dependent on order and predictability in their environment. A crisis that causes prolonged and acute disorder and uncertainty therefore engenders an ever more urgent priority for the most rapid and complete possible restoration of stability and predictability. The quickest and most effective response to that priority is authoritarianism.

Beyond the human need for order is the fact that the very technology that is leading to the crisis of work and leisure augers in favor of authoritarianism. The unprecedented surveillance and tracking capabilities of the electronic communications technology are well known. In the future it may become literally impossible for a human being to escape surveillance. As for leisure as a burden, there is already evidence that among the first human responses to an abundance of leisure and unused energy is a craving for sedation. In part such sedation may be the product of

entertainment. In part it may also be the product of what we have come to call substance abuse, be it alcohol, tobacco, cocaine, or Prozac. In a society where no one can hide and in which any malcontent can willingly or unwillingly submit to sedation, the temptation to totalitarian control would appear to loom large.

The second and more important reason for anticipating an authoritarian response is best termed civic. If huge numbers of adults never have to take real responsibility for making their own way in the world, if their education comes to consist entirely of tutorials in aesthetics and leisure, if their families no longer serve as production units in every traditional sense, then the very values and attitudes that undergird democracy—independence of spirit, responsibility, resourcefulness, honesty, moral integrity—will simply never develop. A majority of people devoted to their own entertainment and idle-time management would far more resemble H. G. Wells' hapless Eloi in *The Time Machine* than the robust practitioners of liberty and self-reliance captured in the writings of Tocqueville, Locke, Montesquieu, and Mill.

This is not, of course, to maintain that the doom of European democracy is certain. Indeed, democracy may well be a prerequisite for solving social problems of the sort and magnitude described here, in the sense that only with a broad political base willing to sacrifice and experiment with new forms of social organization will leaders be able to lead effectively. Neither can one ignore the power of historical memory and political culture. Europe's experience with authoritarianism in this century may well serve to prevent its revival in the next. Democracy is to some extent a habit, and habits, good and bad, are not easily broken. Democracy is also part of Europe's self-definition, and the exertions of new democracies to the east may even have the surprising effect of bolstering by example democracy's prospects farther west.

The only certainties are that the transformation of a key aspect of the human condition is challenging the technologically most advanced nations; that Western Europe in particular is less able to cope with this transformation than the United States; that the required restructuring of society is so radical as to engender social conflict; and that the manner in which Europe resolves this conflict, while unpredictable, will be of utmost consequence to the human future.

Globalizers of the World, Unite!

Daniel Drezner

Benjamin Barber, *Jihad vs. McWorld.* New York: Times Books, 1995.

Francis Fukuyama, *The End of History and the Last Man.* New York: Free Press, 1992.

Samuel Huntington, *The Clash of Civilizations and the Remaking of World Order.* New York: Simon and Schuster, 1996.

Robert Kaplan, *The Ends of the Earth: A Journey at the Dawn of the 21st Century.* New York: Random House, 1996.

Kenichi Ohmae, *The End of the Nation State: The Rise of Regional Economies.* New York: Free Press, 1995.

The past decade has not been kind to the nation-state. Its economic and security functions have been called into question. The advanced industrial states have lost much of their influence over the global economy, a trend epitomized in September 1992 by the collapse of the pound sterling on "Black Wednesday," when a speculator's bet proved stronger than the full faith and credit of the British Treasury. Governments today have little choice but to privatize their economies and pursue rigidly stable macroeconomic policies. Powerful multinational corporations circumvent states, conducting their own foreign affairs and international agreements (Strange 1992). If the leading industrial nations have

Daniel Drezner is an assistant professor of political science at the University of Colorado at Boulder. He has just completed his year as a John M. Olin National Security Fellow at Harvard University's Center for International Affairs.

From the *Washington Quarterly,* Vol. 21, No. 1, Winter 1998, pp. 209-225. © 1998 by the Center for Strategic and International Studies (CSIS) and the Massachusetts Institute of Technology. Reprinted by permission.

found themselves constrained, weaker states have been torn asunder. Culture and ethnicity, thought insignificant during the Cold War, have proven stronger than state institutions in Yugoslavia and the Soviet Union. Many governments face a situation of juridical but not actual sovereignty over their territories (Jackson 1990). All told, the Westphalian system of state sovereignty looks much weaker at the end of this century than at its mid-point.

The nation-state's eroding influence is underscored by the recent spate of books predicting its demise. Kenichi Ohmae argues that the authority invested in nation-states is devolving to regional organizations. For Samuel Huntington, the civilization is replacing the state as the primary unit in global politics. Francis Fukuyama and Benjamin Barber believe that global economic forces are creating a homogeneous world culture, making the state superfluous. Robert Kaplan is the most apocalyptic, claiming that demographic and environmental changes will lead to the end of the nation-state and the beginning of chaos.

These books split along economic and cultural lines. Ohmae, Barber, and Fukuyama focus on globalization—the cluster of political, economic, and technological changes that have reduced barriers to exchange. Huntington and Kaplan emphasize the renewed importance of cultural forces—the growing desire to be part of a tribe or civilization that excludes and barely tolerates the rest of the world. The cumulative effect is akin to a group of doctors bickering about the specific disease but nodding in solemn agreement that the patient is very sick.

Yet, what is striking about these books is not their areas of disagreement, but rather their areas of consensus. All of them echo another philosopher previously considered out of style: Karl Marx. Like Marx, all of these authors are economic determinists. They agree that the global spread of capitalism is eroding the power and autonomy of the nation-state, either through assimilation into a homogeneous global culture or the violent rejection of it. With one important modification—the replacement of class with cultural identity—the modern-day proponents of globalization echo Marx's theories of transnational capital's effect on states, cultures, and individuals developed over a century ago.

The renewed use of Marx is compelling, but ultimately it is not convincing. Undoubtedly, the

All these books echo another philosopher: Karl Marx.

forces of globalization impose stringent constraints on national governments, but they also empower them in new ways. Globalization does not imply the erosion of the nation-state's authority, but rather a change in state strategies and a redirection of state energies. Furthermore, these books share some of the less savory aspects of Marxism—in particular, the rejection of positive social science and the use of grand theories to make policy proposals. Both of these trends deserve to be resisted. The globalization thesis is seductive, but not satisfactory.

The Economic Logic of Globalization

Accusing a book of Marxist leanings does not have the same meaning now that it did during the Cold War. None of these authors calls for a proletarian revolution or the overthrow of the bourgeoisie. Rather, they share Marx's belief that changes in political or social relations are a function of changes in the economic mode of production. Some of these books go further, echoing the Marxist mechanisms through which globalization denudes the state of any autonomy. According to Marx, the globalization of capital is detrimental to the nation-state because it weakens the autonomy of state institutions and dissolves the political bonds between the state and its populace. In *The Communist Manifesto,* Marx and Friedrich Engels note,

> The bourgeoisie, whenever it has got the upper hand, has put an end to all feudal, patriarchal, idyllic relations. It has pitilessly torn asunder the motley feudal ties that bound man to his natural "superiors," and has left remaining no other nexus between man and man than naked self-interest, than callous "cash payment." It has drowned the most heavenly ecstasies of religious fervor, of chivalric enthusiasm, of philistine sentimentalism, in the icy water of egoistic calculation. (Tucker 1978, pp. 475–476)

To some extent, Barber, Fukuyama, Huntington, Kaplan, and Ohmae all accept this logic.[1]

Ironically, the most vigorous acceptance of Marx's logic has come from those on the right of the political spectrum. Fukuyama is the most explicit in acknowledging his intellectual debt to Marx, observing that his explanation is "a kind of Marxist interpretation of history that leads to a completely non-Marxist conclusion." (p. 131) Whereas Marx focused on the breakdown of institutions, however, Fukuyama concentrates on changes at the cognitive level. Because capitalism requires a universally educated labor force, as well as the mobility of factors of production, individuals lose what Fukuyama refers to as "thymos," or their need for recognition by others.

> Individuals must constantly retool for new careers in new cities. The sense of identity provided by regionalism and localism diminishes, and people find themselves retreating into the microscopic world of their families which they carry around with them from place to place like lawn furniture. (p. 325)

The rational part of Fukuyama's individual triumphs over the irrational, thymotic part of the soul. (p. 185)

This change in individuals leads to greater cosmopolitanism and cultural homogeneity as people recognize similar social relationships across borders. The decline of thymos and the recognition of a universal culture eliminates any desire to give one's life for some ancient hatred. The result is an audacious prediction:

> Economic forces encouraged nationalism by replacing class with national barriers and created centralized, linguistically homogeneous entities in the process. These same economic forces are now encouraging the breakdown of national barriers through the creation of a single, integrated world market. The fact that the final political neutralization of nationalism may not occur in this generation or the next does not affect the prospect of its ultimately taking place. (p. 275)

Stripped of any economic or patriotic purpose, the nation-state loses its relevance.

Ohmae's prediction of the nation-state's demise is based on similar grounds but differs slightly in the outcome. He argues that the spread of the marketplace and the rapid pace of technological change weaken the social contact between individuals and nations. The globalization of capital leads to a homogenization of cultures, eliminating differences between nationalities or civilizations. Ohmae refers to this phenomenon as the "Californiaization" of individual preferences, a blending of taste that blurs differences between states and eradicates historical animosities, making interstate war less likely and thus removing one of the nation-state's primary functions. At the same time, the spread of global capital places new economic constraints on the state's role in economic affairs: "Reflexive twinges of sovereignty make the desired economic success impossible, because the global economy punishes twinging countries by diverting investments and information elsewhere." (p. 12)

Ohmae's original contribution is his prediction that, in the future, the natural organizing unit will be "region-states," which can be located within one country, such as Silicon Valley, or across borders, as in Southeast Asia. Regional variations in economic growth within the nation-state generate political and economic conflicts. More dynamic regions start to question the wisdom of subsidizing less dynamic regions within the same country, whereas intraregional ethnic tensions decline: "Indeed, because the orientation of region-states is toward the global economy, not toward their host nations, they help breed an internationalism of outlook that defuses many of the usual kinds of social tensions." (p. 94) Echoing Marx, Ohmae predicts that the global reach of the marketplace will constrain the nation-state and induce a cosmopolitanism that renders it irrelevant.

Barber's description of globalization in *Jihad vs. McWorld* is perhaps the closest in spirit to Marx, although his metaphors are unquestionably juicier. His definition of the global marketplace—what he calls McWorld—is

Barber's description of globalization is perhaps the closest in spirit to Marx.

> that future in shimmering pastels, a busy portrait of onrushing economic, technological, and ecological forces that demand integration and uniformity and that mesmerize peoples everywhere with fast music, fast computers, and fast food—MTV, Macintosh, and McDonald's—pressing nations into one homogeneous global theme park. (p. 4)

His mechanism for McWorld's erosion of the nation-state echoes Marx as well. Globalization creates new sources of economic power and a universal culture, stripping the nation-state of its economic and political rationales.

Jihad vs. McWorld differs from the other books in two respects. First, Barber attaches more importance to multinational corporations, particularly the media conglomerates that control the means of intellectual production. This emphasis places him closer to Marx's vision of monopoly capital than the other authors considered here. Second, Barber recognizes that the disruptive effects of McWorld will lead to an inevitable backlash within each culture; his use of "Jihad" refers to this rejection of modernization and cosmopolitanism. In the end, however, McWorld will win out, or so he says: "My prediction that Jihad will eventually (if not any time soon) be defeated by McWorld rests almost entirely on the long-term capacity of global information and global culture to overpower parochialism and to integrate or obliterate partial identities." (p. 82) In this prediction, Barber has merely updated Marx to the Information Age.

By stressing the direct economic effects of globalization, the first three books implicitly focus their energies on the developed world. In *The Ends of the Earth,* Kaplan looks at a slice of the developing world but comes to the same conclusions about the effects of the global market on the nation-state. More than the other authors, however, Kaplan examines the effect of the global market on states that resist laissez-faire policies. In most cases, he says, it erodes the state's monopoly on coercive violence. Corruption and the pursuit of government favors destroy the coherence of institutions designed to resist the expansion of the free market. He observes, "The border existed to tax the wealthy and to provide jobs and supplemental income for government bureaucrats. It was a wealth-transfer mechanism." (p. 73) In many of the areas he describes, in particular West Africa and Central Asia, little difference seems to exist today between states and armies, armies and militias, militias and criminal gangs. In the developing world, coercive power has become a marketable commodity. The breakdown of the state's monopoly on coercive violence is powerful testimony to the erosion of the nation-state.

The dominant themes in Kaplan's book involve how environmental and demographic change affects cultures and states. His source of ideas is Thomas F. Homer-Dixon (1991), an academic who stresses environmental factors as the cause of conflict. In particular, Kaplan argues that soil erosion and mass urbanization are the main causes of the nation-state's demise. This argument, he thinks, replaces "social-social" theory with "physical-social" theory. He fails to appreciate that the physical factors he mentions are the outcomes of economic causes, namely the spread of industrialization to the developing world. Kaplan's environmental and demographic mechanisms are different, but the causes are still economic and the effect remains the erosion of state power. In the end, his characterization of the modern world economy parallels Marx:

> In a sense, the world economy has become a larger version of pre-revolutionary Iran's, where in the 1960s and 1970s per capita income rose from $200 to $1,000. But the rise was unevenly distributed, and a large subproletariat was created in the process. The result was upheaval. (p. 387)

Although his causal mechanism differs, and although he never acknowledges it, Kaplan shares Marx's economic determinism.

Even Huntington's *Clash of Civilizations,* though the most removed from the theory of globalization, uses some of Marx's argument. Huntington concedes that the spread of the free market has created a homogeneous set of values for the global elite. He refers to this as the Davos Culture, after the World Economic Forum held in Switzerland every year; indeed, his description of this group of people sounds eerily reminiscent of Marx's description of the bourgeoisie:

> They generally share beliefs in individualism, market economies, and political democracy, which are also common among people in Western civilization. Davos people control virtually all international institutions, many of the world's governments, and the bulk of the world's economic and military capabilities. (p. 57)

Huntington differs from the other authors only in arguing that cultural homogenization is restricted to the elite level and fails to trickle down into a more cosmopolitan outlook among non-Western populations.

This does not mean globalization has no effect in Huntington's vision of the world. Rather, he argues that it needs to be parsed into modernization and Westernization. Most of the world embraces the effects of modernization: technological dynamism and the reduction of barriers to economic exchange. Yet, the Western values associated with modernization, such as democracy and individual liberty, generate a backlash that Huntington believes strengthens civilizational, as opposed to national, identities:

> The most obvious, most salient, and most powerful cause of the global religious resurgence is precisely what was supposed to cause the death of religion: the processes of social, economic, and cultural modernization that swept across the world in the latter half of the twentieth century. Long-standing sources of identity and systems of authority are disrupted. People move from the countryside into the city, become separated from their roots, and take new jobs or no job. They interact with large numbers of strangers and are exposed to new sets of relationships. They need new sources of identity. (p. 97)

With this logic, Huntington agrees with the other authors that globalization is eroding the autonomy of the nation-state; any disagreement is over the precise mechanism through which this occurs. Ohmae, Barber, and Fukuyama stress the ability of global capitalism to reduce the nation-state's economic role and to create a genuine cosmopolitanism that erodes its political role. Huntington and Kaplan believe it is in the negative reaction to this cosmopolitanism that identities change.

The Nation-State and the Reaction to Global Capitalism

Just as these authors share Marx's belief in economic determinism to some degree, they also (with the exception of Ohmae) share Marx's use of the dialectic. They acknowledge that the forces of globalization generate social upheaval and resistance to the free market. They further agree that these reactions create new movements led by educated urban elites and consisting of workers alienated by the callousness of capitalism. But at this point, the similarities with Marx, and with each other, end.

Marx believed that capitalism would alienate the laborers from the global economic system, creating a transnational class consciousness of workers. One hundred and fifty years after *The Communist Manifesto,* the new globalizers recognize that cultural identity remains more powerful than class identity. Because cultural identities do not match up well with existing state boundaries, the nation-state is thus caught between the cross-pressures of globalization and the fragmentation produced in reaction to it, weakening state power and sovereignty.

Fukuyama and Ohmae mention the threat of ethnic fragmentation primarily to dismiss it.[2] For them, the economic forces for cosmopolitanism are too great. Barber acknowledges the reaction in his description of Jihad, but he also believes that it is a transient phenomenon. Kaplan and Huntington, on the other hand, devote most of their books to the reaction to globalization.

Of all of the books, Barber's may be the best at describing the interplay between the forces of globalization and fragmentation. He points out that the forces of Jihad are a direct result of the forces of globalization: "Jihad stands not so much in stark opposition as in subtle counterpoint to McWorld and is itself a dialectical response to modernity whose features both reflect and reinforce the modern world's virtues and vices—Jihad via McWorld rather than Jihad versus McWorld." (p. 157) He shrewdly observes that these reactionary movements exploit the same technological advances as those in favor of globalization. Modernization enhances the ability of these rejectionist groups to mobilize. He does not think this will benefit nation-states: "Jihad, even in its most pacific manifestations, almost always turns out to be not simply a struggle on behalf of an ethnic fragment for self-determination, but a compound struggle within that fragment that risks still

greater fragmentation and plenty of confusion as well." (p. 179) He makes the expected references to the Middle East and the former Soviet Union, but to show that Jihad is also a global phenomenon, he also devotes chapters to the United States and Western Europe. In an ironic counterpoint to Ohmae's *The End of the Nation-State,* Barber claims that regional entities will increase their power because of ethnic rather than economic motivations.

> **A**ffirmations of cultural identity would seem to bode well for the nation-state.

Kaplan sums up his empirical conclusions with the following line: "All I had learned so far was that states in West Africa, the Near East, and Central Asia were weakening, and that ethno-religious identities appeared stronger by contrast." (p. 272) Kaplan's descriptions are compelling. West Africa has seen violent ethnic conflicts and a growing resentment of Lebanese immigrants. Turkey and Iran fear the secession of Kurdish and Azeri minorities; Egypt fears the rise of Islamic fundamentalism. From his description, Pakistan is not so much a state as a collection of clans and drug warlords. Everywhere he looks, Kaplan finds states incapable of coping with the environmental and geographic implications of modernization; in their place, new identities are formed, based on religion or ethnicity.

If these observations were confined to the countries south of the equator, then Kaplan's book would have few implications for the more powerful and established nation-states. But he goes further in his conclusions, asserting that these are global problems:

> Many of the problems I saw around the world—poverty, the collapse of cities, porous borders, cultural and racial strife, growing economic disparities, weakening nation-states—are problems for Americans to think about. I thought of America everywhere I looked. We cannot escape a more populous, interconnected world of crumbling borders. (p. 436)

Yet he is extremely pessimistic that the United States or the developed world can do anything about these problems: "We are not in control. As societies grow more populous and more complex, the idea that a global elite like the UN can engineer reality from above is just as absurd as the idea that political 'scientists' can reduce any of this to a *science*." (p. 436) Academic aspersions

447

aside, Kaplan's statement reveals his belief that both globalization and the reaction to it are structural changes that cannot be thwarted by policymakers.

For Huntington, the reaction to modernization and the rejection of "Western" values leads to an erosion of the nation-state's power:

> Political boundaries increasingly are redrawn to coincide with cultural ones: ethnic, religious, and civilizational. Cultural communities are replacing Cold War blocs, and the fault lines between civilizations are becoming the central lines of conflict in global politics. (p. 125)

This occurs through three mechanisms. First, states lose their identity relative to civilizations and thus reject the practices of *realpolitik* that govern the Westphalian world order. They have no choice but to ally with states of the same civilization. Second, many states face internal divisions because they straddle civilizational fault lines, or because their leaders tried in the past to imprint Western values upon their societies and only partially succeeded. The roster of conflicted states includes China, Germany, India, Iran, Japan, Mexico, Russia, South Africa, Turkey, and Ukraine.

Third—and this is where Huntington follows Kaplan's strategy of analyzing international relations to urge a change in U.S. domestic policy—Western civilization faces internal threats from immigration and multi-culturalism:

> Western culture is challenged by groups within Western societies. One such challenge comes from immigrants from other civilizations who reject assimilation and continue to adhere to and propagate the values, customs, and cultures of their home societies. . . . In the name of multiculturalism they have attacked the identification of the United States with Western civilization, denied the existence of a common American culture, and promoted racial, ethnic, and other substantial cultural identities and groupings. (pp. 304–305)

Just as other civilizations are challenging the West, the permeability of state borders has diminished the ability of Western civilization to respond. Huntington, like Kaplan, believes that the developing world's reaction to globalization will spread, tearing apart the advanced industrial states as well.

Critiquing the Last Seduction

Marxism was a seductive philosophy because it attempted to explain, well, *everything*. These books make the same theoretical leap, and the effect, sometimes, is dazzling. In the face of explanations that unite disparate facts and trends, it is tempting to embrace their claims. Yet, rather than join the chorus of mourners for the nation-state, I contend that the arguments for economic determinism do not stand up to empirical or theoretical scrutiny. Empirically, much of the evidence provided in the books is inconclusive. Theoretically, the economic and cultural forces unleashed by globalization impose new constraints on countries, but not a straight-jacket. Globalization also creates new strategies and roles for the nation-state.

Empirically, these books leave many questions unanswered (*The End of History and the Last Man* excepted, as it is primarily a theoretical tract). These books were written for a relatively broad audience and thus skip over much of the drudgery of data collection and fact checking, which leads to some sloppiness. With so much ground to cover, each of the books have their factual *faux-pas*. For example, Kaplan states that the United States actually has less enmity and deeper military, economic, and educational links with Iran than either Japan or Germany. (p. 186) Fukuyama claims that Russian nationalism is neither expansionist nor a powerful force within Russia. (p. 272) Barber includes South Korea as an example of how free markets can be divorced from free political institutions. (p. 184) Huntington asserts an Islamic revival in post-Soviet Central Asia that has yet to be observed by others. (pp. 96–97) And Ohmae categorizes North Korea as having a higher per capita income than China. (pp. 90–91)

Even when the facts are correct, however, they do not necessarily corroborate the authors' claims. Kaplan and Ohmae commit this error in different ways. Kaplan "discovers" that countries with corrupt governments, stagnant economies, and short histories of statehood are falling apart. In other words, he looks only at failed states and concludes that all states are failing. He believes these trends can be generalized to the rest of the world, yet his own descriptions contradict him. In the countries where statehood has a longer tradition, such as Turkey, Iran, and Thailand, Kaplan finds a stronger state and a less fragmented populace. This distinction severs the contagion effect Kaplan wants to ascribe to events in West Africa and Central Asia.

Ohmae makes the mistake of most business gurus: In looking only at the economically successful, he analyzes a biased sample and thus reaches flawed conclusions.[3] Ohmae provides no compelling evidence that information technologies favor regional units of economic organization. Many of the traits that Ohmae describes in successful region-states are also evident in areas that have yet to experience rapid economic growth (Saxenian 1989), implying that the region is not the natural unit of organization across the globe. Furthermore, his East Asian examples present a paradox. On the one hand, he uses the Pacific Rim to show that the nation-state is losing its relevance in the borderless economy. In making this argument, he seems to have ignored the rising defense budgets of most states in the region, the collective effort to suppress internal dissent, and the sovereignty dispute over the Spratly Islands. In the part of the globe where his argument should be the most powerful, the nation-state remains a robust institution.

Barber's description in *Jihad vs. McWorld* is certainly vivid, but his evidence consists of anecdotes, film revenue reports, and rock lyrics, none of which proves his theory that capitalism erodes democracy. Indeed, Robert Putnam (1993) offers a rigorous analysis of the ingredients of a good democracy and concludes that economics has very little to do with it; the bonds of civic association are far more resilient than Barber claims. Barber contradicts himself on the ability of markets to erode state power, railing at Rupert Murdoch for his repeated concessions to the Chinese government. Furthermore, the claim that globalization strips states of their domestic autonomy does not have much empirical support; studies of economic integration suggest that governments have been able to *increase* their role, even in a globalizing economy (Garrett 1995; Hallenberg 1996; Katzenstein 1985).

As for cultural homogenization, Barber's references to movies and MTV are not enough to prove his point. He describes a thin gruel of global culture but ignores the richer cultural stew that all countries, the United States included, possess. In describing the aspects of culture that can move across boundaries, he fails to realize that much of what defines culture is immobile. To Barber's credit, he tries to show the forces of Jihad in the areas where it would be least expected, such as Western Europe and the United States. The problem is, he finds very tenuous support for his thesis. Even in the areas where fragmentation would be expected, such as the former Soviet Union, his knowledge is at best superficial and at worst wrong.[4]

Huntington's book is the best researched of the lot, but his evidence could be interpreted in several ways. For example, to show a resurgent Confucian civilization in East Asia, he liberally quotes Lee Kuan Yew and Mahathir Mohamad asserting the existence of distinct Asian values. Fair enough, but these two are leaders of relatively small countries—Singapore and Malaysia—trying to maintain their internal control; it is not surprising that they would use such rhetoric as a way of increasing their power and prestige. Huntington also uses the length and viciousness of ethnic conflicts as proof that "fault-line" civilizational wars are longer and bloodier than other conflicts. But not all ethnic conflicts are civilizational, as Rwanda and Northern Ireland attest. Wars based along clan lines (Somalia) or ideology (Cambodia) can be just as long and just as bloody.

Huntington's evidence can be interpreted in several ways.

This is not the first time the proponents of the globalization thesis have cried wolf. Marx's predictions about the subjugation of national governments to transnational capital did not occur in the nineteenth century. In 1907, a Prussian official complained: "In our time of international trade, the telephone and the telegram, the owners of 'mobile capital' are in no way bound to a specific residence. If the demands of the state on their performance become too large, then the danger is near that they will brush the Prussian dust from their feet and leave."[5] E. H. Carr (1945) wrote during World War II that state sovereignty "is being sapped by modern technological developments which have made the nation obsolescent as the unit of military and economic organization, and are rapidly concentrating effective decision and control in the hands of great multi-national units." (p. 39) In 1969, noted economist Charles Kindleberger argued that the nation-state "was just about through as an economic unit."[6] None of these predictions came true.

The Nation-State at the New Millennium

Theoretically, the global trends described in these books should enhance both the economic and political role of the nation-state. Economically, the constraints of global finance have three positive effects. First, although states must abdicate certain responsibilities, such as the ownership of corporations and the ability to manipulate the trade-off between inflation and unemployment, most countries were never particularly successful at these tasks to begin with. Government ownership of firms rarely provides the best management, and the inflation/unemployment trade-off is a temporary expedient that breaks down over

449

the long run. In the language of business, shedding these functions empowers states to focus on their core competencies.[7]

Second, rather than the inevitable race to the bottom, globalization can encourage states to coordinate their regulatory policies. The European Union added a social chapter that even Great Britain might join.[8] The North American Free Trade Agreement (NAFTA) imposed more stringent labor and environmental conditions for Mexico. Globally, the Montreal Protocol moved toward the ban of chlorofluorocarbons. Since 1990, the United Nations (UN) has been much more willing to impose multilateral economic sanctions for violations of international norms.[9] States clearly retain the option of interventionist policies in some areas of economic life. Although enforcement is a problem with some of these policies, it is not an insurmountable one. And although coordination can lead to reduced state powers, it can also lead to an enhanced state role (Cohen 1996).

Finally, the increased mobility of capital forces the nation-state to focus on the location of innovation rather than production. This benefits both the state and society. Economists agree that the greatest source of economic growth is technological change (Denison 1974; Abramovitz 1989; Boskin and Lau 1992). A renewed focus on innovation can only expand the economic pie for society. Furthermore, economists also agree that the state can and should play a role in fostering technological innovation. States are assigned tasks, such as the provision of public goods and the establishment of the necessary rules and institutions, that cannot be easily replicated by other actors. Economically, the globalization of markets implies the redirection, not the elimination, of the nation-state's role.

The state's political role also remains. The renaissance of cultural and ethnic identities might spell doom for some nation-states, but not for the nation-state in general. There is a sense in some of these books that ethnic and cultural conflict are the inevitable result of ancient hatreds. In fact, recent work suggests that governments successfully manipulate these ethnic identities to enhance their own power (Gagnon 1995; Chege 1996). Regretfully, this often implies war and bloodshed, but it also shows that states still provide people with their strongest identities. Sometimes this can take relatively benign forms, as in France or the United States. Sometimes, as in Rwanda, it leads to genocide. Furthermore, many ethnic conflicts are not over cultural disagreements, but rather over who controls the machinery of the state. Breakaway groups do not want to abolish the nation-state; they want their own.[10]

The nation-state is not a hostage to ancient hatreds; one of its political roles is to manipulate these identities, and one can hope to direct them toward peaceable ends.

Globalization and its ripple effects do create new constraints for the nation-state. In part, the adaptability of national governments to their new roles explains the varying fortunes of nation-states in this decade. Paradoxically, at the same time as globalizers are claiming the end of the Westphalian system, the United States has increased its relative power and influence. It has strengthened its lead in the military applications of information technologies (Nye and Owens 1996). It has been more willing to use economic statecraft as a policy tool. Beyond its ability to project coercive power, the United States has also increased its co-optive or "soft" power, because the economic changes caused by globalization mirror the preferences of U.S. society and ideology (Nye 1990). Even the collapse of several developing-world states hints at the strength of the great powers. These states collapsed in part because the United States and other former colonizers declined to intervene to prop up failing regimes. The great powers are still capable of performing this function when they choose, as in Haiti and Albania, but the end of the Cold War removed the incentive to intervene everywhere.

Finally, each author makes the mistake of assuming that state sovereignty is an absolute and indivisible commodity. Stephen D. Krasner (1995) notes that the violations of sovereignty that have been observed recently are nothing new; since its inception, the Westphalian norm of absolute state sovereignty has been consistently violated by other states. Even if the nation-state is weakening in the face of global forces, it still has a few centuries of life remaining. Its death is likely to be as slow as its birth.

Social Science and Policymaking

The final connection between the books reviewed here and Marxist philosophy is a disturbing one. Marx scorned the social philosophies of the nineteenth century, arguing that the point was not to explain the world but to change it. The result was a theory that could never be disproven; Marx's successors made amendments to explain away failures, all the while focusing on political change. What is striking about these five authors' books is the varying degrees of scorn they heap on modern social science—and, like Marx's successors, the fact that they use grand theories as a vehicle for radical policy proposals.

The disregard for political science is particularly noticeable in Kaplan and Barber. Kaplan, for example, argues,

A political scientist can do little more than what a journalist does: Go to places where there appear to be interesting linkages . . . and see if the causal relationships exist. From this, some useful ideas or theories might emerge. To call it a science, though, is an overstatement. (p. 413)

Barber comes to a similar conclusion:

The data are too protean to be definitive and the events too vulnerable to distortion by the very probes that effect to explain them to be detachable from the normative frames by which we try to capture them. This is the general problem with pretending that social and political theory can be "scientific." (p. 168)

The other authors are somewhat more generous about the utility of political science, but they reject the accepted theories of international relations as outdated and sterile.

It is a rite of passage for Washington policymakers to bash academics for their scientific pretensions and abstract theorizing. There is certainly enough bad political science to justify it. Nevertheless, it is a dangerous tactic, because it tarnishes a singularly useful purpose of social scientists vis-à-vis policymakers: the role of the critic. Politicians have the incentive to use dubious theories when they are politically expedient (Blinder 1987). Academics test arguments for their theoretical and empirical rigor to filter out those that may be emotionally appealing but wrong. This is useful to policymakers, because it tells them which theories should be ignored and which merit further attention. Scholarly criticism can make a difference. For example, Paul Krugman (1995) has performed an exemplary service in debunking theories of pop internationalism. One wonders whether the accusations against social science made in these books are not self-inoculations against academic criticisms down the line.

Why have so many grand theories been put forward? I would argue that it is a nostalgic, anachronistic search for an American grand strategy. One of the virtues of the Cold War was that the United States had an overarching framework of containment that dictated most of its foreign policy and some of its domestic policies. Many in the policy community look at the frequent chaos of U.S. foreign policy today and conclude that we need a new universal framework. All of these books attempt to provide it, but globalization is

not the constraint on U.S. policy that Soviet power was during the era of bipolarity. Accepting this false analogy would lead to an artificial reduction of U.S. policy options.

Conclusion

These books agree with each other on at least four points. First, the nation-state is losing its influence in world politics. Second, this weakening is caused either directly or indirectly by global market forces. Some argue, akin to Marx, that economic forces directly affect the nation-state by constraining its economic functions and creating a homogeneous global culture that weakens nationalist sentiments. Others argue that economic forces are indirectly responsible, because they generate a cultural backlash that re-ignites older identities not associated with the nation-state. Third, these effects are global; they are not confined to the developed or developing world. Fourth, conventional social science cannot explain these changes.

These arguments challenge conventional paradigms and are genuinely thought-provoking. In the end, however, they are not more persuasive than the original Marxist argument. Whereas much of the description is accurate, it does not imply an erosion of the nation-state's authority, but rather a redefinition of its role in the international system. As a guide for the modern-day constraints on the nation-state, the globalization thesis can serve a useful purpose. Yet, the nation-state has faced constraints since Westphalia, and it has not withered away; some trends these authors mention empower rather than weaken states. As a framework for policy advice, or a map of the future, the globalization thesis leaves a great deal to be desired.

I am grateful to Page Fortna, Mark Lawrence, Timothy Snyder, Jeff Legro, Mary Elise Sarotte, Tim Snyder, and especially James McAllister for their advice. Any errors are my own.

References

Moses Abramovitz, *Thinking About Growth and Other Essays of Economic Growth and Welfare* (Cambridge: Cambridge University Press, 1989).

Alan Blinder, *Hard Heads, Soft Hearts: Tough-Minded Economics for a Just Society* (Reading, Mass.: Addison-Wesley, 1987).

Michael Boskin and Laurence Lau, "Capital, Technology, and Economic Growth," in Nathan Rosenberg, Ralph Landau, and David Mowery, eds., *Technology and the Wealth of Nations* (Stanford: Stanford University Press, 1992).

Edward Hallett Carr, *Nationalism and After* (New York: MacMillan, 1945).

Michael Chege, "Africa's Murderous Professors," *National Interest* 46 (Winter 1996), pp. 32–40.

Benjamin J. Cohen, "Phoenix Risen: The Resurrection of Global Finance," *World Politics* 48 (January 1996), pp. 268–296.

Edward Denison, *Accounting for U.S. Economic Growth, 1929–1969* (Washington, D.C.: The Brookings Institution, 1974).

Richard Falk, "State of Siege: Will Globalization Win Out?" *International Affairs* 73 (January 1997), pp. 123–136.

V. P. Gagnon, "Ethnic Nationalism and International Conflict: The Case of Serbia," *International Security* 19 (Winter 1995), pp. 130–166.

Geoffrey Garrett, "Capital Mobility, Trade, and the Domestic Politics of Economic Policy," *International Organization* 49 (Autumn 1995), pp. 657–688.

Avner Greif, Paul Milgrom, and Barry Weingast, "Coordination, Commitment, and Enforcement: The Case of the Merchant Guild," *Journal of Political Economy* 102 (December 1994), pp. 745–776.

Mark Hallenberg, "Tax Competition in Wilhelmine Germany and Its Implications for the European Union," *World Politics* (April 1996), pp. 324–357.

Thomas Homer-Dixon, "On the Threshold: Environmental Changes as Causes of Acute Conflict," *International Security* 16 (Fall 1991), pp. 76–116.

Robert Jackson, *Quasi-States: Sovereignty, International Relations, and the Third World* (New York; Cambridge University Press, 1990).

Peter Katzenstein, *Small States in World Markets* (Ithaca, N.J.: Cornell University Press, 1985).

Stephen D. Krasner, "Compromising Westphalia," *International Security* 20 (Winter 1995), pp. 115–151.

Paul Krugman, *Pop Internationalism* (Cambridge, Mass.: MIT Press, 1995).

Joseph Nye and William Owens, "America's Information Edge," *Foreign Affairs* 75 (March/April 1996), pp. 20–36.

Mancur Olson, *The Rise and Decline of Nations* (New Haven, Conn.: Yale University Press, 1982).

Thomas Peters and Robert Waterman Jr., *In Search of Excellence: Lessons from America's Best-Run Companies* (New York: Harper and Row, 1982).

Robert Putnam, *Making Democracy Work: Civic Traditions in Modern Italy* (Princeton, N.J.: Princeton University Press, 1993).

Dani Rodrik, *Has Globalization Gone Too Far?* (Washington, D.C.: Institute for International Economics, 1997).

AnnaLee Saxenian, "The Cheshire Cat's Grin: Innovation, Regional Development, and the Cambridge Case," *Economy and Society* 18 (November 1989), pp. 448–477.

Susan Strange, "States, Firms, and Diplomacy," *International Affairs* 68 (January 1992), pp. 1–15.

Robert C. Tucker, ed., *The Marx-Engels Reader* (New York: W. W. Norton, 1978).

Notes

1. This has been observed elsewhere. Falk (1997) notes, "In paradoxical fashion, the Marxist account of the relation between economic and political power seems persuasive only after Marxism has lost its capacity to win adherents to its world view." (p. 135)

2. Fukuyama's tone in *The End of History and the Last Man* is more somber than in his original essay. In his final chapters, he warns that if capitalism leads to the erosion of civil society, individuals will resort to violence to express their thymotic urges. Yet, this warning contradicts his earlier claim that the end of history is the victory of the rational over the thymotic part of the human soul.

3. Another example of this error is Peters and Waterman (1982).

4. For example, his description of Ukraine on pp. 199–200 is badly off; its first president was not "lethally nationalist" and its current one does not have a pro-Russian tilt. Barber clearly derived these characterizations from the 1994 presidential election between Leonid Kuchma and Leonid Kravchuk, but he fails to separate campaign rhetoric from actual policies of either leader.

5. Quoted in Hallenberg (1996), p. 336.

6. Quoted in Cohen (1996), p. 294.

7. I do not want to imply a Panglossian view on globalization's constraints on the state. In the future, it is questionable whether the nation-state will be able to ameliorate the distributional conflicts caused by globalization. Rodrik (1997) provides an excellent account of how globalization can impair the state's ability to fulfill these tasks. Yet, Rodrik also concedes that the state might not be the institution best suited for this task.

8. See Rodrik (1997) for a more pessimistic appraisal of the European Union social chapter.

9. The Security Council has mandated economic sanctions seven times since 1990, as opposed to twice during the UN's first 45 years of existence.

10. The case of Moldova is instructive. Prior to World War II, Moldova was historically part of Romania. Annexed by the Soviet Union in 1945, the alphabet was changed from Roman to Cyrillic, and the republic's language was called Moldavian rather than Romanian. After the break-up, there was a push in Moldova to reunite with Romania. In the end, however, Moldova's leaders decided they did not want to relinquish political power, and therefore spurned any integration with Romania. Even though this state has little history independent of Romania, it survives.

Post–Lawrence–Weber:
Business and Society,
Ninth Edition

Glossary

© The McGraw–Hill
Companies, 1999

Glossary

This glossary defines technical or special terms and may be used by students as a quick and handy reference for terms that may be unfamiliar without having to refer to the specific material(s) where they are used. It also can be a very helpful aid in studying for examinations and for writing term papers where precise meanings are needed.

Acid rain. Rain that is more acidic than normal; occurs when emissions of sulfur dioxide and nitrogen oxides from utilities, manufacturers, and vehicles combine with water vapor in the air.

Acquisition. (see **Corporate merger.**)

Administrative costs. The direct costs incurred in running government regulatory agencies, including salaries of employees, equipment, supplies, and other such items. (See also **Compliance costs.**)

Administrative learning. A stage in the development of corporate social responsiveness during which managers and supervisors learn new practices necessary for coping with social problems and pressures.

Advocacy advertising. A strategy used by companies to promote their social, political, or economic viewpoint through the media.

Affirmative action. A positive and sustained effort by an organization to identify, hire, train if necessary, and promote minorities, women, and members of other groups who are underrepresented in the organization's workforce.

Air pollution. When more pollutants, such as sulfur dioxide or particulates, are emitted into the atmosphere than can be safely absorbed and diluted by natural processes.

Altruism. Acting for the benefit of others at the risk of sacrificing one's self-interest.

American dream. An ideal goal or vision of life in the United States, usually including material abundance and maximum freedom.

Annual meeting. A yearly meeting called by a corporation's board of directors for purposes of reporting to the company's stockholders on the current status and future prospects of the firm.

Anticompetitive merger. A merger of two or more companies that reduces or eliminates competition in an industry or region; usually illegal under U.S. antitrust laws.

Antitrust laws. Laws that promote competition or that oppose trusts, monopolies, or other business combinations that restrain trade.

Arbitration. A method for resolving a dispute between two parties, such as between a business firm and a consumer. In arbitration, a neutral third party, called an arbitrator, hears both sides of the dispute and then makes a final binding decision.

Biodiversity. The variety of living organisms and the range of their genetic makeup.

Biometrics. A field of knowledge that integrates knowledge from biological science and computer science to identify living organisms by identifying their unique genetic patterns.

Biotechnology. The use and combination of various sciences, including biochemistry, genetics, microbiology, ecology, recombinant DNA, and others, to invent and develop new and modified life forms for applications in medicine, industry, farming, and other areas of human life.

Blowing the whistle. (See **Whistle-blowing.**)

Board of directors. A group of persons elected by shareholder votes to be responsible for directing the affairs of a corporation, establishing company objectives and policies, selecting top-level managers, and reviewing company performance.

Bottom line. Business profits or losses, usually reported in figures on the last or bottom line of a company's income statement.

Business. The activity or organizing resources in order to produce and distribute goods and services for society.

Business and society. The study of the relationship of business with its entire social environment.

Business ethics. The application of general ethical ideas to business behavior.

Post–Lawrence–Weber:
Business and Society,
Ninth Edition

Glossary

© The McGraw–Hill
Companies, 1999

Business legitimacy principle. The view that a company must comply with the law and conform to the expectations of its stakeholders in order to be a corporate citizen in good standing.

Carrying capacity. The maximum population that an ecosystem can support. (See also **Limits to growth hypothesis.**)

Cause marketing. A form of philanthropy in which contributions to a nonprofit organization are tied to the use of the donor organization's products or services by the recipient organization's members.

Central state control. A socioeconomic system in which political, social, and economic power is concentrated in a central government that makes all fundamental policy decision for the society.

CERES Principles. A corporate code of conduct, developed by the Coalition for Environmentally Responsible Economies (CERES), that commits signers to sound environmental policies and sustainable use of natural resources. (Formerly known as the Valdez Principles.)

Charity principle. The idea that individuals and business firms should give voluntary aid and support to society's unfortunate or needy persons, as well as to other (nonprofit) organizations that provide community services.

Child care. The care or supervision of another's child, such as at a day-care center; offered as a benefit by some employers to working parents.

Chlorofluorocarbons (CFCs). Manufactured chemicals, used as refrigerants, insulation, solvents, and propellants in spray cans, that are believed to react with and deplete ozone in the upper atmosphere. (See also **Montreal Protocol, Ozone.**)

Cloning. The process of genetically creating an identical cell or organism.

Coalitions. Groups of organizations or corporate stakeholders who work together to achieve a common goal.

Codetermination. A system of corporate governance providing for labor representation on a company's board of directors.

Collaborative partnerships. Companies joining with their key stakeholders to respond better to an important issue or problem by pooling resources.

Command and control regulation. A regulatory approach where the government "commands" companies to meet specific standards (such as amounts of particular pollutants) and "controls" the methods (such as technology) used to achieve these standards. This approach is often contrasted with market-based regulatory approaches where the government establishes general goals and allows companies to use the most cost-effective methods possible to achieve them.

Commercial piracy. The wrongful use of intellectual property, such as software, musical recordings, or clothing designs, for commercial gain.

Commons. Traditionally, an area of land on which all citizens could graze their animals without limitation. The term now refers to any shared resource, such as land, air, or water, that a group of people use collectively. (See also **Global commons.**)

Community. A company's area of local business influence. This includes the people and other stakeholder residing near a business operation.

Community advisory panels (CAPs). Groups of citizens from a local community who meet with corporate officials to discuss issues of common interest about a company's operations, such as plant safety, traffic patterns, and emergency planning.

Community relations. The involvement of business with the communities in which it conducts operations.

Comparable worth. The idea that different kinds of jobs can be equated with each other in terms of difficulty, training required, skills involved, effort made, responsibility involved, and working conditions, for the purpose of equalizing wages paid to people holding jobs approximately equal in these ways.

Competition. A struggle to survive and excel. In business, different firms compete with one another for customers' dollars.

Competition policies. A term used to describe antitrust laws or policies in some nations and trading groups.

Compliance costs. The costs incurred by business and other organizations in complying with government regulations, such as the cost of pollution control machinery or the disposal of toxic chemical wastes. (See also **Administrative costs.**)

Comprehensive Environmental Response, Compensation, and Liability Act (CERCLA). (See **Superfund.**)

Computer hackers. Individuals who break into company databases or other secure information banks to steal and delete information or cause confusion for those trying to use the information.

Concentration (corporate, economic, industrial, market). When relatively few companies are responsible for a large proportion of economic activity, production, or sales.

Post–Lawrence–Weber:
Business and Society,
Ninth Edition

Glossary

© The McGraw–Hill
Companies, 1999

Conglomerate merger. The combination, or joining together, of two or more companies in unrelated industries into a single company. (See also **Horizontal merger, Vertical merger.**)

Consumer bill of rights. Four rights of consumers outlined in a well-known speech by President John F. Kennedy. The four consumer rights Kennedy discussed were the right to safety, the right to be informed, the right to choose, and the right to be heard.

Consumer hot-lines. A telephone line or interactive Web site providing consumers with direct access to a company.

Consumer movement. A social movement that seeks to augment the rights and powers of consumers. (Also known as *consumerism.*)

Consumer protection laws. Laws that provide consumers with better information, protect consumers from possible hazards, or encourage competitive pricing.

Consumer rights. The legitimate claims of consumers to safe products and services, adequate information, free choice, a fair hearing, and competitive prices.

Consumerism. (See **Consumer movement.**)

Corporate crime. Illegal behavior by company employees that benefits a corporation.

Corporate culture. The traditions, customs, values, and approved ways of behaving that prevail in a corporation.

Corporate giving. (See **Corporate philanthropy.**)

Corporate governance. Any structured system of allocating power in a corporation that determines how and by whom the company is to be governed.

Corporate legitimacy. Public acceptance of the corporation as an institution that contributes to society's well-being.

Corporate merger. The combination, or joining together, of two or more separate companies into a single company. (See also **Conglomerate merger, Horizontal merger, Vertical merger.**)

Corporate philanthropy. Gifts and contributions made by corporations, usually from pretax profits, to benefit various types of nonprofit community organizations.

Corporate political agency theory. A theory that holds that politicians are the agents of those who elect or appoint them to office.

Corporate political strategy. Those activities taken by organizations to acquire, develop, and use power to achieve a political advantage or gain.

Corporate power. The strength or capability of corporations to influence government, the economy, and society, based on their organizational resources and size.

Corporate restructuring. The reorganization of a corporation's business units and activities, which often involves the closing of current facilities and reduction of workforce.

Corporate social involvement. The interaction of business corporations with society.

Corporate social policy. A policy or a group of policies in a corporation that define the company's purposes, goals, and programs regarding one or more social issues or problems.

Corporate social responsibility. The idea that businesses are accountable for the effects of their actions and should seek socially beneficial results as well as economically beneficial results.

Corporate social responsiveness. The way firms address social demands initiated by their stakeholders, or actions taken by firms that affect their stakeholders.

Corporate social strategy. The social, political, and ethical parts of a company's plans and activities for achieving its goals and purposes.

Corporate stakeholder. A person or group affected by a corporation's policies and actions.

Corporate strategic management. Planning, directing, and managing a corporation for the purpose of helping it achieve its basic purposes and long-term goals.

Corporate strategic planning. A process of formulating a corporation's basic purpose, long-term goals, and programs intended to achieve the company's purposes and goals.

Corporate takeover. The acquisition, usually by merger, of one corporation by another.

Corporate volunteerism. A program wherein a company engages its employees in community service as a way to improve the company's image as well as serve the communities in which the business operates.

Corporation. Legally, an artificial legal "person," created under the laws of a particular state or nation. Socially and organizationally, it is a complex system of people, technology, and resources generally devoted to carrying out a central economic mission as it interacts with a surrounding social and political environment.

Cost-benefit analysis. A systematic method of calculating the costs and benefits of a project or activity that is intended to produce benefits.

Post–Lawrence–Weber:
Business and Society,
Ninth Edition

Glossary

© The McGraw–Hill
Companies, 1999

Council of Institutional Investors. An organization founded in 1985 that represents the interests of institutional investors.

Crisis management. The use of a special team to help a company cope with an unusual emergency situation that may threaten the company in serious ways.

Cross-media pollution. Pollution that migrates across several different media, such as air, land, or water. For example, hazardous wastes disposed in a dump might leak out, contaminating groundwater, or evaporate, causing air pollution. (Also known as *multimedia pollution.*)

Culpability score. Under the U.S. Corporate Sentencing Guidelines, the degree of blame assigned to an executive found guilty of criminal wrongdoing.

Cultural distance. The amount of difference in customs, attitudes, and values between two social systems.

Cultural shock. A person's disorientation and insecurity caused by the strangeness of a different culture.

Cyberspace. A virtual location where information is stored, ideas are described, and communication takes place in and through an electronic network of linked systems.

Deceptive advertising. An advertisement that is deceptive or misleading; generally illegal under U.S. law.

Defense industry conversion. The process of transforming businesses that once specialized in military production into businesses capable of producing goods and services for civilian or nonmilitary use.

Delaney Clause. An amendment to the Food, Drug, and Cosmetics Act of 1958 that banned all food additives known to cause cancer in humans or animals; repealed in 1996.

Deregulation. The removal of scaling down of regulatory authority and regulatory activities of government.

Design for disassembly. Designing products so that they can be disassembled, and their component parts recycled or reused at the end of their useful life.

Directors. (See **Board of directors.**)

Discrimination (in jobs or employment). Unequal treatment of employees based on *non–job-related* factors such as race, sex, age, national origin, religion, color, and physical or mental handicap.

Diversity (global and cultural). A concept that describes an organization or community composed of people of many racial, cultural, ethnic, religious, and other distinguishing characteristics.

Divestment. Withdrawing and shifting to other uses the funds that a person or group has invested in the securities (stocks, bonds, notes, etc.) of a company. Investors sometimes have divested the securities of companies doing business in countries accused of human rights abuses.

Dividend. A return-on-investment payment made to the owners of shares of corporate stock at the discretion of the company's board of directors.

Downsizing. The reduction of a company's workforce; often part of a corporate restructuring program designed to reduce costs.

Earth Summit. An international conference sponsored by the United Nations in Brazil in 1992 that produced several treaties on global environmental issues. (Also known as the *Conference on Environment and Development.*)

Eco-efficiency. Occurs when businesses or societies are simultaneously economically efficient and environmentally responsible.

Ecologically sustainable organization (ESO). A business that operates in a way that is consistent with the principle of sustainable development. (See also **Sustainable development.**)

Ecology. The study, and the process, of how living things—plants and animals—interact with one another and with their environment.

Ecosystem. Plants and animals in their natural environment, living together as an interdependent system.

Egoist. (See **Ethical egoist.**)

Elder care. The care or supervision of elderly persons; offered as a benefit by some employers to working children of elderly parents.

Electoral politics. Political activities undertaken by business and other interest groups to influence the outcome of elections to public office.

Emissions charges or fees. Fees charged to business by the government, based on the amount of pollution emitted.

Employee stock ownership plan (ESOP). A benefit plan in which a company purchases shares of its own stock and places them in trust for its employees.

Employment-at-will. The principle that workers are hired and retained solely at the discretion of the employer.

Post–Lawrence–Weber:
Business and Society,
Ninth Edition

Glossary

© The McGraw–Hill
Companies, 1999

Encryption. A type of software that scrambles e-mails and files, preventing eavesdroppers from seeing information sent across the Internet and stored in databases.

Enlightened self-interest. The view that social responsiveness and long-run economic return are compatible and are in the interest of business.

Entitlement mentality. A view that a person or group is guaranteed an economic or social benefit by virtue of being a member of the designated group. (See also **Right [human].**)

Environmental audit. A company audit, or review, of its progress toward meeting environmental goals, such as pollution prevention.

Environmental justice. A movement to prevent unfair or inequitable exposure to environmental risk, such as from exposure to hazardous chemicals; or a situation where exposure to such risk is fair and equitable.

Environmental labeling. When government agencies or private organizations label products or packaging judged to be environmentally acceptable.

Environmental partnership. A voluntary, collaborative partnership between or among businesses, government regulators, and environmental organizations to achieve specific environmental goals.

Environmental Protection Agency (EPA). The United States federal government agency responsible for most environmental regulation and enforcement.

Environmental scanning. Examining an organization's environment to discover trends and forces that could have an impact on the organization.

Environmental standards. Standard amounts of particular pollutants allowable by law.

Equal-access rule. A legal provision that requires television stations to allow all competing candidates for political office to broadcast their political messages if one of the candidates' views are broadcast.

Equal job opportunity. The principal that all persons otherwise qualified should be treated equally with respect to job opportunities, workplace conditions, pay, fringe benefits, and retirement provisions.

Ergonomics. Adapting work tasks, working conditions, and equipment to minimize worker injury or stress.

Ethical climate. The prevailing, often unspoken ethical attitudes and beliefs of an organization that tend to guide the behavior of organization members when confronted with an ethical dilemma.

Ethical egoist. A person who puts his or her own selfish interests above all other considerations, while ignoring or denying the ethical needs and beliefs of others.

Ethical relativism. A belief that ethical right and wrong are defined by various periods of time in history, a society's traditions, the specific circumstances of the moment, or personal opinion.

Ethics. A conception of right and wrong conduct, serving as a guide to moral behavior.

Ethics audit. A systematic effort to discover actual or potential unethical behavior in an organization.

Ethics code. A written statement that describes the general value system and ethical rules of an organization.

Ethics committee. A high-level group of executives who provide ethical guidance for employees and are often empowered to investigate and punish ethical wrongdoing at the firm.

Ethnocentric business. A company whose business standards are based on its home nation's customs, markets, and laws.

Ethnocentric perspective. The view that a company is an extension of its home country and owes its loyalty to the home country.

European Union (EU). The political and economic coalition of European countries.

Executive compensation. The compensation (total pay) of corporate executives, including salary, bonus, stock options, and various benefits.

Export of jobs. A loss of jobs in a business firm's home nation, and a creation of new jobs in a foreign nation, caused by relocating part or all of the business firm's operations (and jobs) to the foreign nation.

Expropriation. (See **Nationalization.**)

Family-friendly corporation. A company that removes sex discrimination from all aspects of its operations and that supports both men and women in their efforts to balance work and family responsibilities.

Family leave. A leave of absence from work, either paid or unpaid, for the purpose of caring for a family member.

Fiduciary responsibility or duty. A legal obligation to carry out a duty to some other person or group in order to protect their interest.

Fiscal policy. The patterns of spending and taxation adopted by a government.

Flextime. A plan that allows employees limited control over scheduling their own hours of work, usually at the beginning and end of the workday.

Foreign direct investment (FDI). The investment and transfer of funds by investors in one nation into business activities or organizations located in another nation.

Foreign investment review board. A national government body that is empowered to review and approve or disapprove proposed investments by foreign owners in a nation.

Fraud. Deceit or trickery due to the pursuit of economic gain or competitive advantage.

Free enterprise ideology. A set of beliefs about one way to organize economic life that includes individualism, freedom, private property, profit, equality of opportunity, competition, the work ethic, and a limited government.

Free enterprise system. A socioeconomic system based on private ownership, profit-seeking business firms, and the principle of free markets.

Free market. A model of an economic system based on voluntary and free exchange among buyers and sellers. Competition regulates prices in all free market exchanges.

Functional-area ethics. The ethical problems that typically occur in the various specialized operational areas of business, such as accounting, marketing, and finance.

Functional regulation. Regulations aimed at a particular function or operation of business, such as competition or labor relations.

Future shock. A human reaction to rapid technological change whereby individuals experience difficulty in coping with new conditions of life brought on by new technology.

Gender pay gap. The difference in the average level of wages, salaries, and income received by men and women.

Genetic engineering. (See **Biotechnology.**)

Geocentric business. A company whose business standards and policies are worldwide in outlook including multinational ownership, management, markets, and operations.

Geocentric perspective. The view that businesses are global citizens that should behave and respect the laws and culture of every country in which they do business.

Glasnost. A Russian term used to describe "openness" during the late 1980s and early 1990s when the Soviet Union began to collapse as a political entity.

Glass ceiling. A barrier to the advancement of women, minorities, and other groups in the workplace.

Glass wall. A barrier to the lateral mobility of women, minorities, and other groups in the workplace, such as from human resources to operations.

Global commons. The idea that certain types of natural resources, such as the earth's atmosphere, tropical rain forests, and oceans, are vital for all living organisms. (See also **Commons.**)

Global village. The most remote places on earth are linked together—like a single village—through technological advances that allow faster and more widespread communications.

Global warming. The gradual warming of the earth's climate, believed by some scientists to be caused by an increase in carbon dioxide and other trace gases in the earth's atmosphere resulting from human activity, mainly the burning of fossil fuels.

Government and business partnership. A subtype of socioeconomic system in which government and business work cooperatively to solve social problems. (See also **Public-private partnerships.**)

Grassroots politics. Political activity directed at involving and influencing individual citizens or constituents to directly contact government officials on a public policy issue.

Green consumerism. An attitude of consumers that considers the ecological effects of their purchase, use, and disposal of consumer goods and services.

Green management. An outlook by managers that emphasizes the importance of considering ecological factors as management decisions are made.

Green marketing. A concept that describes the creation, promotion, and sale of environmentally safe products and services by business.

Greenhouse effect. The warming effect that occurs when carbon dioxide, methane, nitrous oxides, and other gases act like the glass panels of a greenhouse, preventing heat from the earth's surface from escaping into space.

Greenmail. The practice of paying a premium over the market price of a company's stock as part of a settlement with investors who wish to take over a company.

Hazardous waste. Waste materials from industrial, agricultural, and other activities capable of causing death or serious health problems for those persons exposed for prolonged periods. (See also **Toxic substance.**)

Post–Lawrence–Weber:
Business and Society,
Ninth Edition

Glossary

© The McGraw–Hill
Companies, 1999

Home country. The country in which a multinational corporation has its headquarters.

Horizontal merger. The combination, or joining together, of two or more companies in the same industry and at the same level or stage of production or sales into a single company. (See also **Conglomerate merger, Vertical merger.**)

Host country. A foreign country in which a multinational corporation conducts business.

Human rights code of conduct. An organization's statement regarding acceptable and unacceptable types of behavior with respect to people's rights to life, liberty, and well-being.

Human rights reasoning. (See **Right [human]**.)

Ideology. A set of basic beliefs that define an ideal way of living for an individual, an organization, or a society.

Individualism. A belief that each individual person has an inherent worth and dignity and possesses basic human rights that should be protected by society. Each person is presumed to be a free agent capable of knowing and promoting his or her own self-interest.

Industrial ecology. Designing factories and distribution systems as if they were self-contained ecosystems, such as using waste from one process as raw material for another.

Industrial policy. Government action to encourage the growth and development of specific industries.

Industrial resource base. The minerals, energy sources, water supplies, skilled labor force, and human knowledge necessary for industrial production.

Industrial society. A society in which the building and mechanical processing of material goods dominates work and employs the largest proportion of the labor force.

Industry-specific regulation. Regulations aimed at specific industries, such as telephone service or railroad transportation, involving control of rates charged, customers served, and entry into the industry.

Inflation. Decline in the purchasing power of money.

Information society. The current phase of technology; emphasizes the use and transfer of knowledge and information.

Insider trading. The illegal practice of buying or selling shares of corporate securities based on fiduciary information which is known only to a small group of persons, such as executives and their friends ("insiders"), and which enables them to make profits at the expense of other investors who do not have access to the inside information.

Institutional investor. A financial institution, insurance company, pension fund, endowment fund, or similar organization that invests its accumulated funds in the securities offered for sale on stock exchanges.

Institutionalized activity (ethics, social responsiveness, public affairs, etc.). An activity, operation, or procedure that is such an integral part of an organization that it is performed routinely by managers and employees. (See also **Organizational commitment.**)

Intellectual property. Ideas, concepts, and other symbolic creations of human intelligence that are recognized and protected under a nation's copyright, patent, and trademark laws.

Interactive model of business and society. The combined primary and secondary interactions that business has with society.

Interactive system. The closely intertwined relationships between business and society.

Intergenerational equity. A term describing the unfairness of one generation's accumulation of debt and tax burdens that will have to be borne by future generations.

Interlocking directorate. A relationship between two corporations that is established when one person serves as a member of the board of directors of both corporations simultaneously.

International regulation. A form of regulation in which more than one nation agrees to establish and enforce the same rules of conduct for international business activities.

Internet (or World Wide Web). A conduit of information systems revolutionizing how business is conducted, students learn, and households operate.

Intranet. Private or limited information network systems cordoned off from public access by software programs called firewalls.

Iron law of responsibility. The belief that those companies who, in the long run, do not use their power in ways that society deems responsible, will tend to lose their power.

Issues management. The systematic method of identification, analysis, priority setting, and response to public issues.

Justice. A mode of ethical reasoning that calls for the fair distribution of benefits and burdens among the people in a society, according to some agreed-upon rule.

Post-Lawrence-Weber:
Business and Society,
Ninth Edition

Glossary

© The McGraw-Hill
Companies, 1999

Knowledge economy. An economy in which new knowledge, in its many forms, is reshaping and transforming old industries and creating new ones.

Labor force participation rate. The proportion of a particular group, such as women, in the paid workforce.

Labor standards. Conditions affecting a company's employees or the employees of its suppliers or subcontractors.

Laissez faire. A french phrase meaning "to let alone," used to describe an economic system where government intervention is minimal.

Laws. A society's formally codified principles that help define right and wrong behavior.

Leveraged buyouts (LBOs). The acquisition of a corporation by a group of investors, often including top executives, that relies on debt financing to pay the purchase price. The value of the company's assets is used as a "lever" to borrow the necessary amount for the purchase.

Life-cycle analysis. Collecting information on the life-long environmental impact of a product in order to minimize its adverse impacts at all stages, including design, manufacture, use, and disposal.

Limits to growth hypothesis. The idea that human society is now exceeding the carrying capacity of the earth's ecosystem and that unless corrective action is taken soon, catastrophic consequences will result. (See also **Carrying capacity.**)

Lobbying. The act of trying to directly shape or influence a government official's understanding and position on a public policy issue.

Market failure. Inability of the marketplace to properly allocate costs to the parties responsible (e.g., of air pollution emissions) or to achieve the benefits associated with free market economics.

Megacorporation. One of the very largest business corporations.

Merger. (See **Corporate merger.**)

Microenvironment of business. The interrelated social, economic, political, and technological segments of society that influence and are affected by a company's actions.

Militarized nondemocratic systems. A socioeconomic system that resembles mixed private and public enterprise, in which the coercive power of the military supports the government.

Mixed state and private enterprise. A socioeconomic system in which government owns some key industrial and financial enterprises but most businesses are owned and operated by private individuals and corporations.

Monetary policy. Government actions to control the supply and demand of money in the economy.

Montreal Protocol. An international treaty limiting the manufacture and use of chlorofluorocarbons and other ozone-depleting chemicals. (See also **Chlorofluorocarbons, Ozone.**)

Moral development stages. A series of progressive steps by which a person learns new ways of reasoning about ethical and moral issues.

Morality. A condition in which the most fundamental human values are preserved and allowed to shape human thought and action.

Most favored nation (MFN). The foreign policy term used to describe any nation with whom the United States has a relationship that is designed to encourage trade by minimizing trade barriers.

Multimedia pollution. (See **Cross-media pollution.**)

Multinational corporation. A company that conducts business in two or more nations, usually employing citizens of various nationalities.

National competitiveness. The ability of a nation to compete effectively with other nations in international markets through the actions of its privately and publicly owned business firms.

National sovereignty principle. A nation is a sovereign state whose laws, customs, and regulations must be respected by people, organizations, and other nations.

Nationalization. Government taking ownership and control of private property with or without compensation. (Also known as *expropriation*.)

New social contract. An evolving view of how a corporation and its stakeholders should act toward one another in light of modern economic and social changes. (See also **Social contract.**)

New World Order. The phrase used to describe relationships among nations following the end of the cold war in the late 1980s.

Nonpoint source. A source of water or air pollution that cannot be easily identified, such as the source of toxic runoff from urban storm drains. (See also **Point source.**)

Nonrenewable resources. Natural resources, such as oil, coal, or natural gas, that once used are gone forever. (See also **Renewable resources.**)

460

Post–Lawrence–Weber:
Business and Society,
Ninth Edition

Glossary

© The McGraw-Hill
Companies, 1999

Occupational crime. Illegal activity by a business employee intended to enrich the employee at the expense of the company.

Occupational segregation. The practice of employing predominantly men or women in a particular job category.

Opportunity costs. The various opportunities that cannot be realized because money is spent for one purpose rather than for others.

Organization commitment. A stage in the development of social responsiveness within a company when social responses have become a normal part of doing business. Therefore, the entire organization is committed to socially responsible actions and policies. (See also **Institutionalized activity.**)

Ozone. A gas composed of three bonded oxygen atoms. Ozone in the lower atmosphere is a dangerous component of urban smog; ozone in the upper atmosphere provides a shield against ultraviolet light from the sun. (See also **Chlorofluorocarbons, Montreal Protocol.**)

Parental leave. A leave of absence from work, either paid or unpaid, for the purpose of caring for a newborn or adopted child.

Paternalistic. Caring for others in need, as a father cares for a child.

Patriarchal society. A society in which men hold the dominant positions in organizations, the society's values reflect and reinforce male-oriented privileges, and women tend to hold subordinate positions.

Perestroika. A Russian term used to describe economic reform and reconstruction during the late 1980s and early 1990s when the Soviet Union began to collapse as a political entity.

Performance-expectations gap. The perceived distance between a corporation's actual performance and the performance that is expected by the corporation's stakeholders.

Perpetual political campaign. The continuous process of raising money, communicating with constituents, and running for reelection.

Philanthropy. (See **Corporate philanthropy.**)

Plant closing laws. Legislation that requires employers to notify employees in advance of the closing of a facility in order to allow time for adjustment, including negotiations to keep the plant open, to arrange an employee buyout, to find new jobs, and so forth.

Pluralism. A society in which numerous economic, political, educational, social, cultural, religious, and other groups are organized by people to promote their own interests.

Point source. A source of water or air pollution that can be easily identified such as a particular factory. (See also **Nonpoint source.**)

Policy decision. A stage in the public policy process when government authorizes (or fails to authorize) a course of action, such as by passing (or failing to pass) a law, issuing a court opinion, or adopting a new regulation.

Policy evaluation. The final stage in the public policy process when the results of a public policy are judged by those who have an interest in the outcome.

Policy formulation. A stage in the public policy process when interested groups take a position and try to persuade others to adopt that position.

Policy implementation. A stage in the public policy process when action is taken to enforce a public policy decision.

Political action committee (PAC). A committee organized according to election law by any group for the purpose of accepting voluntary contributions from individual donors and then making contributions in behalf of candidates for election to public office.

Political cynicism. A climate of public distrust of politics and politicians.

Polluter pays principle (PPP). A principle that states that a polluter should be responsible for paying for the full costs of its pollution, such as through taxes.

Pollution charge. A fee levied on a polluting source based on the amount of pollution released into the environment.

Pollution prevention. (See **Source reduction.**)

Pollution rights. A legal right to emit a specified amount of pollution; such rights may be bought, sold, or held for future use with approval of government regulators.

Polygraph. An operator-administered instrument used to judge the truth or falsity of a person's statements by measuring physiological changes that tend to be activated by a person's conscience when lying.

Populism. A political philosophy that favors grassroots democracy and an economy based on small businesses and farms, and that opposes big business concentration.

Post–Lawrence–Weber:
Business and Society,
Ninth Edition

Glossary

© The McGraw–Hill
Companies, 1999

Predatory pricing. The practice of selling below cost for the purpose of driving competitors out of business; usually illegal under U.S. antitrust laws.

Preferential hiring. An employment plan that gives preference to minorities, women, and other groups that may be underrepresented in an organization's workforce.

Price-fixing. When two or more companies collude to set—or "fix"—the price of a product or service; usually illegal under U.S. antitrust laws.

Primary interactions or involvement. The direct relationships a company has with those groups that enable it to produce goods and services.

Primary stakeholders. The people and groups who are directly affected by a corporation's economic activities and decisions.

Principle of national sovereignty. The idea that the government of each nation is legally entitled to make laws regarding the behavior of its citizens and citizens of other nations who are acting within the nation.

Priority rule. In ethical analysis, a procedure for ranking in terms of their importance the three ethical modes of reasoning—utilitarian, rights, and justice—before making a decision or taking action.

Privacy. (See **Right of privacy.**)

Private property. A group of rights giving control over physical and intangible assets to private owners. Private ownership is the basic institution of capitalism.

Privately held corporation. A corporation that is privately owned by an individual or a group of individuals; its stock is not available for purchase by the general investing public.

Privatization. The process of converting various economic functions, organizations, and programs from government ownership or government sponsorship to private operation.

Product liability. A legal responsibility of a person or firm for the harmful consequences to others stemming from use of a product manufactured, sold, managed, or employed by the person or firm.

Product recall. An effort by a business firm to remove a defective or sometimes dangerous product from consumer use and from all distribution channels.

Productivity. The relationship between total inputs and total outputs. Productivity increases when the outputs of an organization increase faster than the inputs necessary for production.

Profit maximization. An attempt by a business firm to achieve the highest possible rate of return from its operations.

Profit optimization. An attempt by a business firm to achieve an acceptable (rather than a maximum) rate of return from its operations.

Profits. The revenues of a person or company minus the costs incurred in producing the revenue.

Proxy. A legal instrument giving another person the right to vote the shares of stock of an absentee stockholder.

Proxy statement. A statement sent by a board of directors to a corporation's stockholders announcing the company's annual meeting, containing information about the business to be considered at the meeting, and enclosing a proxy form for stockholders not attending the meeting.

Public affairs function. An organization's activities intended to perceive, monitor, understand, communicate with, and influence the external environment, including local and national communities, government, and public opinion.

Public affairs management. The active management of an organization's external relations with such stakeholders as legislators, government officials, and regulatory agencies.

Public issue. A problem or concern of corporate stakeholders that has the potential to become a politicized matter, leading to legislation, regulation, or other formal governmental action.

Public issue life cycle. The sequence of phases through which a public issue may pass.

Public policy. A plan of action by government to achieve some broad purpose affecting a large segment of the public.

Public policy agenda. All public policy problems or issues that receive the active and serious attention of government officials.

Public policy process. All of the activities and stages involves in developing, carrying out, and evaluating public policies.

Public-private partnerships. Community-based organizations that have a combination of businesses and government agencies collaborating to address important social problems such as crime, homelessness, drugs, economic development, and other community issues. (See also **Government and business partnership.**)

Post-Lawrence-Weber:
Business and Society,
Ninth Edition

Glossary

© The McGraw-Hill
Companies, 1999

Public referendum. A citizen's initiative to place a question or resolution on the election ballot for a popular vote.

Public trustee. A concept that a business owner or manager should base company decisions on the interests of a wide range of corporate stakeholders or members of the general public. In doing so, the business executive acts as a trustee of the public interest. (See also **Stewardship principle.**)

Publicly held corporation. A corporation whose stock is available for purchase by the general investing public.

Questionable payments. Something of value given to a person or firm that raises significant ethical questions of right or wrong in the host nation or other nations.

Quotas (job, hiring, employment). An employment plan based on hiring a specific number or proportion of minorities, women, or other groups who may be underrepresented in an organization's workforce.

Rain forest. Woodlands that receive at least 100 inches of rain a year. They are among the planet's richest areas in terms of biodiversity.

Reengineering. The concept of redesigning work systems and organizations in ways that enhance productivity and efficient work activities.

Regulation. The action of government to establish rules by which industry or other groups must behave in conducting their normal activities.

Reinventing government. A phrase used to describe efforts to reengineer, restructure, and reduce the cost of government.

Relationship investing. When large stockholders, usually institutions, form a long-term committed link with a company.

Renewable resources. Natural resources, such as fresh water or timber, that can be naturally replenished. (See also **Nonrenewable resources.**)

Reregulation. The imposition of regulation on activities that were deregulated earlier.

Reverse discrimination. The unintended negative impact experienced by an individual or group as a result of legal efforts to overcome discrimination against another individual or group.

Right (human). A concept used in ethical reasoning that means that a person or group is entitled to something or is entitled to be treated in a certain way. (See also **Entitlement.**)

Right of privacy. A person's entitlement to protection from invasion of his or her private life by government, business, or other persons.

Rule of cost. The idea that all human actions generate costs.

Secondary interactions or involvement. The relationship a company has with those social and political groups that feel the impact of the company's main activities and take steps to do something about it. These relationships are derived from the firm's primary interactions.

Secondary stakeholders. The people and groups in society who are indirectly affected by a corporation's economic activities and decisions.

Sex-role spillover. When men continue to think of women mainly as performing traditional roles as sex partners, homemakers, and childbearers, rather than as co-workers and qualified professionals.

Sexual division of labor. The traditional or accepted allocation of jobs or roles in a society between men and women.

Sexual harassment. Unwanted and uninvited sexual attention experienced by a person, and/or a workplace that is hostile or threatening in a sexual way.

Shareholder. (See **Stockholder.**)

Shareholder resolution. A proposal made by a stockholder and included in a corporation's notice of its annual meeting that advocates some course of action to be taken by the company

Shareholders' lawsuit. A lawsuit initiated by one or more stockholders to recover damages suffered due to alleged actions of the company's management.

Social accountability. The condition of being held responsible to society or to some public or governmental group for one's actions, often requiring a specific accounting or reporting on those activities.

Social audit. A systematic study and evaluation of an organization's social performance. (See also **Social performance evaluation.**)

Social Charter. Social policy developed by countries in the European Union.

Social contract. An implied understanding between an organization and its stakeholders as to how they will act toward one another. (See also **New social contract.**)

Social forecasting. An attempt to estimate major social and political trends that may affect a company's operations and environment in the future.

Social overhead costs. Public and private investments that are necessary to prepare the environment for effective operation of a new business or other major institutions.

Social performance evaluation. Information about an organization's social performance, often contained in a company's annual report to stockholders and sometimes

Post–Lawrence–Weber:
Business and Society,
Ninth Edition

Glossary

© The McGraw–Hill
Companies, 1999

prepared as a special report to management or the general public. (See also **Social audit.**)

Social regulation. Regulations intended to accomplish certain social improvements such as equal employment opportunity or on-the-job safety and health.

Social responsibility. (See **Corporate social responsibility.**)

Social responsibility shareholder resolution. A resolution on an issue of corporate social responsibility placed before stockholders for a vote at a company's annual meeting, usually by social activist groups.

Social responsiveness. (See **Corporate social responsiveness.**)

Society. The people, institutions, and technology that make up a recognizable human community.

Socioeconomic system. The combined and interrelated social, economic, and political institutions characteristic of a society.

Soft money. Funds donated to a political party to support party-building activities such as televised commercials that do not specify a candidate, get-out-the-vote drives, and opinion polling. Soft money is often criticized as a loophole in the political campaign finance laws.

Solid waste. Any solid waste materials resulting from human activities, such as municipal refuse and sewage, industrial wastes, and agricultural wastes.

Source reduction. A business strategy to prevent or reduce pollution at the source, rather than to dispose of or treat pollution after it has been produced. (Also known as *pollution prevention.*)

Special economic zones. Industrial areas in the People's Republic of China that are reserved for foreign companies to establish business operations.

Specialized learning. A stage in the development of corporate social responsiveness within a company during which managers and supervisors, usually with the help of a specialist, learn the new practices necessary for coping with social problems and pressures.

Stakeholder. (See **Corporate stakeholder.**)

Stakeholder coalitions. Temporary unions of a company's stakeholder groups in order to express a common view or achieve a common purpose on a particular issue.

Stakeholder power. The ability of one or more stakeholders to achieve a desired outcome in their interactions with a company.

State-owned enterprise. A government-owned business or industry (e.g., a state-owned oil company).

Stateless corporation. A multinational corporation whose activities are conducted in so many nations as to minimize its dependence on any single nation and enable it to establish its headquarters' activities virtually anywhere in the world.

Stewardship principle. The idea that business managers should act in the interest of all members of society who are affected by their business decisions, thus behaving as stewards or trustees of the public welfare. (See also **Public trustee.**)

Sticky floor. When women, minorities, or other groups are unable to advance in the workplace because they become "stuck" in entry-level, low-paying jobs.

Stockholder. A person, group, or organization owning one or more shares of stock in a corporation. (Also known as *shareholder.*)

Strategic philanthropy. A form of philanthropy in which donor organizations direct their contributions to recipients in order to achieve a direct or indirect business objective.

Strategic rethinking. The process of reconsidering critical business assumptions about what an organization does, business activities it conducts, and in which markets, and how, it will compete.

Strategies of response. (See **Corporate social strategy.**)

Strict liability. A legal doctrine that holds that a manufacturer is responsible (liable) for injuries resulting from the use of its products, whether or not the manufacturer was negligent or breached a warranty.

Superfund. A U.S. law, passed in 1980, designated to clean up hazardous or toxic waste sites. The law established a fund, supported mainly by taxes on petrochemical companies, to pay for the cleanup. (Also known as the *Comprehensive Environmental Response, Compensation, and Liability Act [CERCLA].*)

Sustainable development. A concept that describes current economic development that does not damage the ability of future generations to meet their own needs.

Technology. The tools, machines, skills, technical operations, and abstract symbols involved in human endeavor.

Technology cooperation. Long-term cooperative partnerships between companies in developed and developing countries to transfer advanced technologies.

Telecommunications. The transmission of information via electromagnetic signals.

Telecommuting. Performing knowledge work and transmitting the results of that work by means of computer terminal to an organization's central data bank and management center, while the employee works at home or at some other remote location.

Term limits. Limits on the maximum number of terms in office that an elected official can serve.

Third world nations. Developing nations relatively poorer than advanced industrial nations.

Total quality management (TQM). A management approach that achieves high quality and consumer satisfaction through teamwork and continuous improvement of a product or service.

Toxic substance. Any substance used in production or in consumer products that is poisonous or capable of causing serious health problems for those persons exposed. (See also **Hazardous waste.)**

Tradable allowances. A market-based approach to pollution control in which the government grants companies "rights" to a specific amount of pollution (allowances), which may be bought or sold (traded) with other companies.

Trade association. An organization that represents the business and professional interest of the firms or persons in a trade, industry, or profession, such as medical doctors, chemical manufacturers, or used car dealers.

Trade-offs, economic and social. An attempt to balance and compare economic and social gains against economic and social costs when it is impossible to achieve all that is desired in both economic and social terms.

Trade policy. Actions by government to encourage or discourage commerce with other nations.

Transparency. The degree of openness or visibility surrounding a government's—or other organization's—decision-making process.

Unanimity Rule. In ethical analysis, a procedure for determining that all three modes of ethical reasoning—utilitarian, rights, and justice—provide consistent and uniform answers to an ethical problem or issue.

Urban sprawl. The spread of urban activities into areas that were once suburban and rural land. This usually implies business activities, congestion, and other byproducts of more people and activity.

U.S. Sentencing Guidelines. Official rules to help judges determine the appropriate penalty for criminal violations of federal laws.

U.S. Foreign Corrupt Practices Act. A federal law that specifies penalties for companies that make illegal or questionable payments to officials of other countries.

Utilitarian reasoning. An ethical approach that emphasizes the cost-benefit relationship between actions and their consequences.

Utility (social). A concept used in ethical reasoning that refers to the net positive gain or benefit to society of some action or decision.

Values. Fundamental and enduring beliefs about the most desirable conditions and purposes of human life.

Vertical merger. The combination, or joining together, of two or more companies in the same industry but at different levels or stages of production or sales into a single company. (See also **Conglomerate merger, Horizontal merger.)**

Volunteerism. The uncompensated efforts of people to assist others in a community.

Wall Street. A customary way of referring to the financial community of banks, investment institutions, and stock exchanges centered in the Wall Street area of New York City.

Warranty. A guarantee or assurance by the seller of a product or service.

Water pollution. When more wastes are discharged into waterways, such as lakes and rivers, than can be naturally diluted and carried away.

Whistle-blowing. An employee's disclosure to the public of alleged organizational misconduct, often after futile attempts to convince organizational authorities to take action against the alleged abuse.

White collar crime. Illegal activities committed by corporate managers, such as embezzlement or fraud.

Women's movement. A social movement for the rights of women.

Workplace safety team. A group of workers and managers who seek to minimize the occurrence of workplace accidents.

World Business Council for Sustainable Development (WBCSD). A group of over 125 companies from several nations formed in 1995 to encourage high standards of environmental management and to promote cooperation among businesses, governments, and other organizations concerned with sustainable development.